LIST OF THE OFFICERS OF THE BENGAL ARMY

Printed and bound in Great Britain by Antony Rowe Ltd, Eastbourne

LIST OF THE OFFICERS
OF THE BENGAL ARMY

1758–1834

*Alphabetically Arranged and Annotated
with Biographical and Genealogical
Notices by*

MAJOR V. C. P. HODSON

INDIAN ARMY (RETIRED LIST)
AUTHOR OF 'HISTORICAL RECORDS OF THE VICEROY'S BODY-GUARD'

A - C

PREFACE

A FEW words are necessary in explanation of the scope and limitations of this Biographical Dictionary. The work on which it is based is that known as *Dodwell & Miles's List*, or, to give it the full title, "Alphabetical List of the Officers of the Bengal Army; with the dates of their respective promotion, retirement, resignation, or death, whether in India or in Europe; from the year 1760, to the year 1834 inclusive, corrected to September 30, 1837." This work, dedicated by permission to the Honourable Court of Directors of the East India Company, and published in 1838 by Longman, Orme, Brown & Co., Paternoster Row, London, was compiled and edited by Messrs. Dodwell and Miles, East India Army Agents, 69 Cornhill. The compilers, Edward Dodwell and James Samuel Miles, had been, for thirty and twenty years respectively, in the Civil and Military Pay Dept. at the East India House, the former latterly as Chief Clerk, with Miles as his Assistant. As such, they had special facilities for obtaining the particulars essential to their subject.

Their compilation has, for nearly ninety years, been the standard, in fact the only, printed work purporting to give a complete list of officers who served in the Bengal army between the dates mentioned above. Hence it is the one authority on the subject which is cited in genealogical works, family histories, pedigrees, and other books of this nature. It will be found on the shelves of the Reading Room at the British Museum (2102d) side by side with the works of such well-known genealogists as Joseph Foster, Burke, and other authoritative reference books of a similar class.

Unfortunately, judged by modern standards, *Dodwell & Miles* is out-of-date, and scarcely deserves its reputation as the supreme authority. It is, for one thing, incomplete—necessarily so since no edition subsequent to 1838 has been issued; it is, moreover, often inaccurate in the spelling of proper names both of persons and places; and it contains not a few errors as to facts and dates.

Whilst there is no desire to belittle the merits of a work which has stood alone for the greater part of a century, it is felt, nevertheless, that the time has now come when a revised edition, more extended in its range, may not be out of place. The following pages, which still unfortunately display many an ugly gap, are the outcome of an attempt to rectify some of the errors in *Dodwell & Miles*, and to complete that work in so far as it is possible so to do.

PREFACE

The study of military history and genealogical research are two separate and distinct sciences : the number of military historians who have concerned themselves, otherwise than superficially, with genealogy is small ; few genealogists appear to have studied the former in connexion with their own special subject. It is hoped that both classes may here be able to gather useful items of information.

For purposes of easier reference the genealogical notes have been kept distinct from the purely military details of an officer's career. Thus, anyone wishing solely to ascertain the parentage, birth, marriage, or death of any particular officer may do so without being obliged to wade through a mass of what, to him, may possibly be extraneous matter. Similarly, when the dates of rank or war services of an officer are in question, these particulars will be found unencumbered by matters of mere family interest.

It is recognized, as has already been stated, that many of the following biographies are at present far from complete. Some of the missing details may, it is confidently hoped, be supplied in the lists of Corrigenda and Addenda to be published at the end of succeeding parts of the present work ; and I shall be grateful for any corrections or additional details which may be sent to me, addressed c/o the Publishers.

With regard to the record of service of each officer, details and dates have been obtained from the various records, either in MS. or in print, preserved at the India Office, Whitehall. It has not been considered necessary to add the words " India Office Records " to the list of authorities mentioned at the end of each biography.

But meagre details, in the majority of cases, are available during the eighteenth century ; and particulars as to an officer's war services, and even as to the number of the regiment or battalion in which he served, have not always been easily obtainable. It may here be noted that the number of the regiment as given after an officer's name at the beginning of each biography is that in which he was serving, or on the roll of which he was borne, at the date of his becoming a casualty, either by death, retirement, resignation, transfer to the invalid or pension establishment, or dismissal. Should a comma precede the title of the regiment, it is to be taken as indicating that the officer in question was actually on the strength of that regiment at the date of his death. Transfers of officers of any rank from one battalion to another, and even from one regiment to another, were of frequent occurrence down to May 1824—the date of the final reorganization of the pre-Mutiny Bengal army ; [1] such transfers, in the case of those who attained the rank of Lt. Col., continuing until the end of the period with which we are dealing. Owing to considerations of space it has not always been found

[1] See " Reorganization," *post*.

PREFACE

practicable to mention every regiment in which an officer served during the course of his military career.

Although 1760 is given as the date of commencement of *Dodwell and Miles*, yet it will be noticed, on referring to that work, that the names of a few officers are included whose first commission is anterior to that year. Amongst the *Orme MSS.* preserved at the India Office is to be found a MS. Bengal Army List, dated June 1758. As this is thought to be the earliest complete list of Bengal officers in existence, the year 1758 has been taken as the starting-point of the present work, which is believed to contain the name of every officer (including some 250 not given in *Dodwell & Miles*) who was borne on the rolls of the Bengal army in June 1758, or who entered the Service between that date and 31st December, 1834. This latter date, which coincides with the termination of *Dodwell & Miles*, has, owing principally to considerations of space, been chosen for our present purpose also, instead of what would appear to be a more suitable date, *viz.* the Accession of Queen Victoria.

A word with regard to the genealogical data supplied. The object here has been, not so much to give all available details, as to place searchers in a position to continue the search themselves by referring them to printed pedigrees and other references in genealogical works, biographies, contemporary literature, etc. In cases where a memoir appears in the *D.N.B.* or any other easily-accessible standard work, a minimum of detail has been given here. In every case, however, the authorities cited are such as can be met with in any good reference library, and these should be consulted when further information is desired.

Many of the officers who figure in the following pages were, as is only to be expected, members of families whose genealogy is not to be found in the pages of the *Peerage*, nor in *Landed Gentry*. In such cases, in order to assist identification, the names of relatives mentioned in the Will of the officer in question have been given. In this connexion it is interesting to note the wideness of the circle from which the East India Company drew its Cadets. Nearly every grade of the social scale, from the son of a Marquess to that of a hatter, a wigmaker, and a slop-seller, will be found to be represented. An East India Cadetship, it must be remembered, was a valuable asset ensuring a competence for life with a fair chance, in the eighteenth century, at any rate, of being able to leave India with a substantial fortune. Is it too much to conjecture that the wigmaker or the hatter may have received the Cadetship for his son as a *quid pro quo* from some aristocratic patron capable of pulling strings in Leadenhall Street ?

In addition to the pecuniary advantages, a commission in the Bengal army offered prospects of a military career of sufficiently stirring nature to appeal in no uncertain measure to the youth of Great Britain and Ireland.

There was yet another class by whom, in the earlier days, these Cadetships were eagerly sought as affording the opportunity of a more or less protracted absence from the United Kingdom. Amongst such may be included London Bucks who had "outrun the constable," duellists and other fugitives from justice, as well as illegitimate sons whose presence in England it might be difficult to explain in certain quarters.

As to the personal details of an officer's private life, *i.e.* his parentage, and the dates of birth, baptism, marriage, and death ; these have been derived from various reliable sources, chief amongst which are the certified copies from the original entry in the parish register,[1] and they may be accepted as accurate. When these are at variance with the dates as given in any printed pedigree or biography, a note to that effect has been made. In cases where doubt exists as to the accuracy of any such date, or where there is a reasonable presumption of an officer's parentage which has not yet been capable of actual proof, such statement appears in parentheses preceded by a " ? " and by an expression of doubt.

Difficulty has been experienced in many cases in tracing the date of death of officers who resigned their commissions before they had qualified for a pension, or who were removed from the Service. Of such, no further record has been kept at the India Office. Similarly, there are a few cases of officers, on the Retired List and in receipt of a pension, the date of whose death does not appear to have been notified to the authorities by the relatives or representatives concerned. In such cases the name in question has continued to figure in the list of Retired Officers, possibly for many years after his demise, until, at length, realizing that death must have occurred some years earlier, it has eventually been removed from the list with the remark, " Presumed dead, as nothing has been heard of him for —— years."

Where the approximate date only of birth is known, or where the age at death has been ascertained from obituary notices, or M.I., such date is given in the following pages thus : " *b.* 1780-81," or " *b. c.* 1780." It must be remembered, however, that these dates can be considered as approximate only, the age at death as given in one journal being occasionally at variance with the age as given in another.

With regard to marriages ; no claim to completeness is put forward in this respect, and the omission of any reference to a marriage must not be taken as implying that the officer in question did not contract any marriage, unless it is distinctly stated that he

[1] See " Cadets," *post.*

PREFACE

died unmarried. "*m.* (?)" or "*m.* ——" both indicate that the officer was married, but that his wife's name has not been traced. "(? *m.*)" implies a belief that he was married, although the fact has not been verified by the compiler.

Whilst on this subject, attention may be drawn to a circumstance so frequently noted by writers on social life in India during the period with which we are dealing, *viz.* the great disparity in numbers which existed, in the case of Europeans, between the two sexes. Opportunities for revisiting the land of their birth were few and far between, and when the turn for furlough did at length arrive, officers were not seldom precluded from availing themselves of it owing to the high cost of the return passage. On this account, spinsters of marriageable age did not remain single for long in the East; and so we find that the daughters of officers of the Bengal army, probably born and brought up in India, frequently found husbands from amongst the officers of their fathers' regiments, or at any rate from the same Service. Instances will be found in these pages where no less than six sisters have all thus married Bengal officers, whilst cases of two or three sisters so doing are of comparatively frequent occurrence. In every such case cross-references have been made to the various sons-in-law.

In the interests of historical accuracy it has been found impossible to avoid mention of the award of punishment involving dismissal by Courts Martial or by Civil Courts. It must be remembered, however, that in pre-Mutiny days it was considered necessary to bring officers to trial by Court Martial on the slightest pretext, and on charges which nowadays would hardly be described as dishonourable or unbecoming the character of an officer and a gentleman. The Proceedings of Courts Martial are naturally regarded as confidential, and, as such, are not available for inspection at the India Office. A sufficiently full résumé of the charges and findings can usually be found in the Indian journals of the period, whence they were often copied into the *Asiatic Annual Register*, the *Asiatic Journal*, and other periodicals of a similar nature published in Great Britain. For the convenience of those requiring fuller details, reference to the published account has been supplied. No mention has been made in the following pages of the circumstance of the trial of an officer by Court Martial where, although found guilty, the sentence awarded has not involved suspension or removal from the Service.

In the few cases in which an officer has taken his own life, the fact has been briefly noted together with a reference to the authority for such statement.

The personal history of the lives of nearly 7,000 officers whose names are recorded in this Dictionary is the history of the Bengal

Army from the capture of Calcutta by Suraj-ud-Daulah in 1756 down to the transfer of that Army to the Crown on 1st November, 1858 : to follow intelligently the careers of the former it is essential to possess a rough general knowledge of the latter, and of the battles and sieges in which it took part. This can best be acquired by a perusal of Cardew's *Sketch of the Services of the Bengal Native Army to the year* 1895, compiled in the office of the Adjutant General in India, and published in the office of the Superintendent of Government Printing, Calcutta, in 1903. No more succinct or authoritative account dealing with the whole period under review has ever been published.

In order to avoid unnecessary repetition of dates in the enumeration of the war services of each officer, a general list of all the principal campaigns in which any unit of the Bengal army was engaged, together with the dates of the more important actions and sieges of such campaign, has been compiled for ready reference, and will be found at the end of the Introduction.

The spelling of the names of places in India has always proved a matter of difficulty for the reason that, unless one is prepared to admit the charge of inconsistency, the adoption of the most generally-accepted "Hunterian system" throughout involves the disguising of such well-known names as Cawnpore, Lucknow, Bhurtpore, etc., under the grotesque renderings, Khanpur, Lakhnau, Bharatpur. This has been avoided by spelling all place names exactly as given in the *Times Atlas*, 1923.[1] In the case of battles where the name is not to be found in the gazetteer to this Atlas, the spelling as given in Cardew's *Services of the Bengal Native Army*, alluded to above, has been adhered to.

Books, as we are occasionally reminded by reviewers and others, are of two sorts—those which can be read, and those which cannot. Without any wish to disarm criticism, let it here be admitted at the outset that this book falls into the second category, and that those who, in the expectation of finding much of human interest, take it up and turn its pages, are foredoomed to disappointment. It is intended to be regarded and treated simply as a work of reference.

Finally, an expression of grateful thanks is due to all those from whom I received assistance in its compilation, more particularly to the officials in charge of the Military Records and of the Ecclesiastical Records at the India Office, and to the Staff of the North Devon Athenaeum Library at Barnstaple, from all of whom unfailing courtesy and willing help has ever been forthcoming.

Sept. 1926.   V. C. P. H.

[1] To those acquainted with India some of these spellings will possibly appear to be of dubious correctness, *e.g.* Barasat, Bhagulpur, Khyber.

CONTENTS OF PART I

	PAGE
Preface	v
List of Abbreviations	xiii
Bibliography	xvii
Cadets	xxi
Education	xxiv
Furlough and Leave	xxvi
Genealogical References	xxvii
Glossary	xxix
Lord Clive's Fund	xxxi
Medals	xxxi
Rank	xxxiii
Reorganization	xxxv
Retirement Regulations	xxxviii
Select Picket	xxxviii
Staff	xxxix
Chronological List of Campaigns, Actions, and Sieges	xli
ABBOTT, Augustus—AYTON, James Alexander	1-64
BABER, John—BYRON, George	65-272
CADDELL, Walter—CUTHBERT, Peter	273-436

LIST OF ABBREVIATIONS

(The ordinary abbreviations of degrees and orders are not included.)

A.A.G.   Assistant Adjutant General.
A.A.R.   *Asiatic Annual Register.*
Acad.   Academy.
A.C.G.   Assistant Commissary General.
Actg.   Acting.
A.D.C.   Aide-de-Camp.
Adjt.   Adjutant.
Adjtcy.   Adjutancy.
Adm.   Admiral.
Admon.   Administration.
A.G.   Adjutant General.
A.G.G.   Agent to Governor General.
A.H.Q.   Army Headquarters.
A.J.   *Asiatic Journal.*
A.L.   *Army List.*
Appt.   Appointment.
Apptd.   Appointed.
A.Q.M.G.   Assistant Quartermaster General.
A.R.   *Annual Register.*
Arr.   Arrived.
Art.   Artillery.
Attd.   Attached.
Atty.   Attorney.
Aust.   Australia.
Aux.   Auxiliary.

B.   Barón.
b.   born.
B.M.   British Museum.
B.M. Add. MS.   Additional Manuscripts in the British Museum.
B. & O.   Bihar and Orissa. (Province.)
bapt.   baptized.
Barr.   Barrister.
Bart.   Baronet.
B.C.S.   Bengal Civil Service.
Bde.   Brigade.
Bdr. Gen.   Brigadier General.
Bk. Mr.   Barrack Master.
Bldgs.   Buildings.
Bn.   Battalion.
Bo.   Bombay.

B : P.P.   *Bengal : Past and Present.*
Bt.   Brevet.
bur.   buried.

c. circa.
Cantt.   Cantonment.
Capt.   Captain.
Cav.   Cavalry.
C.C.   Cadet College.
C.D.   Court of Directors (of the East India Company).
cf.   compare.
C.G.   *Calcutta Gazette.*
C.G.H.   Cape of Good Hope.
C.I.   Central India.
C.-in-C.   Commander-in-Chief.
C.J.   Chief Justice.
Cl.   Class.
C.M.   Court Martial.
Col.   Colonel.
Coll.   College.
Comd.   Command.
Comdd.   Commanded.
Comdg.   Commanding.
Comdt.   Commandant.
Comr.   Commissioner.
Comst.   Commissariat.
Comy. Gen.   Commissary General.
Cons.   Consultations.
Coy.   Company.
C.P.   Central Provinces.
cr.   created.
Cresc.   Crescent.
C.S.   Civil Service.

D.   Duke.
d.   died.
D.A.A.G.   Deputy Assistant Adjutant General.
D.A.C.G.   Deputy Assistant Commissary General.
D.A.G.   Deputy Adjutant General.
D.A.Q.M.G.   Deputy Assistant Quartermaster General.
dau.   daughter.
D.C.   Deputy Commissioner.

LIST OF ABBREVIATIONS

d.d. doing duty.
Dept. Department.
D.G. Dragoon Guards.
Dgns. Dragoons.
D.I.B. Dictionary of Indian Biography.
D.I.G. Deputy Inspector General.
Dir. Director.
Dist. District.
Div. Division.
Divl. Divisional.
D.L. Deputy Lieutenant.
D.N.B. Dictionary of National Biography.
D.Q.M.G. Deputy Quartermaster General.
Durani. Durani Empire, Afghan Order of the.
Dy. Deputy.

E. Earl.
Edin. Edinburgh.
ed. educated.
E.I.C.N.S. East India Company's Naval Service.
E.I.Co. East India Company.
E.I.C.S. East India Company's Service.
E.I.M.C. East India Military Calendar.
E.I.R. East India Register.
E.L.I. European Light Infantry.
Ency. Brit. Encyclopaedia Britannica.
Engr. Engineer.
Ens. Ensign.
Est. Establishment.
Eur. European.
Expedn. Expedition.
ext. extinct.

Fenc. Fencible.
F.F. Field Force.
F.M. Field Marshal.
Ft. Foot.
Ft. Wm. Fort William (Bengal).
Fur. Furlough.
Fus. Fusiliers.

Garr. Garrison.
Gaz. Gazette.
G.C.M. General Court Martial.
Gdns. Gardens.
Gds. Guards.

Gen. General.
G.G. Governor General of India.
G.G.B.G. Governor General's Body Guard.
G.M. Gentleman's Magazine.
G.O. General Order.
G.O.C. General Officer Commanding.
G.O.C.C. General Order by Commander-in-Chief.
G.O.G.G. General Order of Governor General.
Govr. Governor.
Govt. Government.
Gren. Grenadier.
Gt. Great.

H.A. Horse Artillery.
H.C.S. Honourable (East India) Company's Service.
H.E.I.C.S. Honourable East India Company's Service.
H.F.B. Heavy Field Battery.
Highlrs. Highlanders.
Hon. Honourable.
Hony. Honorary.
h.p. half-pay.
H.Q. Headquarters.
Hrs. Hussars.

I. Isle.
I.A.L. Indian Army List.
ibid. the same.
I.G. Inspector General.
I.L.N. Illustrated London News.
I.M. Allen's Indian Mail.
I.N. Indian News.
Ind. Indian.
Indep. Independent.
Insp. Inspector.
intest. intestate.
Intr. Interpreter.
I.O.Rec. India Office Records.
Irreg. Irregular.
I.W. Isle of Wight.

J.A.G. Judge Advocate General.
J.P. Justice of the Peace.

K.C. Knight of the Crescent.
K.C.H. Knight Commander of Hanover.
K.H. Knight of Hanover.
kld. killed.
K.S. King's Scholar.

LIST OF ABBREVIATIONS

K.S.F. Knight of San Fernando.
Kt. Knight.

L.C. Light Cavalry.
L.I. Light Infantry.
Lieut. Lieutenant.
Lieut. F. Lieutenant Fireworker.
Lond. Gaz. *London Gazette.*
Lt. Col. Lieutenant Colonel.

M. Marquis.
m. married.
Mag. Magazine.
M.C. Minutes of Council.
m.c. medical certificate.
M.C.S. Madras Civil Service.
Mgte. Magistrate.
M.I. Monumental inscription.
Mil. Militia.
Mily. Military.
M.M.B. Member of Medical Board; also, Member of Military Board.
mos. months.
M.R. Medal Roll.
MS. Manuscript.
M.M. *Monthly Magazine.*

N.C. Native Cavalry.
N.F.P. No further particulars.
N.I. Native Infantry.
N. & Q. *Notes and Queries.*
nr. near.
N.S. New series.
N.S.W. New South Wales.
N.W.F. North-West Frontier (of India).
N.W.P. North-West Province.
N.Z. New Zealand.

Obit. Obituary.
Offg. Officiating.
Ofr. Officer.
Ord. Ordnance.

P.A. Political Agent.
p.a. private affairs.
Paymr. Paymaster.
P.C. Perpetual Curate.
Ped. Pedigree.
Pk. Park.
Pl. Place.
P.M.G. Postmaster General.
Pol. Political.
P.R. Prize Roll.

Preby. Prebendary.
Presdy. Presidency.
Provl. Provincial.
psh. parish.
ptely. privately.
pub. published.
P.W.D. Public Works Department.
P.W.I. Prince of Wales Island (Penang).

Q.M.G. Quartermaster General.
Qmr. Quartermaster.

R.A. Royal Artillery.
R. Adm. Rear Admiral.
R.E. Royal Engineers.
Rec. Records.
Refs. References.
Reg. Register.
Regt. Regiment.
Res. Resigned.
Resdt. Resident.
Ret. Retired.
R.L. Royal Licence.
R.M. Royal Marines.
R.M.A. Royal Military Academy (Woolwich).
R.N. Royal Navy.
Rt. Right.

s. succeeded.
S.A. South Africa.
S.A.C.G. Sub-Assistant Commissary General.
S. & M. Sappers and Miners.
s.c. sick certificate.
Sec. Secretary.
Sergt. Sergeant.
S.M. *Scots Magazine.*
s.n. *sub nomine*
Soc. Society.
s.p. *sine prole.*
sq. square.
S.S. Superintending Surgeon.
S.S.C. Solicitor before Supreme Court (Scotland).
S.S.O. Station Staff Officer.
St. Saint; also, Street.
Subsdy. Subsidiary.
Supt. Superintendent.
Suptg. Superintending.
Supy. Supernumerary.
Surg. Surgeon.

LIST OF ABBREVIATIONS

s.v.   sub voce.
(s.w.).   severely wounded.
T.C.D.   Trinity College, Dublin.
tempy.   temporary.
Terr.   Terrace.

Univ.   University.
unm.   unmarried.
U.P.   United Provinces (of Agra and Oudh).
u.p.a.   urgent private affairs.
u.s.l.   unemployed supernumerary list.

V.   Viscount.
Vol.   Volunteer.
vol.   volume.
V.P.   Vice-President.
v.p.   vita patris, in the lifetime of his father.

(w.).   wounded.
W.I.   West Indies.
wid.   widow.
W.S.   Writer to the Signet.

BIBLIOGRAPHY

(With abbreviated titles used in the text.)

N.B.—The titles, in many cases, have been considerably condensed from the original title pages. Only those works which are quoted in the text are given here.

Alumni Carthusiani, 1614-1872. Edited by Bower Marsh and F. A. Crisp. Privately printed, 1913.

Alumni Dublinenses, 1593-1846. Edited by G. D. Burtchaell and T. U. Sadleir. London, 1924.

Alumni Oxonienses, 1715-1886. Annotated by Joseph Foster. 4 vols., Oxford, 1888.

Alumni Westmonasterienses, 1663-1851. Collected by Joseph Welch. New edition by C. B. Phillimore, London, 1852.

Ancestor, The.

Anderson, William. The Scottish Nation. 3 vols., Edin., 1869.

Bengal : Past and Present (B. : P.P.). The Journal of the Calcutta Historical Soc. 1907-26. (In progress.)

Blundell's School Register, 1770-1882.

Boase. Dictionary of Modern English Biography.

Broome, Capt. A. History of the Bengal Army. London, 1850.

Buckle, Capt. E. Memoir of the Services of the Bengal Art. London, 1852.

Bulloch. Gordons under Arms (being vol. iii. of The House of Gordon), by Mrs. Skelton and J. M. Bulloch. Aberdeen, 1912.

Burke, John. Burke, Sir Bernard. Burke, Ashworth P. See references to genealogical works.

Burton, Major R. G. History of the Hyderabad Contingent. Calcutta, 1905.

Cardew, Major F. G. The Services of the Bengal Native Army. Calcutta, 1903.

Charterhouse School Lists.

Clan Campbell. Records of Clan Campbell in H.E.I.C., 1600-1858, by Major Sir Duncan Campbell, Bt. London, 1925.

Crawford. History of the Indian Medical Service, 1600-1913, by Lt.-Col. D. G. Crawford. 2 vols., London, 1914.

Crockford. Clerical Directory.

BIBLIOGRAPHY

De Rhé-Philipe. Biographical notices of Military Officers ... mentioned in Inscriptions on tombs and monuments in the Punjab ..., compiled by G. W. De Rhé-Philipe. Lahore, 1912.

D.I.B. Dictionary of Indian Biography, by C. E. Buckland. London, 1906.

Dictionnaire Biographique des Genevois et des Vaudois, par Albert de Montet. 2 vols., Lausanne, 1877-8.

D.N.B. Dictionary of National Biography.

Edinburgh Academy Register.

E.I.M.C. The East India Military Calendar, by John Philippart. 3 vols., London, 1823-6.

Eton School Lists, 1791-1877, by H. E. Chetwynd-Stapylton. London, 1885.

Firminger. The Diaries of Three Surgeons of Patna, 1763. Edited for the Calcutta Hist. Soc. by Rev. Walter K. Firminger. Calcutta, 1909.

Forde, Col. L. Lord Clive's Right-hand Man, Francis Forde. London, 1910.

Forrest. Selections from Papers in Foreign Department, by G. W. Forrest. 3 vols., Calcutta, 1890.

Forrest's Clive. The Life of Lord Clive, by Sir George Forrest, C.I.E. 2 vols., London, 1918.

Foster, Joseph. Our Noble and Gentle Families of Royal Descent. 2 vols., London, 1887.

—— Index Ecclesiasticus, 1800-1840. Oxford, 1890.

Frasers of Lovat, History of, by Alexander Mackenzie. Inverness, 1896.

Gardiner. The Admission Registers of St. Paul's School, 1748-1876, by Rev. R. B. Gardiner. London, 1884.

G.E.C. The Complete Peerage, by G. E. Cokayne.

—— The Complete Baronetage, by G. E. Cokayne.

Genealogist, The.

Graduati Cantabrigienses, 1800-1872, by H. R. Luard. Cambridge, 1873.

Grier. Letters of Warren Hastings to his Wife, by S. C. Grier. Edin., 1905.

Harrow School Register, 1800-1911. 3rd edition, London, 1911.

Haydn. The Book of Dignities, by Joseph Haydn. 1890 edition.

Hearseys, The. Five Generations of an Anglo-Indian Family, by Col. Hugh Pearse, D.S.O. Edin., 1905.

Hickey. Memoirs of William Hickey, edited by Alfred Spence. 4 vols., London.

Hill. Bengal in 1756-7 (Indian Records Series), by S. C. Hill. 3 vols., London, 1905.

BIBLIOGRAPHY xix

Hill's Calcutta. List of Europeans in Bengal in 1756, by S. C. Hill. Calcutta, 1902.

Howard & Crisp. Visitation of England and Wales, vols. 1-9 by J. J. Howard and F. A. Crisp, vols. 10-21 by F. A. Crisp. Privately printed, 1893-1921.

Howard & Crisp (Notes). Notes to the above. 12 vols., 1896-1917.

Howard & Crisp's Ireland. Visitation of Ireland, vols. 1-3 by J. J. Howard and F. A. Crisp, vols. 4-6 by F. A. Crisp. Privately printed, 1897-1918.

Innes. History of the Bengal European Regiment, by Lt.-Col. P. R. Innes. 3rd edition, London, 1885.

Kane. List of Officers of R.A., 1716-1869. Revised edition, Woolwich, 1869.

Kirby. Winchester Scholars. London, 1888.

Leslie. List of Officers of the Madras Art., by Lt.-Col. J. H. Leslie, late R.A.

Livre d'Or des Familles Vaudoises, par Henri Delédevant et Marc Henrioud. Lausanne, 1923.

Love. Vestiges of Old Madras, 1640-1800 (Indian Records Series), by Col. H. D. Love. 3 vols., London, 1913.

Military Secretaries to the Governors General and Viceroys, List of. Calcutta, 1908.

Misc. Gen. et Her. Miscellanea Genealogica et Heraldica, edited by J. J. Howard.

Mundy. Journal of a Tour in India, by Capt. Mundy. 2 vols., London, 1832.

Pester. War and Sport in India, 1802-1806; the Diary of Lieut. John Pester. London, n.d. (? 1913).

Repton School Register, 1620-1894. London, 1895.

Robinson. Register of Merchant Taylors' School, 1562-1874, by Rev. C. J. Robinson. 2 vols., 1882-3.

Rugby School Register, 1675-1874. Rugby, 1886.

Seaton. From Cadet to Colonel, by Maj.-Gen. Sir Thomas Seaton. 2 vols., London, 1866.

Selections from Calcutta Gazettes, 1784-1823, by W. S. Seton-Karr and H. D. Sandeman. 5 vols., London, 1864-9.

Shaw. The Knights of England, by W. A. Shaw. 2 vols., London, 1906.

Sherborne Register, 1823-1892, by H. H. House. London, 1893.

Shrewsbury School Register, 1798-1898, by Rev. J. E. Auden.

Spring. List of Officers of the Bombay Art., by Col. F. W. M. Spring, late R.A. London, 1902.

Stubbs. History of the Bengal Art., by Maj.-Gen. F. W. Stubbs. 3 vols., London, 1877-1895.

BIBLIOGRAPHY

Stubbs's List. List of Officers of the Bengal Art., by Maj.-Gen. F. W. Stubbs. Bath, 1892.

Swinton of Kimmerghame Records. Privately printed, Edin., 1908.

Thackeray. The Royal (Bengal) Engineers, by Col. Sir Edward Thackeray, K.C.B., V.C. London, 1900.

Tonbridge School Register, 1826-1910, by H. E. Steed. London, 1911.

Uppingham School Lists.

Vibart. Addiscombe, its Heroes and Men of Note, by Col. H. M. Vibart. 2 vols., London, 1894.

V.B.G. Historical Records of the Viceroy's Body Guárd, by Lieut. V. C. P. Hodson. London, 1910.

Walford. The County Families of the U.K., by Edward Walford. 1st edition, London, 1860.

Westminster School Register, 1764-1883, by G. F. Russell-Barker and A. H. Stenning.

Williams. History of the Bengal Native Inf., by Capt. John Williams. London, 1817.

In addition to the above, various family and county histories have been consulted; also the undermentioned *Obituaries* :

Musgrave's Obit. Harleian Soc. 6 vols., London, 1898-1901.

Bengal Obit. Calcutta, 1848.

Inscriptions on Tombs, Assam, Shillong, 1902.

,, ,, Bengal, by C. R. Wilson, 1896.

,, ,, Bombay, Bombay, 1911.

,, ,, Madras, by J. J. Cotton, 1905.

,, ,, Punjab, by M. Irving, 1910.

Special acknowledgment is due to the authors of the following works, from which a great deal of information has been derived :

B. ; P.P. ; Cardew ; Clan Campbell ; Crawford ; Gordons under Arms ; Stubbs ; Marshall's Genealogist's Guide.

N.B.—Where a book referred to is in dictionary form, or is otherwise fully indexed, the number of the actual page to which attention is to be drawn has been omitted.

CADETS

The following were the "Terms of a Cadet" in 1780. "The Company will Pay Fourteen Pounds for his Passage to India and will make him a Gratuity of Ten Guineas previous to his going on board. On his Arrival in India, he will enter into Pay at Twenty pence a Day,[1] and be promoted to a Commission according to his Rank and behaviour in the Service."

"Country" Cadets, so called in contradistinction to "Europe" Cadets, were those who were already in India when they obtained their appointment as a Cadet. The term did not imply that they had been born or brought up in India, although sometimes this was the fact. In the majority of cases they were young men of exactly similar status to the "Europe" Cadets, who, possibly lacking sufficient interest at the Court of Directors to procure an appointment, came out to India, as "Free Merchants" or in other guises, in the hope of securing the coveted appointment in that country. With a few exceptions, the appointment of these "Country" Cadets ceased after 1786.

"Minor" Cadets. Nominations to Minor Cadetships were occasionally, towards the end of the eighteenth century, given to the sons of deserving officers of the E.I.C.S. In some cases the recipients were actually infants in arms. Although it does not appear that these Minor Cadets ever drew pay as such, the appointment being regarded more in the light of a promise of the grant of a Cadetship when the youth in question should have attained the requisite age, yet the practice was not of long duration.

Fifteen years (afterwards raised to sixteen) was nominally the minimum age for appointment as Cadet. This regulation, however, was not always strictly observed during the eighteenth century; and the following pages will furnish many instances where Cadets overstated their age on embarkation. Before long the Court of Directors decided to demand a copy of the would-be Cadet's birth or baptismal certificate as evidence of age.

The following extracts from "Cadets Regulations" are considered to be of sufficient interest to quote in full.

"At a Court of Directors, held on Wednesday, the 7th December, 1808. RESOLVED, That the age of fifteen, at which period young men

---

[1] Increased to Rs.20 *p.m.* plus half batta at one rupee *p.d.* by M.C. dated 16 June 1786. In 1808 the pay of a Cadet was still further increased to 4s. 2d. *per diem.*

have hitherto been eligible for appointments as cadets for the infantry and cavalry in the Company's service in India, is too early an age; and therefore, in future, the age of sixteen years be the earliest period at which cadets for those corps may be appointed.

The certificates required to be produced by the Act of Parliament, and the Court's several resolutions are as follows, viz.

1st. An extract from the register of the parish wherein the cadet was born or christened, signed by the resident clergyman, and countersigned by the churchwardens.

2nd. A certificate from the father, mother, or nearest of kin to the cadet (or his guardian, in the event of their death), agreeably to the following form. This must be annexed to the above extract.

'I do hereby certify, that the foregoing extract from the register of baptisms of the parish of ——, in the county of ——, contains the date of the birth of my son ——, who is the bearer of this, and nominated a cadet on the —— establishment, by —— Esq.; and I do further declare, that I received the said appointment for my son —— gratuitously, and that no money, or other valuable consideration, has been or is to be paid, either directly or indirectly for the same; and that I will not pay, or cause to be paid, either by myself, by my son, or by the hands of any other person, any pecuniary or valuable consideration whatsoever, to any person or persons who have interested themselves in procuring the said nomination for my son from the Director abovementioned.

'Witness my hand, this —— day of —— in the year of our Lord ——.'

3rd. A letter from the cadet's friend, who actually interests himself in procuring the nomination from the Director, certifying to the following effect, viz.:

'To THE HONOURABLE COURT OF DIRECTORS OF THE UNITED EAST-INDIA COMPANY.

GENTLEMEN,

I do hereby declare, upon my honor, that I received the nomination of a cadet for the —— (infantry or cavalry) from —— Esq. gratuitously, and that I have given it gratuitously to Mr. ——, with whose family and connections I am well acquainted.

I am, GENTLEMEN,

Your most obedient servant.'

Unless the whole of the above papers are delivered in by the cadet he will not be passed.

In the event of no parish register existing or to be found, the beforementioned act of parliament provides as follows, viz.

'That if no such register can be found, an affidavit of that circumstance shall be made by the party himself, with his information and belief, that his age is not under fifteen years, and doth not exceed twenty-two years.'

CADETS   xxiii

The following is the form of the affidavit to be made by the cadet, and sworn to before a magistrate, *viz.*

'I, C. D., presented for the appointment of a cadet by ——, Esq. do make oath and swear, that I have caused search to be made for a parish register, whereby to ascertain my age, but am unable to produce the same, there being none to be found; and, further, I make oath and swear, that from the information of my parents (and other relations) which information I verily believe to be true, that I was born in the parish of ——, in the county of ——, on ——, in the year ——, and that I am not at this time under the age of sixteen, or above twenty-two years.

'Sworn before me,   'Witness my hand, this —— day of ——, this —— day   in the year of our Lord ——. of ——.   'C. D.'

The father, mother, or nearest of kin, must then add their certificates as to the truth of the affidavit, nearly similar to the one ordered to be annexed to the extract from the parish register; and the friend who obtains the nomination for the cadet must likewise furnish him with the declaration above-mentioned.

It is, here necessary to remark, in consequence of several persons having been detected in attempting to pass under false certificates, when they have either been under or above the age prescribed by the act of parliament, that all persons who may in future be nominated cadets, if there is any cause to suspect their certificate has been forged, or alteration made therein, or collusion made use of in obtaining the same, they will, on detection, be immediately dismissed the Company's service, and rendered for ever ineligible to hold any situation or employment in the Company's civil, military, or marine service, either abroad or at home.

Where the person to be appointed a cadet has held a commission in His Majesty's service, for the term of one year at least, or in the militia, or fencible corps when embodied, and shall have joined his regiment, and been called into actual service, or shall have been in the Company of cadets of the royal regiment of artillery, such person is eligible for the appointment of cadet in the Company's service, provided his age does not exceed twenty-five years; of which circumstance he must, nevertheless, produce the several certificates before mentioned, as also his commission, together with a certificate from the war-office, or commanding officer of his regiment, of his having actually joined, and done duty with the regiment for the full term of one year or upwards; and that he was neither dismissed or resigned his regiment in consequence of any misconduct.

Upon the cadet being approved of by the Court, he will be furnished with a card of necessaries for his equipment, and the Court's regulations as to the sums to be paid for his accommodation on board ship. And the Court expect, that he will take his passage in one of the first ships bound to the presidency to which he is appointed. The cadet will also take notice that the commanders are prohibited from demanding or receiving any greater sum than £95, for his accommodation at their table, and the third mates any greater sum than £55, to accommodate him in their mess, exclusive of the Charter-party passage-money to the owners, of £15, which the cadet will be required to pay, in both instances, into the pay-office.

When the cadet is ready to embark, he must apply to Mr. Abington for a certificate of his having passed, who will point out the ship in which he is expected to proceed, which certificate will direct him to the pay-office, where he is to pay in the amount of his passage-money; also to the private-trade office, to receive the order for his baggage; and lastly, to the secretary's-office, where he will obtain the certificate of his appointment. He will then hold himself in readiness to embark, either previous to the ship's departure from Gravesend, or at the last port from whence the ship shall be ordered to take her departure from England.

N.B.—The cadet's baggage is limited to a chest of necessaries, a trunk of necessaries, a liquor case, a hamper of wine, and a cot and bedding."

EDUCATION

WITHOUT taking into consideration the elementary, or non-professional, education of a Cadet,[1] the chief places of military education through which, during the first third of the eighteenth century, a Cadet passed before receiving his Commission were as follows:

Addiscombe. The establishment of a Military Seminary at Addiscombe, near Croydon, was authorized by a resolution of the Court of Directors dated 7 Apr. 1809, but some Cadets had already been in residence from 21 Jan. of that year. It was originally intended for the education of Engineer and Artillery Cadets only, but in 1816 the admission of Infantry Cadets also was sanctioned.

The following brief extracts from the earliest regulations for admission to the Seminary give some idea of the standard of education expected from the entrants. "No Cadet to be admitted under fourteen, or above eighteen years of age." "He must be well grounded in arithmetic, including vulgar fractions, write a good hand, and must have acquired a competent knowledge of the English and Latin grammars." A few years later he was expected to be "able to read and construe Caesar's Commentaries, and be expert in vulgar and decimal fractions," on joining at Addiscombe.

When the Seminary was thrown open for Cavalry and Infantry Cadets, it was laid down, that "Cadets nominated for either of the

---

[1] So far as has been ascertained, only some 5% of the whole received their education at the universities or larger public schools.

above Corps must be 15 (afterwards raised to 16) years of age, and under 22, unless they have held a commission in His Majesty's service for one year, or in the militia or fencibles for the same period, they are then eligible if not more than 25 years of age ; ... "

The first public examination was held on 22 Dec. 1809, when two Cadets for the Bengal Artillery and one for the Bengal Engineers passed out. 509 of the officers whose lives are here recorded received their military education at Addiscombe. The last examination was held on 7 June 1861, and two months later, the Government of India having passed to the Crown, the College and grounds were sold by public auction by order of the Secretary of State for India.

Barasat Cadet College. This institution was inaugurated at Barasat, some sixteen miles from Calcutta, towards the end of 1802. It was intended for the instruction of the cavalry and infantry Cadets of the Bengal army in professional subjects and in Hindustani. It was closed during the Mahratta war, was re-opened in 1806, and was finally closed on 1 Sept. 1811, its methods having proved not altogether successful. Figures for the period 1802-3 are not available ; but during the second phase of its existence some 620 Cadets received instruction at the College. The length of stay at Barasat varied according to the proficiency and industry of the Cadet from a few months only to two years or even longer.

College of Fort William. Founded by Marquis Wellesley, the Governor General, in 1800 for the instruction of young Civil Servants of the E.I.C., the College of Fort William was opened in Calcutta in Nov. 1800, and was abolished on 24 Jan. 1854. Our only concern with it here, beyond the fact that at different times various officers held the appointment of examiner or professor of oriental languages, is due to the fact, that after the closing of the Barasat C.C., junior officers were occasionally permitted to avail themselves of the facilities it afforded for the study of the languages of the country.

R.M.A., Woolwich. Although it appears that twelve Cadets intended for the E.I.C.S. were sent to Woolwich (probably as " Extra Cadets," not resident at the Academy) on 1 Jan. 1797, yet it was not until 1798 that it was determined that the R.M.A. should in future provide officers for the Company as well as for the King's service. These regulations were to be carried into effect from 1 July 1798, and during this first year six Bengal Cadets entered the R.M.A. Between this date and 1809, in which latter year the Cadets destined for India were withdrawn on the opening of the Seminary at Addiscombe, nearly one hundred Bengal Cadets were educated at the Academy, the last having been nominated on 16 Mar. 1808.

The Court of Directors paid at the rate of £100 *p.a.* for each of their Cadets at Woolwich, in addition to a sum of £3,000 for providing the extra accommodation required.

Although some Cadets managed to pass out after eighteen months' residence, in some cases as much as three years elapsed before the Cadet was able to obtain his certificate, the average length of stay being from two to two and a half years.

R.M.C., Marlow. Founded by the Duke of York, the Royal Military College was first opened, in May 1802, in a house rented for the purpose at Great Marlow, Bucks. It was removed in 1812 to its present site at Sandhurst. Five Cadets for the E.I.C.S. were admitted to the College in 1802, sixteen in the following year. During the period 1802-9, in which latter year the E.I.Co. started its own Seminary at Addiscombe, a total of 88 Cadets for India passed through Marlow, of whom about 30 were appointed to Bengal.

FURLOUGH AND LEAVE

AN excellent summary of the furlough and leave rules in force at different periods will be found in Lt.-Col. D. G. Crawford's *History of the Indian Medical Service*, vol. i., chap. xix. A few only of the more important points can here be briefly stated. Previous to 1796 any officer wishing to return to Europe had to resign the Service. He received no pay while absent from duty, though he might be reappointed and permitted to return to India, without detriment to his rank, should he apply for reinstatement in the Service.

The first furlough regulations were issued in 1796, when it was laid down that the period of furlough was to be for three years, reckoning from its date to the day of the return of the officer to his respective Presidency. It was also enacted, "That Subalterns be ten years in India before they can be entitled (except in case of certified sickness) to their rotation to be absent on Furlough."

Shortly afterwards the Court of Directors decided that " No officer on furlough can receive pay for more than two years and a half from the period of his quitting India." In 1811 it was resolved that five years should be the absolute maximum of continued absence from India, allowed on any grounds. Some seven years later it was resolved that " Officers who have not served ten years in India, but whose presence in England is required by urgent private affairs, may be allowed a furlough for one year without pay."

In 1824 furlough to New South Wales was sanctioned on the same terms as to Europe.

GENEALOGICAL REFERENCES

ALL references to Burke's *Landed Gentry of Ireland* are to the latest (1912) edition; those to Burke's *Extinct and Dormant Baronetcies of England, Ireland, and Scotland*, to the 2nd (1844) edition; those to Joseph Foster's *Peerage, Baronetage, and Knightage of the British Empire*, to the 2nd (1881) edition; and those to Walford's *County Families of the U.K.*, are, except where otherwise stated, to the 1st (1860) edition.

As a general rule the reader is referred throughout to the latest edition of Burke's *Landed Gentry* or *Peerage* in which the subject's name is mentioned. In some cases it will be found, on referring to the current (13th) edition, that the family in question still figures in that work even though the particular member of that family with whom we are concerned has dropped out; in other cases no mention of the family will be found in any edition subsequent to that cited as a reference. Even in such cases where the officer has been too remotely connected with a family to secure mention in Burke, or has consistently been omitted owing to premature demise unmarried, or to other causes, reference has, for purposes of identification, been made to the latest edition in which this family appears.

Appended is a list of the various editions of Burke's *Landed Gentry*, and it should be noted that reference will henceforth be made in these pages to the number of the edition, not to the year of issue.

1st edition.	"History of the Commoners," 4 vols., 1837-8. (Quoted throughout as Burke's *Commoners*.)	
2nd edition.	"Dictionary of the Landed Gentry," 3 vols., 1848-9. The 3rd vol. contains a supplement, corrigenda, and a general index. Reprinted in 2 vols., without the index, 1851. (Quoted throughout as Burke's *Landed Gentry*, 2nd edition.)	
3rd edition.	1 vol. n.d. (1858).	
4th edition.	2 vols., 1862-3.	Reprinted in 1868.
5th edition.	2 vols., 1871.	Reprinted in 1875.
6th edition.	2 vols., 1879.	Reprinted in 1882.
7th edition.	2 vols., 1886.	
8th edition.	2 vols., 1894.	
9th edition.	2 vols., 1898.	
10th edition.	1 vol., 1900.	
11th edition.	1 vol., 1906.	
12th edition.	1 vol., 1914.	
13th edition.	1 vol., 1921.	

GENEALOGICAL REFERENCES

Other genealogical works by Burke to which reference will be made are:

Colonial Gentry, vol. i., 1892; vol. ii., 1895.
Family Records, 1 vol., 1897.
The Royal Families of England, Scotland, and Wales. 1 vol., 1876. (A re-issue, in a condensed and remodelled form, of Burke's *Royal Families*, 1851.)
A Visitation of the Seats and Arms of the Noblemen and Gentlemen of Great Britain. 1st series, vol. i., 1852; vol. ii., 1853. 2nd series, vol. i., 1854; vol. ii., 1855.
The Patrician. 6 vols., London, 1846-8.

GLOSSARY

Adawlut, a court of justice.

Batta, an extra allowance made to officers, soldiers, or other public servants, when in the field, or on other special grounds.

Bildar (*Beldar*), an excavator or digging labourer; hence a sapper, miner, or pioneer.

Budgerow, a lumbering, keelless barge, formerly much used by Europeans travelling on the Gangetic rivers.

Chowky (*Choky*), a customs or toll-station; hence the dues levied at such places. *e.g.* Salt Chowkies.

Dacoit, a robber belonging to an armed gang.

Dawk (*Dak*), post; the mail or letter-post.

Doab, the tract of land between two rivers.

Factor, see *Merchant*.

Free Merchant, a non-official European holding a licence from the E.I.C. to trade on his own account.

Ghaut (*Ghat*), a landing-place; a path of descent to a river; a quay, etc. Also, a mountain pass; hence a mountain range. The *O.E.D.* prefers the former spelling.

Golandaz, a native artilleryman; lit. a " cannonball thrower."

Gram, the vetch (*Cicer arietinum*), in most general use all over India as a horse food. Eng. Chick-pea.

Jaghirdar, the holder of a *jaghir* or fief.

Khasias, a hill people occupying the mountains N. of Sylhet.

Khud, a precipitous hillside; also a deep valley.

Kiladar, the commandant of a fort.

Land-waiter, an officer of the customs whose duty is to wait or attend the landing of goods, and to examine, weigh, or measure, and take an account of them. (Webster.)

Merchants (Junior and Senior). " From an early date in the Company's history up to 1833, the members of the Civil Service were classified during the first five years as *Writers*, then to the eighth year as *Factors*; in the ninth and eleventh as *Junior Merchants*; and thenceforward as *Senior Merchants*." (*Hobson-Jobson*.)

Najib, a kind of half-disciplined infantry soldiery under some of the native governments; also at one time a kind of militia under the British.

Nullah (*Nala*), a small ravine, or water-course.

Paik, an armed attendant, an inferior police and revenue officer. In Cuttack the Paiks formerly constituted a local militia.

Portioner, a small laird; Scots law. (*O.E.D.*)

Ryot, a tenant of the soil; an individual occupying land as a farmer or cultivator.

Sebundy (*Sibandi*), "irregular soldiery. A sort of Militia or imperfectly disciplined troops maintained for the garrisons of forts and guards in towns and villages, and for revenue and police duties." (Wilson's *Glossary of Indian Terms*.)

Sudder (*Sadr*), chief; *e.g. Sudder Adawlut*, the chief court of appeal.

Tacksman, one who holds a lease. In the Highlands of Scotland, a tenant of the higher class.

Taluqdar (*Talookdar*), in Oudh, a large landowner.

Thug (*Thag*), a class of robber and assassin who, having strangled their victims, usually travellers on the road, with handkerchiefs, plundered them and buried the bodies.

Tide-waiter, an officer of the customs who watches the landing of goods, to secure the payment of dues.

Wahabis, a puritanical sect of Mohammedan fanatics.

Writer, see *Merchant*. In Scotland, an attorney.

Zemindar, a small landowner.

LORD CLIVE'S FUND

MIR JAFAR KHAN, Nawab of Murshidabad, bequeathed at his death the sum of five lakhs of rupees to Lord Clive as a personal legacy. This sum the latter most generously transferred to the E.I.Co. for the purpose of establishing an Invalid Pension Fund for the Company's military servants and their families. The fund thus inaugurated came into operation on 6 Apr. 1770, when its assets, owing to a donation of three lakhs, given by the then Nawab of Bengal, Saif-ud-Daulah, in 1767, and accumulated interest, stood at nearly ten lakhs. On this sum the Court of Directors, who were to be trustees of the fund, engaged to allow, in perpetuity, interest at the rate of eight per cent. per annum; this interest (amounting to £8,043 13s. 4d.) to be applied in granting pensions to commissioned and warrant officers and soldiers, superannuated or worn out in their service, or to their widows.

In order to be eligible for benefit from this fund (the half-pay of their respective ranks), officers were obliged to make affidavit to the effect that they were not in possession of, nor entitled to, property to a certain amount, such amount varying according to rank from £4,000 in the case of a Colonel to £750 in that of an Ensign.

So early as 1808 the income of the fund was found to be quite inadequate to pay the pensions; and in 1846 the Government of India stated that Lord Clive's Fund existed as such merely in name, having long since been exhausted. In 1887-8 the amount paid in pensions had fallen to £74,000.

MEDALS

ALTHOUGH from the end of the eighteenth century onwards, the E.I.Co. had habitually issued war medals to its native troops, the British officers in its service were not included in the grant.

The first medal awarded to European commissioned officers was that for the capture of Seringapatam in 1799 during the fourth Mysore war.

Out of the fifteen officers who accompanied the expedition to Egypt in 1801, under Sir David Baird, the only one who survived till 1850 received in that year the Military War Medal (commonly called the Peninsula Medal) with clasp "Egypt."

For the capture of Java in 1811 the Prince Regent gave a gold medal, similar to the Peninsula, to all field officers. All British ranks who survived received the Peninsula Medal with clasp " Java " in 1848.

The first general contemporary issue of medals to all ranks, both British and Indian, took place after the first Afghan war of 1839-42. These included medals for Ghuznee (Ghazni); [1] Kelat-i-Gilzie (Kalat-i-Ghilzai) ; defence of Jellalabad (Jalalabad) ; Cabul (Kabul), 1842 (to Gen. Pollock's army) ; Candahar (Kandahar), 1842 (to Gen. Nott's force) ; Ghuznee, Cabul, 1842 ; and Candahar, Ghuznee, Cabul, 1842.

From this period onwards medals were regularly issued for each campaign of importance, as follows :

Campaign in Scinde (Sind), 1843. Three medals : Meeanee (Miani), 1843 ; Hyderabad, 1843 ; Meeanee, Hyderabad, 1843.

Gwalior campaign, 1843. Bronze star for Maharajpoor (Maharajpur) ; bronze star for Punniar (Paniar).

First Sikh war, or Sutlej campaign. Moodkee (Mudki) ; Ferozeshuhur (Ferozshahr) ; Aliwal ; Sobraon. The first battle in which the recipient took part was engraved on the medal, clasps being issued for subsequent ones.

Second Sikh war, or Punjab campaign. Medal inscribed with the word " Punjab," with clasps for Mooltan (Multan) ; Chilianwala ; and Goojerat (Gujerat).

The India Medal, with twenty-one clasps, was granted on 14 Apr. 1851 to the surviving officers who were engaged in the following :

Storm of Allighur (Aligarh), 4 Sept. 1803.
Battle of Delhi, 11 Sept. 1803.
Battle of Laswarree (Laswari), 1 Nov. 1803.
Defence of Delhi, Oct. 1804.
Battle of Deig, 13 Nov. 1804.
Capture of Deig, 23 Dec. 1804.[2]
Nepal War, 1816.
Battle of Seetabuldee (Sitabaldi) and capture of Nagpore (Nagpur), Nov. and Dec. 1817.
Battle of Maheidpoor (Mahidpur), 21 Dec. 1817.
War in Ava (first Burma War), 1824-6.
Siege and storm of Bhurtpoor (Bhurtpore), 1826.

[1] The first name in each case is that which appears on the medal or clasp ; the modern orthography, as employed throughout this work, is given in parentheses.

[2] What was believed to be a unique specimen of this medal, with the five clasps, " Allighur," " Battle of Delhi," " Laswarree," " Battle of Deig," " Capture of Deig," which had been issued to Cornet Patrick Dunbar, *q.v.*, sold for £220 at auction in London on 30 June 1824 : *see*, however, John Greenstreet.

MEDALS

The remaining clasps for operations on the western side of India do not concern us here.

Second Burma War, 1852-4. Medal with clasp "Pegu." This medal, under the designation of the "India Medal of 1854" (the old frontier medal), was afterwards adopted as the decoration for operations in India generally for a period of 45 years.

First China War, 1842 (the Opium War). Medal without clasp issued in 1842.

Second China War, 1857-60. Same medal as the above with clasps: Fatshan, 1857; Canton, 1857; Taku Forts, 1858; Taku Forts, 1860; Pekin, 1860.

Indian Mutiny campaign, 1857-9. Medal with clasps: Delhi; Defence of Lucknow; Relief of Lucknow; Lucknow; Central India.

Campaigns on the N.W.F. By G.G.O. No. 812 of 1869, the India Medal, with a clasp inscribed "North-West Frontier," was granted to all survivors of the troops engaged in the various expeditions on the N.W.F., 1849-1857, from the operations against the Baizai Swatis in the former year down to and including the expedition to the Bozdar Hills in the latter year. As, however, a full list of these minor campaigns is given on p. lv, there is no need to recapitulate them here.

The "Order of the Durani Empire" was instituted by Shah Shuja-ul-Mulk after he had been placed on the throne of Afghanistan by force of British Arms, and was given to a few selected Officers and Politicals. It was withdrawn from British recipients after our departure from that country, but some of the decorations were not handed in.[1]

RANK

THE dates of the various ranks as given in these pages are those of regimental, not army, rank up to and including that of Lieut. Colonel. In the case of Cornets and Ensigns, however, owing to the length of time which sometimes elapsed before a regimental vacancy occurred, or before an officer was first appointed permanently to his regiment, the date of army rank as Ensign, *i.e.* the date of first commission, has been given in parentheses in addition to the date of regimental rank.

Brevet rank. Promotion by brevet was given both as a reward for meritorious service, and for mere length of service. Subaltern officers of fifteen years' service in that rank were automatically promoted to the brevet rank of Captain. For a short period in the

---
[1] *Journal of the United Service Institution of India*, vol. xxxviii. (Oct. 1809), p. 521.

early thirties, Cadets for whom no vacancy had as yet occurred were appointed acting Ensigns after two years of actual service in India.[1] In all cases the date of brevet rank has been ignored here except when such brevet rank happens to be the highest rank attained at the date of casualty.

Some of the titles of rank, now obsolete, call for a few words of explanation.

Lieut. Colonel Commandant, i.e. Colonel regimentally. These officers, owing to the regulation which existed to the effect that the rank of Colonel should not be given till the officers of H.M. Army of similar standing had been promoted, received the pay and emoluments of a regimental full Colonel, without the rank. (G.G.O. of 28 July 1807.)

Capt.-Lieutenant. This rank was abolished in the Artillery and Infantry by G.O.C.C. of 9 Jan. 1819 ; it had already been abolished in the Engineers ten years previously. In the Infantry the Capt.-Lieutenant's commission was held by the senior subaltern of the two Bns., who was placed in charge of the Colonel's Coy.

Lieut.-Fireworker. This rank, peculiar to the Artillery, which was discontinued in the R.A. after 1 Jan. 1771, survived in the Bengal Art. down to the reorganization of the regiment in 1818, after which Fireworkers became 2nd Lieutenants.

Cornet and *Ensign.* These were the designations in use throughout the period with which we are dealing for the most junior rank in the Cavalry and the Infantry respectively. In the Corps of Engineers, Cadets were commissioned as Ensigns down to 1824, after which date the rank was changed to that of 2nd Lieut., to conform to the other scientific branch of the Service.

Brevet Ensign. Towards the close of the eighteenth century the rank of Brevet Ensign was sometimes conferred on deserving European Non-commissioned Officers as a reward for meritorious service. These Bt. Ensigns were usually posted to Sepoy Militia Corps, and were debarred from rising to any higher rank in the Service.

[1] This delay in commissioning Cadets and posting them to regiments is accounted for in this wise. Owing to the great distance between England and India, and, until the forties of the nineteenth century, the slow means of communication between the two countries, it was always considered necessary by the Court of Directors to have a number of young officers, supernumerary to the establishment, waiting in India so as to be ready to fill vacancies the moment they occurred. More particularly was this the case in earlier times, when the European officers were few, and the army was almost constantly on active service. The Barasat Cadet College, during its brief existence, provided the necessary waiting list; but after its abolition there was no reserve of youths in India whence replacements could be drawn as required. Hence this congestion of Cadets " doing duty," acting Ensigns, and unposted Ensigns.

During the first quarter of last century, the average length of service of officers on the Bengal Est. in the various grades was as follows :

Cornet or Ensign to Lieut.	6½ years
Lieut. to Capt.	15 years
Capt. Lt. to Capt.	2¼ years
Capt. to Major	8½ years
Major to Lt. Col.	6 years
Lt. Col. to Col.	12 years

A step of honorary or brevet rank on retirement was first granted by G.G.O. dated Fort William, 23 Mar. 1855. This Order, publishing a military letter from the Court of Directors to the Govt. of India, dated 7 Feb. 1855, contains the following pertinent paragraph : " The names of officers above the rank of captain who have already retired, or may hereafter retire from the service on full pay, are to be retained in the army list in italics ; and officers now on the retired full pay list, or hereafter retiring upon full pay, are to receive a step of brevet rank, but such officers cannot be further promoted." These brevet promotions, which carried with them no increase of pension, were to have effect from 28 Nov. 1854, that being the date assigned to the first promotions of a similar nature made in H.M.S. under the royal warrant of 6 Oct. 1854. A further royal warrant, dated 31 Jan. 1859, the provisions of which need not be recapitulated here, granted improved conditions of promotion to the ranks of Colonel and General officer.

It may here be noted, that although the Indian military service was one of pure seniority, that is to say, the sale and purchase of Commissions was not officially recognized, yet, owing to the slowness in promotion, a practice prevailed for many years during the first half of last century of offering the senior officers of a regiment a substantial sum to induce them to retire. A Major of an infantry regiment, who was willing to retire on obtaining his promotion to that rank, could usually command thirty thousand rupees from his juniors in the regiment. This sum was, of course, levied proportionately to the rank of those who would benefit by the vacancy. Thus the shares levied varied from twelve thousand rupees in the case of the senior Captain to one hundred and fifty in the case of the junior Ensign.

REORGANIZATION

Two only of the numerous reorganizations undergone by the Bengal army during the century terminating with the Mutiny of 1857 can be mentioned here. Both were of major importance, owing to the

REORGANIZATION

changes necessitated thereby in the numbering of regiments and battalions. It will be best to give these changes in tabular form.

REORGANIZATION OF 1796.

(Minutes of Council, 30 May 1796. G.O.C.C., 2 June 1796.)

New Designation.		Old Designation.				
Regiment.	Battalion.	Formed from the				
1st	1st	1st Bn.	and the	Right Wing	of	32nd Bn.
	2nd	13th ,,	,,	Left	,,	,,
2nd	1st	2nd ,,	,,	Right	,,	28th Bn.
	2nd	25th ,,	,,	Left	,,	,,
3rd	1st	3rd ,,	,,	Right	,,	27th Bn.
	2nd	22nd ,,	,,	Left	,,	,,
4th	1st	4th ,,	,,	Right	,,	37th Bn.
	2nd	31st ,,	,,	Left	,,	,,
5th	1st	5th ,,	,,	Right	,,	35th Bn.
	2nd	23rd ,,	,,	Left	,,	,,
6th	1st	6th ,,	,,	Right	,,	36th Bn.
	2nd	20th ,,	,,	Left	,,	,,
7th	1st	7th ,,	,,	Right	,,	24th Bn.
	2nd	16th ,,	,,	Left	,,	,,
8th	1st	8th ,,	,,	Right	,,	33rd Bn.
	2nd	30th ,,	,,	Left	,,	,,
9th	1st	9th ,,	,,	Right	,,	34th Bn.
	2nd	29th ,,	,,	Left	,,	,,
10th	1st	10th ,,	,,	Right	,,	18th Bn.
	2nd	14th ,,	,,	Left	,,	,,
11th	1st	11th ,,	,,	Right	,,	26th Bn.
	2nd	19th ,,	,,	Left	,,	,,
12th	1st	12th ,,	,,	Right	,,	21st Bn.
	2nd	17th ,,	,,	Left	,,	,,

Cavalry. At the date of the reorganization of 1796 the two existing regiments of cavalry were converted from irregular to regular corps. Two more regiments were raised during the course of the next few months, and on the completion of the cavalry brigade to four regiments the Native cavalry was for the first time separated from the infantry and declared a distinct service, its officers being promoted on a general cavalry list. (G.O.C.C. of 2 June 1797.) Shortly after the close of the Third Mahratta War the title "Light Cavalry" was substituted for "Native Cavalry."

REORGANIZATION OF 1824.
(G.G.O. of 6 May 1824.)

Old Number.			New Number.	Old Number.			New Number.
1st	1st Bn.	- -	2nd	18th	1st Bn.	- -	36th
	2nd Bn.	- -	4th		2nd Bn.	- -	37th
2nd	1st Bn.	- -	5th	19th	1st Bn.	- -	38th
	2nd Bn.	- -	22nd		2nd Bn.	- -	39th
3rd	1st Bn.	- -	6th	20th	1st Bn.	- -	25th
	2nd Bn.	- -	19th		2nd Bn.	- -	40th
4th	1st Bn.	- -	7th	21st	1st Bn.	- -	41st
	2nd Bn.	- -	23rd		2nd Bn.	- -	42nd
5th	1st Bn.	- -	11th	22nd	1st Bn.	- -	43rd
	2nd Bn.	- -	20th		2nd Bn.	- -	44th
6th	1st Bn.	- -	3rd	23rd	1st Bn.	- -	45th
	2nd Bn.	- -	18th		2nd Bn.	- -	46th
7th	1st Bn.	- -	13th	24th	1st Bn.	- -	47th
	2nd Bn.	- -	10th		2nd Bn.	-. -	48th
8th	1st Bn.	- -	9th	25th	1st Bn.	- -	49th
	2nd Bn.	- -	24th		2nd Bn.	- -	50th
9th	1st Bn.	- -	8th	26th	1st Bn.	- -	51st
	2nd Bn.	- -	21st		2nd Bn.	- -	52nd
10th	1st Bn.	- -	14th	27th	1st Bn.	- -	53rd
	2nd Bn.	- -	16th		2nd Bn.	- -	54th
11th	1st Bn.	- -	15th	28th	1st Bn.	- -	55th
	2nd Bn.	- -	17th		2nd Bn.	- -	56th
12th	1st Bn.	- -	12th	29th	1st Bn.	- -	57th
	2nd Bn.	- -	1st		2nd Bn.	- -	58th
13th	1st Bn.	- -	26th	30th	1st Bn.	- -	59th
	2nd Bn.	- -	27th		2nd Bn.	- -	60th
14th	1st Bn.	- -	28th	31st	1st Bn.	- -	61st
	2nd Bn.	- -	29th		2nd Bn.	- -	62nd
15th	1st Bn.	- -	30th	32nd	1st Bn.	- -	63rd
	2nd Bn.	- -	31st		2nd Bn.	- -	64th
16th	1st Bn.	- -	32nd	33rd	1st Bn.	- -	65th
	2nd Bn.	- -	33rd		2nd Bn.	- -	66th
17th	1st Bn.	- -	34th	34th	1st Bn.	- -	67th
	2nd Bn.	- -	35th		2nd Bn.	- -	68th

In 1825 (G.G.O. No. 149 of 13 May 1825) two Extra Regiments of Cavalry and twelve Extra Regiments of Infantry were ordered to be raised. The two former became 9th and 10th L.C. in 1826, in which year also the 7th to 12th Extra Inf. Regiments were reduced. The remaining six Extra Regiments became in 1828 the 69th to 74th N.I. The title "Local Horse" was changed to "Irregular Cavalry" by G.G.O. No. 276 of 23 Dec. 1840.

RETIREMENT REGULATIONS

THE following is a short abstract of the regulations governing retirement from the Service. They were instituted in 1793, and remained in force, with minor modifications, for over half a century.

"Every officer after twenty-five years' service in India, three years for one furlough being included, is allowed to retire with the pay of the rank to which he has attained; but such pay is to be the same only as that allowed to officers of infantry."

"Every Lieut. Col., Major, Capt., or Capt. Lt., is allowed to retire with the *half pay* of the rank to which he has attained, in case his health shall not permit him to serve in India."

"A Lieut. having served thirteen, or an Ensign nine years in India, including three years for a furlough, may retire on the *half pay* of his rank, in case his health shall not permit him to serve in India."

"A subaltern officer... having served six years in India, is permitted to retire on the *half pay of Ensign*, if his constitution should be so impaired as to prevent the possibility of his continuing in India."

THE SELECT PICKET

THE "Select Picket," which was in existence from *c.* 1772-5, was composed of Gentlemen Cadets for whom, on first arrival from Europe, there were as yet no vacancies as Ensigns. Such Cadets were formed into a separate Coy. and carried arms like a private soldier. The Select Picket was posted on the right of the advanced guard of the army in the field, and won for itself a distinguished reputation. In M.C., Fort William, of 17 Dec. 1772, are recorded some "Observations by the General on the Establishment of a Select Picquet for the Instruction of the Young Gentlemen Cadets on the Bengal Establishment," amongst which occurs the following sentence. "As this Corps is composed of a Sett of very promising young men, the Characters of such who offer themselves voluntarily in this Country should be strictly scrutinized, some of very indifferent reputation have crept into it, and the removal of such would be of great service to the Picquet."

STAFF APPOINTMENTS

Regimental Staff. From the date of the reorganization of the army in 1796, when the two-battalion regimental system was first introduced, down to 1814, the regimental staff consisted of the following : 1 Col. comdg. the Regt. 1 Adjt. and Qmr. for the whole Regt. 1 Lt. Col. comdg. each Bn. 1 Adjt. for each Bn.

In 1814 the appointment of regtl. Adjt. and Qmr. was abolished, an officer in each Bn. performing subsequently the combined duties of Interpreter and Qmr.

No notice, as a rule, has been taken here of acting, officiating, or temporary regtl. appointments.

Extra-regimental staff appointments. A few of these extra-regimental appointments, eagerly sought after as carrying with them enhanced pay and emoluments, and, in some cases, prospects, may be recorded here.

Superintendent of Mysore Princes. This appointment, which was of a political nature, was one of the most coveted in the Bengal army. It necessitated residence in or near Calcutta, the Princes, sons of Tippoo Sultan, who were taken as state prisoners after the final capture of Seringapatam in 1799, being lodged at Russapuglah in the suburbs of that city. The salary of the officer holding it was, by G.O. of 6 Nov. 1806, and of 20 Apr. 1809, fixed at sicca Rs.1,500 *p.m.*, with the pay and full batta of his regimental rank. At a later period the ex-Amirs of Sind and the Sikh Sirdars were also placed under the charge of this officer.

Stud Department. This Dept., which developed by degrees into the modern Army Remount Dept. in India, was formed in 1794 under the title of " The Board of Superintendence for improving the breed of Cattle," and was placed in charge of a Superintendent. It was enlarged in 1814 by the formation of new branches. In 1845 it consisted of two main branches, one for the C.P. and one for the N.W.P., each under a Supt. with various Asst. and Sub-Asst. Supts. under him.

Political employment, more particularly during Lord Ellenborough's term of office as Governor General. The late Lord Curzon, in his *British Government in India* (ii. 201), notes that " in the Nerbudda territories he (Lord E.) had dismissed the entire body of Civil Servants and replaced them by military officers." Under this heading is included the Dept. for the Suppression of Thuggee.

The Nizam of Hyderabad's army. Service in the Hyderabad Contingent, particularly in the Cavalry, offered many advantages. This was in great measure due to the fact that a Capt. or a Field officer in the Coy.'s army might command a Brigade in the Nizam's army, and a Capt., or even a Lieut., in the Coy.'s army might command a regiment in the Nizam's army.

The Governor General's Body Guard—the *corps d'élite* of the Bengal army from 1773 onwards.

Other appointments were : Comdt. of the Calcutta Native Militia ; Comdt. of the Delhi Palace Guards ; Town and Fort Major of Calcutta (which, from 1793 to 1813, was annexed to the office of J.A.G.) ; Fort Adjt. at Buxar, Chunar, Allahabad, and Fort William ; the Army Comst. Dept. ; the Ordnance Comst. Dept. ; and the Pay Dept., including the appointments of Paymaster and Supt. of Native Pensioners.

Two long-forgotten corps, the very names of which sound odd to modern ears, require brief mention.

The Dromedary Corps, raised in 1815 and disbanded, after performing useful service during the third Mahratta war, on 1 Oct. 1821. (G.O.C.C. of 18 Aug. 1821.)

The Rocket Troop of H.A. This Troop was formed in 1816 (G.G.O. of 13 Sept. 1816), the rockets being 12-pdrs., case or shell, carried mostly on camels until the year 1822, when horses were substituted. It ceased to be distinctively a Rocket Troop by G.G.O. of 13 June 1828. A coloured illustration of both of the above will be found in Fitzclarence's *Journal of a Route across India*, 1817-8, London 1819.

CHRONOLOGICAL LIST

of the more important campaigns, actions, and sieges in which the Bengal army was engaged, 1756-1868. (Compiled principally from Cardew's *Services of the Bengal Native Army*.) The references to the Hon. Sir John Fortescue's *History of the British Army* are given under each campaign. For an extended bibliography of works bearing on the various wars in India and the East, see Francis Edwards's *Military Literature*, pub. 1907-8.

(*Fortescue*, vol. ii. pp. 412-82.)

1756. June 15. Siege of Calcutta by Suraj-ud-Daula, ruler of Bengal.
June 20. Capture of Calcutta. Black Hole.
1757. Jan. 2. Recapture of Calcutta by Lt. Col. Robert Clive.
Feb. 5. Battle of Kasipur (Cossipore) nr. Calcutta; defeat of the Nawab Suraj-ud-Daula by Clive.
Mar. 23. Capture of the French settlement of Chandernagore by Clive.
June 18. Capture of Katwa (Cutwa) by Major Eyre Coote.
June 23. Battle of Plassey.
1758. EXPEDITION TO THE NORTHERN CIRCARS, under Lt.-Col. Francis Forde.
Dec. 8. Battle of Condore. Defeat of the French under the Marquis de Conflans.
Dec. 10. Rajamundry seized.
1759. Feb. 6. Ellore occupied.
Apr. 8. Storm of Masulipatam.
Nov. 25. Battle of Badara (Badra), nr. Chandernagore; defeat of the Dutch by Lt.-Col. Francis Forde.

(*Fortescue*, vol. iii. pp. 49-149.)

1760. WAR WITH SHAH ALAM, afterwards Emperor of Delhi.
Feb. 9. Battle of Masimpur, nr. Patna.
Feb. 22. Battle of Sirpur. Major Caillaud.
Apr. 28. Relief of Patna by Capt. Ranfurlie Knox.
June 16. Battle of Birpur. Capt. Ranfurlie Knox.
1761. Jan. 15. Battle of Suan, S. of Patna. Major John Carnac.
1763. WAR WITH MIR MUHAMMAD KASIM, Nawab of Bengal.
June 24-July 1. Fighting at Patna and Manjhi.
July 17. Defence of convoy nr. Katwa, on Adji R., by Lieut. William Glenn.

CHRONOLOGICAL LIST OF

1763. July 19. Battle of Katwa, nr. Plassey. Major Adams.
Aug. 2. Battle of Gheria. Major Adams.
Sept. 5. Battle of Udhua (Oondwa) Nullah. Major Adams.
Oct. 2. Capture of Monghyr. Major Adams.
Oct. 5 or 10/11. Patna massacre.
Oct. 28. Siege of Patna. Major Adams.
Nov. 6. Capture of Patna.

1764. CAMPAIGNS AGAINST THE NAWABS OF BENGAL AND OUDH (Mir Muhammad Kasim and Shuja-ud-Daulah).
May 3. Battle of Patna. Major John Carnac.
Oct. 16. Cavalry action nr. the Bunas Nullah. Major Hector Munro.
Oct. 23. Battle of Buxar. Major H. Munro.
Dec. 2 and 4. Assaults on fort of Chunar. Major Charles Pemble.

1765. Feb. 8. Surrender of Chunar. Major Giles Stibbert.
Feb. 11. Capture of Allahabad. Sir Robert Fletcher.
May 22. Battle of Kalpi (against the Mahrattas). Sir Robert Fletcher.

1767-9. FIRST MYSORE WAR, against Haidar Ali. Expedition to the N. Circars. Operations in Baramahal and Mysore, under Bdr.-Gen. Joseph Smith.

1768. Feb. Operations in the Nizam's dominions.
May-June. Chicacole and Kimedi, against Narayan Deo.
May 24. Defeat of Narayan Deo.
May 30. Capture of fort of Jalumur.

1769. Operations in the Ganjam district.
1770-3. OPERATIONS AGAINST THE SANIYASIS.
1772-3. OPERATIONS AGAINST THE BHUTIAS IN COOCH BEHAR.
1772. Dec. 21. Storm and capture of Cooch Behar. Capt. John Jones.
1773. Apr. Storm and capture of Dhalimkot.
1774. FIRST ROHILLA WAR.
Apr. 23. Battle of St. George (Miranpur-Katra). Col. Alexander Champion.

1776. OPERATIONS IN THE DOAB, against Mahbub Khan.
June 10. Battle of Korah. Lt.-Col. J. N. Parker.

(*Fortescue*, vol. iii. pp. 428-98.)

1778-84. FIRST MAHRATTA WAR. Detachment under Lt.-Col. Matthew Leslie (afterwards superseded by Col. Thomas Goddard) left Cawnpore in May 1778 for Bombay, returning to Calcutta in Apr. 1784.

1780. Jan. 19. Capture of Dabhoi.
Feb. 10-15. Siege of Ahmedabad.
Feb. 15. Storm and capture of Ahmedabad.
Mar. Operations against Sindhia and Holkar nr. Pawangarh.
Apr. 3. Capture of camp of Sindhia and Holkar.
Dec. 11. Capture of Bassein, after one month's siege.

CAMPAIGNS, ACTIONS AND SIEGES

1781.	Feb.	Forcing of Bhor Ghaut.
	Apr.	Retreat down the Bhor Ghaut.
1780-1.	Operations of Major William Popham's detachment.	
1780.	Apr. 20.	Capture of fort of Lahar.
	Aug. 3.	Storm and capture of Gwalior.
	(Popham relieved by Lt.-Col. Jacob Camac at end of 1780.)	
1781.	Mar. 24.	Action at Mahatpur.
1781-5.	SECOND MYSORE WAR. Expedition to Madras, under Col. Thomas Deane Pearse. Returned in Jan. 1785.	
1781.	Aug. 27.	Battle of Pollilur.
	Sept. 29.	Battle of Sholingarh.
	Oct. 23.	Battle of Virakandalur.
1782.	Jan. 11.	Relief of Vellore.
1783.	June 11.	Siege of Cuddalore.
1781.	CAMPAIGN AGAINST THE RAJAH OF BENARES.	
	Aug. 16.	Outbreak at Benares.
	Aug. 20.	Action at Ramnagar.
	Sept. 4.	Action at Patita. Capt. Thomas Blair.
	Sept.	Capture of Patita. Major William Popham.
	Sept. 20.	Action at Lora. Major William Joseph Crabb.
	Sept. 20.	Action at the Sukrut Pass.
	Nov. 10.	Capture of Bijaigarh, C.I. Major William Popham.
1791.	EXPEDITION TO KEDAH, PENANG. Lieut. Thomas Williamson.	
	Apr. 12.	Action at Point Pria fort, against pirates.

(*Fortescue*, vol. iii. pp. 549-612.)

1790-2.	THIRD MYSORE WAR.	
1790.	Sept. 13.	Action at Satyamangalam.
1791.	Mar. 6-21.	Siege and capture of Bangalore.
	May 14.	Battle of Arikera.
	Sept. 22.	Siege of Nandidrug commenced.
	Oct. 18.	Nandidrug captured.
	Oct. 31.	Storm of Penagra, in the Baramahal.
	Nov. 8.	Unsuccessful assault of Krishnagiri.
	Dec.	Operations before Savandrug.
	Dec. 24.	Storm of Utradrug.
1792.	Feb. 6/7.	Capture of Seringapatam.
1793-4	EXPEDITION TO ASSAM. Capt. Thomas Welsh.	
1793.	Recapture of Gauhati.	
1794.	Apr. 13.	Skirmish nr. Goalpara.
	July.	Troops withdrawn from Assam.
1794.	SECOND ROHILLA WAR. Sir Robert Abercromby.	
	Oct. 26.	Battle of Bitaurah.
1795-6.	CAPTURE OF CEYLON. Col. James Stuart, H.M. 72nd Regt.	
1795.	Dec.	Surrender of Trincomalee.
1796.	Feb. 15.	Colombo capitulated.

(*Fortescue*, vol. iv. pp. 711-68.)

1798-9. FOURTH MYSORE WAR.
1798. Detachment under Major Henry Hyndman sent to Hyderabad.
Oct. 22. Employed in disarming and reducing about 14,000 of the Nizam's troops, formed by M. Raymond and officered by Frenchmen.
1799. Force from Bengal proceeded to Madras by sea, under Maj.-Gen. William Popham.
Mar. 27. Battle of Malavelli.
May 4. Storm and capture of Seringapatam.
The Bengal detachment was subsequently employed under Col. Hon. A. Wellesley in the country on the N. frontier of Mysore, and returned to Bengal in May 1800.
1799. OPERATIONS AGAINST WAZIR ALI, ex-Nawab of Oudh.
Jan. 14. Insurrection at Benares ; murder of Mr. Cherry, the British Resident, and others.
Subsequent operations in the E. districts of Oudh.

(*Fortescue*, vol. iv. pp. 800-63.)

1801. EXPEDITION TO EGYPT. Maj.-Gen. David Baird.
Feb. Bengal detachment sailed from Bombay, returning to India in July and Aug. 1802.
1801. EXPEDITION TO TERNATE, SPICE Is., under Lieut. William Gill.
June 21. Surrender of Ternate fort and island.
1801. DISTURBANCES IN GUMSUR, GANJAM, MADRAS. 1st and 2nd 6th N.I., under Lt.-Col. Bennet Marley.
1801-2. EXPEDITION TO MACAO, CHINA. 4th Coy. 1st Bn. Art., under Capt. Andrew Fraser.
1801. Sailed for Macao.
1802. Nov. Returned to Bengal, no fighting having taken place.
1802-3. OPERATIONS IN THE JUMNA DOAB against refractory zemindars. Known as the " Mud War."
1802. Dec. 12. Siege of Sasni commenced. Lt.-Col. Robert Blair. Against Rajah Bhagwant Singh.
1803. Jan. 14. Sasni unsuccessfully assaulted. Maj.-Gen. Hon. F. St. John ; later Lord Lake.
Feb. 8. Sasni town captured.
Feb. 11. Sasni fort evacuated by the enemy.
Feb. 27. Bijaigarh fort evacuated by the enemy.
Mar. 13. Kachaura fort reduced.
Sept. 30. Thathia fort (Rajah Chattar Sal) unsuccessfully attacked. Lt.-Col. John Guthrie.

(*Fortescue*, vol. v. pp. 138-64.)

1803-4. OPERATIONS IN CEYLON against the King of Kandy. Maj.-Gen. Hay Macdowall. Two Coys. Bengal Art.

CAMPAIGNS, ACTIONS AND SIEGES xlv

1803. Jan. 31. Force left Colombo.
Feb. 21. Occupation of Kandy.
Mar. 14. Taking of Hangeramkatty.
June 26. Massacre of garrison of Kandy.
1804. Oct. Both Coys. Art. left Ceylon.

(*Fortescue*, vol. v. pp. 3-137.)

1803-6. SECOND MAHRATTA WAR (" Lord Lake's campaign ").
1803. Aug. 29. Skirmish at Koil, nr. Aligarh.
Sept. 4. Storm and capture of Aligarh.
Sept. 11. Battle of Delhi.
Oct. 17. Surrender of Agra fort.
Nov. 1. Battle of Laswari.
1803. Operations against Rajah Shamsher Bahadur. Occupation of Bundelkhand by Lt.-Col. Peregrine Powell.
Oct. 12. Action at Kapsa.
Dec. 4. Capture of Kalpi.
1803. Reduction of Cuttack by Lt.-Col. G. W. R. Harcourt, 12th Ft.
Oct. 10. Surrender of Cuttack.
Oct. 14. Assault and capture of Barabati fort.
1803. Minor operations to S.W. of Delhi, under Lt.-Col. George Ball. Reduction of Narnaul, Kanun, and other places.
1803. Operations in the Baghelkhand district.
Nov. 20. Reduction of Chaukandi fort, C.I.
1803. Operations at the head of the Doab, about the Karnal district, under Lt.-Col. William Burn.
1803. Operations on the frontier towards Nagpur, under Lt.-Col. Edward Swift Broughton.
Dec. 31. Capture of Sambalpur.
1804. Jan. Siege of Gwalior. Lt.-Col. Henry White.
Feb. 2. Capture of Gwalior.
May 15. Taking of Rampura. Lt.-Col. Patrick Don.
Operations of Col. Monson's detachment.
July 2. Capture of Hinglaisgarh fort. Major James Sinclair.
July 8-Aug. 31. Retreat of Monson's force to Agra.
Aug. 21-24. Actions with Holkar on Banas R.
1804. Operations in Bundelkhand, under Lt.-Col. W. D. Fawcett.
May 22. Amir Khan cuts off a party of 50 Art. and two Coys. 1/18th N.I. engaged in besieging Bela fort, nr. Kunch.
Fawcett superseded by Lt.-Col. Gabriel Martindell.
July 2. Defeat of Rajah Ram Singh.
July 28. Storm and capture of Jaitpur.
1804. Oct. 8-14. Defence of Delhi. Lt.-Col. William Burn.
Nov. 13. Battle of Deig.
Nov. 17. Surprise of the Mahratta camp at Farrukhabad.
Dec. 24. Capture of Deig.
1805. Jan. 2-Apr. 16. Siege of Bhurtpore (Bharatpur).
Jan. 9. First assault.

xlvi   CHRONOLOGICAL LIST OF

1805.   Jan. 21. Second assault.
        Feb. 20. Third assault.
        Feb. 21. Fourth assault.
        Feb. Attack by enemy on convoy at Kumher, nr. Bhurtpore.
1804.   Operations in Cuttack against the Rajah of Khurda.
        Oct. 19. Action at Dillori. Capt. John Hickland.
        Dec. 7. Storm and capture of Khurda.
1804.   Operations to N. of Delhi against Sher Singh. Lt.-Col. William Burn.
        Nov. 23. Action at Deoband ; defeat of Sher Singh.
1805.   Operations of Capt. Charles Hutchinson's detachment, left behind at Tonk (Rampura) by Monson.
        Jan. 18. Capture of Khataoli.
        Feb. 24. Capture of Bhamangaon.
        Feb. 26. Capture of Karawal.
        Mar. 21. Capture of Dhalra.
1805.   Mar. 2. Cavalry action at Afzalgarh.
1805.   Operations against Rajah Khushal Rao, under Capt. William Henry Royle.
        Apr. 7. Defeat of Khushal Rao at Adalatnagar.
1805-6. Pursuit of Holkar to the Punjab. Lord Lake.
1806.   OPERATIONS AGAINST THE RANA OF GOHAD, C.I., under Lt.-Col. Robert Bowie.
        Feb. 22. Capture of Gohad fort.
1806.   OPERATIONS AGAINST APPARBAL SINGH at Badekh, nr. Kalpi, under Capt. John Owen.
        Oct. 21. Badekh unsuccessfully stormed. Apparbal Singh surrendered shortly afterwards.
1807.   OPERATIONS AGAINST CHAMIR FORT, nr. Kunch, Bundelkhand, under Lt.-Col. Thomas Hawkins.
        Jan. 29. Storm and capture of Chamir fort.
1807.   OPERATIONS IN BUNDELKHAND, under Lt.-Col. Thomas Hawkins.
        Nov. 13. Capture of Sehlehuganj fort, nr. Kaitha, C.I.
1807.   OPERATIONS AGAINST DHUNDIA KHAN, under Maj.-Gen. Richard Mark Dickens, H.M. 34th Ft.
        Oct. 12. Fort Komona invested.
        Nov. 18. Assault of Komona ; fort evacuated the following night.
        Nov. 23. Fort Ganauri invested.
        Dec. 11. Surrender of Ganauri fort.
1807-8. OPERATIONS IN OUDH.
        Mar. Akbarpur taken by storm by Major Henry Anderson O'Donnell.
        Apr. Fort Bhadri subdued by Lt.-Col. Robert Gregory.
        May. Forts Samanpur and Gurha subdued by Lt.-Col. Robert Gregory.
        Oct. Pathar-serai subdued by Major H. A. O'Donnell.

CAMPAIGNS, ACTIONS AND SIEGES xlvii

1808. EXPEDITION TO MACAO, under Capt. Thomas Matthias Weguelin.
Aug. Force, consisting of one Vol. Bn., sailed.
Oct. 20. Landed at Macao.
Dec. 23. Re-embarked for India.
1809. Feb. Force returned to India.
1809. Feb. 16. Attack by Akali Sikhs on Mr. Metcalfe's escort at Amritsar.
1808. Dec. 19. Capture of Hirapur fort, Tikamgarh district, C.I., by Major William Cuppage.
1809. OPERATIONS IN BUNDELKHAND AGAINST LACHMAN DAWA, Chief of Ajaigarh. Lt.-Col. Gabriel Martindell.
Jan. 22. Storm of Rajaoli.
Feb. 13. Surrender of fort of Ajaigarh.
1809. SETTLEMENT OF HARIANA ; operations against the Jats, under Lt.-Col. George Ball.
Aug. 29. Assault and capture of Bhawani.
1809. Autumn. Occupation of Nanpara, in Oudh, without opposition.
1809-10. OPERATIONS IN OUDH, under Lt.-Col. John McGrath.
1810. Jan. 4. Assault of Pragpur, Bahraich district, U.P.
1810-1. OPERATIONS IN BUNDELKHAND AGAINST GOPAL SINGH.
1810. Feb. 18. Action at Parari, nr. Kakarati. Capt. Edward Pitches Wilson.
Mar. 19. Defeat of Gopal Singh at Bichaund. Lt.-Col. Thomas Brown.
Various other minor actions during 1810 and 1811.

(*Fortescue*, vol. vii. pp. 597-629.)

1810. EXPEDITION TO MAURITIUS (I. of France).
Aug. Force, consisting of two Vol. Bns., sailed.
Nov. 29. Disembarked in Grande Baye.
Dec. 1. Port Louis surrendered.
1811. EXPEDITION TO JAVA.
Mar. Force embarked.
Aug. 4. Landed at Chilling-Ching.
Aug. 8. Batavia occupied.
Aug. 10. Action at Weltervreden.
Aug. 26. Capture of fortified lines at Cornelis.
Sept. 16. Action at Jati Ali.
Sept. 17. Surrender of the Island.
1811. OPERATIONS AGAINST THE RAJAH OF BARDI, in Rewah. Lt.-Col. James Tetley.
End of the year. Unsuccessful attack on Bhapawi fort.
1812. REDUCTION OF KALINJAR, 20 m. S.E. of Banda, by Col. Gabriel Martindell.
Feb. 2. Storm of Kalinjar fort.
Feb. 3. Surrender of Kalinjar.

CHRONOLOGICAL LIST OF

1812-3. OPERATIONS IN JAVA, SUMATRA, ETC.
1812. Expedition to Palembang, Sumatra, under Col. Robert Rollo Gillespie, H.M.S.
Mar. 20. Force sailed from Batavia.
Apr. 26. Palembang captured.
June 1. Expedition arrived back at Batavia.
1812. Operations against the Sultan of Mataram, under Col. R. R. Gillespie.
June 20. Capture of Jokyakarta.
1813. Expedition against Sambas, Borneo.
June 28. Capture of Sambas.
Aug. Attack on Ceram, Moluccas.
1813. OPERATIONS IN BAGHELKHAND AGAINST SARNAID SINGH. Lt.-Col. John Withington Adams.
Dec. 4. Storm and capture of Entauri fort.

(*Fortescue*, vol. xi. pp. 109-62.)

1814-5. NEPAL WAR. (First phase.)
1814. Oct. 31. Repulse at Kalanga. (2nd Div.)
Nov. 27. Second unsuccessful assault of Kalanga.
Nov. 30. Kalanga evacuated by the Gurkhas.
Nov.-Dec. Operations against Amar Singh. (1st Div.)
Dec. 27. Unsuccessful attack on Jaithak. (2nd Div.)
1815. Jan. 1. Disasters at Samanpur and Pursa. (4th Div.)
Jan. 3. Unsuccessful attack on Jitpur. (3rd Div.)
Feb.-Apr. Operations in Kumaon.
Apr. 25. Capture of Almora, completing conquest of Kumaon.
Apr. 14-6. Taking of Malaun. (1st Div.)
1816. NEPAL WAR. (Second Phase.)
Feb. 28. Action at Makwanpur. Centre Column, under Sir David Ochterlony.
Mar. 1. Action at Harriharpur. Right Column, under Col. William Kelly, H.M. 24th Ft.
1816. Apr. Insurrection at Bareilly.
1816. CUTTACK INSURRECTION. Operations against Jagbandhu in the Khurda district, under Capt. Philippe Le Fevre.
Apr. 2. Repulse at Ganjpura.
Apr. Subsequent operations under Sir Gabriel Martindell.
1816. OPERATIONS AGAINST THE RAJAH OF BONI, in Celebes, under Major D. H. Dalton.
June 8. Defeat of the Rajah at the entrance of the Baliangan Pass, 8 m. from Macassar.
1817. OPERATIONS AGAINST DYARAM, taluqdar of Hathras, Aligarh district, under Maj.-Gen. Dyson Marshall.
Feb. 12. Investment of Hathras.
Mar. 2. Capture of Hathras fort.
1818. Sept.-Oct. OPERATIONS AGAINST THE BHATTIS OF HARIANA, under Col. John Arnold.

CAMPAIGNS, ACTIONS AND SIEGES xlix

(*Fortescue*, vol. xi. pp. 163-254.)

1817-9. THIRD MAHRATTA WAR. (Pindari War. "Deccan.")
1817. Nov. 26-7. Battle of Sitabaldi.
Dec. 16. Battle of Nagpur.
Dec. 19-24. Siege of Nagpur.
1818. Jan. 29. Storm and capture of Jawad by Maj.-Gen. Thomas Brown.
Mar. 19-24. Siege and capture of Dhamoni by Maj.-Gen. Dyson Marshall.
Apr. 18-26. Siege and storm of Mandala by Marshall.
May 21. Storm and capture of Chanda fort by Bdr.-Gen. John Withington Adams.
June 8-9. Repulse at Satanwara, C.I.
July 1-2. Siege of Taragarh.
July 20. Disaster at Multai. (One Coy. 2/10th N.I. cut up.)
July 27. Capture of Madhurajpura by Lt.-Col. William Augustus Thompson.
Aug. 1. Multai retaken by Major Alexander Cumming.
Aug. 24. Action at Harna. Capt. Thomas Newton.
Aug. Defeat of a large band of the enemy at Junagarhi by Lieut. John Cruikshank.
1819. Operations against the *kiladar* of Asirgarh.
Mar. 17. Siege of Asirgarh begun.
Apr. 6. Surrender of Asirgarh fort.
1820. OPERATIONS IN ROHILKHAND AGAINST BHOJA SINGH.
Mar. Action on banks of the Chuka nullah. Lieut. Aynott Chitty, with detachment of 1st Rohilla Cav.
1821. Feb.-Apr. OPERATIONS AGAINST THE LARKA KOLS IN SINGH-BHUM DISTRICT, B. & O., under Lt.-Col. William Richards.
1821. OPERATIONS AGAINST MAHARAO KISHOR SINGH, of Kotah, Rajputana.
Oct. 1. Action at Mangrol, Kotah.
1822. OPERATIONS IN OUDH AGAINST KASIM ALI KHAN, under Major William Conrad Faithfull.
Feb. 9. Bardgaon bombarded and captured.
1823. OPERATIONS IN JODHPUR TERRITORY, under Bdr. Alexander Knox.
Mar. 17. Capture of Lamba fort.

(*Fortescue*, vol. xi. pp. 269-352.)

1824-6. FIRST BURMA WAR.
1824. Operations in Sylhet and Cachar.
Jan. 17. Action at Bikrampur. Major Thomas Newton.
Feb. 13. Action at Bhadrapur. Capt. Joseph Johnston.
Feb. 21. Repulse at Dudhpatli. Lt.-Col. Herbert Bowen.
Operations in Burma.
May 11. Capture of Rangoon.

CHRONOLOGICAL LIST OF

1824. Dec. 5. Action at Shwe-Dagon Pagoda, Rangoon.
Dec. 15. Action at Kokein.
Operations in Chittagong district.
May 17. Disaster at Ramu. Capt. Thomas Noton.
Operations in Assam.
Mar. Advance of force under Lt.-Col. George Macmorine.
End of year. Advance of force under Lt.-Col. Alfred Richards.
1825. Jan. 29. Occupation of Rangpur by Lt.-Col. Richards.
Operations of Cachar force.
Feb. and Mar. Advance under Bdr.-Gen. Shuldham.
Conquest of Arakan by Bdr.-Gen. Morrison.
Jan. 1. Force marched from Chittagong.
Mar. 29. Attack on Arakan.
Apr. 1. Capture of Arakan.
Operations in Burma.
Mar. 7. Attack on Donabyu.
Apr. 2. Occupation of Donabyu.
Apr. 25. Prome occupied without opposition.
Dec. 1, 2, 5. Prome attacked by the Burmese.
1826. Feb. 9. Action at Paghamyu (Pagan); final defeat of the Burmese.

(*Fortescue*, vol. xi. pp. 353-69.)

1825-6. Operations against Durjan Sal; SIEGE AND CAPTURE OF BHURTPORE by Lord Combermere.
1825. Dec. 5. Operations begun.
1826. Jan. 18. Assault and capture of Bhurtpore.
1829-32. OPERATIONS AGAINST THE KHASIAS.
1829. Apr. 4. Attack on Nonghkhlao, Assam, by Khasias.
Subsequent desultory conflict with the Khasias until 1832.
1830. INCURSION OF SINGPHOS from Hukong into Upper Assam; operations resulting in their expulsion.
1831. WAHABI RISING.
Nov. 19. Defeat and dispersal of the Wahabi fanatics at Hooghly, nr. Calcutta.
1832. OPERATIONS AGAINST THE KOLS, of Chota Nagpur.
1832. OPERATIONS AGAINST THE CHUARS under their leader, Ganga Narayan. Col. John Wells Fast, comdg. Jungle Mehal F.F.
1834. Nov. 20-end of Dec. SHEKHAWAT EXPEDITION, under Bdr.-Gen. R. Stevenson, H.M.S.
1836. RISING IN CUTTACK.
1838-9. REDUCTION OF JHANSI by Maj.-Gen. Sir Thomas Anburey.
1838. Dec. Siege of Jhansi begun.
1839. Jan. 5. Jhansi evacuated by the Rani.
1838-40. FIRST AFGHAN WAR. (First phase.) Lt.-Gen. Sir John Keane, with " Army of the Indus."
1838. Dec. 10. Force left Ferozepore.

CAMPAIGNS, ACTIONS AND SIEGES   li

1839. Feb. 20. Arrived Shikarpur.
      Mar. 16. Entered Bolan Pass.
      Mar. 26. Arrived Quetta.
      Apr. 26. Arrived Kandahar.
      May 8.   Shah Shuja-ul-Mulk installed as Amir of Afghanistan.
      June 27. Left Kandahar.
      July 21. Arrived Ghazni.
      July 23. Storm and capture of Ghazni.
      July 30. March to Kabul.
      Forcing of Khyber Pass and capture of Ali Masjid by Col. Claude Martin Wade.
      Sept. Part of the Bengal troops returned to India with Sir John Keane through the Khyber Pass, arriving at Peshawar in November.
1840. Jan. 1.   Arrived Ferozepore.
      Jan. 2.   " Army of the Indus " broken up.
1839. Operations against Mehrab Khan, the Baluch Khan of Kalat, under Maj.-Gen. Thomas Willshire, H.M.S.
      Nov. 13. Storm and capture of Kalat.
1840. Operations against Sayyid Husain, Padshah of Kunar, under Lt.-Col. Joseph Orchard.
      Jan. 18. Storm of Pashut repulsed.
      Jan. 19. Fort evacuated by the enemy and occupied.
      Operations against the Ghilzais, under Capt. William Anderson.
      May 16.   Action near Tazi, on Turnak R.
      Kalat-i-Ghilzai occupied.
      Aug. 19. Capture of Kajja fort by Lt.-Col. Hugh Massy Wheeler.
      Sept. 18. Action at Bamian. Bdr. William Henry Dennie, H.M. 13th L.I.
      Operations in Kohistan, under Bdr. Sir Robert Sale.
      Sept. 29. Attack on Tutam-dara, nr. Charikar.
      Oct. 3.   Storm of Julgah repulsed; fort evacuated by the enemy.
      Nov. 2.   Action at Parwandara, nr. Ghorband Pass; misbehaviour of two Sqdns. 2nd L.C.
      Nov. 3.   Dost Muhammad Khan, the ex-Amir, surrendered himself at Kabul, and was sent to India.
      Sept.-Oct. Operations in Baluchistan.
      Nov. 3.   Re-occupation of Kalat by Maj.-Gen. William Nott.
1841-2. FIRST AFGHAN WAR. (Second phase.)
1841. Feb. Operations in the Nazian valley, under Col. John Shelton, H.M.S., against the Sangu Khel Shinwaris.
       Apr. Operations against the Ghilzais.
       July. Operations against the Duranis.
       Aug. 5. Defeat of Ghilzais at Karatu by Lt.-Col. Robert Ewbank Chambers.
       Operations of Bdr. Sale's Brigade.

CHRONOLOGICAL LIST OF

1841.
    Oct. 12. Forcing of Kurd Kabul Pass.
    Oct. 28. Forcing of Jagdalak Pass.
    Nov. 13. Sale occupied Jalalabad.
    Nov.-Dec. Occupation and defence of Jalalabad.
    Nov. 1-13. Defence of Charikar.
    Kabul outbreak and disaster.
    Nov. 2. Beginning of the outbreak.

1842.
    Jan. 6. Retreat to Jalalabad through the Khurd Kabul, Tangi Tariki, and Jagdalak passes begun.
    Jan. 13. Complete annihilation of the Kabul force.
    Jan. 19. Repulse in Khyber Pass of force under Bdr. Charles Frederick Wild.
    Jan. 24. Retreat from Ali Masjid to Jamrud of two Bns. under Lt.-Col. George Weyland Moseley.
    Gen. Pollock's advance.
    Apr. 5. Force marched from Peshawar. Khyber Pass forced.
    Apr. 16. Arrived Jalalabad, where Sale's "Illustrious Garrison" had already, on Apr. 7, practically effected its own relief.

1841-2. Defence of Ghazni. Lt.-Col. Thomas Palmer.
1841.
    Nov. 20. Insurgents appeared before Ghazni.
    Dec. 7. Siege begun.
1842.
    Mar. 6. Ghazni surrendered to the enemy; British officers taken prisoner.
    Mar.-May. Fighting round Kandahar. Maj.-Gen. Nott.
    Nott's advance on Kabul.
    Aug. 10. Force left Kandahar.
    Aug. 30. Action at Karabagh, nr. Goaine.
    Sept. 4. Arrived Ghazni.
    Sept. 5. Ghazni evacuated by the enemy.
    Sept. 17. Arrived Kabul (two days after Pollock).
    Pollock's advance on Kabul.
    Aug. 20. Force left Jalalabad.
    Aug. 24. Action at Mamu Khel.
    Sept. 8. Action at Jagdalak.
    Sept. 12-3. Actions at Tazin and Haft Kotal.
    Sept. 15. Arrived Kabul.
    Sept. 22. Our prisoners released and reached Pollock's camp.
    Sept. 29. Capture of Istalif, Kohistan. Maj.-Gen. Sir John McCaskill, H.M.S.
    Oct. Evacuation of Afghanistan.
    Oct. 12. Return march begun.
    Oct. 18. Action on heights above Jagdalak Pass.

1840-2. FIRST CHINA WAR. ("Opium War.")
1840.
    Apr. Expedition sailed.
    July 5. I. of Chusan occupied.

CAMPAIGNS, ACTIONS AND SIEGES

1841.	Jan. 7.	Capture of Fort Chuenpee, situated on an island in Canton R.
	Feb.	Attacks on forts at mouth of Canton R.
	May 24.	Capture of Canton.
1842.	July 21.	Capture of Chin-kiang Foo.
1840-2.	DISTURBANCES IN BUNDELKHAND.	
1840.	Mar. 10.	Capture of Jigni by Lt.-Col. W. F. Beatson.
1841.	Apr.	Storm and capture of Chirgaon, U.P., by Beatson.
1842.	Apr.	Action near Malthon, C.P.
	June.	Action at Panwari, U.P., against Bundela insurgents.
	Dec.	Action at Bhagaura, near Jaitpur, U.P.
1843.	CAMPAIGN IN SIND against the Baluch Amirs. Maj.-Gen. Sir Charles Napier.	
	Feb. 17.	Battle of Miani.
	Mar. 24.	Battle of Hyderabad.
1843.	OPERATIONS AT KAITHAL in the Karnal district.	
	Apr. 9.	Outbreak at Kaithal.
	Subsequent operations in the district.	
1843.	GWALIOR CAMPAIGN.	
	Dec. 29.	Battle of Maharajpur. Right Wing, under Sir Hugh Gough, H.M.S.
	Dec. 29.	Battle of Paniar. Left Wing, under Maj.-Gen. John Grey, H.M.S.
1844-5.	OPERATIONS ON N. SIND FRONTIER against the Hill Tribes.	
1845.	Jan. 15.	Cavalry action at Uch, Bahawalpur.
	Mar. 9.	Reduction of Trakki fort.
1845-6.	FIRST SIKH WAR (Sutlej Campaign).	
1845.	Dec. 18.	Battle of Mudki.
	Dec. 21-2.	Battle of Ferozshahr.
1846.	Jan. 21.	Affair at Badhowal.
	Jan. 28.	Battle of Aliwal.
	Feb. 10.	Battle of Sobraon.
1848-9.	SECOND SIKH WAR (Punjab Campaign).	
1848.	Sept.	Siege of Multan.
	Sept.	Disturbances in the Jullundur Doab.
	Nov. 22.	Affair at Ramnagar.
	Dec. 3.	Action at Sadulapur.
	Dec. 25.	Siege of Multan begun.
1849.	Jan. 2.	Storm of Multan city.
	Jan. 22.	Surrender of Multan.
	Jan. 13.	Battle of Chilianwala.
	Feb. 21.	Battle of Gujerat.
1848-9.	Operations in the Jullundur Doab, under Bdr.-Gen. Hugh Massy Wheeler.	
1848.	Oct. 14.	Capture of Rangar Nagal fort.
	Nov. 22-3.	Capture of Kalalwala.
	Dec. 2.	Action at Amb.
	Dec. 28.	Action at Budi Pind.

CHRONOLOGICAL LIST OF

1849. Jan. 16. Action on the heights of Dalla.
1852-3. SECOND BURMA WAR. Maj.-Gen. Henry Thomas Godwin, H.M.S.
1852. Apr. 5. Capture of Martaban.
Apr. 14. Capture of Rangoon.
May 19. Capture of Bassein.
Oct. Capture of Prome.
Nov. 21. Capture of Pegu.
Dec. 5-14. Siege of Pegu by the Burmese.
Dec. 14. Relief of Pegu.
1853. Feb. 4. Repulse at Donabyu.
Mar. Operations against Myat Toon.
1855. SANTHAL REVOLT. Maj.-Gen. George William Aylmer Lloyd and Bdr.-Gen. Louis Saunders Bird.
July-Dec. Suppression of the revolt.
1857-8. INDIAN MUTINY CAMPAIGN.
1857. May 10. Outbreak of the mutiny at Meerut.
June-Sept. Siege of Delhi.
Sept. 14. Storm and capture of Delhi.
Aug. 25. Battle of Najafgarh.
July-Aug. Havelock's advance from Allahabad to relief of Lucknow.
June-Sept. Defence of Lucknow (first phase).
June 30. Action at Chinhat.
June 30. Defence of Lucknow Residency. Sir Henry Lawrence.
Sept. 25. First Relief of Lucknow by Havelock and Outram.
Sept. 28. Action at Bulandshahr.
Oct. 10. Action at Agra.
Nov. 17. Action at Narnaul.
Sept.-Nov. 18. Defence of Lucknow (second phase).
Nov. 14-8. Second Relief of Lucknow by Sir Colin Campbell.
Dec. Operations of Col. Thomas Seaton's Column.
1857-8. Operations in Central India under Sir Hugh Rose.
1858. Jan. and Feb. Defence of Alambagh. Sir James Outram.
Mar. 2-21. Capture of Lucknow. Sir Colin Campbell.
Apr.-Aug. Rohilkhand campaign.
May-Dec. Oudh campaign.
1858-60. SECOND CHINA WAR.
1858. June. White Cloud Mountain operations.
Aug. Expedition to Namtow.
1859. Jan. Action as Shek-tsin.
EXPEDITIONS ON THE NORTH-WEST FRONTIER.[1]
1849. Dec. Against the Baizais, a Swat clan.
1850. Feb. Against the Kohat Pass Afridis. Sir Charles Napier.
1851-2. Against the Mohmands. Sir Colin Campbell.

[1] See *Campaigns on the North-West Frontier*, by Capt. H. L. Nevill, D.S.O. London, John Murray, 1912.

CAMPAIGNS, ACTIONS AND SIEGES lv

1852.　　Mar.　Against the Ranizais.　Sir Colin Campbell.
　　　　　May.　Against the Utman Khel.
　　　　　Dec.　Against the Waziris.　Major John Nicholson.
1852-3.　Against the Hassanzais of the Black Mountain.　Lt.-Col. Frederick Mackeson.
1853.　　Against the Hindustani Fanatics.
　　　　　Against the Shiranis.
　　　　　Against the Kasranis.　Bdr.-Gen. John Studholme Hodgson.
　　　　　Nov.　Against the Jowaki Afridis.
1854-5.　Against the Mohmands.
1855.　　Against the Aka Khel Afridis.　Lt.-Col. John Craigie-Halkett.
　　　　　Against the Urakzais.　Bdr.-Gen. Neville Bowles Chamberlain.
1855-6.　Operations in the Miranzai and Kurram valleys.　Bdr.-Gen. Neville Bowles Chamberlain.
1857.　　Mar.　Against the Bozdars.　Bde.-Gen. N. B. Chamberlain.
　　　　　July-Aug.　Against the Hindustani Fanatics.　Major John Vaughan.
1858.　　Apr.　Against the Hindustani Fanatics and the Khudu Khel. Maj.-Gen. Sir Sydney John Cotton.
1859-60.　Dec.　Against the Kabul Khel Waziris.　Bdr.-Gen. N. B. Chamberlain.
1860.　　Apr.-May.　Against the Mahsud Waziris.　Bdr.-Gen. N. B. Chamberlain.
1863.　　Ambela expedition.
　　　　　Against the Mohmands.
1868.　　Black Mountain expedition.
　　　　　NORTH-EAST FRONTIER.
1858-9.　Abor expedition.
1860-1.　Sikkim expedition.

A

N.B.—Compound names must be sought under the last element of the compound.

N.B.—An asterisk denotes that the name is omitted from *Dodwell & Miles's List*.

ABBOTT, Augustus (1804-1867). Major General, C.B. Artillery. *b.* London 7 Jan. 1804. Cadet 1818. Admitted 30 Oct. 1819. 2nd Lieut. 16 Apr. 1819. Lieut. 7 Aug. 1821. Capt. 10 May 1835. Major 3 July 1845. Lt. Col. 16 June 1848. Col. 14 Nov. 1858. Maj. Gen. 13 Apr. 1860. *d.* Cheltenham, 25 Feb. 1867. Eldest son of Henry Alexius Abbott, of Blackheath, a retired Calcutta merchant, and Margaret Welsh his wife. Brother of Sir Frederick Abbott, *q.v. m.* 1st, Karnal, 14 Sept. 1835, Charlotte, dau. of Robert Becher (1791-1841), *q.v.* (She died Mussoorie 26 June 1839, aged 21.) *m.* 2nd, Fatehgarh, 23 Mar. 1843, Sophia Frances, 3rd dau. of Capt. Jonathan Hayter ("John") Garstin, H.M. 88th Regt. (*See also* Robert McNair.) Educ. Winchester Coll. Addiscombe Cadet 1818-9.
Services : See *D.N.B.* C.B. 4 Oct. 1842. Durani, 3 cl. Hon. A.D.C. to G.G. 1st Apr. 1842.
Refs. : *D.N.B. D.I.B.* Boase. Vibart, p. 337. *The Times*, 1 Mar. 1867.

ABBOTT, Sir Frederick (1805-1892). Major General, Kt., C.B. Engineers. *b.* Littlecourt, nr. Buntingford, Herts., 13 June 1805. Cadet 1822. Arrived in India 29 Dec. 1823. Ensign 29 Dec. 1823. Lieut. 1 May 1824. Capt. 10 July 1832. Major 23 Dec. 1842. Bt. Lt. Col. 19 June 1846. Retired 1 Dec. 1847. Hon. Maj. Gen. 23 July 1858. *d.* Goshen, Branksome Park, Bournemouth, 4 Nov. 1892.
bapt. Layston, Herts., 17 Dec. 1805. 2nd son of Henry Alexius Abbott, of Blackheath, Kent. Brother of Sir James Abbott, *q.v. m.* Karnal, 14 Feb. 1835, Frances, youngest dau. of Lt. Col. Cox, R.A., and widow of Hubert De Burgh, *q.v.* Addiscombe Cadet 1820-2.

Services : See *D.N.B.* C.B. 27 June 1846. Kt. 9 June 1854.
Refs. : D.N.B. D.I.B. Boase. Vibart, p. 190. *Thackeray,* p. 86. *The Times,* 7 Nov. 1892, p. 10. *Daily Graphic,* 10 Nov. 1892, p. 13 (portrait).

ABBOTT, George (1803-1838). Captain, 15th N.I. *b.* Calcutta 26 Nov. 1803. Cadet 1823. Arrived in India 19 May 1824. Ensign 16 Jan. 1824. Lieut. 13 May 1825. Capt. 10 Jan. 1838. *d.* Sambalpur, B. & O., 1 Apr. 1838.

Son of George Edward Abbott, Head Asst. G.P.O., Calcutta, and Ann Maria his wife, dau. of Rev. Henry Peter Stacy, and sister of Henry Peter Stacy, *q.v.* Brother of Herbert Edward Stacy Abbott, *q.v.*

Services : Cadet R.A. (Warrant from the Duke of Wellington.) Posted as Ensign to 15 N.I. Siege and capture of Bhurtpore; Lieut. 15th N.I. Pioneers 26 Aug. 1828. Adjt. 15th N.I. 17 Apr. 1837. Employed on surveying duty at date of death. Pub. in 1827, "Views of the Forts of Bhurtpore and Weire," 13 litho. plates; also, Calcutta 1830, "Views about Kurrah Manickpore in the Province of Allahabad," Atlas 4to.

Refs : G.M. 1838, ii. 230.

ABBOTT, Henry (1811-1837). Lieutenant, 44th N.I. *b.* Calcutta, 1 June 1811. Cadet 1826. Arrived in India 2 Feb. 1828. Ensign 13 Aug. 1827. Lieut. 14 Mar. 1833. *d.* Goalpara, Assam, 12 Mar. 1837.

Son of John Abbott, Asst. to Messrs. Alexander & Co. of Calcutta, agents. Brother of Peter Abbott, *q.v.* Addiscombe Cadet 1826.

Services : Posted as Ensign to 44th N.I. 1 July 1828. Lieut. d.d. Assam Sebundy Corps, 18 May 1835, and was still serving with that Corps at date of death. No record of active service.

Refs. : M.I. in Goalpara Cemetery.

ABBOTT, Herbert Edward Stacy (1814-1883). Lieut. General, 28th N.I. *b.* Calcutta 19 Nov. 1814. Cadet 1831. Arrived in India 2 July 1832. Ensign 8 Dec. 1831. Lieut. 23 May 1836. Capt. 24 Jan. 1845. Major 11 Nov. 1854. Lt. Col. 22 Aug. 1858. Col. 20 Nov. 1865. Maj. Gen. 13 June 1870. Lt. Gen. 1 Oct. 1877. *d.* 29 Powis Sq., Bayswater, London, 17 May 1883.

bapt. Calcutta 30 Dec. 1814. Son of George Edward Abbott, Head Asst. G.P.O., Calcutta, and Ann Maria his wife, dau. of Rev. Henry Peter Stacy, and sister of Lewis Robert Stacy, *q.v.* Brother of John Richard Abbott, *q.v. m.* Nasirabad, 21 Sept. 1840, Sarah, 4th dau. of Capt. Thomas Masson, late R.A. Addiscombe Cadet 6 Nov. 1830 till 8 Dec. 1831.

THE BENGAL ARMY, 1758-1834

Services : To do duty with 24th N.I. 28 July 1832 ; do. 74th N.I. 6 Oct. 1832. Posted as Ensign to 13th N.I. 19 Dec. 1833. Transfd. to 74th N.I. 24 Jan. 1834. With Jodhpur F.F. 1839-40 ; surrender of fort of Jodhpur. Actg. Adjt. Jodhpur Legion 18 Jan. 1840. Adjt. 74th N.I. 9 Apr. 1840 till 6 June 1843. In charge of Nowgong Div. P.W.D. 14 Dec. 1843. Intr. & Qmr. 74th N.I. 28 May 1844. Mutiny campaign 1857-9 ; present with 74th N.I. at Delhi on outbreak of mutiny, and comdd. the post at the Kashmir gate ; comdd. 2nd Eur. Bengal Fus. in Delhi district Sept. to Nov. 1857 ; served with Saugor F.F. Apr. to July 1858 (Medal with clasp).
Refs. : Boase. *The Times* 19 May 1883. *I.L.N.* 26 May 1883, p. 534.

ABBOTT, Sir James (1807-1896). General K.C.B. Artillery. Retired List. *b.* " The Paragon," Blackheath, Kent, 12 Mar. 1807. Cadet 1822. Arrived in India 29 Dec. 1823. 2nd Lieut. 6 June 1823. Lieut. 28 Sept. 1827. Capt. 4 Aug. 1841. Major 6 Mar. 1854. Lt. Col. 4 July 1857. Col. 18 Feb. 1861. Col. Comdt. 27 Feb. 1877. Maj. Gen. 19 June 1866. Lt. Gen. 27 Feb. 1877. Gen. 1 Oct. 1877. *d.* Ellerslie, Ryde, I.W., 6 Oct. 1896.

3rd son of Henry Alexius Abbott, of Blackheath. Brother of Saunders Alexius Abbott, *q.v. m.* 1st, Calcutta, 8 Feb. 1843, Margaret Ann Harriett, eldest dau. of John Hutchison Fergusson, of Trochraigne, co. Ayr. (She died Asirgarh, C.P. 11 Feb. 1844.) *m.* 2nd, May 1868, Anna Matilda, youngest dau. of Reymond Hervey de Montmorency, *q.v.*
Services : See *D.N.B.* C.B. 24 May 1873. K.C.B. 26 May 1894. Durani, 3 cl.
Refs. : *D.N.B.* *D.I.B.* Boase. *Vibart*, p. 368. *The Times*, 8 Oct. 1896, p. 4.

ABBOTT, John Richard (1811-1888). Lieut. Colonel. 12th N.I. *b.* Calcutta 25 Aug. 1811. Cadet 1827. Arrived in India, 3 June 1828. Ensign 3 Feb. 1828. Lieut. 19 Oct. 1833. Capt. 1 Jan. 1846. Bt. Major 20 June 1854. Retired 13 Aug. 1855. Hon. Lt. Col. 26 Oct. 1855. *d.* 18 Sept. 1888.

Son of George Edward Abbott, of Calcutta, merchant, and Ann Maria his wife, dau. of Rev. Henry Peter Stacy, LL.D. Brother of George Abbott, *q.v. m.* Calcutta, 10 Jan. 1837, Isabella Maria, 2nd dau. of James Nicholson, solicitor. (*See also* George Richard James Meares.)
Services : Posted as Ensign to 12th N.I. 4 Nov. 1828. Arakan Local Bn. 12 Aug. 1837. Junior Asst. to Comr. in Arakan 9 Sept. 1837. Senior do. 27 Oct. 1841 till 1845. First Sikh War ; Feroz-

shahr; Lieut. 12th N.I. (Medal). Fur. 1854. Local Lt. Col. in Turkey, 6 Apr. 1855.

ABBOTT, Peter (1809-1861). Bt. Colonel, 72nd N.I. *b.* Calcutta, 11 Oct. 1809. Cadet 1825. Arrived in India 30 June 1826. Ensign 23 Dec. 1825. Lieut. 16 May 1827. Capt. 1 Dec. 1836. Major 10 May 1853. Lt. Col. 28 Aug. 1857. Bt. Col. 20 June 1857. *d.* Dehra Dun, U.P., 7 Dec. 1861.

bapt. Calcutta 26 Nov. 1809. Son of John Abbott, of Calcutta, merchant. Brother of Henry Abbott, *q.v.*

Services: Ensign d.d. 57th N.I. 8 July 1826. Posted as Ensign to 4th Extra Regt. (became 72nd N.I.). Adjt. Mhairwara Local Bn. 14 Oct. 1829 till 10 Dec, 1836. Served with 2nd L.I. Bn. 1841-3. Tempy. A.A.G. Sirhind Div. 30 Oct. 1843. No record of active service.

ABBOTT, Saunders Alexius (1811-1894). Major General. 51st N.I. *b.* 9 July 1811. Cadet 1828. Arrived in India 22 Mar. 1829. Ensign 12 June 1828. Lieut. 18 Feb. 1838. Capt. 2 Aug. 1850. Major 3 Aug. 1850. Lt. Col. 28 Nov. 1854. Col. 25 Jan. 1861. Retired 27 Oct. 1864. Hon. Maj. Gen. 24 Jan. 1865. *d.* Brighton 7 Feb. 1894.

bapt. Lewisham, Kent, 2 Aug. 1811. 4th son of Henry Alexius Abbott, of Blackheath, and Margaret Welsh his wife, of Monksilver, Somerset. Brother of Augustus Abbott, *q.v. m.* Allahabad, 15 Feb. 1839, Harriot Margaret, eldest dau. of James Johnstone, M.D., Surgeon Bengal Est. Addiscombe Cadet, 5 Aug. 1826 till 12 June 1828.

Services: See *D.N.B.* Ensign d.d. 42nd N.I. 10 June 1829. Posted as Ensign to 51st N.I. 2 Aug. 1832. Extra A.D.C. to G.G. 13 Mar. 1843.

Refs.: D.N.B. D.I.B. Boase. The Times, 9 Feb. 1894, p. 10. *I.L.N.,* 7 Apr. 1894, p. 432.

ABERCROMBIE, John (*d.* 1787). Lieutenant, 25th Bn. Sepoys. Cadet 1778. Ensign 4 June 1778. Lieut. 1 Jan. 1781. *d.* Jilda 8 Sept. 1787.

Services: N.F.P.
Refs.: G.M. 1788, i. 366.

ABERCROMBIE, John (1814-1860). Lieut. Colonel, Artillery. *b.* Wapping, London, E., 31 Aug. 1814. Cadet 1830. Arrived in India 4 Aug. 1831. 2nd Lieut. 10 Dec. 1830. Lieut. 10 Feb. 1840. Capt. 10 Feb. 1849. Bt. Major 7 June 1849. Lt. Col. 6 Dec. 1859. *d.* 7 Vicarage Gdns., Kensington, 4 Jan. 1860.

Son of William Abercrombie, of 33 Cornhill, merchant, and Rachel his wife. Brother of William Abercrombie, q.v. m. Meerut, 7 Oct. 1847, Rosalinda Helena, 4th dau. of John Angelo, q.v. (*See also* Richmond Houghton, John Liptrott, and Edmund Sissmore.) Addiscombe Cadet 1829-30.

Services : First Afghan War 1842 ; Jagdalak, and in the several engagements leading to the re-occupation of Kabul (Medal). Operations at Kaithal, Karnal district, 1843. Adjt. & Qmr. 8th Bde. H.A. 27 Sept. 1845. First Sikh War ; Ferozshahr ; Sobraon ; Adjt. 3rd Bde. H.A. (Medal with clasp). Second Sikh War ; Ramnagar ; Chilianwala ; Gujerat ; D.A.A.G., Art. (Medal with 2 clasps). Mutiny campaign, 1857-9 ; minor operations (Medal). Fur. 1859 till death.
Refs. : G.M. 1860, i. 305. *The Times*, 6 Jan. 1860.

ABERCROMBIE, William (1812-1858). Colonel. Engineers. *b.* Wapping, Middlesex, 12 Sept. 1812. Cadet 1828. Arrived in India 25 May 1830. Ensign 12 June 1828. Lieut. 20 May 1839. Capt. 23 May 1847. Bt. Major 7 June 1849. Bt. Lt. Col. 28 Nov. 1854. Retired 10 May 1857. Hon. Col. 10 May 1857. *d.* his residence, 50 Norland Sq., Notting Hill, London, 22 Apr. 1858.

Son of William Abercrombie, of Wapping, sailmaker, and Rachel his wife. Brother of John Abercrombie, q.v. Addiscombe Cadet 1826 till 12 June 1828.

Services : Supt. of roads, etc., Calcutta, 5 May 1836. Gwalior campaign ; Maharajpur (Bronze star). First Sikh War ; Sobraon (w.) (Medal) ; expedition towards Kashmir under Sir John Littler, q.v., 1846. Second Sikh War ; Multan ; Gujerat ; with the column in pursuit of the Sikh army (Medal with clasp). Executive Engr. Dum-Dum Div., P.W.D., 6 June 1851. Suptg. Engr., P.W.D. 27 Oct. 1854. Fur. s.c. 5 Nov. 1855 till retirement.
Refs. : G.M. 1858, i. 683. *The Times*, 26 Apr. 1858.

ABERNETHY, Alexander (1778-1812). Captain, 27th N.I. *bapt.* St. Mary's, Newington Butts, Surrey, 4 Dec. 1778. Cadet 1797. Ensign 10 Sept. 1798. Lieut. 1 Nov. 1798. Capt. 29 Aug. 1810. *d.* Java, 3 Mar. 1812.

Son of James Abernethy, of Maiden Row, Peterhead, co. Aberdeen, and Elizabeth his wife.
Services : Ensign 2nd Regt. Royal East India Vols. 21 June 1797. Second Mahratta War ; capture of Deig 24 Dec. 1804 (w.) ; Lieut. 1/8th N.I. Transfd. to newly-raised 1/27th N.I. in 1805. Adjt. 1/27th N.I. 1805-10. Operations against Dhundia Khan 1807 ; Komona ; Ganauri ; Lieut. 1/27th N.I. Capt. Lt. 27th N.I. 3 Jan. 1810. Capture of Java 1811 ; Capt. 6th Bn. Bengal Vols.
Refs. : Will dated 13 Mar. 1811 ; proved 19 June 1812.

ACHMUTY or AUCHMUTY, Arthur (1729/30-1793). Colonel, Infantry. *b.* 1729/30. Cadet 1760. Ensign 18 Sept. 1761. Lieut. 26 Aug. 1763. Capt. 20 Dec. 1764. Major 3 Sept. 1768, Lt. Col. 13 Sept. 1779. Col. 28 May 1786. *d.* Dinapore, 6 Dec. 1793, aged 63.

Of Harley St., London. 2nd son of Samuel Achmuty, of Brianstown, co. Longford, and Mary his wife, eldest dau. of John King, of Charlestown, co. Roscommon. *m.* Calcutta, 25 July 1767, Miss Ursula da Cruz. This marriage was solemnized in the R.C. as well as in the English Church. Father of James Achmuty, *q.v.*

Services : Sailed for India on the *Royal Duke* in 1759. Was in England on fur. in 1788-9. N.F.P.

Refs. : Burke's *Landed Gentry*, 2nd edn., p. 2, *s.n.* Achmuty, or Auchmuty, of Brianstown, co. Longford. *Hickey*, iv. 84, 108-10. Will dated London, 9 Mar. 1789.

ACHMUTY or AUCHMUTY, Arthur Forbes (*d.* 1781). Major, Infantry. Lieut. 10 Oct. 1763. Capt. 6 Aug. 1765. Major 19 Dec. 1769. *d.* Nov. 1781 whilst on active service.

Brother of James Achmuty, of Dublin, and of Catherine Gibson, of Sligo.

Services : Transfd. to Bengal army as Lieut. from H.M. 84th Regt. Apptd. to comd. 1st Bn. in 2nd Bde. in 1765. First Mysore War ; comdg. 3rd Bn. Sepoys. First Mahratta War ; operations against Sindhia, 1781 ; with the force under Lt. Col. Grainger Muir, *q.v.*, sent to reinforce Lt. Col. Jacob Camac, *q.v.*

Refs : Burke's *Landed Gentry*, 2nd edn., p. 2, *s.n.* Achmuty or Auchmuty, of Brianstown, co. Longford. Will dated 8 Dec. 1780.

ACHMUTY or AHMUTY, James (*d.* 1773). Ensign, Infantry. Cadet 1770. Ensign 6 Dec. 1771. *d.* Baugerramor (? Bangarmau, U.P.) May 1773.

Services : N.F.P.

ACHMUTY or AHMUTY, James (1775-1864). General, Artillery. *bapt.* Calcutta 21 Oct. 1775. Cadet 1790. Arrived in India 21 June 1791. Fireworker 24 May 1791. Lieut. 6 Sept. 1799. Capt. Lt. 28 May 1804. Capt. 15 May 1807. Major 15 Feb. 1818. Lt. Col. 14 Jan. 1821. Comdt. 29 Aug. 1824. Col. 5 June 1829. Maj. Gen. 28 June 1838. Lt. Gen. 11 Nov. 1851. Gen. 15 Sept. 1855. *d.* his residence, 14 Chesham Pl., Belgrave Sq., London, 12 Jan. 1864, in his 90th year.

4th son of Arthur Achmuty, *q.v.*, and Ursula his wife. *m.* 1st, ———. *m.* 2nd, Cawnpore, 10 Dec. 1805, Miss Anne Fearon, late of Edinburgh.

THE BENGAL ARMY, 1758-1834

Services : Apptd. a " Minor Cadet " in India at a very early age ; struck off by order of the C.D. 2 May 1786. Fur. s.c. 27 July 1797 till 23 Sept. 1799. Second Mahratta War ; battles of Delhi and Deig ; siege of Bhurtpore (India medal). Fur. p.a. 18 Feb. 1808 till 26 Nov. 1811. Served in Chittagong 1812-4. Fur. p.a. 5 Feb. 1825 till death.

Refs. : Burke's *Landed Gentry*, 2nd edn., p. 2, *s.n.* Achmuty, or Auchmuty, of Brianstown, co. Longford. *G.M.* 1864, i. 269. *The Times*, 15 Jan. 1864.

ACKERS, Thomas Pickop (1804- ?). Lieutenant. Artillery. *b.* Liverpool 18 Feb. 1804. Cadet 1820. Arrived in India Sept. 1821. 2nd Lieut. 19 Dec. 1820. Lieut. 1 May 1824. Resigned in England 30 Dec. 1825.

Son of James Ackers, of Liverpool, brewer. Addiscombe Cadet 1819-20.

Services : Sailed for India on the *Marquis of Wellington*. Fur. 1823 till resignation. Posted to 4th Troop 3rd Bde. H.A. in 1825. No record of active service.

ADAIR, Alexander. Captain. Infantry. Cadet 1766. Ensign 1 Dec. 1766. Lieut. 1 Sept. 1768. Capt. 5 Apr. 1773. Resigned 31 July 1775.

Services : N.F.P.

ADAMS, Anthony (*d.* 1815). Lieut. Colonel, 19th N.I. Cadet 1783. Arrived in India 22 Oct. 1783. Ensign 13 Feb. 1785. Lieut. 2 Jan. 1792. Capt. 30 Sept. 1803. Major 16 Sept. 1807. Lt. Col. 31 May 1813. *d.* Karnal, 13 June 1815.

Brother of Samuel Adams, of Ardee, Ireland.

Services : Adjt. 1/6th N.I. 29 May 1800 till 1803. Disturbances in Ganjam 1801 ; Lieut 1/6th N.I. Nepal War 1814-5 ; Lt. Col. 1/6th N.I. in 2nd Div. Transfd. to 19th N.I. in 1815. Sometime Comdt. of the garrison at Delhi. Served continuously in India without taking fur. to Europe.

Refs. : *G.M.* 1816, i. 372. Will dated Karnal, 18 Oct. 1814 ; proved in 1815.

ADAMS, Frederick (1814-1892). Lieutenant. 24th N.I. *b.* 25 Apr. 1814. Cadet 1831. Arrived in India 7 Feb. 1833. Ensign (14 June 1832) 7 Nov. 1832. Lieut. 7 Aug. 1838. Retired in England 19 Aug. 1841. *d.* Chepstow Rd., Croydon, Surrey, 1 June 1892.

bapt. Totnes, Devon, 17 July 1814. 5th son of Samuel Adams, of Totnes (of Hounslow, Barrack Master), and Elizabeth Bentall his wife. Addiscombe Cadet, 5 Feb. 1830 till 14 June 1832.

Services : Ensign d.d. 35th N.I. 20 June 1833. Fur. s.c. 6 mos. to Singapore 3 July 1834. Posted as Ensign to 37th N.I. 11 Feb. 1834 ; transfd. to 24th N.I. 11 Mar. 1834. Fur. s.c. 20 Jan. 1835 till 21 Jan. 1839, and 22 Feb. 1840 till retirement. No record of active service.

Refs. : Burke's *Landed Gentry,* 7th edn., p. 5, *s.n.* Adams, of Bowdon, Devon. *The Times,* 3 June 1892.

ADAMS, John (*d.* 1767). Captain, Engineers. Cadet 1761. Ensign 6 Oct. 1761. Capt. Lt. 30 Dec. 1765. Capt. 30 Dec. 1766. *d.* in India 1767.

Son of Eleanor Adams, and nephew of Richard Adams.

Services : Employed on surveying work in Bengal under James Rennell, *q.v.*

Refs. : Will dated 17 July 1767 ; proved in 1767.

ADAMS, Sir John Withington (1764-1837). Major General, G.C.B. Colonel 16th N.I. *b.* 17 Feb. 1764. Cadet 1780. Arrived in India 30 Apr. 1781. Ensign 22 Mar. 1781. Lieut. 23 June 1781. Capt. 1 Nov. 1798. Major 21 Sept. 1804. Lt. Col. 13 Sept. 1809. Col. 14 Aug. 1819. Maj. Gen. 22 July 1830. *d. unm.* Sabathu, Punjab, 9 Mar. 1837.

Son of ——- Adams and Elizabeth his wife, née Withington, of Manchester. Cousin of Rev. William George Garrett.

Services : Second Rohilla War ; battle of Bitaurah ; Lieut. 10th Bn. Sepoys. Fourth Mysore War ; Malavelli ; siege and capture of Seringapatam ; Capt. 1/10th N.I. (Medal). Second Mahratta War 1805-6 ; Major 2/10th N.I. Comdd. F.F. against the Bhattis, Nov. 1810. Operations in Baghelkhand 1813 ; capture of Entauri ; comdg. Rewah F.F. Third Mahratta War ; Seoni ; Chanda ; comdg. 5th Div. Army of the Deccan. Siege and capture of Bhurtpore 1825-6 ; comdg. 3rd Inf. Bde. To comd. E. frontier 12 June 1826 ; to comd. Muttra and Agra frontier 20 Oct. 1826 ; to comd. Sirhind Div. 26 May 1828. Apptd. Col. 16th N.I. June 1828. C.B. 4 June 1815. K.C.B. 27 Sept. 1831. G.C.B. 10 Mar. 1837 (the day after his death).

Refs. : De Rhé-Philipe. *D.I.B. G.M.* 1837, ii. 659. Will dated 6 Feb. 1830 ; codicil dated 10 Sept. 1834 ; proved 16 June 1837. M.I. at Sabathu.

ADAMS, O. George (*d.* 1781). Lieutenant, 3rd Bengal European Regt. Cadet ——? Ensign 1779. Lieut. 14 Nov. 1780. *d.* Bijaigarh, C.I., 3 Oct. 1781.

Services : Against the Rajah of Benares, 1781, with the force under Major William Popham, *q.v.*

ADAMS, Richard (1754/55-1803). Captain, 16th N.I. *b.* in Ireland 1754/55. Cadet 1780. Arrived in India 4 May 1781. Ensign 22 Mar. 1781. Lieut. 3 July 1781. Capt. Lt. 7 Jan. 1796. Capt. 1798. *d.* at sea 10 July 1803, on board the *Lord Eldon* on his passage to England.
Services : Sailed for India on the *Earl of Dartmouth* 3 June 1780, aged 25. Second Rohilla War ; Bitaurah (w.) ; Lieut 13th Bn. Sepoys. Transfd. to 2/1st N.I. (late 13th Bn.) in 1796. Capt. 2/1st N.I. in July 1798. Fur. 4 Apr. 1803.
Refs. : *Hickey*, iv. 122.

*ADAMS, Robert (1781- ?). Infantry Cadet. *b.* 12 Apr. 1781. Cadet 1795. Never arrived in India. Struck off, not having claimed the appointment.
bapt. Croydon, Surrey, 13 Apr. 1781. Son of John Adams and Sophia his wife.
Refs. : *Philippart MS.*

ADAMS, Samuel (1759/60-1799). Captain, 5th N.I. *b.* Wilts. 1759/60. Cadet 1780. Arrived in India 23 Oct. 1781. Ensign 22 Mar. 1781. Lieut. 2 June 1781. Capt. Lt. 7 Jan. 1796. Capt. 1798. *d.* Ambur, Madras, 20 Mar. 1799.
Services : Sailed for India on the *Essex* 13 Mar. 1781, aged 21. Captured by the enemy on the voyage out to India in 1781. Fourth Mysore War ; served with the force which assembled at Ambur in Feb. 1799 for the invasion of Mysore, under the comd. of Lt. Gen. George Harris. Was Capt. in 5th N.I. in June 1798.

*ADAMSON, Benjamin (1733/34-1763). Fireworker, Artillery. *b.* Norfolk 1733/34. Cadet 1761. Fireworker 18 Sept. 1761. *d.* 5th, 6th or 11th Oct. 1763 : massacred at or near Patna by order of Nawab Mir Muhummad Kasim.
Note : " . . . on the nights of the 5th or 6th and 11th of October 1763, brutally massacred near this spot by the troops of Mir Kasim, Nawab Subahdar of Bengal, under command of Walter Reinhardt *alias* Samru, a base renegade." (M.I. in Patna city.)
Services : N.F.P.
Refs. : *Broome*, p. 365. *Stubbs*, i. 25.

ADDERLEY, Thomas (1747/48-1786). Major. Infantry. *b.* 1747/48. Cadet 1764. Ensign 15 Oct. 1765. Lieut. 15 Jan. 1767. Capt. 23 Sept. 1770. Major 16 Jan. 1781. Dismissed 7 Sept. 1785. *d.* 9 Sept. 1786 : lost at sea at the mouth of the Hooghly R., in the *Severn* packet, on his passage to England.
Son of Thomas Adderley, of London, and Mary his wife. Brother

of William and Mary Adderley. Educ. Merchant Taylors' school ; entered in 1759.
Services : Sailed for India on the *Earl of Elgin* 4 May 1764, aged 16. N.F.P.
Refs. : *Robinson*, ii. 119. *S.M.* 1787, p. 148. Will dated 13 Jan. 1782 ; proved 11 Oct. 1786.

ADDIE, Arthur (*d.* 1781). Lieutenant, Infantry. Cadet 1778. Ensign (?). Lieut. 27 Aug. 1779. *d.* Fatehgarh, Nov. 1781.
Services : N.F.P.

ADDISON, Edmund (*d.* 1784). Fireworker, Artillery. Fireworker 3 July 1782. *d.* Calcutta 23 Nov. 1784.
Services : Second Mysore War ; siege of Cuddalore ; Fireworker with the detachment of Bengal Art., under Lt. Col. T. D. Pearse, which he joined in Mar. 1783.

ADDISON, Hadley (*d.* 1805). Captain, 15th N.I. Cadet 1794. Arrived in India 29 Feb. 1796. Ensign 15 Oct. 1795. Lieut. 25 Oct. 1797. Capt. 29 Oct. 1804. *d.* Muttra 25 Nov. 1805.
Of Hammersmith, Middlesex.
Services : Operations in Jumna Doab 1803 ; Sasni ; Bijaigarh ; Kachaura ; Lieut. 2/15th N.I. Second Mahratta War ; Delhi ; Agra ; Laswari ; Deig ; Bhurtpore (w. in second assault 21 Jan. 1805) ; Lieut. 15th N.I. Capt. 2/15th N.I.

*ADDISON, Henry Robert (1803-1876). Ensign. 22nd N.I. Subsequently Lieut. h.p. 2nd D.G. *b.* Calcutta 25 Aug. 1803. Cadet 1820. Arrived in India June 1821. Ensign 12 Jan. 1821. Resigned in India 2 Aug. 1822. *d.* Albion St., Hyde Park, London, 24 June 1876.
Son of John Addison, B.C.S., Commercial Resident at Rampur Bauleah, Bengal. Brother of Louisa, wife of Lt. Gen. Sir William Sheridan, K.C.H., and of Colette, wife of Gen. Sir Robert Barton, Kt.
Services : Sailed for India on the *Moffat*. Ensign H.M. 65th Ft., 26 Dec. 1821. h.p. 8 Sept. 1825. Cornet 2nd Dragoon Gds. 12 July 1824. Lieut. & Adjt. do. 15 Mar. 1831. h.p. 21 June 1833. Miscellaneous writer. F.S.A. 10 March 1836.
Refs. : *Boase*. *The Times*, 27 June 1876.

*ADNET(T), Joseph (*d.* 1758). Captain, Bengal European Regt. Ensign (H.M. 39th Regt.) (?). Transferred to Bengal European Regt. Lieut. (?). Capt. 13 Dec. 1757. *d.* 9 Dec. 1758 : kld. in action at the battle of Condore.
Services : N.F.P.
Refs. : *Orme MSS India*, xiii. 3639. *Innes*, pp. 70, 91. *Forde*, pp. 21, 100, 101.

ADSTONE, Mark (1744/45- ?). Ensign. Infantry. b. London 1744/45. Cadet 1764. Ensign 27 Dec. 1764. Dismissed 1765.
Services : Sailed for India on the Carnarvon, 20 Feb. 1764, aged 19. N.F.P.

AFTON, John. Cadet. Infantry. Cadet 1770. Resigned 16 Aug. 1772.
Services : N.F.P

AGAR, George Frederick (1792-1829). Captain, 49th N.I. b. Congleton, Cheshire, 8 July 1792. Cadet 1810. Ensign 27 Jan. 1813. Lieut. 15 Nov. 1816. Capt. 28 Dec. 1825. d. Mauritius 4 Aug. 1829.
Natural son of George Agar, Lord Callan, of Fitzroy Sq., London. Brother of Samuel David Agar, q.v.
Services : Cadet d.d. 25th N.I. 1811-3. Posted as Ensign to 1/25th N.I. in 1813. Transfd. as Lieut. to 2/25th N.I. (? Siege and capture of Hathras ; Lieut. 25th N.I.) Third Mahratta War ; Lieut. 25th N.I. Fur. 1821-4. Transfd. to 49th N.I. (late 1/25th) May 1824. First Burma War ; Arakan 1825 ; Lieut. 49th N.I. Fur. s.c. 8 mos. to Malacca 23 Mar. 1827 ; s.c. 20 mos. to N.S.W. via Mauritius 13 Mar. 1829.
Refs. : G.E.C.'s Complete Peerage, new edn., ii. 487. Will dated 29 July 1829 ; proved 5 Mar. 1831.

AGAR, Samuel David (1806-1874). Lieutenant. 55th N.I. b. co. Carmarthen 9 Dec. 1806. Cadet 1825. Arrived in India 13 Mar. 1826. Ensign 16 Sept. 1825. Lieut. 31 May 1835. Resigned in England 5 July 1840. d. Ramsgate 9 Mar. 1874.
Natural son of George Agar, Lord Callan, of Fitzroy Sq., London. Brother of George Frederick Agar, q.v. Ed. at Harrow school 1820/21-1824.
Services : Posted as Ensign to 55th N.I. Fur. u.p.a. 27 June 1831 till 27 Dec. 1833 ; fur. s.c. 5 Jan. 1838 till resignation. No record of active service. Promoted to the brevet rank of Capt. 16 Sept. 1840, before his resignation was known in India : this was subsequently cancelled.
Refs. : Harrow School Register. The Times, 11 Mar. 1874.
Note : He appears to have been baptized as Samuel David, and his names are given thus in the Harrow School Register and in official records. In his brother's Will, however, and in his obit. notice in The Times, he is described as David Samuel Agar.

AGG, James (*d.* 1828 ?). Capt. Lieutenant. Engineers. Cadet 1781. Arrived in India Nov. 1777. Ensign 20 Dec. 1781. Lieut. 3 Nov. 1782. Capt. Lt. 25 Apr. 1797. Retired 11 Dec. 1799. *d.* in England 1828 ?

Of Cheltenham. J.P. and D.L. Gloucs. "Son of a common hard-working stone-mason in Cheltenham."

Note : His name is omitted from the list of Retired Officers in *E.I.R.* after May 1828. It is possible, however, that his death may have occurred in 1826, as his name, which figures in the list of proprietors of E.I. stock corrected to 28 Mar. 1826, is absent from a similar list corrected to 28 Mar. 1827. This, of course, may simply mean that he parted with his holding during his lifetime.

Services : Sailed for India on the *Seahorse* 30 Apr. 1777, going out as an assistant to Col. Henry Watson, *q.v.* " Mr. Agg was, some years after he arrived in Bengal, appointed an Engineer Officer, in which corps he rose to the rank of Captain, when he quitted the service and returned to Europe with a handsome fortune. Soon after he reached England the Court of Directors offered him the situation of Lieutenant-Governor of Saint Helena, which he declined accepting." Designed and built St. John's Church, Calcutta, 1784-7.

Refs. : *Hickey*, ii. 104 ; iv. 474-5.

AGNEW, Alexander Keir (1804-1855). Captain. 6th N.I. *b.* Madras 5 Oct. 1804. Cadet 1820. Arrived in India June 1821. Ensign 16 Dec. 1820. Lieut. 11 July 1823. Capt. 15 Feb. 1836. Retired in India 1 Mar. 1844. *d.* in England, suddenly, 16 Mar. 1855.

bapt. Madras 2 Oct. 1805. Son of Maj. Gen. Patrick Alexander Agnew, Madras Est., and Margaret his wife. Nephew of Col. Mark Wilks, Madras Est. (*D.N.B.*). *m.* Takli, nr. Nagpur, 19 July 1828, Miss Dorothy Watson. (She died 21 May 1864, aged 54.) Addiscombe Cadet 1819-20.

Services : Posted as Ensign to Bengal Eur. Regt. 16 Dec. 1820. Transfd. to 3rd N.I. in 1823 ; to 6th N.I. (late 1/3rd) May 1824. Employed in Nagpur, C.P., 1824-9. Fur. s.c. 11 Jan. 1831 till 3 Oct. 1833. First Afghan War 1842 ; re-occupation of Kabul (Medal) ; Capt. 6th N.I., with 4th Bde. of Force under Sir George Pollock, *q.v.*

Refs. : *G.M.* 1855, i. 546.

AGNEW, John (1791-1820). Lieutenant, 22nd N.I. *b.* Larne, co. Antrim, 26 May 1791. Cadet 1806. Arrived in India 3 Oct. 1807. Ensign 28 Oct. 1807. Lieut. 3 Jan. 1812. *d.* Bargarh, Cuttack district, 29 Apr. 1820.

Son of Patrick Agnew. Brother of Robert Agnew, *q.v.*

Services : Posted as Ensign to 2/22nd N.I. in 1808. Nepal War 1814-5 ; Lieut. 2/22nd N.I. in 4th Div. Nepal War 1816 ; Lieut. 2/22nd N.I. in 3rd Bde., Centre Column.
Refs. : Will dated 17 Apr. 1820 ; proved 10 Nov. 1820. M.I. in Cuttack cemetery (where the date of birth is incorrectly given as 7 July 1793).

AGNEW, Patrick (1789-1824). Captain, 7th L.C. *b.* Ahogill, co. Antrim. *bapt.* 10 Nov. 1789. Cadet 1805. Arrived in India 13 Dec. 1806. Cornet 14 Dec. 1806. Lieut. 1 Oct. 1815. Capt. 1 Jan. 1819. *d.* Kaitha, Bundelhkand, C.I., 2 Oct. 1824.
Son of William Agnew, late of Craigs, Ahogill. Brother of William Agnew, *q.v.*, John Agnew, Mary Church Agnew, and Anne Stewart.
Services : Posted as Cornet to 7th N.C. and remained with that Regt. throughout his service. Settlement of Hariana 1809-10. Nepal War 1814-5 ; in 2nd Div. Siege and capture of Hathras. Third Mahratta War ; Dhamoni ; Mandala ; Multai ; Harna ; in Centre Div.
Refs. : Will dated 28 Mar. 1823 ; codicil dated 15 Jan. 1824 ; proved 3 Jan. 1825.

AGNEW, Robert (1790-1826). Captain, 33rd N.I. *b.* Larne, co. Antrim, 12 May 1790. Cadet 1806. Arrived in India 3 Oct. 1807. Ensign 17 Oct. 1807. Lieut. 16 Aug. 1810. Capt. 1 May 1824. *d. unm.* at sea, 1 Jan. 1826, on board the *Hercules.*
Son of Patrick Agnew. Brother of John Agnew, *q.v.*
Services : Posted as Ensign to 1/16th N.I. in 1808. (? Operations in Bundelkhand 1810-1 ; Lieut. 1/16th N.I.) With 4th Gren. Bn. in 1816. Adjt. 1/16th N.I. 1822-4. Transfd. to 33rd N.I. (late 2/16th) May 1824. First Burma War ; Arakan 1825 ; Capt. 1st Gren. Bn.
Refs. : Will dated 14 Dec. 1825 ; proved 1 Apr. 1826.

AGNEW, William (1778-1823). Lieut. Colonel, 7th N.I. *bapt.* Cullybackey, co. Antrim, 4 Nov. 1778. Cadet 1794. Arrived in India 22 Feb. 1796. Ensign 11 Nov. 1795. Lieut. 14 July 1797. Capt. 8 Apr. 1805. Major 15 May 1815. Lt. Col. 20 Feb. 1821. *d.* 13 Feb. 1823 on board the *William Money* on his passage to England.
Son of William Agnew, of Craigs, Ahogill, co. Antrim. Brother of Patrick Agnew, *q.v.*
Services : Second Mahratta War ; Bundelkhand 1803 ; Kapsa ; Kalpi ; siege and capture of Gwalior 1804 ; Lieut. 2/11th N.I. Capture of Gohad 1806. Reduction of Kalinjar 1812 ; Capt. 2/11th

N.I. Comdg. 1st Gren. Bn. in 1816. Siege and capture of Hathras; Major 2/11th N.I. Third Mahratta War; Major 2/11th N.I., in Centre Div. Transfd. as Lt. Col. to 2/7th N.I. in 1821.
Refs. : Will dated 18 Oct. 1820; codicil dated 22 Dec. 1822; proved 7 Aug. 1823.

AINSLIE, John (*d.* 1817). Lieut. Colonel. 28th N.I. Country Cadet 1781. Admitted 15 Oct. 1781. Ensign 21 July 1782. Lieut. 17 Jan. 1785. Capt. 21 Jan. 1803. Major 26 Jan. 1809. Lt. Col. 25 Jan. 1815. Retired 22 Jan. 1817. *d.* at his residence in Forth Street, Edinburgh, 13 Mar. 1817.
m. 1st, Leith, 30 July 1805, Sarah, dau. of Archibald Geddes, of Leith. (She died 6 June 1813.) Father of John Ainslie, *q.v. m.* 2nd, Drumsheugh, Edinburgh, 3 July 1815, a dau. of William Walker, of Coats.
Services : Bt. Capt. 5th N.I. in 1798. (? Second Mahratta War; Agra; Laswari; capture of Gwalior; Capt. 9th N.I.) Fur. 16 June 1804 till 14 Oct. 1807. Bk. Mr. at Cawnpore Feb. 1808. Fur. 4 Feb. 1814 till retirement. Transfd. as Lt. Col. to 1/28th N.I. in 1815.
Refs. : *G.M.* 1817, i. 374. *S.M.* 1805, p. 726; 1817, i. 309.

AINSLIE, John (1807-?). Ensign. 40th N.I. *b.* Edinburgh 30 May 1807. Cadet 1825. Ensign 13 Feb. 1826. Struck off in India 22 Nov. 1830.
Son of John Ainslie, *q.v.*, and Sarah his first wife. (? *m.* 10 Jan. 1833, Mary Susanna, eldest dau. of John Arthur Borrow, of Woolden Hall, Lancs.)
Services : Ensign d.d. 6th Extra Regt. 8 July 1826. Posted as Ensign to 40th N.I. in 1826. No record of active service.

AIRD, John (1765/66-1792). Lieutenant, Infantry. *b.* 1765/66. Cadet 1780. Ensign 1781. Lieut. 21 Oct. 1782. *d.* in India 31 Mar. 1792.
Services : Approved as Cadet on 15 May 1782, aged 16. To rank as a Cadet of the season 1780.

AIRE, James Ritchie (1792-?). Bt. Captain. 64th N.I. *b.* Leith, Midlothian, 6 Dec. 1792. Cadet 1808. Arrived in India 27 Oct. 1809. Ensign 21 July 1810. Lieut. 16 Dec. 1814. Bt. Capt. 24 Apr. 1824. Discharged from the Service by G.C.M. 24 Apr. 1827.
Son of John Aire, Lieut. R.N., and Christian Ritchie his wife.
Services : Posted as Ensign to 22nd N.I. in 1810. (? Storm of Kalinjar; Ensign 22nd N.I.) Nepal War, 1814-5; Lieut. 6th Coy.

THE BENGAL ARMY, 1758-1834

Pioneers. Served with the Pioneers till 1821. Transfd. as Lieut. to newly-raised 2/30th N.I. in 1815. Comdd. a Beldar Corps 1822-5. Transfd. to 32nd N.I. 11 July 1823 ; to 63rd N.I. (late 1/32nd) May 1824 ; to 64th N.I. in 1824. Siege and capture of Bhurtpore ; Bt. Capt. 64th N.I. (but appears to have been serving at the time with 63rd N.I.).
Refs. : A.J. xxiv. 660-1.

AIREY, Henry Cookson (1810-1866). Lieutenant. 59th N.I. b. Temple-Sowerby, Westmorland, 17 May 1810. Cadet 1827. Arrived in India 15 Oct. 1828. Ensign 16 Apr. 1828. Lieut. 8 Aug. 1837. Resigned in England 25 June 1839. d. 10 May 1866.

Of Kingsthorpe House, Yorks., and latterly of Grosvenor Pl., Bath. 2nd son of Thomas Airey, Capt. 9th East Norfolk Regt., and Julia his wife, 4th dau. of Matthew Atkinson, of Temple-Sowerby, and sister of Richard Atkinson, q.v. m. 20 Dec. 1838, Emily, dau. of William Parke, of Awfield Lodge, Lancs., and Mollance, co. Kirkcudbright.

Services : Ensign d.d. 51st N.I. 20 Nov. 1828. Posted as Ensign to 59th N.I. 4 Mar. 1829. Fur. s.c. 25 Dec. 1836 till resignation. No record of active service

Refs. : Burke's Colonial Gentry, ii. 502. Burke's Family Records, p. 2.

AITCHISON, James (1793-1848). Major. 28th N.I. b. 2 Mar. 1793. Cadet 1810. Admitted 22 Oct. 1811. Ensign 8 July 1813. Lieut. 4 Nov. 1817. Capt. 28 Aug. 1826. Major 30 June 1840. Invalided 30 Nov. 1840. Retired 24 July 1846. d. Broomhill, Lasswade, 27 Dec. 1848.

Son of John Aitchison, merchant in Leith and farmer in Stirling. m. —— .

Services : Ensign Peeblesshire Regt. of Local Militia. Did duty as a Cadet for some months with 2/2nd N.I. until posted as Ensign to that Corps. Operations in Baghelkhand 1813 ; Entauri ; Ensign 2/2nd N.I. Served with 2nd Gren. Bn. 1815-6. Transfd. to 2/14th N.I. 24 May 1816. Third Mahratta War ; siege of Mandala ; Lieut. 14th N.I. Served with Pioneers 1819-27. Engineer, Narbada F.F., 31 Oct. 1820. Transfd. to 28th N.I. (late 1/14th) May 1824. Fur. p.a. 6 Nov. 1827 till 19 July 1830. Fur. s.c. 24 Jan. 1844 till retirement.
Refs. : G.M. 1849, i. 221.

AITKEN, Robert (1804-1839). Captain, Invalid Est. 6th L.C. b. Cupar, co. Fife, 1 Aug. 1804. Cadet 1819. Arrived in India

Feb. 1821. Cornet 23 Aug. 1820. Lieut. 15 Aug. 1823. Capt. 8 May 1833. Invalided 30 Oct. 1837. *d.* at sea on board the *Bedford* 6 Apr. 1839 on his passage to England.

Son of George Aitken, of Cupar, banker.

Services : Sailed for India on the *Boyne* in 1820. Posted as Cornet to 6th L.C. in 1821, and served throughout with that Regt. Siege and capture of Bhurtpore ; Lieut. 6th L.C., in 1st Bde., Cav. Div. Adjt. 6th L.C. 15 Nov. 1832. Fur. s.c. 6 Jan. 1833 till 22 Oct. 1835. Fur. s.c. 13 Jan. 1839.

Refs. : A.J. N.S. xxix. 158. Will dated 11 May 1838 ; proved 26 Oct. 1839.

AKERMAN, James. Major, Infantry. Subsequently Comdt. E.I.C. depot for recruits in I.W. Cadet 1763. Ensign 29 Dec. 1763. Lieut. 27 Feb. 1765. Capt. 5 June 1767. Major 12 Sept. 1779. Resigned 9 Mar. 1780.

Services : First Rohilla War ; battle of St. George ; Capt. comdg. 16th Bn. Sepoys, to the comd. of which Corps he was apptd. on. 29 Nov. 1772. Living in 1804, when he was comdg. the I.W. recruit depot.

ALBRIGHT, James (*d.* 1763). Cadet. Infantry. Subsequently a Free Merchant. Cadet 1762. Resigned 27 Oct. 1762. *d.* 5th, 6th or 11th Oct. 1763 : massacred at or near Patna by order of Nawab Mir Muhammad Kasim. (See note to Benjamin Adamson.)

Services : N.F.P.

Refs. : MS. list preserved at the India Office entitled, " List of Persons killed in the Massacre at Patna, and at other places during the Troubles, 1763." This is certified as " A True List " by John Graham, Secretary, Fort William, 20 Feb. 1764.

ALCOCK, Chambré Brabazon Ponsonby (1809-1844). Captain, Engineers. *bapt.* Bath 24 Feb. 1809. Cadet 1827. Arrived in India 10 June 1828. 2nd Lieut. 16 June 1826. Lieut. 28 Sept. 1827. Capt. 4 Sept. 1839. *d.* Bath 4 Apr. 1844.

Son of George Alcock, of Bath, wine merchant, formerly of Dublin, and Sophia Jane his wife, 2nd dau. of George Lowther, of Kilrue and of Lowther Lodge, co. Dublin. Brother of Richard Ponsonby Alcock, *q.v. m.* Delhi, 17 June 1837, Charlotte Nott, 2nd dau. of B. Hobday, and niece of Sir William Nott, *q.v.* (*See also* William Buttanshaw.) Addiscombe Cadet, 4 Feb. 1825 till 16 Dec. 1825. Chatham, 7 Sept. 1826 till 4 Oct. 1827.

Services : 2nd Lieut. d.d. Sappers and Miners at Aligarh, 25 July 1828. Executive Engr., Mhow, 27 Apr. 1835. Offg. Garrison and Executive Engr. at Delhi in 1837. Suptg. Burdwan and Benares

road in 1838. Fur. s.c. 13 Dec. 1842 till death. No record of active service.
Refs.: Burke's *Landed Gentry*, 11th edn., p. 1055, *s.n.* Lowther, of Shrigley Park, Cheshire. *G.M.* 1844, i. 556. Will dated Hazaribagh, 3 Apr. 1841 ; proved 16 Dec. 1844.

ALCOCK, Richard Ponsonby (1806-1844). Captain, 46th N.I. *b.* Walcot, Somerset, 18 Jan. 1806. Cadet 1824. Arrived in India 13 Sept. 1825. Ensign 29 Apr. 1825. Lieut. 3 Nov. 1827. Capt. (29 Apr. 1840) 18 Sept. 1844. *d.* Mainpuri, U.P., 26 Oct. 1844 : murdered by a band of dácoits when travelling to Agra.

Son of George Alcock, of Bath, wine merchant, formerly of Dublin, and Sophia Jane his wife, 2nd dau. of George Lowther. Brother of Chambré Brabazon Ponsonby, *q.v.* Addiscombe Cadet 1821-3.

Services : Posted as Ensign to 46th N.I. and remained on the roll of that Regt. throughout his service. Fur. s.c. 7 June 1831 till 9 Aug. 1834. Offg. D.A.Q.M.G. 12 June 1837. D.A.Q.M.G., 2 cl., Saugor Div., 24 Apr. 1838. do., 1 cl., 18 Aug. 1841. A.Q.M.G. 13 Jan. 1842. Extra A.D.C. to G.G. 13 Mar. 1843. Gwalior campaign ; Maharajpur (Bronze star).
Refs.: *G.M.* 1845, i. 566. *I.M.*, 4 Jan. 1845, p. 13.

ALCOCK, Thomas (1763-1856). Major. 18th N.I. *b.* 9 June 1763. Cadet 1780. Arrived in India 27 Apr. 1781. Ensign 22 Mar. 1781. Lieut. 5 July 1781. Capt. 29 Apr. 1799. Major 30 Sept. 1803. Retired in England 10 Oct. 1804. *d.* Upper Grosvenor St., London, 15 July 1856, aged 93.

Of Burwood House, Surrey, J.P. and D.L., Lt. Col. Comdt. 3rd Surrey Local Militia. 4th son of William Alcock, of Raunston, Leics., and Mary his wife, sister of Sir Joseph Mawbey, 1st Bart., of Botleys, Surrey. *m.* Bath, 20 Feb. 1802, Hon. Caroline Catherine Letitia, 5th dau. of St. Leger Aldworth, first Viscount Doneraile. (*See also* William Annesley Bailie.) (She died 1 Feb. 1840, aged 66.)

Services : Qmr. 3rd Eur. Bn. in 1790. Transfd. from 2nd Eur. Regt. to 18th N.I. 29 May 1800. Fur. 20 Feb. 1801 till retirement. Subsequently, for many years, Treasurer of the Ordnance in London.
Refs. : Burke's *Landed Gentry of Ireland*, p. 660, *s.n.* Stawell, of Coolmain. Burke's *Peerage*, 1923, p. 738, *s.n.* Doneraile, V. Burke's *Extinct Baronetcies*, 2nd edn., p. 347, *s.n.* Mawbey, of Botleys. *G.M.* 1802, i. 272 ; 1856, ii. 262.

ALDER, Thomas Gilbert (1782-1845). Major. 30th N.I. *bapt.* St. Mary's, Newington Butts, Surrey, 1 Apr. 1782. Cadet 1798. Arrived in India 7 Jan. 1801. Ensign 2 Oct. 1799. Lieut. 28 Oct. 1799. Capt. 26 Jan. 1807. Major 24 Jan. 1819.

Invalided 11 Sept. 1823. Retired 24 Nov. 1826. *d.* Hawley Rd., Kentish Town, 9 Sept. 1845.

Eldest son of Thomas Alder (? of Morris Hall), Comptroller of Customs, and Ann Maria his wife. *m.* 1st, 1815, Bennett, dau.ʳof Capt. Dawes, of the Country ship *Lucy Maria.* (She died Chinsura, Bengal, 24 Mar. 1826.) *m.* 2nd, St. James's, Piccadilly, 20 Sept. 1844, Mary Anne, widow of James Watts, of Tichbourne St., London. (She died 19 Jan. 1864.)

Services : Posted as Lieut. to 2/8th N.I. 15 Apr. 1801. Operations in Jumna Doab 1803 ; Sasni ; Bijaigarh ; Kachaura ; Lieut. 2/8th N.I. Second Mahratta War ; Laswari ; Lieut. 2/8th N.I. Transfd. to newly-raised 24th N.I. in 1805 ; to newly-raised 2/30th N.I. in 1815. Fur. 1812 till 20 June 1815.

Refs. : A.J. 1816, i. *G.M.* 1844, ii. 642 ; 1845, ii. 543.

ALDERSON (*formerly* **LLOYD**), **Christopher** (1790- ?). Ensign. 20th N.I. *b.* London 19 Sept. 1790. Cadet 1809. Arrived in India 2 Aug. 1810. Ensign 26 Feb. 1812. Struck off 22 Nov. 1816.

Of Homerton, Middlesex. Eldest son of William Lloyd, of London, and Kitty Alderson his wife, dau. of Thomas Lever, of Doncaster. Assumed, by R.L., 11 June 1812, the surname of Alderson, in lieu of Lloyd, pursuant to the will of his great-uncle, Christopher Alderson. Cousin-german of Thomas Evans (1776-1812), *q.v.*, and of Sir William Lloyd, Kt., *q.v. m.* Fanny Greig.

Services : Returned to England on fur. 22 Nov. 1811. Promoted to the rank of Lieut. 1 Mar. 1815 : promotion subsequently cancelled.

Refs. : Burke's *Landed Gentry*, 2nd edn., iii. 207, *s.n.* Lloyd, of Brynestyn, co. Denbigh.

ALDERSON, John Christopher (1812-1849). Captain, Invalid Est. 62nd N.I. *b.* Barnstaple, Devon, 2 Feb. 1812. Cadet 1828. Ensign 7 Nov. 1829. Lieut. 2 Nov. 1835. Capt. 22 Mar. 1844. Invalided 20 Mar. 1848. *d.* Calcutta 23 Dec. 1849.

bapt. Barnstaple 3 Feb. 1812. Son of Christopher Richard Alderson, M.D., Surgeon H.M. 95th Regt., and Maria his wife. Addiscombe Cadet 1827-9.

Services : Ensign d.d. 59th N.I. 15 Oct. 1832. Posted as Ensign to 62nd N.I. 22 Dec. 1832, and passed the whole of his service with that Corps. No record of active service. To do duty with Eur. Invalids at Chunar, 2 May 1848.

ALDOUS, William (1793-1869). Lieut. Colonel. 38th N.I. *bapt.* New Buckenham, Norfolk, 22 July 1793. Cadet 1807. Arrived in India 21 Mar. 1809. Ensign 20 Feb. 1809. Lieut. 7 Oct. 1814.

Capt. 22 Apr. 1827. Major 8 Oct. 1836. Retired 30 Mar. 1837. Hon. Lt. Col. 28 Nov. 1854. *d.* Worthing, Sussex, 12 May 1869.

Son of John Aldous. *m.* 1st, Sidmouth, 4 Oct. 1825, Ann Maria, youngest dau. of John Morris, of Staines, Middlesex. (She died 10 Sept. 1827.) *m.* 2nd, Brighton, 22 Mar. 1836, Eliza, youngest dau. of W. Vernon, of North Lodge. (She died Bath, 22 July 1880.)

Services : Barasat C.C. Posted as Ensign to 2/19th N.I. 20 Feb. 1809. (? Nepal War 1814-5 ; Lieut. 2/19th N.I.—name not included in medal roll.) Third Mahratta War ; Lieut. 2/19th N.I., in Reserve Div. Fur. s.c. 14 Feb. 1824 till 24 May 1826. Transfd. to 38th N.I. (late 1/19th) May 1824. Intr. & Qmr. 38th N.I. 28 Dec. 1826. Fur. p.a. 10 Feb. 1830 till 12 Dec. 1831 ; and 20 Sept. 1835 till retirement.

Refs. : A.J. xix. 608 ; N.S. xix. 309. *The Times,* 14 May 1869.

ALEXANDER, James. Fireworker. Artillery. Cadet 1783. Fireworker 10 Mar. 1785. Resigned 20 Feb. 1792.

Services : Adjt. 3rd Bn. Art. in 1790.

ALEXANDER, James (1780-1847). Major General, 74th N.I. *bapt.* Bromley, Kent, 3 Mar. 1780. Cadet 1798. Arrived in India 8 Nov. 1799. Ensign 30 Sept. 1799. Lieut. 28 Oct. 1799. Capt. 13 June 1808. Major 18 Feb. 1820. Lt. Col. 1 May 1824. Col. 1 Dec. 1829. Maj. Gen. 28 June 1838. *d.* Benares 11 Mar. 1847.

Son of Nicholas Alexander and Elizabeth his wife. *m.* (before 1807) Harriet ——. (She died 23 Apr. 1859.) Brother of Thomas Alexander, *q.v.*

Services : Posted as Lieut. to 2/19th N.I. 15 Apr. 1801. Apptd. to Vol. Corps under Major James Maclean, *q.v.*, 21 Dec. 1801. Expedition to Egypt 1801-2. Adjt. 1/10th N.I. 1805-8. Dy. Paymr. Dinapore and Berhampore, 18 Mar. 1808 till 1821. Major 2/19th N.I. Transfd. as Lt. Col. to 48th N.I. 1 May 1824 ; to 39th N.I. ; to raise and command 6th Extra Regt. at Dinapore 21 May 1825. Transfd. to 56th N.I. in 1826. Fur. 11 Feb. 1826 till 23 Nov. 1829. Transfd. to 48th N.I. in 1827 ; to 69th N.I. 1 May 1828 ; to 19th N.I. 13 Jan. 1830 ; to 46th N.I. 8 Jan. 1835 ; to 65th N.I. 12 Jan. 1835. Fur. 14 Jan. 1833 till 23 Dec. 1843. Bdr. 13 Feb. 1843. To comd. at Delhi 23 Apr. 1844. G.O.C. Benares Div. 13 Sept. 1844 till death. Transfd. as Col. to 74th N.I. (late 6th Extra Regt.) 17 Apr. 1845.

Refs. : G.M. 1848, i. 334. Will dated 6 Mar. 1847 ; proved 3 Sept. 1847.

ALEXANDER, Sir James (1803-1888). General, K.C.B. Colonel Comdt. Royal (Bengal) Artillery. *b.* Lambeth, London, 14 Jan. 1803. Cadet 1819. Arrived in India Feb. 1821. 2nd Lieut. 16 June 1820. Lieut. 6 Apr. 1824. Capt. 21 Dec. 1836. Major 1 July 1847. Lt. Col. 25 Feb. 1853. Col. 18 Feb. 1861. Col. Comdt. 21 Jan. 1872. Maj. Gen. 18 May 1856. Lt. Gen. 6 Mar. 1868. Gen. 1 Aug. 1872. *d.* 35 Bedford Pl., Russell Sq., London, 6 June 1888.

m. Ipswich, 28 Apr. 1832, Maria, only dau. of Peter B. Long, of Ipswich. (She died 26 Apr. 1852.). Addiscombe Cadet 1819-20.

Services : Posted as Lieut. to 2nd Troop 3rd Bde. H.A. in 1825. Siege and capture of Bhurtpore (India medal). Served with 3rd Troop 2nd Bde. H.A. 1826-8. Fur. s.c. 19 Nov. 1828 till 5 Nov. 1832. Capt. comdg. 3rd Troop 2nd Bde. H.A. 1838-47. First Afghan War 1842 ; comdg. the Art. with the Force under Maj. Gen. George Pollock, *q.v.* ; forcing of the Khyber Pass ; action at Tezin ; re-occupation of Kabul (Medal). Gwalior campaign ; Maharajpur (Bronze star). First Sikh War ; Badhowal ; Aliwal ; Sobraon (Medal with clasp). Bdr. 2 cl., Lucknow, 23 June 1856. Fur. 1857 till death. Col. Comdt. " F " Bde. R.H.A. 1874-7. C.B. 27 June 1846. K.C.B. 20 May 1871.

Refs. : Boase. *The Times,* 7 June 1888.

ALEXANDER, Nathaniel (1740/41-1792). Captain, Invalid Est. Infantry. *b.* 1740/41. Cadet 1771. Ensign 15 Dec. 1772. Lieut. 14 Mar. 1777. Capt. 14 Mar. 1781. Invalided (?). *d.* Monghyr, Bengal, 31 Jan. 1792, suddenly, in the 52nd year of his age.

Brother of Thomas Alexander, of Long Acre, Middlesex, Charles, Elizabeth Mary, and Ann Alexander, of Manningford Bruce, Wilts.

Services : Comdg. 2nd Bn. Native Invalids at Monghyr in 1790.

Refs. : Will. M.I. in Monghyr cemetery.

ALEXANDER, Samuel (*d.* 1794). Lieutenant, Infantry. From the Bencoolen Est. Ensign Aug. 1786. Lieut. 7 Dec. 1793. *d.* Bencoolen, Sumatra, 13 Sept. 1794.

Services : Reverted to the Bencoolen Est. N.F.P.

ALEXANDER, Thomas (1783-1801). Cadet, Infantry. *bapt.* Bromley, Kent, 7 Mar. 1783. Cadet 1800. Never arrived in India. *d.* 1801 on his passage to India on board the *Earl Howe.*

Son of Nicholas Alexander and Elizabeth his wife. Brother of James Alexander (1780-1847), *q.v.*

THE BENGAL ARMY, 1758-1834 21

ALEXANDER, William (1796-1851). Lieut. Colonel, C.B., 8th L.C. *bapt.* Armagh 8 Apr. 1796. Cadet 1819. Admitted 21 Aug. 1820. Cornet 9 Jan. 1820. Lieut. 1 May 1824. Capt. 30 May 1830. Major 23 July 1839. Lt. Col. 3 Apr. 1846. *d.* Doranda, B. & O., 2 Oct. 1851.

Son of Rev. John Alexander, vicar of Drumsang, co. Westmeath, and Martha his wife, eldest dau. of Henry Thomas Bellingham Ruxton. *m.* 1st, Muttra, 18 July 1823, Anne, dau. of James Kennedy, *q.v.* (*See also* William Charles Birch, Edward Macleod Blair, James Duncan Macpherson, Robert Augustus Master, William Minto.) (She died Muttra, 5 July 1844.) *m.* 2nd, St. James's, Piccadilly, 3 Dec. 1850, Penelope, youngest dau. of William Hooper, of Merton House, co. Hereford.

Services : Cornet H.M. 24th Light Dns. 14 Feb. 1816. Posted as Cornet to 5th L.C. in 1820. Adjt. 5th L.C. 11 Aug. 1823 till 14 June 1827. Comdt. 4th Local Horse 17 Oct. 1838. First Afghan War 1839-42 ; Ghazni 1839 (Medal) ; Kabul 1842 (Medal) ; comdg. 4th Local Horse. First Sikh War ; Mudki ; Ferozshahr ; Aliwal ; Sobraon ; Major 5th L.C. (Medal with 3 clasps). Second Sikh War ; Ramnagar (s.w., lost an arm) ; Bt. Lt. Col. 5th L.C. (Medal). Fur. s.c. 1849-51. Transfd. to 11th L.C. (became 2nd) 27 Mar. 1850 ; to 8th L.C. Nov. 1850. C.B. 24 Dec. 1842. Durani 3 cl. (*Cal. Gaz.* 15 Aug. 1840).

Refs. : Burke's *Landed Gentry*, 9th edn., p. 1293, *s.n.* Ruxton, of Broad Oak, Kent. *Boase. I.M.* 20 Dec. 1850, p. 755.

ALEXANDER, William Charles (1817-1889). Major. 4th European L.C. *b.* 30 Sept. 1817. Cadet 1834. Arrived in India 7 June 1835. Cornet 7 June 1835. Lieut. 16 June 1840. Capt. 9 Oct. 1850. Retired 1 Jan. 1860. Hon. Major 1 Jan. 1860. *d.* 96 Inverness Terr., Hyde Park, London, 24 Aug. 1889.

bapt. Calcutta 4 Jan. 1818. 2nd son of Henry Alexander, B.C.S., M.P. for Barnstaple, a director E.I.C., and Elizabeth Leonora his 1st wife, dau. of Joseph Pringle, Consul Gen. at Madeira. *m.* All Saints, Paddington, 5 Oct. 1865, Ellen Charlotte, only dau. of Thomas Quin, *q.v.*

Services : To do duty with 10th L.C. 19 June 1835. Posted as Cornet to 10th L.C. 24 Aug. 1836. First Afghan War 1842 ; Kabul ; Lieut. 10th L.C. (Medal). Adjt. 2nd Cav., Gwalior Contt., 26 Jan. 1843. Actg. 2nd in comd. 2nd Irreg. Cav. 9 June 1843. Adjt. 2nd Irreg. Cav. 18 May 1844. First Sikh War ; Sobraon ; Adjt. 2nd Irreg. Cav. (Medal). 2nd in comd. 13th Irreg. Cav. 2 Jan. 1846. Second Sikh War ; 13th Irreg. Cav. (Medal). Actg. Comdt. 13th Irreg. Cav. 18 May 1850. Fur. 1854-5. Local Major in Turkey

27 Mar. 1855. Comdt. 11th Irreg. Cav. 22 Sept 1856. Mutiny campaign ; Comdt. 11th Irreg. Cav. (disarmed at Berhampore). Transfd. to 4th Eur. L.C.
Refs. : Foster's *Baronetage*, p. 5. *The Times*, 28 Aug. 1889.

ALEXANDER, William Ferguson (1809-1833). Ensign, 50th N.I. *b.* Bantry, co. Cork, 18 July 1809. Cadet 1826. Arrived in India 11 June 1827. Ensign 13 Feb. 1827. *d.* Bankura, Bengal, 25 Mar. 1833, of fever.
Son of Gen. Alexander. (*Probably* Maj. Gen. William Alexander.)
Services : Operations against the Kols and Chuars in Chota Nagpur 1832-3 ; Ensign 50th N.I. Was doing duty with the Bankura Levy at date of death.
Refs. : A.J. N.S. xii. 113.

ALLAMAND, John Peter (1787-1807). Ensign, unposted. Under instruction at Barasat C.C. *b.* Leicester 31 Jan. 1787. Cadet 1806. Arrived in India 1 Aug. 1807. Ensign 18 Aug. 1807. *d.* Barasat C.C. 27 Oct. 1807.
Son of John Peter Allamand (? of Old Three Cranes, Leicester).

ALLAN, David (1791-1806). Cadet, Infantry. *b.* Edinburgh, 14 May 1791. Cadet 1805. Never arrived in India. *d.* Dec. 1806, on his passage to India, in the wreck of the *Skelton Castle*. Struck off with effect from 5 Nov. 1806.
Son of David Allan, of Edinburgh.
Note : "The *Skelton Castle* sailed from Portsmouth, 24 Sept. 1806, with the *Union* and ' country ' ship *Matilda*. The three ships were reported ' all well on 5 Oct. in lat. 45.55 N., long. 11.38 W.' On 21 Dec. 1806 the *Skelton Castle* appears to have foundered with all her passengers and crew " (*Clan Campbell*, p. 113).
According to a contemporary account, the *Skelton Castle* sailed from Plymouth on or about 24 Sept. 1806, was seen and parted company from the *Union* and the *Matilda* on 10 or 11 Dec. 1806. in lat. 30 S., long. 12 W., and was never seen or heard of again. No less than twenty Bengal Cadets, in addition to two field officers, lost their lives on this occasion.

ALLAN, George (1792-1821). Lieutenant, 7th L.C. *b.* Alloa, co. Clackmannan, 1 Dec. 1792. Cadet 1807. Arrived in India 19 Aug. 1808. Cornet 19 Aug. 1808. Lieut. 31 Dec. 1815. *d.* Karnal 20 Oct. 1821.
Son of James Allan, surveyor of window taxes, and Elizabeth Colvin his wife.
Services : Posted as Cornet to 7th N.C. in 1809. Actg. Adjt.

7th N.C. in 1812; Adjt. do. 1813-5. Nepal War 1814-5; Cornet and Adjt. 7th N.C., in 2nd Div. Siege and capture of Hathras; Lieut. 7th N.C. Third Mahratta War; Dhamoni; Mandala; Multai; Harna; Lieut. 7th N.C., in Centre Div.

ALLARDICE, William. Ensign. Infantry. Cadet 1783. Ensign 23 Mar. 1785. Struck off in England 1791.
Services : Was on fur. in 1790. N.F.P.

*****ALLARDYCE, James George** (1815-1838). 2nd Lieutenant, Engineers. *b.* Bombay 23 Jan. 1815. Cadet 1834. Arrived in India 15 Sept. 1835. 2nd Lieut. 11 June 1833. *d.* Sylhet, Assam, 11 July 1838.
Son of Dr. Allardyce, of Cheltenham. Addiscombe Cadet 1 Aug. 1831 till 11 June 1833. Chatham 27 Mar. 1834 till 13 Feb. 1835.
Services : Posted to Sappers and Miners at Delhi 25 Sept. 1835. To comd. 5th Coy. S. & M. 6 Nov. 1837. Arrived at Sylhet 21 Jan. 1838.
Refs. : M.I. in Sylhet cemetery.

ALLDIN, Joseph James (1775-1834). Lieut. Colonel Comdt., Invalid Est. 48th N.I. *b.* London Bridge 23 Dec. 1775. Cadet 1794. Arrived in India 13 Sept. 1794. Ensign 5 Oct. 1794. Lieut. 1 June 1796. Capt. 21 Sept. 1804. Major 16 Dec. 1814. Lt. Col. 30 June 1819. Lt. Col. Comdt. 1 May 1824. Invalided 16 June 1826. *d.* Bhagulpur, B. & O., 21 Oct. 1834.
bapt. St. Magnus, London Bridge, 22 Jan. 1776. Son of Joseph Alldin and Hannah his wife. Brother of Mrs. Hannah Delmar, of Bridge, nr. Canterbury.
Services : Second Mahratta War; battle of Delhi 11 Sept. 1803 (s.w.); Lieut. 2nd N.I. Adjt. Etawah Sebundy Corps 1804-5. Transfd. as Capt. to newly-raised 2/24th N.I. in 1805. (? Operations in Hariana 1809; Bhawani; Capt. 2/24th N.I.) Major 2/24th N.I. Lt. Col. 2/24th N.I. Transfd. as Lt. Col. Comdt. to 48th N.I. (late 2/24th) May 1824. After transfer to the Invalid Est. he held the appt. of recruiting officer, Tirhut and Bhagulpur, till death.
Refs. : A.J. N.S. xvi. 272. Will dated 2 Aug. 1825; proved 27 Nov. 1834.

ALLEN, Andrew (1785-1819). Bt. Captain, 25th N.I. *b.* Edinburgh 21 Aug. 1785. Cadet 1804. Arrived in India 10 July 1805. Ensign 21 Aug. 1805. Lieut. 21 Aug. 1805. Bt. Capt. 8 Jan. 1818. *d.* Chandpal Ghat, Calcutta, 23 Aug. 1819.
Son of Andrew Allen, of Edinburgh, and Mary Blair his wife.

Services : Posted as Lieut. to 2/25th N.I. in 1806. Expedition to Mauritius 1810 ; Actg. Adjt. 2nd Bengal Vol. Bn. in 3rd Bde. (Lieut. 2/25th N.I.). Comdg. escort to Ava 1812. Actg. S.A.C.G. 24 July 1813. S.A.C.G. 1816 till death.

ALLEN, James. Ensign. Infantry. Cadet (?). Ensign 1764. Dismissed 17 Jan. 1765.

Services : Had been a sergeant in H.M. 84th Regt., was given a Commission in the Bengal Army and apptd. Adjt. of the Eur. Bn.

Refs. : Broome, p. 415.

ALLEN, James (1793-1859). Lieut. Colonel. 7th L.C. b. London 9 Nov. 1793. Cadet 1809. Arrived in India 2 Aug. 1810. Cornet 28 Sept. 1813. Lieut. 1 Sept. 1818. Capt. 2 Oct. 1824. Bt. Major 28 June 1838. Retired 15 Apr. 1840. Hon. Lt. Col. 28 Nov. 1854. d. his residence, the Chantry, Bradford-on-Avon, 1 Apr. 1859.

Son of Thomas Allen.

Services : Cadet d.d. 4th N.I. 1811-3. Posted as Cornet to 7th N.C. 28 Sept. 1813. Nepal War 1814-5 ; Cornet 7th N.C. in 2nd Div. Siege and capture of Hathras ; Cornet 7th N.C. Third Mahratta War ; Dhamoni ; Mandala ; Multai ; Harna ; Lieut. 7th N.C. in Centre Div. Fur. p.a. 10 Sept. 1833 till 7 Dec. 1836. Retired in India on the pension of a Major.

Refs. : G.M. 1859, i. 550. The Times, 6 Apr. 1859.

ALLEN, John (d. 1769). Lieutenant, Infantry. Cadet 1767. Ensign 15 Sept. 1767. Lieut. 28 Apr. 1768. d. 1769.

Services : N.F.P.

ALLEN, Richard. Cadet (? Ensign), Infantry. Cadet 1767. Ensign (?). Resigned 1768.

Services : N.F.P.

ALLEN, Robert Steer (1758-1804). Lieut. Colonel, Pension Est. 11th N.I. b. 1758. Cadet 1778. Arrived in India 10 Dec. 1778. Ensign Dec. 1778. Lieut. 6 Nov. 1779. Capt. 7 Jan. 1796. Major 22 Aug. 1800. Lt. Col. 30 Sept. 1803. Pensioned 1804. d. Cawnpore 30 Oct. 1804.

Son of Robert Allen, of Carey St., London. Ed. St. Paul's school ; admitted 22 Feb. 1769, aged 10.

Services : Sailed for India on the Nassau 7 Mar. 1778, aged 19. First Mahratta War ; with Popham's detachment at capture of Gwalior. Fur. 23 Dec. 1796 till 28 May 1801. Major 11th N.I.

Refs. : Gardiner.

THE BENGAL ARMY, 1758-1834

ALLEY, George Holroyd (1782-1818). Captain, 20th N.I. *b.* psh. of St. Peter, Dublin, *c.* 1782. Cadet 1803. Arrived in India 2 Sept. 1804. Ensign 24 Aug. 1804. Lieut. 21 Sept. 1804. Capt. 3 June 1816. *d.* Penang 26 May 1818.
Son of Rev. Jerome Alley, of Drogheda. *m.* Johanna Christina, dau. of Johannes Plusker, of the Dutch E.I.C.S., head surgeon at Chinsura, Bengal. (*See also* Robert Blisset, Robert Roche, Charles Rowning.) (She died Oct. 1819.) T.C.D. Pensioner, 8 Jan. 1799, aged 17.
Services : Spent the whole of his service with 20th (Marine) N.I. Capture of Java ; Weltervreden ; Cornelis ; Lieut. 1/20th N.I.
Refs. : Alumni Dub. Will dated P.W.I. 25 May 1818 ; proved 18 Sept. 1818.

ALLINGHAM, Edward (1788-1845). Lieutenant. 11th N.I. *b.* London 11 Oct. 1788. Cadet 1807. Arrived in India 19 July 1809. Ensign 19 July 1809. Lieut. 16 Dec. 1814. Retired 28 June 1820. *d.* 13 Mar. 1845.
Youngest son of Thomas Allingham, of the city of London, and Mary his wife, 2nd dau. of John Taylor, of Furseyhurst, I.W. (? *m.* Margaret, who died Kilburn, June 1834.)
Services : Posted as Ensign to 11th N.I. 19 July 1809. Reduction of Kalinjar fort ; Ensign 11th N.I. Lieut. 1/11th N.I. With 3rd Gren. Bn. in 1815. Nepal War 1816 ; Lieut. Champaran L.I. Fur. 1819 till retirement.
Refs. : Burke's *Landed Gentry*, 3rd edn., p. 298, *s.n.* Dickinson, of Farley Hill, Berks.

ALLISON, Edward (1764/65-1804). Captain, 8th N.I. *b.* 1764/65. Cadet 1782. Admitted 12 Nov. 1781. Ensign 7 Feb. 1783. Lieut. 20 Jan. 1790. Capt. 10 June 1803. *d.* Patna 26 Oct. 1804.
Of Burnham, Norfolk.
Services : Sailed for India on the *Worcester* 6 Feb. 1782, aged 17 Bt. Capt. 7 Jan. 1796. Posted to 1st Bengal Eur. Regt. in May 1796. 1st Eur. Regt. in 1798. Operations in Jumna Doab 1802-3 ; Sasni ; Capt. Lt. 8th N.I. (? Second Mahratta War ; Laswari ; Capt. 8th N.I.)
Refs. : Will dated Cawnpore 23 Oct. 1798 ; proved 13 Dec. 1805.

ALPE, Henry (1804-1850). Captain, 41st N.I. *b.* Hardingham, Norfolk, 2 Aug. 1804. Cadet 1822. Arrived in India 20 Oct. 1823. Ensign 11 July 1823. Lieut. 13 May 1825. Capt. 24 Jan. 1845. *d.* Doranda, B. & O., 16 July (? 16 Aug.) 1850.

Son of Col. Hamond Alpe, of Hardingham, and Lucy his wife, younger dau. of Edward Pratt, of Ryston.
Services : Siege and capture of Bhurtpore ; Lieut. 41st N.I. To comd. Police Bn. at Meerut 18 May 1844. Appt. cancelled 11 Sept. 1844. First Sikh War ; Ferozshahr ; Lieut. 41st N.I. (Medal). Fur. 18 Feb. 1847 till 1849.
Refs. : Burke's Landed Gentry, 13th edn., p. 1440, *s.n.* Pratt, of Ryston Hall, Norfolk. *I.M.* 5 Oct. 1850, p. 581.

ALSTON, David (*d.* 1815). Lieutenant. Infantry. Cadet 1772. Ensign 1 Aug. 1776. Lieut. 19 July 1778. Struck off 179—. *d.* Scotland 6 Aug. 1815.
Of Auchterhard.
Services : At home on fur. in 1787 : struck off after 1791, having been absent from India for more than five years. N.F.P.
Refs. : S.M. 1815, p. 875.

*ALSTON, George (*d.* 1763). Lieutenant, Bengal European Regt. Cadet (?). Ensign (?). Lieut. (?). *d.* 1 July 1763 : kld. in action at the battle of Manji ; *or* massacred at or near Patna, 5th, 6th or 11th Oct. 1763, by order of Nawab Mir Muhammad Kasim. (See note to Benjamin Adamson.)
Services : N.F.P.
Refs. : Broome, p. 365. *Innes,* p. 169. M.I. in Patna city.

ALSTON, James Millar (1791-1824). Captain, 40th N.I. *b.* Glasgow 13 June 1791. Cadet 1809. Arrived in India 2 Aug. 1810. Ensign 27 Nov. 1811. Lieut. 30 July 1816. Capt. 1824. *d.* Calcutta 1 Oct. 1824.
Son of John Alston, of Westertown.
Services : Cadet d.d. 4th N.I. 1811-2. Posted as Ensign to 11th N.I. in 1812. Transfd. to newly-raised 2/28th N.I. in 1815. (? Third Mahratta War ; Dhamoni ; Lieut. 2/28th N.I.) Transfd. to 2/20th N.I. at P.W.I. in 1818. Fur. 1820-3. Transfd. to 40th N.I. (late 2/20th) May 1824.
Refs. : S.M. 1825, i. 511.

ALSTON, James Stewart (1810-1848). Captain, 27th N.I. *b.* Moulin, co. Perth, 17 May 1810. Cadet 1825. Arrived in India 22 Oct. 1826. Ensign 21 June 1826. Lieut. 15 Feb. 1829. Capt. 13 Jan. 1842. *d.* Green St., Park Lane, London, 3 Nov. 1848.
2nd son of Major James Alston-Stewart, of Urrard, co. Perth (who assumed the additional surname of Stewart 15 Apr. 1830), and Charlotte his wife. Brother of William Alston (1804-1844), *q.v.*
Services : Posted as Ensign to 27th N.I. 21 June 1826. Served

THE BENGAL ARMY, 1758-1834

with the Pioneer Corps 9 Dec. 1829 till 1831. Adjt. 27th N.I. 13 Dec. 1831 till 1842. First Afghan War 1840-2 ; Ghazni garrison ; Capt. 27th N.I. (Medal). Taken prisoner : released, 22 Sept. 1842. Fur. s.c. 18 Apr. 1843 till 1845. Fur. 1848 till death.

Refs. : Burke's *Landed Gentry*, 7th edn., p. 1743, *s.n.* Stewart, of Urrard, co. Perth. *G.M.* 1848, ii. 664.

ALSTON, William (*d.* 1786). Captain, 2nd Bengal European Bn. Cadet 1769. Ensign 13 Nov. 1769. Lieut. 9 Mar. 1773. Capt. 21 Sept. 1779. *d.* Cawnpore 21 Sept. 1786.

Eldest son of William Alston, of Edinburgh, W.S.

Services : N.F.P.

Refs. : *S.M.* 1787, p. 206.

ALSTON, William (1804-1844). Captain, 68th N.I. *b.* Moulin, co. Perth, 8 Oct. 1804. Cadet 1823. Arrived in India 7 Oct. 1824. Ensign 20 May 1824. Lieut. 2 Jan. 1826. Capt. 3 Oct. 1842. *d.* on board the *Amherst*, off Akyab, 27 Jan. 1844.

Of Urrard, co. Perth. Elder son of Major James Alston-Stewart, of Urrard (who assumed the additional surname of Stewart 15 Apr. 1830), and Charlotte his wife. Brother of James Stewart Alston, *q.v. m.* Narsinghpur, C.P., 7 Apr. 1830, Penelope Crichton, dau. of Samuel Pidding Bishop, *q.v.* (*See also* James Mackay.) (She died Calcutta 29 July 1855.)

Services : Sailed for India on the *Asia* 20 May 1824. Posted as Ensign to 34th N.I. 31 Mar. 1825. Transfd. as Ensign to 68th N.I. in 1825, and remained with that Regt. throughout his service. First Burma War 1825 ; Ensign 68th N.I. Intr. & Qmr. 68th N.I. 31 Aug. 1831 till 9 Dec. 1840. Jodhpur demonstration 1834. Fur. 13 Feb. 1840 till 8 Oct. 1842.

Refs. : Burke's *Landed Gentry*, 7th edn., p. 1743, *s.n.* Stewart, of Urrard, co. Perth. M.I. in Akyab cemetery.

Note : It is doubtful whether he himself ever assumed the additional surname of Stewart.

ALSTON, William Charles (1760/61-1838). Lieut. Colonel. 24th N.I. *b.* 1760/61. Was already in India when apptd. Cadet on 21 Mar. 1779. Ensign 12 Oct. 1779. Lieut. 22 May 1781. Capt. 31 Aug. 1798. Major 21 Sept. 1804. Lt. Col. 23 June 1809. Retired 15 Aug. 1809. *d.* Devonshire St., London, 1 Apr. 1838, aged 77.

Services : Was Adjt. 24th Bn. Sepoys in 1790. Capt. 16th N.I. and Bk. Mr. at Dinapore in 1803-4. Transfd. as Major to newly-raised 24th N.I. in 1804. Fur. 28 Jan. 1805 till retirement.

Refs. : *G.M.* 1838, i. 554. *N. & Q.* 12 S. i. 204. M.I. in St. John's Church, St. John's Wood Rd., London.

ALVES, Gilmour (1775-1801). Lieutenant, Infantry. *b.* Edinburgh Castle *c.* Feb. 1775. Cadet 1794. Arrived in India 22 Feb. 1796. Ensign 7 Oct. 1795. Lieut. 3 Oct. 1796. *d.* Chunar 25 May 1801.
Son of —— Alves, of Edinburgh Castle, later of Askham, Yorks. (*Probably* son of Basil Alves, Fort Major of Edinburgh Castle, who died 4 Apr. 1797.)
Services : N.F.P.
Note : One Gilmour Alves was Ensign H.M. 35 Foot 13 Mar. 1789 (Army rank, 10 Sept. 1788).

AMMOND or AMMON, George (1756/57-1784). Lieutenant, Infantry. *b.* 1756-57. Cadet 1778. Ensign 6 Oct. 1778. Lieut. 13 Oct. 1778. *d.* Jan. 1784, whilst on active service with the Bombay detachment.
A native of Herts. His sole legatee was James Bucknall, third Viscount Grimston.
Services : First Mahratta War 1781-4 ; served with the detachment under Lt. Col. Grainger Muir, *q.v.*, sent to Bombay in 1781 to reinforce Lt. Col. Jacob Camac, *q.v.*
Refs. : Will dated 27 Apr. 1780.

AMOS, Robert (*d.* 1798). Bt. Captain, Infantry. Was already in India when apptd. Cadet on 11 Aug. 1778. Ensign 13 May 1779. Lieut. 18 Jan. 1781. Bt. Capt. 7 Jan. 1796. *d.* Cawnpore 29 Nov. 1798.
Services : N.F.P.

AMPHLETT, Thomas (*d.* 1790). Lieutenant, Infantry. Cadet 1782. Ensign 13 Apr. 1783. Lieut. 12 Mar. 1790. *d.* Dinapore 7 Sept. 1790.
Services : N.F.P.

ANBURY, Sir Thomas (1759/60-1840). Major General, K.C.B., Kt. Engineers. *b.* 1759/60. Cadet 1782. Admitted 30 July 1784. Ensign 12 Nov. 1783. Lieut. 8 Jan. 1796. Capt. 1 Jan. 1806. Major 1 Sept. 1818. Lt. Col. 1 Dec. 1826. Col. 5 June 1829. Lt. Col. Comdt. 9 May 1829. Maj. Gen. 10 Jan. 1837. *d.* Saugor, C.P., 31 Mar. 1840, aged 80.
Son of O. Anbury (who died Thornbury, Gloucs., in 1820). Cousin of Elizabeth Carr of Hamilton Terr., Maida Hill. *m.* Calcutta 16 Feb. 1794, Miss Caroline Dent.
Services : Dy. Comy. of Stores 14 Feb. 1794. Comy. of Stores, Fort William, 1797 till 1808. Fur. 1808 till 1810. Served in Java in 1813 ; in P.W.I. in 1814. Supt. of bldgs. at Barrackpore 1815-6 ; at Delhi 1817. Third Mahratta War. Comdt. newly-

raised Corps of S. & M. 19 Feb. 1819 till 1828. Principal Field Engr. at Cawnpore 1820-4. Siege and capture of Bhurtpore; Chief Engineer. Suptg. Engr., P.W.D., N.W.F., 1829-31. Lt. Col. Comdt. Engineers and Chief Engr., with a seat on the Mily. Board, 2 July 1830. G.O.C. Saugor Div. 24 Nov. 1836 till death. Demonstration against Jhansi Dec. 1838-Jan. 1839; G.O.C. the Force. C.B. 24 Oct. 1818. Kt. 29 Aug. 1827. K.C.B. 20 July 1838.
Refs.: *G.M.* 1840, ii. 558. Will dated 7 Aug. 1838; proved 21 Apr. 1840.

ANDERDON, William Proctor (1781-1859). Captain. 8th N.I. *bapt.* 2 Apr. 1781 (ptely.). Cadet 1796. Arrived in India 9 Oct. 1797. Ensign 24 Oct. 1797. Lieut. 10 Sept. 1798. Capt. 25 Jan. 1809. Retired 8 July 1812. *d.* his residence, St. James's Sq., Bath, 16 Apr. 1859, in his 79th year. Received into the Church at St. Mary Magdalen, Taunton, 10 Sept. 1781.

Son of Ferdinando Anderdon and Mary his wife. Nephew of Edmund Anderdon, mayor of Bath for three successive years. *m.* Queen St. Chapel, Bath, 18 Jan. 1817, Frances, 3rd dau. of John Livesey, of Bath.

Services : Selected in 1801 to raise and train one of the new L.I. Coys. Operations in Jumna Doab 1803; Sasni; Lieut. 8th N.I. Bde. Maj. 2nd Bde., Lord Lake's Army, 26 Aug. 1803. Second Mahratta War; Laswari; capture of Deig 24 Dec. 1804 (s.w. in shoulder); Lieut. and Adjt. 2/8th N.I., Bde. Maj. (India medal). In charge of Cadets in 1805. Capt. Lt. 8th N.I. 23 Feb. 1807. Fur. 22 Jan. 1810 till retirement.

Refs.: *G.M.* 1859, i. 653. *The Times*, 20 Apr. 1859. *Pester, passim.*

ANDERSON, David Dalrymple (1789-1850). Major. 29th N.I. *b.* North Berwick 28 Sept. 1789. Cadet 1804. Arrived in India 6 Apr. 1806. Ensign 23 Mar. 1806. Lieut. 24 Feb. 1807. Capt. 11 July 1823. Major 4 July 1836. Retired in India 6 Apr. 1838. *d.* 13 Sept. 1850.

Son of John Anderson, of Windygard.

Services : (? Nepal War 1814-5; Lieut. 2/14th N.I., with 3rd Div.) Intr. & Qmr. 2/15th N.I. in 1819. Bde. Maj. Cawnpore, 30 June 1820. A.D.C. to Maj. Gen. Sir Gabriel Martindell, *q.v.*, 10 Jan. 1822. Adjt. 2/14th N.I. 15 June 1822 till 19 Aug. 1823. Fort Adjt. at Delhi 21 June 1823 till 1825. Transfd. to 29th N.I. (late 2/14th) May 1824. Bde. Maj., Meerut, 25 June 1825. Siege and capture of Bhurtpore; A.A.G. 2nd Inf. Div. D.A.A.G 2 Sept. 1826. A.A.G., Sirhind Div., 29 Dec. 1829; do. Benares Div., 9 Mar. 1835. Leave to the Cape for two years, 17 Jan. 1836.

LIST OF THE OFFICERS OF

ANDERSON, George (1783-1811). Lieutenant, 15th N.I. *b.* Dublin 14 Aug. 1783. Cadet 1802. Arrived in India 31 Aug. 1803. Ensign 3 Sept. 1803. Lieut. 21 Sept. 1804. *d.* Java 19 Oct. 1811.

bapt. Protestant Dissenters' Chapel, Strand, Dublin. Son of James Anderson, of Dublin, merchant.
Services : Ensign d.d. 9th N.I. in 1804. Posted as Lieut. to 15th N.I. in 1805. Capture of Java ; Lieut. 3rd Bn. Bengal Vols.

ANDERSON, Henry (1779-1810). Captain, 12th N.I. *b.* Clapton, Middlesex, 5 June 1779. Cadet 1798. Arrived in India 23 Nov. 1799. Ensign 17 Nov. 1799. Lieut. 29 May 1800. Capt. 28 Oct. 1808. *d.* Nadia, Bengal, 30 July 1810.

Son of William Anderson and Ann Grisel his wife, dau. of Robert Boardman. Brother of John Anderson (1784-1866), *q.v. m.* (?).
Services : Posted as Lieut. to 1/12th N.I. 15 Apr. 1801. Second Mahratta War ; Agra ; Laswari ; capture of Deig ; Bhurtpore ; Lieut. 1/12th W.I. Operations in Oudh 1808. Served with Pioneers 1808-9.

ANDERSON, Henry (1784-1805). Lieutenant, 14th N.I. *bapt.* Coates 5 Mar. 1784. Cadet 1799. Arrived in India 10 Dec. 1800. Ensign 8 Oct. 1800. Lieut. 17 May 1802. *d.* Fatehpur Sikri, U.P., 22 Sept. 1805.

Son of Dr. Anderson, of Coates, of psh. of St. Cuthbert, Edinburgh.
Services : Posted as Ensign to 1/14th N.I. 17 Apr. 1801, and remained with that Regt. throughout his service. Second Mahratta War ; battle of Delhi ; Agra ; siege and capture of Gwalior ; Lieut. 1/14th N.I.

ANDERSON, James. Lieutenant. Infantry. Cadet 1775. Ensign 29 July 1776. Lieut. 16 July 1778. Struck off 1791.

Brother of David Anderson, B.C.S., President of the Committee of Revenue.
Services : Benares Insurrection 1781. Asst. to his brother, David, as Political Resident with Sindhia 1782-5. Succeeded his brother as Resident in 1785. Was on fur. in 1790.
Refs. : D.I.B. (*s.n.* David Anderson).

ANDERSON, James (1784-1811). Lieutenant, 18th N.I. *b.* Cupar, co. Fife, 13 Dec. 1784. Cadet 1805. Arrived in India 7 Feb. 1807. Ensign 3 Jan. 1807. Lieut. 1 Aug. 1810. *d.* Fatehgarh 22 Mar. 1811.

Son of Bailie James Anderson.
Services : Posted as Ensign to 18th N.I., and served throughout

with that Regt. Was on active service with his Bn. in either Bundelkhand or Hariana in 1809.

ANDERSON, John (*d.* 1772). Lieutenant, Infantry. Cadet 1767. Ensign 15 Sept. 1767. Lieut. 9 Oct. 1769. *d.* Burdwan, Bengal, Jan. 1772.
Services : N.F.P.

ANDERSON, John (*d.* 1820). Lieutenant. Infantry. Cadet 1781. Ensign 21 Aug. 1781. Lieut. 6 June 1783. Resigned 22 Feb. 1792. *d.* Norfolk St., Strand, London, 10 May 1820.
Services : N.F.P.
Refs. : *G.M.* 1820, i. 477.

ANDERSON, John (*d.* 1812). Bt. Major, Bengal European Regt. Cadet 1783. Admitted 29 Oct. 1783. Ensign 27 Jan. 1785. Lieut. 21 Oct. 1791. Capt. 13 July 1803. Bt. Major 25 July 1810. *d.* Colgong, Bengal, 21 Jan. 1812.
m. Howrah, Bengal, 30 Nov. 1787, Mrs. Elizabeth Thomas. His dau. *m.* Browne Roberts, *q.v.*
Services : Lieut. 1st Bengal Eur. Regt. in 1796 ; Capt. Lt. do. 8 Jan. 1798. Second Mahratta War ; Capt. Bengal Eur. Regt.

ANDERSON, John (1784-1866). General. Colonel 61st N.I. *b.* St. James's, Garlick Hythe, London, 14 Dec. 1784. Cadet 1800. Arrived in India 6 Feb. 1802. Ensign 25 Dec. 1801. Lieut. 28 Mar. 1804. Capt. 1 Aug. 1818. Major 14 July 1825. Lt. Col. 3 June 1830. Col. 7 June 1842. Maj. Gen. 20 June 1854. Lt. Gen. 5 Dec. 1855. Gen. 13 Jan. 1864. *d.* 25 Apr. 1866.
Son of William Anderson, of No. 1, Three Cranes Wharf, London, and Ann Grisel his wife, dau. of Robert Boardman. Brother of Henry Anderson (1779-1810), *q.v. m.* 1st, Delhi, 27 Mar. 1806, Miss Mary Morrell. *m.* 2nd, Fatehgarh, 22 Oct. 1827, Anna Moor. (She died 20 Nov. 1874 in her 74th year.)
Services : Posted as Ensign to 19th N.I. in 1803. Transfd. to newly-raised 22nd N.I. in 1804 ; to newly-raised 1/27th N.I. in 1805. Operations against Dhundia Khan 1807 ; Komona ; Lieut. 1/27th N.I. Adjt. 1/27th N.I. 26 Nov. 1811 till 4 Aug. 1818. Nepal War 1814-5 (India medal). 3rd Ceylon Vol. Bn. 1818-9. Fur. 1819. Transfd. to 32nd N.I. in 1823 ; to 63rd N.I. (late 1/32nd) May 1824. Siege and capture of Bhurtpore ; Capt. 3rd Extra Regt. (clasp to India medal). Transfd. to 62nd N.I. 24 Jan. 1831 ; to 8th N.I. 19 Feb. 1834. Fur. s.c. 31 Dec. 1834. Col. 61st N.I. 7 July 1842. Fur. 28 Feb. 1842 till death.
Refs. : *The Times,* 4 May 1866.

ANDERSON, John (1787-1806). Cadet, Infantry *b.* Durness, co. Sutherland, 2 Aug. 1787. Cadet 1805. Never arrived in India. *d.* Dec. 1806, on his passage to India, in the wreck of the *Skelton Castle.* Struck off with effect from 5 Nov. 1806. (See note to David Allan.)

ANDERSON, John (1807-1849). Captain, Artillery. *b.* Westham, Essex, 21 Aug. 1807. Cadet 1824. Arrived in India 23 July 1825. 2nd Lieut. 16 Dec. 1824. Lieut. 26 Apr. 1828. Bt. Capt. 16 Dec. 1839. Capt. 25 Nov. 1843. *d.* 21 Feb. 1849 ; kld. in action at battle of Gujerat.

Son of Alexander Anderson, of London, merchant, and Christian his wife. Brother of William Anderson (1804-1869), *q.v.* Addiscombe Cadet 1823-4.

Services : Posted to 2nd Troop 1st Bde., H.A., 11 Oct. 1828. First Afghan War 1838-9 ; with Army of the Indus ; capture of Ghazni (Medal) ; occupation of Kabul. Fur. p.a. 9 Feb. 1844 till Nov. 1845. First Sikh War ; Sobraon ; Capt. 4th Coy. 3rd Bn. Foot Art. (Medal). To comd. 4th Troop 3rd Bde., H.A., 1846. Second Sikh War ; 1st siege of Multan ; 2nd siege and capture of Multan ; Gujerat (kld.) ; comdg. 4th Troop 3rd Bde., H.A.

Refs. : De Rhé-Philipe. Will dated 20 Nov. 1845 ; proved 19 Mar. 1849. M.I. St. Stephen's, Dum-Dum.

ANDERSON, John (1804-1851). Major, 44th N.I. *b.* Monikie, co. Forfar, 19 Mar. 1804. Cadet 1825. Arrived in India 18 Sept. 1826. Ensign 5 May 1826. Lieut. 3 Sept. 1832. Capt. 26 June 1840. Major 25 Nov. 1850. *d.* Barrackpore 2 Aug. 1851.

bapt. 29 Mar. 1804. Son of George Anderson, tenant in Carlungie.
Services : Fur. s.c. 16 Dec. 1831 till 11 Aug. 1834. Adjt. 44th N.I. 19 Sept. 1838 till 3 Aug. 1840. First Sikh War ; Ferozshahr ; Capt. 44th N.I. (Medal).

ANDERSON, John (1810-1857). Lieut. Colonel, Engineers. *b.* 18 Aug. 1810. Cadet 1827. Arrived in India 10 Jan. 1829. 2nd Lieut. 15 June 1827. Lieut. 28 Sept. 1827. Capt. 8 Nov. 1843. Major 1 May 1855. Lt. Col. 20 Sept. 1857 (his death occurred 9 days earlier). *d.* Lucknow 11 Sept. 1857.

Son of George Anderson, merchant. Brother of James Anderson, of Durie Foundry, co. Fife. *m.* Hazaribagh, B. & O., 5 Oct. 1837, Elizabeth, dau. of Alexander Dingwall, of Ranieston, co. Aberdeen. (*See also* George Thomson (1799-1886.) Ed. Cupar Academy. Addiscombe Cadet 1826-7.

Services : Lieut. d.d. S. & M. at Aligarh 11 Feb. 1829. Asst. to Supt. of Doab canal 16 May 1836. Executive Engr., P.W.D.,

Ramgarh Div., 22 Dec. 1836. First Afghan War 1839 ; Ghazni (Medal). Transfd. from Burdwan to Benares Div., P.W.D., 31 Oct. 1845 ; as Executive Engr. from Delhi to Ambala 2 Oct. 1847. Apptd. Chief Engr., Oudh, 13 June 1856. Mutiny campaign 1857 ; at Lucknow as Chief Engr., Oudh, at outbreak of mutiny ; Chief Engr. during defence of Lucknow till death.
Refs. : *Thackeray,* p. 91. *Boase. I.L.N.,* 1 Aug. 1863, p. 124 (view of memorial monument). Will dated 25 June 1845 ; proved 9 Aug. 1858.

ANDERSON, Philip Cortlandt (1792/93-1842). Major, 64th N.I. *b.* 1792/93. Cadet 1809. Admitted 1810. Ensign 8 Aug. 1812. Lieut. 13 Sept. 1815. Capt. 24 Apr. 1827. Major 17 Jan. 1841. *d.* Jalalabad, Afghanistan, 24 Apr. 1842.

2nd son of John M. Anderson and Mary Ricketts his wife, eldest dau. of Col. Philip Van Cortlandt. *m.* Lucy, dau. of Harry Younge by his first wife. (She died 20 July 1881, aged 76.) Passed by C.D. as Cadet on 11 Mar. 1810, aged 17.

Services : Cadet d.d. 13th N.I. 1811-2. Posted as Ensign to 1/6th N.I. in 1812. Nepal War 1814-5 ; Ensign 1/6th N.I., in 2nd Div. Third Mahratta War ; Lieut. 1/6th N.I., in Reserve Div. Served with the Pioneers 1821-8. First Burma War. Siege and capture of Bhurtpore. Transfd. to 32nd N.I. 11 July 1823 ; to 64th N.I. (late 2/32nd) May 1824. Second in comd. Mhairwara Local Bn. 15 Feb. 1828 till 1836. Bde. Major at Delhi 11 Dec. 1838 till 28 Sept. 1839. Comdt. Delhi Palace Guards 26 Nov. 1839. First Afghan War 1842 ; retreat from Ali Masjid to Jamrud ; forcing of Khyber Pass ; relief of Jalalabad ; Major 64th N.I., with Gen. Pollock's Force.

Refs. : Burke's *Landed Gentry,* 2nd edn., p. 1363, *s.n.* Taylor, of Pennington, Hants.

ANDERSON, Robert. Captain. Infantry. Cadet 1771. Ensign 20 July 1773. Lieut. 16 Mar. 1778. Capt. 9 Oct. 1781. Struck off 1791.
Services : N.F.P.

ANDERSON, Robert (1753-1810). Ensign, Infantry. Subsequently Asst. Surgeon, Bengal Medical Est. *b.* London 1753. Cadet 1781. Ensign 29 Sept. 1781. Resigned combatant Commission 2 Jan. 1782. Asst. Surgeon 2 Jan. 1782. *d.* Jessore, Bengal, 11 Apr. 1810.

Services : Practised as a medical man for over thirteen years before he became a combatant officer. Surgeon's Mate of the *Grosvenor* 1778-9 ; of the *Rochford* 1780. Apptd. Cadet on 9 Jan.

1781, aged 27. Resigned his combatant Commission from the date of his Warrant as Asst. Surgeon.
Refs. : *Crawford*, i. 236, etc.

ANDERSON, Robert. Lieutenant, Infantry. Cadet (?). Ensign (?). Lieut. 1782. Struck off 1788. *Probably identical with the last.*

ANDERSON, Samuel (*d.* 1790). Lieutenant, Infantry. Cadet 1779. Ensign 2 Oct. 1779. Lieut. 2 June 1781. *d.* Calcutta 25 Feb. 1790.
Services : N.F.P.

ANDERSON, Thomas (1764/65-1789). Lieutenant, Infantry. *b.* Ireland 1764/65. Cadet 1780. Arrived in India 15 Nov. 1782. Ensign 1780. Lieut. 26 July 1781. *d.* Cawnpore (? Fatehgarh) 23 Sept. 1789.
m. Alice.
Services : Sailed for India on the *Hillsborough* on 27 July 1780. This ship having been captured by the combined fleets of France and Spain off the N.W. coast of Africa, on 9 Aug. 1780, he spent some time as a prisoner of war in Spain. On his release he returned to England, whence he eventually sailed for India as a Lieut. on the *Worcester*, 6 Feb. 1782, aged 17.
Refs. : *S.M.* 1791, p. 203. Will dated Chunar Ghur 30 July 1788.

ANDERSON, William (1803-1858). Lieut. Colonel, 59th N.I. *bapt.* London 28 Aug. 1803. Cadet 1822. Arrived in India 13 May 1823. Ensign 21 Apr. 1823. Lieut. 9 Dec. 1824. Capt. 3 Oct. 1838. Major 8 May 1853. Lt. Col. 15 Sept. 1856. *d.* Mount Abu, Rajputana, 21 Apr. 1858.
Son of William Anderson, of Piccadilly, London, job master. *m.* Saugor, 5 Mar. 1835, Amelia Mary, 2nd dau. of George Chapman, *q.v.*
Services : Posted as Ensign to 30th N.I. in 1823. Transfd. to 59th N.I. (late 1/30th) May 1824. First Burma War ; Arakan 1825 ; Lieut. 2nd L.I. Bn. (India medal). Adjt. Gardner's Horse 17 Dec. 1825. 2nd in comd. 2nd Local Horse. Adjt. do. till 25 Aug. 1838. Comdt. Shah Shuja's 2nd Cav. 3 Sept. 1838. First Afghan War 1839-42 ; Ghazni (Medal) ; comdg. Shah's 2nd Cav. ; taken prisoner by Mohd. Akbar Khan during the retreat from Kabul ; released 22 Sept. 1842 ; action at Parwan-dara Nov. 1840. 2nd in comd. Jodhpur Legion 29 Sept. 1843. Comdt. and Supt. Sirohi, Rajputana, 25 Nov. 1845 till death. Durani, 3 cl.
Refs. : *The Times*, 14 Oct. 1858.

THE BENGAL ARMY, 1758-1834   35

ANDERSON, William (1804-1869). Colonel, C.B. Artillery. *b.* London 27 Apr. 1804. Cadet 1819. Arrived in India Feb. 1821. 2nd Lieut. 16 June 1820. Lieut. 1 May 1824. Capt. 11 Oct. 1837. Major 9 Aug. 1847. Lt. Col. 6 Mar. 1854. Col. 28 Nov. 1854. Retired 20 Feb. 1855. *d.* Albury Hall, Ware, Hants, 22 Sept. 1869.

Of 19 Gloucester Sq., Hyde Park, London. Son of Alexander Anderson, of London, merchant, and Christian his wife. Brother of John Anderson (1807-1849), *q.v.* *m.* Calcutta, 9 Dec. 1845, Frances Sophia Pattle, youngest dau. of Trevor John Chicheley Plowden, B.C.S. Addiscombe Cadet 1818 till June 1820.

Services : Sailed for India on the *Commodore Hayes* in 1820. Served at Fort Marlbro' 1821-2. Siege and capture of Bhurtpore ; Lieut. 1st Troop 2nd Bde., H.A. (from 3rd Troop 1st Bde.) (India medal). Adjt. & Qmr. 1st Bde. H.A. 26 Mar. 1831. Accompanied Sir H. Fane to Bombay in 1838 with experimental guns for camel draught. Raised two troops of H.A. for service with Shah Shuja. First Afghan War 1838-42 ; Kandahar ; Ghazni ; Kabul ; comdg. Shah's H.A. (Medals). Powder Agent at Ichapur, Bengal, 2 Jan. 1843 till Mar. 1854. Special Commr. to enquire into the Bengal Comst. 1851-2. Presented with the Freedom of the Burgh of Wick 12 Sept. 1862. C.B. 24 Dec. 1842. Durani, 3 cl. (*Calcutta Gaz.* 15 Aug. 1840).

Refs. : The Times, 27 Sept. 1869.

ANDREE, Frederick (1783-1819). Captain, 4th N.I. *bapt.* Enfield 19 Sept. 1783. Cadet 1798. Arrived in India 26 Nov. 1799. Ensign 20 Nov. 1799. Lieut. 29 May 1800. Capt. 19 Dec. 1809. *d. unm.* Sambalpur, B. &. O., 12 Jan. 1819.

Son of Frederick Andree and Anne his wife. Brother of Richard Collyer Andree, *q.v.*

Services : Posted as Ensign to 2/4th N.I. 15 Apr. 1801. Second Mahratta War ; storm of Aligarh 4 Sept. 1803 (w.) ; battle of Deig ; Lieut. 1/4th N.I. Adjt. 1/4th N.I. 1804-5. Adjt. & Qmr. 4th N.I. 1805 till 11th Feb. 1807. Adjt. Invalid Bn. at Allahabad 1809-10. Actg. Agent for manufacture of gunpowder at Allahabad 1811. Fur. 1812-3. Raised 1/30th N.I. at Dinapore in 1815 (G.O. of 11 Jan. 1815). With 4th Gren. Bn. in 1815.

ANDREE, Richard Collyer (1785-1865). General. Colonel 69th N.I. *b.* London 5 June 1785. Cadet 1799. Admitted 5 Jan. 1801. Ensign 5 Nov. 1800. Lieut. 10 May 1802. Capt. 16 Dec. 1814. Major 1 May 1824. Lt. Col. 27 Jan. 1826. Col. 20 June 1836. Maj. Gen. 23 Nov. 1841. Lt. Gen. 11 Nov. 1851. Gen. 2 Nov. 1861. *d.* Stuttgart, Württemberg, 27 Mar. 1865.

bapt. St. Anne's, Westminster, 15 July 1785. Son of Frederick Andree and Anne his wife. Brother of Frederick Andree, q.v.

Services : Second Mahratta War ; Koil ; Aligarh ; Chandausi (led storming party) ; relief of Delhi ; battle and capture of Deig ; Lieut. 4th N.I. Adjt. & Qmr. 4th N.I. 11 Feb. 1807 till 1814. Nepal War 1816 ; Capt. 2/4th N.I., in 4th Bde. Centre Column (India medal with clasps). Fur. 16 Jan. 1817 till 6 Nov. 1819. Employed in comd. of his Regt. in Oudh, in 1819, in the reduction of various forts. Transfd. as Major to 7th N.I. (late 1/4th) May 1824. First Burma War ; Cachar 1825 ; comdg. 7th N.I. in 3rd Bde. of force under Bdr. Gen. Thomas Shuldham, *q.v.* Comdd. 7th N.I. till 1 Nov. 1838. To comd. troops in Rohilkhand and Kumaon 16 July 1835. Fur. 11 Feb. 1838 till death. Transfd. from 7th to 69th N.I. Nov. 1850.

Refs. : The Times, 5 Apr. 1865.

ANDREWS, Charles (1789-1842). Major, 2nd Bengal European Regt. *bapt.* Andover, Hants, 16 Sept. 1789. Cadet 1804. Arrived in India May 1806. Ensign 12 Nov. 1805. Lieut. 17 Sept. 1806. Capt. 18 Aug. 1823. Major 8 Oct. 1839. *d.* Ludhiana 15 Aug. 1842, aged 53.

Eldest son of Major John Andrews, of Andover, and Jane his wife. *m.* (?).

Services : Served at the capture of Cape of Good Hope in Jan. 1806, whilst on his way out to India. Posted as Ensign to 1/5th N.I. June 1806. Transfd. to 2/21st N.I. July 1806 ; to 2/24th N.I. Dec. 1806. Operations against Dhundia Khan 1807 ; Ganauri ; Lieut. 2/24th N.I. Transfd. to newly-raised 1/32nd N.I. Sept. 1823 ; to 64th N.I. (late 2/32nd) May 1824. Tempy. charge of Agra Provl. Bn. 9 Feb. 1828. Fur. s.c. 18 mos. to N.S.W. and Mauritius 13 Feb. 1829. Bde. Major E. Frontier 1831. D.A.A.G. 30 Aug. 1836 till 11 Nov. 1839. Posted to 2nd Eur. Regt. 21 Oct. 1839. Comdd. 2nd L.I. Bn. 12 Nov. 1840 till death.

Refs. : G.M. 1843, i. 554. De Rhé-Philipe. Will dated 3 Jan. 1840 ; proved 12 Mar. 1844.

ANDREWS, James Richard Benson (1809-1902). Captain, Invalid Est. 52nd N.I. *b.* Richmond, Surrey, 21 May 1809. Cadet 1825. Arrived in India 25 Oct. 1826. Ensign 23 May 1826. Lieut. 18 Feb. 1828. Capt. 1 Jan. 1841. Invalided 2 Oct. 1846. *d.* Mussoorie, U.P., 14 Aug. 1902, of acute bronchitis, aged 93.

Son of William Smith Andrews, of Richmond, surgeon. Brother of William Eyre Andrews, *q.v. m.* Chinsura, Bengal, 24 Dec. 1843, Rath Deacle, widow.

Services : Posted as Ensign to 18th N.I. Transfd. as Ensign

THE BENGAL ARMY, 1758-1834 37

to 52nd N.I. 4 Jan. 1827. Fur. s.c. 19 Feb. 1835 till 2 Feb. 1838. No record of active service.

ANDREWS, William Eyre (1808-1854). Bt. Major, 73rd N.I. *b.* Richmond, Surrey, 10 Feb. 1808. Cadet 1824. Arrived in India 6 June 1825. Ensign 23 Jan. 1825. Lieut. 29 Aug. 1826. Capt. 30 June 1843. Bt. Major 11 Nov. 1851. *d.* Agra 22 May 1854.

Son of William Smith Andrews, of Richmond, surgeon. Brother of James Richard Benson Andrews, *q.v. m.* Meerut, 3 Nov. 1851, Ellen Charlotte Mahundee.

Services : Posted as Ensign to 5th Extra Regt. in 1825. Adjt. 73rd N.I. (late 5th Extra Regt.) 2 July 1831, for a short time only. 2nd in comd. Sylhet L.I. 11 Dec. 1839. First Sikh War ; Sobraon ; Capt. 73rd N.I. (Medal). Second Sikh War ; garrison duty in Lahore ; Capt. 73rd N.I. (Medal).

Refs. : I.M. 18 July 1854, p. 378.

ANGELO, Frederick (Joseph John) (1800-1869). Major, Invalid Est. 7th L.C. *b.* London 26 Jan. 1800. Cadet 1819. Admitted 14 June 1820. Cornet 10 Jan. 1820. Lieut. 14 Aug. 1822. Capt. 26 Aug. 1831. Major 26 July 1841. Invalided 28 Sept. 1841. *d.* Ootacamund, Madras, 22 Jan. 1869.

4th son of Anthony Angelo Malevolti Tremamondo, *q.v.*, and Elizabeth Martha Bland his wife. Brother of John (William Thomas) Angelo., *q.v.* His sister *m.* James Steel, *q.v. m.* 15 Dec. 1825, Catherine, 3rd dau. of John M. Anderson, and sister of Philip Cortlandt Anderson, *q.v.*

Services : Directed to join and do duty with G.G.B.G. until further orders 28 June 1820. Posted as Cornet to 7th L.C. in 1821. Adjt. 7th L.C. 2 July 1825 till 29 May 1826. D.J.A.G. Dinapore and Benares Divs. 6 Jan. 1832 ; do. Sirhind Div. 29 Dec. 1835 till 30 Dec. 1840. J.A.G. to Army of the Indus at Ferozepore during the First Aghan War 1838-9. No record of active service.

Refs. : The Ancestor, viii (1904), pp. 1 *sqq. Misc. Gen. et Her.*, 4S. ii. 182-4. *V.B.G.* p. 228. *The Times*, 16 Mar. 1869.

ANGELO, John (1792-1860). Lieut. Colonel, Invalid Est. 8th L.C. (Formerly John William Thomas Angelo TREMAMONDO, but dropped all names except the above in Feb. 1818.) *b.* London 26 Sept. 1792. Cadet 1807. Arrived in India 28 Oct. 1808. Cornet (30 Apr. 1808) 5 May 1810. Lieut. 1 Sept. 1818. Capt. 1 May 1824. Major 30 Oct. 1848. Lt. Col. 21 Oct. 1852. Invalided 27 May 1853. *d.* Dehra Dun, U.P., 29 Mar. 1860.

Eldest son of Anthony Angelo Malevolti Tremamondo, *q.v.*, and

LIST OF THE OFFICERS OF

Elizabeth Martha Bland his wife. Brother of Richard Angelo, *q.v.*
m. Berhampore, Bengal, 27 June 1818, Louisa (Eleanor), dau. of
Major Neate, H.M. 57th Regt. (She died Mussoorie 12 July 1860.)
His daus. *m.* John Abercrombie (1814-1860), Richard Houghton,
John Liptrott, Edmund Sissmore, *q.v.*

Services : Cornet H.M. 22 Light Dns. 1 May 1810. Lieut. do.
14 Nov. 1811. Sold his Commission 16 Sept. 1813. Posted as
Cornet to 3rd N.C. in 1810. Kalinjar 1812. Rewah 1813. Alwar
1814. Fur. s.c. 30 Dec. 1814 till 24 Sept. 1817. Third Mahratta
War. Adjt. 3rd L.C. 20 Nov. 1818 till 17 June 1824. Operations
in Jodhpur 1823 ; Lamba. Siege and capture of Bhurtpore ;
Capt. 3rd L.C. (India medal). Fur. 28 Feb. 1827 till 12 Dec. 1829.
Against the Kols 1832. First Afghan War ; Ghazni (Medal).
First Sikh War ; Aliwal ; Sobraon ; comdg. 3rd L.C. (Medal with
clasp). Comdt. 5th Irreg. Cav. 1848. Transfd. to 8th L.C. Jan.
1853.

Refs. : *The Ancestor,* viii. (1904), pp. 1 *sqq.* *The Times,* 14 May
1860. Will dated 13 Jan. 1854 ; proved 17 July 1860.

ANGELO, Richard (Frederick) (1802-1854). Lieut. Colonel, 34th
N.I. *b.* London 6 Aug. 1802. Cadet 1819. Admitted 21 Nov.
1820. Ensign 5 June 1820. Lieut. 11 July 1823. Capt. 6 Aug.
1835. Major 21 Nov. 1848. Lt. Col. 20 June 1854. *d.* Lucknow
13 Dec. 1854.

5th son of Anthony Angelo Malevolti Tremamondo, *q.v.*, and
Elizabeth Martha Bland his wife. Brother of John Angelo, *q.v.*
m. (before 1832) Elizabeth, dau. of Capt. John Mansell, H.M. 62nd
Foot, subsequently a Knight of Windsor. (She died Delhi 7 Oct.
1840.)

Services : Posted as Ensign to 23rd N.I. Transfd. as Lieut. to
17th N.I. in 1823 ; to 35th N.I. (late 2/17th) May 1824 ; to 34th
N.I. (late 1/17th) 12 July 1824. Intr. & Qmr. 34th N.I. 28 June
1825. Adjt. 34th N.I. 6 Aug. 1825 till 30 June 1828. Fur. s.c.
28 Aug. 1828 till 14 Nov. 1831. Against the Kols in Chota Nagpur
1832-3. Leave to the Cape 9 July 1832 till 11 Jan. 1833. A.D.C.
to G.G. 16 Jan. 1835. Asst. to Agent and Commr. of Delhi 25 Apr.
1840. Comdt. Delhi Palace Guards 6 May 1840 (appt. confirmed
19 Sept. 1841) till 1847. 34th N.I. disbanded for mutiny 20 Mar.
1844. Posted to re-embodied 34th N.I. in 1846. Fur. 18 Feb. 1847
till 1849.

Refs. : *The Ancestor,* viii. (1904), pp. 1 *sqq.* *G.M.* 1855, i. 438.
Will dated Lucknow 16 Nov. 1854 ; proved 22 May 1855.

ANGERSTEIN, John (or AUGUSTINE, Peter) (*d.* 1772). Captain,
Infantry. Cadet 1765. Ensign 25 Aug. 1765. Lieut. 5 Jan.

1767. Capt. 17 Sept. 1770. *d.* Monghyr, B. & O., Jan. 1772 : drowned. (? *Perhaps* related to John Julius Angerstein (*D.N.B.*).)
Note : Names given as John Angerstein in *B.M. Add. MS.*, as Peter Augustine in *Dodwell & Miles.*
Services : N.F.P.
Refs. : B.M. Add. MS. 6050.

ANGUS, James (*d.* 1776). Ensign, Infantry. Cadet 1772. Ensign 20 July 1775. *d.* Belgaum, Bombay, 24 June 1776.
Services : N.F.P.

AN(N)INGSON, Robert. Lieutenant. Infantry. Cadet 1782. Ensign 22 Jan. 1783. Lieut. 1789 (some date between 15 Mar. and 1 July). Struck off in England 1791.
Services : N.F.P.

ANQUETIL, Thomas John (1784-1842). Lieut. Colonel, 42nd N.I. Bdr. General. *bapt.* St. Helier, Jersey, 17 Dec. 1784. Cadet 1803. Arrived in India 29 Apr. 1805. Ensign 25 Mar. 1805. Lieut. 26 Mar. 1805. Capt. 4 Apr. 1818. Major 4 Mar. 1828. Lt. Col. 14 Mar. 1833. *d.* Jagdalak, Afghanistan, 12 Jan. 1842 : kld. in action during the retreat from Kabul.
Son of Thomas Anquetil and Marie Poingdestre his wife.
Services : Posted as Lieut. to 1/22nd N.I. in 1805. Operations in Hariana 1809 ; Bhawani ; Lieut. 1/22nd N.I. Reduction of Kalinjar 1812 ; Lieut. 1/22nd N.I. Third Mahratta War ; Nagpur. Capt. 2/22nd N.I. 3rd Bn. Ceylon Vols. in 1819. Transfd. to 44th N.I. (late 2/22nd) May 1824. First Burma War ; Cachar 1825 ; D.A.Q.M.G. 3 cl. Comdg. Pioneers 27 Sept. 1825 till 1829. Transfd. to 57th N.I. in 1829 ; as Lt. Col. to 44th N.I. 15 Oct. 1833 ; to 4th N.I. 15 Aug. 1834. D.A.G. 7 Aug. 1834 till 22 Jan. 1838. Shekhawat expedition 1834-5 ; A.G. of Bdr. Gen. R. Stevenson's force. Bdr., 2 cl., Oudh Aux. Force, 27 Dec. 1837 till 31 Dec. 1840. Transfd. to 42nd N.I. in 1840. First Afghan War 1841-2 ; comdg. Shah Shuja's force from 28 Mar. 1841 ; comdd. advance column in retreat from Kabul 6 Jan. 1842.
Refs. : D.I.B. M.I. in St. John's Church, Calcutta.

ANSON, Frederick Walpole (1806-1848). Major, 18th N.I. *b.* St. George's, Hanover Sq., London, 21 May 1806. Cadet 1821. Arrived in India 24 Dec. 1822. Ensign 1 Jan. 1823. Lieut. 1 May 1824. Capt. 12 Sept. 1833. Major 1 Aug. 1846. *d.* Royal Hospital, Chelsea, 12 Nov. 1848.
3rd son of Gen. Sir George Anson, G.C.B., Govr. of Chelsea hospital (who was younger brother of Thomas, first Viscount Anson),

and Frances his wife, sister of Sir Frederick Hamilton, Bart. First cousin to George Edward Anson, *q.v. m.* Agra, 25 July 1827, Miss Catherine Hanson, niece of Thomas Chadwick, *q.v.* (*See also* John Theophilus Boileau.) (She died New Zealand 11 June 1880, aged 71.) His dau. *m.* David Wilkie, *q.v.* Winchester scholar 1819 ; left in 1822.

Services : Posted as Ensign to 6th N.I. in 1823. Transfd. as Lieut. to 18th N.I. (late 2/6th) May 1824. Siege and capture of Bhurtpore ; Lieut. 18th N.I. Adjt. 18th N.I. 6 Jan. 1826 till 22 Mar. 1833. Fur. p.a. 9 Jan. 1833 till 5 Sept. 1835. Comdg. C.-in-C.'s escort 1836-7. D.A.A.G., Sirhind Div., 29 Nov. 1839. A.A.G. do. 1 Sept. 1841 till 1845. Comdg. 5th Irreg. Cav. 26 Feb. 1846 till Feb. 1848. Fur. 24 Feb. 1848 till death.

Refs. : Foster's *Peerage,* p. 407, *s.n.* Lichfield, E. *Kirby. G.M.* 1849, i. 102.

ANSON, George Edward (1812-1849). Cornet. Attached to 2nd L.C. Subsequently Keeper of the Privy Purse to Queen Victoria. C.B. *bapt.* Sudbury 14 May 1812. Cadet 1828. Cornet (?). Resigned 13 Jan. 1830. *d.* 8 Oct. 1849.

2nd son of Very Rev. Frederick Anson, D.D., Dean of Chester (who was younger brother of Thomas, first Viscount Anson), and Mary Anne his wife, only dau. of Rev. Richard Levett, of Milford, Staffs. First cousin to Frederick Walpole Anson, *q.v. m.* 2 Oct. 1837, Georgiana Mary, eldest dau. of Edward, third Lord Suffield. Educ. Rugby ; entered in 1826.

Services : Cornet d.d. 2nd L.C. 10 June 1829. He subsequently became Pte. Sec. to Lord Melbourne, First Lord of the Treasury, and afterwards to H.R.H. the Prince Consort. Keeper of the Privy Purse to H.M. Queen Victoria. Treasurer to the Household, and Cofferer to the Prince Consort.

Refs. : Foster's *Peerage,* p. 408, *s.n.* Lichfield, E. Burke's *Peerage,* 1923, p. 2125, *s.n.* Suffield, B. *Rugby School List.*

ANSTICE, Frederick (1790-1819). Lieutenant, 17th N.I. *b.* South Petherton, Somerset, 20 Jan. 1790. Cadet 1806. Arrived in India 3 Oct. 1807. Ensign 9 Aug. 1807. Lieut. 30 Oct. 1811. *d.* Jaun Bazar, Calcutta, 29 Aug. 1819.

Son of William Anstice. *m.* 12 Apr. 1817, Miss Catherine Harvey. *Services :* Posted as Ensign to 1/17th N.I. Capture of Java ; Cornelis 26 Aug. 1811 (w.) ; Lieut. 4th Bengal Vol. Bn. Capture of Jokyakarta June 1812 ; Lieut. 4th Vol. Bn. Continued serving in Java until the island was restored to the Dutch in 1816.. Served in Penang 1818-9.

ANSTRUTHER, Ashford John (1804-1842). Major, 54th N.I. *b.* London 29 Apr. 1804. Cadet 1817. Admitted 19 Sept. 1818. Ensign 15 Sept. 1818. Lieut. 9 Aug. 1819. Capt. 6 Jan. 1832. Major 10 Jan. 1842. *d.* nr. Kabul 13 Jan. 1842 : kld. in action during the retreat.
Son of Hon. David Anstruther, *q.v.*, and Mary his wife. Brother of Robert Lindsay Anstruther, *q.v.*
Services : Lieut. 1/27th N.I. Transfd. to 54th N.I. (late 2/27th) May 1824. Fur. s.c. 11 Nov. 1825 till 12 Nov. 1828. Intr. & Qmr. 54th N.I. 14 July 1829. First Afghan War 1840-2 ; Major 54th N.I.
Refs. : See Hon. David Anstruther.

ANSTRUTHER, Hon. David (1750/51- ?). Lieutenant. Cavalry. *b.* 1750/51. Cadet 1778. Arrived in India 8 Oct. 1778. Ensign 1 Jan. 1778. Lieut. 9 Oct. 1778. Resigned 12 May 1794. *d.* (after 1818).
Of Huntsmore Park, Bucks. 3rd son of Sir Alexander Anstruther, styled Lord Newark, and Jean Leslie his wife, titular Baroness Newark. Elder brother of William Anstruther, third titular Lord Newark. *m.* Kasimbazar, Bengal, Feb.1780, Miss Mary Donaldson,of Allachie, co. Aberdeen. (*See also* George Mence.) Father of Ashford John Anstruther, *q.v.*, and of Robert Lindsay Anstruther, *q.v.*
Services : Comdg. the Nawab Wazir of Oudh's Body Guard *c.* 1785. Was on fur. in 1790.
Refs. : Burke's *Extinct Peerage*, 1883, p. 320, *s.n.* Lord Newark. Burke's *Peerage, s.n.* Carmichael-Anstruther, Bart., and Redesdale, B. Fielding's *New Peerage*, p. 133. *G.M.* 1780, p. 393. *N. & Q.* 4S. iii. 575. *Hickey*, iii.

ANSTRUTHER, Robert Lindsay (1789-1868). Colonel. 6th L.C. *bapt.* Calcutta 24 Dec. 1789. Cadet 1807. Arrived in India 21 Mar. 1809. Cornet (25 Mar. 1809) 18 Jan. 1811. Lieut. 12 Apr. 1817. Capt. 15 Aug. 1823. Major 28 Dec. 1838. Lt. Col. 12 Apr. 1849. Retired 21 Aug. 1849. Hon. Col. 28 Nov. 1854. *d.* 5 Albion Terr., Southampton, 5 Dec. 1868.
Eldest son of Hon. David Anstruther, *q.v.*, and Mary his wife. Brother of Ashford John Anstruther, *q.v. m.* 1st, ——. (She died 25 Aug. 1813.) *m.* 2nd, 13 Dec. 1814, Elizabeth, 2nd dau. of Rev. Charles Gardner, of Stoke Hammond, Bucks. (She died Bath, 11 Jan. 1843.) His dau. *m.* Robert Price, *q.v.*
Services : Posted as Cornet to 6th N.C. in 1811, and served throughout with that Regt. Fur. s.c. 12 Dec. 1813 till 31 Dec. 1816. Third Mahratta War ; Sitabaldi ; Nagpur. Intr. & Qmr. 6th L.C. 18 Sept. 1820. Adjt. 6th L.C. 10 Oct. 1821 till 6 Aug. 1823.

Siege and capture of Bhurtpore (India medal). Fur. p.a. 22 Feb. 1827 till 21 Oct. 1829. Reduction of Jhansi 1838-9. To comd. 6th L.C. 13 Dec. 1839. Fur. s.c. 2 Feb. 1847 till retirement.

Refs. : Burke's *Extinct Peerage*, 1883, p. 320, *s.n.* Lord Newark. Burke's *Peerage*, *s.n.* Carmichael-Anstruther, Bart. Howard & Crisp, xv. 150, *s.n.* Price. *N. & Q.* 4S. iii. 575. *G.M.* 1815, i. 80. *The Times*, 9 Dec. 1868.

APLIN, Christopher D'Oyl(e)y (1787-1833). Captain, 33rd N.I. *bapt.* Banbury, Oxon., 14 Apr. 1787. Cadet 1805. Arrived in India 11 July 1806. Ensign 4 Sept. 1806. Lieut. 4 Apr. 1809. Capt. 25 Dec. 1822. *d.* at sea 13 May 1833.

Son of Oliver Aplin and Mary his wife. *m.* Cawnpore 27 Oct. 1818, Julia, dau. of Sir Dyson Marshall, K.C.B., *q.v.* (*See also* Charles William Brooke, William James (1785-1855), William Larkins Watson, John Winston.) (She died Blackheath 30 Aug. 1837.)

Services : Posted as Ensign to 2/16 N.I. Served with the Pioneer Corps 1809-17. Reduction of Kalinjar. Nepal War 1814-5 ; Bde. Qmr., 2nd Inf. Bde., Dinapore Div. Siege and capture of Hathras ; Actg. A.Q.M.G. Lieut. 2/16th N.I. Third Mahratta War ; siege of Mandala ; Sec. and Persian Intr. to Maj. Gen. Dyson Marshall, *q.v.* D.A.Q.M.G., 2 cl., 16 Oct. 1819. S.A.C.G. 2 Jan. 1821. Capt. 2/16th N.I. Transfd. to 33rd N.I. (late 2/16th) May 1824. A.A.G. 30 Apr. 1825. Siege and capture of Bhurtpore ; Offg. D.A.G. Fur. 9 Nov. 1826 till 26 Oct. 1829, and 25 Aug. 1832 till death.

Refs. : *A.J.* N.S. xi. 96. Will dated Baker St., London, 27 Apr. 1829 ; proved 26 Aug. 1834.

APPACH, John Francis (1790-1818). Lieutenant, 28th N.I. *b.* London 2 Aug. 1790. Cadet 1808. Arrived in India 27 Oct. 1809. Ensign 25 Aug. 1810. Lieut. 23 Nov. 1815. *d.* Rewari 29 Dec. 1818.

Eldest son of John Jacob Appach, of Clapton (naturalized in 1770), and his wife, dau. of Joseph Partridge, of Fenchurch St., London.

Services : Posted as Ensign to 6th N.I. in 1810. Transfd. to 27th N.I. in 1812 ; as Lieut. to newly-raised 1/28th N.I. in 1815. Third Mahratta War ; Madhurajpura ; Lieut. 1/28th N.I. in Reserve Div.

Refs. : *G.M.* 1788, ii. 750 ; 1819, ii. 88.

APPERLEY, Henry (1812-1845). Bt. Captain, Artillery. *bapt.* Stoke Lacy, co. Hereford, 10 Aug. 1812. Cadet 1829. Arrived in India 9 Feb. 1830. 2nd Lieut. 12 June 1829. Rank cancelled and reduced to Cadet (G.G.O. of 31 May 1830) under instructions

THE BENGAL ARMY, 1758-1834   43

from C.D. Apptd. Actg. 2nd Lieut. 27 Feb. 1832. (Service afterwards allowed to count for brevet rank.) Lieut. 25 Apr. 1838. Bt. Capt. 12 June 1844. *d.* Chini, Kanawar, 1 July 1845, whilst on sick leave.
Son of Rev. Thomas Apperley, rector of Stoke Lacy. Brother of Herbert Apperley, *q.v.*
Services : Posted to 4th Coy. 3rd Bn. Foot Art. in Nov. 1833. Transfd. to 2nd Troop 1st Bde. H.A. in Sept. 1838. With Army of Reserve (for Afghanistan) at Ferozepore Oct. 1842 till Jan. 1843. Operations at Kaithal and in the Karnal district 1843.
Refs. : De Rhé-Philipe. Will dated Chini 27 June 1845 ; proved 29 May 1848.

APPERLEY, Herbert (1806-1838). Lieutenant, 6th N.I. *b.* Stoke Lacy, co. Hereford, 29 May 1806. Cadet 1825. Arrived in India 21 Oct. 1826. Ensign 13 June 1826. Lieut. 5 Dec. 1828. *d.* Cuttack 7 Nov. 1838.
Eldest son of Rev. Thomas Apperley, rector of Stoke Lacy. Brother of Henry Apperley, *q.v.* Educ. Eton : in 4th form in 1820.
Services : Served throughout in 6th N.I. Apptd. to tempy. charge of Khurda Paik Coy. 16 Apr. 1838. No record of active service.
Refs. : Eton School Lists. G.M. 1839, i. 333. M.I. at Aligarh.

APPERLEY, William Wynne (1807-1870). Colonel. 3rd European L.C. *b.* Butterley, Salop, 22 Mar. 1807. Cadet 1823. Arrived in India 20 May 1824. Cornet 14 Apr. 1824. Lieut. 13 May 1825. Capt. 1 Mar. 1843. Major 28 Nov. 1854. Bt. Lt. Col. 1 May 1858. Retired 31 Dec. 1861. Hon. Col. 31 Dec. 1861. *d.* Morben, co. Montgomery, 25 Apr. 1870.
Of Morben, co. Montgomery. Son of Charles James Apperley ("Nimrod"—*D.N.B.*), of Beaurepaire, and Elizabeth his wife, younger dau. of William Wynne, of Wern. *m.* Karnal 1 May 1837, Catherina Esther, dau. of Newton Wallace, *q.v.* (*See also* Sir Matthew Richard Onslow, Bart.)
Services : Posted as Cornet to 4th L.C. in 1824. Transfd. to newly-raised 2nd Extra Cav. Regt. 17 June 1825 ; retransfd. to 4th L.C. in 1825. Siege and capture of Bhurtpore ; Cornet 4th L.C. (India medal). Intr. & Qmr. 4th L.C. 2 July 1827. Asst. Stud Dept. 8 Nov. 1838. 2nd Asst. do. 30 Sept. 1840. Sub-Asst. do. 7 July 1843. Asst. 2 cl. 11 June 1850. Fur. 3 Apr. 1852 till 1853. Asst. 1 cl. 1 Sept. 1853. Dy. Supt. Stud Dept. 2 June 1854. Fur. s.c. 30 Apr. 1856 till 1857. Remount Agent at C.G.H. 1857-60. Transfd. to newly-raised 3rd Eur. L.C. in 1858.
Refs. : Burke's *Landed Gentry,* 13th edn., p. 1950, *s.n.* Wynne, of Peniarth, co. Merioneth. *Boase. The Times,* 29 Apr. 1870.

APRICHARD, William (*d.* 1778). Lieutenant, Infantry. Cadet 1769. Ensign 14 June 1770. Lieut. 1 July 1776. *d.* Chhatarpur, C.I., June 1778.

Services : Probably at the date of his death was *en route* from Cawnpore to Bombay with the force marching under Lt. Col. Mathew Leslie for the purpose of participating in first Mahratta War.

APSLEY, Alexander (1756/57- ?). Lieutenant. Infantry. J.A.G., Bengal. *b.* 1756/57. Cadet 1776. Resigned 24 Dec. 1777. Lieut. 4 Sept. 1778. Resigned 10 Oct. 1793.

A native of Ashford, Kent.

Services : Sailed for India on the *Egmont* 1 Jan. 1777, aged 19. Apptd. J.A.G., Bengal, 26 Mar. 1788. Was Town and Fort Major of Calcutta in June 1789, and A.D.C. to G.G. in 1790.

Refs. : Whinyate Family Records.

APSLEY, John (1782-1816). Lieutenant, 4th N.C. *bapt.* Belfast 5 July 1782. Cadet 1800. Arrived in India 24 Aug. 1801. Cornet 4 Jan. 1802. Lieut. 29 Aug. 1810. *d.* at sea, 31 July 1816, on board the *Lord Castlereagh*, on his passage to England.

Son of Robert Apsley, M.D., and Ann his wife.

Services : Posted as Cornet to 4th N.C. Operations in Jumna Doab 1803 ; Sasni ; Bijaigarh ; Kachaura ; Cornet 4th N.C. Second Mahratta War ; Laswari ; Cornet 4th N.C. Transfd. as Cornet to 5th N.C. in 1805 ; retransfd. to 4th N.C. the same year. Dy. Agent for camels and gram 1806-7. Comdg. escort of Resident with Sindhia 1811-2. Fur. 1816.

APTHORP, Charles (1808-1866). Colonel. 41st N.I. *b.* Gumley, Leics., 28 July 1808. Cadet 1824. Arrived in India 8 May 1825. Ensign 9 Jan. 1825. Lieut. 20 May 1827. Capt. 27 Feb. 1846. Major 1 June 1857. Retired 23 May 1859. Hon. Col. 23 May 1859. *d.* Orwell Lodge, Torquay, 22 Jan. 1866.

Son of Rev. Frederick Apthorp, rector of Gumley. *m.* Ipswich, 21 Aug. 1849, Rebecca, dau. of Postle Jackson, of Ipswich.

Services : Sailed for India on the *Hythe* 21 Jan. 1825. Siege and capture of Bhurtpore ; Ensign 41st N.I. (India medal). Arakan Local Bn. 8 Sept. 1837. Adjt. do. 30 Aug. 1838. 2nd in comd. do. 17 Jan. 1839. Fur. s.c. 18 Nov. 1840 till 10 Sept. 1842. Actg. Adjt. 41st N.I. 27 June 1843. First Sikh War ; Ferozshahr ; Sobraon ; Lieut. 41st N.I. (Medal with clasp). Fur. 10 Mar. 1847 till 1849.

Refs. : G.M. 1866, i. 447. *The Times*, 25 Jan. 1866.

THE BENGAL ARMY, 1758-1834

ARABIN, Alfred (1802-1833). Lieutenant, 7th N.I. *b.* London 10 Oct. 1802. Cadet 1821. Arrived in India 15 Apr. 1822. Ensign 24 Oct. 1821. Lieut. 1 May 1824. *d.* Calcutta 1 Sept. 1833.
Son of Gen. William John Arabin, of West Drayton, Middlesex, 2nd Life Guards. *m.* Calcutta, 5 May 1833, Mary, eldest dau. of Sir William Russell, Kt., Chief Justice, Bengal.
Services : Posted as Ensign to 11th N.I. Transfd. to 2/3rd N.I. 31 May 1822 ; to 1/1st N.I. 22 June 1822. Pioneers 28 Dec. 1822 till 12 Oct. 1824. Transfd. to 1/4th N.I. in 1823 ; to 7th N.I. (late 1/4th) May 1824. Siege and capture of Bhurtpore ; Lieut. Pioneers. Adjt. Gorakhpur L.I. in 1826. Posted to 7th (or Hill) Coy. Pioneers 7 Nov. 1826, and served with Pioneers till 1832. Adjt. Pioneers 27 July 1829 till June 1832. Bde. Major at Barrackpore 4 June 1832 till death.
Refs. : Burke's *Landed Gentry,* 6th edn., p. 31, *s.n.* Arabin, of Beech Hill Park, Essex, and Drayton House, Middlesex. Will dated 7 June 1831 ; codicils dated 17 June 1833 and 30 Aug. 1833 ; proved 1 Oct. 1833.

ARBUTHNOTT, Harry (1783-1806). Lieutenant, 2nd N.I. *b.* London 17 Apr. 1783. Cadet 1798. Arrived in India 19 Sept. 1799. Ensign 17 Oct. 1799. Lieut. 28 Oct. 1799. *d.* Agra 15 Aug. 1806.
bapt. Marylebone, London, 27 Apr. 1783. Son of Romeo Arbuthnott and Christiana his wife. Brother of Thomas Arbuthnott, *q.v.*
Services : Posted as Lieut. to 2/2nd N.I. 15 Apr. 1801. Second Mahratta War ; battle of Delhi ; battle and capture of Deig ; siege of Bhurtpore (s.w. in 4th assault on 21 Feb. 1805) ; Lieut. 1/2nd N.I.
Refs. : Burke's *Landed Gentry,* 3rd edn., p. 1319 *s.n.* Whitter, of Devon. *Pester. S.M.* 1807, p. 237. Will dated 13 Aug. 1806 ; proved 14 Dec. 1807.

ARBUTHNOTT, Thomas (1780-1822). Captain, 5th N.I. *b.* London 5 Feb. 1780. Cadet 1800. Arrived in India 17 Sept. 1801. Ensign 14 Nov. 1801. Lieut. 30 Sept. 1803. Capt. 1 Aug. 1818. *d. unm.* Dinapore 1 Aug. 1822.
bapt. Marylebone, London, 29 Feb. 1780. Son of Romeo Arbuthnott and Christiana his wife. Brother of Harry Arbuthnott, *q.v.*
Services : Posted as Ensign to 2/5th N.I. and served throughout with that Regt. Reduction of Kalinjar. Adjt. 1 July 1814 till 27 May 1818. Third Mahratta War ; in Reserve Div.
Refs. : Burke's *Landed Gentry,* 3rd edn., p. 1319, *s.n.* Whitter, of Devon. Will dated Karnal 6 Sept. 1819 ; codicil dated Fatehgarh 10 Dec. 1821 ; proved 16 Sept. 1822.

ARCHBOLD, Edward Cook (1800- ?). Captain. 8th L.C. *b.* Gibraltar 20 Nov. 1800. Cadet 1819. Admitted 25 Sept. 1820. Cornet 20 May 1820. Lieut. 1 May 1824. Capt. 20 May 1835. Resigned 1 Feb. 1836. (Living in 1851 when the India medal was awarded.) Son of Edward Archbold, of London, merchant, formerly of Gibraltar.
Services : Posted as Cornet to 8th L.C. A.D.C. to G.G. 13 Oct. 1823. With G.G.B.G. from 1 Nov. 1823. Extra Asst. to Resident at Nagpur 15 July 1824. First Burma War 1824-5 ; Kokein 15 Dec. 1824 (w.) ; with G.G.B.G. (India medal). Returned to Calcutta in Feb. 1825. Siege and capture of Bhurtpore ; Lieut. 8th L.C. (clasp to India medal). Dy. Paymr. at Benares 18 Jan. 1828. S.A.C.G. 13 June 1828 till 20 Apr. 1830. Fur. p.a. 28 Dec. 1830 till 22 Aug. 1834.
Refs. : V.B.G.

ARCHDEACON, John (*d.* 1792). Captain, 14 Bn. Sepoys. Cadet 1768. Ensign 12 Aug. 1769. Lieut. 25 Jan. 1773. Capt. 4 Jan. 1781. *d.* 6 Feb. 1792 : kld. in action in the attack on Seringapatam.
Brother of James Archdeacon, of co. Limerick, and of Edmund Archdeacon, of Keldrummin, co. Limerick.
Services : Held tempy. comd. of 4th Bn. (being the senior Lieut.) from 3 June 1778, when on active service with the Bombay detachment during first Mahratta War. Was comdg. 14th Bn. in 2nd Bde. in 1790. Third Mysore War ; storm of Seringapatam (kld.) ; comdg. 14th Bn.
Refs. : Williams, pp. 94, 147. Will dated camp, S. of Kisnah river, 21 June 1790. M.I. on cenotaph erected by the Mysore Govt. in Bangalore fort.

ARCHDEAKIN, Edward (*d.* 1790). Ensign, Infantry. Cadet 1783. Ensign 5 Apr. 1785. *d.* Calcutta 10 Mar. 1790.
Services : N.F.P.

ARCHER, Charles (1792-1811). Fireworker, Artillery. *b.* Perth 31 May 1792. Cadet 1808. Arrived in India 7 Dec. 1809. Fireworker 1 Nov. 1809. *d.* at sea 10 July 1811, on board the *Batavia,* with the expedition proceeding to Java.
Son of Charles Archer, of Perth, "late shipmaster, now merchant."
Services : Proceeded with 7th Coy. 1st Bn. Art. on the expedition against the Dutch in Java 1811, but died at sea on the voyage thither.
Refs. : G.M. 1812, i. 594. Will dated 8 Mar. 1811 ; proved 18 July 1812.

THE BENGAL ARMY, 1758-1834 47

ARCHER, John (1784-1808). Lieutenant, 13th N.I. *b.* Penton-Mewsey, Hants, 9 Oct. 1784. Cadet 1803. Arrived in India 2 Dec. 1804. Ensign 4 Nov. 1804. Lieut. 4 Nov. 1804. *d.* Allahabad 15 Mar. 1808.
Services : Posted as Lieut. to 1/13th N.I. in 1805. Operations against Dhundia Khan 1807 ; Komona ; Ganauri ; Lieut. 1/13th N.I.

ARCTANDER, Nicholas M. Captain. Infantry. Was already in India when apptd. Cadet on 26 Nov. 1781. Ensign 1 Aug. 1782. Lieut. 23 Jan. 1785. Capt. 7 Jan. 1796. Resigned 12 Sept. 1796.
Services : N.F.P.

ARDEN, Russell. Lieutenant. Infantry. Cadet (?). Ensign (?). Lieut. 15 Sept. 1768. Resigned 15 Oct. 1776.
Services : N.F.P.

ARDEN, Samuel (1782-1822). Major, 27th N.I. *bapt.* Pipe Ridware, Staffs., 17 Sept. 1782. Cadet 1798. Arrived in India 6 Sept. 1799. Ensign 7 Nov. 1799. Lieut. 21 Apr. 1800. Capt. 22 Feb. 1814. Major 12 May 1820. *d.* Saugor, C.P., 18 Oct. 1822.

4th son of Rev. John Arden, of Longcrofts Hall, Burton-on-Trent, Staffs., and Alathea his wife, dau. of Robert Cotton, of Worcester. *m.* Westbury-upon-Trym, Gloucs., Jan. 1812, Jane Hannah, eldest dau. of James Franklyn, of Bristol, merchant and sometime (1812) mayor of that city. Father of Samuel Arden, *q.v.*, and grandfather of Michael Arthur Bass, first Baron Burton.

Services : Posted as Lieut. to 1/2nd N.I. 15 Apr. 1801. Operations in Jumna Doab 1803 ; Sasni ; Lieut. 1/2nd N.I. Transfd. to newly-raised 2/21st N.I. in 1803. Second Mahratta War ; Monson's retreat (w.) ; Lieut. 2/21st N.I. Transfd. to 1/27th N.I. in 1806. Operations against Dhundia Khan 1807 ; Komona ; Lieut. 1/27th N.I. Fur. 5 Dec. 1809 till 1812. Third Mahratta War ; Madhurajpura ; Capt. 1/27th N.I. with Right Div.

Refs. : Burke's *Landed Gentry*, 9th edn., p. 27, *s.n.* Arden, late of Longcrofts Hall, Staffs. Burke's *Colonial Gentry*, ii. 534. Burke's *Peerage*, 1923, p. 217, *s.n.* Bass, Bart. *Pester. M.M.* 1812, i. 84.

ARDEN, Samuel (1814-1854). Lieutenant. 27th N.I. *b.* Rewari, Punjab, 7 June 1814. Cadet 1830. Arrived in India 29 Dec. 1831. Ensign 9 June 1831. Lieut. 23 July 1837. Retired 15 June 1839. *d.* Calne, Wilts., 23 June 1854.

Eldest son of Samuel Arden, *q.v.*, and Jane his wife. Addiscombe Cadet 1829-31.

Services : To do duty with 6th N.I. 1 Feb. 1832. Posted as Ensign to 27th N.I. 19 Oct. 1833, and spent the remainder of his service with that Regt. Fur. s.c. 8 June 1838 till retirement. Retired on h.p., viz. 4s. p.d. No record of active service.

Refs. : Burke's *Landed Gentry*, 9th edn., p. 27, *s.n.* Arden, late of Longcrofts Hall, Staffs. Burke's *Colonial Gentry*, ii. 534. *G.M.* 1854, ii. 204.

ARDING, Cecil (1806- ?). Lieutenant. 58th N.I. *b.* March Baldon, Oxon., 21 Apr. 1806. Cadet 1824. Arrived in India 13 Mar. 1826. Ensign 16 Sept. 1825. Lieut. 21 May 1827. Resigned 23 Oct. 1837. (Living in 1859.)

Son of Rev. Isaac Richard Arding, rector of March Baldon. *m.* 1st, Wallingford, 26 July 1837, Elizabeth, youngest dau. of Edward Wells. *m.* 2nd, All Saints, Southampton, 5 Oct. 1859, Emma M., dau. of Thomas Creed.

Services : Posted as Ensign to 58th N.I. Actg. Adjt. 58th N.I. 12 Nov. 1828. 7th Coy. Pioneers 27 Oct. 1829. Fur. s.c. 23 Apr. 1835 till resignation. No record of active service.

Refs. : A.J. N.S. xxiv. 56. *I.M.* 17 Oct. 1859, p. 863.

ARMSTRONG, Alexander (or **Michael**). (*d.* 1770). Lieutenant, Infantry. Cadet 1767. Ensign 6 May 1768. Lieut. 19 Dec. 1769. *d.* Calcutta 3 Aug. 1770. *bur.* 4 Aug. 1770.

Note : Christian name given as Alexander in the burial register, as Michael in *Dodwell & Miles*.

Services : N.F.P.

Refs. : Calcutta burial register.

ARMSTRONG, Alexander (1782-1817). Captain, 18th N.I. *b.* Killeshandra, co. Cavan, 1782. Cadet 1799. Arrived in India 23 Oct. 1800. Ensign 7 Sept. 1800. Lieut. 30 June 1802. Capt. 1 Aug. 1810. *d.* Khurda, B. & O., 4 Sept. 1817.

6th son of Robert Armstrong, of Hackwood, co. Cavan, and Dorothy Young his wife.

Services : Posted as Lieut. to 1/18th N.I. 17 Apr. 1801. Second Mahratta War ; Lieut. 18th N.I. Settlement of Hariana 1809 ; Bhawani. Capt. Lt. 18th N.I. 22 Apr. 1809. Capt. 2/18th N.I. Fur. 16 Feb. 1811 till 1813. Nepal War 1816 ; Capt. 8th Gren. Bn., in 2nd Bde., Left Column.

Refs. : Will dated 8 Dec. 1816 ; proved 10 Dec. 1817.

ARMSTRONG, Andrew Bigoe (1802-1824). Lieutenant, 10th N.I. *b.* in India 2 June 1802. Cadet 1818. Ensign (?). Lieut.

THE BENGAL ARMY, 1758-1834 49

28 May 1820. *d.* 21 Feb. 1824 : kld. in action at Dudhpatli, Assam.

Only son of Major Edmund Armstrong, Bo. N.I. (who was 6th son of Andrew Armstrong, of Garry Castle, King's Co., J.P.), and Leonora Lucas his wife. Nephew of Archibald Armstrong, *q.v.*
Services : Ensign d.d. 1/10th N.I. in 1820. With 1/27th N.I. in 1821. Rejoined 1/10th N.I. in 1823. First Burma War ; Assam 1824 (kld.) ; Lieut. N.I.
Refs. : Burke's *Landed Gentry of Ireland,* p. 14, *s.n.* Armstrong, of Garry Castle, King's Co.

ARMSTRONG, Archibald (1763-1791). Lieutenant, Infantry. *b.* 1 Nov. 1763. Cadet 1780. Ensign 1780. Lieut. 1 June 1781. *d.s.p.* Chunar 29 Aug. 1791.

Eldest son of Andrew Armstrong, of Garry Castle, King's Co., J.P., and Elizabeth his wife, only dau. of Capt. James Buchanan, of Craigavern and Dromakill, Scotland. Nephew of James Buchanan, *q.v.*, and uncle of Andrew Bigoe Armstrong, *q.v.*
Services : Sailed for India on the *Duke of Portland* 12 Feb. 1780. N.F.P.
Refs. : Burke's *Landed Gentry of Ireland,* p. 14, *s.n.* Armstrong, of Garry Castle, King's Co.

ARMSTRONG, Augustus (1810-1830). 2nd Lieutenant, Artillery. *b.* Cheshunt, Herts., 19 Apr. 1810. Cadet 1827. 2nd Lieut. 13 Dec. 1827. *d.* Kyaukpyu, Arakan, 5 Nov. 1830, of Arakan fever.

4th son of Rev. William Archibald Armstrong, of Pengelly Lodge, rector of Hykham, Lincs. (who was 1st cousin of Archibald Armstrong, *q.v.*), and Charlotte Eleanor Mary his wife, younger dau. of Richard Hassell. Brother of George Craven Armstrong, *q.v.* Addiscombe Cadet 1826-7.
Services : No record of active service.
Refs. : Burke's *Peerage,* 1923, p. 137, *s.n.* Armstrong, Bart., of Ashfield Pl., London. *A.J.* N.S. v. 36.

ARMSTRONG, David (1790-1815). Cornet, 2nd N.C. *b.* Edinburgh 7 June 1790. Cadet 1808. Arrived in India 1809. Cornet 26 Dec. 1811. *d.* Ludhiana 22 Apr. 1815.

bapt. Queen St., St. Andrew's, Edinburgh, 24 Aug. 1790. Son of Edward Armstrong.
Services : Did duty with 8th N.C. as supernumerary. Posted as Cornet to 2nd N.C. in Jan. 1812. No record of active service.
Refs. : De Rhé-Philipe.

ARMSTRONG, George Craven (1806-1863). Bt. Lieut. Colonel. 47th N.I. *b.* Cheshunt, Herts., 2 Apr. 1806. Cadet 1821. Arrived in India 18 Sept. 1822. Ensign 30 Sept. 1821. Lieut. 13 May 1825. Capt. 12 Mar. 1838. Major 16 Oct. 1851. Bt. Lt. Col. 1853. Retired 15 Dec. 1853. *d.* Vicarage, Willesden, London, N.W., 4 Mar. 1863.

3rd son of Rev. William Archibald Armstrong, of Pengelly Lodge, rector of Hykham, Lincs., and Charlotte Eleanor Mary his wife. Brother of Augustus Armstrong, *q.v. m.* Barrackpore 20 Jan. 1828, Georgiana, youngest dau. of Capt. Philip Hughes, E.I.C.S., of Upper Montague St., Russell Sq., London. Ed. Merchant Taylors' school : entered in July 1816.

Services : Posted as Ensign to Eur. Regt. in 1822. Transfd. to 24th N.I. in 1823 ; to 47th N.I. (late 1/24th) May 1824. This Regt. having mutinied in Nov. 1824, he was transfd. the same month to newly-raised 69th N.I. (became 47th N.I. in 1828). Intr. & Qmr. 69th N.I. 18 Sept. 1826 ; do. 47th N.I. 25 June 1830 till 14 Sept. 1831. (? Operations against the Kols 1831-2.) Fur. s.c. 19 Mar. 1832 till 11 Feb. 1835. 2nd in comd. Ramgarh L.I. Bn. 13 Dec. 1836 till 7 Aug. 1850. Comdt. 4th Sikh Infantry 8 Aug. 1850 till 1853. Second Burma War 1852-3 (s.w.) ; comdg. 4th Sikhs (India medal).

Refs. : Burke's *Peerage*, 1923, p. 137, *s.n.* Armstrong, Bart., of Ashfield Pl., London. *Robinson*, ii. 203. *Boase. A.J.* xxvi. 219. *The Times*, 6 Mar. 1863.

*****ARMSTRONG, John** (*d.* 1763). Ensign, Infantry. Cadet (?). Ensign (?). *d.* 1 July 1763 : kld. in action at the battle of Manji ; *or* massacred at or near Patna, 5th, 6th or 11th Oct. 1763, by order of Nawab Mir Muhammad Kasim. (See note to Benjamin Adamson.)

Services : N.F.P.

Refs. : MS. list preserved at the India Office entitled " List of Persons killed in the Massacre at Patna, and at other places during the Troubles, 1763." *Diaries of Three Surgeons of Patna. Swinton of Kimmerghame Records,* p. 48.

ARMSTRONG, John (*d.* 1769). Lieutenant, Infantry. Cadet 1765. Ensign 7 Nov. 1765. Lieut. 28 May 1767. *d.* in India 1769 : struck by lightning and killed whilst sheltering under a tamarind tree, with his horse's bridle under his arm, during a thunderstorm. His horse also was killed.

Services : N.F.P.

Refs. : *G.M.* 1770, p. 393.

THE BENGAL ARMY, 1758-1834 51

ARMSTRONG, Richard (1788-1859). Major. 73rd N.I. *b.* Durrow, King's Co., 17 Jan. 1788. Cadet 1804. Arrived in India 7 Apr. 1806. Ensign 9 Apr. 1806. Lieut. 19 Mar. 1807. Capt. 13 May 1825. Retired 6 Aug. 1834. Hon. Major 28 Nov. 1854. *d.* Torquay, Devon, 13 Sept. 1859.
Services : Lieut. 2/14th N.I. Served with Pioneer Corps 1809-16. Nepal War 1814-5 ; Nalagarh ; Bilaspur ; Malaun ; Lieut. 4th Coy. Pioneers, in 1st Div. (India medal). Fur. 27 Jan. 1817 till 20 Nov. 1821. Transfd. as Lieut. to 1/14th N.I. 2nd in comd. Cuttack Legion 5 Apr. 1822. Transfd. to 28th N.I. (late 1/14th), May 1824. 2nd Asst. Mily. Auditor Gen. 1823-9. Transfd. to newly-raised 5th Extra Regt. (became 73rd N.I.) in 1825. 1st Asst. Mily. Auditor Gen. 10 Apr. 1829 till 9 Aug. 1832. Leave to China and Cape, July 1830 till 5 Nov. 1832. Fur. s.c. 7 Feb. 1833 till retirement.
Refs. : G.M. 1859, ii. 541. *The Times,* 24 Sept. 1859.

ARMSTRONG, Richard Boswell (*d.* 1800). Captain, 8th N.I. Cadet 1783. Admitted 4 Aug. 1784. Ensign 10 Jan. 1785. Lieut. 10 Dec. 1790. Capt. 8 Jan. 1798. *d.* Calcutta 22 June 1800.
Brother of Joseph Armstrong and Charles Armstrong. *m.* Calcutta, 6 Nov. 1784, Miss Frances White.
Services : Capt. 1/8th N.I. in 1799.
Refs. : Will dated Cawnpore 5 Nov. 1799 ; proved in 1800.

ARMSTRONG, Robert (*d.* 1812). Major, 8th N.C. Cadet 1781. Admitted 26 Feb. 1781. Cornet 31 Aug. 1781. Lieut. 14 June 1783. Capt. 21 Feb. 1801. Major 11 Mar. 1805. Invalided 1812. *d.* at sea, 16 Oct. 1812, on board the *Cornwall,* on his passage to England.
m. Calcutta, 15 Mar. 1798, Margaretta, dau. of Sir James Watson, Kt., serjeant-at-law, sometime judge of the supreme court, Calcutta. (She died London 25 Jan. 1837.)
Services : Lieut. and Bt. Capt. 4th N.C. Capt. Lt. 4th N.C. 29 May 1800. Operations in Jumna Doab 1803 ; Sasni ; Bijaigarh ; Kachaura ; Capt. 4th N.C. Second Mahratta War ; Laswari ; Capt. 4th N.C. Transfd. as Major to newly-raised 8th N.C. in 1805.

ARNAUD, Henry Hawker (1803-1876). Major. 34th N.I. *b.* 16 Sept. 1803. Cadet 1819. Admitted 27 Mar. 1820. Ensign 26 Oct. 1819. Lieut. 28 May 1823. Capt. 17 Dec. 1832. Retired in India 17 Mar. 1844. Hon. Major 28 Nov. 1854. *d.* 28 Gayfield Sq., Edinburgh, 24 May 1876.
bapt. London 14 Oct. 1803. Son of John Arnaud. *m.* Edinburgh, 29 Aug. 1851, Agnes Williamson Thompson, only dau. of Andrew Kedslie, Surgeon E.I.C.S.

Services : Posted as Ensign to 1/12th N.I. in 1820. Transfd. as Lieut. to 2/17th N.I. 4 Feb. 1823 ; to 35th N.I. (late 2/17th) May 1824 ; to 34th N.I. (late 1/17th) 26 June 1824. Against the Kols in Chota Nagpur 1832-3 ; Capt. 34th N.I.
Refs. : *The Times,* 29 May 1876.

ARNOLD, Edward Shippen (1780-1813). Lieutenant, 6th N.C. *b.* Philadelphia, U.S.A., 19 Mar. 1780. Cadet 1799. Arrived in India 12 Jan. 1801. Cornet 12 Feb. 1801. Lieut. 11 Mar. 1805. *d. unm.* Dinapore 17 Dec. 1813.

4th (eldest by second wife) son of Gen. Benedict Arnold (*D.N.B.*) and Margaret his wife, dau. of Edward Shippen, Chief Judge of Pennsylvania. Brother of George Arnold, *q.v.* Granted by sign manual 20 July 1793, a pension of £100 *p.a.* in recognition of his father's services.

Services : Operations in Jumna Doab 1803 ; Sasni ; Bijaigarh ; Kachaura ; Cornet 6th N.C. Second Mahratta War ; Laswari ; pursuit of Holkar ; Cornet 6th N.C. Adjt. 6th N.C. 1804-6. Dy. Paymr. at Muttra 1807 till death.

Refs. : Burke's *Landed Gentry,* 7th edn., p. 44, *s.n.* Arnold, of Little Missenden Abbey, Bucks. *Life of Col. Pownoll Phipps. G.M.* 1814, ii. 399. Will dated 2 May 1813 ; codicil dated 15 Dec. 1813 ; proved in 1814.

ARNOLD, George (1787-1828). Lieut. Colonel, 2nd L.C. *b.* St. John's, New Brunswick, 5 Sept. 1787. Cadet 1803. Arrived in India 4 Dec. 1804. Cornet 11 Mar. 1805. Lieut. 15 Aug. 1809. Capt. 1 Sept. 1818. Major 7 Oct. 1824. Lt. Col. 26 Oct. 1827. *d.* Kalpi, U.P., 2 Oct. 1828.

6th (3rd by second wife) son of Gen. Benedict Arnold (*D.N.B.*) and Margaret his wife, dau. of Edward Shippen, Chief Judge of Pennsylvania. Brother of Edward Shippen Arnold, *q.v. m.* Clapham, 10 Jan. 1826, Ann Martinez, elder dau. of Henry Brown, M.C.S., Commercial Resident at Ramnad. (She *re-m.* Henry Mason, Capt. R.N., on 2 Feb. 1831, and died 29 Oct. 1843, aged 39.) Granted by sign manual, 20 July 1793, a pension of £100 *p.a* in recognition of his father's services. Marlow Cadet.

Services : In 2nd N.C. throughout his service. Adjt. 1 Jan. 1807 till 1816. Nepal War 1814-5 ; in 1st Div. Fort Adjt. and Bk. Mr. at Agra 1817-9. Bk. Mr. Karnal Div. 1820-2. Fur. 1822-6.

Refs. : Burke's *Landed Gentry,* 7th edn., p. 44, *s.n.* Arnold, of Little Missenden Abbey, Bucks. *Life of Col. Pownoll Phipps. Howard & Crisp,* ii. 25, *s.n.* Brown. *G.M.* 1826, i. 80 ; 1829, i. 381. *A.J.* xxvii. Will dated Muttra 18 Sept. 1828 ; proved 2 Jan. 1829.

THE BENGAL ARMY, 1758-1834

ARNOLD, Sir John (1755-1836). Major General, K.C.B. Colonel 10 N.I. *b.* Feb./Mar. 1755. Was already in India when apptd. Cadet on 9 Mar. 1778. Ensign 4 June 1778. Lieut. 16 Nov. 1780. Capt. 16 Dec. 1796. Major 13 July 1803. Lt. Col. 19 Oct. 1805. Col. (4 June 1813) 14 Jan. 1819. Maj. Gen. 12 Jan. 1819. *d.* Barrackpore 8 Oct. 1836, aged 81 years and 7 months. Brother of Mrs. Elizabeth Hatsell, Mrs. Sophia Morton, Mrs. Maria Byrn, and Mrs. Ann Veysie. His daus. *m.* Charles Jackson Doveton, *q.v.*, and William Logie, *q.v.*
Services : Adjt. 1st Bengal Eur. Regt. in 1780, and comdg. coy. of Cadets in Fort William. A.D.C. to Col. Samuel Hampton, *q.v.*, in 1783. A.D.C. and Persian Intr. to Col. John White, comdg. a Bde. at Dinapore (*d.* 1794), *q.v.*, in 1788. Capt. Lt. 3rd Regt. Eur. Inf. 1796-8. Operations in Bundelkhand 1807-9 ; Sehlehuganj ; comdg. 1/19th N.I. Nepal War 1814-5 ; Nalagarh, as Bdr. ; Malaun ; comdg. 1/19th N.I., in 1st Div. Third Mahratta War ; Bdr. comdg. 8th Bde. with the Reserve. Comdd. a force operating against the Bhattis in Hariana Sept. 1818. Col. 19th N.I. 14 Jan. 1819. Comdd. Rohilkhand district 1819-20 ; and Saugor Div. 1823-7. Col. 10th N.I. in 1834. C.B. 3 Feb. 1817. K.C.B. 2 Jan. 1827.
Refs. : *E.I.M.C.* iii. 1. Will dated Barrackpore 22 Aug. 1835 ; proved 14 Oct. 1836. M.I. in old cemetery at Barrackpore.

ARNOLD, Thomas. Lieutenant. Infantry. Cadet 1766. Ensign 6 Sept. 1766. Lieut. 1 Dec. 1767. Resigned 3 Mar. 1768.
Services : N.F.P.

ARNOLD, Thomas (1763/64-1781). Lieutenant, 2nd N.I. *b.* Gloucester 1763/64. Cadet 1780. Ensign 1780. Lieut. 8 July 1780. *bur.* Calcutta 25 June 1781.
Services : Sailed for India on the *London* 12 Feb. 1780, aged 16.

ARNOTT, Frederick Maitland (1759/60-1807). Lieutenant (? Captain). Infantry. *b.* Jamaica 1759/60. Cadet 1777. Arrived in India 2 Nov. 1777. Ensign 9 Feb. 1778. Lieut. 19 Sept. 1779. Resigned 19 Dec. 1787. *d.* Kishunnagar, B. & O. (? Krishnagar, Nadia district, Bengal), 31 Aug. 1807 : beaten to death by Ryots owing to a dispute over some indigo.
Natural son of Hon. Frederick Lewis Maitland, Capt. R.N. (who was 6th son of Charles, sixth Earl of Lauderdale), by a native woman of Jamaica. *m.* 22 Dec. 1785, Harriet D'Oyly, eldest dau. of William Greer, Chief Ofr. of the *Nassau*, East Indiaman. (She was lost at sea on the *Calcutta*, Mar. 1809.)

Services : After resigning the Service he became an indigo planter at " Hurrah, Kissennagur."
Refs. : *Hickey*, ii. 103, 247 ; iv. 353-4. Will dated 7 Dec. 1793 ; proved 19 Nov. 1807.

ARROW, George (1792-1825). Captain, 2nd L.C. *b.* Westminster 11 Aug. 1792. Cadet 1806. Arrived in India 17 Mar. 1808. Cornet 15 Mar. 1808. Lieut. 1 Sept. 1818. Capt. 21 Feb. 1823. *d.* Berhampore, Bengal, 31 Jan. 1825.
Son of Jordan James (*or* Jones) Arrow, joiner to H.M. Board of Works, and Adjt. Westminster Vol. Cav. Brother of James Arrow, *q.v. m.* (?).
Services : Served throughout in 2nd N.C. Nepal War 1814-5, in 1st Div. Adjt. 2nd N.C. 1816-9 ; Qmr. 1819-21. Third Mahratta War ; in Reserve Div. Fur. 15 July 1821 till 1823.
Refs. : Will dated Benares 26 Mar. 1821 ; proved 9 Mar. 1825.

ARROW, James (1786-1819). Captain, 3rd N.I. *b.* London 5 Apr. 1786. Cadet 1800. Arrived in India 26 Oct. 1801. Ensign 2 Dec. 1801. Lieut. 30 Sept. 1803. Capt. 12 Apr. 1815. *d.* at sea, 27 Dec. 1819, between Madras and the Cape.
bapt. St. John Evang., Westminster, 27 Apr. 1786. Son of Jordan James (*or* Jones) Arrow and Elizabeth his wife. Brother of George Arrow, *q.v. m.* Berhampore, 25 Jan. 1806, Mary, dau. of William Palmer (1740-1816), *q.v.*, by Bibi Faiz Bukhsh, a Begum of Delhi. Owned a small estate at Boyne Hill, nr. Maidenhead.
Services : Posted as Ensign to 3rd N.I. and was borne on the roll of that Regt. throughout his service. Lieut. 1/3rd N.I. ; Capt. 2/3rd N.I. A.D.C. to his father-in-law at Berhampore 1806-12. Cantt. Adjt. and Bk. Mr. at Berhampore 21 Jan 1812 till 1819. No record of active service.
Refs. : *G.M.* 1820, i. 476. Will proved 26 May 1820.

ARROWSMITH, Joseph (1780-1802). Ensign, (? 14th N.I.). *bapt.* Upton-on-Severn, Worcs., 22 June 1780. Cadet 1800. Arrived in India 14 Oct. 1801. Ensign 11 Oct. 1801. *d.* Bahraich, U.P., 4 Sept. 1802.
Son of Benjamin Arrowsmith and Margaret his wife.
Services : N.F.P.

ARUNDEL, Yates Richard (*d.* 1770). Ensign, Infantry. Cadet 1769. Ensign 15 Aug. 1769. *d.* Berhampore 11 June 1770.
Services : N.F.P.

THE BENGAL ARMY, 1758-1834

ASHE, Benjamin. Captain. Infantry. Capt. 11 Aug. 1768. Resigned 5 Jan. 1779.
m. Mary, sister of James Moore (1750/51-1785), *q.v.*
Services : Probably transfd. as Capt. from H.M.S. N.F.P.

ASHE, Benjamin (1792-1868). Lieut. Colonel. 62nd N.I. *b.* Bengal July 1792. Cadet 1806. Arrived in India 28 May 1808. Ensign 31 Mar. 1808. Lieut. 6 Mar. 1814. Capt. 13 May 1825. Major 30 May 1841. Invalided 22 Mar. 1844. Retired 13 Nov. 1844. Hon. Lt. Col. 28 Nov. 1854. *d.* Homburg 1 Oct. 1868.
bapt. Bengal July 1792. (*Probably* son of St. George Ashe (1756/57-1843), *q.v.* *m.* Cawnpore, 9 May 1828, Harriet, sister of Capt. Edward Hopper, H.M. 38th Regt. (She died London, 25 Dec. 1882, aged 78.)
Services : Ensign d.d. 2nd N.I. in 1811. With Bengal Eur. Regt. in 1812. Embarked for Java 24 Feb. 1812. To do duty with Amboynese Corps 26 Sept. 1812 ; served with that Corps till 1816. Macassar June 1816 ; assault on entrenchments at the Baliangan Pass. Third Mahratta War ; Lieut. Bengal Eur. Regt. A.D.C. to Maj. Gen. St. George Ashe, *q.v.*, in 1820. Transfd. to 2/31st N.I. 11 July 1823 ; to 62nd N.I. (late 2/31st) May 1824. Intr. & Qmr. 62nd N.I. 22 May 1824. First Burma War ; Arakan 1825 ; Capt. 62nd N.I. (India medal). Fur. p.a. 24 Jan. 1831 till 15 Dec. 1833. Comdd. 62nd N.I. 27 Aug. 1837 till Sept. 1838.
Refs. : Misc. Gen. et Her. 3S. ii. 166.

ASHE, Joseph (*d.* 1797). Captain, Infantry. Country Cadet 1778. Admitted 29 Dec. 1778. Ensign 29 Mar. 1779. Lieut. 1 Feb. 1781. Capt. 7 Jan. 1796. *d.* Bombay 18 Dec. 1797.
Services : N.F.P.

ASHE, St. George (1756/57-1843). Lieut. General. Colonel 46th N.I. *b.* 1756/57. Cadet 1778. Admitted 8 Oct. 1778. Ensign Oct. 1778. Lieut. 3 Nov. 1778. Capt. 7 Jan. 1796. Major 4 Mar. 1800. Lt. Col. 21 Jan. 1803. Col. 1 Jan. 1812. Maj. Gen. 4 June 1814. Lt. Gen. 22 July 1830. *d.* Albany St., Regent's Park, London, 8 Feb. 1843, aged 86.
3rd son of Richard Ashe, of Ashfield, co. Meath, M.P., and Anne Deane his wife. *m.* (?). Father of St. George Ashe, *q.v.* His daus. *m.* Peter Bearsley Hume, *q.v.*, and John Lumsdaine (1782-1805), *q.v.*
Services : Sailed for India on the *Nassau*, 7 Mar. 1778, aged 21. First Mahratta War (s.w.). Second Mahratta War ; Agra ; capture of Gwalior ; Monson's retreat ; comdg. 2/9th N.I. Fur. p.a. 22 Dec. 1808 till Dec. 1811. Apptd. Mily. Comr. in Rohilkhand 21 June 1816. To comd. Rohilkhand district Jan. 1817. To tempy.

comd. of 2nd Div. of Field Army Dec. 1818. To Staff of the Presidency 1 Apr. 1819. Fur. p.a. 11 Jan. 1821 till death.
Refs. : Burke's *Commoners*, ii. 581. *E.I.M.C.* i. 290. *The Times*, 9 Feb. 1843. *G.M.* 1843, i. 330. G.O. of 5 May 1843.

ASHE, St. George (1789-1810). Ensign, 3rd N.I. *b.* Bengal 1789. Cadet 1805. Arrived in India 19 Sept. 1806. Ensign 2 Oct. 1806. *d.* Bhagulpur, B. & O., 19 Nov. 1810.
bapt. Berhampore, Bengal, 27 Mar. 1791. Son of St. George Ashe, *q.v.* (*Probably* brother of Benjamin Ashe (1792-1868), *q.v.*
Services : Apptd. Cadet on 18 Dec. 1805, aged 16. Served throughout with 3rd N.I. No record of active service.

ASHHURST, James Henry (1782-1817). Captain, 11th N.I. *b.* London 5 Aug. 1782. Cadet 1796. Arrived in India 26 Mar. 1800. Ensign 15 Sept. 1799. Lieut. 28 Oct. 1799. Capt. 22 May 1810. *d.* Hoshangabad, C.P., 13 June 1817.
bapt. St. Martin in the Fields, London, 3 Sept. 1782. 3rd son of Sir [1] William Henry Thomas Ashhurst, Kt., one of the justices of the King's bench in England from 1770 to 1800, and Grace his wife, dau. of Robert Whalley, of Oxford, M.D.

[1] *Note :* Kt. according to Burke and Haydn, but not according to Shaw or *D.N.B.*

Services : Posted as Lieut. to 1/11th N.I. 15 Apr. 1801. Second Mahratta War ; Laswari (w.) ; Lieut. 11th N.I., comdg. Lord Lake's escort. Adjt. & Qmr. 11th N.I. 1805-10. Fur. 1812 till 3 Oct. 1715. Dy. Paymr. Nagpur Subsidiary Force (Capt. 1/11th N.I.) in 1817.
Refs. : Burke's *Landed Gentry*, 12th edn., p. 46, *s.n.* Ashhurst, of Waterstock, Oxon. *G.M.* 1818, ii. 186. Will dated camp, Hussingabad, 5 May 1817 ; proved 24 Sept. 1817.

ASHWORTH, John (*d.* 1798). Captain, 3rd Regt. European Inf. Was already in India when apptd. Cadet on 7 June 1781. Ensign 1 July 1782. Lieut. 1 Jan. 1785. Capt. 7 Jan. 1796. *d.* Calcutta 11 Feb. 1798.
Services : Was Adjt. & Qmr. 3rd Bde. in 1790. Fur. 21 Jan. 1794 till 27 Jan. 1798.

ASPINWALL, John Henry (1786-1814). Lieutenant, 7th N.I. *b.* London 18 May 1786. Cadet 1803. Arrived in India 3 Dec. 1804. Ensign 13 Oct. 1804. Lieut. 13 Oct. 1804. *d. unm.* Java 11 July 1814.
Son of Henry Aspinwall, of St. Pancras (Gt. Russell St., Bloomsbury), London, and Ann his wife.

THE BENGAL ARMY, 1758-1834   57

Services : Posted as Lieut. to 7th N.I. Capture of Java ; Lieut. 4th Bengal Vols. Qmr. to 4th Bn. in 1813.
Refs. : Will dated Sourabaya 20 Jan. 1812 ; codicil dated 19 Aug. 1813 ; proved 8 Dec. 1821.

ASTON, Thomas (1782-1839). Ensign. 5th N.I. *bapt.* St. Mildred, Bread St., London, 8 June 1782. Cadet 1799. Arrived in India 24 Dec. 1800. Ensign 8 Sept. 1800. Resigned in India 30 Apr. 1801. *d.* Dawlish, Devon, 6 Dec. 1839.
Son of Thomas Aston and Susanna his wife.
Services : Posted as Ensign to 1/5th N.I. 17 Apr. 1801.
Refs. : *G.M.* 1840, i. 106.

ATKINS, Robert (1744/45-1786). Lieutenant, Infantry. *b.* 1744/45. Cadet 1780. Apptd. Cadet on 14 Mar. 1781, aged 36. Ensign 1780. Lieut. 14 July 1782. *d.* Chittagong 9 Jan. 1786. A native of Scotland.
Services : Sailed for India on the *Deptford*, 26 June 1781, aged 36. N.F.P.

ATKINSON, Charles (1808-1840). Lieutenant, 10th L.C. *bapt.* King's Co. 11 Mar. 1808. Cadet 1827. Arrived in India 28 May 1828. Cornet (25 Dec. 1827) 28 Feb. 1829. Lieut. 12 Apr. 1836. *d.* Nasirabad, Rajputana, 16 June 1840, from the bite of a snake, received four days earlier.
3rd son of Jackson Wray Atkinson, of Cangort, Lt. Col. of the King's Co. Militia, High Sheriff King's Co. 1803, and Sarah his wife, dau. of Richard Caddell, of Downpatrick.
Services : Cornet d.d. 4th L.C. 25 Nov. 1828. Posted as Cornet to 10th L.C. 28 Feb. 1829. Fur. s.c. 15 Jan. 1833 till 13 Feb. 1837. No record of active service.
Refs. : Burke's *Landed Gentry of Ireland*, p. 16, *s.n.* Atkinson, of Cangort, King's Co. *A.J.* 1840. *I.N.* 11 Sept. 1840, p. 77.

ATKINSON, Frederick Dayot (1816-1883). Lieut. General. 2nd European Regt. u.s.l. *b.* Calcutta 23 July 1816. Cadet 1832. Ensign 11 June 1833. Lieut. 3 Oct. 1840. Capt. 12 July 1847. Major 16 Dec. 1859. Lt. Col. 18 Feb. 1861. Col. 18 Feb. 1866. Maj. Gen. 1 Oct. 1877. Lt. Gen. 21 Dec. 1880. *d.* Homesdale, Worthing, Sussex, 23 June 1883.
Son of James Atkinson, Bengal Medical Service, and Jane his wife. *m.* Ghazipur, 26 Feb. 1842, Ann Sophia Mackenzie, widow of Henry Sturrock, *q.v.*, and 4th dau. of Isaac Pereira, *q.v.* (*See also* George Alexander **Barbor** and William **Veysie**.) Addiscombe Cadet 1831-3.

Services : Ensign d.d. 55th N.I. 14 Dec. 1833. Joined the 12th N.I. in May 1834. Transfd. to 2nd Bengal Eur. Regt. as Adjt. in Dec. 1839. Operations against the hill tribes of Sind 1844-5. Fort Adjt. at Allahabad July 1847. 2nd Asst. Sec. in Mily. Dept. Mar. 1848. 1st Asst. Sec. May 1851. Dy. Sec. Mily. Dept. 11 Feb. 1856. Officiated as Mily. Sec. to Lord Canning, the G.G., March to June 1856. Controller of mily. finance 4 Mar. 1862. Returned to Europe Apr. 1874. Transfd. to u.s.l. 1 July 1881.
Refs. : Boase. List of Military Secretaries to the Governors-General and Viceroys, p. 31. *The Times,* 26 June 1883.

ATKINSON, Henry. Lieutenant. Infantry. Cadet (?). Ensign (?). Lieut. 1 Sept. 1768. Resigned 29 Aug. 1770.
Services : N.F.P.

ATKINSON, James (1757/58-?). Major. 23rd N.I. *b.* in Ireland 1757/58. Cadet 1780. Admitted 18 June 1781. Ensign 1780. Lieut. 25 July 1781. Capt. 31 July 1799. Major 21 Sept. 1804. Retired 14 Aug. 1805. (*d.* 1828 ?)

Note : His name disappears from the list of Retired Officers, as published in *E.I.R.*, after the issue dated 15 May 1828. His death may, however, have occurred some years earlier.

Services : Arrived in Madras 5 Jan. 1781, and joined army under Sir Eyre Coote against Haidar Ali of Mysore ; served as a volunteer to end of first campaign. Adjt. 11th N.I. for 15 years. Second Rohilla War 1794 ; battle of Bitaurah. Adjt. & Qmr. 10th N.I. 1796. On service in Hyderabad in 1798, disarming the Nizam's troops officered by Frenchmen ; Capt. Lt. 10th N.I. Capt. Lt. 10 Sept. 1798. Fourth Mysore War ; D.Q.M.G. of Col. Wellesley's Div. ; storm and capture of Seringapatam ; comdg. a flank coy. (Medal). Capt. 5th N.I. Comdd. escort of Admiral Sir Home Popham's embassy to the Arab states 1801-4. Transfd. as Major to 23rd N.I. in 1804. Fur. 19 Jan. 1803 till retirement.
Refs. : E.I.M.C. i. 194.

ATKINSON, Richard (1786- ?). Lieutenant. 6th N.I. *b.* Temple Sowerby, Westmorland, 26 Mar. 1786. Cadet 1803. Arrived in India 1 Dec. 1804. Ensign 8 Oct. 1804. Lieut. 8 Oct. 1804. Pensioned 1 Sept. 1815. Retired 21 Feb. 1821. (*d.* 1830 ?)

Younger son of Matthew Atkinson and Mary his wife, dau. of Rev. George Gilbanks, of Wetherall, Carlisle. Uncle of Henry Cookson Airey, *q.v.*

Note : His name disappears from *E.I.R.* after the issue dated 15 May 1830.

THE BENGAL ARMY, 1758-1834

Services : Posted as Lieut. to 6th N.I. in 1805 and served throughout with that Regt. (? Nepal War 1814-5.)
Refs. : Burke's *Landed Gentry*, 13th edn., p. 47, *s.n.* Atkinson, of Morland Hall, Westmorland.

ATKINSON, William (1787- ?). Lieutenant. Artillery. *b.* 5 Aug. 1787. Cadet 1805. Arrived in India 10 July 1805. Lieut. 4 May 1805. Resigned 25 Nov. 1805.
bapt. Stepney, Middlesex, 1 Oct. 1787. Son of Thomas Atkinson and Ann his wife. Woolwich Cadet : nominated on 13 Apr. 1802 ; obtained his certificate on 25 Jan. 1805.
Services : Sailed for India on the *Surrey*. Returned to England in 1805.

ATKINSON, William Spranger (1756/57-1794). Lieutenant, Infantry. *b.* London 1756/57. Cadet 1777. Ensign 3 Jan. 1778. Lieut. 11 Sept. 1778. *d.* Cawnpore 8 Apr. 1794.
Son of (? William) Atkinson, of Pall Mall, London, apothecary. Brother of Jane, widow of Edward Bishop, of London. Kinsman of Sir William Dunkin, Kt., a puisne judge of the supreme court in Calcutta.
Services : Sailed for India on the *Houghton*, 9 Feb. 1777, aged 20. N.F.P.
Refs. : *Hickey*, iii. 350. Will dated 21 Sept. 1792 ; proved in 1794.

ATTY, William (*d.* 1779). Fireworker, Artillery. Cadet 1778. Fireworker 31 Dec. 1778. *d.* Calcutta 14 Mar. 1779.
Services : N.F.P.

AUBERJONOIS, Anthony Francis Louis (1787-1837). Major. 52nd N.I. *bapt.* Yverdon, canton Vaud, Switzerland, 29 Mar. 1787. Cadet 1809. Arrived in India 3 Oct. 1810. Ensign 26 Oct. 1811. Lieut. 16 Dec. 1814. Capt. 24 Oct. 1825. Major 1 Jan. 1837. Retired 1 Jan. 1837. *d.* at sea 1837, on board the *Royal Saxon*.
Son of Francis Adam Auberjonois, of Yverdon, president of the tribunal of canton Vaud.
Services : Posted as Ensign to 26th N.I. Lieut. 2/26th N.I. With 6th Gren. Bn. in 1815-6. Against the Bhattis of Hariana 1818 ; Lieut. 2/26th N.I. Transfd. to 52nd N.I. (late 2/26th), May 1824. Intr. & Qmr. 52nd N.I. 27 Nov. 1823 till 14 Nov. 1825. (? First Burma War ; Cachar 1825 ; Lieut. 52nd N.I.)
Refs. : *Dict. hist. et biog. de la Suisse*, vol. i. (1921). *Livre d'or des familles vaudoises*. *A.J.* N.S. xxiii. 331.

AUBERT, Jeremiah (1785-1834). Lieut. Colonel, 18th N.I. *b.*
London 3 Dec. 1785. Cadet 1803. Arrived in India 2 Dec. 1804.
Ensign 3 Oct. 1804. Lieut. 3 Oct. 1804. Capt. 14 July 1815.
Major 8 Sept. 1825. Lt. Col. 7 June 1830. *d.* Betul, C.P.
29 July 1834.

Son of Alexander Aubert, of Moorfields, London, a Swiss from
Geneva, and Sarah Clarke his wife. *m.* (before 1818) ?
Services : Posted as Lieut. to 1/19th N.I. in 1805. Operations
in Bundelkhand 1807 ; Sehlehuganj ; Lieut. 1/19th N.I. Fur. s.c.
18 June 1811 till 10 Apr. 1813. Actg. Adjt. 1/19th N.I. 1 Nov. 1814.
Nepal War 1814-5 ; Lieut. 1/19th N.I. in 1st Div. Bde. Major
1st Inf. Bde., Nagpur Subsidiary Force, 14 Nov. 1817. Third
Mahratta War ; Bde. Major. Capt. 1/19th N.I. Operations in
Oudh 1820. Tempy. comd. of Purnea Provl. Bn. 7 June 1824.
Transfd. to newly-raised 2nd Extra Regt. in 1825 ; to 31st N.I. in
1827 ; to 10th and 45th N.I. in 1828 ; as Lt. Col. to 70th N.I.
1 Mar. 1831 ; to comd. 18th N.I. 21 Dec. 1833.

Refs. : Notices généalogiques sur les familles genevoises, par Galiffe,
iii. (1836) 17. *G.M.* 1835, i. 447. *Dict. biog. des genevois et des
vaudois,* par Albert de Montet, i. 16.

AUBERY, John Philip (1771-1808). Captain, 2nd N.I. *b.* London
19 Apr. 1771. Cadet 1791. Admitted 31 Aug. 1791. Ensign
10 Mar. 1792. Lieut. 3 Oct. 1794. Capt. 21 Sept. 1804. *d.*
Calcutta 17 Nov. 1808.

bapt. St. Martin's, Ludgate, London, 19 May 1771. Son of John
Peter Aubery (naturalized in 1775) and Elizabeth his wife.
Services : Lieut. in 3rd Regt. Eur. Inf. 1796-8. Second Mahratta
War ; Aligarh ; battle of Delhi ; Lieut. 2nd N.I. Fur. 5 Mar. 1804
till 27 Sept. 1807.
Refs. : Pester.

AULDJO, Thomas (1790-1808). Ensign, 18th N.I. *bapt.* Aberdeen
10 July 1790. Cadet 1805. Arrived in India 11 July 1806.
Ensign 23 Aug. 1806. *d.* nr. Lucknow 3 Sept. 1808 : kld. by
dacoits.

4th son of Day George Auldjo, of Portlethen, co. Aberdeen.
Services : No record of active service.
Refs. : S.M. 1809, p. 478.

AURIOL, James (1785-1833). Lieut. Colonel, Invalid Est. 21st N.I.
b. London 16 Oct. 1785. Cadet 1800. Arrived in India 17 Oct.
1801. Ensign 28 Sept. 1801. Lieut. 22 Oct. 1802. Capt. 6 Mar.
1814. Major 1 May 1824. Lt. Col. 21 June 1827. Invalided
11 July 1828. *d.* Chunar 13 Sept. 1833.

THE BENGAL ARMY, 1758-1834

bapt. St. Pancras, London, 23 Dec. 1785. Son of James Peter Auriol, of Stratford Pl., London, and Hariot his 1st wife. *m.* 1st (before 1814), ? - (She died 26 Sept. 1819.) *m.* 2nd, St. John's, Calcutta, 19 Sept. 1826, Mary, widow of John Irwin, *q.v.*, and dau. of Thomas Charters, *q.v.*

Services : Second Mahratta War ; battle of Deig ; capture of Deig ; siege of Bhurtpore ; Lieut. Bengal Eur. Regt. Expedition to I. of Macao 1808-9 ; on staff of Major Thomas Matthias Weguelin, *q.v.*, comdg. the force. Transfd. to newly-constituted 2nd Eur. Regt. 1 May 1824. First Burma War ; Arakan 1825. Retransfd. to 1st Eur. Regt. 24 Sept. 1826 ; to 2nd Eur. Regt. 7 Dec. 1826, and finally to 21st N.I. After transfer to the Invalid est., he comdd. the European Invalids at Chunar till death.

Refs. : *A.J.* N.S. xiii. 205. Will dated Chunar 16 May 1833 ; proved 13 Nov. 1833.

AUSTEN, George Powell (1811-1853). Captain, 18th N.I. *b.* co. Dublin 15 Mar. 1811. Cadet 1827. Arrived in India 11 Feb. 1829. Ensign 23 Aug. 1828. Lieut. 16 Jan. 1834. Capt. 1 Aug. 1846. *d.* Ambala 24 May 1853.

Son of Samuel Austen, solicitor. *m.* Bath, 30 Mar. 1841, Anna, eldest dau. of Capt. Clotworthy Gillmor, R.N., of Brock St., Bath. (*See also* Charles Henry Thomas.) His sisters *m.* Crawford Mitford Rees, *q.v.*, and Edward Sunderland, *q.v.* T.C.D. Pensioner 2 Jan. 1826, aged 15.

Services : Ensign d.d. 30th N.I. Posted as Ensign to 18th N.I. in June 1829. Leave s.c. to N.S.W. 24 Sept. 1832 till 18 Feb. 1834. Kicked by a horse and leg broken 3 Jan. 1835. Fur. s.c. 7 Mar. 1839 till 24 Oct. 1841. Second Sikh War ; in garrison at Lahore ; Capt. 18th N.I. (Medal).

Refs. : De Rhé-Philipe. Bath Chron. 11 Aug. 1853.

AUSTIN, Edward Griffith (1812-1861). Bt. Lieut. Colonel. Artillery. *b.* Greenwich 26 Sept. 1812. Cadet 1828. Arrived in India 13 Aug. 1829. 2nd Lieut. 12 Dec. 1828. Lieut. 21 Dec. 1836. Capt. 13 May 1846. Bt. Major 7 June 1849. Bt. Lt. Col. 20 June 1854. Retired 9 June 1856. *d.* S. Bersted, Sussex, 18 Aug. 1861.

Son of Thomas Austin, deputy treasurer of Greenwich Hospital. *m.* Delhi, 8 Feb. 1842, Anna Theresa, 4th dau. of Horace Watson, of Mill Hill, Hendon, Middlesex. Addiscombe Cadet 1 Aug. 1827 till 12 Dec. 1828.

Services : Served with 1st Troop 2nd Bde. H.A. 1836-9 ; with 4th Troop 2nd Bde. 1840 ; with 2nd Troop 2nd Bde. 1841 ; with 3rd Troop 2nd Bde. 1843. Gwalior campaign ; Paniar ; Bde.

LIST OF THE OFFICERS OF

Major H.A. (Bronze star). First Sikh War; Aliwal; Sobraon; Bde. Major 2nd Bde. H.A. (Medal with clasp). Second Sikh War; Sadulapur (s.w.); Gujerat; comdg. No. 10 H.F.B. (Medal with clasp). Comdg. 2nd Troop 3rd Bde. H.A. 1849-53. Fur. 1854 till retirement.

Refs. : *The Times*, 7 Jan. 1862.

AUSTIN, George (*d.* 1789). Captain, Infantry. Cadet 1771. Ensign 25 Mar. 1773. Lieut. 22 May 1778. Capt. 16 Jan. 1784. *d.* Cawnpore 20 July 1789.

Services : N.F.P.

AUSTWICK, William (1762/63-1787). Lieutenant, Infantry. *b.* 1762/63. Cadet 1780. Ensign 27 Sept. 1780. Lieut. 29 June 1781. *d.* at sea 1787.

A native of Berks.

Services : Sailed for India on the *Bridgwater*, 12 Feb. 1780, aged 17. N.F.P.

AVELINE, George (1781-1805). Lieutenant, 1st N.I. *b.* Wortham, Suffolk, 8 May 1781. Cadet 1800. Arrived in India 6 Feb. 1802. Ensign 20 Dec. 1801. Lieut. 30 Sept. 1803. *d.* 13 Feb. 1805 : kld. in action in the Doab.

bapt. Wortham 2 Aug. 1781. Son of William Aveline (*formerly* Adams), of Datchet, Bucks., and Catherine his wife, afterwards Catherine Babbs, of Dorking.

Services : Posted as Ensign to 1st N.I. Operations in Bundelkhand 1804-5 ; Lieut. (? 1/) 1st N.I.

Refs. : Intestate ; admon. granted 9 Apr. 1805.

AWDRY, James (1805-1835). Lieutenant, 55th N.I. *b.* Chippenham, Wilts., 17 Sept. 1805. Cadet 1823. Arrived in India 3 Sept. 1824. Ensign 13 Apr. 1824. Lieut. 13 May 1825. *d.* Bankura, Bengal, 31 May 1835.

Eldest son of William Henry Awdry, of Chippenham (Sec. to John Awdry, of Wotton House, Wilts., Receiver Gen. for Wilts.), and Eliza his wife, dau. of West Hill, M.D., of Devizes.

Services : Served throughout in 55th N.I. Intr. & Qmr. 2 Oct. 1827. At date of death was Junior Asst. to A.G.G. in the Ramgarh district. No record of active service.

Refs. : Burke's *Landed Gentry*, 13th edn., p. 54, *s.n.* Awdry, of Seend, Wilts. *G.M.* 1835, ii. 667.

*AXFORD, Isaac (1742/43-1769). Lieutenant, Infantry. *b.* 1742/43. Cadet (?). Ensign (?). Lieut. 2 Nov. 1765. *d.* in India 1769.

THE BENGAL ARMY, 1758-1834   63

A native of Wilts. Brother of William Axford, of Ludgate Hill, London, grocer, and of Ann Axford.

Note : Possibly either the husband of, or connected by marriage with, Hannah Lightfoot (*D.N.B.*).

Services : Sailed for India on the London, 2 Apr. 1764, aged 21. First Mysore War.

Refs. : *B.M. Add. MS.* 6050. *N. & Q.* 10S. viii. 321, 404, 483. Will dated 22 May 1769 ; filed 3 Oct. 1769.

AXFORD, Richard (1784-1853). Major. 27th N.I. Subsequently H.E.I.C. Recruiting Officer at Liverpool. *b.* Bridgwater, Somerset, 26 Aug. 1784. Cadet 1800. Arrived in India 23 Aug. 1801. Ensign 2 Jan. 1802. Lieut. 2 Nov. 1803. Capt. 1 Jan. 1819. Major 1825. Retired 15 Jan. 1825. *d.* Liverpool 13 Nov. 1853. *bapt.* Bridgwater 30 Dec. 1784. Son of Richard Axford and Frances his wife. *m.* Maria.

Services : Posted as Ensign to 13th N.I. Operations against Dhundia Khan 1807 ; Komona ; Ganauri ; Lieut. 1/13th N.I. Nepal War ; Bt. Capt. 13th N.I. (India medal). Capt. 1/13th N.I. Actg. Dy. P.M.G. 1821-4. Transfd. to 27th N.I. (late 2/13th) May 1824. Fur. 1824 till retirement. Subsequently, till death, employed on H.E.I.C. recruiting service in the Liverpool district.

Refs. : *G.M.* 1854, i. 105.

AYLMER, Hon. James Thomas (1785-1813). Lieutenant, 8th N.I. *bapt.* St. Peter's, Carmarthen, 24 Jan. 1785. Cadet 1802. Arrived in India 12 July 1803. Ensign 29 July 1803. Lieut. 25 Aug. 1804. *d. unm.* Calcutta 5 Aug. 1813.

4th son of Henry, fourth Baron Aylmer, and Catherine his wife, dau. of Sir Charles Whitworth, of Leyborne.

Services : Second Mahratta War ; capture of Deig ; siege of Bhurtpore (w. in 3rd assault on 20 Feb. 1805) ; Lieut. 1/8th N.I. A.D.C. to Maj. Gen. John Smith 1805-6. Adjt. & Qmr. of Eur. Invalids at Chunar in 1808. (? Expedition against Mauritius 1810-1 ; Lieut 2nd Bn. Vols. In 2nd Bn. Vols. in 1811.

Refs. : Burke's *Peerage*, 1923, p. 172, *s.n.* Aylmer, B.

AYTON, James Alexander (1791-1832). Bt. Captain. 17th N.I. *b.* 28 July 1791. Cadet 1806. Arrived in India 6 Oct. 1807. Ensign 22 Oct. 1807. Lieut. 1 May 1813. Bt. Capt. 14 Apr. 1822. Resigned in India 27 Mar. 1824. *d.* 10 Aug. 1832, on his pinnace, nr. Budge-Budge, Bengal.

bapt. Calcutta 24 Oct. 1791. Son of James Ayton and Margaret his wife, sister of Ynyr Burges. Stepson of George Fleming (1760/

61-1818), *q.v.* *m.* Chinsura, Bengal, 16 Oct. 1820, Sophia Thomasin, widow of Henry Manley, *q.v.*, and dau. of his stepfather, George Fleming.

Services : Posted as Ensign to 17th N.I. and remained on the roll of that Regt. throughout his service. Mily. student at Coll. of Fort William July 1812 till 1813. Intr. & Qmr. 2/17th N.I. 1 July 1814. Nepal War 1814-5 ; Lieut. 2/17th N.I. in 3rd Div. Served with the escort to the Resident at Katmandu, Nepal, 1817-9. Actg. Asst. Professor of Persian and Arabic at the Coll. of Fort William 24 Jan. 1820 till 1822.

B

BABER, John (1783-1807). Lieutenant, 8th N.I. *b.* Leather Lane, London, 3 Mar. 1783. Cadet 1801. Arrived in India 19 July 1802. Ensign 9 July 1802. Lieut. 24 May 1804. *d.* Mauritius 16 July 1807.
bapt. St. Andrew's, Holborn, 6 Jan. 1797. Son of Thomas Baber, of Red Lion St., Clerkenwell, and Elizabeth his wife. Ed. St. Paul's school; admitted (not on the foundation) 1790/91; admitted 24 Feb. 1794, aged 11. Pembroke Coll., Oxon.; matric. 4 Nov. 1799, aged 16.
Services : Posted as Lieut. to 8th N.I. (? Second Mahratta War.)
Refs. : Gardiner. *Alumni Oxon.*

BABINGTON, William (1789-1813). Lieutenant, 2nd N.I. *b.* Lochmaben, co. Dumfries, 27 Apr. 1789. Cadet 1804. Arrived in India 10 Mar. 1806. Ensign 31 Mar. 1806. Lieut. 10 Feb. 1807. *d.* Ajaigarh, Bundelkhand, 1 Aug. 1813.
Son of Murray Babington. Woolwich Cadet.
Services : Posted as Lieut. to 2nd N.I. in 1807. No record of active service.

BACKHOUSE, Benjamin (*d.* 1773). Cadet, Infantry. Cadet 1772. *d.* Cawnpore May 1773.
Services : N.F.P.

BACKHOUSE, Edward Barnes (1802-1829). Lieutenant, 7th L.C. *b.* Deal 25 Mar. 1802. Cadet 1819. Cornet 8 June 1820. Lieut. 1 May 1824. *d.* Kalpi, U.P., 27 Sept. 1829.
Son of Rev. John Barnes Backhouse, rector of Upper Deal, and Sarah his wife, youngest dau. of Rev. Ralph Drake Brockman, of Beachborough. Brother of Julius Brockman Backhouse, *q.v.*, and cousin-german of George Brockman, *q.v.*
Services : Posted as Cornet to 7th L.C. Intr. & Qmr. 7th L.C. 29 July 1825 till death. No record of active service.
Refs. : Burke's *Landed Gentry*, 11th edn., p. 199, *s.n.* Brockman, of Beachborough, Kent.

BACKHOUSE, Frederick George (1811-1838). Lieutenant, 68th N.I. *b.* Christ Church, Marylebone, Middlesex, 14 May 1811. Cadet 1828. Arrived in India 21 Mar. 1829. Ensign 12 June 1828. Lieut. 6 Oct. 1832. *d.* Nowgong, Assam, 19 Oct. 1838.

Son of Benjamin Backhouse, Capt. 23rd Foot. Addiscombe Cadet 1826-8.

Services : Posted as Ensign to 68th N.I. 3 June 1829. Assam Local Bn. 29 Jan. 1835. Offg. Adjt. do. 20 Aug. 1835. Against the Singphos from Hukong ; assault of stockade 17 Nov. 1835. Junior Asst. to Comr. in Assam 22 May 1837. Principal Asst. to A.G.G., N.E. frontier, Nowgong Div., 17 Oct. 1838.

Refs. : M.I. in Nowgong cemetery.

BACKHOUSE, Julius Brockman (1804-1867). Lieut Colonel, C.B. Artillery. *b.* Deal, Kent, 12 Sept. 1804. Cadet 1820. 2nd Lieut. 9 June 1821. Lieut. 1 May 1824. Capt. 31 Dec. 1838. Bt. Major 4 Oct. 1842. Retired 1 Apr. 1845. Hon. Lt. Col. 28 Nov. 1854. *d.* Middle Deal 4 Apr. 1867.

Son of Rev. John Barnes Backhouse, rector of Upper Deal, and Sarah his wife, youngest dau. of Rev. Ralph Drake Brockman, of Beachborough. Brother of Edward Barnes Backhouse, *q. v. m.* (?). Addiscombe Cadet 1819-21.

Services : Served with 3rd Troop 2nd Bde. H.A. 1825-33. (? Siege and capture of Bhurtpore (India medal). Fur. p.a. 19 June 1834 till 29 June 1837. Served with the British Legion in Spain, under Sir De Lacy Evans, 1835-6. First Afghan War 1839 ; Ghazni (Medal) ; Bde. Major. Apptd. at Kabul to raise a mountain battery for the Shah's service, for which purpose he returned to India. First Afghan War 1841-2 ; with the Mountain Train. To comd. 5th Troop 1st Bde. H.A. (late Shah Shuja's H.A.) 1843. C.B. 24 Dec. 1842. Durani, 3 cl.

Refs. : Burke's *Landed Gentry*, 11th edn., p. 199, *s.n.* Brockman, of Beachborough, Kent. *G.M.* 1867, i. 689.

BACON, Samuel Ishmael (1786-1819). Bt. Captain, 1st L.C. *b.* Ottery St. Mary, Devon, 7 July 1786. Cadet 1800. Arrived in India 21 Oct. 1801. Cornet 1 Jan. 1803. Lieut. 1 Feb. 1806. Bt. Capt. 8 Jan. 1816. *d. unm.* in camp nr. Tharod, C.I., 23 Nov. 1819.

bapt. Ottery St. Mary 9 Nov. 1786. Son of Dashwood Bacon and Ann Barbera his wife. Cousin of Sir Edmund Bacon, 9th and 10th Bart. of Redgrave, and of Mildenhall, premier baronet of England.

Services : Posted as Cornet to 1st N.C. (? Operations in Jumna Doab 1803 ; Sasni ; Bijaigarh ; Kachaura.) Second Mahratta

THE BENGAL ARMY, 1758-1834

War; Laswari; Cornet 1st N.C. Fur. 27 June 1805 till 17 Aug. 1808. Served with Java L.C. 1814-5. Third Mahratta War; Bt. Capt. 1st N.C.
Refs. : Burke's *Peerage*, 1923, p. 176, *s.n.* Bacon, Bart., of Redgrave. Will dated Muttra 7 Sept. 1819; proved 8 Feb. 1820.

BACON, Thomas (1813-1892). 2nd Lieutenant. Artillery. Subsequently rector of King's Worthy, nr. Winchester. *bapt.* London 8 Sept. 1813. Cadet 1830. Arrived in India 4 Aug. 1831. 2nd Lieut. 10 Dec. 1830. Resigned 28 July 1838. *d.* Torquay, Devon, 19 Feb. 1892, aged 78.
Son of John Bacon, of Sidmouth, Devon, sculptor (*D.N.B.*), and Susannah Sophia his wife. Addiscombe Cadet 1829-30.
Services : Fur. p.a. 29 Mar. 1836 till resignation. No record of active service. Called to the Bar by the Middle Temple 1841. Took holy orders. Deacon 1846. Priest 1847. Canon of Gibraltar 1847. Rector of King's Worthy 1852-72. Author of " First Impressions in India, embracing Five Years' Residence in Bengal and Doab, 1831-6," lithos., 2 vols. 8vo, 1837; also " The Oriental Portfolio," 1841.
Refs. : Boase. *A.J.* N.S. xxii. 317. *Guardian*, 2 Mar. 1892, p. 311.

BACON, William (1786-1839). Bt. Major, 65th N.I. *b.* Dublin 4 Nov. 1786. Cadet 1807. Arrived in India 16 Nov. 1808. Ensign 1 Dec. 1808. Lieut. 16 Dec. 1814. Capt. 13 May 1825. Bt. Major 28 June 1838. *d.* nr. Berhampore, Bengal, 14 Apr. 1839.
Son of Thomas Bacon.
Services : Posted as Ensign to 10th N.I. Third Mahratta War; Lieut. 1/10th N.I. Intr. & Qmr. 2/10th N.I. 8 June 1820. Transfd. to 33rd N.I. 1 Oct. 1823. Actg. Adjt. 33rd N.I. 26 Dec. 1823. Transfd. to 65th N.I. (late 1/33rd) May 1824. Adjt. Capt. Walker's Levy 28 Dec. 1824. Fur. s.c. from P.W.I. 18 Aug. 1826 till 23 Nov. 1829. Fur. s.c. 8 Jan. 1834 till 8 Dec. 1837.

BADDELEY, Henry Clinton (1811-1842). Lieutenant. 61st N.I. *b.* Calcutta 6 May 1811. Cadet 1827. Arrived in India 12 June 1828. Ensign 30 Dec. 1827. Lieut. 13 June 1833. Discharged by G.C.M. 12 Apr. 1837. *d.* Longbottom stockade, Australia, 3 Mar. 1842.
Son of William Clinton Baddeley, *q.v.*, and Catherine Margaretta his wife.
Services : Posted as Ensign to 61st N.I. 4 Nov. 1828. Fur. s.c. 5 Dec. 1832 till 8 Dec. 1833. Served with the Arakan Local Bn.

16 June 1835 till 8 Oct. 1835. No record of active service with the Bengal Army. After his discharge he entered the Persian service, became a Major, and commanded a Regt. against the Russians. After serving for a time in the Russian service, he was employed by the British Envoy at the Court of Persia to carry despatches to Lord Ponsonby in Constantinople, whence he was sent on to Lord Palmerston in London. As a reward for his good work, he was apptd. an Assistant at the convict stockade at Longbottom, in Australia.

Refs. : *Sydney Herald,* 12 Mar. 1842. *Bombay Monthly Times,* June 1842.

BADDELEY, Joseph (*d.* 1787). Lieutenant, Infantry. Cadet 1779. Ensign 21 Dec. 1780. Lieut. 28 May 1781. *d.* Chunar 7 May 1787.

Services : N.F.P.

BADDELEY, William Clinton (1783-1842). Major General, C.B. Colonel 74th N.I. *b.* Bowes, Yorks., 31 Oct. 1783. Cadet 1800. Arrived in India 23 Sept. 1801. Ensign 16 Sept. 1801. Lieut. 23 Jan. 1803. Capt. 16 Dec. 1814. Major 18 Jan. 1823. Lt. Col. 2 May 1824. Col. 14 June 1833. Maj. Gen. 28 June 1838. *d.* Karnal 19 Dec. 1842.

bapt. Bowes 9 Jan. 1801. Son of —— Baddeley and Mary his wife. *m.* 2 Nov. 1809, Miss Catherine Margaretta Sloane, of Cape Town. (*See also* Christopher Baldock.). (She died 14 Jan. 1879, aged 86.) Father of Henry Clinton Baddeley, *q.v.*

Services : Posted as Ensign to 1/5th N.I. Apr. 1802. Transfd. to newly-formed 2/24th N.I. Jan. 1805. Operations at Gohad and in Jumna Doab 1806 ; reduction of Ganauri 1807 ; Lieut. 2/24th N.I. Pioneers Nov. 1807 till Sept. 1813. Operations in Bundelkhand 1808-9 ; Hirapur ; Rajaoli ; Ajaigarh. Capture of Java ; Cornelis ; comdg. 4 Coys. Pioneers. Fort Adjt. at Monghyr Sept. 1813. Nepal War 1814-5 ; with Champaran L.I. in 4th Div. 2nd in comd. 2nd Rohilla Cav. Oct. 1816. Siege and capture of Hathras. To raise and comd. 3rd Rohilla Cav. May 1817. Third Mahratta War ; comdg. 3rd Rohilla Cav. Comdd. Dromedary Corps 17 Jan. 1820 till Aug. 1821. Comdt. 2nd Skinner's Horse, " Baddeley's Frontier Horse " (became 4th Local Horse) 20 Aug. 1821 till June 1824. Siege and capture of Bhurtpore ; Lt. Col. comdg. 31st N.I. Fur. 24 Jan. 1827 till 12 June 1828. Bdr., Nizam's army, May 1833. Comdd. Aurangabad Div. Col. 74th N.I. 9 June 1835. Leave 2 yrs. to China 13 May 1837. C.B. 2 Jan. 1827.

Refs. : *De Rhé-Philipe.* Will dated 4 Feb. 1837 ; proved 26 Apr. 1844.

THE BENGAL ARMY, 1758-1834

BADENACH, Walter (1786-1832). Captain, 57th N.I. *b.* Balmakewan (? Balmacaan, Inverness) 10 Aug. 1786. Cadet 1805. Arrived in India 24 Apr. 1807. Ensign 11 Apr. 1807. Lieut. 23 Mar. 1810. Capt. 1 May 1824. *d.* Kyaukpyu, Arakan, 17 July 1832.
Son of James Badenach.
Services : Barasat C.C. for 14 mos. Posted as Ensign to 10th N.I. Capture of Java ; Lieut. 6th Bn. Bengal Vols. Transfd. to newly-raised 29th N.I. in 1815. Adjt. 2/29th N.I. 4 May 1815 till 1822. Leave to Cape 4 Sept. 1819 till 30 Nov. 1821. Fur. s.c. 23 Apr. 1823 till 12 Mar. 1828. Transfd. to 57th N.I. (late 1/29th) May 1824. Bde. Major at Barrackpore 6 Aug. 1828 ; do. at Dacca 28 Sept. 1829. Senior Asst. to Local Supt. in Arakan 25 Jan. 1831 till death. Author of " Inquiry into the State of the Indian Army, . . . ," London, 1826.
Refs.: A.J., N.S. x. 120. Will dated 4 Dec. 1819 ; admon. 17 Oct. 1832.

BAGNOLD, John (1792-1821). Lieutenant, 13th N.I. *b.* London 7 July 1792. Cadet 1808. Arrived in India 19 July 1809. Ensign 22 July 1809. Lieut. 16 Dec. 1814. *d.* Barrackpore 15 June 1821.
Son of Thomas Bagnold. *m.* 10 Feb. 1821 Miss Marianne Cauty.
Services : Posted as Ensign to 2/13th N.I. Intr. & Qmr. 2/13th N.I. 26 Aug. 1815 till death. Third Mahratta War ; Lieut. 2/13th N.I.
Refs. : M.I. in old cemetery, Barrackpore (where his Christian names are given as John Henry).

BAGOT, Francis (*d.* 1771). Cadet, Infantry. Cadet 1771. *d.* Calcutta 29 Dec. 1771.
Services : N.F.P.

BAGOT, Humphrey (1793-1815). Lieutenant, 19th N.I. *bapt.* 9 May 1793. Cadet 1809. Arrived in India 2 Aug. 1810. Ensign 10 Sept. 1811. Lieut. 16 Dec. 1814. *d.* 15 Apr. 1815 of wounds received in action at Malaun.
4th son of Rev. Walter Bagot, of Pype Hall, Staffs., rector of Blythfield and Leigh (who was brother of William, first Lord Bagot), and Mary Ward his 2nd wife.
Services : Posted as Ensign to 19th N.I. Nepal War 1814-5 ; operations against Amar Singh ; capture of Malaun (kld.) ; Lieut. 19th N.I. in 1st Div.
Refs. : Burke's *Landed Gentry,* 3rd edn., p. 39, *s.n.* Bagot, of Pype Hall, Staffs. M.I. in St. John's Church, Calcutta.

BAGOT, William (1736/37-1770). Infantry. *b.* 1736/37. Cadet 1764. *d.* Calcutta 28 Jan. 1770.

A native of Ireland. (*Possibly* 2nd son of John Bagot, of Ard, King's Co., and Mary Herbert his wife, of Durrow Abbey, King's Co.)

Services : Sailed for India on the *Vansittart*, 4 Mar. 1764, aged 27. N.F.P.

Note : As his name does not appear in a "List of Officers in the Army on the Bengal Establishment, Feb. 1st, 1767," it is probable that he resigned his commission during the Batta mutiny in May 1766, and was subsequently re-admitted.

BAGSHAW, Robert Morris (1769-1807). Captain, 17th N.I. *b.* 2 Sept. 1769. Was already in India when apptd. Cadet on 22 June 1781. Ensign 5 July 1782. Lieut. 3 Jan. 1785. Capt. 13 Jan. 1801. *d.* Karnal 26 Feb. 1807.

Brother of Granby Calcraft Bagshaw and nephew of Robert Hales of St. Anne's Pl., Limehouse, Middlesex. *m.* Calcutta, 14 Mar. 1795, Miss Sarah Hope. (She died 12 Mar. 1840.)

Services : Attached for duty to 1st Bengal Eur. Regt. June 1781 till 1786. Lieut. 11th Bn. Sepoys. Served in P.W.I. 1794-8. Transfd. to newly-formed Marine Bn. July 1795 ; to newly-formed 2/17th N.I. Jan. 1799. Operations in Jumna Doab 1803 ; Kachaura ; Thathia ; Capt. 2/17th N.I. Second Mahratta War ; storm of Aligarh 4 Sept. 1803 (w.) ; battle of Delhi ; defence of Delhi Oct. 1804 ; pursuit of Holkar 1805-6 ; Capt. 2/17th N.I.

Refs. : *De Rhé-Philipe. Pester.* Burke's *Landed Gentry*, 9th edn., p. 218, *s.n.* Calcraft, of Rempstone, Dorset.

BAGSHAW, Stephen. Cadet. Infantry. Cadet 1772. Resigned 6 Nov. 1773.

Services : N.F.P.

BAGSHAWE, Samuel Robinson (1806-1860). Lieut. Colonel. 7th N.I. *b.* Oakes, co. Derby, 28 June 1806. Cadet 1821. Arrived in India 2 Jan. 1823. Ensign 18 Jan. 1823. Lieut. 26 Nov. 1823. Capt. 15 Jan. 1841. Major 7 May 1854. Retired 10 Jan. 1855. Hon. Lt. Col. 16 Mar. 1855. *d.* London 11 May 1860.

6th son of Sir William Chambers Bagshawe (formerly Darling), Kt., M.D., of Oakes and Wormhill Hall, co. Derby, high sheriff co. Derby 1805, and Helen his wife, dau. of Nathaniel Ridgard, of Gainsborough. *m.* Berhampore, Bengal, 6 Dec. 1826, Cornelia Eliza, dau. of Robert Roche, *q.v.* His dau. *m.* James Grant (1807-1859), *q.v.*

Services : Posted as Ensign to 20th N.I. Transfd. as Lieut. to 4th N.I. 9 Feb. 1824 ; to 7th N.I. (late 1/4th) May 1824. Intr. & Qmr. 7th N.I. 28 July 1828. Offg. in Comst. Dept. in 1849. Cantt. Mgte. at Ferozepore 31 Dec. 1849 till 1853. No record of active service.
Refs. : Burke's *Landed Gentry*, 13th edn., p. 60, *s.n.* Bagshawe, of Oakes, co. Derby. *G.M.* 1860, i. 645. *The Times*, 16 May 1860. *Howard & Crisp (Notes)*, iii. 9.

BAILEY, Abraham Jennings (*d.* 1788). Lieutenant, Artillery. Cadet (?). Fireworker 17 Sept. 1779. Lieut. 26 May 1786. *d.* Anupshahr, U.P., 3 Feb. 1788.

Son of —— Bailey, of Sherborne, and brother of T. Bailey, of Blandford, Dorset.
Services : Went out to India as 4th Officer of the *Godfrey*, which sailed from Plymouth on 9 Feb. 1778. Campaign against the Rajah of Benares ; capture of Bijaigarh, C.I. Lieut. 4th Coy. Art.
Refs. : G.M. 1788, p. 1181.

BAILEY, Charles Drummond (1809-1869). Lieutenant. 56th N.I. *b.* 9 June 1809. Cadet 1825. Arrived in India 22 Oct. 1826. Ensign 27 June 1826. Lieut. 13 Feb. 1839. Retired 4 Sept. 1839. *d.* Camden Cresc., Bath, 26 Nov. 1869.

Of Charlton Musgrove, Somerset. J.P. co. Somerset. *bapt.* Gibraltar 25 June 1809. Son of William Bailey, Col. in the army, sometime A.D.C. to Gen. Drummond.
Services : Posted as Ensign to 56th N.I. Actg. Intr. & Qmr. 56th N.I. 18 Apr. 1828 ; do. 36th N.I. 26 May 1829. Fur. s.c. 20 Nov. 1830 till 27 Dec. 1833. A.D.C. to Bdr.-Gen. William Richards, C.B., *q.v.*, comdg. Dinapore Div., 7 Nov. 1834. Actg. Intr. & Qmr. 67th N.I. 7 Apr. 1835 till 20 Feb. 1837. Fur. s.c. 3 Apr. 1837 till retirement. Retired on h.p. of 3s. *p.d.* No record of active service.
Refs. : The Times, 29 Nov. 1869.

BAILIE, William Annesley (1740/41-1821). Lieut. Colonel. Artillery. *b.* 1740/41. Fireworker (Madras) 28 July 1860. 2nd Lieut. (Madras) 3 Jan. 1763. Lieut. (Madras) 23 Jan. 1764. Capt. Lt. (Bengal) 1 Aug. 1765. Capt. 8 Feb. 1767. Major 9 Nov. 1772 (?). Lt. Col. 16 Sept. 1779. Resigned 31 Aug. 1782. *d.* his residence, Green Park Bldgs., Bath, 16 May 1821, aged 80.

Of the family of Bailie, of Inishargy and Ringdufferin, co. Down. *m.* Hon. Elizabeth, 2nd dau. of St. Leger Aldworth, first Viscount Doneraile. (*See also* Thomas Alcock.) (She died in 1831.)
Services : Transfd. from the Madras Art. Resigned during the

Batta mutiny May 1766; readmitted 13 June 1766. First Rohilla War; battle of St. George (w.); Capt. comdg. 2nd Coy. Art. " Captain Baillie and the Gentlemen of his Corps, in the service of the Artillery, gave great satisfaction." (Extract from Col. Champion's Orders of 23 Apr. 1774.) First Mahratta War; Lt. Col. Art. with Col. Thomas Goddard's detachment.
Refs.: Burke's *Landed Gentry of Ireland*, p. 22, *s.n.* Bailie, of Ringdufferin, co. Down. Burke's *Peerage*, 1923, p. 737, *s.n.* Doneraile, V. Leslie's *Madras Art. Bath Chron.* 24 May 1821.

BAILLIE, Alexander Charles (1800-1858). Lieutenant. 58th N.I. *b.* Hyderabad, Madras, 25 Sept. 1800. Cadet 1817. Ensign (?). Lieut. 21 July 1819. Retired 21 May 1827. *d.* 12 Dec. 1858. Son of Alexander Baillie, Lt. Col. Madras Est. Nephew of John Baillie (1773-1833), *q.v.*
Services: Ensign H.M. 81st Foot 24 Apr. 1817; transfd. to h.p. the same day. Lieut. 1/29th N.I. Transfd. to 56th N.I. (late 2/29th) May 1824. Fur. 1825 till retirement. No record of active service.

BAILLIE, Sir Ewen, first baronet (*d.* 1820). Lieut. General. Colonel 23rd N.I. Cadet 1766. Admitted 14 June 1767. Ensign 15 Sept. 1767. Lieut. 8 Apr. 1769. Capt. 4 Apr. 1777. Major 9 May 1781. Lt. Col. 1 Mar. 1794. Col. 1 Jan. 1798. Maj. Gen. 1 Jan. 1805. Lt. Gen. 4 June 1813. *d.s.p.* Brussels 21 Aug. 1820.
2nd son of William Baillie, of Rosehall, Sutherland (who was 2nd son of Alexander Baillie, of Dochfour), and Elizabeth his 1st wife, dau. of Alexander Sutherland, of Clyne, co. Sutherland. *Cr.* a baronet 11 Dec. 1812. Half-brother of Lamington Baillie, *q.v.*, and uncle of George Baillie, *q.v.*
Services: Fur. 30 Dec. 1772 till 2 Nov. 1774. Comdd. 27th Bn. Sepoys in 1777 on its transfer from the service of the Nawab Wazir of Oudh to the Company. This Regt., which became 2/5th N.I. in 1796, was, until its disappearance during the holocaust of 1857, known as "*Baillie-ki-paltan.*" Fur. 30 Nov. 1783 till 11 Oct. 1789; 29 June 1792 till 6 Mar. 1797; 26 Jan. 1803 till 1 Aug. 1805. Apptd. Col. of 13th N.I.; of 23rd N.I. in 1804. Comdg. at the Presidency 1806-7; at Muttra in 1807; at the Presidency 1807-9. Fur. 22 Jan. 1810 till death.
Refs.: Burke's *Family Records*, p. 31. Burke's *Peerage*, 1859, p. 645, *s.n.* Mackenzie, Bart., of Fairburn, co. Ross; 1923, p. 400, *s.n.* Baroness Burton. *S.M.* 1820, ii. 288.

BAILLIE, George (1788-1806). Cadet, Cavalry. *bapt.* Dornoch 23 Apr. 1788. Cadet 1805. Never arrived in India. *d.* Dec. 1806, on his passage to India, in the wreck of the *Skelton Castle.*

Struck off with effect from 5 Nov. 1806. (See note to David Allan.)
2nd son of Mackay Hugh Baillie, of Rosehall, Maj. Gen., late Reay Fencible Inf., and Sarah Witham his wife. Brother of William Baillie (1786-1806), *q.v.*, and nephew of Sir Ewen Baillie, Bart., *q.v.*, and of Lamington Baillie, *q.v.*
Refs. : Burke's *Family Records*, p. 31. *S.M.* 1814, p. 156.

BAILLIE, John (*d.* 1789 ?). Infantry. Cadet 1772. Dismissed by C.M. 30 May 1776. (? *d.* Bath 9 Apr. 1789.)
(? Son of William Baillie, of Rosehall.)

BAILLIE, John (1772-1833). Lieut. Colonel. 4th N.I. *b.* Inverness 10 May 1772. Cadet 1790. Arrived in India 23 Nov. 1791. Ensign 22 Dec. 1793. Lieut. 6 Oct. 1794. Capt. 30 Sept. 1803. Major 2 Jan. 1811. Lt. Col. 14 July 1814. Retired 30 June 1818. *d.* Devonshire Pl., London, 4 Apr. 1833.

Of Leys Castle, Inverness. Younger son of George Baillie, of Leys Castle, and Anne his wife, sister of Col. John Baillie, of Dunain, co. Inverness. His daus. *m.* Henry Francis Caley, *q.v.*, and Thomas Richard Macqueen, *q.v.*

Services : The first professor of Arabic and Persian at the Coll. of Fort William on its institution in 1800. Second Mahratta War. P.A. in Bundelkhand 1803-7 (he left as an heirloom a diamond ring inscribed, " Wellesley public services in Bundelkhand, 1804 "). Resident at Lucknow 1807-15. Lt. Col. 2/4th N.I. Fur. 1815 till retirement. M.P. for Hendon 1820, and for the Burghs of Inverness 1830. Elected a Director of the E.I.C. 28 May 1823. Author of several works, including " A Digest of Mohummudan Law," unfinished, but completed by his son. See *D.N.B.*
Refs. : *D.N.B.* *D.I.B.* Anderson's *Scottish Nation,* i. 180. Burke's *Family Records,* p. 31. *G.M.* 1833, i. 467. *A.R.* lxxv. (1833) 219. Will dated 19 Oct. 1827 ; codicil dated 12 July 1832 ; proved 17 Dec. 1833.

BAILLIE, Lamington (1762/63-1806). Lieut. Colonel, 3rd N.C. *b.* 1762/3. Cadet 1778. Admitted 18 Feb. 1779. Cornet 30 May 1779. Lieut. 1 Feb. 1781. Capt. 7 Jan. 1796. Major 29 May 1800. Lt. Col. 17 July 1801. *d.* Dec. 1806, on his passage to India, in the wreck of the *Skelton Castle.* Struck off with effect from 5 Nov. 1805. (See note to David Allan.)

Son of William Baillie, of Rosehall, co. Sutherland, and Mary his 2nd wife, 2nd dau. of Col. Hugh Mackay, of Bighouse, and niece of Donald, fourth Baron Reay. Half-brother of Sir Ewen Baillie, Bart., *q.v.*, and uncle of George Baillie, *q.v.*

74 LIST OF THE OFFICERS OF

Services : Capt. 1st N.C. Transfd. as Major to 5th N.C. 29 May 1800. Lt. Col. 3rd N.C. Fur. 22 Feb. 1795 till 8 Jan. 1801, and 19 Mar. 1801 till 1806. He was returning from fur. on the *Skelton Castle* at the time of his death.
Refs. : Burke's *Family Records*, p. 31. Burke's *Peerage*, 1923, p. 400, *s.n.* Baroness Burton. Wills dated 18 Mar. 1801 and 31 July 1806 ; proved respectively 18 Jan. 1808 and 9 Aug. 1809.

BAILLIE, Robert (*d.* 1820). Lieut. Colonel. Infantry. Cadet 1768. Ensign 17 Feb. 1769. Lieut. 16 May 1770. Capt. 25 Aug. 1779. Major 1 Mar. 1794. Lt. Col. 8 Jan. 1796. Retired 22 Dec. 1797. *d.* George Sq., Edinburgh, 25 July 1820.
m. (?). His dau. *m.* Innis Delamain, *q.v.*
Services : Second Rohilla War ; battle of Bitaurah ; Capt. comdg. 1st Bn. Sepoys.
Refs. : G.M. 1820, ii. 188. *S.M.* 1820, ii. 192.

BAILLIE, Thomas (*d.* 1779). Captain, 27th Bn. Sepoys. Cadet 1764. Ensign 3 Aug. 1766. Lieut. (?). Capt. 4 Dec. 1772. *d.* Fatehgarh, U.P., 28 Feb. 1779.
Eldest son of Thomas Baillie (said to have been connected with the Baillies of Lamington) and Helen Gordon his wife. Brother of John Baillie. Adoptive father of Edward, a natural son of Edward Butterfield, *q.v.*
Services : N.F.P.
Refs. : N. & Q. 12S. v. 293 ; ix. 83. Will dated Fatehgarh 5 Jan. 1779 ; proved 10 Aug. 1779.

BAILLIE, William (1752/53-1799). Major. Engineers. *b.* 1752/53. Cadet 1777. Ensign (Inf.) 22 Dec. 1777. Lieut. (Engrs.) 7 May 1781. Capt. (?). Major (?). Resigned 1788. *d.* Calcutta 6 June 1799, aged 46.
m. Ann Mary. (She died Calcutta 27 Apr. 1840.)
Services : Transfd. from Inf. to Engineers 9 Mar. 1778. N.F.P.
Refs. : M.I. in S. Park St. cemetery, Calcutta.

BAILLIE, Sir William, first baronet (1782-1854). Lieutenant. 4th N.C. *b.* St. Cuthbert's, Edinburgh, 25 July 1782. Cadet 1798. Arrived in India 19 Aug. 1799. Cornet 6 June 1800. Lieut. 11 Mar. 1805. Struck off 14 Feb. 1818. *d.* Perth 28 Jan. 1854.
First baronet, of Polkemmet. *Cr.* 14 Nov. 1823. Eldest son of William Baillie, Lord Polkemmet, and Margaret his wife, dau. of Sir James Colquhoun, of Luss, 4th Bart. Cousin-german of Joseph William Colquhoun, *q.v. m.* 25 Apr. 1815, Mary Lyon, youngest dau. of James Dennistoun, of Colgrain, co. Dumbarton.

THE BENGAL ARMY, 1758-1834 75

Services : Posted as Cornet to 4th N.C. Operations in Jumna Doab 1803 ; Sasni ; Bijaigarh ; Kachaura. Second Mahratta War ; Aligarh ; Laswari ; Cornet 4th N.C. (India medal with clasp). Fur. 14 Feb. 1813 till struck off after five years' absence from India.
Refs. : Burke's *Peerage*, 1923, p. 182, *s.n.* Baillie, Bart., of Polkemmet. *G.M.* 1854, i.

BAILLIE, William (1786-1806). Cadet, Cavalry. *b.* Inveresk 28 Dec. 1786. Cadet 1804. Never arrived in India. *d.* Dec. 1806, on his passage to India, in the wreck of the *Skelton Castle.* Struck off with effect from 5 Nov. 1806. (See note to David Allan.)
Eldest son of Mackay Hugh Baillie, of Rosehall, Maj. Gen. late Reay Fencible Inf., and Sarah Witham his wife. Brother of George Baillie, *q.v.*, and nephew of Sir Ewen Baillie, Bart., *q.v.*, and Lamington Baillie, *q.v.*
Refs. : Burke's *Family Records*, p. 31. *S.M.* 1814, p. 156.

BAINBRIDGE, Richard (1784-1818). Captain, Invalid Est. 14th N.I. *bapt.* Ponnal, Yorks., 2 June 1784. Cadet 1800. Arrived in India 22 Aug. 1801. Ensign 30 Oct. 1801. Lieut. 12 Jan. 1803. Capt. 1 May 1813. Invalided 26 Aug. 1815. *d. unm.* Aug. 1818.
Son of John Bainbridge, of Crimpe House, nr. Harrogate, and Grace his wife.
Services : Posted as Ensign to 14th N.I. Second Mahratta War ; Lieut. 14th N.I. Adjt. 2/14th N.I. 19 Feb. 1807 till 1813.
Refs. : Will dated Buxar 19 July 1818 ; proved 28 Dec. 1818.

BAINBRIDGE, Thomas Drake (1805- ?). Cornet. Cavalry. *b.* London 8 Nov. 1805. Cadet 1826. Cornet 1827. Resigned 4 Jan. 1828. (Was living in 1845.)
Son of Thomas Bainbridge, of ·Croydon Lodge, Burslow, and Portnells, Surrey, and Queen's Sq., London, merchant, and Anne his wife, dau. of Morgan Waters, of Tyfig, co. Glamorgan. *m.* All Souls, Langham Pl., London, 22 Apr. 1830, Hester M., 2nd dau. of R. Rickards, of Wimpole St., London.
Services : N.F.P.
Refs. : Burke's *Landed Gentry of Ireland*, p. 23, *s.n.* Bainbridge, of Frankfield, co. Cork.

BAINBRIDGE, William Dixon (*d.* 1776). Cadet, Artillery. Cadet (?). Never arrived in India. *d.* Sept. 1776 : lost at sea on his passage to Bombay.

LIST OF THE OFFICERS OF

*BAINBRIDGE, William Isacke Parnell (*d.* 1820). Cadet, Infantry. Unposted. Cadet 1819. Was already in India when appointed. Approved by the Committee 8 Dec. 1819. Withdrawn on 15 Dec. 1819 and sent to Madras. *d.* Rainwar (?), nr. Ghazipur, U.P., 2 May 1820.
Recommended by Capt. William Bazett Isacke, Madras Est.
Refs. : A.J. 1821, i. 62.

BAINE, James (*d.* 1774). Lieut. Fireworker, Artillery. Cadet 1771. Fireworker 24 Feb. 1773. *d.* Calcutta 29 Nov. 1774.
Services : N.F.P.

BAINE, Robert. Cadet. Infantry. Cadet 1771. Resigned 10 Jan. 1773.
Services : N.F.P.

BAINES, Charles Henry (1783-1844). Lieut. Colonel. 23rd N.I. *bapt.* Earls Colne, Essex, 15 July 1783. Cadet 1798. Arrived in India 6 Nov. 1799. Ensign 22 Jan. 1800. Liéut. 29 May 1800. Capt. 16 Dec. 1814. Major 1 May 1824. Lt. Col. 24 Sept. 1826. Retired 3 June 1831. *d.* 14 Springfield Pl., Bath, 15 Feb. 1844.
Son of Thomas Baines and Jane Elizabeth his wife. *m.* Hatch Beauchamp, Somerset, 30 Sept. 1830, Miss Mary Elizabeth Raban, of Gay St., Bath, niece of William Raban, *q.v.* (? dau. of Thomas Raban, of Calcutta. *See also* Edward Cave-Browne.) (She died 7 Sept. 1864.)
Services : Posted as Ensign to 6th N.I. Transfd. as Lieut. to 1/7th N.I. in 1801. On service in Oudh in 1801. Transfd. to 2/13th N.I. 15 Apr. 1801. Second Mahratta War ; Baghelkhand 1803 ; Chaukandi ; pursuit of Holkar ; Lieut. 2/13th N.I. Fur. s.c. 6 Mar. 1806 till 23 July 1807. Apptd. to Corps of Pioneers in Feb. 1809 ; 2nd in comd. do. Mar. 1809 till Feb. 1818. Settlement of Hariana 1809 ; Bhawani. Against the Bhattis 1810. Nepal War 1814-5 ; operations against Amar Singh ; comdg. Pioneers with 1st Div. Nepal War 1816 ; Makwanpur ; with Centre Column. Fur. 16 Dec. 1816 till 19 Dec. 1820. Actg. Fort Adjt. at Buxar Jan. 1821. Sub-Asst. Stud Dept. Sept. 1821 till Aug. 1822. Comdg. Farukhabad Provl. Bn. 8 Nov. 1822 till 7 June 1824. Transfd. as Major to 27th N.I. (late 2/13th) May 1824 ; as Lt. Col. to 6th N.I. 28 Dec. 1826. Leave to St. Helena 2 Jan. 1827 till 6 Dec. 1827. Transfd. to 23rd N.I. 16 Dec. 1830. Fur. s.c. 16 Jan. 1828 till retirement.
Refs. : E.I.M.C. iii. 387. *G.M.* 1844, i. 444.

THE BENGAL ARMY, 1758-1884 77

BAINES, George Veal (1782-1824). Lieut. Colonel, 36th N.I. *b.* Penzance 2 Oct. 1782. Cadet 1799. Arrived in India 1 Dec. 1800. Ensign 26 Sept. 1800. Lieut. 5 Aug. 1802. Capt. 22 May 1811. Major 22 Sept. 1821. Lt. Col. 1 May 1824. *d.* Nasirabad, Rajputana, 22 Sept. 1824.
bapt. Penzance 11 Oct. 1782. Son of Capt. Cuthbert Baines and Lydia his wife. Ed. Charterhouse : admitted a scholar 9 June 1793 ; left before 12 Apr. 1796 to enter the Royal Navy.
Services : Posted as Ensign to 2/18th N.I. Second Mahratta War 1803-6 ; occupation of Bundelkhand 1803 ; Kapsa ; Kalpi ; capture of Gwalior ; capture of Jaitpur 28 July 1804 (w. twice) ; Lieut. 2/18th N.I. Capture of Java ; Cornelis ; Capt. 5th Bn. Bengal Vols. Capt. 2/18th N.I. Operations in Jodhpur 1823 ; Lamba ; Major 1/18th N.I. Posted as Lt. Col. to 36th N.I. (late 1/18th) May 1824.
Refs. : Alumni Carthusiani. E.I.M.C. ii. 361. *G.M.* 1825, i. 478.

BAKER, Edward (*d.* 1794). Lieutenant, Artillery. Cadet 1783. Fireworker 28 Jan. 1785. Lieut. 24 Mar. 1791. *d.* 26 Oct. 1794 ; kld. in action at the battle of Bitaurah, nr. Bareilly, U.P.
Services : Second Rohilla War ; battle of Bitaurah (kld.) ; Lieut. 2nd Coy. 3rd Bn. Art.
Refs. : M.I. in St. John's churchyard, Calcutta.

BAKER, Frederick (1810-1842). Bt. Captain, 9th L.C. *b.* London 23 Jan. 1810. Cadet 1826. Arrived in India 10 Apr. 1827. Cornet 14 Nov. 1826. Lieut. 9 Sept. 1829. Bt. Capt. 14 Nov. 1841. *d.* Ferozepore 17 July 1842.
Son of Robert Baker, of Newbury, Berks., attorney.
Services : Posted as Cornet to 6th L.C. Transfd. to 9th L.C. 25 Nov. 1828. No record of active service.
Refs. : G.M. 1842, ii. 559. *The Times,* 11 Oct. 1842.

BAKER, Godfrey Evan. Captain. 3rd Bengal European Regt. Cadet 1769. Ensign 8 Aug. 1769. Lieut. 2 Dec. 1772. Capt. 18 Nov. 1779. Resigned 18 Dec. 1783.
Services : N.F.P.

BAKER, Godfrey Phipps (1786-1850). Lieut Colonel. 11th N.I. *bapt.* Holy Trinity, Cork, 12 Apr. 1786. Cadet 1800. Arrived in India 8 Feb. 1802. Ensign 1 Oct. 1801. Lieut. 30 Sept. 1803. Capt. 16 Dec. 1814. Major 1 May 1824. Lt. Col. 22 Apr. 1827. Retired in India 21 Jan. 1831. *d.* 4 Aug. 1850.
Eldest son of Hugh Cossart Baker, Capt. 27th Foot, and —— Phipps his wife. Brother of Hugh Cossart Baker, *q.v.,* and nephew

of William Massy Baker, *q.v.* *m.* 22 July 1817, Miss M.L. Dubois de Saran (*probably* dau. of Dubois de Saran, registrar at Chandernagore).
Services : Adjt. 1/19th N.I. in 1804. Adjt. 2/19th N.I. 1805-6. Served with Bengal L.I. Bn. 1811-6. Capture of Java (Medal). Capture of Jokyakarta. Capt. 2/19th N.I. Third Mahratta War ; comdd. a Bde. of Irreg. Inf. and Aux. Horse with Bdr. Gen. Hardyman's detachment from 18 Nov. 1817. To comd. 1st Rampura Local Bn. 4 May 1818. Asst. Mily. Sec. to Govt. 3 Aug. 1822. Transfd. as Major to 38th N.I. (late 1/19th) 25 May 1824. Fur. 13 Aug. 1825 till 27 Nov. 1828. Transfd. as Lt. Col. to 11th N.I. 18 Dec. 1828.
Refs. : Burke's *Landed Gentry of Ireland,* p. 23, *s.n.* Baker, of Lismacue, co. Tipperary.

BAKER, Henry Minson (1785-1819). Lieutenant, 20th N.I. *b.* Bromley St. Leonard, Middlesex, 31 July 1785. Cadet 1805. Arrived in India 7 Feb. 1807. Ensign 5 Jan. 1807. Lieut. 5 Aug. 1811. *d.* at sea, 15 June 1819, on board the *Sesostris.*
Son of James Baker and Martha his wife.
Services : Posted as Ensign to 2/20th N.I. (? Capture of Java ; Lieut. 2/20th N.I.)

BAKER, Hugh Cossart (1792-1862). Major. Artillery. *bapt.* Galway 15 Apr. 1792. Cadet 1808. Arrived in India 7 Dec. 1809. Fireworker 29 Oct. 1809. Lieut. 21 Apr. 1817. Capt. 1 May 1824. Retired 9 July 1835. Hon. Major 28 Nov. 1854. *d.* Notting Hill, London, 21 Sept. 1862.
3rd son of Hugh Cossart Baker, Capt. 27th Foot, and —— Phipps his wife. Brother of Godfrey Phipps Baker, *q.v.* *m.* St. Pancras, London, 8 Dec. 1836, Mary Anne, dau. of James Popplewell. (She died 3 Nov. 1855.) Woolwich Cadet : nominated on 23 July 1806.
Services : Expedition against Mauritius 1810-1 ; Fireworker d.d. with 6th Coy. 1st Bn. Art. ; returned to Bengal in Aug. 1811. Third Mahratta War ; Taragarh ; Madhurajpura ; Lieut. 5th Coy. 1st Bn. Art. Posted to the Rocket Troop in 1819 ; to 1st Troop 2nd Bde. H.A. in 1825 ; to 1st Troop 3rd Bde. in 1832. Fur. p.a. 31 Dec. 1832 till retirement.
Refs. : Burke's *Landed Gentry of Ireland,* p. 23, *s.n.* Baker, of Lismacue, co. Tipperary. *A.J.* N.S. xxii. 68. *G.M.* 1862 ii. 510. *The Times,* 24 Sept. 1862.

BAKER, John. Ensign. Infantry. Cadet 1770. Ensign 6 Dec. 1771. Resigned 30 Nov. 1775.
Services : N.F.P.

THE BENGAL ARMY, 1758-1834 79

BAKER, John Wright (*d.* 1773). Ensign, Infantry. Cadet 1771. Ensign 6 Jan. 1773. *d.* Calcutta 27 Nov. 1773.
Son of Rev. Thomas Baker, rector of Frinstead, Kent.
Services : N.F.P.
Refs. : Will dated Calcutta 24 Nov. 1773 ; proved 12 Dec. 1773.

BAKER, Onslow (1795-1864). Lieut. Colonel. Artillery. *b.* 8 Aug. 1795. Cadet 1813. Admitted 5 Aug. 1814. Fireworker 31 July 1814. Lieut. 1 Sept. 1818. Capt. 24 May 1831. Major 12 July 1844. Lt. Col. 9 Aug. 1847. Retired 10 Feb. 1849. *d.* 5 Nov. 1864.
bapt. Lexden, Essex, 6 Oct. 1795. 4th and youngest son of Sir Robert Baker, 1st Bart., of Dunstable House, Surrey, and of Nicholas Hayne, Devon, and Dinah his wife, dau. of George Hayley, alderman, sheriff, and M.P. for the city of London. Addiscombe Cadet 1811-4.
Services : Nepal War 1816 ; Fireworker, Art. (India medal). Fur. s.c. 10 Jan. 1845. Lt. Col. comdg. 2nd Bn. Foot Art.
Refs. : Burke's *Peerage*, 1923, p. 186, *s.n.* Baker, Bart., of Dunstable House, Surrey. *G.M.* 1864, ii. 807. *The Times*, 9 Nov. 1864.

BAKER, Richard (1785-1806). Cadet, Infantry. *b.* York 6 Oct. 1785. Cadet 1805. Never arrived in India. *d.* Dec. 1806, on his passage to India, in the wreck of the *Skelton Castle*. Struck off with effect from 5 Nov. 1806. (See Note to David Allan.)
bapt. St. Mark's, Coney St., York. Son of James Baker, proctor.

BAKER, William (1775-1825). Lieut. Colonel, 42nd N.I. *bapt.* All Saints, Worcester, 31 Aug. 1775. Cadet 1796. Arrived in India 19 Sept. 1797. Ensign 11 Aug. 1797. Lieut. 11 July 1798. Capt. 2 Feb. 1809. Major 20 Mar. 1821. Lt. Col. 1 May 1824. *d.* Arakan 2 Nov. 1825.
Son of Benjamin Baker and Sarah his wife. *m.* (before 1810) Charlotte Caroline, dau. of Francis Wilford, *q.v.* (*See also* Henry Pelham Davies and George Warden.) (She died Barrackpore 1 Apr. 1856, aged 76.)
Services : Posted as Ensign to 3rd Eur. Regt. Transfd. to 1/4th N.I. in Oct. 1798 ; to 16th N.I. ; to 1/21st N.I. in 1804. Second Mahratta War. Capt. Lt. 21st N.I. 19 Nov. 1807. Posted to 8th Gren. Bn. 8 Mar. 1811. Nepal War 1816 ; Capt. 8th Gren. Bn., in 2nd Bde., Left Column. Major 2/21st N.I. Transfd. as Lt. Col. to 42nd N.I. (late 2/21st) May 1824. First Burma War ; Arakan 1825 ; comdg. 42nd N.I.
Refs. : Will dated 15 Sept. 1823 ; proved 28 Dec. 1825.

BAKER, William (1810-1877). Lieut. Colonel. 4th European L.C. *b.* 22 Oct. 1810. Cadet 1826. Arrived in India 27 Oct. 1827. Cornet (17 June 1827) 24 July 1828. Lieut. 4 Dec. 1832. Capt. 8 May 1849. Bt. Major 20 June 1854. Retired 8 May 1860. Hon. Lt. Col. 8 May 1860. *d.* his residence, 36 Cleveland Sq., Hyde Park, London, 25 June 1877.
bapt. ptely. at Rathconey House, co. Cork, 2 Apr. 1811. 2nd son of William Massy Baker, *q.v.*, and Mary his wife. *m.* Frances Roupell, dau. of James Simpson.
Services : Posted as Cornet to 2nd L.C. 25 Nov. 1828. Transfd. to 9th L.C. 2 Sept. 1831. Adjt. G.G.B.G. 10 July 1834 till 13 June 1840. Sick leave to Cape for 2 yrs. 22 Dec. 1835. Fur. s.c. 13 June 1840 till 1842. Offg. Adjt. 9th L.C. 19 Aug. 1851. Posted to newly-raised 4th Eur. L.C. in 1858.
Refs. : Burke's *Landed Gentry of Ireland*, p. 23, *s.n.* Baker, of Lismacue, co. Tipperary. *V.B.G. The Times*, 26 June 1877.

BAKER, Sir William Erskine (1808-1881). General, K.C.B. Engineers. *b.* Leith 29 Nov. 1808. Cadet 1827. Arrived in India 1 Aug. 1828. 2nd Lieut. 15 Dec. 1826. Lieut. 28 Sept. 1827. Capt. 31 March 1840. Major 15 Jan. 1851. Lt. Col. 21 Aug. 1854. Col. 10 Mar. 1857. Maj. Gen. 2 Aug. 1865. Lt. Gen. 1 Apr. 1874. Gen. 1 Oct. 1877. *d.* The Castle, Barnwell, nr. Weston-super-Mare, 16 Dec. 1881.
bapt. Leith 25 Jan. 1809. 4th son of Joseph Baker, R.N. *m.* Karnal, 29 June 1837, Frances Gertrude, 3rd dau. of Alexander Duncan (1780-1859), *q.v.* His sister *m.* John Colvin, *q.v.* Addiscombe Cadet 4 Feb. 1825 till 16 June 1826. Chatham 4 Feb. 1827 till 28 Dec. 1827.
Services : See *D.N.B.* K.C.B. (Civil) 1 Feb. 1870.
Refs. : D.N.B. D.I.B. Boase. *Thackeray*, p. 162. *Vibart*, p. 415. *The Times*, 20 Dec. 1881.

BAKER, William Massy (1759/60-1829). Lieut. Colonel. 19th N.I. *b.* 1759/60. Cadet 1778. Admitted 10 Dec. 1778. Ensign 1778. Lieut. 5 Nov. 1778. Capt. 7 Jan. 1796. Major 29 May 1800. Lt. Col. 30 Sept. 1803. Retired 18 Feb. 1806. *d.* Fort William, nr. Cork, 12 Nov. 1829.
4th and youngest son of Godfrey Baker, of Cork, and Elizabeth his wife, dau. of Peter Cossart, of Cork. *m.* 19 Feb. 1807, Mary Towgood, only dau. of Rev. Richard Davies, of Dawstown, co. Cork. Father of William Baker (1810-1877), *q.v.*, and uncle of Hugh Cossart Baker, *q.v.*
Services : Sailed for India on the *Gatton* 27 Apr. 1778, aged 18.

Qmr. 2nd Eur. Bn. in 1790. Capt. 1/10th N.I. Fur. 20 Mar. 1796. till 8 Jan. 1801. Transfd. as Major to 19th N.I. 29 May 1800.
Refs. : Burke's *Landed Gentry of Ireland*, p. 23, *s.n.* Baker, of Lismacue, co. Tipperary. *A.J.* xxviii. 761.

BALCETTI, Joseph Gilbert (1788-1814). Cornet, 3rd N.C. *b.* 11 Aug. 1788. Cadet 1805. Arrived in India 16 Nov. 1808. Cornet 23 July 1807. *d.* Berhampore, Bengal, 28 June 1814. *bapt.* St. James's, Westminster, 16 Oct. 1788. Son of Joseph Balcetti and Judith his wife. *m.* Calcutta, 29 Mar. 1813, Miss Helena Lydia Conyers. (She died Calcutta 10 July 1847, aged 54.)
Services : Volunteer in the Bombay Marine in 1803. Volunteer on the *Viper* 1804-5. Transfd. when a Midshipman to Bengal Cavalry. At home, a prisoner on parole, 1806-7. Posted as Cornet to 3rd N.C. No record of active service.

BALDERS, William Henry (1805-1838). Lieutenant, 16th N.I. *b.* West Barsham, Norfolk, 29 Oct. 1805. Cadet 1824. Arrived in India 5 Sept. 1825. Ensign 6 Apr. 1825. Lieut. 8 Dec. 1826. *d.* Delhi 30 June 1838.
Son of Charles Morley Balders, of West Barsham, Major 53rd Regt., and Lady Mary Hare his wife, dau. of first Earl of Listowel.
Services : Posted as Ensign to 16th N.I. Fur. s.c. 10 Feb. 1827 till 1 Sept. 1830. Adjt. 16th N.I. 30 Dec. 1837 till death. No record of active service.
Refs. : Burke's *Landed Gentry*, 6th edn., p. 69, *s.n.* Balders, of West Barsham, Norfolk. *De Rhé-Philipe.*

BALDERSTON, Archibald (1810-1855). Bt. Major, 16th N.I. *b.* Edinburgh 14 Feb. 1810. Cadet 1825. Arrived in India 7 July 1826. Ensign 15 Mar. 1826. Lieut. 2 Nov. 1827. Capt. 8 Oct. 1844. Bt. Major 20 June 1854. *d.* Forfarshire 9 Sept. 1855.
Son of William Balderston, of Edinburgh, W.S. Brother of Dugald Balderston, *q.v.*
Services : Posted as Ensign to 16th N.I. Adjt. 16th N.I. 14 July 1838. First Afghan War 1839-42 ; capture of Ghazni (Medal) ; operations of the Kandahar force (slightly w. on 22 Sept. 1839) ; Lieut. 16th N.I. (Medal). Gwalior campaign ; Maharajpur (s.w.) ; Bt. Capt. 16th N.I. (Bronze star). First Sikh War ; Sobraon (s.w.) ; Capt. 16th N.I. (Medal). Bde. Major at Cawnpore (afterwards at Bareilly) 13 Sept. 1844 till 1855. Fur. 1855 till death.

82 LIST OF THE OFFICERS OF

BALDERSTON, Dugald (1804-1831). Lieutenant, 72nd N.I. *b.* Edinburgh 9 Nov. 1804. Cadet 1820. Admitted 31 May 1821. Ensign 13 Jan. 1821. Lieut. (11 July 1823) 13 May 1825. *d.* Mullye, Bengal, 14 Aug. 1831.

Son of William Balderston, of Edinburgh, W.S. Brother of Robert Balderston, *q.v.*

Services : Posted as Ensign to 2/22nd N.I. Adjt. 2/25th N.I. 15 Apr. 1824. Transfd. to 36th N.I. 28 Feb. 1825. Adjt. do. 28 Apr. 1825. Intr. & Qmr. 72nd N.I. 21 Jan. 1829. Adjt. do. 10 Oct. 1829.

Refs. : M.I. at Mullye.

BALDERSTON, Robert (1803-1826). Lieutenant, 44th N.I. *b.* Edinburgh 21 May 1803. Cadet 1818. Ensign (?). Lieut. 28 Apr. 1821. *d.* Edinburgh 3 May 1826.

Son of William Balderston, of Edinburgh, W.S. Brother of Archibald Balderston, *q.v.*

Services : Ensign d.d. Bengal Eur. Regt. Posted to 2/22nd N.I. in 1821. Transfd. to 43rd N.I. (late 1/22nd) May 1824 ; to 44th N.I. in 1825. Fur. 1825 till death. No record of active service.

Refs. : A.J. xxi. 817.

BALDOCK, Christopher (1779-1827). Lieut. Colonel Comdt., 57th N.I. *b.* St. Peter Port, Guernsey, 9 June 1779. Cadet 1794. Arrived in India 27 Sept. 1795. Ensign 6 Oct. 1795. Lieut. 3 Oct. 1796. Capt. 21 Sept. 1804. Major 28 June 1813. Lt. Col. 4 Mar. 1818. Lt. Col. Comdt. 1 May 1824. *d.* Camberwell, London, 1 Nov. 1827.

bapt. St. Peter Port, Guernsey, 11 June 1779. Son of Christopher Baldock and Catherine Carey his wife. Brother of Robert Walters Baldock, *q.v. m.* 29 Jan. 1816 Miss Margaretta Bruce Sloane. (*See also* William Clinton Baddeley.) (She died 30 May 1874, aged 78.)

Services : Posted as Ensign to 1st Bengal Eur. Regt. 4 May 1796. Transfd. to 17th N.I. Fur. 4 Mar. 1804 till 30 July 1807. Bk. Mr. at Muttra and Meerut 18 Mar. 1808 till 1813. Major 1/17th N.I. Nepal War 1814-5 ; Major 1/17th N.I., in 2nd Div. Lt. Col. 1/17th N.I. Fur. 7 Mar. 1819 till 1822. Transfd. to 29th N.I. in 1822 ; as Lt. Col. Comdt. to 57th N.I. (late 1/29th) May 1824. Fur. 6 Jan. 1825 till death.

Refs. : G.M. 1827, ii. 475.

BALDOCK, John (1809-1845). Captain, 22nd N.I. *b.* Weeley, Essex, 14 Nov. 1809. Cadet 1825. Arrived in India 13 July 1826. Ensign 23 Jan. 1826. Lieut. 4 June 1829. Capt. 19 Jan. 1843. *d.* Guernsey, 3 June 1845.

Son of John Baldock, Paymaster, 79th Regt. *m.* Fatehgarh, 30 Oct. 1838, Mary Ann, 2nd dau. of S. Birch.
Services : Ensign d.d. 57th N.I. 2 Aug. 1826. Posted as Ensign to 22nd N.I. Shekhawat Expedn. ; Lieut. 22nd N.I. Fur. s.c. 12 Sept. 1844 till death.

BALDOCK, Robert Walters (1785- ?). Colonel. 45th N.I. *b.* London 19 Apr. 1785. Cadet 1800. Arrived in India 24 Aug. 1801. Ensign 8 Oct. 1801. Lieut. 30 Sept. 1803. Capt. 22 Jan. 1817. Major 1 May 1824. Lt. Col. 1 Jan. 1828. Retired 21 Jan. 1829. Hon. Col. 28 Nov. 1854. (*d.* 1880 ?)
bapt. St. Clement Danes, London, 6 May 1785. Son of Christopher Baldock and Catherine Carey his wife. Brother of Christopher Baldock, *q.v. m.* Southampton, 27 June 1829, Miss Susannah Harden.
Note : His name appears amongst Retired Officers in the *India List* down to 1880.
Services : Ensign 17th N.I. Pioneers 1809-11. Bde. Major at Dinapore (afterwards at Benares) 9 Mar. 1811 till 1824. Lieut. 1/17th N.I. Capt. 2/17th N.I. Transfd. as Major to 35th N.I. (late 2/17th) May 1824. Fur. 4 Feb. 1825 till retirement. Transfd. as Lt. Col. to 45th N.I. in 1828.
Refs. : *G.M.* 1829, i. 640.

BALDWIN, Philip Homan (*d.* 1811). Captain. Infantry. Cadet 1781. Ensign 14 Aug. 1781. Lieut. 2 June 1783. Capt. 7 Jan. 1796. Resigned 20 Aug. 1799. *d.* 17 June 1811. Of Cloneygowan, Queen's Co.
Services : Lieut. 2nd Bengal Eur. Regt. in 1796. N.F.P.

BALDWIN, Richard Horsmonden (1812-1871). Lieut. Colonel. Artillery. *bapt.* Harrietsham, Kent, 28 Mar. 1812. Cadet 1827. Arrived in India 3 Feb. 1829. 2nd Lieut. 12 June 1828. Lieut. 10 Mar. 1836. Capt. 22 Dec. 1845. Bt. Major 7 June 1849. Retired 1 Feb. 1857. Hon. Lt. Col. 1857. *d.* The Albany, London, 17 Jan. 1871, aged 58.
Son of William Baldwin, of Stide Hill, nr. Maidstone, and Frances his wife. Addiscombe Cadet 1826-8.
Services : Fur. s.c. 8 Nov. 1838 till 11 Oct. 1841. Posted to 1st Troop 1st Bde. H.A. in 1842. Transfd. to 2nd Troop 1st Bde. in 1845. First Sikh War ; Mudki ; Ferozshahr ; Sobraon ; Capt. 2nd Troop 1st Bde. (Medal with 2 clasps). Comdd. 1st Troop 1st Bde. H.A. from 1846 till 1854. N.W. frontier ; against the Ranizais 1852 (India medal of 1854).
Refs. : *The Times,* 20 Jan. 1871.

BALDWIN, Thomas James (1786-1839). Major. 22nd N.I. b. Wigan, Lancs., 30 Dec. 1786. Cadet 1804. Arrived in India 29 Apr. 1805. Ensign 9 May 1805. Lieut. 10 May 1805. Capt. 11 July 1823. Major 6 Sept. 1826. Retired 3 May 1830. d. 28 Jan. 1839.

Eldest son of William Baldwin, of Standishgate, attorney.
Services : Lieut. 2nd N.I. Intr. & Qmr. 1/2nd N.I. 4 May 1815 till 1823. Transfd. to 22nd N.I. (late 2/2nd) May 1824. Fur. 1828 till retirement. No record of active service.

BALE, Sackville (1789-1812). Ensign, 5th N.I. *bapt.* Withyham, Sussex, 2 Dec. 1789. Cadet 1808. Ensign 21 Nov. 1809. d. Calcutta 15 July 1812.

Son of Rev. Sackville Stephens Bale, rector of Withyham. Ed. Westminster 1804-6. K.S.
Services : Posted as Ensign to 5th N.I. No record of active service.
Refs. : Alumni Westmon.

BALFOUR, Alexander (d. 1788). Lieutenant Fireworker, Artillery. Cadet 1781. Fireworker 20 Sept. 1781. d. Baikanthpur, nr. Patna, 1 May 1788 : drowned.
Services : N.F.P.

BALFOUR, Arthur (1752-1817). Major. Infantry. Cadet (?). Ensign 3 Jan. 1767. Lieut. 18 Apr. 1868. Capt. 5 July 1776. Major 1 Feb. 1781. Resigned 22 Dec. 1783. d. London 14 Nov. 1817.

b. Ballingoy, co. Fife, 1752. (*Possibly* the " Arthur Balfour, of Portland Pl., London," who, together with " Francis Balfour, of co. Fife," is mentioned as a " worthy friend " in the Will of Henry Balfour, *q.v.*)
Services : S.M. 1817, ii. 501. M.I. in Marylebone church.

BALFOUR, Francis (d. 1818). Lieutenant. Infantry. Subsequently a Member of the Medical Board, Bengal. Asst. Surgeon 3 July 1769. Ensign (Inf.) 11 July 1769. Lieut. 26 June 1771. Resigned combatant Commission on promotion to Surgeon 10 Aug. 1777. d. Fernie, co. Fife, 7 May 1818.

Of Fernie Castle, co. Fife. 3rd son of Arthur Balfour, of Fernie, and Janet his 2nd wife, dau. of George Patterson, of Dunmuir. m. Miss Balfour, of Dunbog, co. Fife. He purchased Collairnie, Kilmaron, Hilton and Pitladdo from Sir Henry Steuart-Barclay, Bart., in 1790. (*Probably* related to Henry Balfour, *q.v.*)
Services : See *D.N.B.* Head Surgeon 20 Oct. 1786. M.M.B.

THE BENGAL ARMY, 1758-1834   85

15 Jan. 1788. Reverted to Head Surgeon on 20 Apr. 1796, when the Board was reduced from three to two Members. Reappointed to Medical Board 16 Dec. 1800. Retired 16 Sept. 1807. M.D. Edin. 1767. Author of various medical works.
Refs. : D.N.B. *Crawford, passim.* S.M. 1818, i. 598.

BALFOUR, George. Lieutenant. 3rd Bengal European Regt. Cadet 1778. Ensign 1778. Lieut. 28 Aug. 1779. Struck off 12 Feb. 1781.
Services : N.F.P.

BALFOUR, Henry (*d.* 1818). Lieut. Colonel. Artillery. Country Cadet 1779. Admitted 19 Aug. 1779. Fireworker 29 Sept. 1780. Lieut. 27 May 1786. Capt. Lt. 8 Jan. 1796. Capt. 1 July 1801. Major 21 Sept. 1804. Lt. Col. 15 May 1807. Retired 16 Sept. 1807. *d.* Bristol 21 Mar. 1818.

Of Ashley Pl., St. Paul, Bristol. *m.* Bristol, Jan. 1808, Anne, only dau. of —— Gardiner, of Ashley Pl. (? Apsley Pl.). (She died 14 Oct. 1840, aged 69.) His Will mentions his " worthy friends, Francis Balfour, of co. Fife, and Arthur Balfour, of Portland Pl., London."

Services : Campaign against the Rajah of Benares 1781 ; Lieut. Fireworker. (Having been sent for heavy guns, did not return in time to share in prize money for capture of Bijaigarh.) Qmr. 2nd Bn. Art. in 1790. Third Mysore War ; Bangalore ; Lieut. & Qmr. Went to sea for his health in July 1791. Fur. 6 Jan. 1792 till Oct. 2 1795. Capture of Ceylon 1795-6 ; Capt. Lt. 5th Coy. 1st Bn. Art. Posted to 1st Coy. 3rd Bn. 16 June 1797. Fourth Mysore War ; capture of Seringapatam ; Capt. Lt. 2nd Coy. 3rd Bn. Fur. 28 Jan. 1805 till retirement.
Refs. : M.M. 1808, p. 89. S.M. 1818, i. 499. A.J. 1818, i. 427. Will dated 13 July 1813 ; proved 3 Dec. 1818.

BALFOUR, Sir Patrick, eighth baronet (*d.* 1793). Captain, Comdg. 3rd Bn. Sepoys. Cadet 1769. Ensign 1 Mar. 1769. Lieut. 20 Sept. 1770. Capt. 2 Sept. 1779. *d. unm.* Dinapore 5 June 1793, when the baronetcy became dormant.

8th Bart., of Denmiln and Kinnaird, co. Fife. *s.* his brother, Sir John Balfour, 7th Bart., in 1773, and was served heir to his brother 20 Oct. 1779. 2nd son of Sir Michael Balfour, 6th Bart., and Jane his wife, dau. of —— Ross, of Invernethie.

Services : Third Mysore War ; Capt. comdg. 3rd Bn. Sepoys (became 6th N.I. in 1824).
Refs. : G.E.C. *Complete Baronetage,* ii. 396. *E.I.M.C.* ii. 262.

Note : Both *E.I.M.C.* and *Stubbs* state that he was in comd. of 32nd Bn. at battle of Bitaurah 26 Oct. 1794, during Second Rohilla War. The burial register shows that he was bur. at Dinapore on 5 June 1793, and G.E.C. confirms this.

BALL, George (1761-1811). Lieut. Colonel, 6th N.I. Adjutant General, Bengal. *b.* London 1761. Cadet 1777. Admitted 18 Dec. 1777. Ensign 4 Jan. 1778. Lieut. 10 Sept. 1779. Capt. 17 July 1795. Major 31 July 1799. Lt. Col. 1 Jan. 1803. *d. unm.* Chowringhee, Calcutta, 9 Dec. 1811, aged 50.
Son of William Ball, of Ashfont, nr. Staines, and Ellen his wife. Brother of William Ball, *q.v.*
Services : Sailed for India on the *Duke of Portland* 30 Apr. 1777, aged 16. Campaign against the Rajah of Benares ; Ramnagar 10 Aug. 1781 (w.) ; Lieut. 1/6th N.I. ; Bde. Major to Major William Popham's force ; capture of Bijaigarh, C.I., 10 Nov. 1781. Second Rohilla War ; Bitaurah ; Lieut. 20th Bn. Operations in Jumna Doab 1803 ; siege and capture of Sasni ; Lt. Col. comdg. 1/8th N.I. Second Mahratta War ; comdg. a force employed in reducing various forts to S.W. of Delhi 1803 ; battle of Deig ; capture of Deig 24 Dec. 1804 (s.w.) ; Lt. Col. comdg. 3rd Inf. Bde. Comdd. a force employed in the settlement of Hariana 1809 ; capture of Bhawani. A.G., Bengal, Feb. 1810 till death.
Refs. : E.I.M.C. iii. 418 *D.I.B. G.M.* 1813, i. 183. Will dated Calcutta 4 Aug. 1811 ; proved 12 Dec. 1811. M.I. in N. Park St. burial ground, Calcutta.

BALL, William (1777-1826). Lieut. Colonel, Invalid Est. 28th N.I. *b.* Marylebone, Middlesex, 18 July 1777. Cadet 1798. Arrived in India 15 Dec. 1799. Ensign 31 Oct. 1799. Lieut. 12 Nov. 1799. Capt. 6 July 1811. Major 18 Jan. 1822. Lt. Col. 1 May 1824. Invalided 3 Mar. 1826. *d.* Bhagulpur, B. & O., 27 Apr. 1826.
bapt. London 17 Aug. 1777. Son of William Ball and Eleanor his wife. Brother of George Ball, *q.v.*
Services : Posted as Lieut. to 2/14th N.I. 15 Apr. 1801. Second Mahratta War ; operations in Karnal district ; defence of Delhi Oct. 1804 ; Lieut. 2/14th N.I. Adjt. & Qmr. 14th N.I. 1806-7. Capt. Lt. 14th N.I. 13 Jan. 1808. Capt. 1/14th N.I. Actg. Fort Adjt. at Agra 1816-9. Fort Adjt. at Agra 1819-22. Transfd. as Lt. Col. to 28th N.I. (late 1/14th) May 1824.

BAMFIELD, Daniel (1805-1849). Major, 56th N.I. *b.* 1805. Cadet 1821. Arrived in India 1 Aug. 1822. Ensign 26 Feb. 1822. Lieut. 1 May 1824. Capt. 13 Feb. 1839. Major 4 July 1845. *d.* in camp, Chilianwala, 13 Jan. 1849, of wounds received in action the same day.

bapt. St. Ives, Cornwall, 1 Jan. 1806. Son of Daniel Bamfield, of St. Ives, merchant. *m.* Lucknow, 8 Jan. 1829, Christiana, youngest dau. of James Loch, of Lucknow, of the King of Oudh's service. (She died 13 June 1891, aged 83.)
Services : Posted as Ensign to 2/30th N.I. in Oct. 1822. Transfd. to 1/28th N.I. in Sept. 1823 ; to 56th N.I. (late 2/28th) May 1824. Intr. & Qmr. 56th N.I. 14 June 1827 till 17 Dec. 1832. Fur. s.c. 27 Oct. 1833 till 5 Dec. 1836. Intr. & Qmr. 19th N.I. 17 Dec. 1837 till 7 June 1839. Offg. D.J.A.G., Dinapore and Benares Divs., Apr. 1840 till Mar. 1841. First China War 1842 ; capture of Chin-Kiang-foo ; investment of Nanking ; Capt. 2nd Bn. Bengal Vols. (Medal). Mily. Mgte. at Chusan Apr. 1843 till Apr. 1845. Second Sikh War ; passage of the Chenab ; Sadulapur ; Chilianwala (mortally w.) ; Major comdg. 56th N.I.
Refs. : *De Rhé-Philipe.* Will dated Ferozepore 20 Oct. 1848 ; proved 14 Dec. 1850. *A.J.* xx. 755.

BANKS, John Sherbrooke (1811-1857). Major, 33rd N.I. Chief Commissioner of Lucknow. *bapt.* Naas, co. Kildare, 7 Oct. 1811. Cadet 1828. Arrived in India 11 Dec. 1829. Ensign 11 Dec. 1829. Lieut. 5 Oct. 1835. Capt. 29 Jan. 1846. Major 1857. *d.* Lucknow, 21 July 1857, during the siege.

Son of Samuel Banks, of Burton-on-Trent, Physician H.M. Forces, and Lucinda his wife. *m.* Ootacamund, Madras, 13 Oct. 1855, Elizabeth Hutchinson, youngest dau. of Maj. Gen. Robert Bryce Fearon, C.B., D.A.G. in E.I.
Services : See *D.N.B.* Ensign d.d. 33rd N.I. 8 Jan. 1830 ; do. 58th N.I. 12 Mar. 1833. Posted as Ensign to 33rd N.I. 20 Aug. 1833. Intr. & Qmr. 58th N.I. 12 Aug. 1834 till 27 Dec. 1838, and 3 Apr. 1843 till 2 June 1846.
Refs. : *D.N.B. D.I.B.* Boase. *G.M.* 1857, ii. 565. *The Times*, 15 Oct. 1857.

BANNATYNE, George Augustus (1791-1860). Lieutenant. 8th N.I. *b.* Tellicherry, Madras, 30 May 1791. Cadet 1808. Arrived in India 19 July 1809. Ensign 25 July 1809. Lieut. 16 Dec. 1814. Struck off 1819. *d.* his residence, Bathford House, Somerset, 16 Aug. 1860.

Son of James Bannatyne, Maj. Gen. Bombay Est., and Harriet his wife.
Services : Posted as Ensign to 8th N.I. Lieut. 2/8th N.I. Fur. 30 Dec. 1814. Struck off after five years' absence from India. No record of active service.
Refs. : *G.M.* 1860, ii. 439.

BANNERMAN, Alexander (1786-1825). Captain, 20th N.I. *bapt.* Aberdeen 16 Jan. 1786. Cadet 1804. Arrived in India 10 Sept. 1805. Ensign 14 Sept. 1805. Lieut. 15 Sept. 1805. Capt. 17 May 1823. *d.* Arakan 19 July 1825.

Eldest son of Charles Bannerman, advocate (who was younger brother of Sir Alexander Bannerman, of Elsick, co. Kincardine, 6th Bart.), and Margaret his wife, dau. of Patrick Wilson, of Finzeauch. *m.* Cawnpore, 23 Feb. 1822, Penelope, dau. of Joseph Smith. (She *re-m.* Edward Gwatkin, *q.v.*)

Services : Posted as Ensign to 5th N.I. Lieut. 1/5th N.I. S.A.C.G. at Ludhiana 11 July 1812. A.C.G. at Cawnpore 1817 till death. Transfd. to 20th N.I. (late 2/5th) May 1824. (? First Burma War ; Arakan 1825 ; A.C.G.)

Refs. : Burke's *Peerage*, 1923, p. 196, *s.n.* Bannerman, Bart., of Elsick. Will dated Cawnpore 10 May 1822 ; proved 24 Aug. 1825.

BANNERMAN, George (1782-1806). Lieutenant, 18th N.I. *b.* Tullibardine, co. Perth, 16 Jan. 1782. Cadet 1800. Arrived in India 15 Oct. 1801. Ensign 5 Oct. 1801. Lieut. 30 Sept. 1803. *d.* Cawnpore 7 July 1806.

bapt. Blackford, Perth, 10 Mar. 1801. Son of William Bannerman, of Milln, Tullibardine, and Louisa Carrick his 2nd wife.

Services : Posted as Ensign to 18th N.I. Second Mahratta War ; operations in Bundelkhand 1803-4 ; Kalpi ; Jaitpur ; Lieut. 18th N.I.

Refs. : Burke's *Family Records*, p. 38.

BARBER, Charles (*d.* 1770). Ensign, Infantry. Cadet (?). Ensign 7 July 1769. *d.* Calcutta 20 May 1770.

Services : N.F.P.

BARBER, James (1778-1805). Lieutenant, 19th N.I. *bapt.* 4 Oct. 1778. Cadet 1798. Arrived in India 26 Nov. 1800. Ensign 21 Oct. 1799. Lieut. 28 Oct. 1799. *d.* Mirzapur, U.P., 15 Aug. 1805.

Son of James Barber, of Otley, Yorks. *m.* Charlotte.

Services : Posted as Ensign to 1/19th N.I. 15 Apr. 1801. No record of active service.

Refs. : Will dated 18 Aug. 1804 ; proved 30 July 1805.

BARBER, Matthias (*d.* 1774). Captain, Infantry. Cadet 9 Feb. 1765. Ensign 24 Aug. 1765. Lieut. 11 Jan. 1767. Capt. 21 May 1770. *d.* Calcutta 10 Dec. 1774.

Brother of Mary Barber. *m.* (?).

Services : N.F.P.

Refs. : Will dated 17 Nov. 1774 ; proved 16 Dec. 1774.

THE BENGAL ARMY, 1758-1834   89

BARBER, Thomas.   Cadet 12 Feb. 1765.
Services : N.F.P.
Refs. : *B.M. Add. MS.* 6050.

BARBERIE, Cortlandt Skinner (1804-1841).   Captain.   16th N.I.
b. Liverpool 12 Dec. 1804.   Cadet 1821.   Arrived in India 3 Jan. 1823.   Ensign 13 Jan. 1823.   Lieut. 1 May 1824.   Capt. 18 Sept. 1833.   Retired 20 Feb. 1838.   *d.* Brook St., St. James's, London, 4 May 1841.
Younger son of Oliver Barberie, Major, Barrack Dept., and Euphemia (*or* Efiginia) his wife, dau. of Cortlandt Skinner, attorney general of New Jersey.
Services : Posted as Ensign to 10th N.I. Transfd. to 16th N.I. (late 2/10th) May 1824.   First Burma War ; Assam 1824 ; repulse at Dudhpatli 21 Feb. 1824 (s.w. leg amputated) ; Ensign 1/10th N.I.   Adjt. Patna Provl. Bn. 31 May 1824.   Sub-Asst. in Stud Dept. 17 Apr. 1830.   Removed from Stud Dept. 21 Aug. 1834.   2nd in comd. Assam Sebundy Corps 27 June 1835.   Fur. 20 Aug. 1835 till retirement.
Refs. : Burke's *Landed Gentry*, 2nd edn., p. 1362, *s.n.* Taylor, of Pennington, Hants.   *G.M.* 1841, i. 666.

BARBOR, George Alexander (1805-1888).   Major.   8th L.C.   *b.* Oldswinford, Stourbridge, Worcs., 28 Feb. 1805.   Cadet 1820. Arrived in India 8 Oct. 1821.   Cornet 5 May 1821.   Lieut. 13 May 1825.   Capt. 20 Feb. 1838.   Retired 10 July 1844. Hon. Major 28 Nov. 1854.   *d.* 26 Aug. 1888.
Son of George Barbor. *m.* Nasirabad, 12 Jan. 1829, Harriot Eliza, 2nd dau. of Isaac Pereira, *q.v.* (*See also* Henry Sturrock and William Veysie.)
Services : Posted as Cornet to 8th L.C.   Siege and capture of Bhurtpore ; comdd. the detachment of 8th L.C. which captured the usurper Durjan Sal when escaping from Bhurtpore on 18 Jan. 1826 (India medal).   Actg. Adjt. 8th L.C. 26 Mar. 1827.   Fur. p.a. 3 Mar. 1832 till 1 Dec. 1834.   2nd in comd. 3rd Local Horse 26 June 1837 till 1 Aug. 1838.
Refs. : *A.J.* xxviii. 92.

BARCLAY, Alexander (1802-1833).   Lieutenant, 68th N.I.   *b.* Port, co. Perth, 22 Mar. 1802.   Cadet 1822.   Arrived in India 5 July 1823.   Ensign 10 July 1823.   Lieut. 16 Apr. 1825.   *d.* Calcutta 25 Apr. 1833.
Son of Alexander Barclay (who was 5th son of John Barclay, of Georgeton), formerly of Hamburg, later of Gothenburg, Sweden, merchant.

LIST OF THE OFFICERS OF

Services : Posted as Ensign to 68th N.I. First Burma War; Lieut. 68th N.I. Fur. s.c. 1 Apr. 1830 till 21 Mar. 1833.

Refs. : History of the Scottish Barclays, by Leslie Barclay, Folkestone, 1915, p. 77.

BARCLAY, Andrew (1806-1842). Captain, 12th N.I. *b.* London 23 Sept. 1806. Cadet 1822. Arrived in India 21 June 1823. Ensign 6 June 1823. Lieut. 13 May 1825. Capt. 21 Jan. 1837. *d.* Lucknow 24 Aug. 1842.

Son of William Barclay, of Bartholomew Terr., London, tin manufacturer. *m.* Nasirabad, Rajputana, 12 Mar. 1829, Miss Jane Lydia Mullins.

Services : Posted as Ensign to 1st N.I. Transfd. as Ensign to 12th N.I. 13 May 1825. Siege and capture of Bhurtpore; Lieut. 18th N.I. Adjt. 12th N.I. 24 June 1835.

BARCLAY, George (*d.* 1802). Captain, 4th N.I. Country Cadet 1781. Admitted 26 Feb. 1781. Ensign 27 Aug. 1781. Lieut. 11 June 1783. Capt. 4 June 1801. *d.* Cawnpore 9 May 1802.

Services : Lieut. and Bt. Capt. 4th N.I. in 1800. Capt. Lt. 4th N.I. 24 Aug. 1800.

BARCLAY, John (*d.* 1843). Major, Invalid Est. 4th L.C. Cadet 1807. Arrived in India 10 May 1808. Cornet 16 Mar. 1808. Lieut. 15 Sept. 1816. Capt. 6 Mar. 1823. Major 15 Nov. 1837. Invalided 26 Mar. 1838. *d.* Inverness 13 Dec. 1843.

m. 1st, Inverness, 14 Apr. 1820, Helen, youngest dau. of Capt. John Forbes, 9th Veterans, of Telford St., Inverness. (She died Calcutta 10 Mar. 1822.) His dau. *m.* Charles Harris (1817-1889), *q.v. m.* 2nd, Meerut, 12 Oct. 1823, Miss Elizabeth Lowry. (She died Ealing 10 Jan. 1881, aged 78.)

Services : Sailed from England as Midshipman on the *Lord Nelson* in 1807. With 4th L.C. throughout his service. Third Mahratta War. Fur. s.c. 27 Nov. 1818. Adjt. 4th L.C. 29 Dec. 1821 till 25 Apr. 1823. Fell from a height and was severely injured in 1824. Fur. s.c. 12 Jan. 1828 till 29 Jan. 1831, and 19 Jan. 1843 till death.

Refs. : S.M. 1820, i. 485. *G.M.* 1844, i. 221. *The Times,* 19 Dec. 1843.

BARCLAY, Sir William, sixth baronet (1748-1767). Lieutenant, Infantry. *b.* London 22 May 1748. Cadet 1764. Arrived in India Apr. 1765. Ensign 7 Aug. 1765. Lieut. 25 Dec. 1766. *d. unm.* Calcutta 1767.

6th Bart., of Pierston, co. Ayr. *s.* 7 June 1756. *bapt.* St. John's, Westminster, 22 May 1748. Eldest son of Sir William Blois

Barclay, 5th Bart., and Susannah his wife, dau. of William Church, of Gloucester, surgeon.
Services : Sailed for India with Lord Clive on the *Kent* 4 June 1764.
Refs. : Burke's *Peerage,* 1923, p. 198, *s.n.* Barclay, Bart., of Pierston, co. Ayr. *History of the Scottish Barclays,* by Leslie Barclay, Folkestone, 1915.

BARCLAY, William (1756/57-1810). (See **BERKELEY**.)

BARING, James Drummond (1808-1901). Cornet. 1st L.C. *b.* London 3 Dec. 1808. Cadet 1825. Cornet 17 July 1826. Resigned in India 4 Jan. 1828. *d.s.p.* 1 July 1901.
2nd son of Henry Baring, of Somerley, Hants. (who was 3rd son of Sir Francis Baring, 1st Bart., of Larkbeer, Devon, chairman E.I.C. 1792-3), and Maria Matilda his 1st wife, 2nd dau. of William Bingham, of Philadelphia. 2nd cousin of William Baring-Gould, *q.v.*
Services : Cornet d.d. 1st L.C. 4 Jan. 1827. No record of active service.
Refs. : Burke's *Peerage,* 1923, p. 1683, *s.n.* Earl of Northbrook.

BARKER, George (1786-1819). Captain, 12th N.I. *b.* Bacton, Suffolk, 16 Feb. 1786. Cadet 1800. Arrived in India 19 Aug. 1801. Ensign 24 Sept. 1801. Lieut. 13 July 1803. Capt. 14 June 1815. *d.* Muttra 13 July 1819.
Son of —— Barker and Anna Maria his wife. *m.* Dinapore, Aug. 1810, Emma Maria, only dau. of Thomas William Clayton, *q.v.*
Services : Ensign 12th N.I. Second Mahratta War ; siege of Bhurtpore (w. in 1st assault on 9 Jan. 1805 and in 3rd assault on 20 Feb. 1805) ; Lieut. 2/12th N.I. Adjt. 2/12th N.I. 18 Jan. 1805 till 29 July 1815. Operations in Oudh 1807-8 ; Akbarpur ; Patharserai. Nepal War 1816 ; Capt. 2/12th N.I. in 3rd Bde., Centre Column. (? Capture of Hathras ; Capt. 2/12th N.I.) Third Mahratta War ; Dhamoni. Against the Bhattis of Hariana 1818.
Refs. : *Royal Mily. Chron.* 1811, p. 93.

BARKER, George (1789-1859). Lieut. Colonel. 33rd N.I. *b.* London 12 Nov. 1789. Cadet 1808. Arrived in India 24 July 1809. Ensign 15 Aug. 1809. Dismissed for having obtained his appointment by purchase. (M.C. of 21 Mar. 1810.) Reappointed Cadet 1810. Ensign 16 May 1812. Lieut. 17 Apr. 1818. Capt. 7 Jan. 1825. Bt. Major 28 June 1838. Retired 23 Mar. 1840. Hon. Lt. Col. 28 Nov. 1854. *d.* Arundel Villa, Cheltenham, 30 Aug. 1859.

Son of Richard Barker. *m.* 1st, Stirling, 18 Mar. 1828, Eliza, eldest dau. of D. Dobie, of Gartferry, co. Lanark. (She died 26 Nov. 1845, aged 45.) *m.* 2nd, Mary Catherine.
Services : Dismissed 12 May 1809 for having obtained his appt. by purchase. Struck off 31 Mar. 1810. Permitted to remain in India. Reappointed ; admitted to the Service 27 Aug. 1811. Posted as Ensign to 1/16th N.I. Fur. 27 Dec. 1820 till 25 June 1824. Transfd. to 33rd N.I. (late 2/16th) May 1824. Siege and capture of Bhurtpore ; Lieut. 33rd N.I. (India medal). Fur. 20 Dec. 1826 till 23 Nov. 1829. Comdd. 30th N.I. for a short while.
Refs. : *A.J.* xxv. 568. *G.M.* 1859, ii. 430. *The Times,* 3 Sept. 1859. Will dated 15 Aug. 1856 ; codicil dated 17 Nov. 1858 ; proved 3 Mar. 1860.

BARKER, Sir Robert, first baronet (1729 ?-1789). Brigadier General, Kt. Provincial C.-in-C. in Bengal. *b. c.* 1729. Col. 3 May 1765. Bdr. Gen. 24 Mar. 1770. *d.s.p.* Bushbridge, nr. Godalming, 14 Sept. 1789, when the title became extinct.

1st Bart., of Bushbridge, Surrey. *c.* 24 Mar. 1781. *m.* Ann, dau. of Brabazon Hallowes, of Glapwell Hall, co. Derby, sheriff of Derby.
Services : See *D.N.B.* Arrived in India *c.* 1749. 2nd Lieut. Madras Train of Art. 1 Nov. 1753. Lieut. 1753. Capt. Lt. 1756. Accompanied Clive to Bengal in 1756, in comd. of Art. Capt. 4 Jan. 1757. Major 7 Sept. 1761. Assault and capture of Manila 6 Oct. 1762 ; comdg. Art. Col. 1762. Transfd. to Bengal as Col. Resigned the appt. of Provincial C.-in-C. 18 June 1774, and returned to England. M.P. for Wallingford. Kt. 16 Apr. 1764.
Refs. : *D.N.B.* *D.I.B.* Burke's *Extinct Baronetcies,* 1st edn., p. 37. *Leslie.* *G.M.* 1789, ii. 956. *S.M.* 1789, p. 466.

BARLAND, Walter (*d.* 1771). Lieutenant, Infantry. Cadet (?). Ensign (?). Lieut. 1 Sept. 1768. *d.* Patna 26 Oct. 1771.
Brother of Euphemia Barland, of Perth.
Services : N.F.P.
Refs. : Will dated Arrah 15 Nov. 1770 ; proved 28 July 1772.

BARLOW, Andrew Samuel (1781-?). Lieutenant. 3rd N.C. *b.* York 1 May 1781. Cadet 1801. Arrived in India 17 July 1802. Cornet 6 Aug. 1803. Lieut. 4 Apr. 1807. Struck off 1816.

bapt. St. Mary Bishophill, York, 31 May 1781. 7th son of Samuel (Francis) Barlow, of Middlethorpe (who was son of Francis Barlow, of Middle Thorpe, high sheriff of York in 1735), and Mary his wife, dau. of William Thornton, of Thornville.
Services : Posted as Cornet to 3rd N.C. (? Second Mahratta War ; Delhi ; Laswari ; Deig ; pursuit of Holkar ; Cornet 3rd N.C.

THE BENGAL ARMY, 1758-1834 93

Operations against Dhundia Khan 1807; Komona; Ganauri.
Operations in Bundelkhand 1809; Rajaoli; Ajaigarh.) Fur.
9 May 1811 until struck off in 1816 after five years' absence from
India. (? Subsequently took service with the King of Oudh.)
Refs. : *N. & Q.* 1S. vi. 440.

BARNARD, Henry Clapton (1786-1858). Colonel. 41st N.I. *b.* 5
Feb. 1786. Cadet 1805. Arrived in India 11 July 1806. Ensign
26 Aug. 1806. Lieut. 20 Oct. 1808. Capt. 1 May 1824. Major
18 Feb. 1838. Lt. Col. 7 May 1844. Retired 7 Apr. 1845. Hon.
Col. 28 Nov. 1854. *d.* Painswick, Gloucs., 22 May 1858.
bapt. Dunmow, Essex, 12 Apr. 1786, aged 9 weeks 3 days. Son
of John Barnard and Eleanor his wife. *m.* 1st, Bareilly, 29 Mar.
1811, Mary, reputed dau. of Philip D'Auvergne, *q.v.* (She died
Karnal 28 Mar. 1836, aged 42.) Their dau. *m.* John Bontein, *q.v.*
m. 2nd, Calcutta, 15 June 1840, Jane, widow of R. H. S. Reid.
Services : At Barasat C.C. for 9½ mos. Posted as Ensign to
1/26th N.I. Operations in Bundelkhand 1807; Sehlehuganj;
Ensign 1/26th N.I. Intr. & Qmr. 1/26th N.I. 4 May 1815 till
1 May 1824. Third Mahratta War; Lieut. 1/26th N.I., Bde. Qmr.
1st Inf. Bde., 1st Div. Transfd. as Capt to 51st N.I. (late 1/26th)
May 1824. Fur. 15 Dec. 1828 till 19 Sept. 1832. Gwalior campaign;
Paniar; Major 51st N.I. (Bronze star). Transfd. as Lt. Col. to
45th N.I. 12 Aug. 1844.
Refs. : *G.M.* 1858, ii. 91. *The Times*, 2 June 1858.

BARNARD, Isaac (*d.* 1768). Ensign, Infantry. Cadet 1767.
Ensign 15 Sept. 1767. *d.* in India 1768.
Services : N.F.P.

BARNARD, John Gilbert (1797-1822). Lieutenant, Artillery. *b.*
Litcham, Norfolk, 10 Feb. 1797. Cadet 1814. Fireworker
14 Aug. 1817. Lieut. 1 Sept. 1818. *d.* Meerut 17 Nov. 1822.
2nd son of Rev. Thomas Barnard, of Litcham, and Everilda his
wife, 2nd dau. of Sir Mordaunt Martin, of Long Melford, Suffolk,
4th Bart. Addiscombe Cadet 1812-4.
Services : Third Mahratta War; Lieut. 4th Troop H.A.
Refs. : Burke's *Landed Gentry*, 8th edn., p. 91, *s.n.* Barnard, of
Prestbury, Gloucs. *G.M.* 1823, ii. 477.

BARNES, James (*d.* 1783). Ensign, Infantry. Cadet 1782. Ensign
1783. *d.* Madras Harbour, 19 Apr. 1783 : blown up in the
Duke of Athol.
Note : The H.C. ship *Duke of Athol*, Capt. James Rattray,
arrived at Madras on 16 Apr. 1783. Three days later she took fire,

and blew up in the roads. Most of her crew, as well as several officers and men of H.M. Squadron, who went to her assistance, lost their lives.

Services : Sailed from Portsmouth for India in the *Duke of Athol* 11 Sept. 1782.

BARNES, John (1773/74 ?-1812 ?). Lieutenant. Infantry. *b.* 1773/74 ? Cadet (?). Ensign (?). Lieut. 11 June 1790. Resigned 1794. (? *d.* Calcutta 8 Dec. 1821, aged 47.) (? *m.* Margaret.)

Services : Lieut. on the Bencoolen Est. and stationed at Mana, in Sumatra, in 1790. Transfd. as Lieut. to Bengal Est. 11 June 1790.

Refs. : (? M.I. in S. Park St. cemetery, Calcutta, erected by his widow, Margaret.)

BARNES, Walter Richard (1810-?). Captain. 27th N.I. *bapt.* Reigate 11 Mar. 1810. Cadet 1827. Arrived in India 4 July 1828. Ensign 6 Mar. 1828. Lieut. 8 Mar. 1834. Capt. 31 Dec. 1845. Retired 10 Aug. 1847. (Living in 1894.)

Son of Michael William Barnes, of Streatham, and Lady Georgiana Catherine his wife, 2nd dau. of George William, seventh Earl of Coventry.

Services : Posted as Ensign to 58th N.I. 4 Nov. 1828. 7th Coy. Pioneers 9 July 1832. Transfd. to 27th N.I. 12 Oct. 1832. Fur. s.c. 12 Jan. 1838 till 22 May 1841. First Afghan War 1841-2 ; defence and surrender of Ghazni (w.) ; with Gen. Nott's advance from Kandahar ; Lieut. 27th N.I. (Medal). Fur. 10 Feb. 1843 till retirement.

Refs. : Burke's *Peerage,* 1923, p. 602, *s.n.* Coventry, E.

BARNETT, Hugh Laird (1793-1826). Captain, 46th N.I. *b.* Ballymena, co. Antrim, 21 Apr. 1793. Cadet 1808. Arrived in India 27 Oct. 1809. Ensign 10 Oct. 1810. Lieut. 16 Dec. 1814. Bt. Capt. 24 Apr. 1824. Capt. 1825/26. *d. unm.* Aurangabad, Hyderabad, 19 Apr. 1826.

Son of John Barnett, of Randalstown, co. Antrim. Brother of James Barnett, *q.v.,* and of Mary Lockett (*probably* wife of Abraham Lockett, *q.v.*)

Services : Posted as Ensign to 23rd N.I. Lieut. 2/23rd N.I. Third Mahratta War ; Lieut. 2/23rd N.I. Actg. Bk. Mr. at Fort William 1820. 2nd Asst. to the Resdt. at Hyderabad 1821 till death. Transfd. to 46th N.I. (late 2/23rd) May 1824.

Refs. : Will dated Aurangabad 19 Apr. 1826 ; proved 12 May 1826.

BARNETT, James (1792-1819). Lieutenant, 16th N.I. *b.* Randalstown, co. Antrim, 11 Feb. 1792. Cadet 1808. Arrived in India 27 Oct. 1809. Ensign 16 Aug. 1810. Lieut. 16 Dec. 1814. *d.* Calcutta 11 Apr. 1819.
Son of John Barnett, of Randalstown. Brother of Hugh Laird Barnett, *q.v.*
Services : Posted as Ensign to 16th N.I. Lieut. 2/16th N.I. With Resdt.'s escort at Delhi in 1818. No record of active service.
Refs. : M.I. in S. Park St. burial ground, Calcutta.

BARNETT, William (1792-1867). Major. 53rd N.I. *b.* Trelawney, Cornwall, Jamaica, 21 May 1792. Cadet 1809. Ensign 7 Nov. 1811. Lieut. 26 Apr. 1815. Capt. 27 May 1828. Retired 18 Feb. 1839. Hon. Major 28 Nov. 1854. *d.* 12 Westbourne Park Rd., London, 31 Jan. 1867.
Son of William Barnett.
Services : Captured by the enemy on the voyage out to India. Present at the capture of Mauritius Dec. 1810. Wrecked off Sandip I. in Bay of Bengal. Posted as Ensign to 2/27th N.I. Fur. s.c. 19 Jan. 1816 till 9 Feb. 1819. S.A.C.G. 16 Oct. 1819. D.A.C.G., 2 cl., 3 Feb. 1824. Transfd. to 53rd N.I. (late 1/27th) May 1824. A.C.G., 2 cl., 13 June 1828 ; 1 cl. 26 Aug. 1831. Shekhawat Expedn. 1834-5.
Refs. : *G.M.* 1867, p. 399. *The Times*, 4 Feb. 1867.

BARNWELL, Michael (*d.* 1792). Lieutenant, Pension Est. Cadet 1770. Ensign 14 Dec. 1772. Lieut. 13 Mar. 1777. Pensioned 18 Jan. 1781. *d.* in the King's Bench prison, London, 5 Mar. 1792.
Services : N.F.P.
Refs. : *Eur. Mag.* 1792, i. 240.

BARR, William (1812-1876). Major General. Artillery. *b.* London 19 Apr. 1812. Cadet 1829. Arrived in India 30 May 1830. 2nd Lieut. 11 Dec. 1829. Lieut. 1 Aug. 1838. Capt. 9 Aug. 1847. Major 18 Aug. 1858. Lt. Col. 27 Aug. 1858. Col. 24 Nov. 1862. Retired 1 Sept. 1863. Hon. Maj. Gen. 1 Sept. 1863. *d.* Elmdon House, Shanklin, I.W., 9 July 1876.
Son of John Barr and Eliza his wife. *m.* (before 1839) Maria. Addiscombe Cadet 29 Mar. 1828 till 11 Dec. 1829.
Services : Posted to 4th Troop 2nd Bde., H.A., in 1838. First Afghan War 1838-9 ; forcing of Khyber Pass and advance on Kabul ; Lieut. 4th Troop 2nd Bde. (Medal). Transfd. to 3rd Troop 2nd Bde. in 1840. Fur. s.c. 3 Mar. 1842 till 1844. First Sikh War ; Badhowal ; Aliwal ; Sobraon ; Bt. Capt. 3rd Troop 2nd Bde., Actg.

Adjt. 2nd Bde., H.A. (Medal with clasp). Comdd. 1st Troop 2nd Bde., H.A., 1854-7. At Peshawar during the Mutiny. Author of " Journal of march from Delhi to Peshawar and Caubul and Narrative of Operations in the Khyber Pass, 1839," 1844.
Refs. : *The Times*, 15 July 1876.

BARRAT, Savage (*d.* 1772). Ensign, Infantry. Cadet (?). Ensign 5 Aug. 1765. *d.* Monghyr, B. & O., June 1772.
Services : N.F.P.

BARRAUD, Isaac (*d.* 1791). Major, Invalid Est. Artillery. Cadet (?). Fireworker 16 Sept. 1770. Lieut. 10 Jan. 1773. Capt. Lt. 15 Sept. 1779. Capt. 15 Apr. 1781. Major 30 May 1786. Invalided 23 Nov. 1786. *d.* Calcutta 9 Dec. 1791.
m. (before 1778) Susannah.
Services : Was comdg. the Invalid Art. at Budge-Budge in 1785.
Refs. : Will proved in Calcutta.

BARRELL, George (*d.* 1766). Ensign, Infantry. Cadet (?). Ensign 14 Aug. 1765. *d.* in India 1766.
Services : N.F.P.
Refs. : *B.M. Add. MS.* 6050.

BARRETT, John (1754/55-1779). Lieutenant, Artillery. *b.* in Ireland 1754/55. Cadet 1776. Fireworker (?). Lieut. 26 Sept. 1778. *d.* Chunar, U.P., 10 June 1779.
Services : Sailed for India on the *Houghton* 9 Feb. 1777, aged 22. N.F.P.

BARRETT, John (1810-1880). Lieut. General. 37th N.I. Retired List. *b.* Charlton, Kent, 14 Apr. 1810. Cadet 1825. Arrived in India 12 Mar. 1827. Ensign 30 Sept. 1826. Lieut. 8 Oct. 1839. Capt. 26 Apr. 1849. Major 26 Jan. 1861. Lt. Col. 6 Apr. 1863. Col. 18 Feb. 1866. Maj. Gen. 14 Dec. 1871. Lt. Gen. 2 May 1878. Retired List Apr. 1880. *d.* Rawal Pindi 16 Dec. 1880.
Son of William Barrett.
Services : Ensign d.d. 62nd N.I. 26 Mar. 1827. Posted as Ensign to 54th N.I. in May 1827. Transfd. to 45th N.I. 2 Aug. 1832 ; to 25th N.I. 31 July 1837 ; to 2nd Eur. Regt. 21 Oct. 1839. With Army of Reserve for Afghanistan at Ferozepore Oct. 1842 till Jan. 1843 ; Lieut. 2nd Eur. Regt. Transfd. to 37th N.I. 14 Dec. 1842. Second Sikh War ; in garrison at Lahore ; Capt. 37th N.I. (Medal). With 37th N.I. at Benares when it mutinied in July 1857.
Refs. : De Rhé-Philipe.

THE BENGAL ARMY, 1758-1834

BARRETT, Tufnell Carbonell (1810-1856). Lieutenant. 65th N.I. *b.* 6 Jan. 1810. Cadet 1826. Arrived in India 6 Dec. 1827. Ensign 15 May 1827. Lieut. 26 Feb. 1829. Resigned 8 Aug. 1832. *d.* 31 Aug. 1856.

bapt. Milton, nr. Gravesend, Kent, 27 Dec. 1810. Of Shorne, Kent. Eldest son of Samuel Tufnell Barrett, of Bath, Capt. 37th Regt., and Agnes his 2nd wife, dau. of Samuel Sealy, of Magh, co. Kerry. *m.* Bath, 29 May 1832, Mary Anne, only dau. of Benjamin O'Neill Hughes, of Kilcorral, Hill Town, co. Wexford, 56th Regt.

Services : Posted as Ensign to 65th N.I. Fur. s.c. 17 Nov. 1828 till resignation. No record of active service.

Refs. : Burke's *Landed Gentry*, 12th edn., p. 102, *s.n.* Barrett, of Court Lodge, Shorne, Kent.

BARRINGTON, R. Cadet. Infantry. Cadet 1780. Resigned 28 Aug. 1780.

Services : N.F.P.

BARRON, Thomas (1783-1844). Lieut. Colonel. 55th N.I. *b.* St. Andrews, Fife, 28 Oct. 1783. Cadet 1799. Arrived in India 8 Dec. 1800. Ensign 10 Nov. 1800. Lieut. 13 July 1803. Capt. 11 July 1823. Major 13 May 1825. Lt. Col. 22 May 1829. Retired 3 July 1832. *d.* his residence, Wellington Sq., Cheltenham, 25 May 1844.

bapt. St. Andrews 11 Nov. 1783. Son of Professor William Barron and Margaret Stark his wife. A relative of Harry Stark, *q.v. m.* (?).

Services : Posted as Ensign to 2/9th N.I. 17 Apr. 1801. Transfd. to 10th N.I. in 1801. Second Mahratta War ; Lieut. 10th N.I. Adjt. 1/10th N.I. 1805-10. Adjt. & Qmr. 10th N.I. 18 Sept. 1810 till 1814. Intr. & Qmr. 1/10th N.I. 1815. Capt. Lt. 1/10th N.I. 1 Oct. 1815. (? Third Mahratta War ; Capt. Lt. 1/10th N.I.) Fur. 11 Mar. 1821 till 26 Mar. 1824. A.A.G. 11 Jan. 1825 till 5 Dec. 1829. Transfd. as Lt. Col. to 55th N.I. 5 Dec. 1829. Fur. 10 Feb. 1830 till retirement.

Refs. : The Times, 5 June 1844.

BARRY, Henry (1811-1853). Captain, 71st N.I. *b.* 26 June 1811. Cadet 1827. Arrived in India 8 Apr. 1828. Ensign 13 Oct. 1827. Lieut. 3 June 1830. Capt. 24 Jan. 1845. *d. unm.* 28 Dec. 1853 ; kld. in action near Prome, Burma.

2nd son of Henry Greene Barry, of Ballyclough, co. Cork, Maj. Gen. 15th Foot, high sheriff co. Cork, 1821, and Phoebe his wife, dau. of John Armstrong Drought, of Lettybrook, King's Co.

Services : Posted as Ensign to 71st N.I. Fur. s.c. 3 Apr. 1835 till 7 Feb. 1839. Comdt. 1st L.I. Bn. Bundelkhand Legion 30 Jan. 1840. Disturbances in Bundelkhand 1840-1 ; capture of Chirgaon. Comdg. Arakan Bn. 31 Dec. 1847 till death. Mortally wounded nr. Prome on 28 Dec. 1853, " whilst at the head of his Regt. on the march from Rangoon to Prome, having been suddenly attacked by a body of Burmese concealed in a dense forest."

Refs. : Burke's *Landed Gentry of Ireland*, p. 28, *s.n.* Bury-Barry, of Ballyclough, co. Cork. *G.M.* 1854, ii. 200. Will dated 11 Dec. 1838 ; codicil dated 7 Apr. 1841 ; proved 19 June 1858.

BARRY, Willoughby (*d.* 1779). Captain, Infantry. Cadet 1767. Ensign 1 Dec. 1767. Lieut. 11 Oct. 1769. Capt. 24 Feb. 1778. *d.* Chittagong 25 Mar. 1779.

Services : N.F.P.

BARSTOW, John Anderson (1795-1863). Major General. Late 58th N.I. *b.* Ipswich 10 May 1795. Cadet 1811. Arrived in India Aug. 1812. Ensign 13 Aug. 1814. Lieut. 1 June 1817. Capt. 31 Mar. 1831. Major 1 Jan. 1845. Lt. Col. 17 May 1851. Col. 28 Nov. 1854. Maj. Gen. Oct. 1862. *d.* Murree 9 June 1863. Son of Thomas Barstow.

Services : Ensign d.d. 2/9th N.I. Attached for duty to Rangpur Local Bn. in Oct. 1813. Posted to 2/18th N.I. 10 Oct. 1814, but did not join until 1818. Nepal War 1814-6 ; Ensign Rangpur Local Bn. Intr. & Qmr. 2/18th N.I. Oct. 1818 till May 1824. Transfd. to 36th N.I. (late 1/18th) May 1824 ; to 37th N.I. May 1825. Adjt. 37th N.I. June 1825 till May 1831. Siege and capture of Bhurtpore ; Lieut. 37th N.I. (India medal). First Afghan War 1839 ; Bolan Pass 4 May 1839 (s.w.) ; Capt. 37th N.I. (Medal). Fur. s.c. 8 Feb. 1841 till 23 Dec. 1844. Second Sikh War ; in garrison at Lahore ; Major 37th N.I. (Medal). Transfd. as Lt. Col. to 70th N.I. in May 1851 ; to 4th N.I. ; to 57th N.I. in June 1852 ; to 58th N.I. in Apr. 1854. He comdd. this Regt. (which was disarmed during the Mutiny) until it was disbanded in 1860.

Refs. : De Rhé-Philipe. Boase.

BARTHOLOMEW, Charles (1784-1807). Lieutenant, 19th N.I. *b.* Poole, Dorset, 22 Mar. 1784. Cadet 1799. Arrived in India 7 Jan. 1801. Ensign 28 Sept. 1800. Lieut. 14 Dec. 1802. *d.* Barrackpore 25 Mar. 1807.

bapt. Poole 19 May 1784. Son of Charles Bartholomew and Ann his wife.

Services : Posted as Ensign to 2/19th N.I. Lieut. 2/19th N.I. With 1st Vol. Bn. 1804-5. No record of active service.

Refs. : Will proved 30 Sept. 1807.

BARTLEMAN, John (1801-1871). Lieut. Colonel. 44th N.I. b. London 25 Feb. 1801. Cadet 1819. Admitted 15 July 1820. Ensign 14 Feb. 1820. Lieut. 11 July 1823. Capt. 25 Jan. 1837. Major 10 Jan. 1846. Lt. Col. 28 Nov. 1854. Retired 1 Jan. 1855. d. 23 Feb. 1871.
Son of John Bartleman, Major Royal Marines. m. 1st, Edinburgh, 11 Dec. 1828, Mary, only dau. of Angus Macdonald, of Laig, co. Inverness. (She died at sea 5 July 1829, aged 23.) m. 2nd, Linholme, nr. Hamilton, 5 May 1835, Isabella Miller, only dau. of Thomas Boyes, of Wellhall, co. Lanark. (*See* Robert Boyes.) (She died Ambala, 31 Jan. 1844, aged 44.)
Services : Posted as Ensign to 2/19th N.I. Transfd. to 22nd N.I. in 1823. Intr. & Qmr. 44th N.I. (late 2/22nd) 8 May 1826. Fur. 21 Nov. 1827 till 24 Sept. 1829. Adjt. 44th N.I. 18 Mar. 1830. Fur. p.a. 15 Jan. 1833 till 5 Mar. 1836. 2nd in comd. Mhairwara Local Bn. 28 June 1836 till 2 Sept. 1841. Dy. Paymr. Nasirabad (afterwards Sirhind) 15 Sept. 1841. Cashiered by sentence of G.C.M. 25 Nov. 1850. Restored to the Service in 1853. Local Lt. Col. in Turkey 27 Mar. 1855.
Refs. : A.J. xxvii. 125 ; N.S. xvii. 144. I.M. 1851, pp. 3, 8 ; 1855, p. 287.

BARTLETT, William (1806-1863 ?). Lieutenant, Pension Est. 68th N.I. b. East Stoke, Notts., 22 Sept. 1806. Cadet 1825. Ensign 15 Mar. 1826. Lieut. 8 May 1829. Pensioned 30 Apr. 1830. d. 1863 ?
Son of Rev. William Bartlett, vicar of East Stoke, *juxta* Newark, Notts. m. Calcutta, 20 June 1831, Sarah, dau. of Thomas Howitson. (She died Ballygunge, Calcutta, 21 Nov. 1856, aged 66.)
Note : His name disappears from the official *Indian Army and Civil Service List* for Jan. 1864.
Services : Transfd. from 37th N.I. to 68th N.I. 5 Oct. 1826. No record of active service.
Refs. : A.J. N.S. vi. 190.

BARTON, Ezekiel (1781-1855). Lieut. General. Colonel 46th N.I. b. Rougham, Norfolk, 4 Dec. 1781. Cadet 1799. Arrived in India 4 Jan. 1800. Ensign 21 Oct. 1800. Lieut. 8 Apr. 1802. Capt. 16 Dec. 1814. Major 12 Jan. 1825. Lt. Col. 21 Sept. 1828. Col. 22 Jan. 1838. Maj. Gen. 3 Nov. 1841. Lt. Gen. 11 Nov. 1851. d. Irthlingborough House, Higham Ferrers, Northants., 4 June 1855.
Son of George Barton. m. (?).
Services : Posted as Ensign to 1/10th N.I. 17 Apr. 1801. Lieut. 7th N.I. 1804-5. Transfd. to 26th N.I. in 1805. Adjt. & Qmr.

26th N.I. 3 Apr. 1809 till 1814. Capt. 1/29th N.I. Employed as Asst. Surveyor in Nepal and Garhwal 1815-6. A.Q.M.G. 1 Jan. 1817. Siege and capture of Hathras. Third Mahratta War; A.Q.M.G. 4th Div. D.Q.M.G. (with official rank of Major) 25 Feb. 1820. Transfd. to 57th N.I. (late 1/29th) May 1824. Siege and capture of Bhurtpore; Major 57th N.I., D.Q.M.G. of the Army (India medal). Conducted the duties of Q.M.G.'s Dept. with Shekhawati force under Bdr. Stevenson Sept. 1834 till Feb. 1835. Transfd. from 17th N.I. to 73rd N.I. 9 July 1833; to 2nd N.I. 21 Feb. 1835; to 25th N.I. 11 Mar. 1835. Town and Fort Major of Fort William 6 Mar. 1837 till 5 Mar. 1842. Leave s.c. to Cape 22 Dec. 1838 till 17 Nov. 1840. Transfd. from 71st N.I. to 46th N.I. 18 May 1843. Bdr., 2nd cl., 13 Feb. 1844. Fur. 15 Jan. 1845 till death.

Refs. : *G.M.* 1855, ii. 110.

BARTON, John (*d.* 1800). Lieut. Colonel, Artillery. Country Cadet 1777. Admitted 12 Nov. 1777. Fireworker 12 Nov. 1777. Lieut. 1 Oct. 1778. Capt. Lt. 5 Aug. 1784. Capt. 30 May 1786. Major 29 Apr. 1799. Lt. Col. 1 Jan. 1800. *d.* at sea, 30 May 1800, on his passage to Europe.

Services : Second Mysore War, under Lt. Col. Thomas Deane Pearse, *q.v.*; Lieut. 5th Coy. 2nd Bn. Art. Returned to Bengal in Dec. 1783. Third Mysore War; Bangalore, as Capt. Served in Ceylon from 1795 till 1799, when he returned to Bengal on promotion. Fur. 10 Dec. 1799, but died on the voyage home.

Refs. : *G.M.* 1801, i. 572.

Note : *G.M.* gives the date of death as 5 Nov. 1800; *A.A.R.* as Oct. 1800; *Stubbs* as 30 May 1800.

BARTON, Nathaniel Dunbar (1803-1885). Colonel. 3rd European L.C. *b.* London 7 June 1803. Cadet 1821. Arrived in India 25 Sept. 1822. Cornet 1 May 1822. Lieut. 1 May 1824. Capt. 30 Oct. 1837. Major 24 Dec. 1855. Bt. Lt. Col. 18 Mar. 1856. Retired 8 Apr. 1861. Hon. Col. 8 Apr. 1861. *d.* 64 Regency Sq., Brighton, 23 June 1885.

2nd son of Lt. Gen. Charles Barton, Lt. Col. 2nd Life Guards, and Susannah his wife, dau. of Nicholas Weld Johnston, of Bordeaux. *m.* Karnal, 28 Oct. 1831, Honoria Angelina, 2nd dau. of Lt. Col. Alexander Lawrence and sister of Sir Henry Montgomery Lawrence, *q.v.*

Services : Posted as Cornet to 6th L.C. Transfd. to 4th L.C. 8 Nov. 1822. Exchanged to 6th L.C. 14 Feb. 1825. Adjt. 6th Local Horse 28 Jan. 1825 till 14 Mar. 1827. Intr. & Qmr. 6th L.C. 16 Feb. 1830 till 20 Mar. 1834. Fur. s.c. 1 Jan. 1837 till 10 Feb.

THE BENGAL ARMY, 1758-1834 101

1840. Second Sikh War; Chilianwala; Gujerat; Capt. 6th L.C. (Medal with clasp). Transfd. to newly-raised 3rd Eur. L.C. in 1858. Fur. 1859 till retirement.
Refs.: Burke's *Landed Gentry of Ireland*, p. 31, *s.n.* Barton, of The Waterfoot, co. Fermanagh. *The Times*, 30 June 1885.

BARWELL, Augustus Leycester (1802-1844). Ensign. 18th N.I. *b.* Westbourne, Sussex, 27 Aug. 1802. Cadet 1821. Ensign 4 July 1821. Struck off in England 6 Feb. 1824. *d.* his seat, Blackbridge, nr. Milford, 30 Dec. 1844.
6th son of Richard Barwell, of Stanstead Park, Sussex, M.P. for St. Ives and Winchester (*D.N.B.*), and Catherine his 2nd wife. *m.* St. Pancras New Church, 2 July 1829, E. S. West, 3rd dau. of Professor Coleman, of the Royal Veterinary Coll. B.N.C., Oxon.; matric. 15 Jan. 1821, aged 19.
Services: Posted as Ensign to 18th N.I. On fur. in 1823.
Refs.: *Alumni Oxon. G.M.* 1845, i. 332.

BARWELL, Henry Montague (1811-1837). Lieutenant, 59th N.I. *b.* Chittagong 25 July 1811. Cadet 1827. Arrived in India 10 June 1828. Ensign 20 Feb. 1828. Lieut. 22 July 1836. *d.* Shahjahanpur, U.P., 8 Aug. 1837.
2nd son of Edward Richard Barwell, B.C.S., session judge, Jessore. *Services*: Posted as Ensign to 45th N.I. 4 Nov. 1828. Transfd. to 59th N.I. 8 Dec. 1828. Fur. s.c. 23 Jan. 1830 till 18 Nov. 1833. Pte. Sec. and A.D.C. to Lt. Govr. of Agra 20 Mar. till 4 May 1835. No record of active service.
Refs.: M.I. at Shahjahanpur. Will dated 27 Dec. 1835; proved 29 Aug. 1837.

BARWICK, John Isaac (1760/61-?). Lieutenant. Infantry. *b.* 1760/61. Cadet 1779. Ensign 8 July 1779. Lieut. 28 Feb. 1781. Struck off 15 Apr. 1782.
A native of Essex.
Services: Sailed for India on the *Ganges*, 7 Mar. 1779, aged 18. N.F.P.
Note: John Barwick, Corpus Coll. Camb.; B.A. 1789; rector of Boughton, Kent, 17 Nov. 1804; M.A. 1805.

BASELEY, Charles (1806-1854). Bt. Major, 51st N.I. *bapt.* Gayton, Norfolk, 23 Mar. 1806. Cadet 1822. Arrived in India 5 July 1823. Ensign 10 July 1823. Lieut. 19 June 1824. Capt. 30 Jan. 1842. Bt. Major 11 Nov. 1851. *d.s.p.* Rawal Pindi 7 Sept. 1854.
Son of Thomas Warriner Baseley, comptroller of customs, St. Lucia, and Susannah Nelson his wife. Brother of Horace Baseley,

q.v. m. Brompton, Middlesex, 18 Oct. 1849, Marian, 2nd dau. of Charles Harvey Hodson, of Wellingborough.
Services : Posted as Ensign to 26th N.I. Transfd. to 51st N.I. (late 1/26th) May 1824. Fur. s.c. 30 Dec. 1827 till 3 Dec. 1831. Baggage Master to the force in Rajputana 19 Dec. 1834. A.D.C. to Maj. Gen. James Cock, *q.v.*, 24 Aug. 1842. Gwalior campaign; Paniar; Capt. 51st N.I. (Bronze star). Fur. s.c. 21 Feb. 1847 till 1849.
Refs. : Burke's *Family Records*, p. 326, *s.n.* Hodson. Will dated 3 June 1850; proved 9 Jan. 1855.

BASELEY, Horace (1803-1831). Lieutenant, 45th N.I. *b.* Rougham, Norfolk, 1 June 1803. Cadet 1820. Arrived in India May 1821. Ensign 16 Jan. 1821. Lieut. 11 July 1823. *d.* Nimach, C.I., 11 Nov. 1831.

Son of Thomas Warriner Baseley, comptroller of customs, St. Lucia, and Susannah Nelson his wife. Brother of Charles Baseley, *q.v.*
Services : Posted as Ensign to 1/26th N.I. Transfd. to 23rd N.I. 11 July 1823; to 45th N.I. (late 1/23rd) May 1824. (? First Burma War; Cachar 1825; Lieut. 45th N.I.) Adjt. 45th N.I. 8 May 1826 till death.

BASSETT, Thomas Turner (1759/60-1818). Colonel, Invalid Est. 20th N.I. *b.* 1759/60. Cadet 1778. Admitted 12 Feb. 1780. Ensign 28 June 1779. Lieut. 16 Feb. 1781. Capt. 7 Jan. 1796. Major 12 Jan. 1803. Lt. Col. 21 Sept. 1804. Col. 4 June 1813. Invalided 31 Aug. 1809. *d.* Serampore, Bengal, 25 Oct. 1818.

A native of Kent. *m.* (before 1793) Clara. (She died Chandernagore 10 Dec 1855, aged 91)
Services : Sailed for India on the *Ceres*, 16 June 1779, aged 19. Comdg. 3rd Coy. Eur. Invalids in 1790. Capt. 2/1st N.I. in 1798. Second Mahratta War; capture of Deig 24 Dec. 1804 (w.); Lt. Col. comdg. 1/8th N.I. Transfd. to 24th N.I. in 1805; to 26th and 20th N.I in 1806.

*****BAST, John** (*d* 1774). Supernumerary Lieutenant, Infantry *bur.* Calcutta 19 Nov. 1774.
Services : N.F.P.
Refs. : Calcutta burial register.

BATE, Samuel (1776- ?). Lieutenant. Infantry. *bapt.* St. Clement Danes, London, 11 Feb. 1776. Cadet 1794. Arrived in India 22 Feb. 1796. Ensign 20 Oct. 1795. Lieut. 15 Mar. 1797. Dismissed by G.C.M. 19 July 1801.

Son of Samuel Bate and Elizabeth his wife.
Services : Posted as Ensign to 3rd Bengal Eur. Regt. 4 May 1796.

BATEMAN, John (1750/51-1799). Lieut. Colonel, 2nd N.I. *b.* 1750/51. Cadet 1768. Admitted 8 July 1769. Ensign 9 Jan. 1769. Lieut. 19 Dec. 1769. Capt. 15 July 1778. Major 2 Feb. 1784. Lt. Col. 1 Mar. 1794. *d.* Bhagulpur, B. & O., 13 July 1799, aged 48.
Services : N.F.P.
Refs. : M.I. in Bhagulpur cemetery.

BATEMAN, John (1790-1819). Lieutenant, 13th N.I. *b.* Gale, co. Kerry, 18 Oct. 1790. Cadet 1807. Arrived in India 17 Sept. 1808. Ensign 4 Oct. 1808. Lieut. 16 Dec. 1814. *d. unm.* Almora, U.P., 22 July 1819, of typhus fever.
3rd and youngest son of Colthurst Bateman, of Bedford House, nr. Listowel, co. Kerry, J.P., and Jane his wife, dau. of Robert Dobson, of Anngrove, co. Cork.
Services : Posted as Ensign to 13th N.I. Intr. & Qmr. 1st Gren. Bn. in 1815. Subsequently Intr. & Qmr. 1/13th N.I. No record of active service.
Refs. : Burke's *Landed Gentry of Ireland*, p. 32, *s.n.* Bateman, of Bartholey, co. Monmouth. *A.J.* 1820, i. 391. Will dated 23 Mar. 1818 ; proved 14 Aug. 1819.

*****BATEMAN, Jonathan.** Ensign, Infantry. Cadet 1807. Never arrived in India. Ensign 18 Sept. 1808.
Note : Not traced in the India Office : included here on the authority of the Philippart MS., which gives both this man and the following.

BATEMAN, Jonathan (1790-1809). Ensign, Infantry. *bapt.* Penrith, Cumberland, 30 May 1790. Cadet 1807. Arrived in India 16 Nov. 1808. Ensign 2 Nov. 1808. *d.* Calcutta 6 Aug. 1809.
Son of William Bateman and Ann his wife, née Dawson. Ward of Thomas Brougham, *q.v.*
Services : N.F.P.

BATEMAN, Thomas Saunders (1761-1821). Major General. 6th L.C. *b.* 1761. Cadet 1778. Arrived in India 2 Oct. 1778. Cornet Dec. 1778. Lieut. 2 Dec. 1778. Capt. 7 Jan. 1796. Major 29 May 1800. Lt. Col. 13 Nov. 1800. Lt. Col. Comdt. 11 Mar. 1805. Col. 25 July 1810. Maj. Gen. 4 June 1813. *d.* London, 29 Apr. 1821, aged 60.
Son of Rev. Dr. Bateman, of Thorns Hall, nr. Sedbergh, Yorks., and his wife, nearly related to the families of Wharton and Otway, Westmorland. Brother of Rev. Samuel Bateman, of Newbiggin Hall, Cumberland, and of Catherine Gillman.

Services : Sailed for India on the *Nassau*, 7 Mar. 1788, aged 16. Capt. 2nd N.C. in 1798. Transfd. as Major to 3rd N.C. 29 May 1800. Fur. 9 Mar. 1800 till 18 Mar. 1805. Transfd. as Lt. Col. to newly-raised 6th N.C. 13 Nov. 1800. Fur. 22 Dec. 1807 till death.

Refs. : *M.M.* xiv. (1802) 278. *G.M.* 1821, i. 477. *A.J.* 1821, i. 641. Will dated 10 Dec. 1807 ; proved 6 Dec. 1821.

BATSON, William (*d.* 1778). Ensign, Infantry. Cadet 1778. Ensign 1778. *d.* Cawnpore 22 Nov. 1778.

Services : N.F.P.

BATTINE, William (1785-1851). Major General, C.B. Artillery. *b.* Steynton, co. Pembroke, 20 Mar. 1785. Cadet 1803. Arrived in India 27 Sept. 1804. Lieut. 26 Aug. 1804. Capt. Lt. 10 June 1808. Capt. 25 Sept. 1817. Major 1 May 1824. Lt. Col. 1 Dec. 1834. Lt. Col. Comdt. 6 July 1843. Maj. Gen. 23 Nov. 1841. *d.* Mian Mir 21 July 1851.

bapt. Steynton 31 Jan. 1787. Son of William Battine and Dorothy his wife. *m.* Calcutta, 7 Dec. 1829, Louisa Eliza Catherine, dau. of Alexander Haig, of Bath. (She died London, 9 Jan. 1893, aged 84.)

Services : Operations in Bundelkhand 1809-10 ; in Oudh 1810-1. Reduction of Kalinjar 1812. Nepal War 1814-5 ; Kalanga ; Jaithak ; Capt. Lt. 6th Coy. 3rd Bn. Art., later comdg. Art. of 2nd Div. Siege and capture of Hathras ; Capt. Lt. 6th Coy. 3rd Bn. Third Mahratta War ; Bde. Maj. Art. of Centre Div. Grand Army. Fur. 14 Mar. 1821 till 20 May 1825. Siege and capture of Bhurtpore ; Major comdg. 4th Bn. Art. (India medal, with clasps for Nepal and Bhurtpore). Apptd. Principal Comy. of Ord. 23 Jan. 1835. Fur. p.a. 3 Mar. 1843. Bdr., 2 cl., 26 Apr. 1850 ; comdg. at Barrackpore 29 Apr. 1850 ; at Ambala Nov. 1850 ; Divl. Staff, Punjab Div., 7 Jan. 1851.

Refs. : *De Rhé Philipe. A.J.* N.S. ii. 83. *G.M.* 1851, ii. 553.

BATTLEY, Richard Edmond (1802-1837). Captain, 22nd N.I. *bapt.* co. Dublin 30 July 1802. Cadet 1819. Arrived in India 22 Jan. 1821. Ensign 8 July 1820. Lieut. 11 Nov. 1823. Capt. 20 June 1836. *d. unm.* Landaur 21 Sept. 1837.

Eldest son of Thomas Cade Battley, of Willbrook, barr.-at-law, and Belinda his wife, dau. of Rev. Richard Chappell Grange, of Sallymount, co. Wicklow. His sister *m.* George Larkins, *q.v.*

Services : Posted as Ensign to 1/10th N.I. Transfd. as Lieut. to 2nd N.I. 11 July 1823 ; to 22nd N.I. (late 2/2nd) May 1824. Intr. & Qmr. 22nd N.I. 15 June 1826. Fur. 3 July 1829 till 22 Jan. 1833.

THE BENGAL ARMY, 1758-1834   105

Shekhawat expedn. ; Lieut. 22nd N.I. 2nd in comd. 3rd Local Horse 20 Apr. 1835.
Refs. : Burke's *Landed Gentry of Ireland,* p. 35, *s.n.* Battley, of Belvedere Hall, co. Wicklow.

BAUGH, James (1787-1812). Lieutenant, Pension Est. 24th N.I. *bapt.* Ludlow, Salop, 19 Nov. 1787. Cadet 1804. Arrived in India 30 Sept. 1805. Ensign 30 Aug. 1805. Lieut. 31 Aug. 1805. Pensioned 12 Dec. 1809. *d.* Calcutta 18 Nov. 1812.
Son of Robert Walker Baugh (? who was son of Thomas Baugh, of Broad St., Ludlow).
Services : Posted as Lieut. to 24th N.I. in 1806. No record of active service.

BAUGH, Thomas (*d.* 1789). Captain, Engineers. Cadet (?). Ensign (?). Lieut. (?). Capt. 13 May 1786. *d.* Calcutta 18 Aug. 1789.
Services : N.F.P.
Refs. : G.M. 1789, ii. 1147.

BAUMGARDT, Francis Robert (1791-1821). Lieutenant, 2nd N.I. *b.* Calcutta 2 Feb. 1791. Cadet 1805. Arrived in India 19 Sept. 1806. Ensign 1 Oct. 1806. Lieut. 24 Jan. 1809. *d.* Banda, C.P., 24 June 1821, of cholera.
bapt. Calcutta 12 Mar. 1791. Son of John Peter Baumgardt, and Johanna his wife.
Services : Posted as Ensign to 2nd N.I. and served throughout with that Regt. (? Reduction of Kalinjar 1812. Operations in Baghelkhand 1813 ; Entauri ; Lieut. 2/2nd N.I.) Lieut. 2/2nd N.I. in 1815 ; 1/2nd N.I. at death.
Refs. : A.J. 1822, i. 184.

BAWDWIN, Thomas (1740/41-1770). Captain, Infantry. *b.* 1740/41. Cadet 1762. Ensign (?). Lieut. 27 Oct. 1765. Capt. 5 Apr. 1769. *d.* Chittagong 16 Sept. 1770.
A native of London.
Services : Sailed for India on the *Hector* 25 Mar. 1762, aged 21. N.F.P.

BAYLDON, Richard (1780-1844). Bt. Major. 71st N.I. *bapt.* Royston, Yorks., 25 July 1789. Cadet 1806. Arrived in India 25 Nov. 1807. Ensign 19 Oct. 1807. Lieut. 26 Apr. 1813. Capt. 13 May 1825. Bt. Major 10 Jan. 1837. Retired 1 Jan. 1838. *d.* in India 19 Oct. 1844.
Son of Richard Bayldon, of Royston.

Services : Barasat C.C. for 8 mos. Posted as Ensign to 6th N.I.
Adjt. 1/6th N.I. 1 Nov. 1814. Nepal War 1814-5 ; Lieut. 1/6th
N.I., in 2nd Div. Bde. Major to troops on E. frontier 20 Aug. 1822.
Transfd. to 3rd N.I. (late 1/6th) May 1824. First Burma War ;
Assam 1824-5 ; Rangpur. D.A.A.G. 7 June 1825. Posted to
newly-raised 3rd Extra Regt. (became 71st N.I. in 1828) in 1825.
A.A.G. 15 May 1830. A.A.G., Saugor Div., 11 Jan. 1835 ; subsequently A.A.G. Benares Div.

BAYLE, Henry Dundas (1778-1803). Lieutenant, Artillery. *b.*
Edinburgh 25 Oct. 1778. Cadet 1794. Arrived in India 8 Mar.
1797. Fireworker 27 June 1797. Lieut. 20 Feb. 1802. *d.*
24 Jan. 1803, of a wound received at the siege of Sasni on 8 Jan.
bapt. 29 Oct. 1778. Son of John Bayle and Margaret Bigot his
wife.
Services : Fourth Mysore War ; siege and capture of Seringapatam ; Lieut. F. 3rd Coy. 1st Bn. Art. Operations in Jumna
Doab 1802-3 ; siege of Sasni ; Lieut. 4th Coy. 2nd Bn. (s.w.—both
legs shot off on 8 Jan. 1803).
Refs. : S.M. 1804, p. 158. Will dated Etyah 13 Nov. 1802 ;
proved 15 June 1803.

BAYLEY, Brook William (1788-1816). Lieutenant, 18th N.I.
bapt. London 6 Apr. 1788. Cadet 1804. Arrived in India 13 May
1806. Ensign 27 Mar. 1806. Lieut. 18 Feb. 1808. *d.* Cuttack
5 Oct. 1816.
Son of John Bayley.
Services : Posted as Lieut. to 18th N.I. Nepal War 1816 ;
Harriharpur ; Lieut. 1/18th N.I., in 1st Bde., Right Column.
Cuttack insurrection 1816

BAYLEY, William (1788-1826 ?). Captain, Pension Est. 34th N.I.
bapt. Rotherhithe, Surrey, 4 May 1788. Cadet 1805. Arrived in
India 25 July 1807. Ensign 12 July 1807. Lieut. 23 Jan. 1810.
Capt. 1 May 1824. Pensioned 1 July 1825. *d.* 1826 ?
Son of James Bayley and Mary his wife.
Note : His name disappears from the *E.I.R.* after Oct. 1826.
Services : Posted as Ensign to 17th N.I. Nepal War 1814-5 ;
Lieut. 1/17th N.I., in 2nd Div. Transfd. as Capt. to 35th N.I.
(late 2/17th) May 1824. Subsequently transfd. to 34th N.I.

BAYLISS, William (1787-1806). Lieutenant, 5th N.I. *bapt.* New
Brentford, Middlesex, 3 June 1787. Cadet 1804. Arrived in
India 21 July 1806. Ensign 7 Nov. 1805. Lieut. 15 Aug. 1806.
d. Midnapore, Bengal, 15 Oct. 1806.

THE BENGAL ARMY, 1758-1834

Son of William Bayliss.
Services : Posted as Lieut. to 1/5th N.I. No record of active service.

BAZELY, Francis Ruddle (1806-1857). Lieut. Colonel, Artillery. *bapt.* St. James's, Dover, 30 Nov. 1806. Cadet 1822. Arrived in India 26 Mar. 1824. 2nd Lieut. 6 June 1823. Lieut. 28 Sept. 1827. Capt. 1 Mar. 1841. Major 23 Jan. 1854. Lt. Col. 25 June 1857. *d.* Lucknow 25 Sept. 1857 : kld. in action.
3rd son of Capt. Henry Bazely, R.N., and Mary his 2nd wife, dau. of Francis Ruddle, of Queen's Sq., Bloomsbury. *m.* Meerut, 11 Apr. 1835, Susan Denson, of co. Chester. (She died London 21 Aug. 1891, aged 83.) Addiscombe Cadet 10 Aug. 1821 till 6 June 1823.
Services : Siege and capture of Bhurtpore ; 2nd Lieut. 4th Bn. Foot Art. (India medal). Fur. s.c. 12 July 1827 till 1 June 1830. Comy. of Ord. 26 Oct. 1838. Dy. Principal Comy. of Ord. 8 Aug. 1845. Principal Comy. of Ord. 30 Apr. 1855. Indian mutiny ; first relief of Lucknow (kld.).
Refs. : Howard & Crisp, xvii. 125 (with portrait). *G.M.* 1858, i. 224. Will dated 26 Nov. 1853 ; proved 15 July 1858.

BAZETT, Charles Young (1807-1879). Lieut. Colonel. 9th L.C. *b.* St. Pancras, London, 12 Sept. 1807. Cadet 1826. Arrived in India 5 Oct. 1827. Cornet 18 Jan. 1828. Lieut. 29 Nov. 1831. Capt. 28 Oct. 1842. Bt. Major 20 June 1854. Retired 18 July 1855. Hon. Lt. Col. 21 Sept. 1855. *d.* his residence, Springfield, Reading, 20 Sept. 1879.
Son of Richard Bazett, of Broad St., London, East India agent. Brother of Henry Young Bazett, *q.v. m.* Cheltenham, 5 Sept. 1838, Harriet, widow of William Trigge Garrett, *q.v.* (She died 18 Nov. 1887, on her 80th birthday.)
Services : Posted as Cornet to 9th L.C. 25 Nov. 1828, and remained with that Regt. throughout his service. Actg. Intr. & Qmr. 23 July 1833. Fur. p.a. 31 July 1837 till 6 Sept. 1839. Campaign in Sind 1843 ; Miani ; Hyderabad (Medal).
Refs. : A.J. N.S. xxvii. 123. *The Times,* 23 Sept. 1879.

BAZETT, Henry Young (1810-1842). Lieutenant, 5th L.C. *b.* London 24 Sept. 1810. Cadet 1829. Arrived in India 13 Sept. 1830. Cornet 13 Sept. 1830. Lieut. 5 Aug. 1839. *d.* 12 Jan. 1842 : kld. in action in the Jagdalak Pass during the retreat from Kabul.
Son of Richard Bazett, of Broad St., London, East India agent. Brother of Charles Young Bazett, *q.v. m.* Cawnpore, 8 Mar. 1838,

Louisa Colebrook, youngest dau. of John Bruce, Bengal Medical Est.
Services : Cornet d.d. 9th L.C. 30 Sept. 1830. Posted as Cornet to 5th L.C. 9 June 1836. First Afghan War 1840-2 ; defeat of Ghilzais at Karatu 5 Aug. 1841 (w.) ; Lieut. 5th L.C.
Refs. : M.I. St. Peter's, Fort William, Bengal.

BEAGHAN, Francis (1777-1803). Lieutenant, Artillery. *b.* Ruthin, co. Denbigh, 7 Mar. 1777. Cadet 1793. Arrived in India 16 Sept. 1793. Fireworker 12 June 1793. Lieut. 6 Aug. 1801. *d.* 20 Dec. 1803, of wounds received in action at Agra on 10 Oct.
bapt. Ruthin, 19 June 1777. Son of George Edmund Beaghan.
Services : Second Mahratta War ; action before Agra 10 Oct. 1803 (s.w.) ; Lieut. Art. " The intrepidity and courage evinced by Lieutenant Beaghan, of the artillery, employed in the assault, calls for his Excellency's warmest approbation and thanks."
Refs. : Stubbs, i. 218. Undated Will, written at Agra ; proved in 1804.

BEAN, John Dickson Dyke (1801-1847). Major, 23rd N.I. *bapt.* Littlington, Sussex, 10 Oct. 1801. Cadet 1817. Admitted 5 Sept. 1818. Ensign 26 Aug. 1818. Lieut. 1 Aug. 1818. Capt. 20 Jan. 1831. Major 1 Apr. 1846. *d.* Lucknow 8 Aug. 1847.
2nd son of John Bean, of Clapham House, Sussex. *m.* 1st, Miss M. Elias. *m.* 2nd, Almora, 26 July 1826, Miss Maria Faithful. (*See also* Charles Chester, Thomas Robert Fell, and John Moule.)
Services : Posted as Lieut. to 2/4th N.I. Intr. & Qmr. 23rd N.I. (late 2/4th) 17 June 1824 till 3 Feb. 1829. Siege and capture of Bhurtpore. First Afghan War ; Kalat ; Ghazni ; comdg. Shah Shuja's 1st Regt. of Inf. (Medal). Fur. s.c. 1 Dec. 1841 till 17 Oct. 1843. Postmaster at Dinapore 14 Jan. 1846. Durani, 3 cl. (*Lond. Gaz.* 1 Feb. 1842).
Refs. : G.M. 1847, ii. 558. Will dated 12 Aug. 1826 ; proved 7 Aug. 1848.

BEARDMORE, Samuel (*d.* 1779). Lieutenant, Infantry. Cadet 1772. Ensign 5 July 1776. Lieut. 26 June 1778. *d.* in India 16 Oct. 1779.
Services : N.F.P.

BEATSON, Alexander Campbell (1799-1832). Captain, 2nd N.I. *b.* Burntisland, co. Fife, 20 Oct. 1799. Cadet 1817. Admitted 5 Sept. 1818. Ensign 4 Mar. 1818. Lieut. 1 Aug. 1818. Capt. 30 Sept. 1830. *d.* Dinapore 11 Aug. 1832.
Of Rossend, co. Fife. 2nd son and heir of Robert Beatson, of

THE BENGAL ARMY, 1758-1834

Kilrie, Lieut. h.p. 76th Foot, J.P. co. Fife (who was elder brother of Maj. Gen. Alexander Beatson, Govr. of St. Helena (*D.N.B.*)), and Jane his wife, only child of Murdoch Campbell, of Rossend Castle, co. Fife. Brother of Robert Wedderburn Beatson, *q.v.* *m.* 22 Dec. 1831, Eliza, 3rd dau. of John Baird, of Camelon.

Services : Posted as Lieut. to 2/1st N.I. Intr. & Qmr. 2/1st N.I. 25 July 1821. Transfd. to 2nd N.I. (late 1/1st) May 1824. Intr. & Qmr. 2nd N.I. 17 June 1824 till 15 June 1825. Adjt. 10th Extra Regt. 21 May 1825 till its reduction on 1 Apr. 1826. Fur. p.a. 9 Aug. 1829 till 19 May 1832. No record of active service.

Refs. : Burke's *Landed Gentry*, 4th edn., p. 77, *s.n.* Beatson, of Kilrie, co. Fife

*BEATSON, Alexander David (1807-1824). 2nd Lieutenant, Engineers. *bapt.* Frant, Sussex, 7 Apr. 1807. Cadet 1824. Never arrived in India. 2nd Lieut. 17 June 1824. *d. unm.* Chatham 7 Jan. 1825.

Eldest son of Maj. Gen. Alexander Beatson, Madras Est., of Knowle Farm, and Henley, Sussex, Govr. of St. Helena (*D.N.B.*), and Davidson his wife, 2nd dau. of David Reid. Brother of Theodore Francis Broughton Beatson, *q.v.*, and cousin-german of William Fergusson Beatson, *q.v.* Addiscombe Cadet 1822-4.

Services : Died whilst under instruction at Chatham.

Refs. : Burke's *Landed Gentry*, 4th edn., p. 77, *s.n.* Beatson, of Kilrie, co. Fife. *G.M.* 1825, i. 92. *A.J.* xix. 216.

BEATSON, Robert Wedderburn (1801-1848). Captain. 72nd N.I. *b.* Burntisland, co. Fife, 12 July 1801. Cadet 1818. Admitted 10 Feb. 1820. Ensign 10 Aug. 1819. Lieut. 1 Jan. 1821. Capt. 29 July 1835. Invalided 29 Oct. 1838. Retired 1 June 1845. *d.s.p.* 11 Dec. 1848.

3rd son of Robert Beatson, of Kilrie, and Jane his wife. Brother of William Fergusson Beatson, *q.v.*, and cousin-german to Alexander David Beatson, *q.v.* *m.* Carphin House. co. Fife, 5 Jan. 1831, Helen Hay, 2nd dau. of John Raitt, of Carphin.

Services : Posted to 11th N.I. Offg. Adjt. Eur. Invalids at Chunar. Transfd. to 7th N.I. ; to 13th N.I. (late 1/7th) May 1824. Adjt. 13th N.I. 4 Nov. 1824. Bde. Maj. at Cuttack 11 Apr. 1825. Dir. of telegraphs 26 Feb. 1827. 2nd Bn. N.I. Invalids at Chunar 15 July 1828. Fur. s.c. 18 May 1829 till 2 June 1831. Adjt. 72nd N.I. 11 July 1832 till 7 Feb. 1835. Fur. p.a. 4 Mar. 1842 till 23 June 1843. No record of active service.

Refs. : Burke's *Landed Gentry*, 4th edn., p. 77, *s.n.* Beatson, of Kilrie, co. Fife.

BEATSON, Theodore Francis Broughton (1809-1865). Colonel. 4th European L.C. *bapt.* St. Helena 6 Sept. 1809. Cadet 1825. Arrived in India 22 Oct. 1826. Cornet 27 June 1826. Lieut. 29 Aug. 1832. Capt. 14 Oct. 1844. Major 23 July 1858. Lt. Col. 1861. Retired 31 Dec. 1861. Hon. Col. 31 Dec. 1861. *d.* Dieppe, France, 16 Sept. 1865, aged 56.

2nd son of Maj. Gen. Alexander Beatson (*D.N.B.*) and Davidson his wife, 2nd dau. of David Reid, comr. of H.M. customs for Scotland. Brother of Alexander David Beatson, *q.v.* *m.* Chelsea, 22 June 1843, Louisa, his cousin-german, only dau. of Stephen Reid, *q.v.*

Services : Posted as Cornet to 6th L.C. Transfd. as Cornet to 10th L.C. 10 May 1827. Adjt. 10th L.C. 8 Apr. 1834 till 24 Oct. 1840. Leave to N.S.W. and Cape 27 Nov. 1840. First Afghan War 1842 ; Bt. Capt. 10th L.C., with Gen. Pollock's force (Medal). Fur. p.a. 11 Feb. 1843 till 24 Nov. 1843. Gwalior campaign ; Maharajpur ; Bt. Capt. 10th L.C. (Bronze star). Transfd. to newly-raised 4th European L.C. 23 July 1858. Fur. 1859 till retirement.

Refs. : Burke's *Landed Gentry*, 4th edn., p. 77, *s.n.* Beatson, of Kilrie, co. Fife. *A.J.* 3S. i. 331. *G.M.* 1865, ii. 534. *The Times*, 20 Sept. 1865.

BEATSON, William Fergusson (1804-1872). Major General, K.S.F. 4th European Inf. *b.* Rossend Castle, co. Fife, 25 June 1804. Cadet 1819. Admitted 11 Dec. 1820. Ensign 13 July 1820. Lieut. 11 July 1823. Capt. 26 Jan. 1837. Major 18 July 1848. Lt. Col. 15 Nov. 1853. Col. 26 May 1864. Maj. Gen. 8 Jan. 1865. *d.* the Vicarage, New Swindon, Wilts., 4 Feb. 1872.

4th and youngest son of Robert Beatson, of Kilrie, and Jane his wife. Brother of Alexander Campbell Beatson, *q.v.* *m.* Kalpi, U.P., 12 Feb. 1840, Margaret Marian, youngest dau. of Richard Humfrays (or Humphreys), *q.v.* (*See also* William Stuart Beatson and Gavin Young.)

Services : Posted as Ensign to 2/25th N.I. Transfd. to 27th N.I. ; to 54th N.I. (late 2/27th) May 1824. 2nd Gren. Bn. 5 Sept. 1825. Adjt. Bareilly Provl. Bn. 17 Jan. 1826. Adjt. 54th N.I. 14 Mar. 1827. Leave s.c. 1 yr. to N.S.W. 29 July 1828. Fur. 9 Sept. 1832 till 9 July 1837. Served with British Legion in Spain 1835-6 (s.w.), when he held a Commission as Lt. Col. in the service of the Queen of Spain. Permitted to accept and wear Cross, 1st Cl., National and Mily. Order of San Fernando, for actions on 28 May 1836 and 6 July 1836. (*Lond. Gaz.* 12 Sept. 1837.) D.J.A.G. To comd. Bundelkhand Legion. Capture of Jigni and Chirgaon. Against the Hill tribes in Sind 1844-5 ; reduction of Trakki Fort. Bdr. comdg. Nizam's Cav. Div. 4 Mar. 1847 till Mar. 1851. Siege

THE BENGAL ARMY, 1758-1834

and capture of Rai Mhow Nov.-Dec. 1850 ; of Dharur fort Jan.-Feb. 1851. Transfd. to newly-raised 3rd Bengal Eur. Regt. 15 Nov. 1853 ; to 65th N.I. Dec. 1853 ; to 43rd N.I. Dec. 1855. Crimea 1854-5 ; organized the Bashibazouks. Local rank of Maj. Gen. in Turkey 16 Mar. 1855. Gold medal (*Nishan-Iftihar*) from Sultan for services on the Danube. With Heavy Bde. at Balaclava and Inkermann (Medal with 3 clasps). Mutiny campaign ; raised two Regts. of "Beatson's Horse" (Medal). Fur. 1859-64. To comd. Allahabad Div. 3 Oct. 1866 ; Ambala Div. 1869. K.S.F. 12 Sept. 1837.

Refs. : Burke's *Landed Gentry*, 4th edn., p. 77, *s.n.* Beatson, of Kilrie, co. Fife. *D.I.B. Boase. The Times*, 9 Feb. 1872. *I.N.* No. 1, p. 12. *Sketches of some distinguished Anglo-Indians*, by Col. W. F. B. Laurie. *Hist. of the Hyderabad Contingent*, by Col. R. G. Burton.

BEATSON, William Stuart (1788-1837). Lieut. Colonel, 7th L.C. *b.* Stevenston, co. Ayr, 18 Oct. 1788. Cadet 1804. Arrived in India 16 May 1806. Cornet 3 Apr. 1806. Lieut. 1 Sept. 1818. Capt. 13 May 1825. Major 3 May 1829. Lt. Col. 12 Apr. 1836. *d.* at sea, 13 Apr. 1837, on board the *Robarts* on his passage to England.

Son of Lieut. Beatson, of Glasmount (related to the family of Beatson, of Kilrie), and Janet Stewart his wife. *m.* Dinapore, 16 Jan. 1819, Emma, 5th dau. of Richard Humfrays (or Humphreys), *q.v.* (*See also* William Fergusson Beatson and Gavin Young.)

Services : Went out to India in the Fleet with the expedition against the Cape of Good Hope, under Lt. Gen. David Baird 1805-6, and was on actual service at the Cape. Posted as Cornet to 1st N.C. Operations in Bundelkhand 1810-1. Actg. Adjt., Intr. & Qmr., 1st N.C. in 1816. A.D.C. to Maj.-Gen. Sir Thomas Brown, *q.v.*, 1817-8. Third Mahratta War ; D.A.A.G., Centre Div., Lieut. 1st N.C., with official rank of Capt. Posted as Capt. to 10th L.C. 13 May 1825. Siege and capture of Bhurtpore ; D.A.G. of the Army, Capt. 10th L.C., with official rank of Major. A.G. of the Army, with official rank of Lieut. Col., 28 Jan. 1832. Comy. Gen., with official rank of Lt. Col., 29 Nov. 1833. Posted as Lt. Col. to comd. 7th L.C. 12 Apr. 1836.

Refs. : Burke's *Landed Gentry*, 4th edn., p. 76, *s.n.* Beatson, of Kilrie, co. Fife. *G.M.* 1837, ii. 438.

BEATY, Francis (1802-1854). Major, Invalid Est. 1st European L.I. *b.* Stoke Damerel, Devon, 30 Aug. 1802. Cadet 1820. Admitted 31 May 1821. Ensign 13 Jan. 1821. Lieut. 11 July

1823. Capt. 2 July 1833. Major 6 Aug. 1843. Invalided 22 Nov. 1843. d. Mussoorie 27 July 1854.

Son of Francis Beaty, Purser R.N. (who was Purser of H.M.S. *Conqueror* at the battle of Trafalgar). Brother of Henry Beaty, *q.v.*
Services : Posted as Ensign to 1/8th N.I. Transfd. as Lieut. to Bengal Eur. Regt. 11 July 1823. Fur. s.c. 24 Dec. 1824 till 28 Nov. 1827. First Afghan War 1839 ; capture of Ghazni ; Capt. 1st Bengal Eur. Regt. (Medal).

BEATY, Henry (1804-1850). Captain, 62nd N.I. *b.* Stoke Damerel, Devon, 10 July 1804. Cadet 1821. Arrived in India 10 Nov. 1822. Ensign 16 Dec. 1822. Lieut. 13 May 1825. Capt. 30 Mar. 1841. *d.* at sea, 2 Feb. 1850, on board the *Bucephalus*.

Son of Francis Beaty, Purser R.N. Brother of Francis Beaty, *q.v.*
Services : Posted as Ensign to 31st N.I. Intr. & Qmr. 62nd N.I. (late 2/31st) 2 Mar. 1825. First Burma War ; Lieut. 62nd N.I. Fur. s.c. 22 Feb. 1826 till 11 Aug. 1828. Adjt. 62nd N.I. 22 Oct. 1840 till 27 Aug. 1841. P.W.D. in C.P. 27 Feb. 1843. Fur. 1850.

Refs. : *G.M.* 1850, ii. 108.

BEAUCHAMP, Willoughby George (1800-1844). Lieutenant, Pension Est. Bengal European Regt. *b.* Forthampton, Gloucs., 23 Feb. 1800. Cadet 1817. Ensign (?). Lieut. 1 Aug. 1818. Pensioned 27 May 1824. *d.* Monghyr, B. & O., 10 Nov. 1844.

5th son of William Henry Beauchamp-Proctor, of Forthampton (who was youngest son of Sir William Beauchamp-Proctor, 1st Bart., of Langley Park, Norfolk), and Frances Mary his wife, dau. of Rev. William Davie, prebendary of Exeter. *m.* Ellen. (She died Patna 22 Sept. 1857).

Services : Posted as Lieut. to Bengal Eur. Regt. No record of active service.

Refs. : Burke's *Peerage*, 1923, p. 230, *s.n.* Proctor-Beauchamp, Bart., of Langley Park, Norfolk. *I.M.* 16 Nov. 1857, p. 785.

BEAUCLERK, Ferdinand (1811-1829). Cadet, Cavalry. Unposted. *b.* London 19 Feb. 1811. Cadet 1828. *d.* Cawnpore 5 Oct. 1829.

4th and youngest son of Charles George Beauclerk, of St. Leonard's Forest, Horsham, Sussex (who was grandson of Lord Sydney Beauclerk, vice-chamberlain to George II.), and Emily Charlotte his wife, 2nd dau. of William Ogilvie.

Services : Attached as Cadet to 3rd L.C. at Cawnpore. Actg. Cornet d.d. 3rd L.C. 13 July 1829.

Refs. : Burke's *Landed Gentry*, 2nd edn., p. 73, *s.n.* Beauclerk, of St. Leonard's Forest, Horsham. Burke's *Peerage*, 1923, p. 1938, *s.n.* Duke of St. Albans.

BEAUMONT, Ernest Charles Francis (1804-1850). Captain. 32nd N.I. *b.* London 15 June 1804. Cadet 1825. Arrived in India 28 June 1826. Ensign 13 Feb. 1826. Lieut. 16 Oct. 1834. Capt. 24 Jan. 1845. Retired 16 Aug. 1849. *d.* London 23 Aug. 1850. 2nd son of John Thomas Barber Beaumont.
Services : Ensign d.d. 4th Extra Regt. 8 July 1826. Posted as Ensign to 32nd N.I. (? Shekhawat expedn. 1834.) Intr. & Qmr. 32nd N.I. 7 Apr. 1835 till 9 Dec. 1839. Leave to Cape 21 Dec. 1840 till 26 Dec. 1842. Fur. p.a. 6 Mar. 1843 till 1845.
Refs. : G.M. 1850, ii. 448.

BEAVAN, Francis (1810-1842). Lieutenant, 56th N.I. *b.* London 15 Nov. 1810. Cadet 1827. Arrived in India 4 July 1828. Ensign 6 Mar. 1828. Lieut. 8 Oct. 1839. *d.* Hong Kong 8 Nov. 1842.
Son of Hugh Beavan, of Marylebone St., Piccadilly, silversmith, and Anne his wife. Brother of Robert Beavan, *q.v.*
Services : Ensign d.d. 42nd N.I. 31 July 1828. Posted as Ensign to 56th N.I. 4 Nov. 1828. Transfd. to 66th N.I. 2 Aug. 1832. Retransfd. to 56th N.I. Posted to 2nd Bengal Vols. 1 Feb. 1842. First China War ; arrived in China with 2nd Vol. Bn. in June 1842 (Medal).

BEAVAN, Robert (1809-?). Captain. 31st N.I. *b.* London 18 Sept. 1809. Cadet 1825. Arrived in India 7 July 1826. Ensign 15 Mar. 1826. Lieut. 25 May 1829. Capt. 17 Aug. 1839. Dismissed by G.C.M. 3 Apr. 1844.
Son of Hugh Beavan, of London, solicitor (*sic*), and Anne his wife. Brother of Francis Beavan, *q.v. m.* 26 Mar. 1840, Cecilia, dau. of Rev. Henry Drury, of Harrow.
Services : Posted as Ensign to 31st N.I. Fur. from Java 14 Nov. 1831 till 13 Nov. 1834. Fur. s.c. 7 Feb. 1837 till 10 Sept. 1840. Orderly Officer at Addiscombe 25 July 1838. No record of active service.
Refs. : A.J. N.S. xxxii. 78. *I.M.* No. 14, p. 427.

BEAVOIR, W. (*d.* 1773). Ensign, Infantry. Cadet 1771. Ensign 21 Jan. 1773. *d.* Madras Sept. 1773.
Services : N.F.P.

BEAZLY or BEESLY, George (1760/61-1782). Lieutenant, Infantry. *b.* Ireland 1760/61. Apptd. Cadet on 7 Dec. 1780, aged 20. Ensign 6 July 1781. Lieut. 8 Oct. 1782. *d.* Cawnpore 11 Nov. 1782.
Services : Sailed for India on the *Chapman* 13 Mar. 1781, aged 20. N.F.P.

BEBB, formerly LAWRELL, Horatio (1805-1881). Bt. Captain. 3rd L.C. b. London 21 Oct. 1805. Cadet 1823. Cornet 1 May 1824. Lieut. 13 May 1825. Bt. Capt. 1 May 1839. Retired 8 Sept. 1839. d. Edinburgh 1 Oct. 1881.

Of Donnington Grove, Newbury, Berks., and 13 Gloucester Pl., Portman Sq., London. Son of James Lawrell, of Farnborough. Assumed the surname of Bebb in lieu of his patronymic Lawrell, by R.L. 7 June 1850 (*Lond. Gaz.* p. 1599), in compliance with the Will of his uncle, John Bebb, a Director E.I.C.

Services : Posted as Cornet to 3rd L.C. Siege and capture of Bhurtpore ; Lieut. 3rd L.C. (India medal). Operations against the Kols 1832. Fur. 8 Mar. 1838 till retirement.

Refs. : Burke's *Visitation of Seats and Arms*, 1S. ii. 67. *The Times*, 4 Oct. 1881.

*BECHEATON, John (1795/96-1811). Ensign, 9th N.I. b. 1795/96. Cadet (?). Ensign (?). d. Buxar, 31 Jan. 1811, aged 15.

Note : Not traced at the India Office : his name is included here on the authority of the following M.I. in Buxar burial-ground (see *B* : *P.P.* xii. 120) : "Sacred/to the Memory/of Ensign/John Becheaton/of the 9th Regiment Bengal Native Infantry/who died at Buxar on the 31st January/1811. Aged 15 years./This Monument is erected/by his Brother Officers as a mark/of their affection and esteem."

BECHER, Sir Arthur Mitford (1816-1887). General, K.C.B. 61st N.I. b. 7 May 1816. Cadet 1832. Arrived in India 2 Jan. 1834. Ensign 20 Oct. 1833. Lieut. 16 July 1839. Capt. 11 Apr. 1845. Bt. Major 3 Apr. 1846. Bt. Lt. Col. 7 June 1849. Lt. Col. 18 Feb. 1863. Bt. Col. 28 Nov. 1854. Maj. Gen. 29 Apr. 1861. Lt. Gen. 25 June 1870. Gen. 2 June 1877. d. St. Faith's Mede, Winchester, 5 Oct. 1887.

bapt. Benares 27 July 1816. 6th son of George Becher, *q.v.*, and Harriot his 2nd wife. Brother of Septimus Harding Becher, *q.v.* m. Simla, 4 Sept. 1841, Frances Anne, 3rd dau. of Capt. M. W. Ford. (She died 21 Aug. 1888, aged 64.). Addiscombe Cadet 5 Aug. 1831 till 11 June 1833.

Services : Ensign d.d. 33rd N.I. 8 Jan. 1834. Posted to 61st N.I. 24 May 1834. D.A.Q.M.G., 2 cl., 1 Dec. 1838. do., 1 cl., 12 Jan. 1842. First Afghan War 1839 ; Ghazni (Medal). Leave to Cape for 2 yrs. 11 Feb. 1843. A.Q.M.G. 13 Dec. 1844. First Sikh War ; Mudki ; Ferozshahr ; Sobraon ; Capt. 61st N.I., A.Q.M.G. (Medal with 2 clasps). Hon. A.D.C. to G.G. 12 Jan. 1848. Second Sikh War ; Multan ; Gujerat ; Major 61st N.I., A.Q.M.G. (Medal with clasp). D.Q.M.G. 8 Feb. 1850. Q.M.G. 11 June 1852 till 1863.

Indian Mutiny ; Q.M.G. of Army before Delhi (s.w. on 19 June 1857) (Medal with clasp). Permitted to reckon 15 mos. leave as service for pension. Comdd. Sirhind Div. 25 Nov. 1864 till 1869. Fur. 1869 till death. C.B. 21 Jan. 1858. K.C.B. 24 May 1873. Good service Pension 11 Jan. 1865.
Refs. : D.I.B. Boase. *The Times*, 8 Oct. 1887, p. 6.

BECHER, Charles (1776/77-1842). Cornet, Cavalry. Subsequently B.C.S. *b.* 1776/77. Cadet 1793. Arrived in India 25 Sept. 1794. Cornet 1 Dec. 1794. Resigned 25 Nov. 1795. *d.* Nice, France, 16 July 1842, aged 65.

m. 1st, Berhampore, 9 Jan. 1800, Mary Penneck, dau. of Henry Read, *q.v.* (She died 10 Aug. 1805, aged 23.) *m.* 2nd, Calcutta, 1807, Miss Charlotte Humfrays. Father of Charles Grant Becher, *q.v.*, Samuel John Becher, *q.v.*, and Harriet Jane, wife of James Colley Tudor, *q.v.*

Services : Appointed a Writer, B.C.S., 26 Sept. 1795. Became a Senior Merchant. Apptd. Commercial Resident at Radnagore 6 Feb. 1829. Retired 1 May 1836.

Refs. : A.J. N.S. xxxviii. 422.

BECHER, Charles Grant (1811-1859). Bt. Lieut. Colonel, 5th European L.C. *b.* Calcutta 20 Jan. 1811. Cadet 1828. Arrived in India 27 Aug. 1829. Cornet 27 Aug. 1829. Lieut. 12 Nov. 1842. Capt. 10 Oct. 1851. Bt. Major 10 Oct. 1851. Bt. Lt. Col. 28 Nov. 1854. *d.* Indore 2 Apr. 1859.

Son of Charles (Grant) Becher, B.C.S., Commercial Resident at Radnagore, *q.v.*, and Charlotte his 2nd wife. Brother of Samuel John Becher, *q.v. m.* (?). Ed. Sherborne ; left in 1828.

Services : To do duty with 5th L.C. 22 Sept. 1831. Actg. Cornet 27 Oct. 1831, having been more than 2 yrs. in India. To do duty with 4th L.C. 27 Feb. 1832 ; do 5th L.C. 3 Jan. 1835. Offg. Adjt. G.G.B.G. 4 Jan. 1836. To 1st L.C. 9 June 1836. 1st Cav., Oudh Auxy. Force, 27 Dec. 1837. Adjt. do. 19 Feb. 1838. (Became 6th Irreg. Cav. 23 Dec. 1840.) 2nd in comd. 8th Irreg. Cav. 15 Mar. 1842. First Afghan War 1842 ; Tezin ; Kabul ; Istalif ; Cornet 1st L.C. (Medal). Transfd. to 5th L.C. 11 Dec. 1842. On service in Bundelkhand with 8th Irreg. Cav. 20 Dec. 1842. Gwalior campaign ; Paniar ; 2nd in comd. 8th Irreg. Cav. (Bronze star). To comd. 8th Irreg. Cav. 27 June 1845. First Sikh War ; Sobraon (horse w.) ; comdg. 8th Irreg. Cav. (Medal). Posted to newly-raised 5th Eur. L.C. in 1858. Mutiny campaign ; against the rebels in Malwa and C.I. Oct. 1858 till Apr. 1859 (Medal).

Refs. : G.M. 1859, ii. 89. *The Times*, 18 May 1859. V.B.G.

BECHER, George (1780-1837). Colonel, 4th L.C. b. 1 Sept. 1780. Cadet 1794. Admitted 2 Nov. 1795. Cornet 6 Nov. 1795. Lieut. 29 May 1800. Capt. 27 Feb. 1812. Major 1 Sept. 1818. Lt. Col. 1 May 1824. Col. 3 May 1829. d. at sea, 15 Nov. 1837, on board the *Reliance*.

m. 1st, Patna, 10 Aug. 1807, Miss Harriet Barclay. Father of George Richard Prendergast Becher, q.v., and of Henry Murray Becher, q.v. m. 2nd, Harriot Gildart. Father of Arthur Mitford Becher, q.v., and of Septimus Harding Becher, q.v.

Services : Transfd. from Inf. to Cav. Cornet 3rd N.C. Lieut. 5th N.C. Capt. Lt. 5th N.C. 11 Mar. 1805. With G.G.B.G. 26 July 1802 till 12 Mar. 1807. A.D.C. to G.G. 14 Dec. 1805. Dy. Agent for camels and grain 12 Mar. 1807. S.A.C.G. 1 Feb. 1810. A.C.G. 25 July 1812 till 1819. Fur. 1819-21. Transfd. as Lt. Col. to 6th L.C. 12 Feb. 1825. Siege and capture of Bhurtpore ; Lt. Col. comdg. 6th L.C. Transfd. to 3rd L.C. 18 Sept. 1826 ; to 10th L.C. ; to 8th L.C. 15 Aug. 1829. Returned from fur. 22 Oct. 1832. Transfd. to 2nd L.C. 27 Oct. 1832 ; to 5th L.C. 30 Sept. 1834 ; to 7th L.C. 20 Aug. 1835 ; to 4th L.C. Fur. 14 Oct. 1837.

Refs. : V.B.G. A.J. N.S. xxv. 199. Will dated 26 Aug. 1829 ; proved 7 June 1839.

BECHER, George Richard Prendergast (1808-1846). Bt. Captain. 4th N.I. b. in India 26 Sept. 1808. Cadet 1825. Arrived in India 7 July 1826. Ensign 15 Mar. 1826. Lieut. 9 Apr. 1832. Bt. Capt. 15 Mar. 1841. Cashiered 19 May 1845. d. Bareilly 17 Mar. 1846.

bapt. Cawnpore 29 Oct. 1808. Son of George Becher, q.v., and Harriet his 1st wife. Brother of Henry Murray Becher, q.v. m. Bareilly, 13 Sept. 1841, Phoebe Letitia Cecilia, eldest dau. of H. J. F. Berkeley, P.S.A. (She *re-m.* 6 Apr. 1847 William Vincent, q.v.)

Services : Transfd. as Ensign from 38th N.I. to 4th N.I. 10 May 1827. No record of active service.

Refs. : I.M. 1845, p. 445.

BECHER, Henry (1805-1826). Lieutenant, 23rd N.I. b. London 13 May 1805. Cadet 1823. Ensign 14 Jan. 1824. Lieut. 13 May 1825. d. Moradabad, U.P., 12 Apr. 1826.

Son of Robert Becher.

Services : Posted as Ensign to 23rd N.I. Siege and capture of Bhurtpore ; Lieut. 23rd N.I.

BECHER, Henry Murray (1810-1884). Bt. Captain. 50th N.I. b. Cawnpore 25 Dec. 1810. Cadet 1827. Arrived in India 12 Dec. 1828. Ensign 12 June 1828. Lieut. 19 Nov. 1836.

THE BENGAL ARMY, 1758-1834

Bt. Capt. 12 June 1843. Retired 12 Aug. 1847. *d.* Alma Rd., Clifton, 16 Mar. 1884.

Son of George Becher, *q.v.*, and Harriet his 1st wife. Brother of George Richard Prendergast Becher, *q.v.* Addiscombe Cadet 1826-8. *Services :* Ensign d.d. 7th N.I. 20 Jan. 1829. Posted as Ensign to 50th N.I. 3 June 1829. Operations against the Kols 1832-3 ; Ensign 50th N.I. Fur. s.c. 29 July 1833 till 6 Dec. 1836. Leave to N.S.W. for 2 yrs. 5 Mar. 1838. Fur. 28 Feb. 1845 till retirement. *Refs. :* The *Times*, 19 Mar. 1884.

BECHER, Robert (1764/65-?). Lieutenant. Infantry. *b.* 1764/65. Apptd. Cadet on 14 Feb. 1781, aged 16. Ensign 23 May 1781. Lieut. 5 Sept. 1782. Resigned 17 Sept. 1792.

A native of Kent. (*Possibly* father of Henry Becher, *q.v.*) *Services :* Sailed for India on the *Fortitude* 13 Mar. 1781, aged 16. On fur. in 1790. N.F.P. (? Subsequently, until 1808, a merchant at Cawnpore.)

BECHER, Robert (1791-1841). Major, 62nd N.I. *b.* in India Jan. 1791. Cadet 1805. Arrived in India 11 July 1806. Ensign 26 July 1806. Lieut. 13 Sept. 1807. Capt. 21 July 1823. Major 9 Mar. 1837. *d.* Canton, China, 30 May 1841, from over-fatigue.

bapt. Berhampore 27 May 1791. Son of Richard Becher, B.C.S., salt agent at Tamluk, Midnapore. *m.* Elizabeth. (She died Gauhati, Assam, 15 Sept. 1860.) His dau. *m.* Augustus Abbot, *q.v.* *Services :* Posted as Ensign to 1/10th N.I. Adjt. 1/10th N.I. 18 Sept. 1810 till 1818. Bde. Qmr. 1st Inf. Bde., Nagpur Subsidiary Force 14 Nov. 1817. Third Mahratta War. Offg. D.A.Q.M.G. Nagpur Subsidiary Force 1818. D.A.Q.M.G., 3 cl., 24 Oct. 1818. 2 cl., 13 Feb. 1819. 1 cl., 11 Mar. 1820. Transfd. to 2/31st N.I. 21 July 1823 ; to 62nd N.I. (late 2/31st) May 1824. First Burma War ; D.Q.M.G. 2nd A.Q.M.G. 8 June 1832. First China War ; D.Q.M.G.

Refs. : Will dated 11 Apr. 1837 ; proved 1 Oct. 1841.

BECHER, Samuel John (1816-1865). Lieut. Colonel. 11th N.I. *b.* Calcutta 6 Aug. 1816. Cadet 1833. Arrived in India 3 Nov. 1834. Ensign 31 Oct. 1834. Lieut. 30 July 1839. Capt. 13 May 1848. Major (?). Retired 31 Dec. 1861. Hon. Lt. Col. 31 Dec. 1861. *d.* 31 Aug. 1865.

Son of Charles (Grant) Becher, B.C.S., *q.v.*, and Charlotte his 2nd wife. Brother of Charles Grant Becher, *q.v.* *m.* Mehidpur, C.I., 25 Jan. 1844, Fanny C., dau. of Frederick Hervey Sandys, *q.v.*, and Jane Culloden his 1st wife. Ed. Sherborne ; left in 1833.

Services : Ensign d.d. 55th N.I. 10 Nov. 1834 ; do. 19th N.I.

2 Jan. 1835. Posted to 11th N.I. 2 Mar. 1835. Actg. Adjt. 3rd Local Horse 7 Feb. 1839 and 18 Dec. 1840. Adjt. Inf., Bundelkhand Legion, 1 Sept. 1841. Malwa Contingent 29 Dec. 1841. Adjt. Cav., Malwa Contingent, 1 May 1842 till 10 June 1848. Fur. s.c. 9 Aug. 1852 till 1855. No record of active service.

BECHER, Septimus Harding (1817-1908). General. 61st N.I. u.s.l. *b.* 15 July 1817. Cadet 1833. Arrived in India 11 Dec. 1834. Ensign (11 June 1834) 27 Aug. 1834. Lieut. 3 Oct. 1840. Capt. 1 Dec. 1846. Major 18 Feb. 1861. Lt. Col. 18 Feb. 1861. Col. 18 Feb. 1866. Maj. Gen. 1 Oct. 1877. Lt. Gen. 18 Dec. 1880. Gen. 22 Jan. 1889. *d.* Eastbourne, 23 Nov. 1908, aged 91.

bapt. Calcutta 15 Oct. 1817. Son of George Becher, *q.v.*, and Harriot his 2nd wife. Brother of Arthur Mitford Becher, *q.v. m.* Chelsea, 15 May 1849, Augusta Emily, dau. of Augustus Prinsep, B.C.S. Addiscombe Cadet 1 Aug. 1832 till 13 June 1834.

Services : Ensign d.d. 19th N.I. 2 Jan. 1835 ; do. 1st N.I. 22 Jan. 1835. Posted as Ensign to 63rd N.I. 2 Mar. 1835. Transfd. to 61st N.I. 2 June 1835. Actg. Adjt. Kumaon Local Bn. 16 Mar. 1839 and 19 Sept. 1840. P.W.D., Kumaon, 11 Feb. 1841. Adjt. 61st N.I. 14 Jan. 1842 till 13 Feb. 1847. Fur. p.a. 13 Feb. 1847 till 1849. Bde. Major at Barrackpore Oct. 1850. 2nd A.A.G. of the Army 18 Nov. 1850. 1st do. 6 May 1856. Special duty, Mily. Finance Dept., 23 May 1862. No record of active service. Transfd. to u.s.l.

Refs. : The Times, 24 Nov. 1908.

BECK, David Septimus (1812-1835). Ensign, 68th N.I. *bapt.* Coventry, co. Warwick, 2 Mar. 1812. Cadet 1828. Arrived in India 27 Aug. 1829. Ensign 5 June 1829. *d.* 24 Aug. 1835 : drowned at the Great Waterfall, Mhow.

Son of James Beck, of Allesley Park, nr. Coventry, banker at Coventry, and Sarah Coker his wife, only dau. of Simon Adams, of Anstey Hall, co. Warwick. Brother of Francis George Beck, *q.v.* Addiscombe Cadet 1827-8.

Services : Posted as Ensign to 73rd N.I. 7 Jan. 1830. Transfd. to 17th N.I. 20 Aug. 1833 ; to 73rd N.I. 19 Sept. 1833 ; to 68th N.I. 26 Aug. 1834. No record of active service.

Refs. : Burke's *Landed Gentry*, 13th edn., p. 4, *s.n.* Woolcombe-Adams, of Anstey Hall, co. Warwick. *A.J.* N.S. xix. 149, 197.

BECK, Francis George (1806-1836). Lieutenant, 13th N.I. *bapt.* Coventry, co. Warwick, 30 Nov. 1806. Cadet 1825. Arrived in India 4 May 1826. Ensign 12 Jan. 1826. Lieut. 6 June 1828. *d.* Agra 2 Aug. 1836.

Son of James Beck, of Allesley Park, nr. Coventry, banker at Coventry, and Sarah Coker his wife, only dau. of Simon Adams, of Anstey Hall, co. Warwick. Brother of James Henry Beck, *q.v.*
Services : Served throughout with 13th N.I. Actg. Adjt. 21 Dec. 1835. No record of active service.
Refs. : Burke's *Landed Gentry*, 13th edn., p. 4, *s.n.* Woolcombe-Adams, of Anstey Hall, co. Warwick. *G.M.* 1837, i. 335.

BECK, James Henry (1809-1833). Lieutenant, 24th N.I. *bapt.* Coventry 13 July 1809. Cadet 1826. Arrived in India 11 June 1827. Ensign 13 Feb. 1827. Lieut. 2 Jan. 1833. *d.* Bankura, Bengal, 29 Mar. 1833, of jungle fever.
Son of James Beck, of Allesley Park, and Sarah Coker his wife, only dau. of Simon Adams. Brother of David Septimus Beck, *q.v.*
Services : Posted as Ensign to 24th N.I. No record of active service.
Refs. : Burke's *Landed Gentry*, 13th edn., p. 4, *s.n.* Woolcombe-Adams, of Anstey Hall, co. Warwick. *A.J.* N.S. xii. 113.

BECKETT, John Ostlife (1791-1857). Lieutenant. 22nd N.I. *bapt.* Enfield, Middlesex, 5 May 1791. Cadet 1807. Arrived in India 14 Aug. 1808. Ensign 3 Sept. 1808. Lieut. 3 Jan. 1814. Resigned 1 May 1823. *d.* Kidderpore, Calcutta, 3 Aug. 1857.
Eldest son of William Beckett, of Enfield, *q.v.* Brother of William Beckett (1798-1844), *q.v. m.* Calcutta, 14 Sept. 1824, Miss Anna Maria Booth.
Services : Posted as Ensign to 22nd N.I. Mily. student at Coll. of Fort William in 1814. Nepal War 1814-6 ; Lieut. 2/22nd N.I. (India medal). Intr. & Qmr. 2/22nd N.I. 30 Oct. 1815 till 1822. Sec. and Persian translator to O.C. Nagpur Subsidiary Force 1822 till retirement. Apptd. an examiner at Coll. of Fort William 22 Nov. 1827; but resigned after a few months. After retirement was engaged in various mercantile pursuits in India. He first joined the firm of Mercer & Co., then settled at Koil, Aligarh, as indigo planter, subsequently joining the Agra Bank. He was, at the date of his death, Sec. to the Bengal Mily. Orphan Soc.
Refs. : G.M. 1857, ii. 566. Will dated 8 Feb. 1856 ; proved 7 Aug. 1857.

BECKETT, William. Bt. Captain. Infantry. Cadet (?). Ensign 7 Sept. 1781. Lieut. 7 Jan. 1784. Bt. Capt. (?). Struck off 1793.
Of Enfield, brewer. *m.* Enfield, 13 July 1790, ——, dau. of John Ostlife, of Enfield, brewer. Father of John Ostlife Beckett, *q.v.*, William Beckett, *q.v.*, Mary, wife of James Glencairn Burns, *q.v.*, and Jane, wife of Hon. Robert Vernon Powys, *q.v.*

Services : Was on fur. in 1790 and did not return to India. Both his family and that of his wife were connected with the brewing industry in Enfield. After quitting the Service he became a partner in the brewery with his brother-in-law, Francis Ostlife.

Refs. : *G.M.* 1790, ii.

BECKETT, William (1798-1844). Captain, 9th N.I. *b.* Enfield, Middlesex, 7 Jan. 1798. Cadet 1818. Admitted 4 Sept. 1819. Ensign 2 Sept. 1819. Lieut. 17 Jan. 1821. Capt. 25 Sept. 1833. *d.* Allahabad 14 Dec. 1844.

Son of William Beckett, of Enfield, *q.v.* Brother of John Ostlife Beckett, *q.v. m.* Meerut, 26 July 1824, Ann, 2nd dau. of Major Robert Durie, 11th Light Dns. (*See also* Francis Burton Boileau, John Griffin, Henry Roche Osborn, and Charles Samuel Reid.) Father of Ann Ellen, wife of Thomas Riddell, *q.v.*, and of Eliza Mary, wife of Daniel Stansbury, *q.v.*

Services : Posted as Ensign to 1/8th N.I. Adjt. 9th N.I. (late 1/8th) 17 June 1824. Intr. & Qmr. do. 25 Sept. 1825 till 11 Jan. 1834. Officiated for a short period in 1840-1 as 2nd Asst. Mily. Auditor Gen. No record of active service.

Refs. : Will dated 6 July 1832 ; proved 29 Jan. 1845.

BEDELL, William (1764/65-1829). Colonel, Invalid Est. 30th N.I. Comdg. Dacca Provl. Bn. *b.* 1764/65. Cadet 1779. Admitted 14 Sept. 1779. Ensign 12 Sept. 1780. Lieut. 23 Mar. 1781. Capt. 30 Oct. 1797. Major 27 Jan. 1804. Lt. Col. 11 July 1807. Col. 4 June 1814. Invalided 1 Oct. 1815. *d.* Dacca, Bengal, 6 June 1829, aged 64.

A native of Middlesex. *m.* 1st, Calcutta, 8 July 1792, Miss Ann Young. Father of Catherine Jane, wife of Archibald Dickson, *q.v.*, and Lucy Elizabeth, wife of Henry Sibley, *q.v. m.* 2nd, Manjhi, Bihar, 2 Oct. 1798, Anne Eliza, dau. of Henry Revell, B.C.S., and aunt of Henry Patch, *q.v.* (She died Calcutta 31 Aug. 1854.) Father of Harriet, wife of Charles Henry Phelips, *q.v.*, and 2ndly of Philip Brewer, *q.v.*

Services : Sailed for India on the *Ceres* 16 June 1779. Capt. 13th N.I. Transfd. to 27th N.I. in 1805. Fur. 6 Sept. 1806 till 21 Oct. 1809. Transfd. as Lt. Col. to 24th N.I. in 1807 ; to Eur. Regt. in 1808 ; to 8th N.I. in 1810 ; to 4th N.I. in 1814. Comdg. Eur. Invalids 16 Aug. 1816 till 1823. Comdg. Dacca Provl. Bn. 1823 till death.

Refs. : Burke's *Landed Gentry*, 13th edn., p. 1608, *s.n.* Sivright, of South House and Meggatland. *A.J.* xxviii. 734. Will dated 26 May 1829 ; proved 24 June 1829.

THE BENGAL ARMY, 1758-1834 121

BEDFORD, James (1788-1871). Lieut. Colonel. 2nd European Regt. Dy. Surveyor Gen. *bapt.* London 8 Mar. 1788. Cadet 1808. Arrived in India 25 Sept. 1809. Ensign 29 Mar. 1810. Lieut. 16 Dec. 1814. Capt. 13 May 1825. Bt. Major 28 June 1838. Retired 11 Jan. 1843. Hon. Lt. Col. 28 Nov. 1854. *d.* Stoulgrove, Gloucs., 31 Mar. 1871, aged 83.
Youngest son of John Bedford, of Fairlawn, Acton, Middlesex. *m.* Meerut, 20 Sept. 1828, Jane Helen, only dau. of John Troup, of Fir Hall, Nairn, and sister of Colin Troup, *q.v.* (She died Allahabad, 18 Sept. 1836, aged 26.)
Services : Posted as Ensign to 2/24th N.I. Intr. & Qmr. 2/24th N.I. 1818. Transfd. to 48th N.I. (late 2/24th) May 1824. First Burma War ; with Assam F.F. (India medal). Apptd. to Revenue Survey Dept. 15 Dec. 1826. Dy. Surveyor Gen. 11 June 1832. Posted to re-formed 2nd Eur. Regt. 8 Oct. 1839, but remained in the Survey Dept.
Refs. : *A.J.* xxvii. 481. *The Times*, 4 Apr. 1871.

*BEDINGFIELD, John George (1802-?). Cadet. Infantry. Subsequently Capt. H.M. 41st Foot. *b.* London 12 Aug. 1802. Cadet 1819. Never arrived in India.
Son of John Bedingfield, inspector R.N. pay office, J.P. Westminster, Middlesex, and Surrey.
Services : Ensign H.M. 41st Foot 2 Nov. 1820. Lieut. do. 29 June 1824. Capt. do. 5 June 1837. Served in First Burma War.

BEDINGFIELD, Richard Gurdon (1802-1829). Lieutenant, Artillery. *b.* Ditchingham, Norfolk, 5 Sept. 1802. Cadet 1818. 2nd Lieut. 8 Apr. 1819. Lieut. 13 June 1820. *d.* Nongkhlao, Assam, 4 Apr. 1829 : kld. by a party of Kasiyas.
3rd and youngest son of Francis Philip Bedingfield, of Kirklinton Hall, Cumberland (who was youngest son of Philip Bedingfield, of Ditchingham Hall, Norfolk), and Catherine his wife, dau. of Thomas Havers, of Thelton, Norfolk. Addiscombe Cadet 1818-9.
Services : First Burma War ; Assam 1824-5 ; Rangpur.
Refs. : Burke's *Landed Gentry*, 12th edn., p. 127, *s.n.* Bedingfield, late of Bedingfield House, Eye, Suffolk. *Stubbs*, ii. 187. *A.J.* N.S. i. 6. *I.M.* No. 23, p. 80.

BEEK, William George (1804-?). Ensign. 24th N.I. *bapt.* London 3 Oct. 1804. Cadet 1824. Ensign 29 Apr. 1825. Resigned in India 2 Nov. 1827.
Son of James Beek, of Hackney, Middlesex, architect.
Services : Posted as Ensign to 24th N.I.

BEEVOR, Thomas Charles (1793-1818). Lieutenant, 7th N.I.
b. Newton Flotman, Norfolk, 9 Mar. 1793. Cadet 1808. Arrived in India 5 Nov. 1809. Ensign 16 Mar. 1811. Lieut. 16 Dec. 1814. *d. unm.* Agra 15 Dec. 1818.
2nd son of Rev. George Beevor (who was youngest son of Sir Thomas Beevor, 1st Bart., of Hethel, Norfolk), and Jane his wife, eldest dau. of Rev. Arthur Branthwayt.
Services : Posted as Ensign to 7th N.I. Nepal War 1814-5; Lieut. 1/7th N.I., in 2nd Div. (? Third Mahratta War ; Lieut. 1/7th N.I.)
Refs. : Burke's *Peerage*, 1923, p. 245, *s.n.* Beevor, Bart.

BEGBIE, Arthur Pitt (1805-1880). Lieutenant, Pension Est. Artillery. *b.* Hendon, Middlesex, 31 Dec. 1805. Cadet 1823. Arrived in India 16 June 1824. 2nd Lieut. 18 Dec. 1823. Lieut. 28 Sept. 1827. Bt. Capt. 18 Dec. 1838. *d.* Simla 13 July 1880.
Son of Peter Begbie. *m.* (before 1832) (?). His sister *m.* George Poyntz Ricketts, *q.v.* Addiscombe Cadet 1821-3.
Services : (? First Burma War ; 2nd Lieut. Art.)
Note : This statement is made on the authority of Stubbs's *History of the Bengal Artillery*, ii. 189 ; his name, however, does not appear in the official medal roll.

BEGBIE, Patrick (1781-1801). Lieutenant, Infantry. *b.* Culross, co. Fife, 26 Jan. 1781. Cadet 1798. Arrived in India 23 Nov. 1799. Ensign 23 Nov. 1799. Lieut. 29 May 1800. *d.* Midnapore, Bengal, 1 Feb. 1801.
Son of Patrick Begbie, of Castlehill, and Jean Bland (*or* Blane) his wife.
Services : N.F.P.
Refs. : *M.M.* xiii. (1802) 94.

BEGG, Francis (*d.* 1787). Lieutenant, Infantry. Cadet 1781. Ensign 1781. Lieut. Nov. 1782. *d.* Barrackpore 11 Aug. 1787.
Services : N.F.P.

BELCHES, Anthony (*d.* 1780). Captain, Infantry. Cadet 1769. Ensign 19 Dec. 1769. Lieut. 16 Mar. 1773. Capt. 14 Nov. 1779. *d.* Madras 13 Dec. 1780.
Services : N.F.P. (? Capt. 2/1st Bengal Eur. Regt. ; accompanied expedition to Madras for second Mysore war.)

BELL, Alexander (*d.* 1768). Ensign, Infantry. Cadet 1768. Ensign 1 June 1768. *d.* in India 1768.
Services : N.F.P.

BELL, Charles Hamilton (1789-1848). Lieut. Colonel. Artillery. *b.* Coldstream, co. Berwick, 19 Apr. 1789. Cadet 1805. Arrived in India 27 Apr. 1807. Fireworker 5 May 1807. Lieut. 23 July 1807. Capt. Lt. 1 Aug. 1818. Capt. 1 Sept. 1818. Major 17 Jan. 1836. Lt. Col. 25 Mar. 1840. Retired 28 Feb. 1842. *d.* Edinburgh, 20 Apr. 1848.
Of Portobello, Edinburgh. *bapt.* Coldstream 2 May 1789. Son of Rev. Dr. James Bell, minister of Coldstream, and Anna his wife. Brother of John Bell (1791-1842), *q.v. m.* 1st, Agra, 23 May 1820, Sophia Carden, 6th dau. of Thomas Chadwick, of Barnascounce, and sister of Thomas Chadwick, *q.v.* (*See also* Robert Blackall, Gardner Boyd, and George Casement.) *m.* 2nd, Saugor, 5 Apr. 1836, Miss Louisa Smith.
Services : Nepal War 1814-5 ; Lieut. 4th Coy. 1st Bn. Art., with Col. Nicholl's force in Kumaon. Siege and capture of Hathras ; Lieut. 4th Coy. 3rd Bn. Operations against the Bhattis of Hariana 1818 ; Lieut. comdg. 4th Coy. 1st Bn. Operations in Jodhpur 1823 ; capture of Lamba. Fur. 2 Jan. 1830 till 10 July 1832.
Refs. : Burke's *Colonial Gentry*, ii. 587, *s.n.* Chadwick. Intestate ; admon. granted 10 July 1850.

BELL, George Banks (1786-1847). Bt. Colonel, 65th N.I. *b.* Nov. 1786. Cadet 1803. Arrived in India 18 Mar. 1805. Ensign 24 Mar. 1805. Lieut. 25 Mar. 1805. Capt. 11 July 1823. Major 1 Nov. 1830. Lieut. Col. 30 May 1836. Bt. Col. 9 Nov. 1846. *d.* Cloudesley Sq., London, 24 Apr. 1847.
bapt. Hexham, Northumberland, 25 Dec. 1787, aged 13 mos. Son of John Bell, glazier. Brother of John Bell (1781-1800), *q.v.*
Services : Posted as Lieut. to 18th N.I. Transfd. to newly-raised 2/30th N.I. in 1815. Capt. 68th N.I. First Burma War ; Capt. 68th N.I. Bde. Major at Barrackpore 6 July 1825. Fur. s.c. 7 Sept. 1828 till 3 Oct. 1831. Comdd. 68th N.I. 6 Mar. 1835 till 3 Aug. 1836. Transfd. as Lt. Col. to 52nd N.I. 10 July 1836 ; to 13th N.I. 13 Jan. 1838 ; to 46th N.I. 11 Feb. 1844 ; to 65th N.I. Apr. 1846. Fur. m.c. 29 Aug. 1845 till death.
Refs. : G.M. 1847, i. 672.

BELL, James (1809-1883). Lieutenant. 71st N.I. *b.* Dundee 26 Feb. 1809. Cadet 1826. Arrived in India 10 Nov. 1827. Ensign 14 June 1827. Lieut. 13 May 1829. Retired 19 June 1839. *d.* 13 Mar. 1883.
Son of John Bell, of Berwick, merchant.
Services : Posted as Ensign to 71st N.I. Fur. s.c. 19 Dec. 1836 till retirement. No record of active service.

BELL, John. Cadet. Infantry. Cadet 1769. Resigned 5 Sept. 1769.
Services : N.F.P.

BELL, John. Ensign, Infantry. Afterwards Lt. Col. Madras Artillery. Cadet 1780. Ensign 17 Feb. 1781. Transfd. to Madras Est. 15 Oct. 1781.
Services : Lieut. Fireworker, Madras Art., 3 Dec. 1780. Lt. Col. 25 Sept. 1803. Was Lt. Col. comdg. 1st Bn. Art., and senior officer comdg. Seringapatam, during the "Madras mutiny." Cashiered by G.C.M. 8 Mar. 1810.
Refs. : Seton Kerr's *Selections from Calcutta Gazettes*, iv. 85.

BELL, John (*d.* 1791). Lieutenant, Infantry. Cadet 1783. Ensign 24 Jan. 1785. Lieut. 1791. *d.* Chittagong 1 Nov. 1791.
Services : N.F.P.

BELL, John (1781-1800). Lieutenant, 12th N.I. *bapt.* Hexham, Northumberland, 25 Dec. 1781. Cadet 1798. Arrived in India 24 Feb. 1800. Ensign 18 Nov. 1799. Lieut. 29 May 1800. *d.* Chunar 30 July 1800.
Son of John Bell, glazier. Brother of George Banks Bell, *q.v.*
Services : Posted as Lieut. to 12th N.I.

BELL, John (1791-1842). Major. 1st N.I. *b.* Coldstream, co. Berwick, 3 Jan. 1791. Cadet 1808. Arrived in India 27 Oct. 1809. Ensign 31 July 1810. Lieut. 16 Dec. 1814. Capt. 13 May 1825. Major 20 June 1833. Retired 1 Feb. 1837. *d.* 22 Oct. 1842.
Son of Rev. Dr. James Bell, minister of Coldstream. Brother of Charles Hamilton Bell, *q.v.*
Services : Posted as Ensign to 1/12th N.I. Lieut. 1/12th N.I. Transfd. to 1st N.I. (late 2/12th) May 1824. No record of active service.

BELL, John Davidson (1811-1841). Lieutenant, Artillery. *b.* Middlebie, co. Dumfries, 28 Feb. 1811. Cadet 1827. Arrived in India 9 June 1828. 2nd Lieut. 13 Dec. 1827. Lieut. 1 Feb. 1835. *d.* Nimach, C.I., 12 Jan. 1841.
Son of John Bell, of Broadlee, co. Dumfries, farmer. Brother of Thomas Bell, *q.v.* Addiscombe Cadet 1826-7.
Services : Served throughout with Foot Art. Was Adjt. Nimach Div. Art. at date of death. No record of active service.

BELL, Robert. Lieutenant. Infantry. Cadet (?). Ensign 11 May 1779. Lieut. 16 Aug. 1781. Resigned 3 Jan. 1785.
Services : N.F.P.

BELL, Robert (1792- ?). Lieutenant. 17th N.I. *b.* Madras 29 Oct. 1792. Cadet 1811. Ensign 15 Jan. 1814. Lieut. 10 Aug. 1817. Resigned 14 Aug. 1819.
bapt. Trichinopoly 27 Nov. 1792. Son of Gen. Robert Bell, Madras Art., and Sarah his wife.
Services : Posted as Ensign to 2/17th N.I. Nepal War 1814-5 ; Ensign 2/17th N.I., in 3rd Div. Comdg. Art. with Nizam's troops in Berar 1818-9.

BELL, Thomas (1809-1841). Bt. Captain, 2nd N.I. *b.* Middlebie, co. Dumfries, 3 May 1809. Cadet 1825. Arrived in India 10 Mar. 1826. Ensign 12 Oct. 1825. Lieut. 12th Aug. 1834. Bt. Capt. 12 Oct. 1840. *d.* Kandahar 18 Aug. 1841.
Son of John Bell, of Broadlee, co. Dumfries, farmer. Brother of John Davidson Bell, *q.v.*
Services : Posted as Ensign to 15th N.I. Transfd. to 2nd N.I. 27 Aug. 1831. Intr. & Qmr. 2nd N.I. 24 Dec. 1831 till 7 Jan. 1836. First Afghan War 1840-1.
Refs. : *A.J.* N.S. xx. 97.

BELL, William (1792-1836). Captain, Artillery. *b.* Leith 3 Sept. 1792. Cadet 1809. Arrived in India 19 July 1809. Fireworker 7 Nov. 1809. Lieut. 25 Sept. 1817. Capt. 1 May 1824. *d.* Calcutta 21 Dec. 1836.
Son of Charles Bell, of Leith, wine merchant. *m.* 1st (before 1821), (?). (She died 3 Sept. 1826.) *m.* 2nd, Burdwan, 21 Mar. 1827, Miss Eliza Isabella Aldous. (She died 17 July 1829, aged 23.) *m.* 3rd, Calcutta, 10 May 1830, Miss Elenor Howel Stewart. (She died Elwick, nr. Hobart, Tasmania, 14 Aug. 1834.) *m.* 4th, Calcutta, 22 June 1835, Mary, only dau. of James Stewart. His sister *m.* Henry John Wood, *q.v.*
Services : Capture of Java ; Lieut. 1st Coy. 2nd Bn. Art. Jokyakarta. Third Mahratta War ; Dhamoni ; Lieut. 4th Coy. 2nd Bn. Posted to 4th Troop H.A. in 1819. Siege and capture of Bhurtpore ; Lieut. comdg. 2nd Troop 3rd Bde. H.A. Comdd. 1st Troop 1st Bde. 1829-31 ; 2nd Capt. in 1st Troop 2nd Bde. 1832-4. Supt. P.W.D., Cuttack, 15 Jan. 1835.
Refs. : *A.J.* N.S. xix. 39. Will dated Chinsura 7 Dec. 1831 ; proved 27 Dec. 1836.

BELLASIS, John (1761/62-1794). Lieutenant, Infantry. *b.* Shrewsbury 1761/62. Cadet 1777. Ensign 23 Dec. 1777. Lieut. 3 Sept. 1778. *d.* Fatehgarh, U.P., 12 July 1794.
Services : Sailed for India on the *Eagle*, 25 Dec. 1777, aged 15. N.F.P.

BELLASIS, Joseph Harvey (1759-1799). Ensign. Engineers. *b.* 21 May 1759. Cadet 1785. Ensign 1 June 1785. Resigned in India Feb. 1794. *d.* Saunda, Datia State, Dec. 1799 : kld. in action.

bapt. Yattendon, Berks., 21 June 1759. Elder son of Rev. George Bellasis (originally Bellas—resumed the former spelling of his name by Earl Marshal's Warrant, 27 May 1792), D.D., rector of Yattendon, and vicar of Basildon, Berks., and Margaret his 1st wife, dau. of Rev. William Harvey, rector of Pangbourne, Berks. Half-brother of Edward Bellasis, serj.-at-law (*D.N.B.*). *m.* Bengal, 1 June 1785, Sarah (? Juliana), dau. of Capt. Williams, H.E.I.C.S. Queen's Coll., Oxon. ; matric. 12 July 1775, aged 16.

Services : After resigning the Service, he entered that of the Mahratta Chief Ambaji Inglia, for whom he raised four Bns. of Inf. Took part in the storm and capture of Lohar fort, 1797, after which he was discharged. Two years later he again entered Ambaji's service and obtained comd. of two Bns. of Inf. With these he was engaged in the siege of Saunda, Dec. 1799. He was shot through the head in the assault on Lakwa Dada's entrenchment.

Refs. : Howard & Crisp, ii. 57. *G.M.* 1800, ii. 1008 ; 1802, i. 184. *Alumni Oxon. Hindustan under Free Lances,* 1779-1820, by H. G. Keene, pp. 105-7. *European Military Adventurers of Hindustan,* by H. Compton, p. 338.

BELLEW, Christopher Robert (1801-1826). Lieutenant, 37th N.I. *bapt.* Bexley, Kent, 18 Jan. 1801. Cadet 1817. Ensign (?). Lieut. 9 Sept. 1818. *d.* Bareilly 27 July 1826.

3rd son of Robert Bellew, of Ballendiness, Castle Martyr, co. Cork, barr.-at-law (a cadet of the family of Lord Bellew), and Sophia Fowke his wife. Brother of Henry Walter Bellew, *q.v.*, and cousin-german of Patrick Bellew Fitton, *q.v.*

Services : Posted as Lieut. to 1/18th N.I. Intr. & Qmr. do. 1 Oct. 1823. Transfd. to 36th N.I. (late 1/18th) as Intr. & Qmr. May 1824 ; to 37th N.I. as do. 28 June 1825. Siege and capture of Bhurtpore ; Lieut. 37th N.I.

Refs. : Burke's *Commoners,* ii. p. xv, *s.n.* Bellew, of Stockleigh Court, Devon. *A.J.* xxiii. 389. Will dated 25 July 1826 ; proved 23 May 1828.

***BELLEW, Edmund** (1784-1805). Cadet, Artillery. *b.* Martinique, W.I., 16 Nov. 1784. Cadet 1805. Never arrived in India. *d.* at sea, 1 Feb. 1805 : lost in the wreck of the *Earl of Abergavenny* off Portland.

Son of Lawrence Bellew.

THE BENGAL ARMY, 1758-1834 127

BELLEW, Francis John (1799-1868). Captain. 62nd N.I. *bapt.*
Bexley, Kent, 4 Aug. 1799. Cadet 1814. Arrived in India
Aug. 1815. Ensign 20 Aug. 1815. Lieut. 17 May 1816. Capt.
11 July 1823. Retired 10 Apr. 1832. *d.* 2 Sept. 1868.
2nd son of Robert Bellew, of Ballendiness, Castle Martyr, co. Cork,
barr.-at-law, and Sophia Fowke his wife. Brother of Christopher
Robert Bellew, *q.v. m.* Calcutta, 21 Nov. 1818, Anne, only dau. of
Simon Temple, formerly of Hylton Castle, co. Durham. (She died
2 June 1856.)
Services : Posted as Ensign to 1/27th N.I. Third Mahratta
War ; Lieut. 1/27th N.I. Intr. & Qmr. 1/18th N.I. 3 Feb. 1821.
Operations in Jodhpur 1823 ; capture of Lamba ; Lieut. 1/18th
N.I. Transfd. as Capt. to 2/31st N.I. 1 Oct. 1823 ; to 62nd N.I.
(late 2/31st) May 1824. Intr. & Qmr. 1 Oct. 1823 till 8 May 1826.
First Burma War ; Arakan 1825 ; mily. sec. to Bdr.-Gen. J. W.
Morrison, comdg. Arakan F.F. 2 Feb. 1825 (India medal). S.A.C.G.
27 Mar. 1826. Fur. s.c. 31 Mar. 1830 till retirement. Author of
" Memoirs of a Griffin," 2 vols., London, 1845.
Refs. : Burke's *Commoners,* ii. p. xxi. *The Times,* 19 Sept. 1868.

BELLEW, Henry Walter (1803-1842). Bt. Major, 56th N.I. *bapt.*
Bexley, Kent, 2 Jan. 1803. Cadet 1818. Admitted 20 Nov.
1819. Ensign 16 Nov. 1819. Lieut. 1 Jan. 1821. Capt. 28 June
1827. Bt. Major 23 Nov. 1841. *d.* 13 Jan. 1842 : kld. in action
in the Khurd Kabul Pass, Afghanistan.
4th and youngest son of Robert Bellew, of Ballendiness, barr.-at-law, and Sophia Fowke his wife. Brother of Francis John Bellew,
q.v. m. Agra, 17 Aug. 1831, Anna, 3rd dau. of Peter Jeremie, *q.v.*
(*See also* John Turner.)
Services : Posted as Ensign to 2/28th N.I. Transfd. to 56th N.I.
(late 2/28th) May 1824. Intr. & Qmr. 56th N.I. 24 June 1824 till
29 May 1827. Bde. Major Rajputana F.F. 16 Apr. 1828. Offg. in
Q.M.G. Dept. 18 Apr. 1829. Shekhawat expedn. 1834. First
Afghan War ; D.A.Q.M.G. A.Q.M.G. 18 Aug. 1841. 1st A.Q.M.G.
of the Army 12 Jan. 1842.
Refs. : Burke's *Commoners,* ii. p. xv, *s.n.* Bellew, of Stockleigh
Court, Devon. *G.M.* 1842, i. 677. *The Times,* 12 Apr. 1842.

BELLEW, Patrick Edward (1794-1812). Ensign, Engineers. *bapt.*
Walcot, Somerset, 1 May 1794. Cadet 1809. Ensign in Army
15 Nov. 1810. (Supernumerary in Corps.) *d. unm.* in India
7 Dec. 1812.
Eldest son of Robert Bellew, of Ballendiness, barr.-at-law, and
Sophia Fowke his wife. Brother of Christopher Robert Bellew,

q.v., and cousin-german of Patrick Bellew Fitton, *q.v.* Woolwich Cadet 1808-9. Addiscombe Cadet 1809-10.
Services : N.F.P.
Refs. : Burke's *Commoners*, ii. p. xxi, *s.n.* Bellew of Stockleigh Court, Devon.

BELLINGHAM, Henry (1778-1820). Major, 1st N.I. *b.* Castle Bellingham, co. Louth, 5 June 1778. Cadet 1798. Arrived in India 12 Oct. 1799. Ensign 6 Sept. 1799. Lieut. 28 Oct. 1799. Capt. 1 Jan. 1807. Major 5 Dec. 1815. *d.* Murshidabad (? Moradabad) 26 May 1820.

2nd son of Alan Bellingham, of Kilsaran, and Anne his wife, dau. of John Cairnes, of Killyfaddy, co. Tyrone. Younger brother of Sir Alan Bellingham, 2nd Bart., and cousin-german of Henry Tenison Bellingham, *q.v. m.* Gravesend, Kent, 25 Mar. 1809, Henrietta Elizabeth, dau. of Capt. William Cruden, R.N. (She died 13 Mar. 1872.)
Services : Posted as Lieut. to 1/1st N.I. 15 Apr. 1801. Fur. 11 Mar. 1806 till 27 Oct. 1809, and 1814-7. Third Mahratta War ; Major 1st N.I.
Refs. : Burke's *Peerage*, 1923, p. 254, *s.n.* Bellingham, Bart., of Castle Bellingham, co. Louth. *G.M.* 1809, i. 383 ; 1821, i. 90. Will dated Moradabad 15 Jan. 1820 ; proved 8 July 1820.

*****BELLINGHAM, Henry Tenison** (1784-1812). Cadet, Infantry. Subsequently Captain H.M. 4th Foot. *bapt.* Castle Bellingham, co. Louth, 6 Aug. 1784. Cadet 1798. Did not take up his appointment. *d.* 6 Apr. 1812 : kld. in action at Badajoz.

2nd son of Lt. Col. Henry Bellingham (who was eldest brother of Sir William Bellingham, 1st Bart.) and Elizabeth his wife, dau. of Richard Tenison, of Thomastown, co. Louth. Cousin-german of Henry Bellingham, *q.v.*
Services : Ensign 4th (King's Own) Regt. of Foot 10 Sept. 1803. Lieut. 21 Apr. 1804. Capt. 14 Feb. 1811.
Refs. : Burke's *Peerage*, 1923, p. 254, *s.n.* Bellingham, Bart., of Castle Bellingham, co. Louth.

*****BEN, James** (*d.* 1774). Lieutenant, Infantry. Cadet (?). Ensign (?). Lieut. (?). *d.* Calcutta 30 Nov. 1774.
Services : N.F.P.
Refs. : Calcutta burial register.

BENDLEY, Thomas (*d.* 1792). Lieut. Fireworker, Artillery. Cadet 1783. Fireworker 9 May 1785. *d.* 1792.
Services : N.F.P. Was on fur. in 1790.

THE BENGAL ARMY, 1758-1834

BENETT, Frederick (1791-1823). Bt. Captain, 3rd L.C. *b.* Donhead, Wilts., 25 Sept. 1791. Cadet 1806. Arrived in India 1 Aug. 1807. Cornet 26 July 1807. Lieut. 28 Apr. 1818. Bt. Capt. 5 Feb. 1822. *d.* Nasirabad, Rajputana, 30 Sept. 1823.
2nd son of Rev. John Benett, LL.D., rector of Donhead St. Andrew, Wilts., and Frances his wife, sister of Sir Thomas Turton, Bart. *m.* 1811, Miss Henrietta Emilia Knipe, of St. Helena. (*See also* William Burlton.) (She *re-m.* M. P. Cashel, of Lisson Hall, co. Tipperary, and died 8 Aug. 1832.)
Services : Posted as Cornet to 3rd N.C. Fur. 1812-3. Siege and capture of Hathras. Third Mahratta War ; Jawad ; Lieut. 3rd N.C., in Centre Div. Intr. & Qmr. 3rd N.C. 10 Apr. 1819 till death. (? Operations in Jodhpur ; capture of Lamba fort ; Lieut. 3rd L.C.)
Refs. : Burke's *Landed Gentry*, 8th edn., p. 129, *s.n.* Benett, of Pythouse, Wilts. Will dated 12 Feb. 1817 ; proved 28 Oct. 1823.

BENNETT, Frederick (1802/03-1824). Ensign, 45th N.I. *b.* 1802/03. Cadet 1821. Ensign 28 Nov. 1822. *d.* Ramu, Arakan, 16 May 1824 : kld. in action.
Services : Passed by the Committee for a Cadetship on 24 May 1822, aged 19. Posted as Ensign to 1/23rd N.I. (became 45th N.I. in May 1824). First Burma War, operations in Chittagong district, 1824 ; Ramu (kld.) ; Ensign 45th N.I.

BENNETT, George (*d.* 1770). Captain, Infantry. Cadet 1764. Formerly Qmr. Sergeant H.M. 89th Regt. Ensign 29 Dec. 1764. Lieut. 6 Jan. 1766. Capt. 8 Apr. 1769. *d.* Berhampore 1770.
Services : Action near Banas nala (Bonass-nullah) Oct. 1764 ; as Qmr. Sergt. H.M. 89th Regt.
Refs. : Williams, p. 40. Broome, p. 470.

BENNETT, Hector (*d.* 1796). Captain, Invalid Est. Infantry. Cadet 1769. Admitted 26 July 1769. Ensign 19 July 1770. Lieut. 16 Nov. 1772. Capt. 2 Jan. 1781. Invalided (after 1790). *d.* Monghyr, B. &.O., 29 June 1796.
Services : N.F.P.

BENNETT, Henry Whitchurch (1794-1824). Lieutenant, 2nd European Regt. *bapt.* Tavistock, Devon, 4 June 1794. Cadet 1810. Ensign 1 Sept. 1813. Lieut. 13 Aug. 1815. *d.* Nagpur 11 Sept. 1824.
Son of John Bennett, of Tavistock, mercer, and Martha his wife.
Services : Cadet d.d. 9th N.I. 1812-3. Posted as Ensign to Bengal Eur. Regt. 1 Sept. 1813. Transfd. to newly-formed 2nd Bengal Eur. Regt. in May 1824. No record of active service.

BENNETT, John William (1808-1868). Bt. Lieut. Colonel. 1st European Fusiliers. *bapt.* Writtle, Essex, 4 July 1808. Cadet 1828. Arrived in India 1 June 1829. Ensign 6 Jan. 1829. Lieut. 16 Dec. 1835. Capt. 1 Nov. 1824. Bt. Major 20 June 1854. Retired 5 Mar. 1856. Bt. Lt. Col. 29 Apr. 1856. *d.* 23 Nov. 1868.

Son of Rev. Dr. Samuel Bennett, rector of Walton-on-the-Hill, Surrey, and Mary Ann his wife. *m.* Sylhet, 21 Oct. 1833, Sarah, 4th dau. of George Inglis.
Services : Ensign W. Essex Militia 28 Apr. 1825. Ensign d.d. 33rd N.I. 13 July 1829 ; do. 22nd N.I. 1829. Posted as Ensign to Bengal Eur. Regt. 20 Nov. 1829. To do duty with Sylhet L.I. 30 Jan. 1837. First Afghan War 1839 ; capture of Ghazni ; Lieut. Bengal Eur. Regt., with Army of the Indus (Medal). Fur. p.a. 13 Feb. 1841 till 8 July 1842. Fort Adjt., Fort William, and Supt. of Gentlemen Cadets 18 Apr. 1845 till 1852. Fur. s.c. 21 Feb. 1852 till 1854.

BENNETT, Simon William (1803-1832). Lieutenant, Artillery. *b.* Edinburgh 28 May 1803. Cadet 1818. Admitted 17 Nov. 1819. 2nd Lieut. 15 Apr. 1819. Lieut. 14 Jan. 1821. *d.* Dumroy, nr. Dacca, 23 Feb. 1832, suddenly.

Son of John Bennett, F.R.C.S., of Edinburgh, and Mary Ann Ouchterlony his wife.
Services : With Foot Art. throughout his service. Apptd. Bde. Major 12 Sept. 1831 ; posted to E. frontier 16 Sept. 1831. No record of active service.
Refs. : A.J. N.S. ix. 35.

BENNETT, Thomas (1806-1831). Ensign, 9th N.I. *b.* London 11 Oct. 1806. Cadet 1825. Ensign 4 Feb. 1826. *d.* at sea, 13 Mar. 1831, on board the *Orient.*

Son of Thomas Bennett, wine merchant.
Services : Ensign d.d. 57th N.I. 30 June 1826. Posted as Ensign to 9th N.I. Fur. s.c. 15 Jan. 1830 till death. No record of active service.

BURLTON-BENNETT, Francis Edward (1809-1830). 2nd Lieutenant, Engineers. *b.* Calcutta 25 Aug. 1809. Cadet 1828. 2nd Lieut. 15 Dec. 1827. *d.* Aligarh, U.P., 17 Aug. 1830.

2nd son of William Robert Burlton-Bennett, B.C.S., Collector of Rajshahi, Bengal (who was son of Anthony Burlton-Bennett and the Hon. Frances Charlotte his wife, youngest dau. of William, second Viscount Galway). Addiscombe Cadet 1826-7. Chatham 1828.

THE BENGAL ARMY, 1758-1834 131

Services : Posted as 2nd Lieut. to Sappers.
Refs. : M.I. at Aligarh. Will dated 17 Aug. 1830 ; proved 24 Mar. 1831.

BENSON, Bennet (*d.* 1766). Ensign, Infantry. Cadet 1764. Ensign 17 Jan. 1765. *d.* 23 Mar. 1766.
Services : N.F.P.

BENSON, George (1755-1810). Major, Invalid Est. 6th N.I. *b.* 1755. Cadet 1781. Admitted 20 Apr. 1782. Ensign 28 June 1781. Lieut. 1 Oct. 1782. Capt. 8 Dec. 1800. Major 8 May 1806. Invalided 15 Sept. 1807. *d.* Calcutta, 7 Jan. 1810, aged 54.
Son of George Benson, of Salisbury, Wilts.
Services : Sailed for India on the *Northumberland* 26 June 1781. Apptd. Cadet 14 Aug. 1781, aged 25. Lieut. 6th N.I. Capt. Lt. 6th N.I. 29 May 1800. Operations in Baghelkhand 1803 ; Chaukandi ; Capt. 2/6th N.I. Fort Adjt. at Monghyr 1805 till invalided. Comdg. Eur. and Native Invalids at Buxar 1807 till death.
Refs. : *G.M.* 1810, ii. 192. M.I. in S. Park St. burial ground, Calcutta. Will dated Buxar 6 Nov. 1809 ; codicil dated 19 Dec. 1809 ; proved 8 Jan. 1810.

BENSON, Richard (1785-1858). Major General, C.B. Colonel 11th N.I. *b.* Cockermouth, Cumberland, 9 Jan. 1785. Cadet 1805. Arrived in India 11 July 1806. Ensign 8 Aug. 1806. Lieut. 30 Aug. 1809. Capt. 1 May 1824. Major 29 Oct. 1832. Lt. Col. 30 July 1839. Col. 16 July 1849. Maj. Gen. 28 Nov. 1854. *d.* his residence on the lake of Buttermere, Cumberland, 26 Aug. 1858.
Son of Thomas Benson and Isabella his wife.
Services : Posted to 5th N.I. Adjt. 1/5th N.I. 1812. Intr. & Qmr. 1/5th N.I. 1 July 1814 till 1824. Transfd. as Capt. to 11th N.I. (late 1/5th) May 1824. 2nd in comd. 10th Extra Regt. 21 May 1825 till 1 Apr. 1826. Siege and capture of Bhurtpore ; Capt. 11th N.I. (s.w.) (India medal). Asst. sec., Mily. dept., 15 Jan. 1828. Mily. sec. to G.G. 5 Sept. 1828 till 4 Sept. 1833. Fur. s.c. 4 Sept. 1833 till 24 May 1838. Resdt. at Ava, with official rank of Col., 2 June 1838. Lt. Col. 68th N.I. 30 July 1839. Transfd. to 74th N.I. ; to 53rd N.I. ; to 1st N.I. Fur. s.c. 14 Jan. 1840 till 7 Oct. 1843. Dy. sec., Mily dept., 31 Jan. 1844. M.M.B. First Sikh War ; Mudki ; Ferozshahr ; Sobraon (Medal with 2 clasps). Transfd. to 41st N.I. 15 Feb. 1848. Offg. Mily. sec. to Lord Dalhousie 4 Oct. 1848 till 5 Dec. 1849. Col. 11th N.I. 16 July 1849. Fur. s.c. 2 Feb. 1851 till death. C.B. 3 Apr. 1846.
Refs. : *Boase. List of Military Secretaries to the Governors General and Viceroys.*

BENSON, William (1804-1848). Bt. Major, 4th L.C. *b.* Bassenthwaite, Cumberland, 1 Mar. 1804. Cadet 1820. Arrived in India May 1821. Cornet 16 Jan. 1821. Lieut. 7 Mar. 1823. Capt. 15 Nov. 1837. Bt. Major 9 Nov. 1846. *d.* Cawnpore 28 Oct. 1848.

Son of Joseph Benson, of Annan, co. Dumfries, innkeeper and farmer. *m.* Meerut, 16 Feb. 1826, Miss Amelia Ann Wallace (*probably* sister of Newton Wallace, *q.v.*).

Services : Posted as Cornet to 4th L.C. 21 Nov. 1821, and served throughout with that Regt. Intr. & Qmr. 27 July 1825 till 19 Oct. 1830. Siege and capture of Bhurtpore. Fur. s.c. 26 Feb. 1831 till 15 Dec. 1834. First Sikh War ; Mudki ; Ferozshahr ; Sobraon (Medal with 2 clasps).

BENT, Richard (1778- ?). Capt. Lieutenant. 25th N.I. *bapt.* Newcastle-under-Lyme, Staffs., 24 June 1778. Cadet 1795. Arrived in India 2 Feb. 1797. Ensign 5 Dec. 1796. Lieut. 19 Nov. 1797. Capt. Lt. 18 Oct. 1807. Resigned 21 Apr. 1809.

Son of James Bent.

Services : Adjt. 2/7th N.I. 1803-5. Adjt. 2/25th N.I. 1805-6. Operations against the Rana of Gohad 1806 ; capture of Gohad ; Lieut. and Adjt. 2/25th N.I. Fur. 22 Sept. 1806 till resignation.

BENTLEY, F—— P—— (*d.* 1782). Captain. Infantry. Cadet 1768. Ensign 15 Jan. 1769. Lieut. 19 Dec. 1769. Capt. 27 July 1778. *d.* 1782.

Services : Returned to England in the *Nassau*, which arrived in the Downs 14 Sept. 1780. N.F.P.

Refs. : Hickey, ii. 186.

BENTON, William (*d.* 1772). Captain, Infantry. Cadet 1763. Ensign 20 June 1763. Lieut. 6 Feb. 1764. Capt. 2 June 1772. *d.* Calcutta 5 Nov. 1772.

Services : N.F.P.

BERESFORD, John Gorges (1805-1879). Lieutenant. 74th N.I. Subsequently collector of customs at Southampton. *b.* nr. Cork 3 June 1805. Cadet 1823. Arrived in India 3 May 1824. Ensign 9 Jan. 1824. Lieut. 13 May 1825. Retired 9 Nov. 1831. *d.* Ravenswood, Ryde, I.W., 24 Dec. 1879.

4th son of Hon. and Rev. George de la Poer Beresford, rector of Fenagh, co. Leitrim (who was 2nd son of Hon. and Rev. William Beresford, first Baron Decies, archbishop of Tuam), and Susan his wife, 3rd dau. of Hamilton Gorges, of Kilbrew, co. Meath. *m.* Dinapore, 21 Oct. 1826, Matilda Anne, eldest dau. of Major Francis

THE BENGAL ARMY, 1758-1834

Russell Eager, H.M. 31st Regt. Ed. Rugby; entered the school in 1820.
Services : Posted as Ensign to 53rd N.I. Transfd. to newly-raised 6th Extra Regt. (became 74th N.I.) 5 Sept. 1825. Intr. & Qmr. 6th Extra Regt. 14 Feb. 1826. Fur. s.c. 26 Feb. 1829 till retirement. Pensioned on Lord Clive's fund 22 July 1831. Retired on a pension of 2/6 *p.d.* from 9 Nov. 1831. No record of active service.
Refs. : Burke's *Peerage,* 1923, p. 675, *s.n.* Decies, B. *Rugby School List. The Times,* 2 Jan. 1880.

BERESFORD, William (1777-?). Cadet. Infantry. *bapt.* Ashbourne, co. Derby, 12 Mar. 1777. Cadet 1796. Arrived in India 27 Jan. 1798. Resigned 27 Mar. 1798.

4th and youngest son of Richard Beresford, of Ashbourne and Bentley, and Alicia his wife, dau. of Richard Garle, of Leicester. Uncle of Sir Francis Wheler, Bart., *q.v.*
Services : N.F.P.
Refs. : Glover's *Derbyshire,* ii. 46.

BERGUER, John Frederick (1790-1826). Captain, 60th N.I. *b.* Royston, Herts., 9 June 1790. Cadet 1805. Arrived in India 27 June 1807. Ensign 17 July 1807. Lieut. 29 Mar. 1810. Capt. 1 May 1824. *d.* at sea, 10 Dec. 1826, on board the *Eliza* on the voyage to England.

Son of Rev. David Berguer, rector of Everleigh, Wilts., in 1808.
Services : Posted as Ensign to 19th N.I. Transfd. to 30th N.I. in 1815. Intr. & Qmr. 2/30th N.I. 1818. Adjt. 1/30th N.I. 1 June 1819 till May 1824. Transfd. as Capt. to 60th N.I. (late 2/30th) May 1824. Siege and capture of Bhurtpore; Capt. 60th N.I. Sailed from Calcutta on fur. on the *Eliza* 24 Sept. 1826.

BERKELEY, Henry Nicholas Lionel (*d.* 1809). Lieutenant, Invalid Est. Cadet (?). Ensign 4 July 1779. Lieut. 2 Feb. 1781. Invalided 15 Mar. 1787. *d.* Chunar 25 Oct. 1809.

m. 1st, Calcutta, Nov. 1794, Jane Zara. *m.* 2nd, Calcutta, 16 Dec. 1797, Elizabeth Huet.
Services : 1st Coy. Eur. Inf. Invalids in 1790. The last six years, at least, of his life were passed at Chunar.
Pub. in India in 1793 a book of Poems entitled, *Triumph of Magnanimity, etc.*
Refs. : *Calcutta Gaz.* 16 Jan. 1794.

BERKELEY or BARCLAY, William (1756/57-1810). Lieutenant, Infantry. Subsequently Lt. Col. 4th M.N.I. *b* 1756/57 Cadet 1780 Ensign Feb 1781. Removed to Madras Est. 15 Oct. 1781. *d.* Chatrapur, Madras, 25 Sept. 1810, aged 53.

LIST OF THE OFFICERS OF

m. 3 June 1804, Elizabeth Bell. (She died Sept. 1848, aged 70.)
Services : Ensign (Madras) 17 Dec. 1780. Lieut. 17 Apr. 1786.
Adjt. 11th M.N.I. 16 July 1791. Capt. 5 Aug. 1797. Major 15th
M.N.I. 9 May 1802. Lt. Col. 2/4th M.N.I. 3 Feb. 1808.
Refs. : M.I. in Ganjam cemetery.

BERNARD, William Owen (1788-1813). Lieutenant, Artillery.
b. Sutton, Surrey, 20 Dec. 1788. Cadet 1806. Arrived in India
1 Aug. 1807. Fireworker 9 May 1807. Lieut. 31 Mar. 1808.
d. Kaitha, Bundelkhand, 22 Aug. 1813.

Son of John Frederick Bernard and Jane his wife. Woolwich
Cadet ; nominated Cadet for R.M.A. 6 June 1804 ; obtained his
certificate 2 Jan. 1807.
Services : Sailed for India on the *Castle Eden.* No record of
active service.
Refs. : G.M. 1814, i. 408.

BERRIE, Robert (*d.* 1842). Major. 4th N.I. Cadet 1783. Arrived
in India 17 Sept. 1783. Ensign 25 Feb. 1785. Lieut. 9 Dec.
1791. Capt. 30 Sept. 1803. Major 19 Dec. 1809. Retired
2 Jan. 1811. *d.* Unthank, co. Dumbarton, 4 Feb. 1842 (? 3 Apr.
1842).

Of Unthank, psh. of Kirkintilloch, co. Dumbarton. Brother of
William Berrie.
Services : Second Mahratta War ; storm of Aligarh 4 Sept. 1803
(w.) ; (? battle of Deig) ; Capt. 1/4th N.I. Fur. 18 Feb. 1808 till
retirement.
Refs. : Will dated Glasgow 29 Apr. 1837 ; proved 5 Apr. 1843.

BERRY, Charles (*d.* 1804). Captain, 8th N.I. Cadet 1793. Arrived
in India 20 Feb. 1795. Ensign 13 Sept. 1794. Lieut. 8 Jan. 1796.
Capt. 1804. *d.* Fatehgarh, U.P., 23 May 1804.
Of Rathbone Pl., Soho, Middlesex.
Services : (? Operations in Jumna Doab 1802-3 ; Sasni ; Lieut.
8th N.I.)
Refs. : Will dated 21 Nov. 1803 ; proved in 1804.

BERTIE, Thomas (1773-1794). Fireworker, Artillery. *b.* Westminster, London, 16 Sept. 1773. Cadet 1791. Fireworker
7 Sept. 1791. *d.* Aug. 1794 : lost at sea on his passage to Bencoolen, Sumatra.

bapt. St. James's, Westminster, 10 Oct. 1773. Son of Thomas
Bertie and Elizabeth his wife.
Services : N.F.P.

THE BENGAL ARMY, 1758-1834   135

BERTRAM, Thomas (*d.* 1770). Lieutenant, Infantry. Cadet 1767. Ensign 3 Mar. 1768. Lieut. 19 Dec. 1769. *d.* Calcutta 16 Sept. 1770.
Services : N.F.P.

BERTRAM, William (1788-1839). Major. 16th N.I. *b.* Carnwath, co. Lanark, 11 July 1788. Cadet 1803. Arrived in India 18 Mar. 1805. Ensign 3 May 1805. Lieut. 3 May 1805. Capt. 29 Apr. 1823. Major 2 June 1826. Retired 13 Sept. 1829. *d.* Edinburgh 11 June 1839.
Of Nisbet and Kersewell, co. Lanark. 2nd son of William Bertram, of Nisbet and Kersewell, Capt. 7th Dragoon Gds., Col. of Lanarkshire Mil., and Jane his wife, dau. of Sir William Lockhart, 3rd Bart., of Lockhart Hall (now Carstairs), co. Lanark. *m.* 1st, Meerut, 16 June 1811, Maria Ramus. (She died Purnea 19 Feb. 1823.) *m.* 2nd, Meerut, 6 July 1825, Louise Caroline Clementine Deli Bertrand, dau. of Dr. Arnaud de Lapeijre, of Port Louis, I. of Mauritius.
Services : Posted as Lieut. to 10th N.I. Third Mahratta War ; Lieut. 1/10th N.I. Intr. & Qmr. 1/10th N.I. 28 Feb. 1817 till 1822. Bk. Mr. 16th (Purnea) Div. 1822-4. Transfd. to 16th N.I. (late 2/10th) May 1824. Tempy. comdg. Chittagong Provl. Bn. 1824-5 ; comdg. do. 1826-8. Leave s.c. 6 mos. to Mauritius 9 May 1827. Fur. p.a. 13 Dec. 1828 till retirement.
Refs. : Burke's *Landed Gentry*, 13th edn., p. 126, *s.n.* Bertram, of Nisbet, co. Lanark. *A.J.* N.S. xxix. 231.

BESANT, Thomas Henry Gatehouse (1806- ?). Major. 21st N.I. *b.* Dorchester 19 Nov. 1806. Cadet 1823. Arrived in India 7 June 1824. Ensign 21 Feb. 1824. Lieut. 13 May 1825. Capt. 1 July 1841. Retired 21 Aug. 1847. Hon. Major 28 Nov. 1854. *d.* (?).
Son of Thomas Gatehouse Besant, brewer and maltster.
Note : Name removed from the list of Retired Officers, given in *India List*, after July 1878 ; although it continues to figure in the official *Quarterly Bengal Army List* so late as Jan. 1884.
Services : Posted as Ensign to 21st N.I. and served throughout with that Corps. Siege and capture of Bhurtpore (India medal). Intr. & Qmr. 21st N.I. 15 Oct. 1831 till 22 May 1840. S.A.C.G. 9 Mar. 1840. First Afghan War ; Kandahar ; Ghazni ; Kabul ; Bolan Pass, with Gen. Nott (Medal). Invalided 1 July 1844. Fur. m.c. 25 Jan. 1845 till retirement.

BEST, John (*d.* 1774). Lieutenant, Infantry. Cadet 1769. Ensign 15 Feb. 1770. Lieut. 9 Feb. 1773. *d.* Calcutta 11 Dec. 1774.
Services : N.F.P.

136 LIST OF THE OFFICERS OF

BEST, Robert (*d.* 1808). Captain, Artillery. Bencoolen Cadet (?). Fireworker (Bencoolen) 31 Aug. 1786. Lieut. (Bengal) 29 Oct. 1794. Capt. Lt. 20 Sept. 1802. Capt. 17 Sept. 1805. *d.* Calcutta 13 Feb. 1808.
Brother of William Best and of Rebecca Long.
Services : Operations in Jumna Doab 1802-3 ; siege and capture of Sasni ; Bijaigarh ; Kachaura ; Capt. Lt. 3rd Coy. 2nd. Bn. Art. Second Mahratta War ; storm of Aligarh ; Capt. Lt. 3rd Coy. 2nd Bn. Was left in charge of Aligarh fort after its capture.
Refs. : Will dated Aligarh 28 June 1806 ; proved 29 Apr. 1808.

BETHELL, James. Captain. Infantry. Cadet 1764. Ensign 1764. Lieut. 9 Jan. 1767. Capt. 21 Sept. 1770. Dismissed Jan. 1772.
Services : N.F.P.

BETTS, Edward John (1799-1849). Captain, Invalid Est. 70th N.I. *bapt.* Birmingham 8 Aug. 1799. Cadet 1820. Arrived in India May 1821. Ensign 16 Jan. 1821. Lieut. 13 May 1825. Capt. 16 Jan. 1836. Invalided 1 July 1839. *d.* at sea, 10 Feb. 1849, on board the *Barham*.
Son of John Betts, of Birmingham, gold and silver refiner.
Services : Posted as Ensign to 2/17th N.I. Transfd. to 21st N.I. First Burma War ; Arakan 1825 ; Lieut. 1st L.I. Bn. Transfd. to newly-raised 2nd Extra Regt. (became 70th N.I. in 1828) in 1825. Fur. s.c. 5 Jan. 1827 ; leave s.c. 8 mos. to Singapore 27 Jan. 1836 ; fur. s.c. 23 Dec. 1848.

BETTSWORTH, William Henry Robin (1788- ?). Lieutenant. 15th N.I. *b.* London 19 Feb. 1788. Cadet 1803. Arrived in India 3 Dec. 1804. Ensign 23 Oct. 1804. Lieut. 23 Oct. 1804. Struck off 27 Feb 1812.
Son of John Bettsworth.
Services : Posted as Lieut. to 15th N.I. Fur. 27 Aug. 1809. Struck off in England after $2\frac{1}{2}$ years' absence from India. Promoted Capt. 2/15th N.I. 1 Oct. 1815, before information was received in India of his having been struck off. No record of active service.

BEVAN, Henry (1745/46-1807). Major. Infantry. *b.* 1745/46. Cadet 1763. Ensign 21 Sept. 1763. Lieut. 15 July 1764. Capt. 1 Aug. 1766. Major 1775. Retired 1778. *d.* Belmont, Shrewsbury, 25 Nov. 1807, aged 61.
m. Sarah, 2nd dau. of Rev. William Pigott, rector of Edgmond and Chetwynd, Salop.
Services : War with Mir Mohd. Kasim 1763. Battle of Buxar 23 Oct. 1764. Dismissed 13 Feb. 1767. Restored to the Service in

THE BENGAL ARMY, 1758-1834 137

1767. Comdd. 10th Bn. (afterwards 11th N.I.) from 1767 for many years. First Rohilla War; battle of St. George; Capt. comdg. 10th Bn. High sheriff, Salop., 1795; chief mgte., Shrewsbury, 1796.
Refs.: Burke's *Landed Gentry*, 11th edn., p. 1335, *s.n.* Pigott, of Doddershall Park, Bucks. *G.M.* 1807, ii. 1178.

BEVERIDGE, William (1799-1825). Lieutenant, Invalid Est. 18th N.I. *b.* Edinburgh 6 Feb. 1799. Cadet 1819. Was already in India as a "Free Mariner" when apptd. a Cadet. Ensign 19 Jan. 1820. Lieut. 11 July 1823. Invalided 16 Jan. 1824. *d.* Meerut 23 May 1825.
Eldest son of William Beveridge, of Edinburgh, W.S.
Services: Posted as Ensign to 1/17th N.I. Lieut. 17th N.I. 4 Feb. 1823. Transfd. to 18th N.I. 11 July 1823. No record of active service.
Refs.: *S.M.* 1825, ii. 766.

BICKERTON, Henry (*d.* 1775). Captain, Infantry. Cadet (?). Ensign 2 May 1764. Lieut. 17 Aug. 1765. Capt. 4 Dec. 1767. *d.* Belgaum, Bombay, 16 Nov. 1775.
Services: N.F.P.
Refs.: Will dated 8 Aug. 1774; proved 1 Jan. 1776.

BIDDULPH, Edward (1788-1858). Colonel, C.B. Artillery. *bapt.* Birdingbury, co. Warwick, 4 July 1788. Cadet 1805. Arrived in India 27 June 1807. Fireworker 2 May 1807. Lieut. 3 May 1807. Capt. Lt. 27 Jan. 1818. Capt. 1 Sept. 1818. Major 1 Dec. 1834. Lt. Col. 6 Dec. 1839. Retired in India 6 Oct. 1846. Hon. Col. 28 Nov. 1854. *d.* Fitzroy Terr., London, 3 Dec. 1858, aged 70.
3rd son of Sir Theophilus Biddulph, 5th Bart., of Westcombe, Kent, and Hannah his wife, dau. of H. Prestidge. Cousin-german of George Biddulph, *q.v.* *m.* Bareilly, 14 Oct. 1837, Louisa, dau. of Col. Kelly. Ed. Rugby; entered the school in 1802. Woolwich Cadet; nominated to R.M.A. 15 Feb. 1804; obtained his certificate 21 Oct. 1806.
Services: Sailed for India on the *Devaynes*. Fur. 11 Mar. 1822 till 10 Oct. 1824. First Burma War 1824-6; Capt. Foot Art., with Sir A. Campbell's force (India medal). Comdd. 3rd Troop 1st Bde., H.A., 1826-7. Gwalior campaign; Paniar; Lt. Col. comdg. Art. of Left Wing of the Army (Bronze star). First Sikh War; Sobraon; Lt. Col. 2nd Bde. H.A. (Medal). C.B. 2 May 1844.
Refs.: Burke's *Peerage*, 1923, p. 272, *s.n.* Biddulph, Bart., of Westcombe, Kent. *Boase*. *Rugby School List*. *G.M.* 1859, i. 104. *The Times*, 8 Dec. 1858.

BIDDULPH, George (1811-1857). Lieut. Colonel, 45th N.I. b. 19 Jan. 1811. Cadet 1827. Arrived in India 4 Sept. 1828. Ensign 16 Apr. 1828. Lieut. 2 Oct. 1831. Capt. 10 July 1846. Major 10 June 1853. Lt. Col. 1857. d. unm. 17 Nov. 1857 : kld. in action at the 2nd relief of Lucknow.

bapt. ptely. at Birdingbury, co. Warwick, 22 Feb. 1811. 5th and youngest son of Rev. John Biddulph, rector of Frankton, co. Warwick (who was 2nd son of Sir Theophilus Biddulph, 4th Bart.), and Sophia his wife, dau. of Sir Charles William Wheler, Bart. Brother of Trevor Biddulph, *q.v.* Ed. Rugby ; entered the school in 1826.

Services : Ensign d.d. 70th N.I. 5 Nov. 1828. Posted as Ensign to 45th N.I. 4 Mar. 1829. Adjt. 45th N.I. 5 Mar. 1838 till 23 May 1846. First Sikh War ; Mudki ; Ferozshahr ; Bt. Capt. 45th N.I., with 3rd Irreg. Cav. (Medal with clasp). Taken prisoner at Mudki, but so impressed the Sikhs by his undaunted bravery that he was released two days later. 2nd in comd. 3rd Irreg. Cav. 4 May 1846. Second Sikh War ; Chilianwala ; Gujerat ; 3rd Irreg. Cav. (Medal with clasp). Comdt. 3rd Irreg. Cav. 17 Mar. 1851 till 10 Feb. 1854. Fur. 1854 till 13 Aug. 1857. Comdt. Sikh Vols. 24 Aug. 1857.

Refs. : Burke's *Peerage*, 1923, p. 272, *s.n.* Biddulph, Bart., of Westcombe, Kent. *Rugby School List.* *G.M.* 1858, i. 336. *The Times*, 19 Jan. 1858.

BIDDULPH, Trevor (1806-1831). Lieutenant, 45th N.I. b. Birdingbury, co. Warwick, 29 Apr. 1806. Cadet 1825. Arrived in India 23 Dec. 1826. Ensign 21 May 1826. Lieut. 29 Oct. 1830. d. unm. Nimach 2 Oct. 1831.

3rd son of Rev. John Biddulph, rector of Frankton, co. Warwick, and Sophia his wife. Brother of William Biddulph, *q.v.*, and cousin-german of Edward Biddulph, *q.v.* Ed. Rugby ; entered the school at midsummer 1820.

Services : Posted as Ensign to 45th N.I. No record of active service.

Refs. : Burke's *Peerage*, 1923, p. 272, *s.n.* Biddulph, Bart., of Westcombe, Kent. *Rugby School List.* *G.M.* 1832, i. 383.

BIDDULPH, William (1805-1852). Captain. 45th N.I. b. Birdingbury, co. Warwick, 9 Jan. 1805. Cadet 1821. Arrived in India 12 Nov. 1822. Ensign 25 Dec. 1822. Lieut. 21 Oct. 1824. Capt. 27 Jan. 1839. Invalided 10 July 1846. Retired 11 July 1849. d. Elgin 13 Jan. 1852.

2nd son of Rev. John Biddulph, rector of Frankton, and Sophia his wife. Brother of George Biddulph, *q.v.* m. Calcutta, 17 Apr. 1841, Hannah Sarah, eldest dau. of Dr. Nathaniel Wallich, Supt.

THE BENGAL ARMY, 1758-1834 139

of Calcutta botanic gardens (*D.N.B.*). Ed. Rugby ; entered the school in 1818.
Services : Posted as Ensign to 32nd N.I. Transfd. to 23rd N.I. ; to 45th N.I. (late 1/23rd) May 1824. Intr. & Qmr. 45th N.I. 28 Dec. 1827. Adjt. 45th N.I. 13 Dec. 1831. Fur. s.c. 13 Feb. 1838 till 19 Mar. 1841. D.A.A.G., Benares Div., 11 Sept. 1843. 2nd in comd. Sirmoor Bn. Jan. 1845.
Refs. : Burke's *Peerage*, 1923, p. 272, *s.n.* Biddulph, Bart., of Westcombe, Kent. *Rugby School List. G.M.* 1852, i. 313.

BIDWELL, Woodward (1783-1838). Captain. 14th N.I. *b.* Thetford, Norfolk, 22 Feb. 1783. Cadet 1800. Arrived in India 22 Aug. 1801. Ensign 9 Jan. 1802. Lieut. 15 Jan. 1804. Capt. 1 Mar. 1816. Struck off 16 Aug. 1822. *d.* Hammersmith 18 Nov. 1838, of apoplexy.
bapt. St. Mary's, Thetford, 30 June 1784. Son of Shelford Bidwell and Mary his wife.
Services : Posted as Ensign to 14th N.I. Capture of Java ; Lieut. 3rd Bn. Bengal Vols. Qmr. do. 1813-5. Capt. Lt. do. 2 Feb. 1816. Served in Java till 1816, when he returned to Bengal and rejoined 2/14th N.I. as Capt. Was on fur. when struck off in 1822.
Refs. : *G.M.* 1839, i. 104. *A.J.* N.S. xxvii. 340.

BIE, George (*d.* 1796). Capt. Lieutenant, Artillery. Country Cadet 1779. Admitted 19 Aug. 1779. Fireworker 1 Oct. 1780. Lieut. 29 May 1786. Capt. Lt. 8 Jan. 1796. *d.* Serampore 22 Aug. 1796.
(*Probably* son of Col. Ole Bie, Danish governor of Serampore, Bengal, 1789-1805, and brother of Jacob Bie, *q.v.*)
Services : Fur. 4 Apr. 1785 till 20 Feb. 1790. N.F.P.

BIE, Jacob. Ensign. Infantry. Cadet 1781. Ensign 16 Aug. 1781. Resigned at home 14 Feb. 1785.
(*Probably* son of Col. Ole Bie, Danish governor of Serampore, and brother of George Bie, *q.v.*)
Services : N.F.P.

BIGGE, Henry Lancelot (1806-1844). Captain, 66th N.I. *b.* Eslington Hall, Northumberland, 10 May 1806. Cadet 1827. Arrived in India 23 Oct. 1828. Ensign 10 May 1828. Lieut. 13 Mar. 1834. Capt. 1844. *d.s.p.* Barisal, Bengal, 9 Dec. 1844.
3rd son of Charles William Bigge, of Linden, Lt. Col. Northumberland Militia, high sheriff 1802, and Alicia his wife, only dau. of Christopher Wilkinson, of Newcastle-upon-Tyne. Uncle of Rt. Hon. Sir Arthur John Bigge, P.C., first Baron Stamfordham. Ed.

Westminster ; admitted 21 May 1818. K.S., 1820, aged 14. Univ. Coll., Oxon. ; matric. 19 Oct. 1824.
Services : Ensign d.d. 33rd N.I. 20 Nov. 1828. Posted as Ensign to 14th N.I. 4 Mar. 1829. Transfd. to 66th N.I. 4 May 1832. Adjt. Assam L.I. 13 Aug. 1832. Offg. Junior Asst. to the Comr. of Assam 1837 ; principal do. 7 Nov. 1838 till 1843. Leave s.c. to China for 2 years in 1835 ; leave s.c. to China 7 Sept. 1843.
Refs. : Burke's *Landed Gentry*, 13th edn., p. 135, *s.n.* Bigge, late of Foulden Hall. *Alumni Westmon. Alumni Oxon.* Will dated 10 Oct. 1844 ; proved 31 Dec. 1844.

BIGGE, James Rundell (1806-1853). Lieutenant. 3rd N.I. *b.* London 3 Mar. 1806. Cadet 1821. Arrived in India 14 Sept. 1822. Ensign 19 June 1822. Lieut. 11 Sept. 1823. Retired 27 Apr. 1832. *d.* 10 July 1853.

Son of Thomas Bigge, merchant, partner in the firm of Rundell, Bridge & Rundell.
Services : Posted as Ensign to 6th N.I. Transfd. to 3rd N.I. (late 1/6th) May 1824. Intr. & Qmr. 3rd N.I. 8 Feb. 1827 till 11 Feb. 1828. Fur. s.c. 4 Jan. 1830 till retirement. No record of active service.

BIGGS, John Andrew (1787-1844). Major General, Artillery. *bapt.* Cookham, Berks., 28 Mar. 1787. Cadet 1804. Arrived in India 2 Dec. 1804. Lieut. 18 Aug. 1804. Capt. Lt. 17 Dec. 1806. Capt. 1 Aug. 1814. Major 8 Aug. 1821. Lt. Col. 29 Aug. 1824. Col. 28 Apr. 1837. Maj. Gen. 28 June 1838. *d.* Cawnpore 12 July 1844, aged 57.

Son of John Andrew Biggs and Elizabeth his wife. *m.* 30 Aug. 1814 the youngest dau. of Capt. S. P. Mouat(t), R.N., of Southcot Pl., Bath. Father of Mary Anne Drake Mouat, wife of Nathaniel Jones, *q.v.*
Services : (? Capture of Chamir fort 29 Jan. 1807.) Nepal War 1816 ; Capt. comdg. 7th Coy. 2nd Bn. Art. To comd. newly-raised 5th Troop H.A. July 1817. Third Mahratta War ; Jawad ; comdg. 5th Troop. Siege and capture of Bhurtpore ; Lt. Col. comdg. 1st Bn. Foot Art. Fur. p.a. 26 Nov. 1830 till 17 Dec. 1832, and 22 Feb. 1840 till 17 Oct. 1843. Apptd. to comd. at Ambala, as Bdr. 2 cl., 24 May 1844, and was on his way there when he died.
Refs. : I.M. 12 Sept. 1844, p. 528. M.I. St. Stephen's, Dum-Dum.

BIGGS, Thomas (*d.* 1770). Fireworker, Artillery. Cadet (?). Fireworker 4 Oct. 1769. *d.* Calcutta 16 Oct. 1770.
Services : N.F.P.

THE BENGAL ARMY, 1758-1834   141

BIGNELL, Moring Agnew (1808-1844). Ensign. 63rd N.I. Subsequently a pleader, Sudder Adawlut, Calcutta, and Dy. Supt. of legal affairs. *b.* 3 Sept. 1808. Cadet 1829. Arrived in India 27 Mar. 1830. Ensign 10 Oct. 1829. Resigned 31 Dec. 1830. *d.* Calcutta 23 Jan. 1844.
bapt. London 12 Nov. 1808. Son of William Bignell, of Torrington, Devon, and Anne his wife. Brother of William Bignell, *q.v. m.* Calcutta, 24 May 1838, Sophia Amelia Alphonsina, dau. of Robert McClintock, of Calcutta, merchant, and sister of George Frederick McClintock, *q.v.* (She *re-m.* 20 Jan. 1852 William A. Parker, of Edinburgh.)
Services : To do duty with 63rd N.I. 5 Apr. 1830. No record of active service.
Refs. : M.I. in Circular Rd. burial ground, Calcutta.

BIGNELL, William (1798-1831). Captain, 63rd N.I. *b.* Hammersmith 25 July 1798. Cadet 1815. Admitted 6 Sept. 1816. Ensign 8 May 1816. Lieut. 11 July 1823. Capt. 28 Mar. 1831. *d.* at sea 10 May 1831.
Son of William Bignell and Anne his wife. Brother of Moring Agnew Bignell, *q.v. m.* St. John's, Calcutta, 2 Nov. 1822, Miss Georgiana Watts. (She died Peckham, Surrey, 29 Oct. 1857.)
Services : Third Mahratta War ; Ensign 8th N.I. Intr. & Qmr. 1/8th N.I. 18 Sept. 1821. Transfd. to 32nd N.I. July 1823 ; to 63rd N.I. (late 1/32nd) May 1824. Intr. & Qmr. 63rd N.I. 6 July 1824. Siege and capture of Bhurtpore ; Lieut. 63rd N.I. Leave s.c. for 18 mos. to Mauritius and the Cape 4 May 1831.
Refs. : *A.J.* N.S. vi. 190.

BIGNELL, William Phillips (1803-1852). Captain, 69th N.I. *bapt.* Banbury, Oxon., 13 Sept. 1803. Cadet 1826. Arrived in India 13 Oct. 1827. Ensign 8 May 1827. Lieut. 1 Dec. 1836. Capt. 11 Sept. 1845. *d.* Musanagar, nr. Cawnpore, 17 Nov. 1852 ; bur. at Cawnpore 18 Nov. 1852.
Son of Richard Bignell, of Middleton-Stoney, Oxon., solicitor, and Emily his wife. *m.* Saugor, 2 Feb. 1838, Miss Mary Kyd Duckett Kyd, ward of Duncan Presgrave, *q.v.* His sister *m.* John Arthur James, *q.v. Note :* Christian names given in the marriage register as William Edward Phillips. Ed. at Westminster ; admitted 11 Jan. 1815 ; left midsummer 1817.
Services : Ensign .Oxford Mil. 31 Mar. 1826. Posted as Ensign to 1st Extra Regt. (became 69th N.I.) 3 Jan. 1828. Served in P.W.D. Adjt. 69th N.I. 2 Apr. 1845. Bde. Major 3 July 1845. Fur. s.c. 18 Feb. 1847 till 1849. Whilst comdg. the escort in attendance on the Lieut. Govr., he was seized with a spasmodic

attack in the stomach on 16 Nov. 1852, and died the following morning.
Refs. : *Westminster School Register* (where date of birth is given as 13 Sept. 1801). *I.M.* 1852, pp. 730, 738. Will dated Feb. 1849 ; proved 3 Mar. 1853.

BINGLEY, Frederick (*d.* 1787). Ensign, Infantry. Cadet 1782. Ensign 18 Feb. 1783. *d.* Dinajpur, Bengal, 2 Sept. 1787.
Services : N.F.P.

BINGLEY, Thomas Brooke (1797-1842). Lieutenant. Artillery. *b.* 2 Dec. 1797. Cadet 1814. Fireworker 14 Aug. 1817. Lieut. 1 Sept. 1818. Struck off 23 June 1827. *d.* Dunkirk, France, 20 Nov. 1842.
bapt. St. Clement Danes, Strand, London, 4 Jan. 1798. Son of Thomas Bingley and Charlotte his wife. *m.* Calcutta, 22 May 1818, Anne, eldest dau. of Sir John Horsford, K.C.B., *q.v.* (She died 20 Oct. 1860.) Addiscombe Cadet 1812-4.
Services : (? Third Mahratta War ; Lieut. Foot Art.) Posted to 3rd Troop H.A. in 1820. Transfd. to 1st Troop in 1821 ; to 6th Troop in 1824 ; to 1st Troop 2nd Bde. in 1825. Siege and capture of Bhurtpore ; Lieut. 1st Troop 2nd Bde., serving with 4th Troop 3rd Bde. Struck off for quitting the country without leave. Subsequently went to Russia.
Refs. : *A.J.* N.S. xxxix. 451.

BINNS, Isaac (*d.* 1791). Captain, Artillery. Cadet 1777. Fireworker 30 Mar. 1778. Lieut. 2 Oct. 1778. Capt. Lt. 19 Oct. 1784. Capt. 31 May 1786. *d.* Calcutta 11 Nov. 1791.
m. 1st, Calcutta, 22 May 1787, Catherine Atwood, widow. *m.* 2nd, Calcutta, 19 July 1790, Miss Henrietta Priscilla Caroline Carter.
Services : N.F.P.
Refs. : Will dated 9 Nov. 1791.

BINNY, Alexander (1758-1833). Lieutenant. Infantry. *b.* 1758. Cadet 1781. Ensign 8 Aug. 1782. Lieut. 28 Jan. 1785. Resigned 1 Apr. 1794. *d.* St. Andrews, co. Fife, 24 Oct. 1833.
Of St. Andrews. 2nd son of Alexander Binny, of Forfar, and Isobel Dickson his wife. Grandson of Alexander Binny, provost of Forfar. *m.* Calcutta, 4 May 1796, Elizabeth Amelia, eldest dau. of William Jackson, attorney, register of the supreme court, Calcutta, and sister of James Nesbitt Jackson, *q.v.*
Services : After resigning the Service he appears to have joined the firm of Cockerell, Trail, Palmer & Co., Calcutta.
Refs. : *Howard & Crisp*, xxi. 65. *S.M.* 1796, p. 864. *G.M.*

1796, ii. 1113. Portrait in oils lately in possession of the widow of Robert Fergusson McTier, the grandson.

BINNY, Charles (1796-1818). Lieutenant, 1st N.I. *bapt.* Tannadice, co. Forfar, 31 Oct. 1796. Cadet 1813. Ensign (25 Sept. 1814) 5 June 1815. Lieut. (?). *d.* Saugor 7 Aug. 1818.
Son of David Binny, farmer.
Services : Posted as Ensign to 2/1st N.I. Siege and capture of Hathras. Third Mahratta War ; Dhamoni.

BIRBECK, William (1787-1812). Ensign, 8th N.I. *bapt.* Penrith, Cumberland, 26 May 1787. Cadet 1806. Arrived in India 25 Nov. 1807. Ensign 6 Oct. 1807. *d.* 20 Aug. 1812.
Son of William Birbeck and Betty his wife, née Dawson.
Services : Posted as Ensign to 8th N.I. Expedition against Mauritius 1810 ; Ensign 2nd Bn. Bengal Vols.

BIRCH, Frederick William (1804-1857). Bt. Lieut. Colonel, 41st N.I. *b.* Calcutta 1 Apr. 1804. Cadet 1820. Admitted 23 July 1821. Ensign 7 Jan. 1821. Lieut. 11 July 1823. Capt. 8 Oct. 1839. Major 8 Dec. 1852. Bt. Lt. Col. 20 June 1854. *d.* Sitapur, U.P., 3 June 1857 : kld. by mutineers.
Son of Richard Comyns Birch, B.C.S., P.M.G., Bengal, and Frances Jane his wife, dau. of William Rider, granddau. of J. Z. Holwell (*D.N.B.*), and step-dau. of Martin Yorke, *q.v.* Brother of Sir Richard James Holwell Birch, *q.v. m.* Lucknow, 7 July 1825, Miss Jean Walker. (She died Multan 9 July 1852.)
Services : Posted as Ensign to 1/9th N.I. Transfd. to 2/21st N.I. in 1823 ; to 41st N.I. (late 1/21st) May 1824. First Burma War ; Arakan 1825 ; Lieut. 1st Gren. Bn. Intr. & Qmr. 41st N.I. 18 Feb. 1831. Supt. Calcutta Police 1 Jan. 1836. Supt. Police and of salt chokies 1840. Senior mgte. of the town of Calcutta in 1846. Reverted to regtl. duty in 1849.
Refs. : G.M. 1857, ii. 466.

BIRCH, George (1781-1855). Major. 46th N.I. *b.* 25 Aug. 1781. Cadet 1798. Arrived in India 22 Oct. 1799. Ensign 25 Oct. 1799. Lieut. 28 Oct. 1799. Capt. 28 Sept. 1810. Major 11 July 1823. Retired 15 Jan. 1824. *d.* Folkestone 23 Feb. 1855.
Of Clare Park, Crondall, Hants. *bapt.* S. Thoresby, Lincs., 28 Aug. 1781. Son of Rev. Thomas Birch, D.D., and Mary his wife, née Wright. *m.* 15 June 1831, Lydia Diana, dau. of Samuel Francis Dashwood, of Stanford, Notts.
Services : Posted to 2/10th N.I. 15 Apr. 1801. Adjt. 1/10th N.I. in 1804. Transfd. to 23rd N.I. in 1804. Second Mahratta War ; defence of Delhi Oct. 1804 ; Lieut. comdg. a Najib. Bn. Adjt. &

Qmr. 23rd N.I. 1804-10. At Ludhiana 1812-4. Capt. 1/23rd N.I. Pol. dept., Asst. to Sir David Ochterlony, *q.v.*, 1816-22. Fur. 1822 till retirement. Transfd. to 46th N.I. (late 2/23rd) in May 1824, before his retirement was notified in India.

Refs. : Burke's *Landed Gentry*, 13th edn., p. 140, *s.n.* Birch, of Clare Park, Crondall, Hants. *E.I.M.C.* ii. 497. *G.M.* 1855, i. 445.

BIRCH, George Roydes (1807-1864). Lieutenant. Pensioner on Lord Clive's fund. Artillery. *b.* Calcutta 7 July 1807. Cadet 1824. Arrived in India 5 Sept. 1825. 2nd Lieut. 16 Dec. 1824. Lieut. 4 Apr. 1829. Pensioned 24 June 1833. *d.* 8 Mar. 1864.

bapt. Calcutta 31 July 1807. Son of John Brereton Birch, 1st mgte., Calcutta, and Anna Maria his 2nd wife, née Mann. Brother of Thomas Charles Birch, *q.v.*, and nephew of John Zephaniah Mill Birch, *q.v. m.* 15 Aug. 1839, Sophia, 3rd dau. of Sir William Russell, 1st Bart., of Charlton Park, Gloucs., grand-dau. of James Doddington Sherwood, *q.v.*, and cousin-german of John Russell, *q.v.* Addiscombe Cadet 17 May 1822 till 1824.

Services : Posted to 1st Troop 2nd Bde., H.A., in 1826 ; transfd. to 2nd Troop 1st Bde. in 1827. Fur. s.c. 27 Jan. 1827 till 23 Oct. 1830, and 4 Jan. 1831 till pensioned. No record of active service. Subsequently took holy orders, and became Sec. to the Turkish Missions Aid Soc.

Refs. : Burke's *Peerage*, 1904, p. 1352, *s.n.* Russell, Bart., of Charlton Park. *G.M.* 1864, i. 533. *The Times*, 10 Mar. 1864.

BIRCH, John (1794-1819). Lieutenant, 14th N.I. *b.* 7 Oct. 1794. Cadet 1810. Ensign 7 Apr. 1813. Lieut. 2 Feb. 1816. *d.* in India Mar. 1819.

Son of Rev. Richard Birch, of Widdington, Essex, sometime rector of N. Fambridge, Essex.

Services : Cadet d.d. 25th N.I. 1812-3. Posted as Ensign to 1/14th N.I. (? Third Mahratta War ; Dhamoni ; Mandala ; Garhakota ; Lieut. 1/14th N.I.)

BIRCH, John Zephaniah Mill (*d.* 1794). Lieutenant, 2nd Bengal European Bn. Cadet 1782. Ensign 27 Mar. 1783. Lieut. 3 Mar. 1790. *d.* 26 Oct. 1794 : kld. in action at the battle of Bitaurah.

Son of William Birch and Sarah his wife, dau. of John Zephaniah Holwell, governor of Bengal (*D.N.B.*). Uncle of George Roydes Birch, *q.v.*

Services : Second Rohilla War ; Bitaurah (kld.) ; Lieut. 2nd Eur. Bn.

Refs. : Will dated Rajmahal 4 Dec. 1793 ; proved 6 Jan. 1795. M.I. in St. John's churchyard, Calcutta.

THE BENGAL ARMY, 1758-1884

BIRCH, Sir Richard James Holwell (1803-1875). Lieut. General, K.C.B. 2nd European Fusiliers. *b.* Calcutta 26 Jan. 1803. Cadet 1820. Admitted 23 July 1821. Ensign 7 Jan. 1821. Lieut. 11 July 1823. Capt. 29 Mar. 1836. Major 31 Oct. 1849. Lt. Col. 10 Dec. 1854. Bt. Col. 20 June 1854. Maj. Gen. 4 May 1858. Retired 31 Dec. 1861. Hon. Lt. Gen. 31 Dec. 1861. *d.* Venice 25 Feb. 1875.

Son of Richard Comyns Birch, B.C.S., and Frances Jane his wife, dau. of William Rider, sheriff of Calcutta 1757. Brother of Frederick William Birch, *q.v. m.* 1st, Delhi, 2 Nov. 1831, Elizabeth Cuninghame, dau. of Sir Jeremiah Bryant, Kt., *q.v. m.* 2nd, 1868, Mary, dau. of Capt. George P. Burden.

Services : See *D.N.B.* Adjt. 17th N.I. 19 May 1827. J.A.G. 10 Mar. 1841. Gwalior campaign ; Maharajpur (Bronze star). First Sikh War ; Mudki ; Ferozshahr ; Sobraon (Medal with 2 clasps). Second Sikh War ; Chilianwala ; Gujerat (Medal with clasp). C.B. 9 June 1849. K.C.B. 18 May 1860.

Refs. : *D.N.B. D.I.B. Boase.*

BIRCH, Robert (1799-1825). Lieutenant, 24th N.I. *b.* Glynn, co. Antrim, 20 July 1799. Cadet 1819. Ensign 3 Apr. 1820. Lieut. 8 Apr. 1823. *d.* Arakan 20 July 1825.

Son of Rev. (? George) Birch. (? T.C.D. ; pensioner 7 July 1817, aged 17.)

Services : Posted as Ensign to 1/9th N.I. Transfd. as Lieut. to 8th N.I. in 1823 ; to 24th N.I. (late 2/8th) May 1824. First Burma War ; Arakan 1825 ; Lieut. 1st L.I. Bn.

Refs. : (? *Alumni Dub.*)

BIRCH, Thomas Charles (1814-1857). Captain, 31st N.I. *b.* Bengal 10 Nov. 1814. Cadet 1832. Arrived in India 21 June 1833. Ensign 21 June 1833. Lieut. 27 Mar. 1837. Capt. 31 Mar. 1851. *d.* Allahabad 6 June 1857 : kld. by mutineers.

3rd and youngest son of John Brereton Birch and Anna Maria his 2nd wife. Brother of George Roydes Birch, *q.v.*, and nephew of John Zephaniah Mill Birch, *q.v. m.* Calcutta, 29 May 1838, Dorothy, youngest dau. of James Curtis, B.C.S., civil and session judge, Hooghly. *m.* 2nd, Allahabad, 25 Sept. 1851, Caroline F., dau. ot J. Amesbury. Addiscombe Cadet 15 Apr. 1831 till 14 Dec. 1832.

Services : Ensign d.d. 55th N.I. 24 July 1833. Posted as Ensign to 31st N.I. 24 May 1834. Adjt. 31st N.I. 11 Apr. 1840 till 9 June 1848. Operations against the Kols 1836-7. First Afghan War 1839 ; storm and capture of Kalat ; (? Ghazni) ; Lieut. 31st N.I. (Medal). Gwalior campaign ; Maharajpur ; Lieut. 31st N.I. (Bronze star). Second Sikh War ; Chilianwala ; Gujerat ; Offg.

S.A.C.G. (Medal with clasp). Santhal revolt. Fort Adjt., Allahabad, 6 May 1848 till death.
Refs. : *I.M.* 1851, p. 673. *G.M.* 1857, ii. 346.

BIRCH, William Charles (1805-1869). Lieut. Colonel. 5th N.I.
b. Stoke-on-Trent, Staffs., 21 Feb. 1805. Cadet 1823. Arrived in India 29 Oct. 1824. Ensign 28 June 1824. Lieut. 5 Feb. 1826. Capt. 31 Dec. 1840. Major 15 Nov. 1853. Retired 31 Dec. 1856. Hon. Lt. Col. 31 Dec. 1856. *d.* Merton, Surrey, 11 Oct. 1869.
3rd son of Edmund John Birch, of Fradswell Hall, Staffs., banker at Stafford, and Anna Maria his wife, dau. of John Yates, of Shelton. *m.* Nasirabad, 25 May 1841, Harriet, 7th dau. of James Kennedy, *q.v.* (*See also* William Alexander.) Ed. Rugby; entered the school at midsummer 1820.
Services : Posted as Ensign to 5th N.I. 31 Mar. 1825. Adjt. 5th N.I. 9 Feb. 1835 till 15 Feb. 1837. Asst. to the supt. for suppression of *thuggee* 19 July 1838 till 1849. D.C., Shahpur, 13 Apr. 1849 till 1853. Fur. 1853-5.
Refs. : Burke's *Landed Gentry*, 10th edn., p. 126, *s.n.* Birch, late of Armitage, Staffs. *Rugby School List. The Times*, 13 Oct. 1869.

BIRD, Edward (*d.* 1825). Captain. Infantry. Cadet 1779. Arrived in India 20 Mar. 1779. Ensign 17 Sept. 1779. Lieut. 2 May 1781. Capt. Lt. 7 Jan. 1796. Capt. 1798. Retired in England 7 Nov. 1798. *d.* Southampton 1 Dec. 1825.
Of St. Mary's, Southampton. *m.* (?).
Services : Third Mysore War; Penagra; assault of Krishnagiri 8 Nov. 1791 (s.w.); Lieut. 7th Bn. Sepoys.

BIRD, George. Cadet. Infantry. Cadet 1771. Dismissed 31 Dec. 1772.
Services : N.F.P.

BIRD, Henry Frederick (*d.* 1790). Lieutenant, Infantry. Cadet 1779. Ensign 11 Sept. 1799. Lieut. 28 Apr. 1781. *d. unm.* 17 May 1790.
Son of John Bird, of London.
Services : N.F.P.
Refs. : Will.

BIRD, John. Ensign. Infantry. Cadet 1770. Ensign 9 Dec. 1771. Resigned Dec. 1771.
Services : N.F.P.

BIRD, John Jenkins (1757-1837). Lieut. Colonel, Invalid Est. Bengal European Regt. b. Mar. 1757. Cadet 1782. Arrived in India 15 Nov. 1782. Ensign 18 Apr. 1783. Lieut. 17 Mar. 1790. Capt. Lt. 7 Jan. 1796. Capt. 13 July 1803. Major 6 Aug. 1810. Lt. Col. 4 June 1814. Invalided 1 Sept. 1815. d. Hazaribagh, Bengal, 30 Jan. 1837, aged 79 yrs. and 9 mos.

A native of Ireland. Son of " Count Loiseau," a French émigré, formerly an officer in the loyal Guards, who was son of an Irishman named Bird, attached to the French court.[1] m. Marie L'Herondell (*perhaps* dau. of Francis L'Herondell (formerly de la Tremouille) of Calcutta, attorney, and Mary Le Clere his wife.) (*See also* Robert Francis.) (She died Arrah, 14 Jan. 1840, aged 70.) His daus. m. Aynott Chitty, q.v., John Holbrow, q.v., and Frederick Young, q.v. Father of Louis Saunders Bird, q.v.

Services : Sailed for India on the *Worcester* 6 Feb. 1782. Served in 16th N.I. 1804-14. Comdg. Native Invalids at Monghyr 1816-20 ; comdg. Cawnpore Provl. Bn. 1820 ; comdg. Saharanpur Provl. Bn. 1821-30. At Buxar 1831-2. Resided at Berhampore from 23 Nov. 1833 ; at Hazaribagh from 31 Mar. 1835 till death.

Refs. : Gen. *Frederick Young*, by L. H. Jenkins, pp. 70-1. Will dated Ghazipur 29 May 1832 ; proved 14 Mar. 1837.

[1] *Note :* This statement appears in Mrs. L. Hadow Jenkins' Memoir of her father, Gen. Frederick Young, q.v., pub. in 1923. It must, however, be regarded as of doubtful accuracy, dates being irreconcilable.

BIRD, John Lewis. Lieutenant of Invalids.
m. Rozena Reid.
Services : N.F.P.
Refs. : Will dated Dec. 1781, when on the point of returning to England.

BIRD, Louis Saunders (1792-1874). Lieut. General. Colonel 23rd N.I. b. Chittagong 6 Nov. 1792. Cadet 1807. Arrived in India 16 Nov. 1808. Ensign 8 June 1808. Superseded and former rank cancelled 21 Nov. 1809. Resigned 20 Aug. 1811. Readmitted. Ensign 12 Dec. 1812. Lieut. 16 Dec. 1814. Restored to his original rank as Cadet, 4th class, 1807, and Bt. Capt. 4 June 1823. (G.O. No. 76 of 11 Mar. 1825.) Capt. 5 Apr. 1825. Major 18 June 1840. Lt. Col. 12 Sept. 1846. Col. 17 Apr. 1856. Maj. Gen. 4 Mar. 1858. Lt. Gen. 22 Feb. 1870. d. Clevedon, Somerset, 17 Apr. 1874.

Son of John Jenkins Bird, q.v. m. 1st (before 1815), (?). m. 2nd, Meerut, 3 Sept. 1840, Susan, 3rd dau. of Solomon Earle, q.v.

Services : Suspended whilst at Barasat C.C. and sent to Europe. Served as a vol. with H.M. 22nd Foot during his suspension, and was present at capture of Mauritius in Dec. 1810. Promoted Ensign in H.M.S. for his good service, and returned to Bengal in Mar. 1811. Restored to the Service 27 Feb. 1811. Posted as Ensign to 8th N.I. Nepal War 1816 ; Lieut. 8th N.I. (India medal). Under Bdr. Nation in Oudh 1816-7. Third Mahratta War ; Lieut. 8th N.I. Adjt. 1/8th N.I. 24 Nov. 1817 till 1824. Bundelkhand 1821. Hariana 1824-5. Adjt. 24th N.I. 17 June 1824 till 4 May 1825. D.J.A.G. at Cawnpore 14 May 1830. Against the Kols 1832-3. Asst. to A.G.G., S.W. frontier. Principal Asst. Comr. Chota Nagpur. First Sikh War ; Mudki ; Ferozshahr ; Badhowal ; Aliwal (Medal with 2 clasps). Transfd. from 24th N.I. to 1st Eur. Fus. Jan. 1851 ; to 5th N.I. 11 Sept. 1852 ; to 13th N.I. 1 Dec. 1852 ; to 56th N.I. July 1855 ; to 40th N.I. 5 Aug. 1855 ; to 50th N.I. Oct. 1855 ; to 23rd N.I. July 1856. Bdr. 2 cl. 28 July 1855. Santhal revolt ; comdg. Santhal F.F. Jan. 1856 till 1 Jan. 1857. Fur. 1857 till death.

Refs. : *D.I.B.* *The Times*, 20 Apr. 1874.

BIRD, Luke (1783-1802). Ensign, 6th N.I. *bapt.* Penrith, Cumberland, 30 July 1783. Cadet 1800. Arrived in India 11 Feb. 1802. Ensign 20 Oct. 1801. *d.* Dinapore 26 Nov. 1802.
Son of Isaac Bird, cabinet maker, and Dorothy his wife.
Services : N.F.P.

BIRD, Robert Wilberforce (1814-1888). Major. 4th N.I. *b.* Benares 25 May 1814. Cadet 1834. Arrived in India 16 July 1835. Ensign 24 Feb. 1835. Lieut. 31 Mar. 1841. Capt. 1 July 1848. Retired 1 Apr. 1856. Hon. Major 1 Apr. 1856. *d.* Great Malvern 29 Apr. 1888.

Of Barton House, Shipston-on-Stour. J.P. for Suffolk and cos. Gloucester, Worcester, and Warwick, lord of the manor of Barton-on-the-Heath, Moreton-in-Marsh. Son of Robert Mertins Bird, B.C.S., member of the Sudder board of revenue, Allahabad (who was son of Robert Bird, of Taplow, Bucks.), and Jane his wife, dau. of Rev. David Brown, provost of Coll. of Fort William, Bengal. *m.* Elizabeth Maria. (She died Leamington 15 Dec. 1893.)

Services : Ensign d.d. 12th N.I. 21 July 1835 ; do. 65th N.I. 24 Aug. 1835. Posted to 4th N.I. 24 Sept. 1835. Actg. Intr. & Qmr. 13th N.I. 27 May 1840. Junior Asst. to Comr. in Saugor 24 Mar. 1841. Leave s.c. to Cape 28 Feb. 1842. Asst. to A.G.G., S.W. frontier, 22 Jan. 1844. First Asst. to Resdt. at Lucknow 25 Feb. 1846 ; do. to Supt., Ajmere, 28 Apr. 1852.

Refs. : *Walford*, 1900, p. 86. *The Times*, 2 May 1888.

BIRD, William Charles Lewis (1781/82-1850). Lieut. Colonel. 2nd N.I. *b.* 1781/82. Cadet 1797. Arrived in India 29 Oct. 1798. Ensign 2 Oct. 1798. Lieut. 1 Nov. 1798. Capt. 30 Sept. 1808. Major 20 Oct. 1818. Lt. Col. 15 Feb. 1824. Invalided 15 Feb. 1824. Retired 15 Jan. 1836. *d.* Howland St., London, 5 Dec. 1850, aged 68.

Formerly William Charles Lewis : granted permission to assume the surname of Bird, 15 Dec. 1810. (*Lond. Gaz.* of 3 Mar. 1809.) Son of Lt. Col. William Bird (formerly Lewis). *m.* 1st. St. Pancras, London, May 1810, Miss Pamela Aldous, of Upper Fitzroy St., London. (She died London, 18 Jan. 1837, aged 48.) Father of William Hays Lewis Bird, *q.v. m.* 2nd, St. Pancras, 18 June 1838, Anne Charlotte, dau. of Dr. John White, Assist. Surg. 17th Light Dns., and widow of Capt. David Jones, E.I.C.S.

Services : Second Mahratta War ; battle of Delhi ; Lieut. 2nd N.I. Fur. 18 Feb. 1808 till 1810. Reduction of Kalinjar ; Capt. 2/2nd N.I. Operations in Baghelkhand 1813 ; Entauri ; Capt. 2/2nd N.I. Comdg. Burdwan Provl. Bn. 1825-7. Fur. 1827 till Mar. 1831. Comdg. 2nd Bn. Native Invalids. Comdt. at Buxar 20 May 1831 till 1835.

Refs. : M.M. 1810, i. 498. A.J. N.S. xxii. 205 ; xxvi. 284. G.M. 1851, i. 104.

BIRD, William Hays Lewis (1813-1839). Ensign, 12th N.I. *b.* 18 May 1813. Cadet 1829. Arrived in India 31 May 1830. Ensign (11 Dec. 1829) 23 Apr. 1830. *d.* Margate 26 Sept. 1839. *bapt.* Calcutta 14 Oct. 1813. Son of William Charles Lewis Bird, *q.v.,* and Pamela his wife. Addiscombe Cadet 1828-9.

Services : Ensign d.d. 68th N.I. 7 June 1830 ; do. 38th N.I. 23 Sept. 1831. Disturbances at Bamanghati, B. & O., Apr.-June 1832 ; with 38th N.I. Actg. Ensign 16 July 1832, having been more than two yrs. in India. Leave s.c. to Cape 5 Mar. 1833 till 20 May 1835. Posted to 12th N.I. 20 Aug. 1833. Fur. s.c. 15 Jan. 1836 till 30 Jan. 1838, and 22 Jan. 1839 till death.

Refs. : A.J. N.S. xxx. 263.

BIRKETT, Thomas (1788-1836). Captain, 6th N.I. *bapt.* Moresby, Cumberland, 29 Nov. 1788. Cadet 1808. Arrived in India 3 Nov. 1809. Ensign 20 Nov. 1810. Lieut. 20 July 1814. Capt. 24 Feb. 1826. *d.* Barrackpore 15 Feb. 1836.

Son of John Birkett.

Services : Posted as Ensign to 3rd N.I. Nepal War 1814-5 ; Lieut. 2/3rd N.I. in 1st Div. Transfd. to 6th N.I. (late 1/3rd) May 1824. Adjt. 6th N.I. 17 June 1824 till 8 May 1826. Siege and capture of Bhurtpore. Bde. Major at Agra 25 Nov. 1830.

Refs. : A.J. N.S. xx. 178.

150 LIST OF THE OFFICERS OF

BIRRELL, David (1757/58-1800). Major, Cavalry. *b.* in Scotland 1757/58. Cadet 1778. Admitted 2 Oct. 1778. Cornet 1778. Lieut. 4 Nov. 1778. Capt. 7 Jan. 1796. Major 23 June 1799. *d.* Fatehgarh, U.P., 15 June 1800.
Son of —— Birrell and his wife, ——, a Ramsay, of Balmain. Brother of George Birrell, *q.v.*
Services : Campaign against the Rajah of Benares 1781 ; action at Patita. Fur. 16 Jan. 1789 till 27 Sept. 1793.
Refs. : Family information. *G.M.* 1801, i. 83.

BIRRELL, David (1801-1878). General. Bengal European Regt. *b.* Edinburgh 15 Sept. 1801. Cadet 1817. Admitted 5 Sept. 1818. Ensign 30 Aug. 1818. Lieut. 20 Oct. 1818. Capt. 26 Apr. 1827. Major 10 Nov. 1843. Lt. Col. 1 Mar. 1850. Col. 20 July 1859. Maj. Gen. 25 Apr. 1858. Lt. Gen. 1 Mar. 1870. Gen. 23 July 1876. *d.* 28 Oct. 1878.
Son of George Birrell, *q.v.* Brother of James Ramsay Birrell, *q.v. m.* Edinburgh, 15 July 1831, Matilda Mary Linning, dau. of Dr. James Woodman, physician at Bognor, Sussex.
Services : Borne on the roll of the Bengal Eur. Regt. for upwards of 33 yrs. First Burma War (India medal). Fur. p.a. 4 Jan. 1830 till 6 Mar. 1833. First Afghan War 1839-40 ; capture of Ghazni ; Capt. Eur. Regt. with Army of the Indus ; operations in the Waziri valley (Medal). First Sikh War ; Ferozshahr (horse kld. under him) ; Sobraon, comdg. a Bde. (Medal with clasp). Fur. s.c. 10 Mar. 1848 till 1849. Transfd. to 51st N.I. Jan. 1851 ; to 50th N.I. 1 Dec. 1854 ; to 52nd N.I. Jan. 1855 ; to 72nd N.I. 4 July 1857. Fur. s.c. 20 Feb. 1855 till death. Durani, 3 cl., 28 Mar. 1845.
Refs. : Boase. A.J. N.S. v. 239. *The Times,* 30 Oct. 1878. M.I. in Winchester Cathedral.

BIRRELL, George (*d.* 1830 ?). Captain. Infantry. Cadet 1772. Ensign Mar. 1773. Lieut. (?). Capt. 17 Oct. 1780. Out of the Service in 1784. (? *d.* Edinburgh 22 Dec. 1830.)
Son of —— Birrell and his wife, née Ramsay. Brother of Thomas Birrell, *q.v. m.* (*c.* July) 1797, Helen, dau. of Rev. —— Pairman, of Elie, co. Fife. Father of David Birrell, *q.v.*, and of James Ramsay Birrell, *q.v.*
Services : N.F.P.
Refs. : S.M. 1797, p. 635. (? *A.J.* N.S. iv. 114.)

BIRRELL, James Ramsay (1803-1853). Major, 11th N.I. *b.* Edinburgh 27 Mar. 1803. Cadet 1818. Admitted 27 Mar. 1820. Ensign 20 Sept. 1819. Lieut. 1 Aug. 1822. Capt. 29 Oct. 1832. Major 13 Oct. 1851. *d.* Allahabad 26 July 1853, of cholera.

Son of George Birrell, *q.v.*, and Helen his wife. Brother of David Birrell (1801-1878), *q.v.* *m.* Edinburgh 12 Feb. 1839, Ellen Ramsay, dau. of Bdr.-Gen. Robert McDowall, Madras Est.
Services : Posted as Ensign to 1/5th N.I. Transfd. as Lieut. to 11th N.I. (late 1/5th) May 1824. Adjt. 2nd Gren. Bn. 4 Oct. 1824. Fur. s.c. 10 Feb. 1825 till 5 Nov. 1827, and 20 Jan. 1837 till 18 Nov. 1839. Bde. Major at Cawnpore 11 Nov. 1843. First Sikh War ; Ferozshahr ; Capt. 11th N.I. (Medal).
Refs. : *A.J.* N.S. xxviii. 249. *I.M.* 1853, p. 546. Will dated 15 Dec. 1847 ; proved 2 Sept. 1853.

BIRRELL, Thomas. Lieutenant. 1st Bengal European Bn. Cadet 1776. Ensign 21 Mar. 1777. Lieut. 16 Aug. 1778.
Son of —— Birrell and his wife, ——, a Ramsay of Balmain. Brother of George Birrell, *q.v.*
Services : On fur. in 1790. N.F.P.
Refs. : Family information.

BISCOE, Joseph (1808-?). Lieutenant. 40th N.I. *b.* Bletchingley, Surrey, 13 Oct. 1808. Cadet 1825. Ensign 9 Sept. 1825. Lieut. 9 Sept. 1826. Resigned 10 May 1831.
3rd son of Joseph Seymour Biscoe, of Clifton, Gloucs., and Stephana his 2nd wife, dau. of Ven. John Law, D.D., archdeacon of Rochester. Cousin-german of Joseph William Edwin Biscoe, *q.v.* *m.* twice. Addiscombe Cadet 1824-6.
Services : Posted as Ensign to 40th N.I. Fur. 1829 (G.O. of 19 Dec. 1828) till resignation. Subsequently settled in Australia.
Refs. : Burke's *Landed Gentry*, 13th edn., p. 146, *s.n.* Biscoe, of Newton, Inverness.

BISCOE, Joseph William Edwin (1800-1827). Lieutenant, 3rd L.C. *bapt.* Broad Clyst, Devon, 24 May 1800. Cadet 1819. Cornet 3 Apr. 1820. Lieut. 16 July 1823. *d.s.p.* London, 24 Mar. 1827.
3rd and youngest son of John Edwin Biscoe, of Limpsfield, sometime of Bruges, and Mary Ann Pettingall his 2nd wife. Cousin-german of Joseph Biscoe, *q.v.* *m.* Mary Maclennan. Educ. at Westminster ; admitted 26 Apr. 1813 ; left in 1813.
Services : Posted as Cornet to 3rd L.C. (? Operations in Jodhpur 1823 ; capture of Lamba fort ; Cornet 3rd L.C.) Fur. 1824 till death.
Refs. : Burke's *Landed Gentry*, 13th edn., p. 146. *s.n.* Biscoe, of Newton, Inverness. *Westminster School Register.*

BISHOP, George Thomas (1800-1827). Lieutenant, 9th L.C. *b.* London 4 Apr. 1800. Cadet 1818. Cornet 9 July 1819. Lieut. 20 Oct. 1821. *d.* at sea, 5 Dec. 1827, on board the *Roxburgh Castle*.

Son of Charles Bishop. *m.* St. John's, Calcutta, 26 Nov. 1824, Harriet D'Oyly Robertson, widow. (She died Chandernagore 29 May 1841.) Ed. Eton; 5th form in 1814.
Services : Cornet d.d. 8th L.C. Posted as Cornet to 7th L.C. Fur. 22 Oct. 1821 till 1824. Transfd. to newly-raised 1st Extra Regt. (became 9th L.C.) 17 June 1825. Siege and capture of Bhurtpore; Lieut. 9th L.C.
Refs. : Eton School Lists. A.J. xxv. 568.

BISHOP, George William (1810-1899). General. 23rd N.I. u.s.l. *b.* in India 1 Feb. 1810. Cadet 1825. Arrived in India 25 Sept. 1826. Ensign 26 Apr. 1826. Lieut. 20 June 1828. Capt. 28 May 1843. Major 10 July 1852. Lt. Col. 31 May 1857. Col. 17 Sept. 1866. Maj. Gen. 6 Mar. 1868. Lt. Gen. 20 Mar. 1876. Gen. 1 Oct. 1877. *d.* Ormsby House, Littlehampton, Sussex, 17 July 1899, aged 89.
bapt. Delhi 18 Dec. 1812. Son of Samuel Pidding Bishop, *q.v. m.* Delhi, 6 Feb. 1839 (? 6 Nov. 1838), Mary Ann Romer, eldest dau. of Lt. Col. Meadows, H.M. 5th Regt.
Services : Posted as Ensign to 44th N.I. 5 Oct. 1826. Transfd. to 3rd Extra Regt. (became 71st N.I.) 10 Oct. 1826. Intr. & Qmr. 71st N.I. 3 Sept. 1829. Fur. p.a. 3 Jan. 1837 till 24 June 1840. Comdd. Local Sebundy Corps of S. & M. at Darjeeling. P.W.D. at Darjeeling 20 May 1843 till 1851. Leave s.c. to N.S.W. 3 June 1851. Fur. s.c. 1 Feb. 1856 till 1857. Transfd. to 23rd N.I. in 1857. No record of active service. Transfd. to u.s.l.
Refs. : Boase. G.M. 1839, i. 89. *The Times,* 19 July 1899.

BISHOP, Henry (1815-1841). Lieutenant, 62nd N.I. *b.* Meerut 13 Oct. 1815. Cadet 1834. Arrived in India 5 June 1835. Ensign 24 Feb. 1835. Lieut. 3 Oct. 1840. *d.* Nimach, C.I., 8 Aug. 1841.
Son of —— Bishop, of Blackheath (*probably* Samuel Pidding Bishop, *q.v.*) Ed. Tonbridge 1824-31.
Services : Ensign d.d. 71st N.I. 12 June 1835. Posted as Ensign to 62nd N.I. 24 Sept. 1835. No record of active service.
Refs. : Tonbridge School Register. G.M. 1842, i. 231.

BISHOP, John. Capt. Lieutenant. Artillery. Cadet 1764. Fireworker 27 Dec. 1764. 2nd Lieut. 1 Apr. 1769. Lieut. Mar. 1770. Capt. Lt. 6 May 1772. Resigned 31 Jan. 1774.
Services : N.F.P.

BISHOP, Matthew. Lieutenant. Infantry. Cadet 1769. Ensign 6 May 1770. Lieut. 5 Mar. 1773. Resigned 16 Aug. 1773.
Services : N.F.P.

THE BENGAL ARMY, 1758-1834   153

BISHOP, Samuel Pidding (1783-1833). Lieut. Colonel, 27th N.I. *bapt.* Stanwell, Middlesex, 11 Jan. 1783. Cadet 1799. Arrived in India 2 Dec. 1800. Ensign 3 Jan. 1800. Lieut. 29 May 1800. Capt. 12 May 1811. Major 11 July 1823. Lt. Col. 22 Apr. 1825. *d.* Hansi, Punjab, 26 Sept. 1833.
Son of Thomas Bishop and Margaret his wife. *m.* Calcutta 20 Dec. 1805, Miss Frances Major. Father of George William Bishop, *q.v.*
Services: Lieut. d.d. 2/19th N.I. Dec. 1800. Posted to 1/6th N.I. 15 Apr. 1801. Disturbances in Cuttack 1801; Lieut. 1/6th N.I. With 2nd Bn. Bengal Vols. 1804-6. Nepal War 1814-5, Capt. 1/6th N.I., in 2nd Div. Third Mahratta War; Capt. 1/6th N.I., in Reserve Div. To take charge of Saharanpur Provl. Bn. 9 Mar. 1821. To comd. Delhi Palace Guards 3 Oct. 1821. To raise and comd. 3rd Extra Regt. at Mainpuri 21 May 1825. Transfd. to 68th N.I. 20 Dec. 1828; to 27th N.I. Aug. 1829.
Refs.: De Rhé-Philipe. *G.M.* 1834, i. 454.

BLACK, Alexander (*d.* 1767). Capt. Lieutenant, Artillery. Cadet R.A. 1 June 1760. Fireworker R.A. 26 Oct. 1761. Capt. Lt. Bengal Art. 20 Aug. 1765. *d.* Allahabad 10 June 1767.
Services: Transfd. from the Royal Art. Resigned in May 1766 during the mutinous combination against Clive's new batta regulations. Re-admitted 13 June 1766. N.F.P.

BLACK, Alexander (1787-1818). Captain, 8th N.I. *b.* Kirkcaldy, co. Fife, 19 June 1787. Cadet 1802. Arrived in India 29 Aug. 1803. Ensign 1 Sept. 1803. Lieut. 27 Aug. 1804. Capt. 20 Sept. 1816. *d.* in camp, Jubbulpore, C.P., 8 Nov. 1818.
bapt. 12 July 1787. Son of Dr. John Black and Margaret Wemyss his wife.
Services: Ensign d.d. 12th N.I. Posted as Lieut. to 8th N.I. Second Mahratta War. Lieut. Java Inf. Vols. 1813-5. 3rd Vol. Bn. 1816. Third Mahratta War; Mandala; Capt. 2/8th N.I.
Refs.: *S.M.* 1819, i. 584.

BLACK, Andrew (1759/60-1794). Lieutenant, Infantry. *b.* in Ireland 1759/60. Cadet 1781. Apptd. Cadet 16 May 1781. Ensign 6 Apr. 1781. Lieut. 28 July 1782. *d.* Chunar 6 Oct. 1794.
m. Berhampore, Bengal, 10 Nov. 1791, Charlotte, dau. of Simon Droz(e), B.C.S. (*See also* Thomas Hawkins.)
Services: Sailed for India on the *Deptford*, 26 June 1781, aged 21. N.F.P.

BLACK, Charles (1809-1838). Lieutenant, 17th N.I. *b.* Islington, Middlesex, 5 July 1809. Cadet 1825. Arrived in India 16 May 1826. Ensign 5 Nov. 1825. Lieut. 4 June 1831. *d.* Ludhiana, 1 Nov. 1838, in consequence of a fall from his horse.
Son of Alexander Black, of Bury St. Edmunds.
Services : Posted as Ensign to 17th N.I. in May 1826, joined in Nov., and served throughout with that Regt. No record of active service.
Refs. : De Rhé-Philipe. G.M. 1839, i. 333.

BLACK, Peter (*alias* **Patrick**) (1762/63-1818). Lieut. Colonel. 6th N.C. *b.* in Scotland 1762/63. Cadet 1780. Admitted 5 May 1781. Cornet 1780. Lieut. 29 July 1781. Capt. 29 May 1800. Major 22 Jan. 1802. Lt. Col. 11 Mar. 1805. Retired 29 Aug. 1810. *d.* Dee-mount, nr. Aberdeen, 28 Oct. 1818.
m. Aberdeen, Apr. 1811, Jane, dau. of William Young, of Sheddocksley. (She died 23 Dec. 1859, aged 74.)
Services : Sailed for India on the *Grosvenor*, 3 June 1780, aged 17. Lieut. 2nd N.C. (? Second Rohilla War ; Bitaurah ; Lieut. 2nd N.C.) Transfd. to 1st N.C. after June 1798. Capt. Lt. and Adjt. 1st N.C. before May 1800. Operations in Jumna Doab 1803 ; Sasni ; Bijaigarh ; Kachaura ; Major 1st N.C. Second Mahratta War ; Major 1st N.C. Agent for purchase of Govt. horses 1804-5. Transfd. as Lt. Col. to 6th N.C. in 1805. Agent for Cav. horses 1806. Fur. 17 Feb. 1808 till retirement.
Refs. : G.M. May 1811 ; 1818, ii. 571. *S.M.* 1818, ii. 588.

BLACK, Robert (1785-1804). Ensign, 11th N.I. *b.* Templemoyle, Londonderry, 7 Feb. 1785. Cadet 1802. Arrived in India 9 July 1803. Ensign 31 July 1803. *d.* Rampura 20 Aug. 1804.
Son of Robert Black.
Services : Ensign d.d. 12th N.I. Posted as Ensign to 11th N.I., but probably never joined. Second Mahratta War ; (? Monson's retreat, with 12th N.I., during which he died.)

BLACK, Samuel (*d.* 1799). Lieut. Colonel, 3rd N.C. Cadet 1769. Cornet 31 Aug. 1769. Lieut. 30 Oct. 1771. Capt. 6 Nov. 1780. Major 1 Mar. 1794. Lt. Col. 3 Oct. 1796. *d.* Patna 22 June 1799 : drowned while attempting to swim ashore from a leaking boat.
m. Margaret, elder dau. of Major Jerome Noble, 28th Irish Regt. of Foot, and cousin of Samuel Noble, *q.v.* (*See also* John Powell (died 1804).)
Services : Posted to newly-raised G.G.B.G. in 1773. First Rohilla War ; battle of St. George ; Lieut. G.G.B.G. Left that

Corps at some date between May 1777 and June 1778. Fur. 28 Nov. 1785 till 9 Oct. 1789. Comdt. at Buxar 1793-6. Comdd. newly-raised 3rd N.C. from 1796 till death.
Refs. : Burke's *Landed Gentry of Ireland*, p. 513, *s.n.* Noble, of Glassdrummond, co. Fermanagh. *V.B.G. G.M.* 1800, i. 394.

BLACK, Thomas (1786-1812). Lieutenant, 20th N.I. *b.* Dublin July 1786. Cadet 1803. Arrived in India 3 Dec. 1804. Ensign 22 Nov. 1804. Lieut. 22 Nov. 1804. *d.* Barrackpore 22 Sept. 1812.
Son of Thomas Black, merchant, and Isabella his wife. Marlow Cadet.
Services : Posted as Lieut. to 20th N.I. At P.W.I. 1806-7 ; at Malacca 1811-2.

BLACK, Thomas Montague (1789-1827). Captain, 58th N.I. *b.* Dublin Aug. 1789. Cadet 1804. Arrived in India 16 May 1806. Ensign 1 Feb. 1805. Lieut. 1 Feb. 1805. Capt. 6 Nov. 1822. *d.* Udaipur, Rajputana, 16 Nov. 1827.
Nearly related to John Evans (1802-1886), *q.v.*
Services : Posted as Lieut. to 1st N.I. Transfd. to 2/29th N.I. in 1815. Fur. 1819-20. Transfd. to 58th N.I. (late 2/29th) May 1824. Siege and capture of Bhurtpore ; Capt. 58th N.I. Comdd. Udaipur Escort 1825 till death.
Refs. : Will dated Udaipur 10 May 1822 ; proved 22 Jan. 1828.

BLACK, William (*d.* 1781). Captain, 3rd Bengal European Regt. Cadet 1769. Ensign 2 Mar. 1769. Lieut. 29 Mar. 1771. Capt. 4 Sept. 1779. bur. Calcutta 29 Nov. 1781.
Services : N.F.P.

BLACKALL, Robert (1787-1863). Lieut. General. Colonel 13th N.I. *b.* Desertmartin, co. Londonderry, 1787. Cadet 1805. Arrived in India 11 July 1806. Ensign 15 July 1806. Lieut. 4 Nov. 1807. Capt. 11 July 1823. Major 21 June 1830. Lt. Col. 22 Apr. 1836. Col. 18 July 1848. Maj. Gen. 20 June 1854. Lt. Gen. 18 Dec. 1860. *d.* 20 Apr. 1863.
Son of Robert Blackall and Letitia his wife. *m.* 1st (before 1809), Catherine, dau. of W. Lewis, Bo.C.S. *m.* 2nd, Midnapore, Bengal, 3 Nov. 1812, Elizabeth, 4th dau. of Thomas Chadwick, of Barnascounce, 18th Light Dns., and sister of Thomas Chadwick, *q.v.* (*See also* Charles Hamilton Bell.) (She died Dacca 2 Jan. 1835.) His daus. *m.* John William Carter, *q.v.*, and Joseph Graham, *q.v.*
Services : At Barasat C.C. for 9½ mos. Posted as Ensign to 25th N.I. Siege and capture of Hathras ; Lieut. 1/25th N.I. Third

Mahratta War; Lieut. 1/25th N.I. Adjt. Bareilly Provl. Bn. Capt. 2/25th N.I. Transfd. to 50th N.I. (late 2/25th) May 1824. To tempy. comd. of Agra Provl. Bn. 7 June 1824. 2nd Nassiri Bn. 19 June 1828. Comdd. Pioneer Corps 17 Jan. 1829 till 23 Oct. 1831. Against the Kols 1832-3; Major 50th N.I. Comdd. 50th N.I. Col. 2nd Eur. Bengal Fus. 18 July 1848. Col. 13th N.I. 1859. Fur. 17 Jan. 1851 till death.
Refs.: Burke's *Colonial Gentry*, ii. 587, *s.n.* Chadwick. *Boase.*

BLACKBURN, Richard Edward (1806-1825). Ensign, 42nd N.I. *b.* Kalkapur, Murshidabad, Bengal, 22 Apr. 1806. Cadet 1823. Ensign 14 Jan. 1824. *d.* Arakan 11 June 1825.
Son of Samuel Blackburn, indigo manufacturer, and Maria his wife.
Services: Posted as Ensign to 42nd N.I. First Burma War; Arakan 1825; Ensign 42nd N.I.

BLACKER, Edward (*d.* 1776). Lieutenant, Infantry. Cadet 1767. Ensign 1 Dec. 1767. Lieut. 12 Oct. 1769. *d.* Fyzabad, U.P., Dec. 1776.
Son of George Blacker, of Drogheda. Brother of Lieut. William Blacker, Madras Est., and distantly related to George Blacker, *q.v.*
Services: N.F.P.
Refs.: Will dated, "Camp before Seckranny fort," 25 Dec. 1776; codicil dated 27 Dec. 1776; filed 5 Mar. 1777; proved 20 June 1777.

BLACKER, George (1784-1815). Captain, 17th N.I. *b.* Carrick, co. Armagh, 27 Dec. 1784. Cadet 1799. Arrived in India 11 Dec. 1800. Ensign 7 Aug. 1800. Lieut. 24 Aug. 1800. Capt. 16 Dec. 1814. *d.* Saharanpur 31 Aug. 1815.
2nd son of the Very Rev. Stewart Blacker, of Carrickblacker, dean of Leighlin, archdeacon of Dromore, etc., and Eliza his wife, dau. of Sir Hugh Hill, Bart., M.P. for Londonderry. *m.* Anne, dau. of William Sloane, *q.v.*
Services: Posted to 2/17th N.I. 17 Apr. 1801. Operations in Jumna Doab 1803. Second Mahratta War. Adjt. & Qmr. 17th N.I. 30 Sept. 1804 till 11 Aug. 1813. Capt. Lt. 17th N.I. 28 Jan. 1813. Nepal War 1814-5; Jitpur; Capt. 2/17th N.I., in 3rd Div.
Refs.: Burke's *Landed Gentry of Ireland*, p. 45, *s.n.* Blacker, of Carrickblacker, Armagh. *G.M.* 1816, i. 633.

BLACKER, Stewart (*d.* 1770). Ensign, Infantry. Cadet 1769. Ensign 28 Aug. 1769. *d.* Calcutta 1 Sept. 1770; bur. the following day.

(*Probably* one of the 21 children of William Blacker, of Carrickblacker and Brookend, co. Armagh, and Letitia his wife, dau. of Henry Cary, of Dungiven Castle.)
Services : N.F.P.
Refs. : (? Burke's *Landed Gentry of Ireland*, p. 45, *s.n.* Blacker, of Carrickblacker and Woodbrook, co. Wexford.)

BLACKNEY, James (1781/82-1857). Colonel. 5th N.I. *b.* 1781/82. Cadet 1798. Arrived in India 20 Sept. 1799. Ensign 26 Nov. 1799. Lieut. 29 May 1800. Capt. 6 Nov. 1812. Major 6 Jan. 1823. Lt. Col. 1 May 1824. Retired 21 May 1829. Hon. Col. 28 Nov. 1854. *d.* Dunleckney, co. Carlow, 12 Dec. 1857, aged 75.
Son of James Blackney. Brother of John Francis Blackney, *q.v.*, of Walter Blackney, of Ballyellen, M.P. for co. Carlow, and of Jane, wife of Francis Kyan, *q.v.*
Services : Posted to 1/17th N.I. 15 Apr. 1801. Nepal War 1814-5 ; Capt. 1/17th N.I., in 2nd Div. (India medal). Capt. Lt. 17th N.I. 30 Oct. 1811. Capt. 2/17th N.I. in 1822. Transfd. as Lt. Col. to 35th N.I. (late 2/17th) May 1824. Siege and capture of Bhurtpore ; Lt. Col.. comdg. 35th N.I. (clasp to India medal). Transfd. to 5th N.I. 30 Oct. 1826. Fur. 15 Dec. 1826 till retirement.
Refs. : M.I. in Dunleckney psh. church.

BLACKNEY, John Francis (1783-1815). Captain, 22nd N.I. *b.* 1783. Cadet 1798. Arrived in India 20 Sept. 1799. Ensign 23 Oct. 1799. Lieut. 28 Oct. 1799. Capt. 11 Mar. 1811. *d. unm.* Samanpur, 1 Jan. 1815, aged 31 : kld. in action against the Gurkhas.
Son of James Blackney. Brother of James Blackney, *q.v.*
Services : Posted to 2/8th N.I. 15 Apr. 1801. (? Operations in Jumna Doab 1803 ; Sasni ; Bijaigarh ; Kachaura ; Lieut. 2/8th N.I.) Transfd. to 2/22nd N.I. in 1804. Second Mahratta War ; siege of Bhurtpore (w. in 3rd assault on 20 Feb. 1805) ; Lieut. 2/22nd N.I. Capt. Lt. 22nd N.I. 17 Jan. 1809. Nepal War 1814-5 ; Samanpur (kld.) ; Capt. 2/22nd N.I., in 4th Div.
Refs. : M.I. in Majoiganj cemetery, Sitamarhi, B. & O. Will dated 2 Dec. 1814 ; proved in 1815.

BLACKWELL, Jonathan (*d.* 1819). Lieutenant. Infantry. Cadet 1779. Ensign 27 Aug. 1779. Lieut. 14 Apr. 1781. Struck off 1791. *d.* 23 Mar. 1819.
Of Ampney Park, Gloucs.
Services : On fur. in 1790. N.F.P.
Refs. : *G.M.* 1819, i. 378.

BLACKWOOD, William (1810-1861). Major. 59th N.I. *b.* Edinburgh 8 Feb. 1810. Cadet 1825. Arrived in India 26 Oct. 1826. Ensign 2 June 1826. Lieut. 14 May 1832. Capt. 8 Aug. 1845. Retired 10 June 1850. Hon. Major 28 Nov. 1854. *d.* Ainslie Pl., Edinburgh, 8 Apr. 1861.

3rd son of William Blackwood, of Belville, bookseller and founder of the firm of Wm. Blackwood & Sons, the Edinburgh publishers. *m.* Lucknow, 22 Jan. 1834, Emma, elder dau. of George Moore, *q.v.* (She died Edinburgh, 7 Nov. 1881, aged 70.)

Services : Posted as Ensign to 59th N.I. Adjt. 59th N.I. 15 June 1830 till 2 Feb. 1841. 2nd in comd. Sylhet L.I. 12 Feb. 1841. Fur. 10 Dec. 1847 till retirement. No record of active service.

Refs. : *G.M.* 1861, i. 589. *The Times,* 11 Apr. 1861.

BLADEN, Charles (1770- ?). Fireworker. Artillery. *b.* 10 June 1770. Cadet (?). Fireworker 18 May 1792. Resigned 6 Dec. 1793.

bapt. St. Leonard's, Shoreditch, Middlesex, 1 July 1770. Son of John Bladen, of Norton Folgate, Middlesex, and Hannah his wife.

Services : Resigned in order to go home on fur. : as he did not return to India he was struck off by G.G.O. of 18 May 1797.

BLAGDON, Edward (1788-1806). Ensign, Infantry. Unposted. *b.* Puddington, Devon, 12 Oct. 1788. Cadet 1804. Arrived in India 17 Apr. 1806. Ensign 12 Mar. 1806. *d.* Barasat, 6 Aug. 1806, whilst under instruction at the Cadet College.

Son of Peter Blagdon. Ed. Blundell's ; admitted 2 Oct. 1798, aged 10 ; left 29 June 1800.

Refs. : *Blundell's School Register.*

BLAGRAVE, George (1787-1806). Cadet, Infantry. *bapt.* Reading 12 Mar. 1787. Cadet 1804. Never arrived in India. *d.* at sea, 9 Mar. 1806, on board the *Jane, Duchess of Gordon*, on his passage to India.

(*Probably* one of the younger sons of John Blagrave, of Watchfield, psh. of Shrivenham, and Frances his wife, eldest dau. of Anthony Blagrave.)

Refs. : (? Burke's *Landed Gentry*, 13th edn., p. 151, *s.n.* Blagrave, of Calcot Park, Berks.)

BLAIR, Charles Devaynes (1804-1860). Lieut. Colonel, C.B. Invalid Est. 8th L.C. *b.* London 27 July 1804. Cadet 1821. Arrived in India 17 May 1822. Cornet 5 May 1821. Lieut. 1 May 1824. Capt. 23 Dec. 1831. Major 4 Nov. 1839. Lt. Col. 20 Apr. 1849. Invalided 20 Oct. 1852. *d.* Simla 27 Sept. 1860.

Son of Thomas Blair. *m*. 1st, Meerut, 4 May 1826, Miss Martha Cordelia Creighton. (*See also* William Ramsay.) (She died Nasirabad 23 Oct. 1840.) *m*. 2nd (?). (She died Kartarpur 12 May 1848.)
Services : Posted as Cornet to 3rd L.C. Transfd. to newly-raised 2nd Extra Regt. (became 10th L.C.) 17 June 1825. Siege and capture of Bhurtpore ; Lieut. 10th L.C. (India medal). Intr. & Qmr. 10th L.C. 26 May 1829 till Dec. 1831. First Afghan War 1842 ; Major comdg. 10th L.C., with Gen. Pollock's force (Medal). Comdd. 10th L.C. 1 Nov. 1838 till 3 Feb. 1843. Gwalior campaign ; Maharajpur ; comdg. 10th L.C. (Bronze star). Leave to N.S.W. and Cape 2 Mar. 1845 till May 1847. Second Sikh War ; Jullundur Doab ; Major 10th L.C. Transfd. to 7th L.C. 6 Mar. 1851 ; to 8th L.C. Feb. 1852. C.B. 24 Dec. 1842.
Refs. : *De Rhé-Philipe*.

BLAIR, Edward Macleod (1803-1842). Captain, 5th L.C. *b*. Shikohabad, U.P., 13 May 1803. Cadet 1819. Arrived in India Oct. 1820. Cornet 24 May 1820. Lieut. 1 May 1824. Capt. 1 Sept. 1834. *d*. 12 Jan. 1842 : kld. in action in the Jagdalak Pass.
2nd son of Sir Robert Blair, K.C.B., *q.v.*, and Herculina Eliza his wife. Brother of Thomas Blair (1791-1873), *q.v. m*. Muttra, 2 Aug. 1824, Susanna, dau. of Lt.-Gen. James Kennedy, C.B., *q.v.* (*See also* William Alexander.) (She perished in the Cawnpore massacre June 1857.)
Services : Posted as Cornet to 5th L.C. Jan. 1821, and remained with that Regt. throughout his service. Operations in Kotah 1821 ; Mangrol, with Haraoti F.F. Bde. Major to troops in Bundelkhand 11 June 1825. Intr. & Qmr. 5th L.C. 12 July 1825 till 25 Aug. 1826. First Afghan War 1840-2 ; in the Ghilzai country 1841 ; Kabul-Jalalabad retreat ; action in Jagdalak Pass (kld.).
Refs. : *De Rhé-Philipe*. *G.M.* 1842, ii. 334. M.I. in St. Michael's, Bath, and St. Peter's, Fort William, Bengal.

BLAIR, James (1792-1847). Lieut. Colonel, 5th N.I. Brigadier, Nizam's Army. *b*. co. Kincardine 7 Nov. 1792. Cadet 1809. Arrived in India 3 Oct. 1810. Ensign 19 Feb. 1812. Lieut. 16 Dec. 1814. Capt. 30 Aug. 1825. Major 17 Apr. 1832. Lt. Col. 2 Dec. 1838. *d*. at sea, 12 Aug. 1847, on board the *Madagascar*.
Son of James Blair, of Stonehaven, merchant, Capt. 8th N. British Mil., and Elizabeth his wife, dau. of Alexander Taylor-Imrie, of Lunan, co. Forfar. *m*. Bareilly, 1 Mar. 1827, Charlotte Cecilia, 5th dau. of Jacob Vanrenen, *q.v.* (*See also* Christopher Godby, William Conway-Gordon, Charles Griffiths, and John Satchwell.)

LIST OF THE OFFICERS OF

Services : Barasat C.C. 6 mos. ; left Apr. 1811. Cadet d.d. 2/9th N.I. Posted as Ensign to 15th N.I. Rewah 1812-3. Nepal War ; Lieut. 2/15th N.I., in 4th Div. Acting Intr. & Qmr. 6th Gren. Bn. Siege and capture of Hathras ; Lieut. 2nd Gren. Bn. 2nd in comd. 1st Rohilla Cav. 1817-23. Third Mahratta War. Comdt. 3rd (or Blair's) Local Horse 6 May 1823. Transfd. to 30th N.I. (late 1/15th) May 1824. Apptd. to Nizam's army 13 Mar. 1835. Siege of Barurgi, Hyderabad, Sept. 1841. Transfd. to 8th N.I. ; to 65th N.I. 4 May 1844 ; to 5th N.I. Sept. 1845. Comdd. Nizam's Cav. Div.

Refs. : Burke's *Landed Gentry*, 13th edn., p. 965, *s.n.* Blair-Imrie, of Lunan House, co. Forfar. *Hist. of the Hyderabad Contingent*, p. 124. *Bath Chron.* 9 Dec. 1847. Will dated 28 Feb. 1844 ; proved 16 Nov. 1848.

BLAIR, Peter (*d.* 1792). Lieutenant, Infantry. Cadet 1782. Ensign 4 Mar. 1783. Lieut. 18 Feb. 1790. *d.* Anupshahr, U.P., 10 June 1792.

Services : N.F.P.

Refs. : *S.M.* 1793, p. 205.

BLAIR, Robert (*d.* 1774). Ensign, 17th Bn. Sepoys. Cadet 1769. Ensign 27 Sept. 1770. *d.* Chitarpur, B. & O., 19 July 1774.

Son of —— Blair, of Dunskey, co. Wigtown. Brother of Clementina Blair.

Services : N.F.P.

Refs. : Will dated 19 Mar. 1773 ; proved 9 Feb. 1775.

BLAIR, Sir Robert (1754/55-1837). General, K.C.B. 2nd N.I. *b.* 1754/55. Cadet 1771. Arrived in India 23 Oct. 1771. Ensign 29 Jan. 1773. Lieut. 3 Apr. 1777. Capt. 29 May 1781. Major 1 Mar. 1794. Lt. Col. 31 July 1799. Col. 27 Mar. 1804. Maj. Gen. 25 July 1810. Lt. Gen. 12 Aug. 1819. Gen. 14 Jan. 1837. *d.* Harley House, Bath, 10 Feb. 1837, in his 83rd year.

Son of Daniel Blair, of Burntisland, and Barbara his wife, dau. of Sir John Whitefoord, of Milntoun. Brother of Thomas Blair (died 1833), *q.v.*, and Capt. William Blair, R.N. (*D.N.B.*), cousin of William Blair, *q.v. m.* Dinapore, 25 Mar. 1790, Herculina Eliza, dau. of Hercules Durham, *q.v.* (She died London 7 Aug. 1822.) Father of Edward Macleod Blair, *q.v.*, and of Thomas Blair (1791-1873), *q.v.* His daus. *m.* Henry Clayton, *q.v.*, William Kennedy, *q.v.*, Thomas Reynolds, *q.v.*, William Swinton, *q.v.*, John Waterfield, *q.v.*

Services : First Mahratta War ; with Goddard's force ; comdd. 5th Bn. 1781-2. A.D.C. to William Blair, *q.v.*, 1786-8. Comdt. 1/2nd N.I. 1798. Operations in Jumna Doab 1802-3 ; siege and capture of Sasni ; comdg. the force. Second Mahratta War ; Koil ;

THE BENGAL ARMY, 1758-1834

battle of Delhi ; capture of Agra ; Lt. Col. comdg. 1/2nd N.I.
Comdg. in Cuttack 1808. G.O.C. Presidency Div. 16 Nov. 1812.
Fur. 23 Dec. 1817 till death. K.C.B. 7 Apr. 1815.
Refs. : *E.I.M.C.* ii. 288. *D.I.B. N. & Q.*, 7S. v. 15 ; 8S. iii. 58, 136. *G.M.* 1837, ii. 85.

BLAIR, Thomas (*d.* 1833). Captain. Infantry. Cadet 1768. Ensign 25 July 1769. Lieut. 22 Nov. 1772. Capt. 13 Nov. 1780. Struck off 1791. *d.* Inchinnan, co. Renfrew, 20 Oct. 1833.
Son of Daniel Blair, of Burntisland, and Barbara his wife, dau. of Sir John Whitefoord, of Milntoun. Brother of Sir Robert Blair, *q.v.*, and cousin of William Blair, *q.v.* (? *m.* Matilda, who *re-m.* Taunton, 18 Feb. 1836, Capt. Maher, of Woodlands.)
Services : Apptd. to comd. 1/6th N.I. in 1781. Campaign against the Rajah of Benares ; Patita, comdg. the force ; action at Lora, under Major William Joseph Crabb, *q.v.* Apptd. Sec. and Persian Intr. to his cousin, William Blair, in 1786. Returned to Scotland in 1789.
Refs.: *E.I.M.C.* iii. 214. *N. & Q.*, 7S. v. 15 ; 8S. iii. 58, 136, 204. *G.M.* 1833, ii. 555.

BLAIR, Thomas. Lieutenant. Infantry. Cadet 1772. Ensign 2 July 1776. Lieut. 23 June 1778. Pensioned 19 Aug. 1778.
Services : N.F.P.

BLAIR, Thomas (1791-1873). Captain. Artillery. *b.* in India 1 Nov. 1791. Cadet 1809. Arrived in India 7 Dec. 1809. Fireworker 2 Nov. 1809. Lieut. 25 Sept. 1817. Capt. 1 May 1824. Retired 30 June 1829. *d.* his residence, 46 Queen's Gdns., London, 28 Dec. 1873.
bapt. Calcutta 21 Nov. 1791. Eldest son of Sir Robert Blair, *q.v.*, and Herculina Eliza his wife. Brother of Edward Macleod Blair, *q.v. m.* Walcot, Bath, 6 Mar. 1838, Mary, widow of Col. Francis Philip Stewart, Madras Est. Woolwich Cadet ; nominated for R.M.A. 8 Jan. 1806.
Services : A.D.C. to his father 27 Feb. 1812 till 1816. Adjt. & Qmr. 2nd Bn. Foot Art. 27 June 1816 till 1822. Fur. 1823-6, and 1828 (arrived in England 9 June 1828) till retirement. No record of active service.
Refs. : *A.J.* N.S. xxv. 300. *The Times*, 1 Jan. 1874. M.I. in St. Michael's, Bath.

BLAIR, William (1729/30-1814). Colonel. Infantry. *b.* 1729/30. Entered the Bengal Army as a Major 2 Sept. 1768. Lt. Col. 26 Feb. 1778. Col. 10 Dec. 1781. Resigned 19 Jan. 1788. *d.* Stratford Pl., London, 27 Apr. 1814, aged 84.

Son of John Blair, of Balthayock, co. Perth. Brother of Rev. John Blair, LL.D., the chronologist (*D.N.B.*), and cousin of Sir Robert Blair, *q.v.* *m.* St. Martin-in-the-Fields, London, 3 Mar. 1768, Jane, 3rd dau. of Hon. Roderick Mackenzie (? second) son of John, second Earl of Cromartie, and Sarah Allen his wife. (She died 22 Jan. 1808 ; bur. in Greenwich church.)
Services : Apptd. Govr. of Chunar fort *c.* 1780.
Refs. : *S.M.* 1768, p. 165. *N. & Q.* 7S. v. 15 ; 8S. iii. 58, 136, 204, vi. 206. *G.M.* 1814, i. 519.

BLAIR, W. (*d.* 1771). (?). *d.* Dinapore July 1771.
Services : N.F.P.

BLAKE, Benjamin (1788-1838). Bt. Major, 47th N.I. *b.* Portsmouth 6 Aug. 1788. Cadet 1805. Arrived in India 19 Sept. 1806. Ensign 17 Sept. 1806. Lieut. 23 June 1809. Capt. 1 May 1824. Bt. Major 10 Jan. 1837. *d.* Siwa oasis, Egypt, 12 Mar. 1838, on his way to England.
Son of George Blake. *m.* (before 1824) (?).
Services : Barasat C.C. for ten mos. Posted as Ensign to 24th N.I. Fur. p.a. 17 Jan. 1817 till 24 Nov. 1821. Transfd. to 47th N.I. (late 1/24th) May 1824. Employed on survey work. Fur. 22 Jan. 1826 till 22 Nov. 1830, and 6 Nov. 1837 till death. No record of active service.
Refs. : *A.J.* N.S. xxviii. 69.

BLAKE, Erroll (Ignatius) (1803-1827). Lieutenant, Artillery. *b.* 8 Nov. 1803. Cadet 1820. Arrived in India Mar. 1822. 2nd Lieut. 9 June 1821. Lieut. 1 May 1824. *d.s.p.* Karnal 3 Sept. 1827, of cholera.
bapt. Oranmore, Galway, 15 Dec. 1803. 3rd son of Henry James Blake, Col. Galway Mil., and Anne his wife. Younger brother of Joseph Henry, third Baron Wallscourt.
Note : The second Christian name, Ignatius, which appears on his baptismal certificate, is not given by any other authority.
Services : First Burma War 1824-6 ; capture of Kokein ; posted to the " Rocket Troop " July 1825 ; comdd. the Rocket detachment at storm and capture of Melloon. Apptd. Adjt. Karnal and Sirhind Div. of Art. 23 Dec. 1826.
Refs. : Burke's *Peerage*, 1905, p. 1621, *s.n.* Wallscourt, B. De Rhé-Philipe.

BLAKE, George (1791-1860). Lieut. Colonel, Invalid Est. Artillery. *b.* Dover 8 Jan. 1791. Cadet 1807. Arrived in India 21 Mar. 1809. Fireworker 27 Mar. 1809. Lieut. 26 June 1813.

THE BENGAL ARMY, 1758-1834   163

Capt. 18 Oct. 1822. Major 24 Apr. 1838. Lt. Col. 15 Jan. 1844.
Invalided 1 Dec. 1847. *d*. nr. Darjeeling 6 Nov. 1860.
Son of William Blake. Woolwich Cadet ; nominated for R.M.A.
27 Nov. 1805.
Services : Nepal War 1814-5 ; Lieut. 6th Coy. 2nd Bn. Foot Art.,
with 1st Div. Nepal War 1816. Posted to newly-raised 6th
(Native) Troop H.A. in 1817, and was in comd. till Jan. 1818.
Third Mahratta War ; battle and siege of Nagpur. To comd. 3rd
Troop 2nd Bde. H.A. 1825. Siege and capture of Bhurtpore ;
Capt. comdg. 3rd Troop 2nd Bde. (India medal with clasps for
Nepal and Nagpur). Transfd. to 2nd Troop 2nd Bde. in 1827, and
remained in comd. till 1837. Major 1st Bn. Foot Art. ; Lt. Col.
9th Bn. Art. Comdg. Invalids at Chunar during the Mutiny.

BLAKE, Muirson Trower (1809-1857). Bt. Major, 54th N.I.
b. Berhampore 24 Nov. 1809. Cadet 1826. Ensign 7 Jan. 1827.
Lieut. 4 Sept. 1839. Capt. 18 July 1848. Bt. Major 20 June
1854. *d*. Gwalior 14 June 1857 : kld. by mutineers.
Son of William Blake, *q.v. m*. Lucknow, 9 Mar. 1831, Charlotte
Adeline Judith, youngest dau. of Mordaunt Ricketts, B.C.S.,
Resident at Lucknow. (*See also* John Fitzgerald.) Ed. Harrow
1820/21 till 1824. Addiscombe Cadet 1824 till 20 June 1826.
Services : Posted as Ensign to 56th N.I. Actg. Adjt. 4th Local
Horse 12 Dec. 1831. Asst. Surveying Ofr. and Comdt. of escort to
Capt. Robert Boileau Pemberton's (*q.v.*) Mission to Bhutan and
Tibet 1836. Disturbances in Bundelkhand 1841-2 ; capture of
Chirgaon ; 2nd in comd. Sindhia's Reformed Contingent. Transfd.
to 54th N.I. 14 Dec. 1842. Gwalior campaign ; Paniar (Bronze
star). Comdt. 2nd Inf., Gwalior Contingent, 13 Jan. 1844 till
death. Killed whilst endeavouring to prevent his Regt. from
mutinying.
Refs. : Foster's *Peerage*, p. 591, *s.n.* St. Vincent, V. *Harrow
School List*.

BLAKE, Thomas Gage (1805-?). Ensign. 67th N.I. *b*. 1805.
Cadet 1825. Ensign 11 Feb. 1826. Resigned in India 16 Nov.
1827. *d. unm.* (?).
bapt. Midhurst, Sussex, 10 Apr. 1805. 5th son of Sir James
Henry Blake, 3rd Bart., of Langham, Suffolk, and Louisa Elizabeth
his wife, dau. of Gen. the Hon. Thomas Gage.
Services : Posted as Ensign to 67th N.I. No record of active
service.
Refs. : Burke's *Peerage*, 1923, p. 284, *s.n.* Blake, Bart., of Langham, Suffolk.

BLAKE, William (1780-1821). Major, 13th N.I. *b.* London 24 June 1780. Cadet 1798. Arrived in India 5 Sept. 1799. Ensign 7 Oct. 1799. Lieut. 28 Oct. 1799. Capt. 29 Aug. 1810. Major 5 May 1821. *d.* Benares 23 Sept. 1821.

Son of Benjamin Blake and Ann his wife. *m.* Mary Anne Woolsey. Father of Muirson Trower Blake, *q.v.*, and of Anne Rachel, wife of James Caulfeild, *q.v.*

Services : Posted to 2/13th N.I. 15 Apr. 1801. Fur. 30 Mar. 1805 till 17 Mar. 1808. Adjt. Burdwan Provl. Bn. 1809-11. Mily. Sec. to V.P. and Dy. Govr. (Lt. Gen. George Hewett) 1811. Bareilly insurrection 1816 ; Capt. 1/13th N.I. On survey duty in W. Provinces 1818-9.

Refs. : Will dated 23 Sept. 1821 ; proved 5 Oct. 1821.

*BLAKE, William Powney (1795/96-1814). Cadet, Infantry. *b.* 1795/96. (Aged 16 in 1812.) Cadet 1813. Was already in India when apptd. Cadet. *d.* Titalya, Bengal, 19 Aug. 1814.

Services : "Mr. William Powney Blake, now in India, to be appointed a Cadet, but not to take rank till the time he would be ranked if he had proceeded to the Seminary." (Original Correspondence of 24 Feb. 1813.)

BLANCHE, Samuel (*d.* 1774). Lieutenant, Infantry. Cadet 1766. Ensign 1 Dec. 1767. Lieut. 21 Oct. 1769. *d.* Bisauli, U.P., 26 June 1774.

Services : N.F.P.

BLANCKENHAGEN, Henry (1776-1813). Captain, Bengal European Regt. *bapt.* Lutheran Church, Trinity Lane, London, 11 June 1776. Cadet 1794. Arrived in India 20 Apr. 1797. Ensign 28 Oct. 1795. Lieut. 25 Apr. 1797. Capt. 21 Sept. 1804. *d.* 30 Aug. 1813 : kld. in action against the Malays during an attack on the I. of Ceram.

Son of Theophilus Christian Blanckenhagen, of Dutch descent (naturalized in 1770), and Elizabeth his wife. *m.* Dinapore, 11 Oct. 1802, Miss Caroline Matilda Hariot. (She and her seven children were all drowned in the wreck of an East Indiaman on their passage to England.)

Services : Lieut. 1st Bengal Eur. Regt. Second Mahratta War 1804-5 ; Capt. Eur. Regt. Expedition to Macao 1808-9 ; Capt. Eur. Regt., and Paymr. to the detachment. In Amboyna 1811 ; raised and comdd. the Amboyna Corps from amongst the Malays of the island. Attack on Ceram, Moluccas, Aug. 1813 (kld.).

Refs. : *N. & Q.* 8S. xi. 377. *G.M.* 1814, ii. 299. Will dated Calcutta 19 Oct. 1810 ; proved 7 May 1819.

BLAND, Henry James (1789-1883). Major. 9th N.I. *b.* London 20 Nov. 1789. Cadet 1806. Arrived in India 21 July 1807. Ensign 6 Aug. 1807. Lieut. 22 Aug. 1812. Capt. 1 May 1824. Retired 13 June 1832. Hon. Major 28 Nov. 1854. *d.* 22 Aug. 1883. Son of Thomas Bland.
Services : Barasat C.C. for 10 mos. Posted as Ensign to 8th N.I. Expedition to Mauritius 1810 ; Ensign 2nd Bn. Bengal Vols. Nepal War 1814-5 ; Lieut. 1/8th N.I., in 4th Div. Nepal War 1816 ; Lieut. 1/8th N.I., in 2nd Bde., Left Column (India medal). Adjt. 2/8th N.I. 8 Apr. 1818 till 17 June 1824. Third Mahratta War ; Lieut. 8th N.I. Transfd. as Capt. to 9th N.I. (late 1/8th) May 1824. Fur. p.a. 9 Aug. 1829 till retirement.

BLANDFORD, Robert (1752/53-1787). Lieutenant, Infantry. *b.* 1752/53. Cadet 1781. Apptd. Cadet 20 Feb. 1781. Ensign 12 July 1781. Lieut. 12 Oct. 1783. *d.* Barrackpore 24 Aug. 1787. A native of Gloucs.
Services : Sailed for India on the *Lord Mulgrave*, 26 June 1781, aged 28. N.F.P.

BLANE, George Rodney (1791-1821). Captain, Engineers. *b.* London 7 Jan. 1791. Cadet 1806. Arrived in India 17 Mar. 1808. Ensign 18 Mar. 1808. Lieut. 5 Nov. 1810. Capt. 1 Sept. 1818. *d.s.p.* Ludhiana 18 May 1821.
3rd son of Sir Gilbert Blane, 1st Bart., Physician in Ordinary to George III, and Elizabeth his wife. Ed. Charterhouse ; admitted scholar 6 May 1802. Marlow Cadet.
Services : Nepal War 1814-5 ; first attack on Kalanga 31 Oct. 1814 (s.w.) ; second attack and capture of Kalanga 27 Nov. 1814 ; operations round Nahan ; Surveyor and Asst. Field Engineer, in 2nd Div. Apptd. Executive Officer and Supt. of bldgs. at Ludhiana 1819, and, in addition, May 1820, Supt. of canals in Delhi territory.
Refs. : Burke's *Peerage*, 1905, p. 167, *s.n.* Blane, Bart., of Blanefield, co. Ayr. *De Rhé-Philipe. A.J.* xiv. 228. *Alumni Carthusiani.*

BLANE, Robert (*d.* 1798). Lieut. Colonel. 13th Bn. Sepoys. Cadet (?). Ensign (?). Lieut. 23 Aug. 1765. Capt. 9 Dec. 1767. Major 20 Mar. 1780. Lt. Col. 4 Dec. 1782. Retired before 1791. *d.* Burghfield, Berks., 18 Jan. 1798.
Services : Comdd. 14th Bn. in 1773. In Jan. 1781, when the 14th was formed into a Regt. of two Bns. and renumbered the 13th Regt. (eventually became 4th N.I.), he again got command. Second Mysore War ; Major comdg. 13th N.I.
Refs. : *Williams*, p. 77. *G.M.* 1798, i. 89. *S.M.* 1798, p. 214. *M.M.* 1798, p. 79.

BLANSHARD, John (1782-?). Lieutenant. 6th N.I. *bapt.* St. Mary, Newington Butts, Surrey, 8 Aug. 1782. Cadet 1798. Arrived in India 19 Sept. 1799. Ensign 9 Oct. 1799. Lieut. 28 Oct. 1799. Resigned in England 25 Mar. 1803. *d.* before 1842.

Son of John Atkinson Blanshard, Capt. E.I.C.S., and Harriet his wife, elder dau. of Roger Henry Gale, of Scruton Hall, Yorks. *m.* Jane Eleanora. (She died his widow 12 Jan. 1842.)
Services : Posted to 1/6th N.I. 15 Apr. 1801. N.F.P.
Refs. : Burke's *Landed Gentry*, 2nd edn., p. 261, *s.n.* Coore, of Scruton Hall, Yorks.

BLANSHARD, John Henry (1805-1881). Major, Invalid Est. 63rd N.I. *b.* Northallerton, Yorks., 3 Sept. 1805. Cadet 1823. Arrived in India 8 Oct. 1824. Ensign 11 May 1824. Lieut. 13 May 1825. Capt. 14 Oct. 1841. Major 19 Jan. 1855. Invalided 31 Dec. 1855. *d.* 26 Apr. 1881.

Son of Richard Blanshard, E.I.C.N.S., a mgte. co. York. *m.* (?).
Services : Sailed for India on 11 May 1824. Posted as Ensign to 63rd N.I. 31 Mar. 1825. Siege and capture of Bhurtpore (India medal). Fur. p.a. 7 Jan. 1836 till 25 June 1839. First Sikh War ; Ferozshahr ; Sobraon ; Capt. 63rd N.I. (Medal with clasp).

BLAQUIERE, William (*d.* 1783). Ensign, 1st Bengal European Regt. Cadet (?). Ensign 1782. *d. unm.* Calcutta 23 Sept. 1783 : kld. by William Gore, *q.v.*, in a duel.
Services : N.F.P.
Refs. : Will dated 22 Sept. 1783.

BLEMAN, Joseph. Lieutenant. Infantry. Cadet 1782. Ensign 27 Apr. 1783. Lieut. 21 Mar. 1790. Resigned 14 Dec. 1791.
Services : N.F.P.

BLENCOWE, John (1802-1831). Lieutenant, 38th N.I. *b.* Dersingham, Norfolk, 6 Aug. 1802. Cadet 1820. Admitted 24 Mar. 1821. Ensign 24 Sept. 1820. Lieut. 11 July 1823. *d.* Bath 21 Dec. 1831.

2nd son of Henry Prescott Blencowe, of Blencowe (of Bath), and Rebecca his wife, eldest dau. of Edward Everard, of Lynn, Norfolk.
Services : Posted as Ensign to 1/26th N.I. Transfd. to 19th N.I. in 1823 ; to 38th N.I. (late 1/19th) May 1824. Adjt. 38th N.I. 19 Oct. 1825 till 17 Jan. 1831. Fur. p.a. 16 Mar. 1831 till death. No record of active service.
Refs. : Burke's *Landed Gentry*, 12th edn., p. 180, *s.n.* Blencowe, of Thoby Priory, Essex.

BLENKINS, Frederick Augustus (1791-1813). Ensign, 16th N.I. *b.* Waltham Holy Cross, Essex, 22 June 1791. Cadet 1807. Arrived in India 21 Mar. 1809. Ensign 10 Feb. 1809. *d.* Delhi 14 Feb. 1813.
Son of William Blenkins.
Services : Posted as Ensign to 2/16th N.I. Operations in Bundelkhand 1809-11 ; Ensign 2/16th N.I.

BLENKINSOP, Edward (1807-1837). Ensign, 34th N.I. *bapt.* Eton College 18 Oct. 1807. Cadet 1825. Arrived in India 4 Sept. 1826. Ensign 15 Apr. 1826. *d.* Chaibasa, Singhbhum district, Bengal, 29 Sept. 1837 : murdered by a Sowar of the 5th Local Horse, to whom he had awarded extra drill for insubordinate conduct.
Son of Rev. Henry Blenkinsop, chaplain of Eton College, afterwards rector of Christ Church, Monmouth. *m.* (?).
Services : Posted as Ensign to 21st N.I. 5 Oct. 1826. Transfd. to 34th N.I. 12 Oct. 1826. To do duty with Ramgarh L.I. 19 Dec. 1836. To take charge of two Rissalahs of 5th Local Horse, attached to Ramgarh L.I. 14 Apr. 1837. He was still an Ensign after eleven years' service.
Refs. : A.J. N.S. viii. 205. *G.M.* 1838, i. 558.

*****BLEWITT, John** (*d.* 1763). Ensign, Infantry. Cadet (?). Ensign (?). *d.* 5th, 6th or 11th Oct. 1763 : massacred at or near Patna by order of Nawab Mir Muhammad Kasim. (See note to Benjamin Adamson.)
Services : N.F.P.
Refs. : See John Armstrong (died 1763).

*****BLEWITT, Samuel** (*d.* 1763). Ensign, Infantry. Cadet (?). Ensign (?). *d.* 5th, 6th or 11th Oct. 1763 : massacred at or near Patna by order of Nawab Mir Muhammad Kasim. (See note to Benjamin Adamson.)
Services : N.F.P.
Refs. : See John Armstrong (*d.* 1763).

BLISSET, Robert (1787-?). Captain. 18th N.I. *b.* London 15 Jan. 1787. Cadet 1804. Arrived in India 11 July 1806. Ensign 25 Apr. 1806. Lieut. 16 Sept. 1807. Capt. 11 July 1823. Retired 15 Nov. 1828. *d.* 1836 ?
Son of Charles Blisset and Mary his wife. *m.* 1st, Berhampore, 23 Mar. 1811, Johanna Margaritta, widow of —— Plusker. *m.* 2nd, Meerut, 12 June 1823, Sophia Jacoba, dau. of Jacob Plusker, and widow of Charles Rowning, *q.v.*
Note : His name disappears from the *E.I.R.* after Jan. 1836.

Note : His Christian names appear as Robert Tibbs in the marriage register.
Ed. Merchant Taylors' ; entered in Jan. 1800.
Services : Posted as Ensign to 6th N.I. Nepal War 1814-5 ; Lieut. 2/6th N.I., in 1st Div. Operations in Kotah ; Mangrol ; Lieut. 2/6th N.I. Transfd. to 18th N.I. (late 2/6th) May 1824. Fur. to N.S.W. 18 Mar. 1825 till retirement.
Refs. : Robinson.

BLOIS, Thomas Francis (1807-1871). Lieut. Colonel. 11th N.I. *b.* Elvington, Yorks., 13 Dec. 1807. Cadet 1823. Arrived in India 19 May 1824. Ensign 17 Jan. 1824. Lieut. 13 May 1825. Capt. 20 Jan. 1841. Major 26 July 1853. Retired 12 Oct. 1856. Hon. Lt. Col. 12 Oct. 1856. *d.* 26 Charles St., St. James's, London, 16 Jan. 1871.

4th and youngest son of Sir Charles Blois, 6th Bart., and Clara his wife, dau. of Jocelyn Price, of Camblesworth Hall, Yorks.
Services : Posted as Ensign to 11th N.I. Attached to 2nd Gren. Bn. 5 Sept. 1825. First Burma War ; Arakan 1825 ; Lieut. 2nd Gren. Bn. (India medal). Adjt. 11th N.I. 11 Oct. 1827 till 14 Nov. 1833. A.D.C. to G.G. 23 Oct. 1833 till 7 Jan. 1835. Sub-Asst. in Stud Dept. 25 Sept. 1834. Dy. Paymr., Meerut circle, 7 Jan. 1835 till 1853. First Sikh War ; Sobraon ; Capt. 11th N.I. (Medal). Fur. 1855 till retirement.
Refs. : Burke's *Peerage*, 1923, p. 290, *s.n.* Blois, Bart., of Cockfield Hall, Suffolk. *The Times*, 19 Jan. 1871.

BLOOD, Michael (1795-1831). Lieutenant, 17th N.I. *b.* Shankill, co. Armagh, 27 Aug. 1795. Cadet 1818. Admitted 27 Mar. 1820. Ensign 20 Sept. 1819. Lieut. 22 Aug. 1821. *d. unm.* Fatehgarh, U.P., 4 June 1831.

4th son of Richard Blood, of Bannvale, co. Down, and Jane Maria his wife, dau. of Capt. Thomas Shaw.
Services : Ensign H.M. 82nd Foot 24 Mar. 1813. Lieut. 27 Aug. 1815. h.p. 15 Mar. 1816. Posted as Ensign to 2/11th N.I. in 1820. Transfd. to 17th N.I. (late 2/11th) May 1824. No record of active service.
Refs. : Burke's *Landed Gentry of Ireland*, p. 57, *s.n.* Blood, late of Cranagher, co. Clare.

BLOTT, James (1781-1813). Lieutenant, 18th N.I. *bapt.* Wilton, Hunts, 14 July 1781. Cadet 1801. Arrived in India 7 July 1802. Ensign 11 July 1802. Lieut. 25 May 1804. *d.* at sea 15 May 1813.

Son of James Blott and Sarah his wife.

THE BENGAL ARMY, 1758-1834

Services: Posted as Lieut. to 18th N.I. (? Second Mahratta War; Bundelkhand; Lieut. 18th N.I.) Fur. 31 Jan. 1805 till 5 Dec. 1810.

BLUETT, William Henry Clarke (1790-1829). Lieutenant, 45th N.I. *b.* Holcombe Rogus, Devon, 20 Mar. 1799. Cadet 1823. Arrived in India 10 Oct. 1824. Ensign 23 May 1824. Lieut. 5 Dec. 1827. *d.* Saugor, 6 May 1829, of fever.

2nd son of William Bluett and Elizabeth Maria his wife, dau. of John Clarke, of Halton, Cornwall.

Services : Lieut. 4th Regt. Jersey Mil. 3 Feb. 1823. Posted as Ensign to 16th N.I. 31 Mar. 1825. Transfd. to 45th N.I. 6 Apr. 1825. No record of active service.

Refs. : Burke's *Landed Gentry*, 12th edn., p. 168, *s.n.* Bluett, of Tor Mohun, Devon, formerly of Holcombe Court. *A.J.* xxviii. 604.

BLUNDELL, George Snow (1795-1853). Bt. Major. 51st N.I. *b.* 1795. Cadet 1810. Admitted 27 Aug. 1811. Ensign 13 Nov. 1813. Lieut. 1 Oct. 1816. Capt. 28 Nov. 1826. Bt. Major 23 Nov. 1841. Retired 30 Jan. 1842. *d.* North Town House, Taunton, 26 Mar. 1853, aged 57.

bapt. Taunton 17 Dec. 1795. Son of William Blundell, *q.v.*, and Mary his wife. *m.* Taunton 5 May 1835, Augusta Catherina, youngest dau. of John Rickards, of Ailstone Hill, Hereford. (She died 5 Sept. 1884, aged 76.) Ed. Blundell's, 20 Aug. 1806 till 16 Dec. 1808.

Services : Posted as Ensign to 1/26th N.I. Third Mahratta War; Lieut. 1/26th N.I., in Left Div. With 3rd Bn. Ceylon Vols. in Ceylon 1818-9. Actg. Adjt. 1/26th N.I. 11 Sept. 1820. Transfd. to 51st N.I. (late 1/26th) May 1824. Adjt. 51st N.I. 31 May 1824. Fur. p.a. 26 Jan. 1828 till 9 Jan. 1831. Fur. s.c. 20 Dec. 1832 till 27 Oct. 1835. D.J.A.G. 1 Dec, 1838.

Refs. : *Blundell's School Register.* G.M. 1853, i. 564. *Bath Chron.* 31 Mar. 1853. Will dated 26 Feb. 1853; proved 21 Jan. 1854.

BLUNDELL, William (1751/52-1838). Lieutenant. Artillery. *b.* 1751/52. Cadet 1778. Fireworker 2 Oct. 1778. Lieut. 4 July 1782. Resigned in England 20 Feb. 1790. *d.* Taunton, Somerset, 6 Mar. 1838, aged 86.

m. Mary Ann. (She died 14 Dec. 1804, aged 36.) Father of George Snow Blundell, *q.v.*

Services : Second Mysore War 1781-5; Lieut. 5th Coy. 2nd Bn. Art.

Refs. : *A.J.* N.S. xxv. 300. M.I. in St. Mary Magdalene. Taunton.

BLUNT, Henry James (1807-1836). Ensign, 48th N.I. *bapt.*
Woodford, Essex, 1 Apr. 1807. Cadet 1825. Arrived in India
19 Dec. 1826. Ensign 19 June 1826. *d.* Sitapur, U.P., 18 July
1836.

Son of John Blunt, of Upper Bedford Pl., London, merchant.
m. Calcutta, 10 Feb. 1831, Eliza Jane, eldest dau. of Edward Brown,
q.v.

Services : Posted as Ensign to 48th N.I., and served throughout
with that Regt. Wahabi rising 1831.

BLUNT, James Tillyer (1765/66-1834). Captain. Engineers. *b.*
1765/66. Cadet 1783. Ensign 15 Feb. 1785. Lieut. 25 Apr.
1797. Capt. 1 Jan. 1806. Retired 9 Feb. 1810. *d.* Womford
Hill, Heavitree, Devon, 20 Oct. 1834, aged 68.

m. Calcutta, 3 Sept. 1796, Miss Mary Bristow. (*See also* Robert
Hyde Colebrooke.) (She died 6 June 1849, aged 70.) Ed. Merchant
Taylors' ; entered in 1773.

Services : Employed on surveying duty. Asst. Engr. at Monghyr.
Again employed on survey work. Third Mysore War ; capture of
Seringapatam. Bk. Mr. at Fort William 1798 till 1803. Second
Mahratta War ; operations in Cuttack ; storm and capture of
Khurda. Bk. Mr. at Fort William 1805-7. Fur. 1807 till retirement.

Refs. : *Robinson,* ii. 138. *E.I.M.C.* iii. 290. *Bath Chron.* 31 Oct.
1834.

BLYTH, William Wren (1805-1824). Lieutenant, 44th N.I. *bapt.*
Solihull, co. Warwick, 28 Jan. 1805. Cadet 1822. Ensign 11 July
1823. Lieut. 1824. *d.* Dacca 16 Aug. 1824.

Son of Rev. Thomas Blyth, of Knowle, co. Warwick, sometime
rector of Whitchurch, co. Warwick.

Services : Posted to 44th N.I. in May 1824. No record of active
service.

BODINGFIELD, Henry. Lieutenant. Infantry. Cadet 1783.
Ensign 1783. Lieut. 1788. Struck off 1788.

Services : N.F.P.

BOGLE, Sir Archibald, Kt. (1805-1870). Major General. 5th N.I.
b. Dumbarton 18 Aug. 1805. Cadet 1822. Arrived in India
17 May 1823. Ensign 13 Mar. 1823. Lieut. 13 May 1825. Capt.
14 Aug. 1832. Major 4 Oct. 1844. Lt. Col. 17 Feb. 1851. Col.
28 Feb. 1854. Maj. Gen. 2 Aug. 1862. *d.* 90 Westbourne Terr.,
London, 12 June 1870.

Son of Andrew Bogle, merchant. *m.* 25 June 1828, Miss Maynard

Eliza Grange, niece of Sir Charles D'Oyly, 7th Bart. (She died Howrah, nr. Calcutta, 29 June 1831.) Ed. Harrow; entered the school 1818/19, left 1820/21.

Services : Posted as Ensign to 1st N.I. Transfd. to 2nd N.I. (late 1/1st) May 1824. First Burma War; Assam 1824-5; occupation of Rangpur; Lieut. d.d. 57th N.I. (India medal). D.A.G., Dinapore Div., 1827. To comd. Arakan Bn. and Police Corps 20 June 1828. Asst. to Supt. in Arakan 21 Aug. 1829. Defeat of Dewangiri (Bhutan) Rajah 1836. Comr. of Arakan 16 May 1837. Second Burma War; capture of Martaban; capture of Rangoon 14 Apr. 1852 (s.w.) (Medal); at recapture of Beeling stockade Apr. 1853. Apptd. Comr. in Tenasserim and Martaban 30 Dec. 1852. Transfd. as Lt. Col. to 74th N.I. in 1852; to 22nd N.I. Nov. 1853; to 48th N.I. Mar. 1854; to 16th N.I. Oct. 1854; to 14th N.I. Apr. 1855; to 42nd N.I.; to 5th N.I. Kt. 9 Dec. 1853.

Refs. : Harrow School List. Boase. D.I.B. A.J. xxvi. 740. *Walford. The Times,* 16 June 1870.

BOGLE, George (1761/62-1813). Lieutenant. Infantry. *b.* 1761/62. Cadet 1781. Ensign 25 July 1781. Lieut. 2 Jan. 1782. Struck off 1788. *d.* Old Burlington St., London, 11 Nov. 1813, in his 52nd year.

Of Effingham House, Surrey.

Services : N.F.P.

BOILEAU, Alexander Henry Edmonstone (1807-1862). Major General, Engineers. *b.* Calcutta 3 Feb. 1807. Cadet 1824. Arrived in India 8 May 1825. 2nd Lieut. 17 June 1824. Lieut. 7 Feb. 1827. Capt. 20 May 1839. Bt. Major 19 Aug. 1847. Lt. Col. 1 May 1849. Col. 8 June 1856. Maj. Gen. 18 Oct. 1860. *d.* Cawnpore, 30 June 1862, of dysentery.

bapt. Calcutta 13 Feb. 1807. Posthumous son of Thomas Boileau, of Calcutta, notary public, and Leah his wife, dau. of Lt. Col. Ebenezer Jessop, of Albany, N.Y. Brother of John Theophilus Boileau, *q.v.,* and cousin-german to Solomon Boileau, *q.v. m.* 1st, Agra, 3 Feb. 1834, Charlotte, dau. of William Hanson. (*See also* Frederick Walpole Anson and John Theophilus Boileau.) (She died Barrackpore, 29 Apr. 1840, aged 26.) *m.* 2nd, Paignton, Devon, 5 Sept. 1850, Matilda Grace, 2nd dau. of Alexander Tovey, 20th Regt. Addiscombe Cadet 1823-4.

Services : Posted to S. & M. at Cawnpore 2 July 1825. Siege and capture of Bhurtpore; comdd. two Coys. of S. & M. during the storm (India medal). Shekhawat Expedition 1834. Fur. s.c. 5 July 1850 till 1852. Suptg. Engr. P.W.D., N.W.P., 3 May 1854. Chief Engr. P.W.D., Nagpur territory, 1 Apr. 1856. Comdt. Engrs.

Refs. : Foster's *Baronetage*, p. 56, *s.n.* Boileau, Bart. Burke's *Landed Gentry*, 5th edn., p. 1395, *s.n.* Tovey-Tennent, of Overton and Poole. Boase. *G.M.* 1862, ii. 369. *The Times*, 16 Aug. 1862.

BOILEAU, Francis Burton (1806-1888). Major General. Artillery. *b.* 18 Feb. 1806. Cadet 1822. Arrived in India 20 Oct. 1823. 2nd Lieut. 6 June 1823. Lieut. 28 Sept. 1827. Capt. 12 Aug. 1841. Major 10 Mar. 1854. Lt. Col. 10 July 1857. Col. 18 Feb. 1861. Retired 20 Feb. 1863. Hon. Maj. Gen. 20 Feb. 1863. *d.* Castelnau, Bognor, Sussex, 6 Apr. 1888.

Representative of the Lords of Castelnau, France. *bapt.* Winchelsea, Sussex, 7 May 1806. Son of Simeon Peter Boileau, of Baltinglass, of the Notts. Mil. (who was cousin-german of Solomon Boileau, *q.v*), and Hannah his wife, dau. of Annesley De Rinzy, of co. Wicklow. Brother of Henry Cunningham Boileau, *q.v. m.* Agra, 17 June 1834, Sarah, youngest dau. of Major Robert Durie, 11th Light Dns. (*See also* William Beckett (1798-1844). Addiscombe Cadet 1821-3.

Services : Posted to newly-raised 3rd Troop 1st Bde. H.A. 1826. Siege and capture of Bhurtpore ; 2nd Lieut. 4th Troop 2nd Bde. (from 3rd Troop 1st Bde.) (India medal). Served with 4th Troop 3rd Bde. H.A. 1826-34. Transfd. to 1st Troop 2nd Bde. in 1834 ; to 3rd Troop 3rd Bde. in 1836. Fur. s.c. 12 Jan. 1838 till 31 Dec. 1840. First Sikh War ; Badhowal ; Aliwal ; Capt. comdg. 2nd Coy. 7th Bn. Foot Art. (Medal).

Refs. : Foster's *Baronetage*, p. 55, *s.n.* Boileau, Bart. Burke's *Peerage*, 1904, p. 173, *s.n.* Boileau, Bart., of Tacolnestone Hall, Norfolk. *The Times*, 10 Apr. 1888.

BOILEAU, Henry Cunningham (1804-1852). Bt. Major, 28th N.I. *b.* Winchelsea, Sussex, 29 Nov. 1804. Cadet 1820. Admitted 27 May 1821. Ensign 13 Jan. 1821. Lieut. 11 July 1823. Capt. 6 Nov. 1832. Bt. Major 9 Nov. 1846. *d.* Dinapore 22 Aug. 1852.

Son of Simeon Peter Boileau, of Baltinglass, and Hannah his wife. Brother of Francis Burton Boileau, *q.v.* Addiscombe Cadet 1819-20.

Services : Posted as Ensign to 2/24th N.I. Transfd. to 14th N.I. in 1823 ; to 28th N.I. (late 1/14th) May 1824. Leave s.c. 8 mos. to Singapore 11 Mar. 1825. Supt. and Paymr. of Invalids at Benares, Dinapore, and Monghyr, 27 Mar. 1840 till death. No record of active service.

Refs. : Foster's *Baronetage*, p. 55, *s.n.* Boileau, Bart.

BOILEAU, John Peter (1787-1838). Bt. Colonel, Artillery. *b.* 27 Nov. 1787. Cadet 1804. Arrived in India 14 Aug. 1804. Lieut. 19 Aug. 1804. Capt. Lt. 26 Mar. 1807. Capt. 17 Feb.

THE BENGAL ARMY, 1758-1834 173

1815. Major 22 Nov. 1821. Lt. Col. 28 Sept. 1827. Bt. Col. 18 June 1831. *d.* Cape Town, S.A., 6 Mar. 1838.
Son of Solomon Boileau, cashier of the Dublin bank, and Lieut. 76th Foot, and Dorothea his 1st wife, dau. of Francis Gladwell, of Dublin, merchant. Brother of Solomon Hugh Richard Boileau, *q.v.*, and uncle of Henry Cunningham Boileau, *q.v.* *m.* Meerut, 3 July 1823, Mary, dau. of John Clarke.
Services : Posted to 1st Troop H.A. in 1806. Transfd. to 2nd Troop in 1809. Comdd. as Capt. Lt. the H.A. attached to the Java L.C. Comdd. 1st Troop H.A. 1816-20. Siege and capture of Hathras. Third Mahratta War. To comd. Nagpur Div. of Art. 23 Dec. 1823. Principal Dy. Comy. of Ord. 19 Nov. 1824 till 17 Mar. 1826. Bt. Col. comdg. 1st Bde. H.A. at Meerut. Leave s.c. to Cape for 2 yrs. 16 Jan. 1838.
Refs. : Foster's *Baronetage*, p. 55, *s.n.* Boileau, Bart. *G.M.* 1838, ii. 110. Will dated Calcutta 24 Nov. 1827 ; codicils dated 8 June 1831 and 30 Mar. 1835 ; proved 4 Dec. 1838. M.I. in Cape Town cemetery.

*BOILEAU, John Peter (1790-1818). Lieutenant, 18th N.I. Comdg. Nepal Residency Escort. *bapt.* St. Bridget's, Dublin, 10 Jan. 1790. Cadet 1804. Arrived in India 10 Sept. 1805. Ensign 2 Oct. 1805. Lieut. 26 Oct. 1805. *d. unm.* Patna 1 Dec. 1818.
Son of John Theophilus Boileau, of Bride St., Dublin, merchant, and Jane his wife, dau. of H. Wilson, of Dublin, merchant. Brother of Solomon Boileau, *q.v.*, and cousin-german of John Peter Boileau, *q.v.*, and of Sir John Peter Boileau, 1st Bart.
Services : Posted as Ensign to 18th N.I. Served with Lt. Col. Ochterlony's detachment in 1809. To comd. escort of Major Paris Bradshaw, *q.v.*, 7 Feb. 1814. Nepal War 1814-5 ; received a deep sabre cut in a personal contest with a Nepalese Subadar, whom he slew, 24 Nov. 1814. Comdd. Nepal Residency Escort of Lt. Col. Paris Bradshaw till death.
Refs. : Burke's *Peerage*, 1923, p. 300, *s.n.* Boileau, Bart., of Tacolnestone Hall, Norfolk. Will dated 25 Sept. 1817 ; proved 5 Apr. 1819.

BOILEAU, John Theophilus (1805-1886). Major General. Engineers. *b.* Calcutta 26 May 1805. Cadet 1821. Arrived in India 24 Sept. 1822. Ensign 19 Dec. 1820. Lieut. 1 May 1824. Capt. 18 June 1831. Major 1 Jan. 1843. Lt. Col. 5 May 1846. Col. 1 May 1855. Retired 10 Mar. 1857. Hon. Maj. Gen. 29 May 1857. *d.* 31 Ladbroke Sq., London, 7 Nov. 1886.
bapt. Calcutta 19 Aug. 1805. Elder son of Thomas Boileau, of

Calcutta, and Leah his wife. Brother of Alexander Henry Edmonstone Boileau, *q.v.*, and cousin-german of John Peter Boileau (both), *q.v.* m. Agra, 23 Apr. 1829, Anne, dau. of William Hanson. (*See also* Frederick Walpole Anson.) Addiscombe Cadet 1819-20.

Services : In charge of the Observatory at Simla Oct. 1840 till retirement. Suptg. Engineer, N.W.P., Feb. 1848. Chief Engineer, N.W.P., 1 May 1854 till retirement. Comdt. Engineers Apr. 1855. Consulting Engr. for Rajputana 12 Dec. 1856. No record of active service. Private 1st Middlesex Rifles 1860-6. F.R.S.

Refs. : Foster's *Baronetage*, p. 56, *s.n.* Boileau, Bart. Boase. *The Times*, 9 Nov. 1886. *I.L.N.* 20 Nov. 1886, p. 550 (portrait). Portrait by Sydney Hodges at the Soldiers' Daughters' Home.

BOILEAU, Solomon (1800-1825). Lieutenant, 32nd N.I. *bapt.* Dublin 6 Apr. 1800. Cadet 1817. Ensign (?). Lieut. 1 Jan. 1819. *d. unm.* Cawnpore 14 Dec. 1825.

Son of John Theophilus Boileau, of Dublin, merchant, and Jane his wife. Brother of John Peter Boileau (1790-1818), *q.v.*, and cousin-german of John Theophilus Boileau, *q.v.*, Sir John Peter Boileau, 1st Bart., and Simeon Boileau, of Wales. (? T.C.D. ; Pensioner 3 Nov. 1817.)

Services : Posted as Lieut. to 1/16th N.I. Intr. & Qmr. do. 27 Nov. 1823. Transfd. to 32nd N.I. (late 1/16th) May 1824. No record of active service.

Refs. : Burke's *Peerage*, 1923, p. 300, *s.n.* Boileau, Bart., of Tacolnestone Hall, Norfolk. (? *Alumni Dub.*) Will dated 6 Dec. 1825 ; proved 18 Jan. 1826.

BOILEAU, Solomon Hugh Richard (1781-1810). Capt. Lieutenant, 3rd N.C. *bapt.* St. Paul's, Dublin, 9 Nov. 1781. Cadet 1797. Arrived in India 10 Sept. 1798. Cornet 1 Nov. 1798. Lieut. 29 May 1800. Capt. Lt. 5 Dec. 1807. *d. unm.* Partabgarh, U.P., 11 Apr. 1810.

Son of Solomon Boileau, of Dublin, and Dorothea his 1st wife. Brother of John Peter Boileau, *q.v.*, cousin-german of John Peter Boileau (1790-1818), *q.v.*, and uncle of Francis Burton Boileau, *q.v.*

Services : Posted as Ensign to 2nd Eur. Regt. Sept. 1798. Transfd. to 2/7th N.I. Oct. 1798. Transfd. as Cornet to 3rd N.C. Nov. 1798, and remained with that Regt. till death. Fur. 29 Jan. 1800 till 26 Oct. 1801. Operations in Jumna Doab 1803 ; Sasni ; Bijaigarh ; Kachaura. Second Mahratta War 1803-6 ; battle of Delhi ; Laswari ; battle of Deig ; pursuit of Holkar to the Punjab. Adjt. 3rd N.C. 1805 till death.

Refs. : Burke's *Peerage*, 1923, p. 300, *s.n.* Boileau, Bart., of Tacolnestone Hall, Norfolk.

THE BENGAL ARMY, 1758-1884　　175

BOISRAGON, Charles Henry (1804-1838). Captain, 72nd N.I.
b. Walcot, Somerset, 27 Apr. 1804. Cadet 1821. Arrived in India 20 Aug. 1822. Ensign 5 June 1822. Lieut. 9 Aug. 1824. Capt. 19 Aug. 1835. *d.* Etawah, U.P., 7 Feb. 1838.

Eldest son of Henry Charles Boisragon, M.D., of Walcot, and of Cheltenham, and Mary Annetta his wife, only dau. of John Gascoyne Fanshawe, of Parsloes and Wyersdale, J.P. co. Essex. *m.* Cawnpore, 25 Apr. 1827, Ellen Gardner, dau. of William George Maxwell, *q.v.* (*See also* Charles Ekins, John Craigie-Halkett, Peter La Touche, George Freer Holland, William Henry Ryves.) His dau. *m.* James Drummond (1808-1852), *q.v.* Ed. Eton 1814-20; K.S. 1817.

Services : Ensign 25th N.I. Adjt. 16th N.I. 29 June 1824. Intr. & Qmr. 4th Extra Regt. (became 72nd N.I.) 28 Dec. 1826. Adjt. 72nd N.I. 7 Feb. 1835.[1]

Refs. : Eton School List. Burke's *Landed Gentry,* 13th edn., p. 607, *s.n.* Fanshawe, of Parsloes.

[1] *Note : Eton School List* credits him with service in the First Burma War.

BOLAND, William Henry Robson (1805-1896). Major. 7th N.I.
b. Walcot, Somerset, 14 Apr. 1805. Cadet 1821. Arrived in India 23 Sept. 1822. Ensign 29 Aug. 1822. Lieut. 13 May 1825. Capt. 29 Aug. 1837. Retired 1 June 1843. Hon. Major 28 Nov. 1854. *d.* Versailles, France, 19 Aug. 1896.

Eldest son of Col. John Boland, Capt. h.p. Scotch Bde., Inspecting Field Officer at Bristol.

Services : Posted as Ensign to 2/6th N.I. in 1822. Transfd. to 2/20th N.I. ; to 2/23rd N.I. ; to 4th N.I. ; to 7th N.I. (late 1/4th) May 1824. Adjt. 7th N.I. 6 July 1831 till 2 Mar. 1836. Asst. to A.G.G. & Comr., Saugor and Narbada territories, 22 Mar. 1836. 1st Junior do. 18 Nov. 1840.

Refs. : The Times, 24 Aug. 1896.

BOLINGBROOK, William (*d.* 1777). Captain, Infantry. Cadet 17 Feb. 1765. Ensign 24 Feb. 1765. Lieut. 13 Dec. 1766. Capt. 13 Oct. 1769. *d.* Berhampore, Bengal, 24 Apr. 1777.
Services : N.F.P.

BOLTON, George (1788-1828). Captain, 2nd Bengal European Regt. *b.* Dinapore 3 June 1788. Cadet 1803. Arrived in India 15 Aug. 1804. Ensign 12 Sept. 1804. Lieut. 21 Sept. 1804. Capt. 1 Jan. 1819. *d.* Landown 13 June 1828.

Eldest son of Thomas Bolton, *q.v.,* and Sarah his wife. *m.* Berhampore, 1 Mar. 1818, Miss Fanny Ahmuty. (She died 26 May 1885, aged 79.)

Services : Posted as Ensign to Bengal Eur. Regt. Served in Java and Macassar 1813-6. Transfd. to newly-formed 2nd Eur. Regt., May 1824. First Burma War ; Capt. 2nd Eur. Regt.

BOLTON, Theophilus (Park) (1792-1838). Bt. Major, 47th N.I. *b.* Benares 8 Jan. 1792. Cadet 1806. Arrived in India 14 Oct. 1807. Ensign 5 Nov. 1807. Lieut. 3 Mar. 1813. Capt. 2 May 1824. Bt. Major 10 Jan. 1837. *d.* Agra 2 Mar. 1838.
bapt. Cawnpore 8 Jan. 1793. Son of Thomas Bolton, *q.v.*, and Sarah his wife. Brother of George Bolton, *q.v.*
Note : The second Christian name appears in his baptismal certificate, but not in any other official record.
Services : Barasat C.C. for one year. Posted as Ensign to 24th N.I. (? Hariana ; capture of Bhawani ; Ensign 2/24th N.I.) Adjt. 2/24th N.I. 4 May 1815 till 1824. Offg. Intr. & Qmr. do. 29 Jan. 1824. Transfd. to 47th N.I. (late 1/24th) May 1824. On this Regt. mutinying in Nov. 1824 he was posted to newly-raised 69th N.I. (became 47th in 1828). 2nd in comd. 12th Extra Regt. 21 May 1825 till its reduction on 1 Apr. 1826. Comdg. C.-in-C.'s escort in 1828. To comd. 2nd Nassiri Bn. 20 June 1828. Bde. Major in Oudh 12 Apr. 1836 till 21 Dec. 1836.

BOLTON, Thomas (*d.* 1794). Major, 18th Bn. Sepoys. Cadet 1768. Ensign 16 Jan. 1769. Lieut. 16 May 1770. Capt. 16 Dec. 1778. Major 5 Feb. 1784. *d.* 26 Oct. 1794 : kld. in action at the battle of Bitaurah, nr. Bareilly, U.P.
m. Calcutta, 23 Dec. 1784, Miss Sarah Rowe. Father of George Bolton, *q.v.*, and of Theophilus Bolton, *q.v.*
Services : Second Rohilla War ; battle of Bitaurah (kld.) ; Major comdg. 18th Bn. " This officer is described as having possessed uncommon strength : when surrounded by overwhelming numbers, he slew several of the enemy, until his treacherous sword shivered in his hand, and he fell covered with wounds."
Refs. : E.I.M.C. Williams, p. 152. *A Tour in India,* by Capt. Mundy, ii. 13. M.I. in St. John's churchyard, Calcutta.

BOLTON, Thomas William (1804-1846). Captain, 2nd N.I. *b.* Norwich 11 June 1804. Cadet 1821. Arrived in India Sept. 1822. Ensign 13 Sept. 1822. Lieut. 1 May 1824. Capt. 30 Apr. 1835. *d.* Ferozepore 7 Jan. 1846, of wounds received at the battles of Mudki and Ferozshahr.
Son of John Bolton, of Leicester, excise officer. *m.* Barrackpore, 21 Aug. 1830, Miss Mary French Duncan. (She died 20 Apr. 1884.)
Services : Posted as Ensign to 2/19th N.I. Oct. 1822. Transfd. to 2/16th N.I. Sept. 1823 ; to 2nd N.I. 31 Oct. 1825. Fur. s.c.

THE BENGAL ARMY, 1758-1884

9 Nov. 1826 till 10 Nov. 1829. Adjt. 2nd N.I. 29 July 1831 till 28 May 1835. Fur. p.a. 20 Jan. 1838 till Jan. 1841. First Afghan War 1842; relief of Kalat-i-Ghilzai, May; recapture of Ghazni 5 Sept. 1842; Nott's advance on Kabul; Capt. 2nd N.I. with force under Maj. Gen. England (Medal). Gwalior campaign; Maharajpur; Capt. 2nd N.I. (Bronze star). First Sikh War; Mudki (s.w.); Ferozshahr (s.w.); Capt. 2nd N.I.
Refs. : *De Rhé-Philipe.*

BOMFORD, Robert. Captain. Infantry. Cadet 1771. Ensign 17 Dec. 1772. Lieut. 16 Mar. 1777. Capt. 16 Mar. 1781. Struck off 1793.
N.B.—The following is conjectural only:
(Of Rahinstown, co. Meath. Eldest son of Stephen Bomford, J.P., of Rahinstown, and Elizabeth his wife, dau. of Stephen Sibthorpe, of Brownstown, co. Louth. *m.* 1792, Maria, dau. of Hon. James Massy Dawson, and grand-dau. of Hugh, first Lord Massy.)
Services : On fur. in 1790. N.F.P.
Refs. : (? Burke's *Landed Gentry of Ireland,* p. 60, *s.n.* Bomford, of Oakley Park, Meath.)

BOMFORD, Stephen (1754/55 ? -1782). Lieutenant, Infantry. *b.* Dublin 1754/55 ? Cadet 1778. Ensign 1778. Lieut. 13 Sept. 1779. bur. Madras 2 Feb. 1782.
(? Son of David Bomford, merchant.) (? T.C.D.; Pensioner 10 July 1773, aged 18.)
Services : N.F.P.
Refs. : (? *Alumni Dub.*) Madras burial register.

BONHAM, George William (1797-1853). Lieut. Colonel, 50th N.I. *b.* on board H.C. Extra Ship *Minerva* 17 July 1797. Cadet 1813. Admitted 5 Aug. 1814. Ensign 28 Nov. 1814. Lieut. 1 Aug. 1818. Capt. 13 May 1825. Major 1 Jan. 1844. Lt. Col. 18 June 1850. *d.* Benares, 14 July 1853.
Eldest son of Capt. George Bonham, E.I.C.N.S., Comdr. of the *True Briton,* East Indiaman, and Paulina his 1st wife, dau. of William Lushington. Half-brother of Sir Samuel George Bonham, K.C.B., 1st Bart. (*D.N.B.*). *m.* Piccadilly, London, 2 Aug. 1845, Frances Elizabeth, eldest dau. of C. R. Preston, late of Blackmore Priory, Essex.
Services : Posted as Ensign to 2/13th N.I. Nepal War; Ensign 8th N.I. (India medal). Transfd. to 1/19th N.I. 3 Oct. 1816. Third Mahratta War; Ensign 19th N.I. Transfd. as Lieut. to 2/20th N.I. in Aug. 1818; to 40th N.I. (late 2/20th) May 1824. Fur. 27 Sept. 1826 till 24 Nov. 1829. Fur. s.c. 31 Oct. 1841 till

1845. Transfd. as Lt. Col. to 68th N.I. in July 1850 ; to 50th N.I. 6 Nov. 1851.
Refs. : Burke's *Peerage*, 1923, p. 305, *s.n.* Bonham, Bart. *G.M.* 1853, ii. 537. *I.M.* 1853, p. 580.

BONJOUR, Noë Antoine Abraham (1731-1807). Lieutenant, Artillery. Subsequently Lt. Col. Madras Est. *b.* Avenches, Canton Vaud, Switzerland, 1731. Cadet 1756. Lieut. 2 Dec. 1757. *d.* Bellerive, Switzerland, 1807.
Seigneur de Bellerive.
Services : Sailed for Madras on the *Tavistock* in 1756. Resigned as Lt. Col. and returned to his native country towards the end of 1775. In 1777 he purchased the seigneurie of Bellerive for 120,000 livres, became souspréfet of the district in 1798, and in 1803 was elected a Member of the first Grand Conseil vaudois.
Refs. : *Love*, ii. 597 ; iii. 71-3. *E.I.M.C.* i. 5, 6, 8. *Dict. hist. et biog. de la Suisse*, vol. ii. *Dict. hist. du canton de Vaud*, par E. Mottaz (1914).

BONNAKER, Thomas (1735/36-1765). Captain, Bengal European Regt. *b.* Evesham, Worcs., 1735/36. Cadet 1761. Ensign 11 Dec. 1761. Lieut. 30 Aug. 1763. Capt. 20 Dec. 1764. *d.* in India Apr. 1765.
Brother of Ann Bon(n)aker, of Bradely Green, nr. Turnham, Worcs., and brother-in-law of William Acton, of Bongworth, nr. Evesham.
Services : Sailed for India on the *Hawke*, 17 Jan. 1761, aged 25. Campaign against Mir Mohd. Kasim and Shuja-ud-Daulah 1764 ; battle of Patna ; Capt. Eur. Regt.
Refs. : Will dated, " Camp on banks of Carramnass (Karamnasa R.) under comd. of Capt. McLean," 2 Apr. 1764 ; proved 22 Nov. 1765.

BONTEIN, James (1786-1828). Captain, 1st L.C. *b.* London 4 Oct. 1786. Cadet 1806. Arrived in India 21 July 1807. Cornet 24 July 1807. Lieut. 1 Sept. 1818. Capt. 13 May 1825. *d.s.p.* Calcutta, 24 Oct. 1828.
2nd son of Lt. Col. Sir James Bontein, Kt., Gentleman of the Privy Chamber to George III, and Alice Trant his wife. Uncle of John Bontein, *q.v.*
Services : Posted as Cornet to 1st N.C. Operations in Bundelkhand 1810-11. Third Mahratta War ; Lieut. 1st N.C., in Right Div. Against the Bhattis of Hariana 1818. Actg. Adjt. 1st L.C. 1819-20. Intr. & Qmr. 1st L.C. 10 Apr. 1819 till 6 Oct. 1825.

THE BENGAL ARMY, 1758-1884

Refs.: Burke's *Landed Gentry*, 13th edn., p. 767, *s.n.* Bontein-Cunninghame-Graham, of Ardoch, co. Dumbarton. Will dated 26 Apr. 1828; proved 5 Oct. 1828.

BONTEIN, John (1809-1878). Lieut. Colonel. 37th N.I. *b.* London 12 Feb. 1809. Cadet 1825. Arrived in India 24 Jan. 1827. Ensign 17 Aug. 1826. Lieut. 7 Feb. 1837. Capt. 27 June 1846. Major 20 Mar. 1857. Lt. Col. 26 Jan. 1861. Retired 8 Mar. 1861. *d.* 22 Ledbury Rd., Bayswater, London, 17 Aug. 1878.

Eldest son of Edward Trant Bontein, Capt. 92nd Highlrs., and Anna Maria his 1st wife, dau. of John Sims. Nephew of James Bontein, *q.v. m.* Agra, 21 Sept. 1835, Elizabeth Mary, 2nd dau. of Henry Clapton Barnard, *q.v.*

Services: Posted as Ensign to 51st N.I. Asst. in Surveyor Gen.'s Dept. 9 Oct. 1838. Transfd. to 37th N.I. 14 Dec. 1842. Adjt. 37th N.I. 17 Apr. 1844 till 10 June 1845. Fur. s.c. 14 Jan. 1845 till 1847. Second Sikh War; in garrison at Lahore; Capt. 37th N.I. (Medal). Bde. Major 3rd Bde. Gen. Godwin's force 24 Aug. 1852. Comdt. Dum-Dum Musketry Depot. Comdt. Sikh Vols. 27 July 1857 till 15 Aug. 1857, when he resigned and returned to the Musketry Depot.

Refs.: Burke's *Landed Gentry*, 13th edn., p. 767, *s.n.* Bontein-Cunninghame-Graham, of Ardoch, co. Dumbarton. *The Times*, 21 Aug. 1878.

BORLASE, Charles Bonython (1782-1819). Captain, 2nd L.C. *b.* Penzance 22 Oct. 1782. Cadet 1798. Arrived in India 20 Sept. 1799. Cornet 22 June 1800. Lieut. 11 Mar. 1805. Capt. 1 Sept. 1818. *d. unm.* Nasirabad, Rajputana, 26 Sept. 1819.

bapt. Penzance 30 Nov. 1782. Only son of John Bingham Borlase, M.D., and Ann Edwards his wife.

Services: Posted as Cornet to 2nd N.C. Second Mahratta War; battle of Delhi; Laswari; battle of Deig; Cornet 2nd N.C. Nepal War 1814; Lieut. 2nd N.C., in 1st Div. Third Mahratta War; Bde. Major 4th Bde. Comdg. 2nd Local Cav. in 1819.

Refs.: *Genealogist*, N.S. ii. 288. Will dated 3 Jan. 1819; proved 20 Oct. 1819.

BORRODAILE, George (1805-1835). Lieutenant, 49th N.I. *b.* Streatham, Surrey, 23 Dec. 1805. Cadet 1825. Arrived in India 25 June 1826. Ensign 16 Feb. 1826. Lieut. 27 May 1832. *d.* Calcutta 8 Jan. 1835.

Son of Thomas Borrodaile, of Cateaton St., London, merchant, late of Streatham.

Services : Ensign d.d. 46th N.I. 8 July 1826. Posted as Ensign to 68th N.I. Actg. Adjt. 68th N.I. 30 May 1829 and 9 June 1830. Transfd. to 49th N.I. 4 May 1832. Pioneers 9 July 1832 till 16 Oct. 1833. Bde. Major at Barrackpore 16 Oct. 1833 till death. No record of active service.

Refs. : G.M. 1835, i. 670. Will dated Mainpuri 1 May 1832 ; proved 10 Jan. 1835. M.I. in S. Park St. burial ground, Calcutta.

BORTHWICK, Thomas (1740/41-1769). Captain, Infantry. *b.* in Scotland 1740/41. Cadet 1764. Ensign 27 Dec. 1764. Lieut. Jan. 1766. Capt. 8 Apr. 1769. *d.* Dacca, 7 Aug. 1769, aged about 29 years.

Services : Sailed for India on the *Devonshire*, 20 Feb. 1764, aged 23. N.F.P.

Refs. : M.I. in English cemetery at Dacca (where the name is given as Borthwice.)

*BOSANQUET, Frederick Bernard (1812-1897). Bt. Captain. 16th N.I. *b.* London 15 Nov. 1812. Cadet 1829. Arrived in India 26 Mar. 1832. Ensign (17 June 1830) 19 Oct. 1833. Lieut. 20 Feb. 1838. Bt. Capt. 17 June 1845. Resigned 10 Oct. 1847. *d.* Belleville, Watcombe, Torquay, 7 Jan. 1897.

7th and youngest son of Samuel Bosanquet, of the Forest House, Essex, and Dingestow Court, co. Monmouth, and Laetitia Philippa his wife, younger dau. of James Whatman, of Vintners, Kent. *m.* 24 July 1855, Elizabeth Fanny Catherine, 2nd dau. of Lieut. Thomas James Raikes Barrow, R.N., of Stroud, Gloucs.

Services: Serving abroad on H.M.S. *Comet* when nominated Cadet. To do duty with 54th N.I. 30 Apr. 1832 ; do 73rd N.I. 18 Feb. 1833. Posted to 16th N.I. 19 Oct. 1833. Actg. Adjt. Hariana L.I. 1 May 1838. Actg. Intr. & Qmr. 48th N.I. 9 Feb. 1839. Comdg. Shah Shuja's Atchikzai Horse at Kila Abdulla Apr. 1839. First Afghan War ; Quetta 1839-41 (s.w. in left hand at Quetta 7 July 1840). Granted a gratuity of 6 mos. pay. Fur. p.a. 26 Aug. 1843 till 16 July 1844.

Refs. : Burke's *Landed Gentry*, 13th edn., p. 174, *s.n.* Bosanquet, of Dingestow Court. Foster's *Families of Royal Descent*, i. 206. *The Times*, 12 Jan. 1897.

BOSCAWEN, Hugh Augustus (1779/80-1820). Major, 27th N.I. *b.* 1779/80. Cadet 1795. Arrived in India 22 Oct. 1796. Ensign 31 Oct. 1796. Lieut. 30 Oct. 1797. Capt. 1 Jan. 1810. Major 17 May 1816. *d.* in camp, nr. Hoshangabad, C.P., 11 May 1820, of cholera.

Eldest son of Hugh Boscawen, of Half Moon St., Piccadilly, afterwards of S. Newton, Wilts. *m.* Sophia. (She died 26 Sept.

1819.) Father of Hugh Augustus Boscawen, *q.v.* His daus. *m.* George Edward Hollings, *q.v.*, and James Duff. (See Appendix.) *Services :* Lieut. 7th N.I. in 1798. Second Mahratta War; storm of Aligarh 4 Sept. 1803 (w.); Lieut. 2/17th N.I. Transfd. to 27th N.I. in 1805. Adjt. Purnea Provl. Bn. 1807-9. Capt. 2/27th N.I. (? Third Mahratta War; Madhurajpura; Major 1/27th N.I.)
Refs. : Bath Chron. 28 Dec. 1820. Will dated Narsinghpur, C.P., 19 Mar. 1820; proved 8 July 1820.

BOSCAWEN, Hugh Augustus (1805-1881). Colonel. 54th N.I. *b.* Cawnpore 2 Apr. 1805. Cadet 1821. Arrived in India 28 May 1822. Ensign 4 July 1821. Lieut. 1 May 1824. Capt. 10 Jan. 1842. Major 15 Nov. 1853. Bt. Lt. Col. (?). Retired 29 Aug. 1854. Hon. Col. 28 Nov. 1854. *d.* 19 St. Stephen's Rd., Westbourne Park, London, 29 Dec. 1881.

Son of Hugh Augustus Boscawen, *q.v.*, and Sophia his wife. *m.* 1st, Barrackpore, 8 Aug. 1831, Sophia, eldest dau. of William C. Hollings, of Calcutta, merchant, and sister of George Edward Hollings, *q.v.* (She died Calcutta 15 Feb. 1842, aged 32.) *m.* 2nd, Dum-Dum, 10 July 1843, Ellen Maria, dau. of Benjamin Fergusson. (She died London, 7 Feb. 1882, aged 56.)

Services : Posted as Ensign to 27th N.I. Transfd. to 54th N.I. (late 2/27th) May 1824. Intr. & Qmr. 2nd L.I. Bn. 14 Oct. 1824. First Burma War; Arakan 1825; Lieut. 2nd L.I. Bn. (India medal). Adjt. Magh Levy 18 Nov. 1825. Adjt. Calcutta Native Mil. 28 Oct. 1831. Asst. Sec. Govt. of India, Mily. Dept., 4 May 1840 till 28 Apr. 1841. Sec. to Clothing Board 1841-53. Fur. 1853 till retirement.

Refs. : The Times, 2 Jan. 1882.

BOSWELL, Alexander Carre (1814-1888). Major. 19th N.I. *b.* Edinburgh 3 Jan. 1814. Cadet 1833. Arrived in India 15 Aug. 1834. Ensign 7 July 1834. Lieut. 28 May 1837. Capt. 1 Mar. 1849. Invalided 1 Nov. 1850. Retired 1 Oct. 1861. Hon. Major 1 Oct. 1861. *d.* 7 June 1888.

Son of Alexander Boswell, of Edinburgh, W.S., and Mary Sandeman his wife. Brother of John Sandeman Boswell, *q.v.*, and cousin-german of Bruce Roxburgh, *q.v. m.* Landour, U.P., 28 Sept. 1852, Mary Anne, dau. of T. Coxton. (She died 5 Nov. 1893, aged 85.)

Services : Ensign d.d. 19th N.I. 20 Aug. 1834. Posted as Ensign to 59th N.I. 5 Nov. 1834. Transfd. to 19th N.I. 28 Dec. 1835. Rising in Cuttack 1836; Ensign 19th N.I. Fur. m.c. 25 Jan. 1845 till 1847.

BOSWELL, Bruce (1805-1855). Major. 2nd N.I. *b.* Edinburgh 18 Feb. 1805. Cadet 1820. Arrived in India Sept. 1821. Ensign 5 May 1821. Lieut. 11 Sept. 1823. Capt. 28 June 1831. Major 1 Jan. 1843. Invalided 4 Oct. 1844. Retired 4 July 1849. *d.s.p.* 105 Princes St., Edinburgh, 21 Oct. 1855.

Of Crawley Grange, Bucks. Son of William Boswell, advocate and sheriff of co. Berwick, and Elizabeth his wife, dau. of James Boswell, of Auchinleck, the biographer of Johnson. *m.* Dinapore, 20 Apr. 1831, Anne, eldest dau. of Lawford Tronson, of Newry.

Services : Posted as Ensign to 1/25th N.I. Transfd. to 1st N.I. in 1823 ; to 2nd N.I. (late 1/1st) May 1824. First Burma War ; Arakan 1825 ; Lieut. 2nd L.I. Bn. (India medal). Fur. s.c. 24 Dec. 1825 till 22 Nov. 1828. Adjt. 2nd N.I. 16 Oct. 1830 till 29 July 1831. Asst. to Supt. of Arakan 1831-4. Fur. p.a. 16 Jan. 1838 till 12 Dec. 1840.

Refs. : Burke's *Landed Gentry*, 5th edn., p. 128, *s.n.* Boswell-Williams, of Crawley Grange, Bucks. *G.M.* 1855, ii. 669.

BOSWELL, John Sandeman (1810-1840). Captain, Invalid Est. 19th N.I. *b.* Edinburgh 29 July 1810. Cadet 1825. Arrived in India 4 Jan. 1827. Ensign 14 Aug. 1826. Lieut. 27 Nov. 1827. Capt. 28 May 1837. Invalided 29 July 1840. *d.* Saharanpur, U.P., 29 Oct. 1840.

Son of Alexander Boswell, of Edinburgh, W.S., and Mary Sandeman his wife. Brother of Alexander Carre Boswell, *q.v.*

Services : Posted as Ensign to 19th N.I. Actg. Adjt. Bareilly Provl. Bn. Fur. s.c. 25 Dec. 1836 till 14 Mar. 1840. No record of active service.

Refs. : *G.M.* 1841, i. 558. *The Times*, 24 Jan. 1841.

BOTT, John (1805-1842). Captain, 5th L.C. *b.* London 30 Mar. 1805. Cadet 1823. Arrived in India 7 June 1824. Cornet 7 June 1824. Lieut. 13 May 1825. Capt. 5 Aug. 1839. *d.* 12 Jan. 1842 : kld. in action in the Jagdalak Pass during the retreat from Kabul.

Son of John Bott, of Queen Charlotte Row, New Rd., London, Sec. to Privy Purse of William IV. *m.* Cawnpore, 28 July 1838, Elizabeth, dau. of Richard Murcott Satchwell.

Services : Posted as Cornet to 5th L.C. and served throughout with that Regt. Intr. & Qmr. 2 Oct. 1827 till 19 Mar. 1834. Fur. p.a. 8 Jan. 1835 till 17 Dec. 1837. First Afghan War 1840-2.

Refs. : Burke's *Peerage*, 1923, p. 1421, *s.n.* Loder, Bart. M.I. in St. Peter's, Fort William, Bengal.

THE BENGAL ARMY, 1758-1834   183

BOUJANNAR or BOUJONNAR, John (*d.* 1800). Lieut. Colonel, Infantry. Cadet 1769. Admitted 13 Sept. 1769. Ensign 28 Sept. 1769. Lieut. 24 Mar. 1773. Capt. 22 Jan. 1781. Major 1 Mar. 1794. Lt. Col. 30 Oct. 1797. *d.* at sea on board the *Manship* on his passage to England; bur. at St. Helena 28 Apr. 1800.
m. Berhampore, 24 Sept. 1787, Jane, sister of Henry Leadbeater, of the city of London, and aunt of William Edward Leadbeater, *q.v.*
Note: His name is variously spelled Boujanier, Boujonner, Boujannar, Boujonnar, and, in the bur. register, Boujonnaer. His nationality is uncertain.
Services: N.F.P.
Refs.: *G.M.* 1800, ii. 697; 1801, i. 376. Will dated Calcutta 22 Dec. 1799; proved 11 Dec. 1800.

BOULTON, Charles (1806-1860). Major, Invalid Est. 47th N.I. *b.* Durham 15 July 1806. Cadet 1822. Arrived in India 24 June 1823. Ensign 23 May 1823. Lieut. 13 May 1825. Capt. 15 Apr. 1838. Major 15 Dec. 1853. Invalided 31 Jan. 1854. *d.* Motueka, nr. Nelson, N.Z., 27 Apr. 1860.
5th son of William Boulton, of Leicester, banker. *m.* Calcutta, 4 Dec. 1828, Miss Charlotte Emily Corfield. (She died Brompton, Middlesex, 23 June 1843.)
Services: Posted as Ensign to 24th N.I. Transfd. to 47th N.I. (late 1/24th) May 1824. This Regt. having been disbanded for mutiny in Nov. 1824, he was posted to newly-formed 69th N.I., which was renumbered 47th in 1828. Operations against insurgents near Cuttack 1833; Lieut. 47th N.I. Fur. 11 Sept. 1833 till 23 July 1836. First China War; Capt. 1st Bn. Bengal Vols. (Medal). Fur. s.c. 6 Jan. 1843 till 1845, and 20 Mar. 1856 till death.
Refs.: Will dated Auckland 21 Dec. 1859; proved 21 Nov. 1860.

BOULTON, Charles (1812-1839). Lieutenant, Artillery. *b.* East Teignmouth, Devon, 14 Sept. 1812. Cadet 1829. Arrived in India 9 Feb. 1830. 2nd Lieut. 12 June 1829. Rank cancelled and reduced to Cadet, G.G.O. 31 May 1830, under instructions from C.D. Apptd. Actg. 2nd Lieut., G.G.O. 27 Feb. 1832. Service afterwards allowed to count for brevet rank. Lieut. 7 Mar. 1838. *d.* Jaunpur, U.P., 13 Dec. 1839.
Son of Henry Boulton, of Chudleigh, Devon. Brother of Richard Boulton, *q.v.* Addiscombe Cadet 1827-9.
Services: No record of active service. Was on fur. p.a. in 1836.

BOULTON, Richard (1815-1878). Major. 7th L.C. *bapt.* E. Teignmouth, Devon, 16 Dec. 1815. Cadet 1834. Arrived in India 16 July 1835. Cornet 7 June 1835. Lieut. 15 May 1840. Capt. 21 Aug. 1849. Retired 23 Mar. 1857. Hon. Major 23 Mar. 1857. *d.* Middleton Tyas, Richmond, Yorks., 20 Jan. 1878, from a fall from his horse.

Son of Henry Boulton, of E. Teignmouth, and Emily his wife. Brother of Charles Boulton (1812-1839), *q.v. m.* 10 Aug. 1846, Caroline Charlotte, eldest dau. of Mr. and the Hon. Mrs. Charles Boulton, of Sussex St., Kemp Town, Brighton.

Services : Cornet d.d. 8th L.C. 21 July 1835. Posted to 7th L.C. 26 July 1836. Intr. & Qmr. 7th L.C. 6 Dec. 1839 till 1846. Fur. s.c. 21 Nov. 1845 till 1846. Second Sikh War ; Jullundur Doab ; Lieut. 7th L.C., with Bdr.-Gen. Wheeler's force (Medal). Offg. D.J.A.G., Peshawar Div., 29 Sept. 1852.

Refs. : The Times, 24 Jan. 1878.

BOURDIEU, James (1790-1841). Lieut. Colonel, 22nd N.I. *b.* New York 24 Nov. 1790. Cadet 1806. Arrived in India 15 Mar. 1808. Ensign 11 Mar. 1808. Lieut. 12 June 1813. Capt. 1 May 1824. Major 10 Dec. 1834. Lt. Col. 26 Sept. 1841. *d.* Mussoorie, U.P., 24 Dec. 1841.

m. Agra, 17 June 1813, Miss Harriet Jacques. (*See also* John Landon Jones, and John Swinton.)

Services : Barasat C.C. for 5½ mos. Posted as Ensign to 22nd N.I. (? Reduction of Kalinjar 1812 ; Ensign 1/22nd N.I.) With 7th Gren. Bn. in 1815. Qmr. of Bde. 2nd Inf. Bde., Nagpur Subsdy. Force, 14 Nov. 1817. Third Mahratta War ; Nagpur ; Lieut. 1/22nd N.I. Transfd. to 43rd N.I. (late 1/22nd) May 1824. Fur. s.c. 5 July 1824 till 20 Oct. 1825. (? First Afghan War 1838-40 ; Major 43rd N.I.) Transfd. as Lt. Col. to 22nd N.I. 2 Nov. 1841.

Refs. : Will dated 19 Sept. 1838 ; proved 24 May 1842.

BOURDILLON, Brownlow Cole (1806-?). Lieutenant. 2nd L.C. *b.* Walthamstow, Essex, 18 Dec. 1806. Cadet 1825. Arrived in India 18 Mar. 1826. Cornet 28 Sept. 1825. Lieut. 26 Oct. 1827. Resigned 11 Nov. 1840. Living in Jan. 1895.

Eldest son of Brownlow Bourdillon, of Pulteney St., Bath, and Eliza his wife, dau. of C. Cole, of Paston, nr. Peterborough. Gt. grandson of Gideon Bourdillon, of Geneva, who settled in London in 1737 and was naturalized in 1740. *m.* 1st, 1844, Marguerite Altermatt, of Soleure, Switzerland. *m.* 2nd, Orbe, Switzerland, 20 Oct. 1853, Amélie, eldest dau. of Rev. Jean Victor Daniel Jacques, of Montagny, canton Vaud.

THE BENGAL ARMY, 1758-1834   185

Services : Posted as Cornet to 2nd L.C. Fur. 17 Mar. 1831 till 10 Nov. 1834. Fur. s.c. 26 Jan. 1837 till June 1839. Fur. 17 Mar. 1840 till resignation, which was owing to ill-health. No record of active service.
Refs. : Notices généalogiques sur les familles genevoises, par Galiffe, vi. (1892) 166. *Howard & Crisp,* i. 12, s.n. Cole (Dicker), formerly of Moreton Hampstead, Devon.

BOURKE, Thomas (*d.* 1788). Lieutenant, Infantry. Cadet 1772. Ensign 8 Aug. 1776. Lieut. 25 July 1778. *d.* Monghyr 21 Feb. 1788.
Services : First Rohilla War ; battle of St. George ; Cadet in the "Select Picket."
Refs. : G.M. 1788, ii. 751.

BOURKE, Walter (*d.* 1788). Major, Comdt. 28th Bn. Sepoys. Cadet 1768. Ensign 2 Jan. 1769. Lieut. 19 Dec. 1769. Capt. 12 July 1778. Major 30 Jan. 1784. *d.* Allahabad, 15 Feb. 1788, in his budgerow on the river.
m. Calcutta, 17 Mar. 1777, Catherine, widow of Christian Uldrick Hansen, *q.v.*
Services : N.F.P.
Refs. : G.M. 1788, ii. 751. *Hickey,* ii. *passim.*

BOURNE, John. (*See* **BOWEN, John.**)

BOWE, William (1790-1829). Captain, 16th N.I. *bapt.* Harworth, Notts., 12 Apr. 1790. Cadet 1805. Arrived in India 9 Sept. 1806. Ensign 9 Oct. 1806. Lieut. 24 Jan. 1809. Capt. 1 May 1824. *d.* St. Helena, 31 Jan. 1829, on his way to England.
Son of Rev. William Bowe, of Harworth, and Anne his wife.
Services : Posted as Ensign to 10th N.I. Lieut. 1/10th N.I. 3rd Gren. Bn. 1815-6. Third Mahratta War ; Lieut. 1/10th N.I. Fur. 5 Feb. 1820 till 1822. Transfd. to 16th N.I. (late 2/10th) May 1824. Fur. s.c. 1828.
Refs. : A.J. xxvii. 522.

BOWEN, Herbert (1780-1851). Major General, C.B. Colonel 19th N.I. *bapt.* Shankill, co. Armagh, 20 Feb. 1780. Cadet 1795. Arrived in India 3 Mar. 1797. Ensign 17 Nov. 1796. Lieut. 30 Oct. 1797. Capt. 13 Sept. 1807. Major 30 Oct. 1817. Lt. Col. 29 Apr. 1823. Col. 28 Nov. 1826. Maj. Gen. 28 June 1838. *d.* Montagu Sq., London, 16 Oct. 1851, aged 71.
Son of Thomas Bowen, of Lurgan, and Ann his wife. *m.* (before 1816) Anne. (She died Boulogne 17 Dec. 1854.) His niece *m.* George Simson Lawrenson, *q.v.*

Services : Midshipman R.N. 1793-5, and was present in several actions, including that of Adm. Sir William Cornwallis with the French fleet in June 1795. Second Mahratta War ; Adalatnagar ; Lieut. 1/10th N.I. Settlement of Hariana 1809 ; capture of Bhawani ; Capt. 1/10th N.I. Capture of Java ; Weltervreeden ; Cornelis ; Capt. 6th Bn. Bengal Vols. (Medal). Comdd. 3rd Gren. Bn. Third Mahratta War ; Major comdg. 1/10th N.I., in 5th Div. of Army of the Deccan. First Burma War ; Cachar 1824 ; repulse at Dudhpatli 21 Feb. 1824 (w.) ; Lt. Col. comdg. 1/10th N.I. Transfd. to 14th N.I. (late 1/10th) May 1824 ; to 3rd N.I. 21 Nov. 1826 ; to 34th N.I. 18 Feb. 1828. Returned from fur. in June 1830. Operations against the Kols in Chota Nagpur 1832. Apptd. Bdr. 12 Nov. 1832. Transfd. to 55th N.I. 10 Sept. 1834 ; to 19th N.I. in 1842. Fur. m.c. 5 Sept. 1839 till death. C.B. 20 July 1838.
Refs. : *E.I.M.C.* iii. 109. *G.M.* 1851, ii. 667. *I.M.* 1 Nov. 1851, p. 635.

*BOWEN, John (*d.* 1763). 2nd Lieutenant, Artillery. Cadet 1762. Fireworker 1763. 2nd Lieut. 18 Sept. 1763. *d.* 5th, 6th or 11th Oct. 1763 : massacred at or near Patna by order of Nawab Mir Muhammad Kasim. (See note to Benjamin Adamson.)
Note : Probably identical with John Bourne, *q.v.*, and with John Brown (died 1763), *q.v.* Three authorities give the name as Bowen, three as Brown. Stubbs gives two separate individuals, Bowen and Brown.
Services : N.F.P.
Refs. : MS. list in India Office, dated 20 Feb. 1764. *Stubbs,* i. 25. *Firminger,* p. 71.

BOWER, George James (1795-1840). Infantry Cadet. Subsequently Captain H.M. 62nd Foot. *b.* London 14 Aug. 1795. Cadet 1812. Resigned 20 Nov. 1813. *d.* Gillingham 22 June 1840.

Son of Charles Bower. Foster-brother to H.R.H. the Princess Charlotte of Wales. Ed. Repton ; entered the school in Aug. 1809.
Services : Ensign 14th Foot 2 Nov. 1813. Lieut. 34th Foot (3 Apr. 1815) 1 Jan. 1818. Capt. 62nd Foot 17 Aug. 1832. Had 26 years' Indian service, including Third Mahratta War, and siege and capture of Bhurtpore.
Refs. : *Repton School Register.* *G.M.* 1840, ii. 219. *A.J.* N.S. xxxii. 360.

BOWERBANK, Edward (1788-1811). Lieutenant, 21st N.I. *b.* London 18 June 1788. Cadet 1805. Arrived in India 19 Sept. 1806. Ensign 24 Sept. 1806. Lieut. 2 Feb. 1809. *d.* Chiswick, 31 May 1811, at the house of his brother, Rev. Thomas Bowerbank,

vicar of Chiswick, " after excruciating suffering of more than two years, brought on by fatigue and the effects of the climate."
Youngest son of Rev. Edward Bowerbank, rector of Croft and Barningham, Yorks., and Prebendary of Lincoln.
Services : Posted as Ensign to 21st N.I. Fur. s.c. 17 July 1810 till death.
Refs. : G.M. 1811, i. 676.

BOWIE, Robert (*d.* 1814). Bt. Colonel, 22nd N.I. Cadet 1778. Admitted 11 Aug. 1778. Ensign 6 May 1778. Lieut. 12 Jan. 1781. Capt. 25 Apr. 1797. Major 13 July 1803. Lt. Col. 21 Sept. 1804. Bt. Col. 4 June 1813. *d.* Agra 3 Jan. 1814. Brother of Jane, wife of Alexander Manson, and uncle of John Manson, *q.v. m.* Elizabeth Coventry. (She *re-m.* Baron F. de Stein, of Kochberg, and died 15 June 1843.)
Services : Second Mysore War 1781-4 ; Lieut. 26th Bn. Sepoys. Third Mysore War ; Lieut., with the Bengal detachment under Lt. Col. John Cockerell, *q.v.* Fur. 19 July 1797. Landed at Madras on return from fur. on 19 Feb. 1799, and proceeded to join the army before Seringapatam. Fourth Mysore War ; capture of Seringapatam (Gold medal). Capt. 10th N.I. Comdg. Farrukhabad Sebundy Corps in 1803. Transfd. as Lt. Col. to 22nd N.I. in 1804 ; to 24th N.I. in 1805. Operations against the Rana of Gohad 1806 ; capture of Gohad ; Lt. Col. comdg. the whole force of five Bns. Fur. 21 Nov. 1806 till 21 Oct. 1809. Transfd. to 26th N.I. in 1807 ; to 24th N.I. in 1809 ; to 23rd N.I. in 1810 ; to 22nd N.I. in 1812. Was comdg. at Agra at death.
Refs. : E.I.M.C. iii. 109. *S.M.* 1814, p. 800. Will dated Agra, 24 Dec. 1813 ; proved 15 Mar. 1814.

BOWLES, Charles. Captain. 32nd Bn. Sepoys. Cadet 1765. Ensign 6 Nov. 1765. Lieut. 29 May 1767. Capt. 27 June 1771. Resigned 2 Nov. 1780.
Services : Raised at Cawnpore in July 1778 a new Bn. of Inf., numbered the 32nd (became 22nd N.I. in 1824), called after him " Bole-ki-Paltan."
Refs. : Williams, p. 88.

BOWRING, John (1783-1810). Lieutenant, 12th N.I. *bapt.* Corscombe, Dorset, 21 July 1783. Cadet 1800. Arrived in India 22 Aug. 1801. Ensign 14 Oct. 1801. Lieut. 12 Sept. 1803. *d.* Kishenganj, Purnea district, Bengal, 9 May 1810.
Son of Joseph Bowring and Frances his wife.
Services : Posted as Ensign to 12th N.I. Second Mahratta War ; Agra ; Laswari ; Monson's retreat (w. on 27 Aug. 1804) ; Lieut. 1/12th N.I. Adjt. & Qmr. 12th N.I. 1807 till death.

BOWYER, Cornelius (1783-1855). Lieut. Colonel, C.B. 3rd N.I. *bapt.* Kirk Arbay, I. of Man, 28 Aug. 1783. Cadet 1799. Arrived in India 2 Aug. 1800. Ensign 9 Sept. 1800. Lieut. 9 Nov. 1801. Capt. 7 Oct. 1814. Major 11 Sept. 1823. Lt. Col. 9 July 1825. Retired 20 May 1829. *d.* Ostend, Belgium, 12 Feb. 1855.

2nd son of Richard Atkins-Bowyer (who assumed, under the will of Sir Richard Atkins, Bart., of Clapham, Surrey, the prefix surname of Atkins) and Elizabeth his wife, dau. of —— Brady. Brother of James Bowyer, *q.v.* *m.* Dover, 29 Aug. 1836, Caroline, dau. of Comdr. Simon Hopkinson, R.N.

Services : Posted as Ensign to 1/19th N.I. 17 Apr. 1801. 1st Vol. Bn. 1805-6. Operations in Bundelkhand 1807 ; Sehlehuganj. Adjt. 1/19th N.I. 5 Nov. 1807 till 1812. Capt. Lt. 19th N.I. 10 Sept. 1811. Transfd. to 2/30th N.I. in 1815. Fur. 1816-7. Served in Ceylon with 1st Ceylon Vol. Bn. 1818-9. Bk. Mr. 9th, Bundelkhand, Div. 1820-3. Transfd. to 60th N.I. (late 2/30th) May 1824. Siege and capture of Bhurtpore ; Lt. Col. comdg. 60th N.I. (India medal). Transfd. to 69th N.I. in 1826 ; to 3rd N.I. 7 Nov. 1828. Fur. 1828 till retirement. C.B. 2 Jan. 1827.

Refs.: Burke's *Peerage*, 1923, p. 323, *s.n.* Bowyer, Bart., of Denham Court, Bucks. *Boase. G.M.* 1855, i. 443. *A.J.* N.S. xxi. 121.

BOWYER, James (1786-1804). Lieutenant, 12th N.I. *bapt.* St. Matthew's chapel, Douglas, I. of Man, 1 Mar. 1786. Cadet 1802. Arrived in India 25 July 1803. Ensign 26 July 1803. Lieut. 25 Aug. 1804. *d.* 24 Dec. 1804 : kld. in action at the capture of the fortress of Deig.

3rd and youngest son of Richard Atkins-Bowyer and Elizabeth his wife. Brother of Cornelius Bowyer, *q.v.*

Services : Posted as Ensign to 1/12th N.I. Second Mahratta War ; battle of Deig ; capture of Deig ; Lieut. 1/12th N.I. The day before the battle of Deig, being left sick in camp when his Regt. went in pursuit of Holkar, he wrote to Col. Monson for permission to join H.M. 76th Regt. as a volunteer for the day ; and the latter replied he would make him his A.D.C.

Refs. : Burke's *Peerage*, 1923, p. 323, *s.n.* Bowyer, Bart., of Denham Court, Bucks. *East India United Service Journal*, ii. 458.

BOX, Thomas (1806-1845). Captain, 1st Bengal European L.I. *bapt.* Buckingham 17 May 1806. Cadet 1822. Arrived in India 13 May 1823. Ensign 10 May 1823. Lieut. 18 Aug. 1824. Capt. 27 July 1836. *d.* 21 Dec. 1845 : kld. in action at battle of Ferozshahr.

Son of Thomas Box. *m.* Karnal, 17 Dec. 1842, Miss Julia Frances Victoria Bang. (She died Sabathu, 28 July 1844, aged 28.)

THE BENGAL ARMY, 1758-1834

Services: Posted as Ensign to 2/18th N.I. in Oct. 1823. Transfd. to 37th N.I. (late 2/18th) May 1824; to 1st Eur. Regt. in Oct. 1824. Siege and capture of Bhurtpore; Lieut. 1st Eur. Regt. First Afghan War 1839-40; capture of Ghazni (Medal); occupation of Kabul; attack on Pashut; Capt. 1st Eur. Regt. With Army of Reserve at Ferozepore Oct. 1842 till Jan. 1843. Comdt. Depot 1st Eur. L.I. 28 Nov. 1842. First Sikh War; Ferozshahr (kld.); Capt. 1st Eur. L.I. He was shot through the head and killed as he was leading his men to the assault of the Sikh entrenchments. Durani, 3 cl.

Refs.: *De Rhé-Philipe. Innes*, 358, 380, 392.

BOYCE, Benjamin. Fireworker. Artillery. Cadet 1781. Fireworker 15 Aug. 1782. Resigned 28 Dec. 1788.

Services: First Mahratta War; joined Gen. Goddard's detachment in Dec. 1782; returned sick to Bengal in Mar. 1783.

BOYD, Alexander (1817-1880). Lieut. General. Comdt. 35th N.I. *b.* Meerut 13 Dec. 1817. Cadet 1834. Arrived in India 7 June 1835. Ensign 21 Jan. 1835. Lieut. 27 Dec. 1841. Capt. 15 Aug. 1847. Major 1 Jan. 1862. Lt. Col. 12 Sept. 1866. Col. 18 Feb. 1866. Maj. Gen. 1 Oct. 1877. Lt. Gen. 16 Jan. 1880. *d.* Yvery House, Fareham, Hants, 24 Jan. 1880.

2nd son of Mossom Boyd, *q.v.*, and Isabella his wife. Brother of Brooke Boyd, *q.v. m.* 31 July 1849, Lucy Eliza Naylor. (She died Fareham, 11 Feb. 1880, aged 51.)

Services: Ensign d.d. 57th N.I. 12 June 1835. Posted to 18th N.I. 24 Sept. 1835. Transfd. to 5th N.I. 17 Oct. 1837; to 2nd Bengal Eur. Regt. 8 Oct. 1839. Against the Hill tribes in Sind 1844-5; Lieut. 2nd Bengal Eur. Regt. Second Sikh War; Ramnagar; passage of Chenab; Chilianwala; Gujerat (w.); pursuit of Afghans to Khyber Pass; Capt. 2nd Bengal Eur. Regt. (Medal with 2 clasps). Comdd. four Coys. 2nd Eur. Bengal Fus. in operations against the rebel chief Moung-Goung-Gee 1854-5. Mutiny campaign; comdd. 2nd Bengal Fus. at Badli-ki-Serai 8 June 1857, and during all the operations before Delhi; storm and capture of the city (Medal with clasp); comdd. a Column in the Delhi district in 1859.

Refs.: *The Times*, 28 Jan. 1880, 6*d.*

BOYD, Brooke (1816-1900). General. 68th N.I. u.s.l. *b.* Meerut, 12 Nov. 1816. Cadet 1834. Arrived in India 7 June 1835. Ensign 12 Dec. 1834. Lieut. 13 Nov. 1836. Capt. 20 May 1846. Major 20 Apr. 1855. Lt. Col. 15 May 1859. Col. 19 Oct. 1868. Maj. Gen. 18 Apr. 1871. Lt. Gen. 1 Oct. 1877. Gen. 1 Dec. 1888. *d.* 5 The Lawn, St. Leonards-on-Sea, 17 Nov. 1900.

Eldest son of Mossom Boyd, *q.v.*, and Isabella his wife. Brother of Alexander Boyd, *q.v.* *m.* Dedham, Essex, 7 Nov. 1850, Mary Adelaide, youngest dau. of Charles Smith, of Northampton. *m.* 2nd, Dehra Dun, 26 Feb. 1856, Albina, dau. of Thomas Cox. Addiscombe Cadet 1 Feb. 1833 till 12 Dec. 1834.

Services : Ensign d.d. 57th N.I. 12 June 1835. Posted to 68th N.I. 24 Sept. 1835. Operations against the Bhils in Malwa in 1836. A.D.C. to his father 3 May 1839. Fur. s.c. 17 Jan. 1843 till 1845. First Sikh War ; Sobraon ; Lieut. 68th N.I. (Medal). Fur. 10 Nov. 1849 till 1851. Second Burma War ; Pegu ; Capt. 68th N.I. (Medal with clasp). Mutiny campaign ; Bundelkhand 1858, with Gen. Whitlock's column.

Refs. : Boase. *The Times*, 20 Nov. 1900. *Annual Register*, 1901, p. 146.

BOYD, Charles (1800-1822). Lieutenant, 13th N.I. *b.* Wexford 7 Nov. 1800. Cadet 1818. Ensign 24 July 1819. Lieut. 12 June 1821. *d. unm.* Dacca 14 June 1822.

3rd son of James Boyd, of Rosslare, co. Wexford, J.P., and Elizabeth his wife, only dau. of Col. Walter Hore, of Harperstown. Cousin of Hon. Walter Hore-Ruthven, *q.v.*

Services : Ensign d.d. 23rd N.I. Posted as Ensign to 2/13th N.I. No record of active service.

Refs. : Burke's *Landed Gentry*, 5th edn., p. 137, *s.n.* Boyd, of Rosslare, co. Wexford.

BOYD, Francis Turnley (1796-1867). Major. 65th N.I. *b.* 19 Nov. 1796. Cadet 1813. Admitted 30 July 1814. Ensign 30 July 1814. Lieut. 1 Oct. 1815. Capt. 26 Feb. 1829. Retired 1 Jan. 1844. Hon. Major 28 Nov. 1854. *d.* Ballycastle, co. Antrim, 11 Feb. 1867 (? 9 Apr. 1867).

2nd son of Ezekiel Davys Boyd, of Ballycastle, and Catherine his wife, dau. of Francis Turnley. Brother of Hugh Boyd, *q.v.* *m.* Berhampore, 5 June 1834, Jean Charlotte, eldest dau. of James Meik, M.D., M.M.B., Bengal. (*See also* John Augustus Schalch.)

Services : Posted as Ensign to 15th N.I. Intr. & Qmr. 2/15th N.I. 27 Jan. 1820. Adjt. 2/15th N.I. 17 Feb. 1821. Transfd. to 33rd N.I. 6 Oct. 1823 ; to 65th N.I. (late 1/33rd) May 1824. Apptd. to Stud Dept. S.A.C.G. ; D.A.C.G., 2 cl., 11 Dec. 1829 ; do 1 cl., 20 Aug. 1832 ; A.C.G., 2 cl., 12 Apr. 1837. First Afghan War ; Kabul ; prisoner in Badiabad fort ; released 21 Sept. 1842 (Medal). A.C.G., 1 cl., 9 Oct. 1838.

Refs. : Burke's *Landed Gentry*, 4th edn., p. 140, *s.n.* Boyd, of Ballycastle, co. Antrim. *G.M.* 1867, i. 404.

BOYD, Gardner (1789-1829). Captain, 50th N.I. *bapt.* Londonderry 20 June 1789. Cadet 1803. Arrived in India 4 Dec. 1804. Ensign 8 Nov. 1804. Lieut. 8 Nov. 1804. Capt. 1 Jan. 1821. *d.* Karnal 12 Mar. 1829.

m. Midnapore, 3 Nov. 1812, Arabella, 5th dau. of Thomas Chadwick, of Barnascounce. (*See also* Charles Hamilton Bell.) His dau. *m.* John Macdonald (1807-1872), *q.v.*

Services : Posted as Ensign to 1/2nd N.I. 14 Apr. 1805. Transfd. to newly-raised 1/25th N.I. 22 June 1805. Operations against the Rana of Gohad 1806 ; capture of Gohad ; Lieut. 1/25th N.I. Expedition to Mauritius 1810 ; Lieut. 1st Bn. Bengal Vols. On service in the Khurda district 1814 ; Lieut. 1/25th N.I. Siege and capture of Hathras. Third Mahratta War ; Lieut. 1/25th N.I., with Right Div. of the Grand Army. Transfd. to 50th N.I. (late 2/25th) May 1824. Offg. Fort Adjt. at Allahabad Oct. 1827 till Apr. 1828.

Refs. : De Rhé-Philipe. Burke's *Colonial Gentry*, ii. 587, *s.n.* Chadwick.

BOYD, George (1757/58-?). Lieutenant. Infantry. *b.* in Ireland 1757/58. Cadet 1782. Ensign 13 Mar. 1783. Lieut. 25 Feb. 1790. Resigned 30 Jan. 1793.

Services : Sailed for India on the *Earl Talbot*, 6 Feb. 1782, aged 24. N.F.P. (? Became an indigo planter at Nadia, Bengal.)

BOYD, Hugh (1803-1876). Major General. 59th N.I. *bapt.* co. Antrim 14 Feb. 1803. Cadet 1823. Arrived in India 19 May 1824. Ensign 17 Jan. 1824. Lieut. 27 Mar. 1826. Capt. 5 Nov. 1841. Major 20 Sept. 1849. Lt. Col. 28 Nov. 1854. Bt. Col. 28 Nov. 1857. Retired 31 Dec. 1861. Hon. Maj. Gen. 31 Dec. 1861. *d.* 24 Dec. 1876.

3rd and youngest son of Ezekiel Davys Boyd, of Ballycastle, and Catherine his wife. Brother of Francis Turnley Boyd, *q.v. m.* 1st, Meerut, 8 Oct. 1839, Matilda Campbell, youngest dau. of Major John Grant, 97th Foot, of Auchterblair, Inverness, and sister of Sir Patrick Grant, *q.v.* (She died Calcutta 9 Mar. 1852.) *m.* 2nd, 11 Nov. 1856, Frances Millicent, 2nd dau. of Conway Richard Dobbs, of Castle Dobbs, co. Antrim.

Services : Posted as Ensign to 62nd N.I. First Burma War ; Arakan 1825 ; Ensign 62nd N.I. (India medal). Siege and capture of Bhurtpore ; Ensign 15th N.I. (Clasp to India medal). Intr. & Qmr. 62nd N.I. 2 May 1826. Transfd. to 15th N.I. in 1826. Adjt. Calcutta Native Mil. 22 Nov. 1828. Sub-Asst. in Stud Dept. 19 June 1829 till 25 June 1835. Paymr. of Native Pensioners at Barrackpore 1 June 1835. Paymr. and Supt. of Native Pensioners

at Meerut 13 Feb. 1837 till 1849. Leave s.c. to Cape 13 Feb. 1844.
Transfd. to 56th N.I. in April 1855 ; to 13th N.I. in July 1855 ; to
59th N.I. in Feb. 1857. Fur. p.a. 11 June 1855 till 1857.
Refs. : Burke's *Landed Gentry*, 4th edn., p. 140, *s.n.* Boyd, of
Ballycastle, co. Antrim.

BOYD, Mossom (1781-1865). General. 53rd N.I. *bapt.* Londonderry 26 June 1781. Cadet 1795. Arrived in India 3 Mar. 1797. Ensign 3 Mar. 1797. Lieut. 30 Oct. 1797. Capt. 18 Oct. 1807. Major 21 May 1816. Lt. Col. 11 June 1822. Lt. Col. Comdt. 13 May 1825. Col. 5 June 1829. Maj. Gen. 28 June 1838. Lt. Gen. 11 Nov. 1851. Gen. 9 Apr. 1856. *d.* 6 Dawson Pl., Bayswater, London, 8 Apr. 1865.

(*Probably* son of Mossom Boyd, an officer of customs, who was 4th son of John Boyd, of Letterkenny.) Cousin-german of Robert Boyd, *q.v.* *m.* 1st, Jan. 1815, Isabella, 2nd dau. of Brooke Chambers, of Rock Hill, J.P., high sheriff of Donegal in 1798. Father of Alexander Boyd, *q.v.*, Brooke Boyd, *q.v.*, and of three other sons who also attained the rank of General. *m.* 2nd, Lyme Regis, 14 Jan. 1834, Charlotte, widow of John Moore Adolphus Lucas, *q.v.* (She died 22 June 1867.)

Services : Approved as Cadet 27 July 1796. With 1st Bengal Eur. Regt. in 1798. Second Mahratta War ; Aligarh ; battle of Delhi ; Laswari ; Lieut. 2/15th N.I. (India medal). Expedition to Mauritius 1810 ; Capt. 1st Bn. Bengal Vols. Actg. Bde. Major 28 Apr. 1812. Fur. 12 Feb. 1813 till 18 Sept. 1815. Third Mahratta War ; Major 25th N.I. Fur. 7 Sept. 1820 till 15 Oct. 1822. Bdr. comdg. at Delhi 7 Nov. 1828. Fur. 21 Dec. 1829. Divl. Staff, Sirhind Div., 9 Mar. 1839. Fur. 17 Jan. 1843 till death.

Refs. : Burke's *Landed Gentry of Ireland*, p. 67, *s.n.* Boyd, of Ballymacool, Donegal. *Boase. The Times*, 11 Apr. 1865. *A.J.* N.S. xiii. 135.

BOYD, Robert (1805-?). Lieutenant. 65th N.I. *b.* Templemore, co. Londonderry, 7 Dec. 1805. Cadet 1824. Arrived in India 5 Apr. 1825. Ensign 13 Oct. 1824. Lieut. 9 Apr. 1826. Resigned 9 Nov. 1831.

Son of Archibald Boyd, treasurer of the city and co. of Londonderry, and Anne MacNeill his wife, of the Colonsay family. Brother of Archibald Boyd, dean of Exeter (*D.N.B.*), and cousin-german of Mossom Boyd, *q.v.*

Note : Capt. Robert Boyd, late of the barque *Rob Roy, d.* Calcutta, 30 June 1843, aged 38.

Services : Posted as Ensign to 65th N.I. Fur. p.a. 27 June 1827. No record of active service.

Refs. : Burke's *Landed Gentry of Ireland*, p. 67, *s.n.* Boyd, of Ballymacool, co. Donegal.

BOYD, William (1785-1804). Lieutenant, 15th N.I. *b.* Londonderry 15 Jan. 1785. Cadet 1799. Arrived in India 29 Jan. 1801. Ensign 19 Oct. 1800. Lieut. 13 July 1803. *d.* Muttra, 26 Nov. 1804, of wounds received at the battle of Deig on 13 Nov.
Services : Posted as Ensign to 1/8th N.I. 17 Apr. 1801. Transfd. as Ensign to 15th N.I. Second Mahratta War ; battle of Delhi ; Agra ; Laswari ; battle of Deig (s.w.) ; Lieut. 15th N.I.

BOYDELL, Thomas. Ensign. Engineers. Cadet 1784. Ensign 22 Feb. 1785. Resigned 17 Feb. 1792.
Services : N.F.P.

BOYES, Robert (1788-1834). Captain. 13th N.I. *b.* 9 Jan. 1788. Cadet 1806. Arrived in India 21 July 1807. Ensign 29 July 1807. Lieut. 11 June 1812. Capt. 22 Oct. 1824. Retired 20 Oct. 1825. *d.* Edinburgh 10 Nov. 1834.
Son of John Boyes, of Willhall, Hanullen, co. Lanark.
Services : Posted as Ensign to 5th N.I. (? Reduction of Kalinjar 1812.) Lieut. 2/5th N.I. (? Third Mahratta War ; Lieut. 2/5th N.I.) Fur. 1823 till retirement. Transfd. to 11th N.I. (late 1/5th) May 1824 ; to 13th N.I. in 1825.
Refs. : *A.J.* N.S. xvi. 79.

BOYLON, John. Capt. Lieutenant. Artillery. Cadet (?). Fireworker 1 Dec. 1757. Lieut. 18 Sept. 1761. Capt. Lt. 1761. Dismissed 29 Mar. 1764.
Services : N.F.P.

BOYS, William John Edward (1809-1854). Captain, 6th L.C. *b.* Verdun-sur-Meuse 18 Jan. 1809. Cadet 1825. Arrived in India 9 May 1826. Cornet 18 Jan. 1826. Lieut. 18 Aug. 1834. Capt. 3 Apr. 1848. *d.* Almora, U.P., 21 Mar. 1854.
bapt. Verdun-sur-Meuse 4 Dec. 1809. Son of Edward Boys, of Deal, Capt. R.N. *m.* Cawnpore, 13 Nov. 1832, Sophia Mary, 3rd dau. of Major Benjamin Halfhide, H.M. 44th Foot. (*See also* William Hughes Hall.)
Services : Posted as Cornet to 8th L.C. 26 Sept. 1826. Transfd. to 6th L.C. 2 Sept. 1831. Intr. & Qmr. 6th L.C. 20 Mar. 1834 till 21 Dec. 1838, and 23 June 1841 till 1846. Second Sikh War ; Chilianwala (w.) ; Gujerat ; Capt. 6th L.C. (Medal with clasp).
Refs. : *I.M.* 1854, p. 251. Will dated 20 Feb. 1849 ; proved 25 July 1854.

BRACE, Edward (1803-1871). Bt. Captain. 48th N.I. *b.* London 25 Aug. 1803. Cadet 1818. Admitted 27 Mar. 1820. Ensign 20 Sept. 1819. Lieut. 21 Apr. 1823. Bt. Capt. 20 Sept. 1834. Retired 22 June 1838. *d.* Heron Lodge, nr. Worcester, 15 Sept. 1871.

Son of Thomas Brace, of Surrey St., Strand, London, solicitor.

Services : Posted as Ensign to 1/24th N.I. Transfd. to 48th N.I. (late 2/24th) May 1824. Fur. p.a. 13 Apr. 1830 till 5 Nov. 1832, and 8 Feb. 1838 till retirement. No record of active service.

Refs. : *The Times*, 19 Sept. 1871.

BRACKEN, Chase (1800-1827). Lieutenant, 45th N.I. *b.* London 26 Dec. 1800. Cadet 1818. Was already in India when apptd. Ensign 18 Aug. 1819. Lieut. 11 July 1823. *d.* Betul, U.P., 26 Nov. 1827.

2nd son of Rev. Thomas Bracken, of Ickenham, and Mary his wife, youngest dau. of Richard Chase, of Kensington Sq., London. Brother of John Bracken, *q.v.* *m.* Kempsey, Worcs., 29 Sept. 1825, Jane Anne, dau. of Col. Ludovick Grant (1749/50-1830), *q.v.*, of Bank House, Kempsey.

Services : Was an Assistant in the firm of Messrs. Alexander & Co., Calcutta, in which his brother Thomas, *q.v.*, was a partner, 1819. Posted as Ensign to 1/19th N.I. Mily. student at Coll. of Fort William 1820-1. Transfd. to 23rd N.I. in 1823 ; to 45th N.I. (late 1/23rd) May 1824. (? First Burma War ; Chittagong 1824 ; Cachar 1825 ; Lieut. 45th N.I.). Fur. 1825-6.

Refs. : *S.M.* 1825, ii. 638.

BRACKEN, John (1806-1850). Captain, 29th N.I. First Asst. Adjt. General. *b.* Ickenham, Middlesex, 26 Feb. 1806. Cadet 1821. Arrived in India 2 Jan. 1823. Ensign 2 Jan. 1823. Lieut. 25 Feb. 1825. Capt. 12 Aug. 1838. *d.* Simla, 10 Nov. 1850, of typhus.

3rd son of Rev. Thomas Bracken and Mary his wife. Brother of Thomas Bracken, *q.v.* *m.* 1st, Calcutta, 20 Aug. 1829, Louisa, 4th dau. of Sir Herbert A. D. Compton, Kt. (*D.N.B.*). (She died Calcutta, 18 Apr. 1838, aged 25.) *m.* 2nd, Liverpool, 27 June 1839, Mary Egerton, eldest dau. of Egerton Smith, of Liverpool, founder of the *Liverpool Mercury*.

Services : Posted as Ensign to 2/19th N.I. in Mar. 1823. Transfd. to 2/14th N.I. in Sept. 1823 ; to 29th N.I. (late 2/14th) May 1824. Fur. s.c. 27 Nov. 1826 till 27 Sept. 1828. Adjt. 29th N.I. 29 Apr. 1830. Leave s.c. to Cape 30 Dec. 1831 till Jan. 1833. Fur. s.c. 26 Sept. 1833 till 13 Aug. 1836, and 11 May 1838 till 18 Nov. 1839. Bde. Major at Barrackpore Nov. 1842 till Nov. 1843. Comdd. 2nd

Assam Sebundy Corps from 1 Mar. 1844 till its disbandment in Oct. 1844. Bde. Major, Oudh, 14 Mar. 1845 ; do. at Barrackpore Nov. 1845. D.A.A.G., Saugor Div., 20 Aug. 1847. Offg. A.A.G. of the Army, 1849 ; 2nd A.A.G. of the Army, 1849 ; 1st A.A.G. of the Army, and offg. D.A.G. at A.H.Q., 6 May 1850. No record of active service.

Refs. : De Rhé Philipe. *G.M.* 1851, i. 222. *A.J.* N.S. xxix. 340. *I.M.* 1851, pp. 3, 5. Will dated Simla 9 Nov. 1850 ; proved 14 Feb. 1852.

BRACKEN, Thomas (1791-1850). Cadet. Cavalry. *b.* Stutton, Suffolk, 10 Sept. 1791. Cadet 1810. Resigned 20 Sept. 1811. *d.* Calcutta 16 Dec. 1850.

Eldest son of Rev. Thomas Bracken, of Ickenham, Middlesex, and Mary his wife. Brother of Chase Bracken, *q.v.* *m.* in India, 1 Sept. 1818, Miss Rebecca Sewell. (She died Darjeeling 27 Sept. 1844.) Univ. Coll. Oxon. ; matric. 18 Mar. 1807. Queen's Coll. Oxon. ; B.A., 1810.

After completing his Oxford career he went out to India in 1813 as a " free mariner." Joined the firm of Alexander & Co., merchant-bankers, and in 1818 became a leading partner, which position he continued to hold until 1832, when the firm failed in a sum of three million sterling. Subsequently elected sec. and treasurer of the Bank of Bengal. One of the six original proprietors of the Bank of Hindostan, and sometime sheriff of Calcutta. Retired in 1847 and came to England, but returned later to Calcutta. A frequent contributor to the periodical press in Calcutta.

Refs. : Alumni Oxon. *G.M.* 1851, i. 440. *I.M.* 4 Feb. 1851, p. 61.

BRADBRIDGE, John. (*See* **BROADBRIDGE**.)

BRADBY, Edward Taylor (1789-1826). Captain, 4th Extra Regt. *bapt.* Hamble, Hants, 12 Nov. 1789. Cadet 1804. Arrived in India 11 July 1805. Ensign 10 Aug. 1805. Lieut. 12 Aug. 1805. Capt. 7 June 1819. *d.* Allahabad 19 Sept. 1826.

Son of John Bradby. *m.* Mary. (She died 14 Apr. 1884, aged 84.) Father of Rev. Edward Henry Bradby, D.D., headmaster of Haileybury Coll. 1868-83.

Services : Posted as Lieut. to 4th N.I. Nepal War 1816 ; Lieut. 2/4th N.I., in 4th Bde., Centre Column. Capt. 1/4th N.I. Fur. 13 Dec. 1819 till 1822. Transfd. to 7th N.I. (late 1/4th) May 1824. Bde. Major 3rd Bde., Cachar Force, 23 Dec. 1824. First Burma War ; Cachar 1825 ; Capt. 7th N.I., Bde. Major. Transfd. to newly-raised 4th Extra Regt. in 1825.

Refs. : *G.M.* 1827, i. 477. Will dated Goormah, nr. Dudhpatli, Assam, 18 Jan. 1825 ; proved 21 Dec. 1826.

BRADDON, Richard (1783-1837). Major, Invalid Est. 11th N.I.
bapt. Lifton, Devon, 3 Nov. 1783. Cadet 1800. Arrived in India 25 Oct. 1801. Ensign 25 Oct. 1801. Lieut. 30 Sept. 1803. Capt. 1 Apr. 1818. Major 13 May 1825. Invalided 7 Dec. 1827. *d. unm.* Chittagong, 22 July 1837.

Eldest son of Henry Braddon, of Skisdon, Devon, and Sarah Phillis his wife, dau. of William Clode, of Camelford. His niece *m.* James Henry Chowne, *q.v.*

Services : Posted as Ensign to 5th N.I. Capt. Lt. 1/5th N.I. 16 Dec. 1814. Capt. 1/5th N.I. Transfd. to 11th N.I. (late 1/5th) May 1824. Siege and capture of Bhurtpore ; Major 11th N.I. Comdg. Chittagong Provl. Bn. 1828-31. At Dacca 1832-7.

Refs. : Burke's *Landed Gentry*, 13th edn., p. 193, *s.n.* Braddon, of Skisdon, Devon. *G.M.* 1838, i. 221.

BRADFORD, Cornelius (*d.* 1785). Captain, Infantry. Cadet 1771. Ensign 5 Feb. 1773. Lieut. 24 Feb. 1778. Capt. 1 Oct. 1781. *d.* Buxar 9 Nov. 1785.
Services : N.F.P.

BRADFORD, Sir John Fowler (1805-1889). General, K.C.B. 2nd European L.C. *b.* London 28 Feb. 1805. Cadet 1820. Arrived in India Sept. 1821. Cornet 5 May 1821. Lieut. 1 May 1824. Capt. 27 Apr. 1833. Major 4 Apr. 1844. Lt. Col. 20 Oct. 1852. Col. 20 June 1854. Maj. Gen. 23 July 1858. Lt. Gen. 25 June 1870. Gen. 19 Dec. 1876. Retired 31 Dec. 1877. *d.* 40 Norfolk Sq., London, 11 Apr. 1889.

Son of Edward Chapman Bradford, Capt. E.I.C.S. Nephew of John Yardley Bradford, *q.v. m.* Sultanpur, Benares, 13 Feb. 1824, Eliza Martha Maria, 2nd dau. of Sir William Ouseley, Kt., and sister of Richard Ouseley, *q.v.* (*See also* John Augustus Scott.) (She died 18 Jan. 1875.)

Services : Posted as Cornet to 1st L.C. Intr. & Qmr. 1st L.C. 6 Oct. 1825 till 13 Mar. 1832. Fur. p.a. 26 Jan. 1837 till 10 May 1840. First Afghan War 1842 ; in the several engagements leading to the re-occupation of Kabul ; Capt. 1st L.C., with Gen. Pollock's force (Medal). Gwalior campaign ; Maharajpur (Bronze star). First Sikh War ; Aliwal (Medal). Second Sikh War ; passage of the Chenab ; Chilianwala ; Gujerat (Medal with 2 clasps). Comdg. Meerut Div. as Bdr. Gen. 14 May 1858. C.B. 9 June 1849. K.C.B. 20 May 1871.

Refs. : Boase. Foster's *Knightage*, p. 700. Foster's *Baronetage*. p. 477, *s.n.* Ouseley, Bart. *The Times*, 12 Apr. 1889. *I.L.N.*, 20 Apr. 1889, p. 512 ; 11 May 1889, p. 608.

THE BENGAL ARMY, 1758-1834   197

BRADFORD, John Yardley (1758/59-1841). Major. 21st N.I. b. London 1758/59. (? 1760/61.) Cadet 1782. Admitted 15 Nov. 1782. Ensign 25 Feb. 1783. Lieut. 13 Feb. 1790. Capt. 30 Sept. 1803. Major 25 Apr. 1808. Retired 8 Sept. 1809. d. Montagu Sq., London, 8 Apr. 1841, aged 82 (? 81).
Uncle of Sir John Fowler Bradford, K.C.B., q.v. His sister Harriet m. Kenneth Callandar, of Craigforth, co. Stirling : their dau. m. Rev. Sir Charles Hardinge, 2nd Bart.
Services : Sailed for India on the *Worcester* 6 Feb. 1782, aged 20 (*sic*). Lieut. 8th N.I. Transfd. to 1/18th N.I. 29 May 1800 ; as Capt to 21st N.I. in Sept. 1803. Second Mahratta War ; Capt. 21st N.I. Fur. 23 Feb. 1807 till retirement.
Refs. : Burke's *Peerage*, 1923, p. 1096, *s.n.* Hardinge, Bart. *G.M.* 1841, i. 554. Will dated 3 May 1824, with various codicils ; proved 8 Feb. 1843.

BRADLEY, John (1750 ?-1795). Captain, Infantry. b. 1750 ? Cadet 1769. Admitted 26 July 1769. Ensign 30 July 1769. Lieut. 26 Nov. 1772. Capt. 15 Jan. 1781. d. unm. Midnapore, Bengal, 7 Dec. 1795 (? aged 45).
Brother of Mary, wife of John Kay, of White Lion Court, Bishopsgate, Middlesex, and of Ann, wife of John Larkins, of Sevenoaks, Kent.
Services : In 1795 was comdg. 30th Bn. (eventually became 24th N.I.). N.F.P.
Refs. : Will.

BRADLEY, Matthew (1761-1786). Lieutenant, Infantry. b. London 1761. Cadet 1781. Ensign 25 May 1781. Lieut. 29 Aug. 1782. d. Fatehgarh, U.P., 15 Oct. 1786.
Services : Apptd. Cadet 20 Dec. 1780, aged 19. N.F.P.

BRADLEY, Thomas. Captain. Infantry. Cadet 1771. Ensign 13 Dec. 1772. Lieut. 12 Mar. 1777. Capt. 12 Mar. 1781. Resigned on pension 22 Feb. 1782.
Services : N.F.P.

BRADSHAW, Paris (1764-1821). Lieut. Colonel, 7th N.I. b. in Ireland 1764. Cadet 1781. Admitted 12 Nov. 1781. Ensign 30 June 1781. Lieut. 3 Oct. 1782. Capt. 31 July 1800. Major 18 Apr. 1810. Lt. Col. 16 Dec. 1814. d. Bankipore 9 Aug. 1821.
m. 1805, Charlotte Maria, eldest dau. of Andrew Wilson Hearsey, q.v., and sister of Sir John Bennet Hearsey, K.C.B., q.v. (*See also* William Broome Salmon.) (She died Folkestone, 30 Aug. 1848, aged 61.) Brother of George Bradshaw.

Services : Lieut. 1/8th N.I. Second Mahratta War. Asst. Resdt. at Lucknow 1806-18. Nepal War 1814-6 ; P.A. on Saran frontier. Transfd. as Lt. Col. to 1/7th N.I. in 1814. Fur. 1818-20. Apptd. Resdt. at Lucknow in 1821, but did not live to reach that place.
Refs. : "The Hearseys," pp. 217-20. *N. & Q.*, 8S. viii. 348. Will dated 5 June, 1820 ; proved 18 Dec. 1821.
Note : A rumour was current at the time to the effect that he had been poisoned with diamond dust at the instigation of the King of Oudh, whom he is supposed to have offended by the refusal of a gift.

BRADSHAW, Samuel (1757/58-1839). General. Colonel 3rd N.I. *b.* 1757/58. Country Cadet 1771. Admitted 18 July 1771. Ensign 21 Mar. 1773. Lieut. 18 May 1778. Capt. 13 Jan. 1784. Major 30 Oct. 1797. Lt. Col. 29 May 1800. Col. 25 Apr. 1808. Maj. Gen. 4 June 1811. Lt. Gen. 19 July 1821. Gen. 28 June 1838. *d.* York Terr., Regent's Pk., London, 28 Nov. 1839, in his 82nd year.
m. 1st, Patna, 19 Feb. 1801, Polly, dau. of Christopher Keating, B.C.S., senior judge of the provincial court of appeal at Patna. (She died 14 Oct. 1806, aged 23.) *m.* 2nd, Walcot church, Bath, 18 May 1815, Miss Sophia Hoadly Ashe, of Bath.
Services : Major 2/13th N.I. Apptd. to newly-raised 1/17th N.I. on its formation in 1798. This Bn., which eventually became 34th N.I., was known as " Bradshaw-ki-Paltan " after him. Major 17th N.I. Lt. Col. 17th N.I. Lt. Col. Comdt. 17th N.I. 12 June 1807. Col. 25th N.I. 25 Apr. 1808. Transfd. to 7th N.I. in 1808 ; to 11th N.I. ; to 3rd N.I. 22 Dec. 1827. Fur. 22 Jan. 1810 till death.
Refs. : *G.M.* 1815, i. 642 ; 1840, i. 104. *A.J.* N.S. xxxi. 91.

BRADSHAW, William Rigby (1784/85-1842). Ensign. 22nd N.I. *b.* 1784/85. Cadet 1805. Arrived in India 11 Nov. 1806. Ensign 26 Sept. 1806. Resigned in India 8 Aug. 1808. *d.* Prince's St., Hanover Sq., London, 25 Nov. 1842.
Services : Apptd. Cadet 4 Mar. 1806, aged 21. Posted as Ensign to 22nd N.I. No record of active service.
Refs. : *G.M.* 1843, i. 104.

BRADY, John (1806-1826). 2nd Lieutenant, Artillery. *b.* Belfast 5 Oct. 1806. Cadet 1823. 2nd Lieut. 7 Feb. 1824. *d.* Dum-Dum 13 May 1826.
Ward of Samuel Thompson, of 26 Bury St., St. James's, London. Addiscombe Cadet 1821-3.
Services : First Burma War ; joined the force in Burma in Oct. 1825.

BRANDON, John (1787-1866). Lieut. Colonel. 69th N.I. *b.* London 4 Jan. 1787. Cadet 1805. Arrived in India 11 July 1806. Ensign 27 Aug. 1806. Lieut. 25 Nov. 1807. Capt. 13 May 1825. Major 1 Dec. 1836. Retired 1 Dec. 1836. Hon. Lt. Col. 28 Nov. 1854. *d.* 2 Boys Hill Terr., Cheltenham, 24 Aug. 1866.
Son of David Brandon. *m.* Elizabeth Frances. (She died 19 Nov. 1873, aged 74.)
Services : At Barasat C.C. for 10 mos. Posted as Ensign to 23rd N.I. Intr. & Qmr. 2/23rd N.I. 27 Oct. 1814 till 1819. Third Mahratta War ; Lieut. 2/23rd N.I. Fur. 28 Dec. 1819 till 26 June 1823. Transfd. as Capt. to 46th N.I. (late 2/23rd) 1 May 1824. First Burma War ; Chittagong 1824 ; Ramu ; Capt. 46th N.I. (India medal). Transfd. as Capt. to newly-raised 1st Extra Regt. (became 69th N.I. in 1828) 13 May 1825.
Refs. : *G.M.* 1866, ii. 555.

BRANDON, Joseph (1800-1820). Ensign, Infantry. Unposted. *b.* Hackney, Middlesex, 16 Oct. 1800. Cadet 1819. Ensign (?). *d.* Calcutta 31 July 1820.
Son of D. Brandon.
Services : N.F.P.

BRANDT, Joseph (*d.* 1792). Lieutenant, Infantry. Cadet 1782. Ensign 5 May 1783. Lieut. 19 May 1790. *d.* Berhampore, Bengal, 12 Nov. 1792.
Services : N.F.P.

BRAZIER, John (*d.* 1772). Cadet, Infantry. Cadet 1771. *d.* Bankipore, B. & O., 22 June 1772.
Services : N.F.P.

BREMER, Thomas Mountsteven (1801-1837). Lieutenant, 33rd N.I., and Lieutenant h.p. 60th Rifles. *b.* London 6 Oct. 1801. Cadet 1825. Arrived in India 27 Oct. 1826. Ensign 26 Apr. 1826. Lieut. 25 Jan. 1829. *d. unm.* Jubbulpore 14 Nov. 1837.
Eldest son of William James Hughes Bremer, Comdr. R.N., and Catharine Saumarez his wife, dau. of Thomas Mountsteven, of Bodmin, Cornwall. Nephew by marriage of Henry Fox Calcraft, *q.v.*
Services : Ensign 53rd Foot 9 Dec. 1819. Lieut. 60th Rifles 17 Feb. 1825. Lieut. h.p. 60th Rifles 13 Apr. 1826 till death. Posted as Ensign to 33rd N.I. Adjt. 33rd N.I. 11 Oct. 1827. Leave to Cape for 2 yrs. 15 Nov. 1832. No record of active service.
Refs. : Burke's *Landed Gentry*, 2nd edn., p. 139, *s.n.* Bremer, of the Priory, Devon. Will dated Jubbulpore 3 Nov. 1837 ; proved 29 Dec. 1837.

BREMNER, Charles Stewart (1809-1840). Lieutenant, 64th N.I.
 b. Newcastle-on-Tyne 7 July 1809. Cadet 1827. Arrived in
 India 14 Oct. 1828. Ensign 20 May 1828. Lieut. 13 Mar. 1835.
 d. Landour, U.P., 20 May 1840.
 Son of Charles Bremner, of 3 Ramsay Gdns., Edinburgh, W.S.,
 dy. solicitor of stamps. m. Calcutta, 23 Apr. 1834, E——, only
 dau. of William Philips Price, q.v.
 Services : Ensign d.d. 13th N.I. 20 Nov. 1828. Posted as Ensign
 to 64th N.I. 4 Mar. 1829. Actg. Adjt. 18 Apr. 1840. No record of
 active service.

BREMNER, John (d. 1773). Lieutenant, Infantry. Cadet (?).
 Ensign 17 Sept. 1769. Lieut. 20 Mar. 1773. d. Jaunpur (Benares),
 U.P., 2 Oct. 1773.
 Father of Anne Bremner, of Fortrose, Scotland.
 Services : N.F.P.
 Refs. : Will dated Jaunpore 27 Sept. 1773 (" to be sent to Henry
 Davidson, Esq., of Tulloch ") ; proved 4 Feb. 1774.

BRENNAN, Ambrose (d. 1807). Major, 5th N.I. Cadet 14 Sept.
 1779. Ensign 1779. Lieut. 25 May 1781. Capt. 31 Aug. 1798.
 Major 21 Sept. 1804. d. in England 30 Mar. 1807.
 Services : Fur. 31 Jan. 1805 till death. N.F.P.

BRERETON, William Bolton (d. 1771). Captain, Infantry. Cadet
 (?). Ensign (?). Lieut. (?). Capt. 11 June 1766. d. Calcutta
 22 Apr. 1771.
 (*Possibly* son of Capt. William Bolton Brereton who, as a Lieut.,
 comdd. the lower deck battery of the *Kent* at the siege of Chandernagore 23 Mar. 1757.)
 Services : N.F.P. Was probably one of those who were given
 Commissions by Lord Clive in order to replace the officers who
 resigned during the Batta mutiny.

BRETON, Frederick (d. 1791 ?). Captain. Infantry. Cadet 1770.
 Ensign 22 Dec. 1772. Lieut. 25 Mar. 1777. Apptd. to act as
 Surgeon 1 Jan. 1779. Reverted to combatant Commission (?).
 Capt. 23 Mar. 1781. Resigned in England Dec. 1790. (? d.
 Bourn, Cambs., 22 Nov. 1791.)
 Son of Peter Breton, of an old and noble Norman family. Brother
 of Thomas Breton, q.v.
 Services : Adjt. to Major Carnac's detachment in 1778, when he
 was apptd. to act as Surgeon to the detachment. (*Mily. Cons.*
 of 1 Jan. 1779, where the name is given as Britton.) Was on fur.
 in 1790.

Refs. : Crawford, i. 230-1. *G.M.* 1791, ii. 1160 (where the name is given as Briton.) Burke's *Landed Gentry*, 2nd edn., p. 211, *s.n.* Cherry, of Buckland.

BRETON, Thomas (*d.* 1783). Lieut. Colonel, Infantry. Cadet 1764. Ensign 2 Aug. 1764. Lieut. 24 Aug. 1765. Capt. 11 Dec. 1767. Major 21 Mar. 1780. Lt. Col. 5 Dec. 1782. *d.* Barrackpore 18 June 1783.

Son of Peter Breton. Brother of Frederick Breton, *q.v.*, of John Breton, Capt. R.N., and of Peter Breton, of Southampton, merchant. Cousin of George Frederick Cherry, B.C.S.

Services : N.F.P.

Refs. : Burke's *Landed Gentry*, 2nd edn., p. 211, *s.n.* Cherry, of Buckland. Will. M.I. in old cemetery, Barrackpore.

BRETT, John (1787-1820). Lieutenant, 24th N.I. *b.* London 17 Aug. 1787. Cadet 1807. Arrived in India 14 Sept. 1808. Ensign 2 Oct. 1808. Lieut. 16 Dec. 1814. *d.* Sarguja, Bengal, 8 June 1820.

Son of Samuel Brett, of Peckham. *m.* (before 1815) (?).

Services : Posted as Ensign to 24th N.I. Lieut. 1/24th N.I. Nepal War 1814-5 ; Lieut. Ramgarh Bn., in 4th Div. Served with Ramgarh Bn. from 1814 till death. Adjt. 1819.

Refs. : G.M. 1821, i. 90.

BREWER, Philip (1783-1859). Colonel. 69th N.I. *bapt.* Exeter 17 Feb. 1783. Cadet 1803. Arrived in India 11 Mar. 1805. Ensign 23 Mar. 1805. Lieut. 24 Mar. 1805. Capt. 1 Aug. 1818. Major 18 Apr. 1829. Lt. Col. 10 May 1834. Retired 21 Jan. 1840. Hon. Col. 28 Nov. 1854. *d.* 11 Clarendon Rd., Kensington Pk., London, 28 July 1859, aged 77.

Son of John Brewer. *m.* Dacca, 15 Sept. 1829, Harriet, dau. of William Bedell, *q.v.*, and widow of Charles Henry Phelips, *q.v.*

Services : Posted as Lieut. to 2/24th N.I. in 1806. (? Operations in Hariana 1809 ; capture of Bhawani ; Lieut. 2/24th N.I.) Intr. & Qmr. 2nd Gren. Bn. 1815-6. Capt. Lt. 24th N.I. 10 Aug. 1816. Transfd. to newly-raised 2/32nd N.I. 11 July 1823 ; to 64th N.I. (late 2/32nd) May 1824 ; to 69th N.I. 4 Nov. 1836. Fur. 25 Jan. 1837 till 1839.

Services : G.M. 1859, ii. 316.

BREWSTER, David Edward (1815-1878). (*See* **BREWSTER-MACPHERSON.**)

BRICE, James (1764/65 ?-1808 ?). Lieutenant. Infantry. *b.* 1764/65 ? Cadet 1781. Ensign 31 May 1781. Lieut. 14 Sept. 1782. Struck off 178-. (? *d.* Calcutta, 28 Oct. 1808, aged 43.)

Services : (? After resignation he became Asst. in the powder manufactory at Pultah. Sheriff of Calcutta in 1800.)
Refs. : (? M.I. in S. Park St. burial ground, Calcutta.)

BRICKELL, William. Lieut. Fireworker. Artillery. Cadet 1781. Fireworker 3 Oct. 1781. Resigned 24 July 1783.
Services : N.F.P.

BRIDGE, George (1778-1812). Captain, 23rd N.I. *bapt.* St. Nicholas, Harwich, 5 Aug. 1778. Cadet 1798. Arrived in India 22 Nov. 1799. Ensign 1 Sept. 1799. Lieut. 28 Oct. 1799. Capt. 1 June 1808. *d. unm.* 17 Oct. 1812.
Son of Capt. Cyprian Bridge and Sarah his wife.
Services : Posted as Lieut. to 1/12th N.I. 15 Apr. 1801. Second Mahratta War ; Agra ; Laswari ; Lieut. 1/12th N.I. Transfd. to 23rd N.I. in 1804. Capture of Java 1811 ; Capt. 6th Bn. Bengal Vols.
Refs. : Will dated on board the *Windham* 29 July 1811 ; proved 23 Oct. 1812.

BRIDGE, William (1810-1840). Lieutenant, 62nd N.I. *b.* Beaminster, Dorset, 26 Mar. 1810. Cadet 1827. Arrived in India 15 Oct. 1828. Ensign 16 Apr. 1828. Lieut. 23 May 1834. *d.* Nimach, C.I., 4 Oct. 1840.
Son of Richard Bridge and Ann his wife.
Services : Ensign d.d. 43rd N.I. 14 Jan. 1829. Posted as Ensign to 62nd N.I. 4 Mar. 1829. Adjt. 16 Aug. 1833 till death. Fur. p.a. 16 Sept. 1840, but did not live to avail himself of it. No record of active service.

BRIDGMAN, Perceval (1811-1835). 2nd Lieutenant, Artillery. *b.* Barbados I. 26 Sept. 1811. Cadet 1828. Arrived in India 23 May 1829. 2nd Lieut. 12 Dec. 1828. *d.* at sea, 17 Apr. 1835, on board the *City of Edinburgh.*
Son of John Bridgman, of Versailles, and Catharine his wife. *m.* Agra, 10 Oct. 1834, Jane, 3rd dau. of Major Robert Joseph Debnam, H.M. 13th L.I. (*See also* Henry Shaw Stewart, and William Murray Stewart.) (She *re-m.* Calcutta, 14 May 1836, Theodore Dickens.) Brother of John Hall Bridgman, and of Maria, 1st wife of Theodore Dickens. Addiscombe Cadet 1827-8.
Services : Employed on survey work. Leave s.c. to China 23 Aug. 1832 till 31 May 1833. Fur. s.c. 27 Feb. 1835. Posted to 4th Troop 2nd Bde. H.A. in 1835.
Refs. : G.M. 1835, ii. 222. Will dated Midnapore 3 Feb. 1835 ; proved 13 Aug. 1835.

THE BENGAL ARMY, 1758-1834 203

BRIDG(E)MAN, Simon (or Simeon) (*d.* 1787). Lieutenant, Infantry. Cadet 1778. Ensign 1778. Lieut. 5 Feb. 1779. *d.* Sumatra June 1787.
Services : N.F.P.
Refs. : Will.

BRIETZCKE, Charles (1758/59-1807). Lieut. Colonel, 6th N.I. *b.* London 1758/59. Cadet 1778. Ensign 23 June 1779. Lieut. 14 Feb. 1781. Capt. 30 Oct. 1797. Major 2 Nov. 1803. Lt. Col. 8 May 1806. *d.* Khurda, B. & O., 22 Feb. 1807.
m. Cawnpore, July 1794, Eliza, dau. of Christopher Green, *q.v.* (She died Calcutta, 11 July 1851, aged 77.) His dau. *m.* John Frederick Sanford, *q.v.*
Services : Sailed for India on the *True Briton* 16 June 1779, aged 20. Adjt. 7th Bn. in 1st Bde. in 1790. Capt. 6th N.I. Disturbances in Ganjam 1801 ; Capt. 1/6th N.I. Reposted as Lt. Col. to 1/6th N.I. in 1806.

BRIETZCKE, George (*d.* 1812). Lieutenant. Infantry. Cadet 1778. Ensign June 1778. Lieut. 5 Sept. 1779. Resigned 8 Dec. 1791. *d.* Calcutta 3 July 1812.
Services : According to William Hickey he served in the Second Rohilla War, being wounded at the battle of Bitaurah on 26 Oct. 1794. If this is correct, he must have been re-admitted to the Service after resigning in 1791. From 1803 till 1810 he was sec. to the Orphan Soc. in Calcutta.
Refs. : Hickey, iv. 122.

BRIETZCKE, George John (1809-1840). Lieutenant, 49th N.I. *b.* London 14 Sept. 1809. Cadet 1829. Arrived in India 23 Apr. 1830. Ensign 23 Apr. 1830. Lieut. 31 Dec. 1836. *d.* Nimach, C.I., 16 Jan. 1840.
Youngest son of George Purcas Brietzcke, clerk in the office of the Sec. of State, Home Dept., and Susannah his wife, eldest dau. of Sir Justinian Isham, 7th Bart., of Lamport, Northants. Nephew of Richard Betenson Dean, chairman of the board of customs. Ed. Charterhouse 1822.
Services : Ensign d.d. 13th N.I. 7 June 1830. Fur. s.c. 3 Dec. 1831 till 11 Dec. 1834. Posted to 49th N.I. 20 Aug. 1833. No record of active service.
Refs. : Charterhouse School List. The Times, 18 Mar. 1840. *G.M.* 1840, i. 668.

BRIGGS, Alexander. Lieut. Fireworker, Pension Est. Artillery. Cadet 1781. Fireworker 19 Sept. 1781. Resigned on pension 21 Jan. 1786.
Services : N.F.P.

BRIGGS, William (1792-1828). Lieutenant, 20th N.I. *b.* Largo, co. Fife, 1 Nov. 1792. Cadet 1811. Ensign 1 May 1814. Lieut. 1 Apr. 1818. *d.* Bhagwangola, Murshidabad, 8 Apr. 1828, on board his boat.

2nd son of David Briggs, of Strathairly and Lochty, co. Fife, formerly of Calcutta, and Mary Lauderdale his wife, dau. of John Robertson, writer in Edinburgh.

Services : Posted as Ensign to 1/5th N.I. in 1814. Lieut. 2/5th N.I. Third Mahratta War ; Lieut. 2/5th N.I. Transfd. to 20th N.I. (late 2/5th) May 1824. Intr. & Qmr. 20th N.I. 14 July 1825 till death.

Refs. : Burke's *Landed Gentry*, 13th edn., p. 200, *s.n.* Briggs, of Strathairly, co. Fife. *A.J.* xxvi. 610. Will undated ; proved 23 May 1828.

BRIGGS, William Thomas (1809-1838). Lieutenant, 74th N.I. *b.* London 25 Sept. 1809. Cadet 1825. Arrived in India 7 Aug. 1826. Ensign 11 Feb. 1826. Lieut. 31 May 1829. *d.* Nyagaon, Bengal, 30 Apr. 1838.

Son of John Thomas Briggs, asst. sec. to the commissioners for victualling H.M. Navy.

Services : Posted as Ensign to 6th Extra Regt. (became 74th N.I.). Intr. & Qmr. 74th N.I. 28 Oct. 1834. S.A.C.G. 31 Dec. 1834. Asst. to A.G.G., Saugor & Narbada territories, 21 Jan. 1835.

Refs. : G.M. 1839, i. 222.

BRIND, Frederick (1802-1857). Bt. Colonel, C.B. Artillery. *b.* London 22 Mar. 1802. Cadet 1819. Arrived in India Mar. 1821. 2nd Lieut. 16 June 1820. Lieut. 1 May 1824. Capt. 7 Mar. 1838. Major 1 Jan. 1848. Lt. Col. 31 Dec. 1854. Bt. Col. 20 June 1854. *d.* Sialkot, 10 July 1857, having been mortally wounded the day before by a mutineer of 9th L.C.

Son of Walter Brind, of Paternoster Row, London, ribbon manufacturer and silk merchant. Brother of Sir James Brind, *q.v. m.* Karnal, 9 Sept. 1837, Henrietta Sarah, dau. of Sir Robert Henry Sale, G.C.B. (*See also* John Elphinstone Bruere, George Dysart, Rowley John Hill, and John Leigh Doyle Sturt.)

Services : Fur. June 1824 till 9 Mar. 1828, during which he was employed at Addiscombe from 2 Aug. 1826 till 24 June 1827. Adjt. & Qmr. 3rd Bde. H.A. Feb. 1837 till Apr. 1838. Gwalior campaign ; Paniar ; Capt. comdg. 1st Troop 3rd Bde. H.A. (Bronze star). First Sikh War ; Mudki ; Ferozshahr ; Sobraon ; Bt. Major comdg. 1st Troop 3rd Bde. (Medal with 2 clasps). Second Sikh War ; Ramnagar ; passage of Chenab ; Chilianwala ; Gujerat ; Bt. Lt. Col. comdg. 2nd Bde. H.A. (Medal with 2 clasps). Apptd. Bdr. in

THE BENGAL ARMY, 1758-1834   205

Mar. 1856 and posted to Sialkot. Was comdg. at Sialkot when the mutiny broke out there on 9 July 1857, and was one of the first victims of the outbreak. C.B. 9 June 1849.
Refs. : De Rhé-Philipe.

BRIND, Sir James (1808-1888). General, G.C.B. Colonel Comdt. Artillery. *b.* London 10 July 1808. Cadet 1826. 2nd Lieut. 3 July 1827. Lieut. 15 Oct. 1833. Capt. 3 July 1845. Major 26 June 1856. Lt. Col. 18 Aug. 1858. Col. 18 Feb. 1861. Col. Comdt. 3 Oct. 1867. Maj. Gen. 1 June 1867. Lt. Gen. 1 Oct. 1877. Gen. 1 Oct. 1877. *d.* Brighton 3 Aug. 1888.
Son of Walter Brind. Brother of Frederick Brind, *q.v. m.* 1st, Meerut, 20 Apr. 1833, Jane (Joanna), eldest dau. of Joseph Conway Waller. (She died Ambala 29 Dec. 1849.) *m.* 2nd, Simla, 11 Sept. 1852, Mary Georgiana, dau. of Benjamin Carter. (She died Peshawar 2 Mar. 1854.) *m.* 3rd, Ootacamund, 24 Oct. 1861, Georgina, dau. of Rev. Henry George Philips, vicar of Mildenhall. (She died Simla in 1862 : kld. by a fall with her horse down the *khud.*) *m.* 4th, 1867, Jane, elder dau. of Rev. Daniel Henry Maunsell, of Ballybriggan, co. Dublin. (She died 6 Nov. 1868.) *m.* 5th, 16 Oct. 1873, Eleanor Elizabeth Lumley, 5th dau. of Rev. Henry Thomas Burne, of Grittleton, Wilts. (She died Bath, Mar. 1924.)
Services : See *D.N.B.* C.B. 24 Mar. 1858. K.C.B. 2 June 1869. G.C.B. 24 May 1888. Good Service Pension 11 Jan. 1865.
Refs. : Burke's *Landed Gentry of Ireland,* p. 468, *s.n.* Maunsell, of Ballywilliam, co. Limerick. *D.N.B. D.I.B. Boase. Vibart,* p. 421. *The Times* 6 Aug. 1888. Foster's *Families of Royal Descent,* i. 355.

BRISBANE, Andrew (*d.* 1773). Lieutenant, Infantry. Cadet 1767. Ensign 1 Dec. 1767. Lieut. 20 Oct. 1769. *d.* Calcutta 22 Dec. 1773.
Services : N.F.P.

BRISBANE, Thomas (*d.* 1778). Lieutenant, Infantry. Cadet (?). Ensign 20 Nov. 1771. Lieut. 3 Aug. 1776. *d.* 21 Oct. 1778.
Note : In Dodwell & Miles's List his initials are given as H. W. Thomas is believed to be correct. One W. H. Brisbane died Calcutta 28 Oct. 1818.
Services : N.F.P.

BRISCOE, Horton (1741-1802). Major General. Comdt. 1st Bengal European Regt. *b.* 1741. Cadet 1763. Ensign 25 Aug. 1763. Lieut. 15 Apr. 1764. Capt. 28 July 1766. Major 25 Feb. 1778. Lt. Col. 4 Dec. 1781. Col. 19 Jan. 1788. Maj. Gen. 20 Dec. 1793. *d.* Calcutta 25 Dec. 1802, aged 61.

3rd son of Rev. John Briscoe, D.D., of Crofton Hall, Cumberland, rector of Orton, and vicar of Aspatrie, and Catherine his wife, dau. of John Hylton, of Hylton Castle. Brother of William Musgrave Briscoe, q.v., and of Sir John Briscoe, 1st Bart. m. 1st, Calcutta, 9 Feb. 1769, Miss Maria Howett. m. 2nd, 28 July 1774, Miss Millicent (Millisant) Jane Banks.

Services : Sailed for India on the *Plassey* 2 Jan. 1763. Resigned the Service Aug. 1766 (? during the " Batta mutiny "); re-admitted the same year. Comdt. G.G.B.G. 27 Jan. 1777 till 6 Apr. 1778. Apptd. to comd. a Bn. of Sepoys 4 Apr. 1780. Comdg. at Chunar in 1790. Comdt. 4th Bde. at Cawnpore in 1793. Apptd. to comd. at Barrackpore 30 May 1796. Comdt. 1st Bengal Eur. Regt. in Apr. 1799.

Refs. : Burke's *Peerage*, 1923, p. 344, *s.n.* Brisco, Bart., of Crofton, Cumberland. *V.B.G. G.M.* 1803, ii. 880. M.I. in S. Park St. burial ground, Calcutta.

BRISCOE, John (1761/62-1779). Ensign, Infantry. *b.* in Cumberland 1761/62. Cadet 1778. Arrived in India 8 Oct. 1778. Ensign Dec. 1778. *d. unm.* Cawnpore 1 Mar. 1779.

2nd son of Musgrave Briscoe, Capt. in the army, and Mary his wife, only dau. of Edward Dyne, of Coghurst and Lankhurst, Sussex. Cousin-german of Horton Briscoe, *q.v.*

Services : Sailed for India on the *Nassau*, 7 Mar. 1778, aged 16. N.F.P.

Refs. : Burke's *Commoners*, iii. 237, *s.n.* Brisco, of Coghurst, Sussex.

BRISCOE, John J. (1764/65-1792). Lieutenant, Artillery. *b.* 1764/65. Cadet 1783. Fireworker 3 Jan. 1785. Lieut. 16 Dec. 1790. *d.* Calcutta, 2 Nov. 1792, aged 27.

Services : Third Mysore War ; Bangalore ; Seringapatam ; Lieut. 2nd Coy. 2nd Bn. Art., Offg. Adjt.

Refs. : M.I. in S. Park St. burial ground, Calcutta.

BRISCOE, William Musgrave (*d.* 1765). Ensign, Infantry. Cadet 1764. Ensign 4 Aug. 1765. *d.* 1765 : kld. in action at a mud fort, under Col. Martin.

4th son of Rev. John Briscoe, D.D., and Catherine his wife. Brother of Horton Briscoe, *q.v.*, and cousin-german of John Briscoe, *q.v.*

Services : N.F.P.

Refs. : Burke's *Peerage*, 1923, p. 344, *s.n.* Briscoe, Bart., of Crofton, Cumberland.

THE BENGAL ARMY, 1758-1834 207

BRISTOW, Cerjat Michael (1811-1839). Lieutenant, 71st N.I. *b.* Calcutta 31 Oct. 1811. Cadet 1827. Arrived in India 8 Feb. 1829. Ensign 13 Aug. 1828. Lieut. 1 July 1838. *d. unm.* Nimach, C.I., 22 Mar. 1839.

3rd son of George Bristow, Lt. Col. Gren. Gds., page of honour to Queen Charlotte, afterwards pte. sec. to the Marquis Wellesley, and Elizabeth Lacy his wife, dau. of Lt. Col. Howe, of Bath. Brother of George William Grant Bristow, *q.v.* His sisters *m.* James Henry Daniell, *q.v.*, and Thomas Dundas, *q.v.*

Services : Posted as Ensign to 70th N.I. 3 June 1829. Transfd. to 71st N.I. 30 Nov. 1831. Actg. Adjt. 19 July 1832 ; Offg. Intr. & Qmr. 16 May 1833 ; Actg. Adjt. 3 Jan. 1835 ; Intr. & Qmr. 19 Jan. 1839. No record of active service.

Refs. : Burke's *Landed Gentry*, 5th edn., p. 146, *s.n.* Bristow, of Broxmore Park, Wilts.

BRISTOW, Charles (*d.* 1772). Ensign, Infantry. Cadet 1771. Ensign 12 May 1772. *d.* Calcutta 28 May 1772.

Services : N.F.P.

BRISTOW, D'Oyly Richard (1815-1861). Captain. Artillery. *b.* Calcutta 3 July 1815. Cadet 1833. Arrived in India 15 Aug. 1834. 2nd Lieut. 13 Dec. 1833. Lieut. 22 Feb. 1841. Capt. 1 July 1851. Retired 1 Sept. 1858. *d.* 10 Mar. 1861.

Son of William Bristow, of the salt agency, Calcutta, and Sophia his wife. Godson of Sir John Hadley D'Oyly, 8th Bart., B.C.S. Brother of Edward Wynne Bristow, *q.v.*, and of Mary Anne, wife of Frederick Summers Macmullen, *q.v. m.* 1st, Benares, 4 June 1840, Frances Sibley, youngest dau. of F. Bean, of Camberwell. *m.* 2nd, Paddington, London, 25 Apr. 1846, Louisa, 3rd dau. of Charles Coleman, M.D., of Maidstone. Addiscombe Cadet 3 Feb. 1832 till 13 Dec. 1833.

Services : Served throughout with Foot Art. Fur. s.c. 4 Apr. 1843 till 1846. No record of active service.

BRISTOW, Edward Wynne (1817-1863). Captain, Invalid Est. 1st N.I. *b.* Calcutta 22 Mar. 1817. Cadet 1834. Arrived in India 24 July 1835. Ensign 12 Dec. 1834. Lieut. 6 July 1837. Capt. 1 Feb. 1850. Invalided 4 Jan. 1856. *d.* Heavitree, nr. Exeter, 17 June 1863, of chronic disease of the liver.

Son of William Bristow and Sophia his wife. Brother of D'Oyly Richard Bristow, *q.v. m.* Darjeeling, 22 Oct. 1845, Catherine Osborne, 2nd dau. of Samuel Smith, of Calcutta, publisher. Addiscombe Cadet 8 Mar. 1833 till 12 Dec. 1834.

Services : Posted as Ensign to 71st N.I. 24 Sept. 1835. Transfd.

LIST OF THE OFFICERS OF

to 1st N.I. 13 Feb. 1836. Fur. s.c. 21 Jan. 1848 till 1850. No record of active service.
Refs. : *G.M.* 1863, i. 810. *The Times*, 20 May 1863.

BRISTOW, George William Grant (1809-1892). Lieut. Colonel. 71st N.I. *b.* Calcutta 25 Jan. 1809. Cadet 1827. Arrived in India 7 Feb. 1829. Ensign 13 Aug. 1828. Lieut. 7 Jan. 1836. Capt. 1 Apr. 1847. Bt. Major 20 June 1854. Lt. Col. 28 Nov. 1854. Retired 30 Dec. 1854. *d.* St. Aubyn's, Southsea, 6 Jan. 1892.
bapt. Calcutta 16 Feb. 1809. 2nd son of Lt. Col. George Bristow and Elizabeth Lacy his wife. Brother of Cerjat Michael Bristow, *q.v. m.* 1st, Calcutta, 13 Nov. 1832, Isabella, 3rd dau. of Maj.-Gen. Colin Campbell, comdg. the forces at the Cape of Good Hope. *m.* 2nd, Chesham Bois, 21 July 1852, Miss Susan Kent.
Services : Posted as Ensign to 71st N.I. 3 June 1829. Actg. Adjt. 19 Oct. 1830. Adjt. 13 July 1832 till 1 June 1847. Postmaster at Shahjahanpur 1 May 1841. Second Sikh War ; Jullundur Doab ; Capt. 71st N.I., with Bdr.-Gen. Wheeler's force (Medal). Fur. s.c. 7 Feb. 1852 till retirement.
Refs. : Burke's *Landed Gentry*, 5th edn., p. 146, *s.n.* Bristow, of Broxmore Park, Wilts. *The Times*, 14 Jan. 1892.

BRITTEN, George Ernst (1795-1845). Lieutenant. 62nd N.I. *b.* London 14 Oct. 1795. Cadet 1816. Ensign (?). Lieut. 1 Aug. 1818. Resigned 6 Sept. 1825. *d.* Alpha Pl., Regent's Pk., London, 5 Aug. 1845.
Eldest son of Thomas Britten, of Forest Hill, Kent, merchant. *m.* Calcutta, 4 Mar. 1820, Margaret, youngest dau. of P. Goullet, of Heavitree, Devon.
Services : Ensign d.d. 7th N.I. Transfd. as Lieut. to 24th N.I. in 1819 ; to 1/20th N.I. in 1820 ; to newly-formed 31st N.I. 11 July 1823 ; to 62nd N.I. (late 2/31st) May 1824. Fur. 1825 till resignation. No record of active service.
Refs. : *A.J.* x. 494. *G.M.* 1845, ii. 322.

BRITTRIDGE, Richard Blechynden (1788-1861). Major. 13th N.I. *b.* Calcutta 18 Feb. 1788. Cadet 1809. Admitted 8 Nov. 1811. Ensign 26 Oct. 1811. Lieut. 25 May 1817. Capt. 1 Apr. 1830. Retired in India 18 Feb. 1839. Hon. Major 28 Nov. 1854. *d.* in India 8 Aug. 1861.
bapt. Calcutta 5 May 1788. Son of Richard Brittridge, of Calcutta, engraver and silversmith, afterwards indigo manufacturer, and Mary his wife. *m.* Sitapur, U.P., 8 Feb. 1824, Miss Eliza Jane De Courcy.
Services : Was at Benares when nominated Cadet. Posted as Ensign to 2/7th N.I. Third Mahratta War ; Lieut. 7th N.I., in

Reserve Div. Intr. & Qmr. 2/7th N.I. 17 Aug. 1819 till 1824. Transfd. to 13th N.I. (late 1/7th) May 1824. Intr. & Qmr. 13th N.I. 17 June 1824 till 18 Oct. 1830.

BROADBENT, James (1733/34- ?). Ensign. Infantry. *b.* London 1733/34. Cadet 1764. Ensign 28 Sept. 1766. Resigned 1 May 1776.
Services : Sailed for India on the *Vansittart*, 4 Mar. 1764, aged 30. N.F.P.

BROADBENT, Thomas Wheeler (1778/79-1826). Major, 22nd N.I. *b.* Page Hall, Ecclesfield, Yorks., 1778/79. Cadet 1802. Arrived in India 16 Oct. 1803. Ensign 11 Sept. 1803. Lieut. 25 Aug. 1804. Capt. 1 Aug. 1818. Major 14 Jan. 1826. *d.* Dinapore, 6 Sept. 1826, of a bilious fever.
Son of Thomas Broadbent. Nephew of "Aunt Pemberton," uncle of William Booth. Owned property in Staffs. and Yorks. *m.* 1st (before 1809) (?). (She died Dinapore 21 May 1825.). *m.* 2nd, Dinapore, 1 June 1826, Miss Antonia Milliken.
Services : Posted as Ensign to 22nd N.I. in 1804. Transfd. to 2nd N.I. in 1805. Bde. Major at Cawnpore 1807-14 ; at Berhampore 1814-5 ; at Meerut 1815-9 ; in Bundelkhand 1820 ; at Dinapore 1823. Transfd. to 22nd N.I. (late 2/2nd) May 1824. D.A.A.G. at Dinapore 28 Jan 1825 till death.
Refs. : Burke's *Visitation of Seats and Arms*, 1S. i. 82. *A.J.* xxiii. 529. Will dated 24 June 1824 ; proved 29 Sept. 1826.

BROADBRIDGE or BRADBRIDGE, John (*d.* 1761). Captain, Artillery. Cadet R.A. 1743. Fireworker R.A. 29 Oct. 1755. 2nd Lieut. R.A. 2 Apr. 1757. Capt. Lt. Bengal Art. 6 June 1757. Capt. 19 Sept. 1758. *d.* Calcutta 16 Oct. 1761.
Note : Kane's *List of Officers, R.A.*, and the burial register both give the name as Bradbridge : Mily. Records give Broadbridge.
Services : N.F.P.
Refs. : Kane, No. 224.

BROADBROOK, John (1738 ?-1763). Captain, Bengal European Bn. (? *bapt.* St. Anne's, Calcutta, 15 July 1738.) Volunteer in 1757. Ensign (Bengal) 22 May 1757. Lieut., in England (H.M. 39th), 1758. Lieut. (Bengal) 1758. Capt. Lt. 20 Sept. 1759. Capt. 18 Sept. 1761. *d.* 5 Sept. 1763 : kld. in action at the Udhua Nullah, B. & O.
(*Probably* son of Capt. James Broadbrook, of Calcutta, and Elianor (Elinor) his wife.) *m.* (before 1762) (?).
Services : N.F.P.
Refs. : S. C. Hill's *Siege of Calcutta*, pp. 14-5.

LIST OF THE OFFICERS OF

BROADFOOT, William (1810-1841). Lieutenant, Bengal European Regt. *b.* Kirkwall, Orkney Is., 10 July 1810. Cadet 1826. Arrived in India 22 Sept. 1827. Ensign 8 Feb. 1827. Lieut. 2 July 1833. *d.* Kabul 2 Nov. 1841 : kld. in the Residency during the outbreak that day.

Son of Rev. William Broadfoot, of Kirkwall, minister of a Scotch church in London.

Services : Posted as Ensign to 1st Bengal Eur. Regt. Fur. s.c. 18 June 1833 till 4 Dec. 1836. Adjt. 30 Dec. 1837. Comdd. Hazara Pioneers. First Afghan War 1838-41. Apptd. 2nd in comd. 4th Gurkha Inf. of Shah Shuja's army 31 May 1839 ; storm and capture of Ghazni 23 July 1839 (w.) (Medal) ; pursuit of Amir Dost Mohomed ; operations in the regions of the Hindu Kush 1839-40 with the Gurkha Regt. Political employ 1840 ; apptd. Offg. Political Asst. Resident at Kabul under Sir Alexander Burnes.

Refs. : De Rhé-Philipe. Innes, pp. 353, 360.

BROADHURST, formerly NICHOLS, Thomas (*d.* 1812). Major General. Colonel 5th N.I. Cadet 1765. Ensign 12 Sept. 1766. Lieut. 2 Dec. 1767. Capt. 29 Mar. 1773. Major 26 Jan. 1781. Lt. Col. 1 Sept. 1793. Col. 3 May 1796. Maj. Gen. 29 Apr. 1802. *d.* Drayton Lodge, nr. Market Drayton, Salop., 5 Nov. 1812.

Formerly Nichols : adopted the surname of Broadhurst by R.L. dated 10 Aug. 1809. (*Lond. Gaz.* pp. 1258, 1384.)

Services : Fur. 14 Dec. 1780 till 24 Nov. 1783. Col. 5th N.I. 25 Apr. 1797. Fur. 26 Jan. 1802 till death.

Refs. : G.M. 1812, ii. 592. S.M. 1813, p. 78.

BROCKMAN, George (1811- ?). Lieutenant. 24th N.I. *b.* Cheriton, Kent, 23 Mar. 1811. Cadet 1826. Arrived in India 13 Oct. 1827. Ensign 8 May 1827. Lieut. 29 Mar. 1833. Resigned in India 1 Jan. 1838.

8th son of Rev. Julius Drake Brockman, rector of Cheriton and vicar of Newington, and Harriet his wife, dau. of Rev. Thomas Locke, of Newcastle, co. Limerick. First cousin of Julius Brockman Backhouse, *q.v.*

Services : Posted as Ensign to 24th N.I. Offg. Intr. & Qmr. 19 Apr. 1833. No record of active service. After resigning the Service he became a settler in Western Australia.

Refs. : Burke's *Landed Gentry*, 12th edn., p. 241, *s.n.* Brockman, of Beachborough, Kent.

BRODERIP, Henry Francis (1796-1829). Lieutenant, 38th N.I. *b.* Bristol 18 Apr. 1796. Cadet 1820. Arrived in India Nov. 1821. Ensign 11 June 1821. Lieut. 1 May 1824. *d.* Barrackpore 11

THE BENGAL ARMY, 1758-1834   211

July 1829 : kld. in a duel by Lieut. Low (? John Handcock Low, *q.v.*).
Son of William Brodcrip, M.D., of Clifton.
Services : Ensign H.M. 64th Foot 6 Jan. 1820. Posted as Ensign to 7th N.I. in 1822. Transfd. to 19th N.I. in 1823 ; to 38th N.I. (late 1/19th) May 1824. No record of active service.
Refs. : *A.J.* N.S. i. 33. M.I. in old cemetery, Barrackpore.

BRODHURST, John (1788-1831). Captain, Artillery. *b.* Manchester 26 Dec. 1788. Cadet 1805. Arrived in India 19 Sept. 1806. Lieut. 9 Apr. 1806. Capt. Lt. 25 Sept. 1817. Capt. 1 Sept. 1818. *d. unm.* 9 Oct. 1831 : drowned whilst bathing in the Surma R. at Sylhet, Assam.
bapt. Protestant Dissenters' chapel, Manchester, 24 Apr. 1789. Youngest son of Francis Brodhurst, of Manchester, and Charlotte Barrow his wife, of Knutsford. Nephew by marriage of Sir Robert Wigram, 1st Bart.
Services : Served throughout with Foot Art. Fur. s.c. 27 Jan. 1817 till 19 Feb. 1821, and 11 Mar. 1824 till 10 Nov. 1828. No record of active service.
Refs. : Family information. Will dated Dum-Dum 12 May 1821 ; proved 28 Jan. 1832. M.I. in Dronfield psh. churchyard.

BRODIE, David Hay (1809-1831). Ensign, 13th N.I. (? 15th N.I.) *b.* Westminster 29 Jan. 1809. Cadet 1826. Arrived in India 6 Nov. 1827. Ensign 14 June 1827. *d. unm.* Nongkhlao, Sylhet, Assam, 22 Apr. 1831, of fever.
3rd son of Thomas Brodie, W.S. Brother of Thomas Brodie, *q.v.*
Services : Posted as Ensign to 46th N.I. Transfd. to 13th N.I. 21 Mar. 1829. Sylhet L.I. 2 June 1830. Tempy. comdg. the Shawm Musketeers, Khasi Hills. (? Transfd. to 15th N.I. in 1831.)
Refs. : Burke's *Landed Gentry*, 13th edn., p. 213, *s.n.* Brodie, of Lethen, Nairn. *A.J.* N.S. vi. 138. M.I. in English cemetery at Cherrapunji, Assam.

BRODIE, Edward (1782-1847). Lieutenant. 12th N.I. Subsequently Senior Chaplain, Bengal Ecclesiastical Est. *bapt.* Piercefield, St. Arvans, co. Monmouth, 21 Apr. 1782. Cadet 1798. Arrived in India 24 Nov. 1799. Ensign 27 Oct. 1799. Lieut. 28 Oct. 1799. Resigned 6 Jan. 1803. *d.* Versailles, France, 10 Apr. 1847.
4th son of William Brodie of Bath (who was descended from Joseph Brodie, of Mayne and Muiresk, the 7th son of David Brodie, of Brodie), mgte. at the Gt. Marlborough St. police office, London, and Mary his wife, dau. of Thomas Assheton Smith, of Ashley, co.

Chester. *m.* in France, 1835, Mlle. Vacossin. Ed. Winchester; scholar, 1793 ; left in 1797. Trinity Hall, Camb. ; B.A. 1807.

Services : Posted as Ensign to 2/12th N.I. 15 Apr. 1801. No record of active service. Took holy orders. Apptd. Chaplain on the Bengal Est. 7 May 1813. Chaplain at Benares, subsequently at Dinapore. Retired as a Senior Chaplain 14 July 1825.

Refs. : Burke's *Landed Gentry*, 4th edn., p. 1735, *s.n.* Brodie, of Eastbourne, Sussex. Family information. *Kirby. G.M.* 1847, ii. 103. *Graduati Cantab.*

BRODIE, Thomas (1805-1879). Lieut. Colonel. 5th N.I. *b.* 23 May 1805. Cadet 1826. Arrived in India 29 Oct. 1827. Ensign 25 May 1827. Lieut. 12 Nov. 1842. Capt. 26 Feb. 1851. Bt. Major 20th June 1854. Retired 9 Aug. 1854. Hon. Lieut. Col. 11 May 1855. *d.* Edinburgh 27 Nov. 1879.

bapt. Holborn, Middlesex, 2 Jan. 1806. 2nd son of Thomas Brodie, W.S. Brother of David Hay Brodie, *q.v. m.* Barnbarroch House, co. Wigtown, 20 Sept. 1855, Janet, only dau. of William Haig. Ed. Westminster ; admitted 14 Sept. 1819.

Services : Posted as Ensign to 1st N.I. 30 Jan. 1828. Transfd. to 45th N.I. 2 Aug. 1832. Actg. Adjt. Sylhet L.I. 3 Aug. 1832. Junior Asst. to A.G.G., N.E. frontier. Transfd. to 10th N.I. 24 Sept. 1835. Principal Asst. to A.G.G., N.E. frontier, 16 May 1837 till 1852. Transfd. to 2nd Bengal Eur. Regt. 8 Oct. 1839 ; to 5th N.I. 14 Dec. 1842. Fur. 9 Feb. 1852 till retirement.

Refs. : Burke's *Landed Gentry*, 13th edn., p. 213, *s.n.* Brodie, of Lethen, Nairn. *Westminster School Register* (where the date of birth is given as 23 May 1806).

BROHIER, John. Captain. Artillery. Chief Engineer. 2nd Lieut., Madras Art., 8 Dec. 1749. Capt., Madras Art., 11 May 1753. Chief Engineer and Capt. Train of Madras Art. Aug. 1753. Transfd. to Bengal June 1757. Dismissed 1760.

Services : Arrived in Calcutta in July 1757 in order to lay out the new fort. In 1760 he was placed in arrest in consequence of frauds that had come to light in connexion with the works at Fort William. Having been released on parole, he absconded during the night of 29/30 July 1760 and escaped to Ceylon, where he appears to have settled.

Refs. : Love, ii. 524, 585-6. *Leslie,* No. 15.

BROMLEY, Nathaniel Barrett (1785-?). Lieutenant. Artillery. *b.* Clerkenwell, Middlesex, 22 June 1785. Cadet 13 Feb. 1806. Arrived in India 11 July 1806. Lieut. 10 Apr. 1806. Resigned in India 2 Feb. 1808.

Son of Nathaniel Warner Bromley, of Gray's Inn, London, and of Badmondisfield Hall, Wickhambrook, Suffolk, and Sarah Wright his wife. *m.* Calcutta, 11 Nov. 1806, Miss Sarah Anne Morgan.
Services : N.F.P.
Refs. : *Howard & Crisp*, v. 136, *s.n.* Bromley.

BROOKE, Charles William (1784-1836). Bt. Colonel, 14th N.I. *b.* Burdwan, Bengal, 28 Sept. 1784. Cadet 1800. Admitted 13 Nov. 1801. Ensign 13 Oct. 1801. Lieut. 30 Sept. 1803. Capt. 21 Oct. 1815. Major 30 May 1824. Lt. Col. 1 Apr. 1828. Bt. Col. 22 Jan. 1834. *d.* Fatehgarh, U.P., 22 Apr. 1836.
Son of Thomas Brooke, B.C.S., head asst. and registrar at Burdwan. *m.* Meerut, 10 July 1808, Charlotte, dau. of Sir Dyson Marshall, K.C.B., *q.v.* (*See also* Christopher D'Oyly Aplin.) (She died Krishnagar, Bengal, 19 Nov. 1830, aged 40.) His daus. *m.* Richmond Houghton, *q.v.*, and Henry Augustus Morrieson, *q.v.*
Services : Ensign 11th N.I. Lieut. 1/23rd N.I. Adjt. 1/23rd N.I. 1806. Operations against Dhundia Khan 1807 ; siege and capture of Komona (w.) ; Lieut. 1/23rd N.I. Bde. Qmr. to Lt. Col. Ochterlony's detachment in 1809. Adjt. & Qmr. 23rd N.I. 20 Mar. 1810 till 1814. Actg. S.A.C.G. 5 Aug. 1814. Capt. 1/23rd N.I. S.A.C.G. 22 Dec. 1815 ; A.C.G., 2 cl., 12 Dec. 1823 till 28 May 1825. Transfd. as Major to 46th N.I. (late 2/23rd) May 1824. Fur. 1 Jan. 1826 till 26 Oct. 1829. Transfd. as Lt. Col. to 55th N.I. in 1828 ; to 69th N.I. ; to 63rd N.I. 5 Dec. 1829 ; to 47th N.I. 7 Dec. 1833 ; to 14th N.I. 8 Sept. 1835. To comd. troops in Oudh 8 Feb. 1835.
Refs. : *Walford* (1900), 127, *s.n.* Brooke, of Weston Priory, Somerset. *A.J.* N.S. xxi. 109. Will dated 28 Feb. 1836 ; proved 10 Sept. 1836.

BROOKE, Francis Cissen (1809-1886). Major. 7th N.I. *b.* St. Helena Mar. 1809. Cadet 1825. Arrived in India 24 Jan. 1827. Ensign 17 Aug. 1826. Lieut. 8 Oct. 1832. Capt. 24 Jan. 1845. Retired 1 Aug. 1853. Hon. Major 28 Nov. 1854. *d.* Cheltenham 3 Nov. 1886.
bapt. St. Helena 16 July 1809. Son of Thomas Henry Brooke, sec. to the council and actg. govr. of St. Helena, and Miss Brabazon his 2nd wife. Grand-nephew of Robert Brooke, *q.v. m.* Plymouth, 25 Mar. 1846, Katherine, younger dau. of Henry Drake, and granddau. of Henry Drake, of Barnstaple. Addiscombe Cadet 1824-6.
Services : Posted as Ensign to 7th N.I. Adjt. 7th N.I. 16 May 1838 till 1844. Fur. 5 Mar. 1844 till 1846. No record of active service.
Refs. : Burke's *Landed Gentry of Ireland*, p. 72, *s.n.* Brooke, of Dromavana, co. Cavan. *The Times*, 8 Nov. 1886.

BROOKE, Sir George (1791-1882). General, K.C.B. Colonel Comdt. Artillery. *b.* Bristol 3 Apr. 1791. Cadet 1807. Arrived in India 14 Sept. 1808. Fireworker 18 Apr. 1808. Lieut. 21 Feb. 1810. Capt. 25 Aug. 1821. Major 27 Jan. 1837. Lt. Col. 28 Feb. 1842. Col. Comdt. 22 July 1851. Col. 10 Sept. 1852. Maj. Gen. 28 Nov. 1854. Lt. Gen. 19 June 1866. Gen. 24 May 1870. *d.* 15 Charles St., St. James's Sq., London, 31 Dec. 1882.
Son of Henry Brooke, of Bristol. *m.* Meerut, 22 Mar. 1820, Catharine, dau. of Peter Cochrane. Woolwich Cadet; nominated to R.M.A. 1 May 1805.
Services : Bundelkhand 1809-10. Nepal War 1814-5; Nalagarh; Ramgarh; Malaun; Lieut. 4th Coy. 3rd Bn. Foot Art. (India medal). Served with Rocket Troop 1816-9. Siege and capture of Hathras. Third Mahratta War. Fur. 17 May 1821. Siege and capture of Bhurtpore; Capt. 4th Coy. 1st Bn., Dy. Comy. Ord. (blown up) (Clasp to India medal). First Sikh War; Mudki; Ferozshahr; Sobraon; in the two former of which actions he comdd. the whole of the Art. (Medal with 2 clasps). Second Sikh War; Ramnagar; Chilianwala; Gujerat (Medal with 2 clasps). Bdr. comdg. at Ambala 12 July 1852, afterwards at Meerut. Fur. s.c. 17 Apr. 1856 till death. C.B. 3 Apr. 1846. K.C.B. 13 Mar. 1867.
Refs. : Boase. Foster's *Knightage*, p. 701. *S.M.* 1820, ii. 478. *The Times*, 3 Jan. 1882, p. 7. *I.L.N.* (portrait).

BROOKE, George Perry (1810-1844). Bt. Captain, 68th N.I. *b.* Dublin 6 July 1810. Cadet 1825. Arrived in India 4 Jan. 1827. Ensign 14 Aug. 1826. Lieut. 27 Aug. 1832. Bt. Capt. 14 Aug. 1841. *d.* at sea, 14 Apr. 1844, on board the *Prince of Wales*.
bapt. 15 Aug. 1810. 5th and youngest son of William Brooke, M.D., of Dromavana, Dublin, and of Culmaine House, co. Monaghan, and Angel his wife, dau. of Capt. Edward Perry, of co. Tyrone. Kinsman of Robert Brooke, *q.v.*
Services : Posted as Ensign to 68th N.I. Actg. Adjt. 68th N.I. 17 July 1832, and 30 Oct. 1835. Adjt. 68th N.I. 25 July 1838. Fur. 2 yrs. to Cape 1 Mar. 1844.
Refs. : Burke's *Landed Gentry of Ireland*, p. 73, *s.n.* Brooke, of Dromavana, co. Cavan. Will dated Calcutta 20 Feb. 1844; proved 16 Aug. 1844.

BROOKE, Harold Kynnesman Mapletoft (1810-1867). Cadet, Infantry. *b.* in India 8 July 1810. Cadet 1825. Resigned 10 May 1828. *d.* Blagdon Villa, nr. Taunton, 29 June 1867.
Of Hinton Abbey, Somerset. *bapt.* Agra 18 Dec. 1810. 2nd son of James Henry Brooke, *q.v.*, and Anne his 1st wife. Brother of

THE BENGAL ARMY, 1758-1834 215

Robert Digby Brooke, *q.v. m.* Charterhouse Hinton, 14 Nov. 1832, Margaret Louisa Symonds, of Hinton Abbey, only dau. of Capt. George Clarke Symonds. T.C.D. ; Pensioner 6 July 1829, aged 19. *Services :* To do duty as Ensign with 65th N.I. 2 Mar. 1827.
Refs. : Burke's *Landed Gentry of Ireland,* p. 72, *s.n.* Brooke, of Dromavana, co. Cavan. Burke's *Landed Gentry,* 8th edn., p. 224, *s.n.* Brooke, of Hinton Abbey, Somerset. *Bath Chron.* Nov. 1832. *The Times,* 4 July 1867. *Alumni Dub.*

BROOKE, Henry (*d.* 1771). Cadet, Infantry. Cadet 1770. *d.* Berhampore, Bengal, 17 Aug. 1771.
Services : N.F.P.

BROOKE, Henry Stuart (1798-1820). Lieutenant, 22nd N.I. *b.* in Bengal 24 Aug. 1798. Cadet 1814. Arrived in India Sept. 1815. Ensign 23 Aug. 1815. Lieut. 4 Apr. 1818. *d.* Khurda, Cuttack, 3 Apr. 1820.
Eldest son of Thomas Brooke, B.C.S., judge at Benares, and Ann Maria his wife, née Stuart. Brother of Sir James Brooke, *q.v.* Addiscombe Cadet 1814.
Services : Posted as Ensign to 1/30th N.I. Transfd. to 22nd N.I. in 1816. At home 1816-7. No record of active service.
Refs. : A.J. x. 614. M.I. in Cuttack cemetery.

BROOKE, Sir James (1803-1868). Lieutenant. 18th N.I. Rajah of Sarawak. K.C.B. *b.* Secrole, Benares, 29 Apr. 1803. Cadet 1818. Admitted 23 Oct. 1819. Ensign 11 May 1819. Lieut. 25 Aug. 1821. Struck off 13 Dec. 1827. *d.* his residence, Burrator, Devon, 11 June 1868.
2nd son of Thomas Brooke, B.C.S., and Ann Maria his wife. Brother of Henry Stuart Brooke, *q.v.* Ed. Norwich Grammar School.
Services : See *D.N.B.* Posted as Ensign to 2/6th N.I. Transfd. to 18th N.I. (late 2/6th) May 1824. First Burma War ; Rangpur (s.w.) ; S.A.C.G. (India medal). Granted a wound pension of £70 *p.a.* Fur. 30 July 1825 till struck off. K.C.B. (Civil) 27 Apr. 1848. D.C.L. Oxon. 25 Nov. 1847.
Refs. : D.N.B. D.I.B. Boase. Ency. Brit., 11th edn., iv. 644. Burke's *Landed Gentry,* 13th edn., p. 214, *s.n.* Brooke, of Horton, Gloucs. *Walford. Alumni Oxon. The Times,* 12 June 1868. Portrait (engraving by G. Raphael Ward from a painting by Sir Francis Grant) in India Office library.

BROOKE, James Henry (1781/82-1821). Major, Artillery. *b.* 1781/82. Cadet 1796. Arrived in India 28 Aug. 1798. Fireworker 6 Sept. 1799. Lieut. 21 Feb. 1802. Capt. Lt. 21 Dec.

1804. Capt. 21 Feb. 1810. Major 1 Sept. 1818. *d.* Chowringhee, Calcutta, 21 Nov. 1821, of apoplexy, aged 39.

Eldest son of Robert Brooke, *q.v. m.* 1st, Bath, 15 Mar. 1805, Anne, dau. of Robert Patton, *q.v.,* govr. of St. Helena (*D.N.B.*). Father of Harold Kynnesman Mapletoft Brooke, *q.v.,* and of Robert Digby Brooke, *q.v. m.* 2nd, Calcutta, 23 Jan. 1813, Mrs. Isabella Patton.

Services : Fourth Mysore War ; siege and capture of Seringapatam (w.) ; 2nd Coy. 3rd Bn. Art. (Medal). Fur. 24 Dec. 1802 till 12 May 1806. Operations in Bundelkhand 1808-9 ; Hirapur ; Ajaigarh ; Capt. Lt. comdg. Art. Comdd. newly-raised 3rd Troop H.A. 1809-17. Nepal War 1814-5 ; Kalanga ; Bt. Major 3rd Troop, in 2nd Div. Siege and capture of Hathras. Third Mahratta War ; with 1st Div. of Grand Army. Against the Bhattis of Hariana 1818. Comdg. Golandaz Bn. 1818 till death.

Refs. : Burke's *Landed Gentry of Ireland,* p. 72, *s.n.* Brooke, of Dromavana, co. Cavan. *S.M.* 1805. *A.J.* xiii. 489.

BROOKE, Robert (*c.* 1746-1811). Colonel. Infantry. Governor of St. Helena. *b. c.* 1746. Cadet 1764. Ensign 14 Aug. 1764. Lieut. 25 Aug. 1765. Capt. 10 Dec. 1767. Lt. Col. 1787. Col. (?). *d.* his residence, Somerset Pl., Bath, 25 Jan. 1811, in his 65th year.

Of Prosperous, co. Kildare. 5th and youngest son of Robert Brooke and Honor his wife, dau. of Rev. Henry Brooke, rector of Kinawley, co. Fermanagh. *m.* Mrs. Wynne, née Mapletoft. (She died Cork 26 Mar. 1824.) Father of James Henry Brooke, *q.v.,* and grand-uncle of Francis Cissen Brooke, *q.v.*

Services : See *D.N.B.* Was A.D.C. to Col. William Smith (1726/27-1767), *q.v.,* in 1767. Resigned as Capt. 14 Apr. 1775 ; subsequently promoted to Col.

Refs. : Burke's *Landed Gentry of Ireland,* p. 72, *s.n.* Brooke, of Dromavana, co. Cavan. *A.J.* N.S. xix. 181-4. *D.N.B. D.I.B. G.M.* 1811, i. 190. *Bath. Chron.* 30 Jan. 1811. *N. & Q.* 12S. vi. 321.

BROOKE, Robert Digby (1806-1827). Lieutenant, 9th L.C. *b.* Calcutta 21 Apr. 1806. Cadet 1823. Cornet 9 Jan. 1824. Lieut. 13 May 1825. *d.* Lucknow 26 Apr. 1827.

Eldest son of James Henry Brooke, *q.v.,* and Anne his 1st wife. Brother of Harold Kynnesman Mapletoft Brooke, *q.v.* Addiscombe Cadet 1823-4.

Services : Posted as Cornet to 6th L.C. Transfd. as Lieut. to newly-raised 1st Extra Regt. (became 9th L.C.) 13 May 1825. Siege and capture of Bhurtpore ; Lieut. 9th L.C.

Refs. : Burke's *Landed Gentry of Ireland,* p. 72, *s.n.* Brooke, of Dromavana, co. Cavan.

THE BENGAL ARMY, 1758-1834 217

BROOKHOLDING, Thomas (1791-1809). Cadet, Infantry. *b.* Worcester 7 Dec. 1791. Cadet 1808. Never arrived in India. *d.* at sea 18 Nov. 1809 : kld. on board the *Windham* in action with the French frigate *La Manche.*
Son of Thomas Brookholding and Mary his 2nd wife.

BROOKS, James (1790-1818). Lieutenant, 20th N.I. *b.* London 6 May 1790. Cadet 1804. Arrived in India 4 Aug. 1806. Ensign 28 Apr. 1806. Lieut. 14 Oct. 1807. *d.* Barrackpore 10 June 1818.
Son of William Brooke. *m.* Elizabeth.
Services : Posted as Ensign to 20th N.I. Comdg. Sebundy Corps at Port Marlborough 1810-12. Lieut. 2/20th N.I. at Malacca in 1816.
Refs. : Will dated Malacca 22 Feb. 1816 ; proved 7 July 1818.

BROOKS, Joseph (1779-1840). Lieutenant. 17 N.I. *b.* Liverpool 17 Jan. 1779. Cadet 1799. Arrived in India 12 Mar. 1801. Ensign 16 Mar. 1801. Lieut. 13 July 1803. Resigned 22 Jan. 1810. *d.* his house in Everton 9 Mar. 1840.
Of Everton, nr. Liverpool. *bapt.* St. Peter's, Liverpool, 4 Feb. 1779. Son of Joseph Brooks, of Fazakerley St., Liverpool, merchant. *m.* Cawnpore, 25 May 1803, Hon. Amabel, 2nd dau. of Gerard, first Viscount Lake. His dau. m. Robert Grange, *q.v.*
Services : Posted as Ensign to 2/17th N.I. Operations in Jumna Doab 1803. (? Second Mahratta War ; Lieut. 2/17th N.I.) Adjt. & Qmr. 17th N.I. Bde. Major at Dinapore in 1805 ; at Barrackpore in 1806. Garrison Storekeeper, Fort William, in 1806. D.Q.M.G. 1807 till retirement.
Refs. : Burke's *Peerage,* 1859, p. 1122, *s.n.* Lake, V. *S.M.* 1804, p. 399. *A.J.* N.S. xxxi. 435.

BROOK(E)S, Thomas (1759/60-?). Lieutenant. Infantry. *b.* 1759/60. Cadet 1781. Ensign 26 May 1781. Lieut. 9 Sept. 1782. Struck off 1788.
A native of Gloucs.
Services : Sailed for India on the *Locko,* 13 Mar. 1781, aged 21. N.F.P.

BROOKS, William (1778-1834). Colonel, 41st N.I. *b.* 14 Jan. 1778. Cadet 1795. Arrived in India 13 Feb. 1797. Ensign 22 Oct. 1796. Lieut. 30 Oct. 1797. Capt. 4 June 1807. Major 7 Nov. 1818. Lt. Col. 15 Feb. 1824. Lt. Col. Comdt. 2 Aug. 1828. Col. 5 June 1829. *d.* Stafford, 5 Apr. 1834 : committed suicide by shooting himself with a pistol (coroner's verdict—Insanity).

Of the Dean's Hill Meadows, nr. Stafford. *bapt.* St. Mary's, Stafford, 18 Jan. 1778. Son of Francis Brooks and Ann his wife. Brother of F. Brooks, town clerk of Stafford.

Services : With the Marine Bn. in P.W.I. 25 Mar. 1802 till June 1803. With 3rd Bn. Bengal Vols. 1811-5. Capture of Java. Expedition against Sambas, Borneo. Occupation of Garhakota, C.P., which surrendered to him on 5 July 1820 ; Major 2/9th N.I. Transfd. as Lt. Col. to 21st N.I. (late 2/9th) May 1824. Fur. s.c. 2 Feb. 1825 till 1 June 1828. Transfd. to 31st N.I. 7 Dec. 1826 ; to 41st N.I. 29 Nov. 1828. Fur. 12 Dec. 1828 till death.

Refs. : *G.M.* 1834, i. 560. *A.J.* N.S. xiv. 59. Will dated Stafford 27 July 1833 ; proved 17 Feb. 1835.

Note : His natural dau., Anne., *m.* Oct. 1847, William Palmer, the Rugeley poisoner (*D.N.B.*), and was poisoned by him in 1854. Her mother, Mary Thornton, who died 18 Jan. 1849, is also supposed to have been poisoned by him.

BROOKSBANK, William (1779-1797). Ensign, Infantry. Unposted. *b.* London 30 Jan. 1779. Cadet 1795. Arrived in India 3 Apr. 1797. Ensign 8 Apr. 1797. *d.* Barrackpore 16 Aug. 1797.

Son of Stamp Brooksbank, of Chesterfield St., Mayfair, and Anne his wife, dau. of Thomas Gataker, of Kensington, Middlesex. R.A. Cadet at Woolwich.

Services : N.F.P.

Refs. : Burke's *Landed Gentry*, 12th edn., p. 247, *s.n.* Brooksbank, of Healaugh, Yorks. Burke's *Peerage*, 1923, p. 357, *s.n.* Brooksbank, Bart., of Healaugh.

BROOME, Arthur (1810-1871). Major General, C.S.I. Artillery. *b.* Christchurch, Surrey, 7 Feb. 1810. Cadet 1827. Arrived in India 9 June 1828. 2nd Lieut. 13 Dec. 1827. Lieut. 9 July 1835. Capt. 3 July 1845. Major 14 Sept. 1857. Lt. Col. 27 Aug. 1858. Col. 29 Apr. 1861. Maj. Gen. 6 Mar. 1868. *d.* at sea, 27 Mar. 1871, on board the *Australia*, between Bombay and Suez.

Son of John Broome, of Gt. Marlow, Bucks. *m.* Calcutta, 7 Apr. 1840, Julia Leonora, dau. of Robert Kent, *q.v.* (She died 21 July 1888.) Addiscombe Cadet 1826-7.

Services: Leave s.c. 6 mos. to sea 25 Apr. 1829. 1st Troop 1st Bde. H.A. in 1836. A.D.C. to G.G. 21 Aug. 1838. 3rd Troop 2nd Bde. 1840-2. 1st Asst. Sec., Mily. Board, 24 Feb. 1840. Supt. Cossipore Foundry 16 Nov. 1846 till 1864. Offg. Chief of Mily. Finance Dept. Controller Gen. of Mily. Expenditure 1 Apr. 1864. C.S.I. Author of " History of the Rise and Progress of the Bengal Army," Vol. I. (all pub.), Calcutta, 1850.

Refs. : Boase. *The Times*, 11 May 1871.

BROOME, Ralph (d. 1805). Captain. 1st Bengal European Regt.
Cadet 1771. Ensign 14 Jan. 1773. Lieut. 8 Apr. 1777. Capt.
2 Apr. 1781. Resigned 5 Feb. 1785. d. Bath, June 1805.
m. 1798, Charlotte, dau. of Dr. Charles Burney, younger sister
of Madame D'Arblay (D.N.B.), and widow of Clement Francis,
Surgeon, Bengal Est.
Services : After resignation he became Judge Advocate in India.
Author of " Elucidation of Hastings' Trial " ; " Letters of Simpkin
the Second . . . "
Refs. : M.M. (1805) xix. 626.

BROUGHAM, Henry (1813-1839). Cornet, 4th L.C. b. Edinburgh
7 Feb. 1813. Cadet 1831. Arrived in India ·22 Dec. 1832.
Cornet 22 Dec. 1832. d. Karnal 10 Oct. 1839.
Eldest son of John Waugh Brougham and Margaret his wife, dau.
of James Rigg, of Morton, N.B. Nephew of Henry, first Lord
Brougham and Vaux. Addiscombe Cadet 13 Aug. 1830 ; removed
to Cav. 8 Feb. 1832.
Services : Cornet d.d. 10th L.C. 27 Jan. 1833 ; do. 8th L.C.
17 Nov. 1834. Posted to 4th L.C. 9 June 1836. No record of
active service.
Refs. : Burke's *Peerage*, 1848, p. 135, s.n. Brougham and Vaux, B.
De Rhé-Philipe. G.M. 1840, i. 223.

BROUGHAM, Thomas (1762/63-1819). Major. 13th N.I. b. 1762/
63. Cadet 1780. Admitted 19 Mar. 1781. Ensign 22 Mar. 1781.
Lieut. 16 Aug. 1781. Capt. 27 Mar. 1800. Major 28 Sept. 1804.
Retired 18 Apr. 1805. d. Edinburgh 3 July 1819.
Of Mostyn Hall, Penrith, Cumberland. J.P. co. Cumberland.
m. Isabella Hay. (She died 30 Oct. 1870, aged 90.)
Services : Sailed for India on the *Rochford*, 3 June 1780,
aged 17. Landed at Madras on arrival in India as a Cadet and did
duty with the army at Madras from 10 Jan. 1781. Capt. 4th N.I.
Transfd. to 1/13th N.I. 21 Apr. 1800. Fur. 7 Feb. 1803 till retirement.
Refs. : Burke's *Colonial Gentry*, i. 80. G.M. 1819, ii. 91. S.M.
1819, ii. 200. Will proved in 1820.

BROUGHTON, Edward Robert (1784-1830). Major. 21st N.I.
b. Edinburgh 8 Nov. 1784. Cadet 1800. Arrived in India
14 Oct. 1801. Ensign 18 Nov. 1801. Lieut. 30 Sept. 1803.
Capt. 4 June 1817. Major 7 Mar. 1826. Retired 16 May 1829.
d. Cross Hall, co. Berwick, 3 Oct. 1830.
Of Cross Hall. bapt. 30 Mar. 1785. Son of Bryan Broughton,
Lieut. of Marines, and Helen Cunningham his wife. Related to

(? nephew of) Robert Broughton (1759/60-1832), *q.v.* *m.* Agnes, dau. of William Hunter, of Glenmoriston, co. Peebles.
Services : Posted as Ensign to 9th N.I. Ramgarh Bn. in 1804. Adjt. do. 1806-9. Adjt. & Qmr. 9th N.I. 1 June 1809 till 1814. Intr. & Qmr. 1/9th N.I. 1 July 1814. S.A.C.G. in 1816. Superintending construction of new Jagannath road 1818-23. Supt. of roads in Cuttack 1823-5. Transfd. to 21st N.I. (late 2/9th) May 1824. Siege and capture of Bhurtpore ; Capt. 21st N.I. Fort Adjt. at Fort William in 1826. Fur. p.a. 5 Jan. 1827 till retirement.
Refs. : A.J. N.S. iii. 174. Will dated Edinburgh 17 Aug. 1829 ; proved 21 June 1831.

BROUGHTON, Edward Swift (1757/58-1827). Major General. Colonel 13th N.I. *b.* 1757/58. Cadet 1778. Arrived in India 11 Aug. 1778. Ensign Dec. 1778. Lieut. 11 Oct. 1778. Capt. 1 June 1796. Major 29 May 1800. Lt. Col. 30 Sept. 1803. Col. 1 Jan. 1812. Maj. Gen. 4 June 1814. *d.* Edinburgh, 25 Dec. 1827.
Of Rossend Castle, Burntisland, co. Fife. Brother of Robert Broughton, *q.v.* *m.* St. Helena, 19 Aug. 1809, Barbara, 2nd dau. of Robert Beatson, of Kilrie, and sister of Alexander Campbell Beatson, *q.v.* (She died 24 Apr. 1828.) His dau. *m.* Thomas Graham Dundas, *q.v.*
Services : With 3rd Bn. Sepoys in 1780. Third Mysore War ; with the Bengal detachment under Lt. Col. John Cockerell, *q.v.* Posted to 2nd Bengal Eur. Regt. in 1800. Expedition to Egypt 1801-2 ; Major comdg. Vol. Bn. Apptd. to comd. Ramgarh Bn. in Aug. 1802. Second Mahratta War ; comdg. a detachment operating on the frontier towards Nagpur 1803 ; capture of Sambalpur. Fur. 18 Feb. 1806. Lieut. Govr. of St. Helena 4 July 1808 till Mar. 1813.
Refs. : E.I.M.C. i. 284. *Hist. of I. of St. Helena.* N. & Q. 8S. viii. 168. G.M. 1828, i. 271.

BROUGHTON, Edward Wilson (1788-1814). Lieutenant, 19th N.I. *b.* Fountainbridge 22 Oct. 1788. Cadet 1805. Arrived in India 11 July 1806. Ensign 14 Sept. 1806. Lieut. 20 July 1808. *d.* 2 Nov. 1814, of wounds received during the assault of Kalanga fort on 31 Oct.
Son of Edward Broughton, accomptant of excise, and Cecilia Brown his wife.
Services : Posted as Ensign to 19th N.I. Expedition to Mauritius 1810 ; Lieut. 2nd Vol. Bn. With Ramgarh Bn. in 1812. Nepal War 1814 ; Lieut. 2/19th N.I., in 2nd Div.
Refs. : M.I. in St. John's church, Calcutta.

THE BENGAL ARMY, 1758-1834

BROUGHTON, John Delves (1813-1836). Lieutenant, 67th N.I. *b.* 6 May 1813. Cadet 1828. Arrived in India 11 Nov. 1829. Ensign 11 Nov. 1829. Lieut. 18 Dec. 1834. *d.* Dinapore 28 June 1836 : drowned in the Ganges by the upsetting of a boat.
bapt. Cheadle, co. Chester, 16 May 1813. 3rd son of Rev. Sir Henry Delves Broughton, 8th Bart., of Broughton, Staffs., rector of Cheadle, and Mary his wife, only dau. of John Pigott, of Capard.
Services : To do duty with 7th N.I. 11 Jan. 1830. Actg. Ensign 17 Dec. 1831, having been more than two yrs. in India. Posted as Ensign to 67th N.I. 26 Jan. 1833. No record of active service.
Refs. : Burke's *Peerage*, 1923, p. 360, *s.n.* Broughton, Bart., of Broughton, Staffs. *A.J.* N.S. xxi. 253.

BROUGHTON, Robert (1760/61-1832). Lieut. Colonel. 26th N.I. *b.* in Scotland 1760/61. Cadet 1781. Arrived in India 15 May 1782. Ensign 19 June 1781. Lieut. 24 Sept. 1782. Capt. 30th June 1802. Major 8 June 1806. Lt. Col. 28 Apr. 1812. Retired 1 June 1818. *d.* Charlotte St., Portland Pl., London, 9 Nov. 1832, aged 72.
Brother of Edward Swift Broughton, *q.v.*, and related to Edward Robert Broughton, *q.v.*
Services : Apptd. Cadet on 14 Feb. 1781, aged 19. Lieut. 1/1st N.I. Capt. Lt. 1/1st N.I. 29 May 1800. Fur. 9 Mar. 1800 till 31 July 1804. Capt. 1/1st N.I. Transfd. to newly-raised 24th N.I. in 1805 ; as Lt. Col. to 2/26th N.I. in 1812. Fur. 1816 till retirement.
Refs. : *G.M.* 1832, ii. 483. *A.J.* N.S. ix. 197. Will dated 21 Jan. 1831 ; proved 12 July 1834.

BROUGHTON, Thomas (*d.* 1792). Ensign, Engineers. Cadet 1784. Ensign 13 May 1785. *d.* Calcutta 26 July 1792.
Services : N.F.P.

BROUGHTON, Thomas Duer (1778-1835). Colonel, 28th N.I. *b.* Bristol 8 Mar. 1778. Cadet 1795. Arrived in India 3 Mar. 1797. Ensign 25 Nov. 1796. Lieut. 30 Oct. 1797. Capt. 20 Oct. 1805. Major 4 Mar. 1816. Lt. Col. 11 June 1822. Lt. Col. Comdt. 13 May 1825. Col. 5 June 1829. *d.* Dorset Sq., London, 16 Nov. 1835.
bapt. St. James's, Bristol, 7 Apr. 1778. Son of Rev. Thomas Broughton, rector of St. Peter's, Bristol, and Jane his wife. *m.* St. George's, Hanover Sq., London, 20 Sept. 1814, Georgiana Sophia, eldest dau. of John (Ezechiel) Des Champs, afterwards Chamier, of Grosvenor Pl., London, Member of Council at Madras. Ed. Eton ; entered in 1791 ; K.S. in 1793.
Services : See *D.N.B.* Fourth Mysore War ; siege and capture of Seringapatam ; Lieut. 1st Bn. Bengal Vols. Adjt. of Gent.

Cadets in 1803. Adjt. & Qmr. 1st Bn. Bengal Vols. 1804-5. Fur. 1811 till Aug. 1815, and 1826 till death. Transfd. from 16th to 28th N.I. 30 Oct. 1826. Author of "Letters written in a Mahratta Camp during the year 1809...," London, 1813, 4to, etc.
Refs. : D.N.B. D.I.B. Burke's *Visitation of Seats and Arms*, 1S. i. 34, *s.n.* Chamier. *E.I.M.C.* i. 169. *Eton School List. G.M.* 1814, ii. 392 ; N.S. v. 203.

BROWN, Alexander (*d.* 1792). Ensign, Infantry. Subsequently Lieutenant, Madras Est. Cadet 1780. Ensign 9 Mar. 1781. *d.* Tanjore, Madras, 10 May 1792.
Services : Transfd. to Madras Est. 15 Oct. 1781. Ensign, Madras, 20 Dec. 1780. Lieut., Madras, 17 Apr. 1786.
Refs. : M.I. in St. Peter's cemetery, Tanjore.

BROWN, Alexander (1780-1838). Lieut. Colonel. 25th N.I. *bapt.* Pitsligo, co. Aberdeen, 3 Oct. 1780. Cadet 1800. Arrived in India 22 Aug. 1801. Ensign 27 Nov. 1801. Lieut. 13 July 1803. Capt. 24 Mar. 1816. Major 13 May 1825. Lt. Col. 4 Mar. 1830. Retired 18 June 1834. *d.* Upper Gloucester Pl., London, 8 Oct. 1838, of apoplexy, aged 61 (coroner's verdict—"Died by the visitation of God").

Son of John Brown, of Boghead, Pitsligo, and Margaret Duguid his wife. *m.* (?). (She died 2 Aug. 1825.)
Services : Posted as Ensign to Bengal Eur. Regt. Second Mahratta War ; Deig (s.w.) ; siege of Bhurtpore (w. in 1st assault on 9 Jan. 1805) ; Lieut. Bengal Eur. Regt. Fur. s.c. 5 Nov. 1814 till 30 Sept. 1817. Siege and capture of Bhurtpore ; Major 1st Bengal Eur. Regt. Transfd. to 44th N.I. 29 Dec. 1828 ; to 25th N.I. 15 Oct. 1833. Fur. 31 Jan. 1832 till death.
Refs. : G.M. 1838, ii.

BROWN (*recte* **BRAUN** or **BRUN**), **Béat-Louis** (1718-1792). Captain. Infantry. Subsequently H.B.M. Secretary and Chargé d'Affaires to the Swiss Confederation at Berne. *b.* Berne, Switzerland, 1718. Cadet 1756. Ensign 28 Jan. 1758. Lieut. 27 July 1759. Capt. 9 Oct. 1763. Resigned 1766. *d.* Berne 1792.

The last representative of an ancient Neuchâtel family which settled at Berne in the middle of the seventeenth century. Son of —— Braun (or Brun) and his wife, née Werth. *m.* 1767, Albertine, dau. of the celebrated Albrecht de Haller by his 3rd wife, Amélie Teichmeyer.
Services : Sailed for India on the *Grantham* in 1756. British Sec. and Chargé d'Affaires at Berne from 1776 till death.
Refs. : Biographie Neuchâteloise, par F. A. M. Jeanneret et J. H. Bonhôte, Locle, 1863, vol. i. *Dict. hist. et biog. de la Suisse,* ii. (1921).

BROWN, Charles (1807-1887). (*See* **BROWN-CONSTABLE.**)

BROWN, Clements (1765/66-1838). Major General, C.B. Colonel Comdt. Artillery. *b.* 1765/66. Cadet 1783. Admitted 9 July 1784. Ensign 3 Feb. 1785. Fireworker (3 Feb. 1785) 1 Feb. 1789. Lieut. 1 Dec. 1794. Capt. Lt. 25 Dec. 1802. Capt. 28 Feb. 1806. Major 21 Apr. 1817. Lt. Col. 2 Aug. 1819. Lt. Col. Comdt. 1 May 1824. Col. 5 June 1829. Maj. Gen. 10 Jan. 1837. *d.* Benares, 24 Apr. 1838, aged 72.

Brother of Simon Richardson Brown, *q.v. m.* Ann Helena. (*See* Henry Grace.) (She died Mortimer, Berks., 11 June 1838.)

Services : Transfd. from Inf. to Art. in 1789. Third Mysore War ; Satyamangalam ; Bangalore ; Utradrug. To Madras, Aug.-Oct. 1793, for siege of Pondicherry ; Lieut. F. 4th Coy. 3rd Bn. Second Rohilla War ; Bitaurah. Selected on 4 Dec. 1800 to comd. the experimental troop of H.A. Expedition to Egypt 1801 ; Lt. comdg. experimental troop (1st Troop H.A.). Second Mahratta War ; capture of Deig ; siege of Bhurtpore ; comdg. 1st Troop H.A. Comy. of Ord. 23 Jan. 1806. Fur. 26 Feb. 1810 till Jan. 1812. Agent for gun carriages at Allahabad 23 June 1814 till 1824. Siege and capture of Bhurtpore ; Bdr. comdg. H.A. Bdr. 3 Oct. 1828. Comdt. Bengal Art., with a seat on Mily. Board, 23 Sept. 1831. To comd. Benares Div. Aug. 1836. C.B. 2 Jan. 1827.

Refs. : Stubbs, ii. 246-51. *G.M.* 1838, ii. 342. *A.J.* N.S. xxvi. Will dated 12 Sept. 1837 ; proved 3 Dec. 1838. M.I. at Benares.

BROWN, Edmund John (1814-1848). Bt. Captain, Engineers. *b.* Kensington, London, 13 Mar. 1814. Cadet 1831. Arrived in India 8 June 1832. 2nd Lieut. (8 June 1832) 7 June 1836. Lieut. 20 May 1839. Bt. Capt. 11 June 1845. *d.* Bombay, 9 Nov. 1848, of liver complaint.

Son of Richard Brown, of Kensington, principal clerk, War Office. Addiscombe Cadet 28 Mar. 1828 till 11 June 1830. Chatham 13 Aug. 1830 till 3 Aug. 1831.

Services : Posted to S. & M. in June 1832. Adjt. 31 Dec. 1836. Political employ. Asst. to P.A., Upper Sind, 1839. Campaign in Sind 1843 ; Miani ; Hyderabad ; A.D.C. to Sir Charles Napier (Medal). Sec. to Govt. of Sind 2 Sept. 1843 till death.

Refs. : *I.M.* 1848, p. 742.

BROWN, Edward (1755/56-1826). Captain. Artillery. *b.* Jamaica 1755/56. Country Cadet 1777. Admitted Sept. 1777. Fireworker 12 Nov. 1777. Lieut. 29 Sept. 1778. Capt. Lt. 5 July 1784. Capt. 29 May 1786. Invalided 8 July 1787. Retired 21 Mar. 1804. *d.* Cavendish Pl., Bath, 26 Nov. 1826.

m. Chunar, U.P., 23 Dec. 1793, Miss Ann Brown. His dau. *m.* Henry James Blunt, *q.v.*
Services : Sailed for India on the *Houghton*, 9 Dec. 1777, aged 21. Second Mysore War 1781-5 (w.) ; Adjt. Art. Comdg. Art. Invalid Coy. at Chunar, and Comy. Ord. in 1790. Fur. 22 Jan. 1802 till retirement.
Refs. : G.M. 1826, ii. 573.

BROWN, George (1734/35-1767). Lieutenant, Infantry. *b.* in Scotland 1734/35. Cadet 1764. Ensign 5 June 1764. Lieut. 20 Aug. 1765. *d.* Calcutta 26 Oct. 1767.
Services : Sailed for India on the *Pitt*, 21 Mar. 1763, aged 28. N.F.P.

BROWN, George (1790-1806). Cadet, Infantry. *b.* London, 4 June 1790. Cadet 1805. Never arrived in India. *d.* Dec. 1806, on his passage to India, in the wreck of the *Skelton Castle*. Struck off with effect from 5 Nov. 1806. (See note to David Allan.)

BROWN, Henry (1798-1864). Lieutenant. 51st N.I. Pensioner on Lord Clive's fund. Subsequently Colonel and Chief Recruiting Officer for E.I.C. in London. *b.* Huntingdon 29 Jan. 1798. Cadet 1817. Admitted 21 July 1818. Ensign 13 June 1818. Lieut. 1 Aug. 1818. Capt. 10 Jan. 1834. Major (Local rank) 1841. Lt. Col. 13 Jan. 1852. Col. (?). *d.* Quadrant, Regent St., London, 29 Feb. 1864.
Son of Richard Brown, M.D.
Services : Posted as Ensign to 26th N.I. Transfd. to 51st N.I. (late 1/26th) May 1824. Fur. s.c., *via* Persia, 1 Apr. 1822 till 6 May 1825. Fur. s.c. 1 Sept. 1826. Retired on a pension of 2/6 *p.d.* 18 May 1831. Actg. Subaltern at E.I.C. Chatham Depot 16 May 1827. Paymr. at Chatham 28 July 1837. Adjt. do. in 1838. 2nd in comd. and Bk. Mr. 1841. Recruiting Ofr. in London 1847. Granted the local and tempy. rank of Lt. Col. 13 Jan. 1852, whilst employed on recruiting service in London and on other mily. duties. No record of active service.
Refs. G.M. 1864, i. 539.

BROWN, James (*d.* 1788). Captain, Infantry. Cadet 1771. Ensign 28 Mar. 1773. Lieut. 25 May 1778. Capt. 19 Feb. 1784. *d.* Monghyr, B. & O., 22 Sept. 1788.
Services : N.F.P.
Refs. : S.M. 1789, p. 205.

BROWN, James. Ensign. Infantry. Cadet 1783. Ensign 1783. Struck off 1788.
Services : N.F.P.

BROWN, James (1786-1806). Lieutenant, 25th N.I. *b.* Melrose, co. Roxburgh, 4 Feb. 1786. Cadet 1803. Arrived in India 14 Aug. 1804. Ensign 5 Aug. 1804. Lieut. 21 Sept. 1804. *d.* nr. Arrah, U.P., 20 May 1806.
Son of David Brown and Ann Hepburn his wife.
Services : Posted as Lieut. to 25th N.I. in 1805. (? Capture of Gohad 1806 ; Lieut. 25th N.I.)

BROWN, John (*d.* 1763). Lieut. Fireworker, Artillery. Cadet 1761. Fireworker 1761. *d.* 5th, 6th or 11th Oct. 1763 : massacred at or near Patna by order of Nawab Mir Muhammad Kasim. (See note to Benjamin Adamson.)
Note : See note to John Bowen.
Services : N.F.P.

BROWN, John (*d.* 1775). Captain, Infantry. Cadet 1764. Ensign 6 Jan. 1765. Lieut. 11 Dec. 1766. Capt. 11 Oct. 1769. *d.* Dinapore, 4 Jan. 1775.
Uncle of Thomas Stibbert.
Services : N.F.P.
Refs. : Will dated 27 Nov. 1774 ; proved 27 Mar. 1776.

BROWN, John (*d.* 1776). Ensign, Infantry. Cadet 1771. Ensign 10 Feb. 1773. *d.* Serampore, Bengal, Oct. 1776.
Services : N.F.P.

BROWN, John (1759/60-?). Lieutenant. Infantry. *b.* in Scotland 1759/60. Cadet 1777. Ensign Dec. 1778. Lieut. 12 Oct. 1779. Resigned 17 Jan. 1785.
Services : Sailed for India on the *Mount Stewart*, 9 Feb. 1778, aged 18.

BROWN, John (1791-1826). Captain, 31st N.I. *b.* 1791. Cadet 1807. Arrived in India 14 Aug. 1808. Ensign 26 Aug. 1807. Lieut. 19 Feb. 1812. Capt. 1 May 1824. *d.* 18 Jan. 1826, aged 34 : kld. in action at the assault of Bhurtpore.
m. Dinapore, 4 Mar. 1821, Miss Charlotte Wilkinson.
Services : Apptd. Cadet on 22 Dec. 1807, aged 15. Posted as Ensign to 15th N.I. in 1810. Lieut. 1/15th N.I. Adjt. 6th Gren. Bn. in 1816. Intr. & Qmr. 2/15th N.I. in 1818. Third Mahratta War ; Asirgarh ; Lieut. 2/15th N.I. Adjt. 2/15th N.I. 27 Jan. 1820. Adjt. 1/15th N.I. in 1823. Transfd. as Capt. to 31st N.I. (late 2/15th) May 1824. Siege and capture of Bhurtpore (kld.) ; Capt. 31st N.I.
Refs. : G.M. 1826, ii. 381. Will dated 8 Dec. 1825 ; proved 27 Sept. 1831.

BROWN, John Fletcher. Lieut. Fireworker. Artillery. Cadet (?).
Fireworker 15 Sept. 1767. Dismissed 1769.
Services : N.F.P.

BROWN, John Lens (1807-1826). Ensign, 29th N.I. *b.* Northampton 17 Feb. 1807. Cadet 1823. Ensign 21 Feb. 1824. *d.* Bareilly, U.P., 4 Sept. 1826.
bapt. All Saints, Northampton, 24 Aug. 1807. Son of William Brown, of Northampton, merchant, and Frances his wife. Brother of Peach Brown, *q.v.* Ed. St. Paul's school ; admitted 22 Apr. 1816, aged 9.
Services : Posted as Ensign to 29th N.I. No record of active service.
Refs. : *Gardiner.*

BROWN, Joseph (*d.* 1787). Lieutenant, Infantry. Cadet 1778. Ensign (?). Lieut. 23 Oct. 1778. *d.* 28 Mar. 1787.
Services : N.F.P.

BROWN, Lawrence Constable (1803-1829). Lieutenant, Pension Est. 53rd N.I. *b.* Petrograd 1 Jan. 1803. Cadet 1821. Ensign 26 Feb. 1822. Lieut. 2 Sept. 1824. Pensioned 20 Mar. 1829. *d.* Calcutta 21 Dec. 1829.
Son of Lawrence Constable Brown, Russia merchant. Brother of Charles Brown-Constable, *q.v.*
Services : Posted as Ensign to Bengal Eur. Regt. in 1823. Transfd. to 27th N.I. in 1823 ; to 53rd N.I. (late 1/27th) May 1824. No record of active service.
Refs. : *A.J.* N.S. ii. 98.

BROWN, Peach (1802-1851). Lieut. Colonel, 6th N.I. *b.* Northampton 20 Nov. 1802. Cadet 1818. Admitted 26 June 1819. Ensign 22 June 1819. Lieut. 27 June 1820. Capt. 27 Apr. 1831. Major 12 Aug. 1838. Lt. Col. 23 Dec. 1844. *d.* Agra 12 Oct. 1851.
Son of William Brown and Frances his wife. Brother of John Lens Brown, *q.v. m.* Martha.
Services : Posted as Ensign to 2/14th N.I. Intr. & Qmr. 29th N.I. (late 2/14th) 24 Nov. 1824 till 21 Dec. 1827. Fur. s.c. 23 Jan. 1835 till 30 Dec. 1836. Fur. 5 May 1846 till 1849. Transfd. to 6th N.I. in 1849. No record of active service.
Refs. : Will dated 7 Aug. 1849 ; proved 18 Nov. 1851. *G.M.* 1852, i. 106.

BROWN(E), Robert (1768/69-1805). Captain, Artillery. *b.* 1768/69. Cadet 1783. Admitted 4 Aug. 1784. Fireworker 20 May 1785. Lieut. 21 Feb. 1794. Capt. Lt. 25 Feb. 1802. Capt. 29 Dec. 1804. *d.* Calcutta, 9 July 1805, aged 36.

THE BENGAL ARMY, 1758-1834 227

Son of John Brown(e), of Glasgow, merchant. Brother of Thomas Mayne Browne.
Services : Fourth Mysore War ; Seringapatam ; Lieut. & Qmr. Art. To Madras, Aug.-Oct. 1793, for siege of Pondicherry ; Lieut. d.d. 4th Coy. 1st Bn., as Adjt. Qmr. 3rd Bn. Art. in 1803 till death. *Refs.* : *S.M.* 1806, p. 78. *A.A.R.* viii. Intestate ; admon. granted 8 Aug. 1805. M.I. in S. Park St. burial ground, Calcutta.

BROWN, Samuel (*d.* 1789). Lieutenant, Infantry. Cadet 1781. Ensign 26 July 1781. Lieut. 21 Jan. 1785. *d.* Berhampore, Bengal, 14 Jan. 1789.
Services : N.F.P.

BROWN, Samuel (*c.* 1774-1805). Captain, 24th N.I. *b.* Belfast *c.* 1774. Cadet 1793. Admitted 8 Dec. 1794. Ensign 7 Oct. 1794. Lieut. 1 July 1796. Capt. 19 May 1803. *d. unm.* in England 26 Dec. 1805.
Services : Apptd. Cadet on 16 Apr. 1794, "aged about 20." Fur. 18 Aug. 1802 till death. N.F.P.
Refs. : Will dated Calcutta 12 Apr. 1802 ; proved 30 July 1806.

BROWN, Simon Richardson (1779-1807). Captain, 9th N.I. *bapt.* Donagh, co. Monaghan, 20 Dec. 1779. Cadet 1795. Arrived in India 6 Mar. 1797. Ensign 16 Nov. 1796. Lieut. 30 Oct. 1797. Capt. 3 June 1807. *d.* 18 Nov. 1807 : kld. in action at the assault of Komona.
Brother of Clements Brown, *q.v.*
Services: Lieut. 9th N.I. At Malacca in 1805-6. Operations against Dhundia Khan 1807 ; Komona (kld.) ; Capt. 1/9th N.I.
Refs. : Will dated 13 Oct. 1807 ; proved 14 Jan. 1808.

BROWN, Sir Thomas (*d.* 1838). Lieut. General, K.C.B. Colonel 2nd L.C. Cadet 1775. Admitted 14 Sept. 1777. Cornet 14 Sept. 1779. Lieut. 1 May 1781. Capt. 23 June 1799. Major 16 June 1800. Lt. Col. 22 Jan. 1802. Col. 4 June 1811. Maj. Gen. 4 June 1814. Lt. Gen. 27 May 1825. *d.* Thames Ditton 19 May 1838.
Son of Lt. Col. Arthur Browne, 58th Foot, of Knockduffe House, Kinsale. Brother of Marmaduke Williamson Browne, *q.v. m.* Fort Marlbro', Sumatra, 8 Sept. 1796, Jane Jenkins. His dau. *m.* James Franklin, *q.v.*
Services : Apptd. a Cadet by the C.D. 8 Dec. 1775. Operations in Jumna Doab 1802-3 ; Sasni ; Bijaigarh ; Kachaura ; Lt. Col. comdg. 2nd N.C. Second Mahratta War ; sieges of Aligarh and Agra ; action at Koil ; battles of Delhi and Laswari ; comdg. 2nd N.C. ; battle of Deig ; comdg. Cav. Bde. ; siege of Bhurtpore ;

Afzalgarh. Apptd. to comd. 1st N.C. in 1807. Bundelkhand 1810-1 ; defeat of Gopal Singh at Bichaund 19 Mar. 1811. Reduction of Kalinjar 1812 ; comdg. covering force. Fur. p.a. 2 Jan. 1815 till May 1816. Siege and capture of Hathras ; comdg. the Cav. Third Mahratta War ; comdg. Centre Div. of the Grand Army ; pursuit of Pindaris 1818 ; comdg. a detached force ; capture of Jawad 29 Jan. 1818. Comdg. Dinapore Div. Comdt. at Buxar 26· Aug. 1822. Fur. 10 Jan. 1827 till death. Col. 2nd L.C. 30 Sept. 1834. K.C.B. 23 July 1823.

Refs. : E.I.M.C. i. 253. G.M. 1838, ii. 321. A.J. N.S. xxvi. 127. Burke's *Landed Gentry*, 7th edn., p. 233, *s.n.* Browne, of Riverstown, co. Cork.

BROWN, Thomas Crockat (1759/60-1793). Captain, Engineers. *b.* in Scotland 1759/60. Cadet (?). Ensign 9 Apr. 1777. Lieut. (?). Capt. Lt. (?). Capt. 3 Aug. 1782. *d.* at sea 18 Oct. 1793.

Son of Thomas Brown of Johnston-Burn. Brother of Capt. Henry Brown, 3rd Bombay N.I., and of Capt. Adam Brown, 7th Madras N.I.

Services : Sailed for India on the *Triton*, 19 Apr. 1776, aged 16. N.F.P.

Refs. : S.M. 1794, p. 236. Will dated 28 Apr. 1792.

BROWN(E), Ulysses (*d.* 1798). Bt. Captain, Infantry. Cadet 1782. Ensign 1 Jan. 1783. Lieut. 7 Feb. 1788. Bt. Capt. 7 Jan. 1796. *d.* Bhagulpur, B. & O., 4 Nov. 1798.

Services : Formerly in H.M. Horse Guards. N.F.P.

Refs. : *Hickey*, iii. 142.

***BROWN, Valentine.** Cadet. Artillery. Cadet 14 June 1767. Apptd. in England, but never commissioned.

Refs. : Stubbs's *List of Officers of the Bengal Art.*

BROWN, William (1795-1845). Bt. Major, 69th N.I. *b.* Stewarton, co. Ayr, 29 Dec. 1795. Cadet 1813. Admitted 28 Oct. 1814. Ensign (16 Dec. 1814) 5 June 1815. Lieut. 17 May 1816. Capt. 15 Oct. 1828. Bt. Major 23 Nov. 1841. *d.* Sukkur, Sind, 11 Sept. 1845.

Son of Andrew Brown, writer.

Services : Posted as Ensign to 19th N.I. Asst. Revenue Surveyor at Delhi 29 Dec. 1822. Transfd. to 1st Extra Regt. (became 69th N.I.) in 1826. Revenue Surveyor at Saharanpur 17 Nov. 1826, and passed the greater part of his service in the Survey Dept. Operations on N. Sind frontier against the Hill tribes 1844-5.

Refs. : Will dated 17 Jan. 1844 ; proved 19 Jan. 1846.

BROWNE, Adderley Thomas (1809-1829). 2nd Lieutenant, Artillery. *b.* Rincurran, co. Cork, 10 Oct. 1809. Cadet 1827. 2nd Lieut. 13 Oct. 1827. *d.* Cawnpore 15 Sept. 1829.
Son of Lt. Col. Arthur Browne, Lt. Govr. of Charles Fort, Kinsale, and Dorothea Anne his wife, dau. of Rev. Thomas Adderley Browne, rector of Rincurran, and niece of Sir George Sackville Browne, *q.v.* Brother of George Sackville Henry Browne, *q.v.*, and of Amelia St. George, wife of William Douglas Littlejohn, *q.v.* Addiscombe Cadet 1825-7.
Services : No record of active service.
Refs. : Burke's *Landed Gentry*, 7th edn., p. 233, *s.n.* Browne, of Riverstown, co. Cork.

BROWNE, Birnie (1796-1855). Bt. Colonel, Artillery. *b.* Edinburgh 22 Sept. 1796. Cadet 1815. Arrived in India Aug. 1816. Fireworker 14 Aug. 1817. Lieut. 1 Sept. 1818. Capt. 25 July 1832. Major 3 July 1845. Lt. Col. 1 Dec. 1847. Bt. Col. 28 Nov. 1854. *d.* Peshawar 30 Oct. 1855.
2nd son of Birnie Browne, of Leith, wine merchant, and Catherine Grace his wife, 2nd dau. of John Creswell, of Creswell, Northumberland. *m.* St. John's, Calcutta, 2 Aug. 1826, Miss Maria Jane Christiana. (*See also* James Read, and William Henry Terraneau.) His dau. *m.* Colin Troup, *q.v.* Addiscombe Cadet 29 Sept. 1812 till 13 Nov. 1815.
Services : Served in P.W.I. from June 1818 till 1822. Apptd. to Revenue Survey Dept. Nov. 1822. First Burma War ; Arakan 1825 ; D.A.Q.M.G. (India medal). Gwalior campaign ; Maharajpur ; Capt. comdg. 1st Coy. 4th Bn. Art. and No. 17 Light Field Battery (Bronze star). To comd. Art. at Saugor 24 July 1845. Comdd. Art. Div. at Ferozepore Aug. 1846 till Aug. 1847. Lt. Col. comdg. 2nd Bn. Foot Art. at death.
Refs. : De Rhé-Philipe. Burke's *Landed Gentry*, 6th edn., p. 388, *s.n.* Creswell, of Creswell, Northumberland.

BROWNE, Clement Read (1812-1892). Colonel. 60th N.I. *b.* 14 Jan. 1812. Cadet 1826. Arrived in India 6 Nov. 1827. Ensign 14 June 1827. Lieut. 12 July 1833. Capt. 21 Nov. 1845. Major 17 Mar. 1859. Bt. Lt. Col. 18 Feb. 1861. Retired 31 Dec. 1861. Hon. Col. 31 Dec. 1861. *d.* 8 Queen's Villas, Windsor, 12 Jan. 1892.
bapt. Calcutta 24 May 1812. Son of John Brown, Surgeon, Bengal Medical Est., and Charlotte his wife. Brother of John Swinton Browne, *q.v.*, and of Georgiana Fortescue, 2nd wife of Thomas Hutton (1807-1874), *q.v. m.* Delhi, 4 Sept. 1834, Isabella, youngest dau. of Hugh Davidson, *q.v.* (She died Brighton, 19 Feb. 1860, aged 46.)

Services : Posted as Ensign to 60th N.I. Offg. Intr. & Qmr. 3rd N.I. 24 Dec. 1831. Arakan Local Bn. 29 Jan. 1835. Asst. to A.G.G., Saugor & Narbada, 18 Feb. 1835. D.C., 1 cl., Saugor, 30 Sept. 1841. Served as Pol. Ofr. with a Bde. of Madras troops under Bdr. Watson 1842-3, sent to put down an insurrection in the Saugor & Narbada territories. Fur. to Cape and N.S.W. for 2 yrs. 12 Dec. 1844. D.C., 1 cl., Cis-Sutlej territory, 11 Feb. 1847. D.C. Jhelum Div. Mutiny campaign; accompanied the troops under Col. Ellis, H.M. 24th Regt., sent to disarm the 14th N.I. at Jhelum on 7 July 1857 ; was present during the fight and had his charger wounded.

Refs. : A.J. N.S. xvi. 195. *The Times,* 15 Jan. 1892.

BROWNE, Edward (1782-1824). Captain, 59th N.I. *b.* Galway 11 Oct. 1782. Cadet 1799. Admitted 16 Oct. 1800. Ensign 14 Nov. 1800. Lieut. 1 Jan. 1803. Capt. 6 July 1818. *d.* at sea, 9 Dec. 1824, on board the *Louisa.*

bapt. Galway 1 Nov. 1782. Younger son of Edward Browne, of Ardskea, co. Galway. *m.* Calcutta, 15 Mar. 1808, Sarah, dau. of Henry Swinhoe, of Calcutta, solicitor, and sister of Samuel Swinhoe, *q.v.* (*See also* Gilbert Nichollets, and Sir William Nott.)

Services : Posted as Ensign to 2/13th N.I. 17 Apr. 1801. With Ramgarh Bn. 1812-4. (? Nepal War 1814 ; Lieut. Ramgarh Bn., in 4th Div.) Transfd. as Capt. Lt. to newly-raised 2/30th N.I. in 1815 ; to 59th N.I. (late 1/30th) May 1824.

Refs. : N. & Q. 9S. i. 153.

BROWNE, Sir George Sackville (*d.* 1828). Lieut. General, K.C.B. Colonel 23rd N.I. Cadet 1774. Admitted 2 Nov. 1774. Ensign 4 July 1776. Lieut. 30 July 1778. Capt. 9 Dec. 1793. Major 1 Nov. 1798. Lt. Col. 13 June 1801. Col. 25 July 1810. Maj. Gen. 4 June 1813. Lt. Gen. 27 May 1825. *d.* Brussels 1 Jan. 1828.

Of 26 York Pl., later of 73 Gloster Pl., London. Younger son of Rev. St. John Browne, D.D., and Amelia his wife, dau. of Edward St. George. Grand-uncle of Adderley Thomas Browne, *q.v. m.* (?). His dau. *m.* Sir William Casement, K.C.B., *q.v.*

Services : A.D.C. to Col. Horton Briscoe, *q.v.,* in 1790. Major 15th N.I. Posted as Lt. Col. to 1/4th N.I. 13 June 1801. Second Mahratta War ; storm of Aligarh 4 Sept. 1803 (w.) ; Lt. Col. comdg. 1/4th N.I. Comdg. at Agra in 1808. Transfd. to 27th N.I. in 1808 ; to 6th N.I. in 1809 ; to 17th N.I. in 1810. Fur. 9 Mar. 1811 till death. Col. 14th N.I. 4 May 1812 ; Col. 23rd N.I. in 1824. K.C.B. 7 Apr. 1815. D.C.L. Oxon. 12 June 1823.

Refs. : Burke's *Landed Gentry of Ireland,* p. 78, *s.n.* Browne, of

THE BENGAL ARMY, 1758-1834 231

Riverstown, co. Cork. *G.M.* 1828, i. 94. *Alumni Oxon.* Will dated 6 Aug. 1821; codicil dated Brussels 15 Dec. 1827; proved 5 Jan. 1830. Portrait, by Hobday, of Bristol, sometime in the possession of his dau., Mrs. Amelia St. George Dyer.

BROWNE, George Sackville Henry (1813-1886). Lieutenant. 70th N.I. *b.* Rincurran, co. Cork, 18 Sept. 1813. Cadet 1831. Arrived in India 27 Oct. 1832. Ensign (8 Dec. 1831) 19 May 1833. Lieut. 8 Oct. 1839. Retired 17 Aug. 1840. *d.* 23 Jan. 1886.
Son of Lt. Col. Arthur Browne and Dorothea Anne his wife. Brother of Marmaduke Williamson Browne, *q.v.* Addiscombe Cadet 1830-1.
Services : Ensign d.d. 64th N.I. 22 Nov. 1832. Posted as Ensign to 14th N.I. 19 Dec. 1833. Transfd. to 70th N.I. 10 Oct. 1837. Fur. s.c. 17 Feb. 1838 till retirement. No record of active service.
Refs. : Burke's *Landed Gentry*, 7th edn., p. 233, *s.n.* Browne, of Riverstown, co. Cork.

BROWNE, Henry (1798-1881). Lieutenant. 44th N.I. *b.* Galway June 1798. Cadet 1817. Ensign (?). Lieut. 27 Nov. 1819. Retired 16 Jan. 1823. *d.* 9 Oct. 1881.
Son of Domn. (? Dominic) Browne.
Services : Posted as Lieut. to 2/22nd N.I. in 1820. Mily. student at Coll. of Fort William in 1821. Fur. 1822 till retirement. Transfd. to 44th N.I. (late 2/22nd) May 1824, before his retirement had been notified in India.

BROWNE, Henry Cumming Ayscough (1801-1818). Ensign, Infantry. Unposted. *b.* Burlescombe, Devon, 15 Mar. 1801. Cadet 1817. Ensign (?). *d.* Calcutta 4 Oct. 1818.
Son of Major Thomas Browne, of Canonsleigh House, Devon.
Services : N.F.P.
Refs. : M.I. in S. Park St. burial ground, Calcutta. Lyson's *Devonshire* (vol. vi.), p. 91.

BROWNE, James (1743/44-1792). Lieut. Colonel, Infantry. *b.* 1743/44. Cadet 1765. Ensign 10 Nov. 1765. Lieut. 2 May 1767. Capt. 30 June 1771. Major 19 Jan. 1781. Lt. Col. 2 Feb. 1788. *d.* Dinapore 22 June 1792, aged 58.
m. Calcutta, 16 Dec. 1789, Miss Catherine Charlotte Raper. (She *re-m.* Charles Fraser, *q.v.*). Father of James Edward Browne, *q.v.*
Services : Collector of the Jungleterry district (Santhal Parganas) in 1773. To comd. 14th Bn. Sepoys (formerly 24th) from 1777.

Sent on an embassy to Shah Alam at Delhi. Apptd. Agent and Minister at the court of Delhi 20 Aug. 1782 (Cons. of 3 Mar. 1783). Recalled in 1785 when Warren Hastings left for England. Pub. in 1787 *Indian Tracts.*
Refs. : Forrest, iii. *passim. D.I.B. Williams,* p. 70.

BROWNE, James Edward (1790-1813). Cornet, 6th N.C. *bapt.* Calcutta 16 Dec. 1790. Cadet 1807. Arrived in India 14 Sept. 1808. Cornet 18 Sept. 1808. *d.* Sultanpur, Benares, 27 Sept. 1813.

Son of James Browne, *q.v.,* and Catherine Charlotte his wife. Half-brother of William Fraser (1800-1825), *q.v.*
Services : Posted as Cornet to 6th N.C. Qmr. 6th N.C. 1813 till death. No record of active service.

BROWNE, James Rolfe (1803-1825). Lieutenant, 27th N.I. *b.* Canterbury 23 Dec. 1803. Cadet 1819. Ensign 10 Jan. 1820. Lieut. 3 June 1822. *d.* Barrackpore 22 Sept. 1825.

Son of Alderman Browne.
Services : Posted as Ensign to 2/13th N.I. Transfd. to 26th N.I. (late 1/13th) May 1824. First Burma War ; Arakan 1825 ; Lieut. 26th N.I. Transfd. to 27th N.I. in 1825.

BROWNE, John (*d.* 1790). Lieutenant, Infantry. Cadet 1781. Ensign 1781. Lieut. 18 Sept. 1782. *d.* Bencoolen 15 Apr. 1790.
Services : N.F.P.

BROWNE, John Swinton (1806-1834). Captain, 66th N.I. *b.* Monghyr, Bengal, 30 Aug. 1806. Cadet 1822. Arrived in India 25 Oct. 1823. Ensign 11 July 1823. Lieut. 13 May 1825. Capt. 23 July 1832. *d.* Kyaukpyu, Arakan, 5 Apr. 1834, of a bilious fever.

bapt. Monghyr 28 Dec. 1806. Son of Surgeon John Brown and Charlotte his wife. Brother of Clement Read Browne, *q.v.*
Services : Posted to 66th N.I. Magh Sebundy Corps 7 Jan. 1832. Junior Asst. in Arakan 25 Sept. 1832. No record of active service.
Refs. : A.J. N.S. xvi. 66. M.I. at Kyaukpyu.

BROWNE, Marmaduke Williamson (1776-1833). Colonel, Artillery. *bapt.* Kilnagross, co. Cork, 19 Jan. 1776. Cadet 1790. Admitted 31 Aug. 1790. Fireworker 17 June 1792. Lieut. 21 Feb. 1801. Capt. Lt. 21 Sept. 1804. Capt. 14 Feb. 1808. Major 1 Sept. 1818. Lt. Col. 7 Aug. 1821. Lt. Col. Comdt. 28 Sept. 1827. Col. 5 June 1829. *d.* Taplow, Bucks., 31 June 1833.

Son of Lt. Col. Arthur Browne, 58th Foot, of Knockduffe House, Kinsale. Brother of Sir Thomas Brown, K.C.B., *q.v.,* of Adderley

THE BENGAL ARMY, 1758-1834

Thomas Browne, *q.v.*, of Andalusia, mother of Arthur Alexander, tenth Earl of Carnwath, *q.v.*, and of Margaret, whose daus. *m.* Hon. Harry Burrard Dalzell, *q.v.*, and Richard Horsford, *q.v. m.* 1st, Calcutta, 14 Mar. 1806, Miss Maria Bellett Roberts. (She died Easterland House, nr. Wellington, Somerset, 15 Feb. 1828.) *m.* 2nd, Trinity church, Marylebone, 23 Sept. 1830, Charlotte Mary, widow of Henry Droz, B.C.S.

Services : Second Mahratta War ; Aligarh ; Delhi ; Agra ; battle of Deig ; sieges of Deig and Bhurtpore ; Qmr. to the Art. Bde. Major of Art. Mar. 1806 till Jan. 1809. Dy. Comy. Ord. Jan. 1809. Principal do. 19 May 1818. Comy. of Ord. 1 Nov. 1821. One of the Agents for Army Clothing Nov. 1809 till Jan. 1822. Fur. Jan. 1822 till 1826. Fur. s.c. 12 Jan. 1827 till death.

Refs. : E.I.M.C. i. 168. *G.M.* 1833, ii. 271. *A.J.* N.S. iii. 120.

BROWNE, Richard Veale (1773-1807). Capt. Lieutenant, 7th N.I. *b.* London 29 Oct. 1773. Cadet 1794. Arrived in India 26 Feb. 1796. Ensign 3 Dec. 1795. Lieut. 30 Oct. 1797. Capt. Lt. 20 July 1805. *d.* Kishenganj, Bengal, 20 Oct. 1807.

bapt. All Hallows, Mark Lane, London, 20 Dec. 1773. Son of Francis Browne and Hannah Myles his wife.

Services : Lieut. 7th N.I. Served in 2nd Vol. Bn. 1804-5. (? Second Mahratta War.)

BROWNE, Samuel (1807-1852). Major, 66th or Gurkha Regt. *b.* London 9 Oct. 1807. Cadet 1825. Arrived in India 2 Feb. 1826. Ensign 10 Sept. 1825. Lieut. 27 May 1828. Capt. 15 Nov. 1837. Major 13 Aug. 1850. *d.* in camp at Abazai, nr. Peshawar, 10 May 1852, of sunstroke.

Son of George Henry Browne, of Winchmore Hill, London. *m.* 1st, Cawnpore, 3 Sept. 1839, Mary Ann, dau. of Thomas Dundas, *q.v.* (She died at sea, 10 Feb. 1848, aged 27.) *m.* 2nd, Edmonton, 17 Oct. 1849, Sarah Eleanor, eldest dau. of James Benton, of London, solicitor.

Services : Posted as Ensign to 66th N.I. Fur. s.c. 31 Jan. 1848 till 1850. 66th N.I. having been disbanded for mutiny in Feb. 1850, he was posted in Mar. 1850 to the newly-numbered 66th (or Gurkha) Regt. This Regt., originally designated the 1st Nasiri Bn., now (1926) forms part of the 1st King George's Own Gurkha Rifles. Served with the force under Sir Colin Campbell against the Utman Khel May 1852 ; Major 66th or Gurkha Regt.

Refs. : G.M. 1852, ii. 321.

CAVE-BROWNE, Edward (1779-1841). Lieut. Colonel. 44th N.I. *b.* 15 Nov. 1779. Cadet 1800. Arrived in India 24 Aug. 1801. Ensign 24 Dec. 1801. Lieut. 5 Mar. 1804. Capt. 16 June 1816.

Major 1 May 1824. Lt. Col. 1 Apr. 1828. Retired 27 May 1828. *d.* Taunton 26 July 1841.

bapt. Stretton-en-le-Field, co. Derby, 27 Dec. 1779. 5th and youngest son of John Cave (who took the name of Browne, by act of parliament, in 1752) and Catherine his 2nd wife, dau. of Thomas Asteley, of Wood Eaton, Staffs. Brother of Sir William Cave-Browne-Cave, 9th Bart., of Stanford, and uncle of Rev. Wilmot Cave-Browne-Cave, *q.v. m.* Agra, 8 Oct. 1815, Anne, dau. of Thomas Raban, of Calcutta, attorney, and sister of Richard Raban, *q.v.* (She died 11 July 1876, aged 82.)

Services : Ensign 5th N.I. Transfd. as Lieut. to 22nd N.I. in 1804. Settlement of Hariana 1809 ; Bhawani ; Lieut. 1/22nd N.I. Adjt. 1/22nd N.I. 17 Mar. 1810 till 1816. Reduction of Kalinjar 1812. Third Mahratta War 1817-8 ; Nagpur ; Capt. 1/22nd N.I. Tried by G.C.M. at Hoshangabad, 25 July 1818, on a charge of having during the night of 12/13 May 1818 suffered the escape of Appa Sahib, the ex-Rajah of Nagpur, a State prisoner, expressly and particularly committed to his charge. He was found Not Guilty, and honourably acquitted. In charge of the Inf. Levy at Cawnpore 1822-3. Transfd. as Major to 44th N.I. (late 2/22nd) May 1824. (? First Burma War ; Cachar 1825 ; Major 44th N.I.) Fur. 1826 till retirement.

Refs. : Burke's *Peerage*, 1923, p. 471, *s.n.* Cave-Browne-Cave, Bart. Howard & Crisp, ix. 21.

BROWNLOW, George Arthur (1805-1869). Lieut. Colonel. 3rd L.C. *b.* 16 July 1805. Cadet (Inf.) 11 Feb. 1825. Arrived in India 5 Sept. 1825. Transfd. to Cav. 23 July 1825. Cornet 13 Mar. 1826. Lieut. 4 June 1826. Capt. 30 Oct. 1848. Bt. Major 11 Nov. 1851. Retired 31 Dec. 1851. Hon. Lt. Col. 28 Nov. 1854. *d.* Upper Norwood 8 May 1869.

bapt. Walcot, Somerset, 14 Aug. 1805. 5th son of Lt. Col. Charles Brownlow, of Lurgan, and Caroline his wife, dau. of Benjamin Ashe, of Bath. Younger brother of the Rt. Hon. Charles Brownlow, first Baron Lurgan, and cousin-german of William Brownlow, *q.v. m.* Cawnpore, 12 Apr. 1828, Cornelia Paulina Henrietta, youngest dau. of Thomas Sandby (*D.N.B.*), of Great Lodge, Old Windsor, and sister of George Taylor Seton Sandby, *q.v.* (*See also* William Joseph Loder.) (She died London, 31 Aug. 1893, aged 83.)

Services : Posted as Ensign to 41st N.I. Siege and capture of Bhurtpore ; Ensign 41st N.I. (India medal). Transfd. as Cornet to 3rd L.C. 1 Apr. 1826. D.A.A.G., Benares Div., 14 Feb. 1835. Operations against the Kols 1832. First Afghan War ; Ghazni ; Lieut. 3rd L.C. (Medal). A.A.G., Saugor, 10 Feb. 1840. Fur. p.a.

8 Feb. 1841 till 11 Oct. 1842. Bde. Major at Ferozepore 10 Apr. 1843. First Sikh War; Aliwal; Sobraon; Bt. Capt. 3rd L.C. (Medal with clasp).
Refs.: Burke's *Peerage*, 1923, p. 1454, *s.n.* Lurgan, B. *The Times*, 12 May 1869.

BROWNLOW, William (1802-1881). Captain. 46th N.I. *bapt.* Dublin 22 Aug. 1802. Cadet 1821. Arrived in India 24 Nov. 1822. Ensign 13 Sept. 1822. Lieut. 12 Aug. 1824. Capt. 29 Aug. 1833. Retired 26 May 1835. *d.* Bagot St., Dublin, 18 July 1881.

Of Knapton House, Queen's Co. J.P. Queen's Co.; D.L. co. Monaghan. Eldest son of Rev. Francis Brownlow and Lady Katherine his wife, 6th dau. of Anthony, eighth Earl of Meath. Cousin-german of George Arthur Brownlow, *q.v. m.* 1835, Charlotte, dau. of William Browne, of Brown's Hill, co. Carlow. Ed. Harrow 1817 till 1820/21.

Services: Posted as Ensign to 17th N.I. Transfd. to 2/23rd N.I.; to 46th N.I. (late 2/23rd) May 1824. First Burma War; operations in Sylhet, Cachar, and Assam; Lieut. 46th N.I. (India medal). A.D.C. to G.G. 1 July 1826. S.A.C.G. 7 Mar. 1828. Fur. p.a. 21 Jan. 1833 till retirement.

Refs.: Foster's *Peerage*, p. 432, *s.n.* Lurgan, B. *Harrow School List. The Times*, 20 July 1881.

BROWNRIGG, John Studholme (1786-1853). Captain. 8th N.I. Subsequently M.P. for Boston. *b.* London 17 Mar. 1786. Cadet 1800. Arrived in India 24 Aug. 1801. Ensign 17 Nov. 1801. Lieut. 30 Sept. 1803. Capt. 1 Feb. 1815. Resigned in India 30 Apr. 1820. *d.* Ashford Lodge, Middlesex, 21 Sept. 1853.

bapt. St. George's chapel, Windsor Castle, 27 May 1786. 3rd and youngest son of John Studholme Brownrigg, Lieut. 38th Foot, and Lydia Eames his wife, of Boston, Mass. Nephew of Gen. Sir Robert Brownrigg, 1st Bart. (*D.N.B.*). *m.* Calcutta, 11 Dec. 1812, Elizabeth Rebecca, eldest dau. of James Henry Casamaijor, M.C.S. (She died 6 July 1865.)

Services: Lieut. 12th N.I. Second Mahratta War; Laswari; Lieut. 12 N.I. (India medal). Transfd. to 8th N.I. Adjt. & Qmr. 8th N.I. 1805 till 12 Mar. 1810. A.C.G. 1810. Capture of Java; Capt. 2/8th N.I., Dy.C.G. (Medal). Sec. Mily. Board 14 Feb. 1813 till resignation. He subsequently became a merchant in London. M.P. for Boston 9 Jan. 1835 till 23 July 1847.

Refs.: Foster's *Baronetage*, p. 79. Burke's *Peerage*, 1923. p. 366, *s.n.* Brownrigg, Bart. *Boase. G.M.* 1853, ii. 539. Will dated 6 Aug. 1847; proved 28 June 1854.

BROWNRIGG, Robert Shaw (1790-1831). Captain. 14th N.I. *bapt.* Dublin 3 Apr. 1790. Cadet 1808. Admitted 25 Sept. 1809. Ensign 8 Dec. 1810. Lieut. 1 Oct. 1815. Capt. 5 Oct. 1825. Retired 27 Sept. 1828. *d.* in Ireland 17 Dec. 1831.

Son of Richard Fleetwood Brownrig(g). *m.* 1st, 12 Mar. 1818. Miss Emilie M. A. Bidard. *m.* 2nd, Port Louis, Mauritius, 7 Jan. 1824, Miss Blanche Coralie de Cere.

Services : Ensign 15th N.I. Transfd. to 1/10th N.I. in 1811. Intr. & Qmr. 1/10th N.I. 9 Jan. 1816. D.A.Q.M.G., 3 cl., 1816 ; do., 2 cl., 1818. S.A.C.G. 1819. Leave to Mauritius 1822-4. Transfd. to 14th N.I. (late 1/10th) May 1824. Dy.A.C.G. 1825. Fur. 1826 till retirement.

BRUCE, David (1786-1843). Major. 26th N.I. *b.* Inveresk, Midlothian, 23 Sept. 1786. Cadet 1805. Arrived in India 11 July 1806. Ensign 29 Aug. 1806. Lieut. 9 Sept. 1808. Capt. 1 May 1824. Major 23 Apr. 1834. Retired in India 1 Jan. 1837. *d.* Arndean House, co. Perth, 6 May 1843.

Son of Alexander Bruce, of Musselburgh, surgeon. *m.* Takli, nr. Nagpur, 29 July 1824, Margaret, dau. of Rev. Dr. Duncan, minister of Ratho. (She died Delhi 23 July 1833.)

Services : Posted as Ensign to 1/13th N.I. Actg. S.A.C.G. 22 May 1813. Nepal War. S.A.C.G. 19 Jan. 1816. Third Mahratta War ; Lieut. 1/13th N.I., S.A.C.G., 5th Div. A.C.G., Nagpur Subsidiary Force, 1821. Transfd. as Capt. to 26th N.I. (late 1/13th) May 1824. First Burma War ; Arakan 1825 ; Capt. 1st L.I. Bn. Siege and capture of Bhurtpore ; Capt. 26th N.I., A.C.G. Comdt. Delhi Palace Guards 1 Nov. 1831 till 17 Oct. 1834.

Refs. : *G.M.* 1843, i. 671.

BRUCE, Henry (*d.* 1784). Captain, 35th N.I. Cadet 1770. Ensign 5 Dec. 1772. Lieut. 18 Aug. 1776. Capt. 7 Mar. 1781. *d. unm.* Cawnpore 8 Aug. 1784 ; bur. the same day.

Elder son of William Bruce, of Cowden, co. Perth, and Janet his wife, only dau. of Henry Bruce, of Clackmannan. Brother of William Bruce (*d.* 1807), *q.v.*

Services : N.F.P.

Refs. : Burke's *Commoners*, iv. 619, *s.n.* Bruce, of Clackmannan and Cowden, co. Perth. *G.M.* 1785, i. 403. *S.M.* 1785, p. 257.

BRUCE, Joseph (1741/42-1778). Captain, Infantry. *b.* Clapham, Surrey, 1741/42. Cadet 1764. Ensign 23 Feb. 1765. Lieut. (?). Capt. 15 Nov. 1769. *d.* Moradabad, U.P., 9 Oct. 1778.

Services : Sailed for India on the *Vansittart*, 4 Feb. 1764, aged 22.

N.F.P. Not in the Army List of 1 Feb. 1767. (? *Probably* resigned during the Batta mutiny of May 1766, being subsequently readmitted.)

BRUCE, Louis (1791-1845). Lieut. Colonel, 12th N.I. *b.* London 19 Nov. 1791. Cadet 1807. Arrived in India 16 Nov. 1808. Ensign 30 Nov. 1808. Lieut. 17 Aug. 1814. Capt. 1 May 1824. Major 21 Jan. 1837. Lt. Col. 10 Apr. 1843. *d.* Ferozepore, 31 Dec. 1845, from the effects of a wound received at the battle of Ferozshahr on 21 Dec.

Son of Basil Bruce. *m.* Agra, 19 July 1819, Miss Elizabeth Scott. (She died Brighton 4 Mar. 1851.)

Services : Barasat C.C. from Nov. 1808 till Nov. 1809. Posted as Ensign to 2/12th N.I. 1 Aug. 1809. Nepal War 1814-5 ; Lieut. 2/12th N.I., in 3rd Div. Nepal War 1816 ; Makwanpur ; Lieut. 2/12th N.I., in 3rd Bde., Centre Column. Siege and capture of Hathras. Third Mahratta War ; Lieut. 2/12th N.I., in Right Div. Against the Bhattis of Hariana 1818. Adjt. 2/12th N.I. 17 Aug. 1820 till June 1824. Transfd. to 12th N.I. (late 1/12th) May 1824. First Burma War ; Arakan 1825 ; Capt. 1st L.I. Bn. Fur. s.c. 29 Apr. 1839 till 10 Sept. 1840. Apptd. to comd. 1st L.I. Bn. 12 Oct. 1840. With Army of Reserve for Afghanistan at Ferozepore Oct. 1842 till Jan. 1843. Reposted as Lt. Col. to 12th N.I. 16 Aug. 1843. First Sikh War ; Ferozshahr (s.w.—arm amputated); Lt. Col. comdg. 12th N.I.

Refs. : De Rhé-Philipe. M.I. in St. Paul's Cathedral, Calcutta.

BRUCE, Michael (*d.* 1770). Lieutenant, Infantry. Cadet (?). Ensign (?). Lieut. 5 Sept. 1768. *d.* Patna 6 May 1770.
Services : N.F.P.

BRUCE, Robert (1753/54-1796). Lieut. Colonel, Artillery. *b.* 1753/54. Country Cadet 1770. Admitted 21 Aug. 1770. Fireworker 15 Mar. 1771. Lieut. 28 Oct. 1773. Capt. Lt. 17 Sept. 1779. Capt. 16 Apr. 1781. Major 31 May 1786. Lt. Col. 20 Aug. 1794. *d.* Dinapore, 4 Nov. 1796, aged 42.

Of the ancient family of Bruce of Earlshall. Brother of John Bruce, historiographer to the E.I.C. (*D.N.B.*), and of Margaret Stuart. (? *Possibly* related to Robert Bruce (*d.* 1814), *q.v.*, who was exor. of his Will.)

Services : Operations against the Bhutias in Cooch Behar 1772-3 ; storm and capture of Dhalimkot ; Lieut. comdg. detachment of Art. Dy. Comy. Ord. at Fort William in 1776. First Mahratta War 1778-81 ; joined Popham's detachment in 1781. Campaign against the Rajah of Benares 1781 ; Bijaigarh ; Capt. Lt. comdg.

LIST OF THE OFFICERS OF

the Art. Fur. 8 Jan. 1785 till 15 Aug. 1791. Second Rohilla War; Bitaurah; Lt. Col. 3rd Bn. Art., comdg. the Art.
Refs.: *G.M.* 1797, ii. 615. *S.M.* 1797, p. 431. *John Company*, by Sir William Foster, C.I.E., p. 239. Will dated Cawnpore 3 Aug. 1796.

BRUCE, Robert (*d.* 1814). Lieut. General. Colonel 16th N.I. Cadet 1771. Admitted 26 Sept. 1771. Ensign 2 Jan. 1773. Lieut. 28 Mar. 1777. Capt. 25 Mar. 1781. Major 14 Sept. 1796. Lt. Col. 1 Feb. 1799. Col. 2 Nov. 1803. Maj. Gen. 25 July 1810. Lt. Gen. 4 June 1814. *d.* Elstree, Herts., 21 Sept. 1814.

Brother of Helen Bruce, and of Isobel, wife of James Cockburn, of the Linen Hall, Edinburgh. *m.* (*c.*) 20 July 1805, Miss Charlotte Elizabeth Segar.

Services: Sec. and Persian Intr. to Col. G. B. Eyres, *q.v.*, in 1790. Second Rohilla War; Bitaurah; A.D.C. to Col. George Burrington, *q.v.* (s.w.). Comdd. in 1799 the Corps of Hindustani Cav. known as "Bruce's Independent Regt. of Cav.," employed in the suppression of disturbances created by Wazir Ali. Fur. 8 Mar. 1803 till death.

Refs.: *Hickey*, iv. 122. *G.M.* 1814, ii. 402. *A.A.R.* i. 164. Will dated 22 Dec. 1813; proved 2 Nov. 1827.

Note: "Orders by Major General Stuart, 4th April, 1799. Major General Stuart has much pleasure in expressing his approbation of the expert gallantry of the officers and men of the independent regiment of cavalry, who were engaged with the enemy yesterday evening, and requests that Lieut. Colonel Bruce will give them his thanks."

BRUCE, Robert (Robertson) (1789-1819). Lieutenant, 1st N.I. *b.* Edinburgh 19 May 1789. Cadet 1807. Arrived in India 25 Oct. 1808. Ensign 9 Nov. 1808. Lieut. 10 June 1814. *d.* Mirzapur, U.P., 25 Dec. 1819, after a few hours' illness.

Son of Daniel Bruce. *m.* Catherine Barron, dau. of William Spottiswoode, of Glenfernate, co. Perth. (She *re-m.* Henry Lechmere Worrall, *q.v.*).

Services: Posted as Ensign to 1st N.I. Lieut. 1/1st N.I. Adjt. 1st Gren. Bn. in 1815. Fur. 1817. No record of active service.

Refs.: Burke's *Visitation of Seats and Arms*, 2S. i. 18. *S.M.* 1820, i. 584.

BRUCE, Thomas. Ensign. Infantry. Cadet (?). Ensign 17 Sept. 1765. Resigned 1766.

Services: N.F.P. (? *Probably* resigned in May 1766 during the Batta mutiny.)

BRUCE, William (d. 1783). Major, Infantry. Cadet 1767. Ensign 16 Sept. 1767. Lieut. 14 Apr. 1769. Capt. 6 Apr. 1777. Major 7 May 1781. d. Calcutta 1 May 1783.

Son of David Bruce, of Kinnaird, co. Stirling, and Marion his wife, dau. of James Graham, of Airth. Brother of James Bruce, of Kinnaird, the African explorer (D.N.B.).

Services : First Mahratta War ; capture of Gwalior 1780 ; Capt. comdg. 4th Bn., led the storming party.

Refs. : Burke's *Landed Gentry,* 5th edn., p. 163, *s.n.* Bruce, of Kinnaird, co. Stirling. *Mundy,* ii. 72.

BRUCE, William (d. 1807). Lieutenant. Artillery. Cadet 1778. Fireworker 31 Oct. 1778. Lieut. 29 Jan. 1784. Struck off 1793. d. 22 Jan. 1807.

Of Cowden, co. Perth. Younger son of William Bruce, of Cowden, and Janet his wife. Brother of Henry Bruce, *q.v.* m. Margaret, eldest dau. of Dr. Robert Oliver.

Services : Second Mysore War ; Lieut. F. 5th Coy. 2nd Bn. Art. On fur. in 1790.

Refs. : Burke's *Commoners,* iv. 619, *s.n.* Bruce, of Clackmannan and Cowden, co. Perth.

*BRUCE, ——. Ensign, Bengal European Regt. Cadet (?). Ensign Jan. 1758. Dismissed by C.M. Apr. 1759.

Services : Siege and assault of Masulipatam 8 Apr. 1759 ; Ensign Bengal Eur. Regt. Was apptd. one of four Prize Agents after the capture of that place. He was tried by C.M. the same month on a charge of receiving bribes from some native merchants to whom part of their effects had been restored, was found guilty, and sentenced to dismissal.

Refs. : Orme *MSS., India* xiii. 3639. *Forde,* p. 198.

BRUERE, Charles Fleeming (1812-1857). Major, 13th N.I. *b.* Bedfont, Middlesex, 7 Nov. 1812. Cadet 1828. Arrived in India 6 Oct. 1829. Ensign 5 June 1829. Lieut. 9 June 1838. Capt. 22 July 1846. Major 10 Mar. 1855. d. Lucknow 4 Sept. 1857 : kld. in action.

Son of James Bruere, of Bedfont (of Stanwell), Capt. in the army (*probably* James Bruere, *q.v.*), and Mary his wife. Brother of John Elphinstone Bruere, *q.v.* m. Fatehgarh, 5 July 1847, Jane Lucy Holt, dau. of John Holt White, *q.v.*

Services : Posted as Ensign to 13th N.I. 2 Aug. 1832. Fur. s.c. 30 Jan. 1831 till 19 Nov. 1833. Adjt. 13th N.I. 29 May 1839 till 3 Dec. 1841. Second Sikh War ; passage of Chenab ; Gujerat ; Capt. 13th N.I. (Medal). Indian Mutiny ; defence of Lucknow (kld.).

LIST OF THE OFFICERS OF

BRUERE, James. Ensign. Infantry. (? Subsequently Captain 3rd Dns.) Cadet 1782. Ensign (?). Resigned 15 Feb. 1783.
N.B.—The following is conjectural only : (? Of Bedfont and Stanwell, Middlesex. *m.* Mary. Father of Charles Fleeming Bruere, *q.v.*, and of John Elphinstone Bruere, *q.v.*).
Services : (? Lieut. 60th (or R. American) Regt. of Foot 6 Apr. 1785. Capt. 3rd Dragoons in 1801.)

BRUERE, John Elphinstone (1801-1842). Captain, 13th N.I. *b.* Edinburgh 13 Mar. 1801. Cadet 1817. Admitted 10 Oct. 1818. Ensign 15 Sept. 1818. Lieut. 1 Aug. 1818. Capt. 13 Aug. 1835. *d.* Nasirabad, Rajputana, 6 Sept. 1842, of liver disease.
Son of James Bruere, of Bedfont, and Mary his wife. Brother of Charles Fleeming Bruere, *q.v. m.* Dinapore, 15 Dec. 1828, Mary Harriet, eldest dau. of Maj. Gen. Sir Robert Henry Sale, G.C.B. (*D.N.B.*). (*See also* Frederick Brind.)
Services : Posted as Lieut. to 7th N.I. Transfd. to 13th N.I. (late 1/7th) May 1824. Intr. & Qmr. 13th N.I. 1 Sept. 1826 ; Adjt. do. 22 Oct. 1827. Fort Adjt. at Monghyr 1 June 1829. Bde. Major, Rajputana F.F., 6 Oct. 1838. Comdt. Kotah Contingent 22 July 1840.
Refs. : G.M. 1843, i. 111. *The Times*, 12 Nov. 1842. Will dated Ajmere 20 May 1838 ; proved 13 Dec. 1842.

BRYANT, Edward Pinckard (1809-1893). Lieut. Colonel. 68th N.I. *b.* London 4 Apr. 1809. Cadet 1825. Arrived in India 10 Mar. 1826. Ensign 25 Sept. 1825. Lieut. 17 Nov. 1827. Capt. 27 Jan. 1844. Bt. Major 11 Nov. 1851. Invalided 21 Nov. 1851. Retired 7 Jan. 1859. Hon. Lt. Col. 7 Jan. 1859. *d.* 59 West Hill, St. Leonards-on-Sea, 9 Oct. 1893.
bapt. 25 Dec. 1810. Son of Edward Bryant, surgeon, of South Bank, Regent's Pl., London. *m.* Mhow, 20 May 1835, Miss Sarah Anne Johnson. (She died 19 Feb. 1886, aged 74.) Ed. Merchant Taylors' ; entered in Dec. 1819.
Services : Posted as Ensign to 49th N.I. in 1826. Transfd. to 68th N.I. 4 May 1832. Adjt. 68th N.I. 10 Aug. 1836. Fur. p.a. 6 July 1838 till 22 Nov. 1839. First Sikh War ; Sobraon ; Capt. 68th N.I. (Medal).
Refs. : Robinson. The Times, 10 Oct. 1893.

BRYANT, George (1792-1882). Captain. 55th N.I. *b.* Westminster 3 Mar. 1792. Cadet 1806. Arrived in India 25 Nov. 1807. Ensign 7 Nov. 1807. Lieut. 29 Nov. 1810. Capt. 1 May 1824. Invalided 23 May 1828. Retired 19 Aug. 1831. *d.* 8 Mar. 1882.

THE BENGAL ARMY, 1758-1834   241

Son of William Bryant.
Services : Posted as Ensign to 13th N.I. 6th Vol. Bn. 1811-6.
Capture of Java 1811 (Medal). Transfd. to newly-raised 2/28th
N.I. in 1815. Second Mahratta War ; Dhamoni ; Lieut. 2/28th
N.I. Transfd. to 55th N.I. (late 1/28th) May 1824. Fur. s.c. 9 Jan.
1829 till retirement.

BRYANT, Sir Jeremiah (1783-1845). Major General, Kt., C.B.
Colonel 1st European L.I. *bapt.* Biggleswade, Beds., 14 June
1783. Cadet 1798. Arrived in India 7 Jan. 1800. Ensign
18 Dec. 1799. Lieut. 29 May 1800. Capt. 22 Jan. 1812. Major
11 July 1823. Lt. Col. 13 May 1825. Col. 27 June 1835. Maj.
Gen. 3 Nov. 1841. *d.* Grove Lodge, Richmond, 10 June 1845.
Son of Edward Bryant and Susannah his wife. *m.* in England,
2 Jan. 1823, Mary Anna, dau. of Henry Churchill, of Gloucester Pl.,
Portman Sq., London. (*See also* John Craigie (1786-1840).)
Services : Posted as Ensign to 1st Bengal Eur. Regt. 15 Apr.
1801. Served in Oudh. Second Mahratta War ; Bundelkhand
1803, with force under Lt. Col. Powell ; battle of Deig 13 Nov. 1804
(w.—lost right arm). Bde. Major at Calcutta 22 Jan. 1807 till 1815.
Town and Fort Major, Fort William, 1815. Asst. Sec., Mily. Board
1816. J.A.G. 24 Jan. 1817 till 14 Sept. 1835. Third Mahratta
War ; J.A.G. of Grand Army. Deputed to England on duty
1822-4. Transfd. as Major to 65th N.I. in 1824. Siege and capture
of Bhurtpore ; Lt. Col. 65th N.I., J.A.G. Leave s.c. 6 mos. to
Singapore 8 Aug. 1828. Transfd. to 19th N.I. ; to 14th N.I. ; to
1st Bengal Eur. L.I. Fur. 7 Feb. 1835 till death. Kt. 16 Sept. 1829.
C.B. 20 July 1838. Elected a Director of E.I.Co. 26 Feb. 1841.
Refs. : D.I.B. G.M. 1823, i. 82 ; 1845, ii. 533. *I.M.* 1845,
p. 361. Will proved 14 May 1847.

BRYCE, David (1790-1828). Lieutenant. 6th N.I. Subsequently a
merchant in Calcutta. *b.* Jamaica 11 Nov. 1790. Cadet 1808.
Arrived in India 15 Dec. 1809. Ensign 13 Aug. 1811. Lieut.
28 Nov. 1814. Resigned in India 2 Mar. 1822. *d.* at sea, 18 July
1828, on board the *Thomas Grenville,* on his passage from Bengal.
Son of David Bryce, of Jamaica, and Janet his wife. *m.* Calcutta,
4 Apr. 1811, Johanna, dau. of John Long, Col. Royal Marines.
Services : Posted as Ensign to 6th N.I. Asst. Professor of
Persian at Coll. of Fort William 1814 till Feb. 1815. Nepal War
1815 ; Lieut. 2/6th N.I., in 1st Div. Intr. & Qmr. 2/6th N.I.
13 July 1815. Asst. Professor at Coll. of Fort William 7 Aug. 1818
till resignation. Joined the firm of Cruttenden, McKillop & Co.,
merchants in Calcutta.
Refs. : A.J. xxvi. 389.

H.B.A.   Q

BUCHAN, Alexander (d. 1792). Fireworker, Artillery. Cadet 1783. Fireworker 11 May 1785. d. 7 Feb. 1792 : kld. in action at Sibbald's redoubt in the attack on Seringapatam.

9th and youngest son of John Buchan, of Letham, co. Haddington, and Anne his 2nd wife, sister of George Broun, of Coalston, co. Haddington, a lord of session. Half-brother of Sir George Buchan, 1st Bart.

Services : Third Mysore War ; Bangalore ; Seringapatam (kld.) ; Lieut. F. 1st Coy. 2nd Bn. Art.

Refs. : Foster's *Baronetage*, p. 83, *s.n.* Buchan-Hepburn, Bart., of Smeaton Hepburn, co. Haddington. Name on cenotaph erected by the Mysore Govt. in Bangalore fort.

BUCHANAN, James (1752-?). Major. Infantry. b. 1752. Cadet 1767. Ensign 14 Jan. 1767. Lieut. 29 Sept. 1769. Capt. 1 Jan. 1778. Major 19 Sept. 1781. Struck off 1791.

Younger son of James Buchanan, Lieut. 18th Foot, and Catherine his wife, dau. of Philip Henzell. Brother of William Buchanan, *q.v.* m. Jan. 1793, Honor, dau. of James Grant. Uncle of Archibald Armstrong, *q.v.*

Services : On fur. in 1790. N.F.P.

Refs. : Burke's *Commoners*, iv. 340, *s.n.* Armstrong, of Gallen, King's Co.

BUCHANAN, Robert Hamilton (1785-1816). Captain, 24th N.I. b. London 20 Mar. 1785. Cadet 1799. Arrived in India 7 Jan. 1801. Ensign 30 Aug. 1800. Lieut. 10 Apr. 1801. Capt. 16 Dec. 1814. d. unm. Ghazipur 10 May 1816.

bapt. St. Clement Danes, London, 20 June 1786. Son of Robert Hamilton Buchanan, Lieut. Royal North British Fus., and Cornelia his wife, dau. of Commodore Tinker. Nephew of Francis Hamilton Buchanan (*D.N.B.*).

Services : Posted as Lieut. to 2nd Bengal Eur. Regt. 17 Apr. 1801. Marine Regt. (became 20th N.I.) in 1803. P.W.I. in 1804-5. Transfd. to newly-raised 24th N.I. in 1805. Adjt. & Qmr. 24th N.I. 5 Feb. 1810 till 1813. Capt. 2/24th N.I. 2nd Gren Bn. in 1816.

Refs. : Burke's *Landed Gentry*, 13th edn., p. 230, *s.n.* Hamilton-Buchanan, of Spittal and Leny, co. Dumbarton. Will dated 27 Aug. 1812 ; proved in 1816.

BUCHANAN, Walter (1789-1822). Lieutenant, 4th L.C. b. Harmondsworth, Middlesex, 14 Nov. 1789. Cadet 1808. Arrived in India 21 Oct. 1809. Cornet 7 Dec. 1812. Lieut. 1 Sept. 1818. d. at sea 20 Feb. 1822, on board the *Partridge*, on his passage to England.

Son of Robert Buchanan and Mary his wife.
Services : Cadet d.d. 21st N.I. 1811-13. Posted as Cornet to 5th N.C. in 1813. Fur. 1813. Leave to Cape in 1816. Transfd. as Cornet to 4th N.C. in 1817. (? Third Mahratta War ; Jawad ; Cornet 4th N.C.) Fur. s.c. 1821.

BUCHANAN, William (1748-1767). Ensign, 3rd Bn. Sepoys. *b.* 1748. Cadet 1766. Ensign 18 Sept. 1766. *d. unm.* 10 June 1767.
Elder son of James Buchanan, Lieut. 18th Foot, and Catherine his wife. Brother of James Buchanan, *q.v.*
Services : N.F.P.
Refs. : Burke's *Commoners*, iv. 340, *s.n.* Armstrong, of Gallen, King's Co.

*BUCK, George (1738/39-1760). Fireworker, Artillery. *b.* London 1738/39. Cadet 1758. Fireworker 13 Mar. 1758. *d.* 9 Feb. 1760 : kld. in action at the battle of Masimpur, nr. Patna.
Services : N.F.P.

BUCK, John (1792-1864). Lieutenant. Artillery. Subsequently perpetual curate of Houghton, Cumberland. *b.* London 24 Feb. 1792. Cadet 1808. Arrived in India 28 Oct. 1808. Fireworker 26 July 1809. Lieut. 8 June 1816. Retired 16 Apr. 1819. *d.* Belton House, Pentford, nr. Bristol, 5 May 1864.
Son of Jarvis Buck.
Services : No record of active service. After retirement he became minister of a Baptist congregation in Oxford St., London. Queen's Coll. Camb. ; B.A. 1825 ; LL.B. 1830 ; LL.D. 1835. Took holy orders. Curate of St. Botolph's, Cambridge. Chaplain Liverpool gaol 2 Mar. 1838. Perpetual curate of Houghton 1849.
Refs. : G.M. 1864, i. 804. *Graduati Cantab.*

BUCKE, Nathaniel (1779-1825). Lieut. Colonel, 26th N.I. *bapt.* ptely. 7 May 1779. Cadet 1798. Arrived in India 12 Dec. 1800. Ensign 6 Jan. 1800. Lieut. 29 May 1800. Capt. 4 Aug. 1811. Major 18 Aug. 1823. Lt. Col. 13 May 1825. *d.* Calcutta 8 Sept. 1825.
bapt. in church, Holbrook, Suffolk, 28 Sept. 1779. Son of Nathaniel Bucke and Anne his wife.
Services : Posted to 1/16th N.I. 15 Apr. 1801. Operations in Jumna Doab 1803 ; Thathia ; Lieut. 1/16th N.I. Operations in Bundelkhand 1807 and 1810-1. Capt. Lt. 16th N.I. 17 Oct. 1810. Adjt. & Qmr. 16th N.I. 27 Oct. 1810 till 4 Aug. 1811. Transfd. to newly-raised 1/30th N.I. in 1815. Fur. 1817-20. Transfd. as Major

to 32nd N.I. 11 July 1823; to 64th N.I. (late 2/32nd) May 1824. Major comdg. 1st L.I. Bn. 1824-5. First Burma War; Arakan 1825; comdg. 1st L.I. Bn. Posted as Lt. Col. to 26th N.I. 13 May 1825.

Refs. : *G.M.* 1826, i. 286. Will dated 23 Jan. 1812; proved 3 Oct. 1825. M.I. in S. Park St. burial ground, Calcutta.

BUCKLE, Edmond (1808-1846). Captain, Artillery. *b.* Clifton, Somerset, 7 Jan. 1808. Cadet 1823. Arrived in India 30 Mar. 1825. 2nd Lieut. 17 June 1824. Lieut. 28 Sept. 1827. Capt. 2 Jan. 1843. *d.* Point de Galle, Ceylon, 19 Sept. 1846, on his passage to England.

Son of Richard Buckle, of Bristol, customs surveyor. *m.* Calcutta, 10 Nov. 1840, Anne Sarah Maria, eldest dau. of Lieut. Gen. Sir Jasper Nicolls, K.C.B. (*D.N.B.*). Addiscombe Cadet 1822-4.

Services : First Burma War; Arakan 1825. A.D.C. to Maj. Gen. Sir Jasper Nicolls 15 Jan. 1829. Posted to 3rd Troop 1st Bde. H.A. in 1834. Dy. Comy. Ord. 6 May 1835; Comy. Ord. 12 Jan. 1836. A.A.G., Dum-Dum, 10 June 1840 till death. Posted to 4th Troop 2nd Bde. in 1843; to 1st Troop 2nd Bde. 24 July 1845. Author of " Memoir of the Services of the Bengal Art. "; posthumous, London, 1852; edited by Sir John Kaye, *q.v.*

Refs. : Will dated Dum-Dum, 3 Aug. 1844; proved 9 Mar. 1847.

BUCKLEY, Frederick (1786-1853). Colonel, 70th N.I. *bapt.* Polebrook, Northants., 14 Apr. 1786. Cadet 1803. Arrived in India 15 Aug. 1804. Ensign 7 Aug. 1804. Lieut. 21 Sept. 1804. Capt. 1 Jan. 1819. Major 7 June 1830. Lt. Col. 10 Apr. 1836. Col. 9 Nov. 1846. *d.* Bareilly, U.P., 14 July 1853.

Son of William Buckley and Mary his wife. Brother of William Buckley, *q.v. m.* St. John's, Calcutta, 16 Jan. 1823, Miss Jane Cox.

Services : Settlement of Hariana; capture of Bhawani 29 Aug. 1809 (w.); Lieut. 2/18th N.I. Adjt. 1/18th N.I. in 1817. Intr. & Qmr. 2/18th N.I. in 1818. Fur. 27 July 1819 till 4 Oct. 1822. Transfd. to 37th N.I. (late 2/18th) May 1824; to newly-raised 2nd Extra Regt. (became 70th N.I.) in 1825. A.D.C. to Sir Gabriel Martindell, *q.v.*, 23 Feb. 1826. Transfd. to 14th N.I. 7 May 1836; to 55th N.I. 25 Feb. 1840; to 74th N.I. 21 Jan. 1843. Col. 14th N.I. 28 Mar. 1848; 70th N.I. June 1853. Bdr. 2 cl., comdg. Ambala district, 10 Jan. 1851; comdg. Rohilkhand district 1 Nov. 1851 till death.

Refs. : Boase. *I.M.* 20 Sept. 1853, p. 539. Will dated Bareilly 3 Nov. 1852; proved 13 Sept. 1853.

BUCKLEY, John (*d.* 1774). Captain, Infantry. Cadet (?). Ensign 29 Dec. 1764. Lieut. 3 Dec. 1766. Capt. 13 Apr. 1769. *d.* in camp 7 Oct. 1774.
Son of Joseph Buckley, of Draycott, nr. Sudbury, co. Derby. Brother of Joseph and Catharine Buckley.
Services : First Rohilla War ; battle of St. George.
Refs. : Will dated 21 Apr. 1774 ; proved 26 Jan. 1775.

BUCKLEY, William (1784-1852). Major. 5th L.C. *bapt.* Polebrook, Northants., 15 Mar. 1784. Cadet 1804. Arrived in India 12 Sept. 1805. Cornet 11 Sept. 1805. Lieut. 30 Apr. 1811. Capt. 1 Oct. 1819. Major 1 Sept. 1834. Retired 14 Dec. 1835. *d.* Old Bond St., London, 18 Mar. 1852.
Son of William Buckley and Mary his wife. Brother of Frederick Buckley, *q. v.*
Services : With 5th N.C. throughout his service. Against the Pindaris 1817. Third Mahratta War. Operations in Kotah 1821 ; Mangrol. Fur. 17 Jan. 1828 till 17 Sept. 1831.
Refs. : *G.M.* 1852, i. 531.

BUCKNALL, James (*d.* 1775). Lieutenant, Infantry. Cadet 1763. Ensign 1764. Lieut. 29 Mar. 1771. bur. Calcutta 20 Nov. 1775.
Services : N.F.P. (? *Probably* resigned in May 1766 during the Batta mutiny, being subsequently re-admitted.)

BUDD, George Rowcroft (1810-1858). Major. 3rd L.C. *b.* London 27 May 1810. Cadet 1825. Arrived in India 22 Oct. 1826. Cornet 13 June 1826. Lieut. 1 Nov. 1838. Bt. Capt. 13 June 1841. Retired 5 June 1851. Hon. Major 28 Nov. 1854. *d.* 13 Norfolk Cresc., London, 12 Dec. 1858.
Son of Thomas Hayward Budd, of 34 Bedford Row, London, solicitor, and Maria Ann his wife.
Services : Posted as Cornet to 3rd L.C. Operations against the Kols 1832. Actg. Intr. & Qmr. 3rd L.C. 2 Jan. 1833. Fur. s.c. 21 Jan. 1838 till 28 Dec. 1840, and 8 Feb. 1841 till 11 Oct. 1842. First Sikh War ; Aliwal ; Sobraon ; Bt. Capt. 3rd L.C. (Medal with clasp).
Refs. : *G.M.* 1859, i. 106. *The Times*, 14 Dec. 1858.

BUDD, Henry Poulett (1813-1843). Lieutenant, 17th N.I. *b.* London 20 Oct. 1813. Cadet 1829. Arrived in India 15 Nov. 1830. Ensign (25 June 1830) 19 Oct. 1833. Lieut. 8 Oct. 1839. *d.* Calcutta, 12 Jan. 1843, on board his budgerow nr. Govr. Gen.'s ghat.

2nd son of Edward Hayward Budd, of Elcombe House, Wroughton, Wilts., and Maria his wife. Cousin of Thomas Budd, of 34 Bedford Row, London, solicitor.

Services : 2nd N.I. 5 Jan. 1831. Actg. Ensign 5 Dec. 1832, having been more than two yrs. in India. Posted to 17th N.I. 19 Oct. 1833. Actg. Intr. & Qmr. 20th N.I. 16 Mar. 1837. Intr. & Qmr. 17th N.I. 22 Feb. 1840. No record of active service.

Refs. : *G.M.* 1843, ii. 110. *The Times,* 3 May 1843. Will dated 24 Nov. 1842 ; proved 17 Oct. 1843.

BUDWORTH, Joseph (1756-1815). *See* **PALMER.**

BUIST, George (1807-1842). Lieutenant, 10th L.C. *b.* Falkland, co. Fife, 2 Aug. 1807. Cadet 1827. Arrived in India 1 June 1828. Cornet 25 Feb. 1829. Lieut. 17 Feb. 1836. *d.* Jalalabad, Afghanistan, 29 July 1842 : kld. in action.

Son of Rev. George Buist, vice-rector, university of St. Andrews, and Margaret Fermie his wife. *m.* St. Andrew's, Calcutta, 20 Aug. 1829, Isabella Jane, dau. of Capt. Masson, of St. Andrews, co. Fife.

Services : Served throughout with 10th L.C. First Afghan War 1842 ; with Gen. Pollock's force.

BULLER, Spencer Wellington (1811-1886). Captain. 66th N.I. *b.* London 4 Apr. 1811. Cadet 1831. Arrived in India 7 Nov. 1832. Ensign 7 Nov. 1832. Lieut. 15 Nov. 1837. Capt. 13 Nov. 1845. Retired 19 July 1849. *d.* 20 Lansdown Terr., Cheltenham, 10 Dec. 1886.

Of Upwood, Hunts. 5th son of Cornelius Buller, of London, merchant, a govr. of bank of England, and Mary his wife, 4th dau. of Richard Down, of the city of London, banker. Cousin-german of Edward Kyrle Money, *q.v.* *m.* 5 Aug. 1851, Laura, youngest dau. of Rear-Adm. Sir Richard Hussey, K.C.B., and grand-niece of Vere Warner Hussey, *q.v.* (She died 23 Apr. 1879.)

Services : Posted to 66th N.I. 24 May 1834. Fur. s.c. 26 Jan. 1837 till 11 Nov. 1839, and 19 Jan. 1846 till retirement. No record of active service.

Refs. : Foster's *Peerage,* p. 148, *s.n.* Churston, B. Burke's *Landed Gentry,* 11th edn., p. 1200, *s.n.* Moubray, of Cockairnie and Otterston, co. Fife. *The Times,* 14 Dec. 1886.

BULLER, William (1803-1826). Ensign, 58th N.I. *b.* Colyton, Devon, 22 Nov. 1803. Cadet 1824. Arrived in India 15 May 1825. Ensign 14 Nov. 1824. *d.* Agra 12 June 1826.

Son of Rev. Richard Buller, rector of Lanreath, and Anna Sophia his wife, dau. of James Templer, of Stover, and sister of Charles Templer, *q.v.*

THE BENGAL ARMY, 1758-1834   247

Services : Posted as Ensign to 19th N.I. Transfd. to 58th N.I. in 1825. Siege and capture of Bhurtpore ; Ensign 58th N.I.
Refs. : Burke's *Landed Gentry*, 13th edn., p. 234, *s.n.* Buller, of Erle Hall, Devon.

BULLIVANT, John (*d.* 1792). Lieutenant, Infantry. Cadet 1779. Ensign 1 July 1779. Lieut. 22 Feb. 1781. *d.* Chandernagore, Bengal, 16 Aug. 1792.
Services : On fur. in 1790. N.F.P.

BULLOCK, John (*d.* 1805). Captain, 23rd N.I. Cadet 1781. Ensign 9 Aug. 1781. Lieut. 20 June 1783. Capt. 21 Jan. 1803. *d. unm.* Sasni, U.P., 25 Feb. 1805.
Services : Lieut. 9th N.I. Capt. Lt. 9th N.I. 4 Sept. 1800. Transfd. to newly-raised 23rd N.I. in 1803. Capt. comdg. at Sasni in 1805.
Refs. : Will dated Sasni, 23 Feb. 1805 ; proved 17 May 1805.

BULLOCK, William (*d.* 1765). Lieutenant, Infantry. Cadet (?). Ensign (?). Lieut. 4 Aug. 1765. *d.* in India 1765.
Services : Transfd. as Lieut. from H.M.S. N.F.P.

BUNBURY, Matthew Alexander (1791-1841). Major, 40th N.I. *b.* Edinburgh 29 Apr. 1791. Cadet 1807. Arrived in India 16 Nov. 1808. Ensign 8 Nov. 1808. Lieut. 16 Dec. 1814. Capt. 27 Nov. 1823. Major 16 Nov. 1835. *d.* Sagauli, B. & O., 1 Sept. 1841.

Son of Abraham Bunbury, of Ireland, late Capt. 62nd Foot (*probably* of Kilfeacle, co. Tipperary : *see* Abraham Roberts, and Hamilton George Maxwell). " Eldest son of Mrs. Bunbury, of Clifton." *m.* Calcutta, 18 Sept. 1810, Miss Isabella Brady. (She died Jan. 1869.) His daus. *m.* John Erskine (1810-1846), *q.v.*, and John Grant Gerrard, *q.v.*
Services : Barasat C.C. for 8 mos. Posted as Ensign to 20th N.I. Capture of Java ; Ensign 1/20th N.I. Intr. & Qmr. 1/20th N.I. 14 Mar. 1816 till 26 Feb. 1824. Transfd. to 40th N.I. (late 2/20th) May 1824. Garrison Storekeeper at Poona. Supt. of convicts at P.W.I. Fur. from Singapore 9 Dec. 1830 till 15 Nov. 1832. Comdg. 40th N.I. from Mar. till June 1837.
Refs. : G.M. 1841, ii. 667.

BUNCE, John (1809-1845). Captain, 48th N.I. *b.* Calcutta 2 July 1809. Cadet 1824. Arrived in India 19 Mar. 1826. Ensign 9 Sept. 1825. Lieut. 23 May 1834. Capt. 1 Oct. 1840. *d.* Ludhiana 12 May 1845.
bapt. Calcutta 30 Dec. 1809. Son of John Bunce, Surgeon,

Bengal Medical Est., and Louisa his wife. Brother of William Thomas Bunce, *q.v.*
Services : Posted as Ensign to 48th N.I. Operations against the Bhils 1827-8. Fur. s.c. 27 June 1832 till 25 Oct. 1834. Actg. Intr. & Qmr. 31st N.I. 15 Dec. 1838. First Afghan War ; Ghazni ; capture of Kalat ; Lieut. 48th N.I. (attd. 31st N.I.) (Medal).
Refs. : I.M. 1845, p. 406.

BUNCE, Thomas (1747/48-1766). Ensign. Infantry. *b.* Canterbury, Kent, 1747/48. Embarked for India as an Ensign 1764. Dismissed by C.M. 1765. *d.* Calcutta 26 May 1766.
Services : Sailed for India on the *Devonshire,* 20 Feb. 1764, aged 16. N.F.P.

BUNCE, William Thomas (1813-1835). 2nd Lieutenant, Engineers. *b.* Cawnpore 10 June 1813. Cadet 1832. Arrived in India 19 Oct. 1833. 2nd Lieut. (?). *d.* Delhi 16 Oct. 1835.
Son of John Bunce, Surgeon, and Louisa his wife. Brother of John Bunce, *q.v.* Addiscombe Cadet 12 Feb. 1830 till 14 June 1832. Chatham 3 Aug. 1832 till 11 May 1833.
Services : Posted to S. & M. at Delhi 28 Oct. 1833 ; to 1st Coy. S. & M. 3 Jan. 1834 ; to H.Q. do. at Delhi 30 June 1834. Shekhawat expedition 1834 ; Asst. Field Engr. with Bdr.-Gen. Stevenson's force.
Refs. : A.J. N.S. xix. 296.

BUNCOMBE, John (1802-1845). Captain, 2nd Bengal European Regt. *bapt.* Trull, Somerset, 20 Dec. 1802. Cadet 1820. Arrived in India Nov. 1821. Ensign 20 May 1821. Lieut. 16 Nov. 1823. Capt. 13 Apr. 1831. *d.* at sea 4 Feb. 1845.
Son of Robert Buncombe, of Trull, gentleman farmer.
Services : Posted as Ensign to 2/20th N.I. Transfd. to 1/10th N.I. in 1823 ; to 14th N.I. (late 1/10th) May 1824. First Burma War ; operations in Sylhet and Cachar 1824 ; Bikrampur ; Lieut. 1/10th N.I., with force under Major Thomas Newton, *q.v.* Transfd. to 2nd Bengal Eur. Regt. 8 Oct. 1839. Fur. s.c. 4 Dec. 1841 till 1844.

BUNYON, Joseph (1792-1829). Bt. Captain, 74th N.I. *b.* London 27 Feb. 1792. Cadet 1809. Admitted 21 Feb. 1811. Ensign 22 Jan. 1812. Lieut. 24 Apr. 1816. Bt. Capt. 22 Jan. 1827. *d.* Chittagong 4 Nov. 1829.
Son of Charles Bunyon, spirit merchant.
Services : Cadet d.d. 25th N.I. in 1811. Ensign Bengal Eur. Regt. in 1812. Served in Java in 1812, at Berhampore in 1813.

Transfd. to 1/12th N.I. in 1815. 2nd Ceylon Vol. Bn. 1818-9.
Adjt. 1/12th N.I. in 1820. Transfd. to 1st N.I. (late 2/12th) May
1824 ; to newly-raised 6th Extra Regt. (became 74th N.I.) in 1825.

BUREAU, Alexander William (d. 1808). Lieutenant, 1st N.C.
Cadet 1798. Arrived in India 25 Nov. 1799. Cornet 3 June 1800.
Lieut. 22 Jan. 1802. d. Cawnpore 26 Oct. 1808 : kld. on parade
owing to his horse falling with him while the Regt. was drilling
at the gallop.

(? *Possibly* son of William Bureau, inspecting surgeon, E.I.C.S.
Home Est.)

Services : Cornet 1st N.C. Operations in Jumna Doab 1803 ;
Sasni ; Bijaigarh ; Kachaura. Second Mahratta War ; Laswari ;
Lieut. 1st N.C.

Refs. : G.M. 1809, i. 477. Will dated 12 Apr. 1806 ; proved
9 Nov. 1808.

BURFORD, George (1801-1829). Lieutenant, 27th N.I. b. London,
23 Jan. 1801. Cadet 1820. Ensign 3 Sept. 1821. Lieut. 1 May
1824. d. Benares 15 Feb. 1829.

Son of Jonathan Sommers Burford. m. Chittagong, 6 Dec. 1824,
Miss Ann Hall White.

Services : Posted as Ensign to 19th N.I. in 1822. Transfd. to
13th N.I. in 1823 ; to 26th N.I. (late 1/13th) May 1824. First
Burma War ; Arakan 1825 ; Lieut. 26th N.I. Transfd. to 27th
N.I. in 1825. Adjt. 27th N.I. 14 Feb. 1826 till death.

Refs. : Will dated 25 Jan. 1825 ; proved 24 Mar. 1829.

BURGES, George (1789-1827). Captain, 5th L.C. b. Bristol
10 Nov. 1789. Cadet 1807. Arrived in India 19 Aug. 1808.
Cornet 21 Aug. 1808. Lieut. 1 Sept. 1818. Capt. 1 Mar. 1823.
d. at sea, May 1827, on board the *Sarah*, on his passage to Bombay.

Son of Daniel Burges. m. Kaitha, U.P., 2 Mar. 1826, Maria,
4th dau. of Goddard Richards, q.v. (*See also* Arthur Wheatley.)
Ed. Blundell's ; admitted 16 Feb. 1803, aged 12 ; left 15 Dec. 1806.

Services : Posted as Cornet to 5th N.C. in 1809. Java Light
Cav. 1812-5. S.A.C.G. 1815. Third Mahratta War ; Lieut. 5th
N.C. (? Operations in Kotah 1821 ; Mangrol ; Lieut. 5th L.C.)
Fur. s.c. 18 May 1827.

Refs. : *Blundell's School Register.* A.J. xxiv. 673.

BURGESS, BENJAMIN (1785-1804). Lieutenant, 4th N.I. b.
Leicester 4 Feb. 1785. Cadet 1800. Arrived in India 19 Aug.
1801. Ensign 18 Dec. 1801. Lieut. 30 Sept. 1803. d. 13 Nov.
1804 : kld. in action at the battle of Deig.

250 LIST OF THE OFFICERS OF

bapt. St. Martin's, Leicester, 8 Feb. 1785. Eldest son of Francis Burgess, of Leicester, and Bridget his wife.
Services : Second Mahratta War ; storm of Aligarh 4 Sept. 1803 (w.) ; battle of Deig (kld.) ; Lieut. 1/4th N.I.
Refs. : G.M. 1805, i. 486. Intestate ; admon. granted 11 Sept. 1805.

BURGESS, Thomas. Captain. Infantry. Cadet 1769. Ensign 1769. Lieut. 24 Nov. 1772. Capt. 18 Sept. 1780. Resigned 9 Dec. 1782.
Services : N.F.P.

BURGH ("*alias* BRUGH "), Andrew (*d.* 1804). Captain, 8th N.I. Cadet 1781. Admitted 7 July 1781. Ensign 8 July 1782. Lieut. 5 Jan. 1785. Capt. 12 Jan. 1803. *d.* Fatehgarh (? Sikandra) 26 Aug. 1804 : kld. in action during Monson's retreat.
Brother of John Burgh or Brugh, Surgeon 5th N.I. (who also was kld. at Sikandra three days later), and nephew of Niel Campbell. *m.* Mary.
Services : Lieut. 2/3rd N.I. in 1798. Adjt. 3rd Vol. Bn. 26 Nov. 1798. Fourth Mysore War ; siege and capture of Seringapatam ; Lieut., Adjt. 3rd Vol. Bn. Operations in Jumna Doab 1803 ; Sasni ; Capt. 8th N.I. Second Mahratta War ; Monson's retreat 1804 (kld.) ; Capt. 8th N.I.
Refs. : S.M. 1806, p. 78. Will dated 8 Dec. 1803 ; proved 19 Feb. 1805.

BURGH, William D'Oyly (1783-1841). Major General. Colonel 44th N.I. *b.* Calcutta 12 Mar. 1783. Cadet 1799. Arrived in India 12 Jan. 1801. Ensign 20 Sept. 1800. Lieut. 30 May 1803. Capt. 27 July 1808. Major 9 Aug. 1816. Lt. Col. 14 July 1823. Lt. Col. Comdt. 14 July 1825. Col. 5 June 1829. Maj. Gen. 28 June 1838. *d.* Barrackpore 26 Dec. 1841.
Son of John Burgh, of Torrington, Devon, formerly of Calcutta (who *m.* Elizabeth Mary Cumberlege). Godson of Sir John Hadley D'Oyly, 6th Bart., B.C.S. Ed. Blundell's ; admitted 5 Feb. 1798 ; left 29 June 1799.
Services : Posted as Ensign to 2/15th N.I. 17 Apr. 1801. Operations in Jumna Doab 1803 ; Sasni ; Bijaigarh ; Kachaura ; Ensign 15th N.I. Second Mahratta War ; battle of Delhi ; Agra ; Laswari ; battle of Deig ; Lieut. 15th N.I. Capt. Lt. 15th N.I. Nov. 1807. Capt. 1/15th N.I. Third Mahratta War 1819 ; siege and capture of Asirgarh ; Major 1/15th N.I. Transfd. to 11th N.I. 13 Jan. 1823. Lt. Col. Comdt. 1st Extra Regt. 14 July 1825. Transfd. as Col. to 19th N.I. 5 Dec. 1829 ; to 69th N.I. 13 Jan. 1830 ; to 57th N.I.

27 Oct. 1832 ; to 44th N.I. 9 Jan. 1833. Bdr. comdg. Rohilkhand district 28 Jan. 1833. Bdr. 1 cl., to comd. Rajputana F.F. 20 Dec. 1834. Gen. Staff, comdg. Presidency Div., 17 Apr. 1839.
Refs. : Will dated 16 Mar. 1841 ; proved 31 Dec. 1841. M.I. in old cemetery at Barrackpore.

BURGHALL, George (1739-1821). Capt. Lieutenant. Artillery. *b.* 1739. From Royal Artillery. (*No.* 362 *on Kane's List.*) Lieut. 4 July 1761. Capt. Lt. 13 Sept. 1763. Dismissed 12 Mar. 1765. *d.* Somers Town, London, Aug. 1821.
Son of George Burghall, of Bunbury, co. Chester. Magdalen Hall, Oxon. ; matric. 14 Mar. 1788, aged 48.
Services : Cadet, R.A., 1 Jan. 1759. Fireworker, R.A., 20 July 1759. Resigned in 1762. Sailed for India on the *Deptford*, 2 Jan. 1763, as Lieut. of Art., aged 23. Resigned 23 Dec. 1763 ; re-admitted in 1764.
Refs. : Alumni Oxon. *A.J.* xii. 413.
Note : One George Burghall was granted a pension by Sign Manual of £300 *p.a.* on 13 Mar. 1793.

BURKE, William. Captain. 19th N.I. Cadet 1783. Arrived in India 20 Sept. 1783. Ensign 22 Mar. 1785. Lieut. 31 Mar. 1793. Bt. Capt. 8 Jan. 1798. Capt. 21 Sept. 1804. Retired 12 Mar. 1806.
Note : His name appears in the list of Retired Officers for the last time in *E.I.R.* of Jan. 1851.
Services : Lieut. 5th N.I. in 1798. Adjt. 1/12th N.I. before 29 May 1800. Transfd. to 19th N.I. Adjt. & Qmr. of Eur. Invalids 1803-5.

BURKINYOUNG, Frederick White (1808-1842). Lieutenant, 5th N.I. *b.* London 19 Sept. 1808. Cadet 1826. Arrived in India 10 Nov. 1827. Ensign 14 June 1827. Lieut. 25 Dec. 1834. *d.* 13 Jan. 1842 : kld. in action during the retreat from Kabul.
Son of Frederick Burkinyoung, of 34 Allsop's Bldgs., London, merchant and agent, and Martha his wife. *m.* Saugor, 14 Nov. 1835, Charlotte Maria, eldest dau. of William Broome Salmon, *q.v.*, and niece of Sir John Bennett Hearsey, K.C.B., *q.v.* (She *re-m.* 7 June 1843, Arthur Samuel Mills, Bengal Army.)
Services : Posted as Ensign to 5th N.I. Adjt. 5th N.I. 5 Apr. 1841. First Afghan War 1840-2.
Refs. : M.I. in St. Peter's church, Fort William, Bengal.

BURLTON, Philip Bowles (1803-1829). Lieutenant, Artillery. *bapt.* Ravenstock 18 Dec. 1803. Cadet 1820. Arrived in India Oct. 1821. 2nd Lieut. 19 Dec. 1820. Lieut. 1 May 1824. *d.* Nongkhlao, Khasi Hills, Assam, 4 Apr. 1829 : kld. by Khasiahs.

252 LIST OF THE OFFICERS OF

5th and youngest son of William Burlton, of Wykin Hall, Leics., and Donhead Hall and Ravenstock House, Wilts. Brother of William Burlton, *q.v.* Addiscombe Cadet 1819-20.

Services : First Burma War ; Assam. Served in Assam continuously till death. Explored the sources of the Brahmaputra and Irawadi.

Refs. : D.I.B. *Stubbs,* ii. 186-7. *G.M.* 1829, ii. 477. *A.J.* xxviii. 594, 732.

BURLTON, William (1793-1870). Colonel, C.B. 8th L.C. Commissary Gen., Bengal. *bapt.* Fonthill-Gifford, Wilts., 13 Aug. 1793. Cadet 1807. Arrived in India 21 Mar. 1809. Cornet 13 Aug. 1811. Lieut. 1 Sept. 1818. Capt. 7 Mar. 1823. Major 26 Mar. 1838. Lt. Col. 13 Jan. 1842. Retired 10 Aug. 1850. Hon. Col. 28 Nov. 1854. *d.* Oaklands, Middlesex, 10 Nov. 1870, in his 78th year.

Of Oaklands. Son of William Burlton, of Wykin Hall, Leics. Brother of Philip Bowles Burlton, *q.v. m.* 1st, 23 Mar. 1819, Anna Maria, dau. of Capt. William Knipe, St. Helena Est. (*See also* Frederick Benett.) (She died in 1820, aged 19.) *m.* 2nd, Cawnpore, 28 Dec. 1829, Jane Eliza, 2nd dau. of Powell Thomas Comyn, *q.v.*

Services : Barasat C.C. for 8 mos. Posted as Cornet to 4th N.C. Adjt. 4th N.C. 1817-20. Third Mahratta War ; Cornet 4th N.C. S.A.C.G. 18 Sept. 1820. First Burma War 1824-6 (India medal). D.A.C.G., 2 cl., 3 Oct. 1825 ; do., 1 cl., 2 May 1826. A.C.G., 2 cl., 3 Oct. 1828 ; do., 1 cl., 14 Sept. 1831. Comy. Gen. 12 Apr. 1837. M.M.B. 17 Nov. 1843. Gwalior campaign ; Maharajpur (Bronze star). Transfd. from 5th to 7th L.C. 20 Apr. 1844. Fur. s.c. 10 Feb. 1848 till retirement. C.B. 3 Apr. 1846.

Refs. : Boase. *The Times,* 12 Nov. 1870.

BURN, Henry Pelham (1807-1882). Major General. 4th European Inf. *b.* Dirleton, co. Haddington, 13 Nov. 1807. Cadet 1823. Arrived in India 16 Aug. 1824. Ensign 16 Aug. 1824. Lieut. 13 May 1825. Capt. 6 July 1837. Major 16 Jan. 1855. Lt. Col. 13 Mar. 1859. Bt. Col. 15 Oct. 1857. Retired 31 Dec. 1861. Hon. Maj. Gen. 31 Dec. 1861. *d.* 4 Inverness Terr., Paddington, 1 Jan. 1882.

Son of John Burn, of Kingston, and Pelham Maitland his wife. *m.* Lahore, 15 Jan. 1852, Lucy Young, dau. of William Hickey. (She died 15 Dec. 1888, aged 56.)

Services : Posted as Ensign to 1st N.I. Adjt. Agra Provl. Bn. 8 May 1828. Intr. & Qmr. 1st N.I. 27 July 1829. Adjt. do. 28 Sept. 1829 till 8 Feb. 1838. Comdd. 2nd, or Khyber, Rangers 1 Oct. 1838. First Afghan War 1840-2 ; Jalalabad (Medal) ; re-

occupation of Kabul (Medal) ; S.A.C.G. to 3rd Inf. Bde. under Nott 21 July 1842 ; comdd. force sent from Kabul for capture of Istalif. Fur. 24 Dec. 1844. Second Sikh War ; served as D.A.G. with force sent across the Jhelum R. in pursuit of Shere Singh and the Afghans ; Bt. Major 1st N.I. (Medal). Supt. of Army Clothing, Bengal, 1 June 1854. Mutiny campaign ; comdd. 1st Bengal Eur. Fus. on 14 Sept. 1857 ; afterwards Mily. Govr. of Delhi.
Refs. : *The Times*, 5 Jan. 1882, 6e ; 6 Jan. 1882, 7f.

BURN, William (*d.* 1814). Major General. Colonel 14th N.I. Cadet 1771. Arrived in India 26 Dec. 1771. Ensign 29 Jan. 1773. Lieut. 3 Jan. 1778. Capt. 5 June 1781. Major 13 Sept. 1797. Lt. Col. 31 July 1799. Lt. Col. Comdt. 21 Sept. 1804. Col. 25 Apr. 1808. Maj. Gen. 4 June 1811. *d.* Exeter 11 Apr. 1814. Of Colleton Cresc., Exeter.
Services : " Campaigns of Sir Eyre Coote and Lord Cornwallis." Major 1/1st N.I. Second Mahratta War ; in the Karnal district 1803 ; comdg. 2/14th N.I. ; defence of Delhi Oct. 1804 ; comdg. the force, under the Resident, Sir David Ochterlony, *q.v.* ; action with Holkar at Shamli 30 Oct. 1804 ; operations to N. of Delhi in Saharanpur district Nov. and Dec. 1804 ; action at Deoband 23 Nov. 1804. Fur. 24 Feb. 1807 till death.
Refs. : *E.I.M.C.* ii. 495. *G.M.* 1814, ii. 86. *M.M.* 1814, i. Will dated 2 June 1813 ; proved in 1815.

BURNE, William (*d.* 1814). Ensign, doing duty with 14th N.I. Cadet 1811. Ensign (?). *d.* Allahabad 10 Oct. 1814.
3rd son of Thomas Burne, of Walworth, stockbroker. Addiscombe Cadet 1811-12.
Services : Ensign d.d. 1/14th N.I. N.F.P.
Refs. : *G.M.* 1815, i. 645.

BURNELL, George. Captain. Infantry. Cadet 1771. Ensign 8 Mar. 1773. Lieut. (?). Capt. 17 Oct. 1781. Resigned 22 Jan. 1784.
Services : N.F.P.

BURNET, James (*d.* 1774). Captain, Artillery. Transfd. as Capt. from H.M.S. *Folly* Sept. 1768. *d.* Berhampore 11 June 1774.
Son of James Burnet(t), of Aberdeen, and Isabel his wife.
Services : N.F.P.
Refs. : Will dated 10 June 1774 ; proved 15 Nov. 1774.

BURNET, John (*d.* 1808). Lieut. Colonel, 13th N.I. Cadet 1778. Admitted 9 Mar. 1778. Ensign 1778. Lieut. 24 Aug. 1779. Capt. 7 Sept. 1796. Major 21 Feb. 1801. Lt. Col. 5 Nov. 1803. *d.* Allahabad 2 Mar. 1808.

Son of George Burnet, late of the Strand, London.
Services: Major 10th N.I. Transfd. as Lt. Col. to Bengal Eur. Regt. in 1805; to 1/13th N.I. Operations against Dhundia Khan 1807; Komona; Ganauri; Lt. Col. 1/13th N.I., Bdr. comdg. 2nd Bde.
Refs.: *G.M.* 1809, i. 182.

BURNET, John (1764-1832). Colonel, C.B. 35th N.I. *b.* in Scotland 1764. Cadet 1781. Admitted 18 Oct. 1781. Ensign 4 May 1781. Lieut. 21 Aug. 1782. Capt. 29 May 1800. Major 23 Feb. 1807. Lt. Col. 22 Aug. 1812. Lt. Col. Comdt. 11 July 1823. Col. 5 June 1829. *d.* Dacca 15 Oct. 1832.
m. 24 Nov. 1825, Mrs. Primrose Ann Miller.
Services: Approved as Cadet 7 Dec. 1780, aged 16. In 2/8th N.I. in 1800. To take charge of Marine Bn. at Barrackpore 28 Nov. 1801. Nepal War 1816; Lt. Col. 2/8th N.I. comdg. 4th Bde., Centre Column. Comdg. at Saugor 1 June 1820 till 30 Mar. 1821. To comd. E. frontier 20 Oct. 1826. C.B. 21 Dec. 1816.
Refs.: *G.M.* 1833, ii. 190.

BURNETT, Charles James Francis (1805-1846). Bt. Major, 2nd Bengal European Regt. *b.* co. Aberdeen, 8 Mar. 1805. Cadet 1821. Arrived in India 25 July 1822. Ensign 23 Feb. 1822. Lieut. 9 Nov. 1824. Capt. 15 Aug. 1842. Bt. Major 3 Apr. 1846. *d.* Ferozepore, 30 Apr. 1846, from the effects of a wound received at the battle of Ferozshahr on 21 Dec. 1845.
Son of John Burnett, of the I. of Man, afterwards of Hobart, Tasmania.
Services: Posted to 2/27th N.I. in Oct. 1822. Transfd. to 1/9th N.I. in Sept. 1823; to 2/9th N.I. in Oct. 1823; to 8th N.I. (late 1/9th) May 1824. Leave s.c. to Penang Aug. 1825 till Aug. 1826; to N.S.W. and Mauritius Mar. 1829 till May 1831. Adjt. Mhairwara Local Bn. Dec. 1836 till Nov. 1839. With Rajputana F.F. Transfd. to 2nd Bengal Eur. Regt. 8 Oct. 1839. Fur. to N.S.W. 18 Aug. 1840 till Sept. 1842. 2nd in comd. Hariana L.I. 10 Dec. 1842. Bde. Major Ferozepore 1 Oct. 1844. First Sikh War; Ferozshahr (w.); Bde. Major 7th Bde., 4th Div., and Actg. D.A.A.G. of the Div. Bde. Major 8th Inf. Bde. Jan. 1846. D.A.A.G. Feb. 1846, and posted to Saugor Div., which appt. he never took up owing to his wound.
Refs.: *De Rhé-Philipe*. Will dated 28 Apr. 1846; proved 5 Aug. 1846.

BURNETT, Francis Claude (1809-1888). Major General. Artillery. *b.* Coylton, co. Ayr, 2 Oct. 1809. Cadet 1827. Arrived in India 19 Mar. 1828. 2nd Lieut. 4 Nov. 1827. Lieut. 15 Oct. 1834.

THE BENGAL ARMY, 1758-1884

Capt. 3 July 1845. Major 27 June 1857. Lt. Col. 27 Aug. 1858. Col. 18 Feb. 1861. Retired 10 Mar. 1863. Maj. Gen. 10 Mar. 1863. *d.* Gadgirth, co. Ayr, 15 Feb. 1888.

Of Gadgirth, J.P. 3rd and youngest son of Joseph Burnett, of Gadgirth, *q.v.*, and Margaret his wife. Brother of James Burnett, *q.v. m.* 1st, Paul, Cornwall, 18 Oct. 1836, Anne Emily, dau. of Capt. Wooldridge, R.N. *m.* 2nd, 1863, Mary, dau. of Maj. Gen. John Grant, Bombay Art. Addiscombe Cadet 1825-7.

Services : Posted to 4th Troop 2nd Bde. H.A. in 1830 ; to 2nd Troop 1st Bde. in 1838 ; to 1st Troop 3rd Bde. in 1838. Fur. s.c. 30 Mar. 1835. Adjt. & Qmr. 3rd Bn. Foot Art. 1 Dec. 1843. Second Sikh War ; with Bdr.-Gen. Wheeler's force in Jullundur Doab (Medal). To comd. 2nd Troop 2nd Bde. H.A. in 1853.

Refs. : Burke's *Landed Gentry,* 8th edn., p. 256, *s.n.* Burnett, of Gadgirth, co. Ayr. *Walford. The Times,* 18 Feb. 1888.

BURNETT, James (1805-1832). Lieutenant, 44th N.I. *b.* Inveresk 25 Oct. 1805. Cadet 1821. Arrived in India 14 Sept. 1822. Ensign 17 June 1822. Lieut. 1 May 1824. *d.* Bareilly 3 Sept. 1832.

Eldest son of Joseph Burnett, *q.v.*, and Margaret his wife.

Services : Posted as Ensign to 22nd N.I. Transfd. to 44th N.I. (late 2/22nd) May 1824. Intr. & Qmr. 44th N.I. 31 Jan. 1831. No record of active service.

Refs. : Burke's *Landed Gentry,* 8th edn., p. 256, *s.n.* Burnett, of Gadgirth, co. Ayr.

BURNETT, John Hamilton (1811-1845). Bt. Captain, 16th N.I. *b.* Manners, co. Peebles, 10 Feb. 1811. Cadet 1827. Arrived in India 15 Oct. 1828. Ensign 16 Apr. 1828. Lieut. 13 Jan. 1834. Bt. Capt. 16 Apr. 1843. *d.* 21 Dec. 1845 : kld. in action at the battle of Ferozshahr.

4th son of James Burnett, of Barns, co. Peebles, "Chief of his name," and Christian Catherine his wife, 2nd dau. of Robert Lee, of Greenock, merchant. Brother of Robert Lee Burnett, *q.v.*

Services : Ensign d.d. 54th N.I. 20 Nov. 1828. Posted to 16th N.I. 4 Mar. 1829. Adjt. Jodhpur Legion 11 May 1836 till 4 Sept. 1838. Intr. & Qmr. 16th N.I. 13 Sept. 1838 till 7 July 1845. First Afghan War 1839-42 ; occupation of Kandahar ; capture of Ghazni (Medal) ; with force under Gen. Nott 1841-2 ; relief of Kalat-i-Ghilzai ; recapture of Ghazni ; Lieut. 16th N.I. Gwalior campaign ; Maharajpur ; Bde. Qmr. 3rd Inf. Bde. (Bronze star). S.S.O. at Etawah Feb. 1844 till July 1845. First Sikh War ; Mudki ; Ferozshahr (kld.) ; Bt. Capt. 16th N.I., Bde. Major 4th Inf. Bde.

Refs. : Burke's *Landed Gentry,* 2nd edn., iii. 51, *s.n.* Burnett, of Barns, co. Peebles. *De Rhé-Philipe.*

BURNETT, Joseph (1752/53-1833). Bt. Lieut. Colonel. Artillery. *b.* 1752/53. Cadet (?). Fireworker 8 Sept. 1776. Lieut. 23 Sept. 1778. Capt. Lt. 14 Feb. 1784. Capt. 27 May 1786. Major 25 Apr. 1797. Bt. Lt. Col. 1 Jan. 1798. Retired 6 June 1798. *d.* 10 Oct. 1833, aged 80.

Of Gadgirth, co. Ayr. *m.* Gadgirth, 8 June 1801, Margaret, younger dau. of Rev. John Steele, minister of Stair. Father of Francis Claude Burnett, *q.v.*, of James Burnett, *q.v.*, and of Margaret, wife of Patrick Byres, of Tonley, *q.v.*

Services : N.F.P.

Refs. : Burke's *Landed Gentry*, 8th edn., p. 256, *s.n.* Burnett, of Gadgirth, co. Ayr. *S.M.* 1801, p. 447.

BURNETT, Robert Lee (1805-1843). Captain, 54th N.I. (attached to 16th N.I.). *b.* 23 Mar. 1805. Cadet 1820. Arrived in India Aug. 1821. Ensign 16 Aug. 1821. Lieut. 20 Aug. 1823. Capt. 23 July 1838. *d.* Ferozepore, 29 Jan. 1843, in consequence of wounds received at Ghazni and Jagdalak.

2nd son of James Burnett, of Barns, co. Peebles, and Christian Catherine his wife. Brother of John Hamilton Burnett, *q.v.*

Services : Posted to 2/8th N.I. in Nov. 1821. Transfd. to 2/27th N.I. Sept. 1823 ; to 54th N.I. (late 2/27th) May 1824. First Burma War ; Assam (name not given in P.R.). Operations against the Kols in Chota Nagpur 1832. Adjt. 54th N.I. 27 Sept. 1832 till Sept. 1838. First Afghan War 1840-2 ; defence of Ghazni (s.w. on 7 Mar. 1842—lost sight of one eye) ; taken prisoner 10 Mar. 1842 ; released on 21 Sept. 1842 ; attached to 16th N.I. ; action on heights above Jagdalak Pass 18 Oct. 1842 (s.w.).

Refs. : Burke's *Landed Gentry*, 2nd edn., iii. 51, *s.n.* Burnett, of Barns, co. Peebles. *De Rhé-Philipe.*

BURNEY, George (1803-1870). Major General. 10th N.I. *b.* Calcutta 25 Feb. 1803. Cadet 1818. Admitted 16 Sept. 1819. Ensign 14 Sept. 1819. Lieut. 25 May 1821. Capt. 11 Nov. 1833. Major 26 Feb. 1846. Lt. Col. 6 Jan. 1852. Bt. Col. 28 Nov. 1854. Col. 15 June 1862. Maj. Gen. 17 Apr. 1863. *d.* Dehra Dun, U.P., 25 Mar. 1870.

Son of Richard Thomas Burney, headmaster of the Orphan school at Kidderpore, Calcutta, who was half-brother of Madame D'Arblay (Fanny Burney), and Jane Ross his wife. Brother of Henry Burney, *q.v. m.* Barrackpore, 25 Oct. 1831, Frances, dau. of Charles Jackson Doveton, *q.v.*

Services : Posted as Ensign to 2/19th N.I. Actg. Intr. & Qmr. do. 21 Oct. 1823 ; actg. Adjt. do. 22 Nov. 1823. Served in Sylhet 1824. Transfd. to 38th N.I. (late 1/19th) May 1824. Intr. & Qmr.

38th N.I. 23 Jan. 1828. Asst. to his brother Henry, *q.v.*, at Ava, and comdg. his escort 11 Jan. 1830. Comdd. Arakan Local Bn. 22 May 1837 till 10 July 1838. First Afghan War 1840-2 ; Capt. 38th N.I. with Gen. Nott's force. Comdd. 38th N.I. 21 Aug. till 13 Dec. 1840, and 14 May 1842 till 6 Feb. 1843 (Medal). First Sikh War ; Sobraon ; Major 38th N.I. (Medal). Fur. 1850-1. Transfd. as Lt. Col. to 32nd N.I. in Feb. 1852 ; to 56th N.I. 5 Aug. 1855. Second China War ; comdg. 65th N.I.

Refs. : *The Times*, 4 May 1870.

BURNEY, Henry (1792-1845). Lieut. Colonel, 5th N.I. *b*. Calcutta 27 Feb. 1792. Cadet 1807. Arrived in India 14 Aug. 1808. Ensign 30 Aug. 1808. Lieut. 15 Aug. 1813. Capt. 11 July 1823. Major 23 Dec. 1828. Lt. Col. 17 Jan. 1834. *d*. at sea, 4 Mar. 1845, on board the *Maidstone*, on his passage to England.

Of Hamilton Terr., St. John's Wood, London. 2nd son of Richard Thomas Burney and Jane Ross his wife. Brother of James Christian Burney, *q.v.* *m.* Penang, 30 June 1818, Janet, niece of John Alexander Bannerman, govr. of P.W.I.

Services : At Barasat C.C. for 7 mos. Posted as Ensign to 20th (Marine) Bn. Capture of Java ; Ensign 1/20th N.I. Intr. & Qmr. 1/20th N.I. 1 July 1814. Adjt. 1/20th N.I. 1816 till 16 Sept. 1820. Served in P.W.I. with 1/20th N.I. Mily. Sec. to govr. of P.W.I. 3 Apr. 1818. P.A. with Siamese States 1825. Political employ in Penang. Resdt. at court of Ava. Major 25th N.I. Lt. Col. 16th N.I. Transfd. to 28th N.I. 5 May 1842 ; to 5th N.I. 23 Mar. 1843. Fur. 17 Jan. 1845. Author of "An Account of the Mission sent to the King of Siam by the Governor-General of India, in 1825-6."

Refs. : *A.J.* N.S. v. 15. *G.M.* 1845, ii. 102. M.I. in Mission burial ground, Park St., Calcutta.

BURNEY, James Christian (1797-?). Lieutenant. 16th N.I. *b*. 25 Dec. 1797. Cadet 1819. Ensign 10 July 1820. Lieut. 11 July 1823. Retired 5 Aug. 1826.

bapt. Calcutta 16 Mar. 1798. Son of Richard Thomas Burney and Jane Ross his wife. Brother of John Burney, *q.v.*

Note : His name appears in the list of Retired Officers for the last time in *E.I.R.* of 13 May 1828.

Services : Ensign H.M.S. Posted as Ensign to 2/1st N.I. Transfd. as Lieut. to 10th N.I. 11 July 1823 ; to 16th N.I. (late 2/10th) May 1824. Fur. 1824 till retirement.

BURNEY, John (1799-?). Lieutenant. 13th N.I. *b*. Calcutta Jan. 1799. Cadet 1819. Was already in India when apptd. Cadet. Ensign 20 July 1820. Lieut. 11 July 1823. Retired 6 June 1828.

LIST OF THE OFFICERS OF

Son of Richard Thomas Burney, of Calcutta, and Jane Ross his wife. Brother of Richard Burney, *q.v.*
Note : His name appears in the list of Retired Officers for the last time in *E.I.R.* of Jan. 1830.
Services : Ensign 1/17th N.I. Transfd. as Lieut. to 7th N.I. 11 July 1823 ; to 13th N.I. (late 1/7th) May 1824. Fur. 1826 till retirement. No record of active service.

BURNEY, Richard (1790-1845). Captain. 24th N.I. *b.* Calcutta 30 Dec. 1790. Cadet 1807. Arrived in India 14 August 1808. Ensign 23 Aug. 1808. Lieut. 8 June 1814. Capt. 22 Oct. 1824. Resigned 5 Apr. 1825. *d.* Cunningham Pl., St. John's Wood, London, 30 Nov. 1845 ; bur. in chapel of Christ's Coll., Camb.
Eldest son of Richard Thomas Burney and Jane Ross his wife. Brother of George Burney, *q.v.* Christ's Coll., Camb. ; B.A. 1822 ; M.A. 1839.
Services : Posted as Ensign to 8th N.I. Java Inf. Vols. in 1812. Lieut. 2/8th N.I. 6th Vol. Bn. in 1815. Asst. to Resdt. at Samarang, Java, in 1816. Fur. 19 Nov. 1817 till 1822. (? Operations in Hariana 1824 ; Lieut. 2/8th N.I.) Transfd. to 24th N.I. (late 2/8th) May 1824.
Refs. : *G.M.* 1846, i. 104. M.I. in Mission burial ground, Calcutta. *Graduati Cantab.*

BURNS, James Glencairn (1794-1865). Lieut. Colonel. 3rd N.I. Subsequently an inspector of factories. *bapt.* Dumfries 13 Aug. 1794. Cadet 1810. Admitted 3 Dec. 1811. Ensign 26 Oct. 1813. Lieut. 28 June 1817. Capt. 13 July 1827. Major 19 Apr. 1839. Retired 8 July 1839. Hon. Lt. Col. 28 Nov. 1854. *d.* Cheltenham, 18 Nov. 1865, from the effects of an accident.
3rd son of Robert Burns, excise officer (the poet), and Jean Armour his wife. *m.* 1st, Meerut, 28 Apr. 1818, Miss Sarah Robinson. (She died 7 Nov. 1821.) *m.* 2nd, Nasirabad, 21 June 1828, Mary, eldest dau. of William Beckett, of Enfield, *q.v.* (*See also* Hon. Robert Vernon Powys.)
Services : Posted as Ensign to 1/6th N.I. Nepal War 1814-5 ; Ensign 1/6th N.I., in 2nd Div. (India medal). Third Mahratta War ; Lieut. 6th N.I., in Centre Div., and later with Maj. Gen. Brown's force. S.A.C.G. with executive charge of Nimach F.F. Operations in Jodhpur territory 1823 ; capture of Lamba fort. D.A.C.G., 1 cl., 12 Dec. 1823. Transfd. to 3rd N.I. (late 1/6th) May 1824. Fur. 11 Feb. 1831 till 4 July 1833. Bde. Major 4th Inf. Bde., Rajputana, 27 Sept. 1834. Apptd. in 1841 a sub-inspector of factories in the U.K. by the Marquis of Normanby.
Refs. : *The Times*, 21 Nov. 1865. *G.M.* 1865, p. 146. *I.N.*

No. 12, p. 276. *Edinburgh Courant. I.L.N.* 2 Dec. 1865, p. 547. Portrait, engraved by J. Rogers, pub. by George Virtue, 1838.

BURNS, John (*d*. 1778). Lieutenant, Infantry. Cadet 1767. Ensign 18 Dec. 1770. Lieut. 11 July 1776. *d*. Bankipore, B. & O., 4 Feb. 1778.
Services : N.F.P.

BURNTHWAITE, Simon (1752/53-1786). Lieutenant, Infantry. *b*. London 1752/53. Cadet 1781. Ensign 21 June 1781. Lieut. 25 Sept. 1782. *d*. Fatehgarh, U.P., 15 Oct. 1786.
Services : Apptd. Cadet on 7 Feb. 1781, aged 28 ; sailed for India on the *Chapman*, 13 Mar. 1781, aged 28. N.F.P.

BURRELL, Littellus (1753-1827). Major General. Colonel 42nd N.I. *b*. 1753. Cadet 1779. Admitted 20 Mar. 1779. Ensign 10 Oct. 1779. Lieut. 20 May 1781. Capt. 31 Aug. 1798. Major 27 Jan. 1804. Lt. Col. 19 Nov. 1807. Col. 4 June 1814. Maj. Gen. 19 July 1821. *d. unm*. Notting Hill, London, 30 Sept. 1827.
Brother of William Burrell, of Calcutta, auctioneer, of Henry, and of Anne, wife of Thomas Currie Smith.
Services : See *D.N.B.* Enlisted as a volunteer private in 1769, when about 16 years of age. Sailed for India on the *Vansittart* 22 Feb. 1770. Served as private, corporal, and sergeant in 2nd Bengal Eur. Inf. Subsequently sergeant major in 18th Bn. Sepoys.
Refs. : D.N.B. D.I.B. G.M. 1827, ii. 640. Will.
Note : In his Will his Christian name appears as Littelus, in that of his brother William as Littellus. The latter spelling is also given in *G.M.* and in the various issues of *E.I.R.*, and would appear to be correct, although *D.N.B.* favours Litellus.

BURRINGTON, George (*d*. 1794). Colonel, Infantry. Transfd. as Capt. from H.M.S. 1 Sept. 1768. Major 1780. Lt. Col. 23 June 1783. Col. 7 Dec. 1793. *d*. 26 Oct. 1794 : kld. in action at the battle of Bitaurah, nr. Bareilly.
m. Dunnichen, co. Forfar, 3 Oct. 1776, Helen, 3rd dau. of John Dempster, of Dunnichen. His grand-dau. *m*. Thomas D'Oyly, *q.v.* Relative of Thomas Whinyates, *q.v.*
Services : 1st Bengal Eur. Bn. and comdg. at Monghyr in 1790. Second Rohilla War ; Bitaurah (kld.) ; Col. comdg. the Reserve.
Refs. : Burke's *Landed Gentry*, 5th edn., p. 342, *s.n.* Dempster, of Dunnichen, co. Forfar. *Whinyates Family Records. S.M.* 1776, p. 560. Will ; proved in 1795. M.I. in St. John's churchyard, Calcutta.

BURROUGHS, Frederick William (1806-1879). General. 17th N.I. *b.* London 2 May 1806. Cadet 1824. Arrived in India 29 June 1825. Ensign 8 Jan. 1825. Lieut. 19 Oct. 1827. Capt. 1 Oct. 1841. Major 9 Sept. 1856. Lt. Col. 27 Dec. 1859. Col. 5 Sept. 1862. Maj. Gen. 9 Apr. 1868. Lt. Gen. 24 May 1877. Gen. 18 July 1879. *d.* 56 Warrington Cresc., London, 13 Nov. 1879.

Son of Sir William Burroughs, of Castle Bagshaw, co. Cavan, judge of the supreme court of Calcutta. Cousin-german of William Burroughs, *q.v.* *m.* Fatehgarh, 21 Mar. 1830, Caroline, only dau. of Charles Adolphus Mary de Peyron, *q.v.* (She died 31 Mar. 1863.)
Services: Served throughout with 17th N.I. Fur. s.c. 5 Feb. 1843. First Sikh War; Badhowal; A.D.C. to Gen. Littler, *q.v.* Second Sikh War; Ramnagar, as A.A.G. of Div.; and with force under Gen. Wheeler at the capture of heights of Dalla (Medal). Comdt. Bhagulpur Hill Rangers Jan. 1855.
Refs.: Burke's *Landed Gentry*, 13th edn., p. 248, *s.n.* Burroughs, of Rousay, co. Orkney. Boase. *The Times*, 2 Jan. 1880. *I.L.N.* 10 Jan. 1880, p. 46.

BURROUGHS, Lewis (1796-1871). Major. Artillery. *b.* Dunboe, co. Londonderry, 5 July 1796. Cadet 1813. Admitted 5 Aug. 1814. Lieut. 1 Sept. 1818. Capt. 30 July 1831. Retired 11 Oct. 1837. Hon. Major 28 Nov. 1854. *d.* Clifton 16 Nov. 1871.

Brother (or cousin-german) of William Burroughs, *q.v.*, and nephew of Sir William Burroughs, first and last Bart., of Castle Bagshaw, a puisne judge of the supreme court at Calcutta. Addiscombe Cadet 1811-4.
Services: Dy. Comy. Ord. 25 Sept. 1819; Comy. Ord. 5 Nov. 1823. Fur. s.c. 2 yrs. to Cape 31 Dec. 1830, and 11 Apr. 1835 till retirement. No record of active service.
Refs.: *The Times*, 18 Nov. 1871. (*See* Burke's *Extinct Baronetcies*, p. 93, *s.n.* Burroughs, Bart., of Castle Bagshaw.)

BURROUGHS, William (1787-1853). Colonel, 59th N.I. *b.* Laracor, co. Meath, June 1787. Cadet 1804. Arrived in India 10 Feb. 1805. Ensign 8 Oct. 1805. Lieut. 22 Nov. 1805. Capt. 11 July 1823. Major 19 June 1831. Lt. Col. 27 Sept. 1837. Col. 29 July 1848. *d.* his residence, Rothesay House, Cheltenham, 7 June 1853.

Son of Medlycott Burroughs, an officer in the army, and Mary Moorcroft his wife, widow of Capt. Morrison. Cousin-german of Frederick William Burroughs, *q.v.* *m.* 11 Mar. 1820, Charlotte Mary, dau. of Bennett Marley, *q.v.* (*See also* James McCraken.) (She died Camden House, Cheltenham, 3 Oct. 1881, aged 81.)
Services: Posted as Lieut. to Bengal Eur. Regt. Bk. Mr. at

Cawnpore 3 June 1816. Third Mahratta War ; Baggage Master 1st Div. Paymr. of Invalid Pensioners at Allahabad 30 June 1818 till 1 Aug. 1819. Fort Adjt. at Allahabad 7 Oct. 1826. Fur. 28 Jan. 1832 till 25 Oct. 1834. Transfd. to 29th N.I. 29 Jan. 1838. Fur. 12 Aug. 1843 till 23 Nov. 1844. Transfd. to 61st N.I. 18 Dec. 1844. Fur. s.c. 10 Nov. 1846 till death. Col. 59th N.I. 29 July 1848.
Refs. : Burke's *Extinct Baronetcies*, p. 93, *s.n.* Burroughs, Bart., of Castle Bagshaw. Boase. *G.M.* 1853, ii. 102.

BURROW(S), John (1763/64-1799). Captain, Infantry. *b.* London 1763/64. Cadet 1781. Ensign 19 May 1781. Lieut. 2 Sept. 1782. Capt. 7 Jan. 1796. *d.* Calcutta, 25 Aug. 1799, in the hospital for insane persons.
Services : Apptd. Cadet on 7 Mar. 1781, aged 17 ; sailed for India on the *Northumberland*, 26 June 1781, aged 17. Fur. 9 Jan. 1786 till 18 Nov. 1789. Lieut. 2nd Bengal Eur. Regt. in 1796.

BURROW(S), Robert Fable (*d.* 1793). Lieutenant, Infantry. Cadet 1778. Ensign 1778. Lieut. 22 Nov. 1780. *d.* Barrackpore 4 June 1793.
Services : N.F.P.
Refs. : Will dated 21 May 1793 ; proved in 1793.

BURROWES, Alexander (*d.* 1792). Lieutenant, Infantry. Cadet 1779. Ensign 20 Mar. 1780. Lieut. 25 May 1781. *d.* Berhampore, Bengal, June 1792.
Services : N.F.P.

BURROWES, Cosby (1801-1829). Lieutenant, 45th N.I. *b.* London 8 Dec. 1801. Cadet 1817. Ensign (?). Lieut. 1 Aug. 1818. *d.* Sehore, C.I., 9 Dec. 1829.
Son of Cosby Burrowes, B.C.S., sometime mgte. at Jessore (a cadet of the family of Burrowes, of Stradone House, co. Cavan), and Charlotte his wife. Brother of Robert Burrowes, *q.v. m.* Calcutta, 20 Nov. 1825, Sophia Mary, eldest dau. of John Wilkie, *q.v.* (*See also* William Riddell.) She *re-m.* James Stainback Winfield, *q.v.* Addiscombe Cadet 1816-8.
Services : Posted as Lieut. to 1/23rd N.I. Fur. 1823-4. Transfd. to 45th N.I. (late 1/23rd) May 1824. (? First Burma War ; Cachar 1825 ; Lieut. 45th N.I.)
Refs. : M.I. at Mirzapur.

BURROW(E)S, Peter (*d.* 1807). Lieut. Colonel, 5th N.I. Cadet 1778. Admitted 13 July 1778. Ensign 24 Apr. 1779. Lieut. 5 Jan. 1781. Capt. 25 Apr. 1797. Major 16 Nov. 1802. Lt. Col. 21 Sept. 1804. *d.* Calcutta 21 Nov. 1807. *m.* (?).

Services : On fur. in 1790. Capt. Lt. 1st Bengal Eur. Regt. in 1796. Capt. 2/5th N.I. in 1797.
Refs. : Will dated 21 Oct. 1807 ; proved 24 Nov. 1807.

BURROWES, Robert (1797-1824). Lieutenant, Artillery. *b.* London 28 Aug. 1797. Cadet 1814. Arrived in India Sept. 1815. Fireworker 14 Aug. 1817. Lieut. 1 Sept. 1818. *d.* Agra 28 Dec. 1824.

Son of Cosby Burrowes, B.C.S., and Charlotte his wife. Brother of Cosby Burrowes, *q.v. m.* Agra, 9 Sept. 1819, Miss Catherine Anderson. Addiscombe Cadet 1812-4.

Services : Third Mahratta War ; Lieut. 2nd Coy. 1st Bn. Foot Art. (doing duty with 6th Coy. 3rd Bn.). Posted to 4th Troop H.A. in 1823.

Refs. : Will dated Fatehgarh 25 Sept. 1819 ; proved 9 Mar. 1825.

BURT, Charles Henry (Pomfret) (1809-1867). Lieut. Colonel. 64th N.I. *b.* Bridgwater, Somerset, 11 Nov. 1809. Cadet 1825. Arrived in India 14 Dec. 1826. Ensign 21 July 1826. Lieut. 8 Oct. 1827. Capt. 24 Jan. 1842. Bt. Major 20 June 1854. Retired 23 June 1859. Hon. Lt. Col. 23 June 1859. *d.* his residence in Brighton 17 Apr. 1867.

5th son of Rev. Charles Henry Burt, vicar of Cannington, Somerset, minister of Queensborough, Kent, and chaplain in ordinary to H.R.H. the Duke of Sussex, K.G. Brother of Thomas Seymour Burt, *q.v. m.* 1st, Elizabeth Mary, eldest dau. of G. Williams, of Portland Terr., Regent's Pk., London. (She died 6 Nov. 1843.) *m.* 2nd, Calcutta, 29 Mar. 1849, (Jane) Ellen, dau. of William Wood. (She died Darjeeling, 28 Nov. 1853, aged 23.)

Services : Posted as Ensign to 64th N.I. Fur. p.a. 4 Feb. 1837 till 25 Jan. 1840. First Afghan War ; Ali Masjid ; forcing of Khyber Pass ; and subsequent operations of Gen. Pollock's force ; Capt. 64th N.I. (Medal). Fur. m.c. Oct. 1845. Fur. 1858 till retirement.

Refs. : The Times, 26 Nov. 1838 ; 22 Dec. 1838 ; 19 Apr. 1867. *G.M.* 1867, i. 822.

BURT, Henry Walker (1805-1864). Lieut. Colonel. 46th N.I. *b.* Edinburgh 23 July 1805. Cadet 1823. Arrived in India 8 Oct. 1824. Ensign 11 May 1824. Lieut. 2 Nov. 1825. Capt. 1 Mar. 1838. Bt. Major 11 Nov. 1851. Retired 10 Feb. 1855. Hon. Lt. Col. 1 May 1855. *d.* 115 George St., Edinburgh, 31 Dec. 1864.

Son of Robert Burt, of Edinburgh, physician. Brother of James Ranald Burt, *q.v.*

THE BENGAL ARMY, 1758-1834   263

Services : Posted as Ensign to 46th N.I. 31 Mar. 1825. First Burma War ; Lieut. 46th N.I. (India medal). Adjt. 46th N.I. 25 Aug. 1826 till 12 Dec. 1838. Bde. Major, Meywar F.F., 22 Mar. 1834. Dy. Paymr., Sirhind Circle, 5 Mar. 1846 till retirement.
Refs. : *G.M.* 1865, i. 258. *The Times*, 4 Jan. 1865.

BURT, James Ranald (1811-1846). Bt. Captain, 6th L.C. *b.* Edinburgh 27 May 1811. Cadet 1827. Arrived in India 27 Oct. 1827. Cornet 3 Dec. 1828. Lieut. 19 Nov. 1835. Bt. Capt. 24 Oct. 1842. *d.* Ferozepore 8 May 1846.

Son of Robert Burt, of Edinburgh, physician, and Louisa Macdonald his wife. Brother of Henry Walker Burt, *q.v.*, and nephew of Maj.-Gen. John Macdonald.

Services : d.d. 8th L.C. 4 June 1828 ; d.d. 1st L.C. 24 Sept. 1828. Posted as Cornet to 2nd L.C. Transfd. to 3rd L.C. 26 Jan. 1829 ; to 6th L.C. 2 Sept. 1831. Adjt. 6th L.C. 5 Jan. 1833 till 8 Dec. 1836. Fur. s.c. 15 Aug. 1837 till 29 June 1840, and 11 Sept. 1842 till 1844. No record of active service.

BURT, Thomas Seymour (1805-1890). Major. Engineers. *b.* London 31 Mar. 1805. Cadet 1824. Arrived in India 23 Dec. 1825. 2nd Lieut. (?). Lieut. 1 May 1824. Capt. 22 Jan. 1834. Major 29 Dec. 1843. Dismissed by G.C.M. 19 Aug. 1847. *d.* Cotmandene, Dorking, 8 Mar. 1890.

Son of Rev. Charles Henry Burt, vicar of Cannington. Brother of Charles Henry Burt, *q.v.*, and nephew of William Burt, miscellaneous writer (*D.N.B.*). Addiscombe Cadet 1821-3.

Services : Fur. p.a. 17 Jan. 1834 till 18 Jan. 1838, during which time he served with the British Legion in Spain as Major of Engineers. Ex. Engr., Allahabad Div., 18 Aug. 1843 ; Suptg. Engr., in Sind, 18 Oct. 1844. Tried by G.C.M. at Allahabad, 24 June 1847, and sentenced to dismissal. Author of " Views in India," a poem entitled " Christianity," and various papers on scientific subjects. F.R.S. 17 Mar. 1836.
Refs. : Boase. *I.M.* No. 87, p. 613. *N. & Q.* 12S. iii. 183. *The Times*, 11 Mar. 1890.

BURTON, Charles Æneas (1812-1857). Bt. Major, 40th N.I. *b.* Dinapore 6 Feb. 1812. Cadet 1827. Arrived in India 3 Feb. 1829. Ensign 23 Aug. 1828. Lieut. 5 July 1836. Capt. 2 June 1845. Bt. Major 20 June 1854. *d.* Kotah, 15 Oct. 1857 : kld. by mutineers.

bapt. Dinapore 19 Feb. 1813. Eldest son of Charles William Burton, *q.v.*, and Mary Anne his wife. *m.* 1st, London, 1 Mar. 1832, Elizabeth Jane, widow of H. Bradley. (She died

Aligarh 18 Nov. 1833.) *m.* 2nd, (?). (She died Jullundur, 18 May 1881, aged 81.)
Services : Posted as Ensign to 8th N.I. 3 June 1829. Fur. s.c. 9 May 1831 till 13 Mar. 1833. Transfd. to 40th N.I. 2 Aug. 1832. Leave to Cape 28 Mar. 1837 till 22 Jan. 1839. Actg. Intr. & Qmr. 28th N.I. 5 Aug. 1840. Asst. to Agent and Comr. of Delhi 14 Apr. 1841 till 31 Mar. 1843. Actg. Intr. & Qmr. 73rd N.I. 17 Mar. 1843 ; do. 1st L.C. 11 Sept. 1843. Gwalior campaign ; Maharajapur ; with 1st L.C. (Bronze star). Asst. to A.G.G., Rajputana, 10 June 1848. P.A. Kotah 15 Aug. 1845 ; at Haraoti, Kotah, 15 Mar. 1849 ; at Jaipur 3 May 1855 ; at Haraoti 19 Sept. 1856 till death.
Refs. : Burke's *Landed Gentry*, 2nd edn., p. 168, *s.n.* Burton, of Mount Anville, co. Dublin. *G.M.* 1858, i. 112.

BURTON, Charles William (1780-1816). Captain, 8th N.I. *bapt.* Iffley, 23 Apr. 1780. Cadet 1800. Arrived in India 6 Feb. 1802. Ensign 3 Sept. 1801. Lieut. 10 June 1803. Capt. 16 Dec. 1814. *d.* Mirzapur, U.P., 30 Oct. 1816.

3rd son of Rev. James Burton, D.D., chaplain in ordinary to George III and George IV, senior canon of Christchurch, and Mary Anne his wife, dau. of Robert Jenner, D.C.L. *m.* Calcutta, 6 June 1810, Mary Anne, dau. of John Borthwick Gilchrist, LL.D. (*D.N.B.*). She *re-m.* Metcalf Stanwix Hogg, *q.v.* Father of Charles Æneas Burton, *q.v.*

Services : Ensign 8th N.I. Operations in Jumna Doab 1803 ; Sasni. Second Mahratta War ; capture of Deig ; siege of Bhurtpore ; Lieut. 1/8th N.I. Adjt. 1/8th N.I. 18 Jan. 1805 till 1 July 1814. Capt. 2/8th N.I. Nepal War 1816 ; Capt. 5th Gren. Bn., in 2nd Bde. Left Div.
Refs. : Burke's *Landed Gentry*, 2nd edn., p. 168, *s.n.* Burton, of Mount Anville, co. Dublin. *G.M.* 1817, i. 646. Will dated 15 Feb. 1816 ; proved in 1816.

BURTON, Frederick. Lieutenant. Infantry. Cadet 1779. Ensign 23 Aug. 1779. Lieut. 26 Mar. 1781. Struck off before 1790.
Services : N.F.P.

BURTON, Richard (*d.* 1780). Captain, Infantry. Cadet 1767. Ensign 15 Sept. 1767. Lieut. 24 Apr. 1769. Capt. 8 May 1777. bur. Madras 17 Mar. 1780.

Son of Richard Burton, of Gt. Stukeley, Hunts., and Susannah his wife. Brother of John Burton, Lieut. Gen. R.A.
Services : N.F.P.
Refs. : Will dated 15 Mar. 1780.

BURTON, Richard (d. 1781). Lieutenant, Artillery. Cadet 1778. Lieut. 6 Oct. 1778. bur. Cawnpore 6 Feb. 1781.
Services : N.F.P.

BURTON, Richard Button (1797-1864). Captain. 39th N.I. b. Egham, Surrey, 5 Apr. 1797. Cadet 1813. Admitted 21 Oct. 1814. Ensign 5 June 1815. Lieut. 11 Jan. 1818. Capt. 30 Sept. 1827. Retired 12 June 1832. d. London, 6 Mar. 1864.
Son of Thomas Burton, farmer.
Services : Posted as Ensign to 2/19th N.I. Third Mahratta War ; Lieut. 2/19th N.I., in Reserve Div. Transfd. to 39th N.I. (late 2/19th) May 1824. Arrived in Calcutta, mentally deranged, 12 May 1829. Fur., as insane, 2 Feb. 1830.
Refs. : G.M. 1864, i. 541. The Times, 10 Mar. 1864.

BURTON, William (1763-1817). Lieut. Colonel, Invalid Est. 30th N.I. b. 1763. Cadet 1781. Admitted 24 Sept. 1781. Ensign 30 Mar. 1781. Lieut. 21 July 1782. Capt. 21 Apr. 1800. Major 25 Mar. 1806. Lt. Col. 10 Dec. 1811. Invalided 1 Oct. 1815. d. Dacca, 27 Nov. 1817, aged 53.
A native of Middlesex. m. Cawnpore, 29 June 1800, Miss Charlotte Topham. (She died Dacca 11 July 1809.)
Services : Apptd. Cadet on 14 Dec. 1780, aged 18 ; sailed for India on the *Chapman*, 13 Mar. 1781, aged 18. Operations in Jumna Doab 1803 ; Sasni ; Bijaigarh ; Kachaura ; Capt. 15th N.I. Second Mahratta War ; battle of Deig ; Agra ; Laswari ; Capt. 15th N.I. Bde. Major at Berhampore 1804-6. Transfd. to newly-raised 1/25th N.I. in 1805. Expedition to Mauritius 1810-1 ; Major comdg. 1st Vol. Bn. Lt. Col. 25th N.I. Transfd. to newly-raised 30th N.I. in 1815. Comdg. Dacca Provl. Bn. at death.
Refs. : Will dated 9 Aug. 1805 ; codicil dated 10 Aug. 1810 ; proved 22 Jan. 1818. M.I. in Dacca cemetery.

BUSH, James Tobin (1810-?). Lieut. Colonel. 24th N.I. b. Bristol 28 Mar. 1810. Cadet 1827. Arrived in India 15 Oct. 1828. Ensign 16 Apr. 1828. Lieut. 16 July 1833. Capt. 24 Jan. 1845. Major 17 Apr. 1856. Retired 1 May 1857. Hon. Lt. Col. 1 May 1857. (? Living in 1893.)
3rd son of Robert Bush, of Clifton, merchant, and —— his wife, dau. of Gen. Tobin. m. Calcutta, 13 Oct. 1834, Rose Cordelia, eldest dau. of William McQuhae, *q.v.* (*See also* John William Collin Chalmers, William Richard Maidman, and Peter Arnold Torckler.)
Services : Ensign d.d. 24th N.I. 18 Nov. 1828. Transfd. to 12th N.I. Posted as Ensign to 24th N.I. 12 Apr. 1829. Operations against the Chuars 1832 ; Ensign 24th N.I. Fur. s.c. 9 June 1839

till 13 Dec. 1841. 2nd in comd. Kotah Contingent 26 June 1844 till 8 Jan. 1851.
Refs. : Burke's *Colonial Gentry*, ii. 590. Burke's *Family Records*, 131.

BUSH, Richard Yeat(e)s Brown (1811-1885). Colonel. 13th N.I. *b.* London 17 Oct. 1811. Cadet 1827. Arrived in India 26 Oct. 1828. Ensign 19 May 1828. Lieut. 18 Aug. 1834. Capt. 1 Feb. 1841. Major 12 Jan. 1853. Lt. Col. 15 July 1857. Retired 31 Dec. 1861. Col. 31 Dec. 1861. *d.* his residence, 55 York Terr., London, 10 Jan. 1885.

4th son of Thomas Bush, of Garratt House, Wandsworth, hop merchant, and Harriet his wife, dau. of —— Brown. *m.* St. George's, Bloomsbury, 20 May 1835, his cousin Grizell(e), 4th dau. of Richard Bush, of Wandsworth and Woodford, Essex, and Prudence Wigg his 1st wife. (She died 1 June 1890.)

Services : Ensign d.d. 65th N.I. 13 Dec. 1828. Posted as Ensign to 65th N.I. 4 Mar. 1829. Fur. s.c. 31 Jan. 1832 till 27 Oct. 1835. Adjt. 29 May 1839 till 17 Mar. 1841. Fort Adjt. at Allahabad 25 Jan. 1845. Fur. 21 Feb. 1848 till 1851. Fur. 1858. Transfd. to 13th N.I. in 1859. Permitted to reckon 3 yrs. leave as service for pension, occasioned by sickness or wounds contracted on, or by, service.

Refs. : *History of the Wilmer Family*, p. 231. *The Times*, 13 Jan. 1885.

BUSHBY, Ewen (*d.* 1793). Lieutenant, Infantry. Cadet 1779. Ensign 13 Sept. 1779. Lieut. 30 Apr. 1781. *d.* Calcutta 5 Feb. 1793.

Brother of Austin Bushby.
Services : N.F.P.
Refs. : Will dated 3 Jan. 1787.

BUSHBY, John (*d.* 1780). Lieutenant, Infantry. Cadet 1771. Ensign 24 Dec. 1773. Lieut. 21 Mar. 1777. bur. Calcutta 24 Oct. 1780.
Services : N.F.P.

BUTLER, Charles (1774-1805). Captain, 11th N.I. *b.* St. Bartholomew's, London, 1774. Cadet 1793. Arrived in India 16 Feb. 1795. Ensign 21 Sept. 1794. Lieut. 8 Jan. 1796. Capt. 21 Sept. 1804. *d.* Hyderabad 7 Apr. 1805.

Services : (? Second Mahratta War ; Lieut. 11th N.I.) With Resdt.'s escort at Hyderabad 1804 till death.
Refs. : Intestate ; admon. granted 13 Dec. 1805.

BUTLER, Daniel (*d.* 1784). Major, Artillery. Cadet (from Madras) 1765. Fireworker 16 Nov. 1765. 2nd Lieut. 2 Apr. 1769. Lieut. 5 Mar. 1770. Capt. Lt. 6 May 1772. Capt. 17 Apr. 1775. Major 1 Dec. 1782 ? *d.* Cawnpore 30 June 1784 ; bur. there 3 July 1784.
Son of Norton Butler, of Ireland.
Services : First Rohilla War ; battle of St. George ; Capt. Lt. Art.
Refs. : Broome, p. 581. Will.

BUTLER, Edward William (*d.* 1819). Lieut. Colonel, Artillery. Cadet 1783. Admitted 27 Sept. 1783. Fireworker 24 Apr. 1785. Lieut. 21 May 1793. Capt. Lt. 22 Feb. 1802. Capt. 21 Sept. 1804. Major 26 Aug. 1813. Lt. Col. 1 Sept. 1818. *d.* Agra 1 Aug. 1819.
m. Calcutta, 28 Oct. 1806, Harriet, widow of Charles Christie (*d.* 1805), *q.v.* His dau. *m.* James Nicolson, *q.v.*
Services : Third Mysore War ; Utradrug ; Seringapatam ; Lieut. F. 1st Coy. 2nd Bn. Art. On service to Madras June-Oct. 1794 ; Lieut. 4th Coy. 2nd Bn. Second Mahratta War ; capture of Deig ; siege of Bhurtpore ; Capt. comdg. 4th Coy. 2nd Bn., Bde. Major. Fur. 8 Feb. 1807 till 22 Oct. 1809. Capture of Jokyakarta 1812. Siege and capture of Hathras ; Major Foot Art. Third Mahratta War ; Taragarh ; Madhurajpura ; Nasridah ; Lt. Col. comdg. Art. Reserve.
Refs. : Will dated Ajmer, Rajputana, 29 June 1818 ; proved 21 Aug. 1819.

BUTLER, James. Ensign. Engineers. Cadet (?). Ensign 19 Sept. 1764. Dismissed 8 Feb. 1767.
Services : N.F.P.

BUTLER, John (1804-1872). Lieut. General. 11th N.I. *bapt.* Tenby, co. Pembroke, 7 Sept. 1804. Cadet 1820. Admitted 2 July 1821. Ensign 12 Jan. 1821. Lieut. 11 July 1823. Capt. 1 Jan. 1837. Major 12 Oct. 1845. Lt. Col. 3 Oct. 1851. Bt. Col. 28 Nov. 1854. Maj. Gen. 3 Apr. 1863. Lt. Gen. 9 Dec. 1871. *d.* Simla 30 Apr. 1872.
Son of John Butler, of Bath. *m.* Calcutta, 16 Nov. 1824, Miss Ann Elizabeth Gunn. (She died in 1872, aged 70.)
Services : Posted to 2/13th N.I. 26 Oct. 1821. Transfd. to 1/6th N.I. in Sept. 1823. Offg. Bde. Major, Chittagong, 26 Apr. 1824. Transfd. to 3rd N.I. (late 1/6th) May 1824. Adjt. 3rd N.I. 14 July 1825 till Jan. 1837. D.A.A.G. Saugor Div. 16 June 1841 ; A.A.G. do. 8 Sept. 1843 till Nov. 1845. Second Sikh War ; Jullundur

Doab; Rangar Nagal; Kalalwala; heights of Dalla; Major comdg. 3rd N.I. (Medal). Comdd. a detachment employed in disarming the Sikh population of the Bari Doab in 1849. Lt. Col. comdg. 3rd N.I. 8 Nov. 1851 till June 1857, when it mutinied at Phillaur. Against the Hassanzais of the Black Mtn. 1852-3; comdg. a column under Col. Mackeson, *q.v.* (Medal). Transfd. to 4th Eur. Regt. in Sept. 1858; to 11th N.I. in Oct. 1858.
Refs. : De Rhé-Philipe. Boase.

BUTLER, John (1809-1874). Colonel. 55th N.I. *bapt.* Bramshott, Hants, 31 Dec. 1809. Cadet 1825. Arrived in India 21 Sept. 1826. Ensign 2 Mar. 1826. Lieut. 11 July 1836. Capt. 2 May 1845. Major 14 Nov. 1854. Lt. Col. 27 Aug. 1858. Retired 9 Oct. 1859. Hon. Col. 9 Oct. 1859. *d.* Empshott Terr., nr. Petersfield, 22 May 1874, aged 64.

Son of James Butler, of Liphook. *m.* Gauhati, Assam, 21 Oct. 1841, Cecilia, eldest dau. of William Simonds, *q.v.*

Services : Posted as Ensign to 55th N.I. To do duty with 17th N.I. 26 Mar. 1827. Fur. s.c. 4 Jan. 1832 till 26 Sept. 1834. Actg. Intr. & Qmr. 55th N.I. 10 Oct. 1834. Assam Sebundy Corps 27 Mar. 1837 till 4 Sept. 1837. Intr. & Qmr. 55th N.I. 20 Dec. 1837. Actg. 2nd in comd. Assam L.I. 11 Nov. 1840 till 27 July 1841. Junior Asst. to Comr. of Assam 22 Feb. 1842; Principal do. 8 Oct. 1845; do., 1 cl., 21 Oct. 1848. Dy. Comr., Assam, 20 May 1857. No record of active service. Author of "Travels and Adventures in the Province of Assam during a residence of 14 years," map, plan, and 8 litho. plates, 8vo, 1855; and "A Sketch of Assam; with some account of the Hill tribes," London, 1847.

Refs. : The Times, 27 May 1874.

BUTLER, Whitwell (1761/62-1798). Captain, Infantry. *b.* 1761/62. Cadet 1777. Admitted 18 Dec. 1777. Ensign 8 Feb. 1778. Lieut. 18 Sept. 1778. Capt. 7 Jan. 1796. *d.s.p.* Chunar, U.P., 2 Aug. 1798.

4th son of James Butler, of Priestown, co. Meath, and Dorothea his wife, dau. of Sir Richard Steele, 1st Bart.

Services : Sailed for India on the *Duke of Portland,* 30 Apr. 1777, aged 15. N.F.P.

Refs. : Burke's *Landed Gentry,* 7th edn., p. 270, *s.n.* Butler, of Priestown, co. Meath. Will dated 28 Nov. 1790; proved in 1798.

BUTLER, William (1786-1819). Lieutenant, 11th N.I. *bapt.* Carlow, 10 Mar. 1786. Cadet 1805. Arrived in India 7 Feb. 1807. Ensign 28 Dec. 1806. Lieut. 17 Jan. 1810. *d.* St. Helena 25 Mar. 1819.

Son of James Butler, of Carlow, and Deborah his wife.
Services : Posted as Ensign to 11th N.I. Reduction of Kalinjar 1812. Siege and capture of Hathras 1817 ; Lieut. 2/11th N.I. Third Mahratta War.
Refs. : Will dated St. Helena 20 Mar. 1819 ; proved 1 Jan. 1820.

BUTLER, William Augustus (1805-1838). Lieutenant, 22nd N.I. *b.* Roscommon *c.* Aug. 1805. Cadet 1824. Arrived in India 18 Nov. 1825. Ensign 13 May 1825. Lieut. 6 Sept. 1826. *d. unm.* Beawar, Ajmer, 9 Dec. 1838.
3rd son of Augustus Richard Butler-Danvers and Eliza Bizarre his 2nd wife, dau. of Humphrey Sturt, of Critchill House, Dorset. Half-brother of George John Danvers Butler, fifth Earl of Lanesborough.
Services : Posted as Ensign to 22nd N.I. Fur. s.c. 10 Jan. 1833 till 5 Mar. 1836. No record of active service.
Refs. : Burke's *Peerage*, 1923, p. 1329, *s.n.* Earl of Lanesborough.

BUTTANSHAW, William (1791-1847). Captain. 7th N.I. *b.* 10 Aug. 1791. Cadet 1810. Admitted 16 Aug. 1811. Ensign 5 Mar. 1813. Lieut. 22 June 1816. Capt. 16 Mar. 1826. Retired 15 Jan. 1841. *d.* Lee Park, Blackheath, 17 June 1847.
bapt. West Peckham 11 Sept. 1791. Son of John Buttanshaw, of W. Peckham, paper manufr. *m.* Saugor, 13 Oct. 1827, Maria Mary Anne, dau. of B. Hobday, and niece of Sir William Nott, *q.v.* (*See also* Chambré Brabazon Ponsonby Alcock.) (She died 2 June 1856.)
Services : Posted as Ensign to 1/4th N.I. Bde. Major, Saugor, 18 Oct. 1820. Asst. Bk. Mr., Saugor Div. Transfd. to 7th N.I. (late 1/4th) May 1824. Fur. s.c. 20 Feb. 1834 till 26 Dec. 1836. D.J.A.G., Cawnpore Div., 14 Sept. 1838. No record of active service.
Refs. : Will dated 24 June 1845 ; admon. 4 Mar. 1848. *G.M.* 1847, ii. 217.

BUTTERFIELD, Edward (*d.* 1776). Captain, Infantry. Cadet 1766. Ensign 16 Sept. 1766. Lieut. 1 Dec. 1767. Capt. 2 Apr. 1773. *d. unm.* Kora, U.P., Oct. 1776.
Services : N.F.P.
Refs. : Will dated 21 Sept. 1776 ; proved 26 Mar. 1777.

BUTTICAZ, George William (1788-1818). Capt. Lieutenant, 2nd N.I. *bapt.* Harrow 21 June 1788. Cadet 1803. Arrived in India 2 Dec. 1804. Ensign 3 Nov. 1804. Lieut. 3 Nov. 1804. Capt. Lt. 15 Nov. 1817. *d.* Lohoo Ghat, Almora district, U.P., 15 Nov. 1818.
Son of Rev. James Butticaz, of a Swiss family from Montreux,

canton Vaud, French master at Harrow school till 1805. Ed. Harrow ; entered in 1798 ; left in 1803.
Services : Posted as Lieut. to 6th N.I. Nepal War 1814-5 ; Lieut. 2/6th N.I., in 1st Div. With newly-raised 2nd Nassiri Bn. from 1815 till death.
Refs. : Harrow School Register. G.M. 1819, i. 654.

BUXTON, Bentley (1796-1825). Lieutenant, Engineers. *b.* Leicester 26 Sept. 1796. Cadet 1815. Ensign 25 Apr. 1817. Lieut. 1 Sept. 1818. *d.* Singapore 28 Feb. 1825.
bapt. 28 Oct. 1796. Son of Thomas Bentley Buxton, of North America, and Anne his wife. Addiscombe Cadet 1811-4.
Services : Employed on survey work in Cuttack 1818 till 1822. Bk. Mr. at Ghazipur in 1823. Asst. to Supt. of public bldgs. in lower provinces 1823 till death.

BYERS, John Lawson (1785-1815). Lieutenant, 6th N.C. *b.* Bowness, Cumberland, 13 May 1785. Cadet 1804. Arrived in India 10 Dec. 1805. Cornet 13 Sept. 1805. Lieut. 18 Jan. 1811. *d.* Kaitha 27 Aug. 1815.
Son of John Byers, customs officer.
Services : Posted as Cornet to 6th N.C. Settlement of Hariana 1809 ; Bhawani 29 Aug. 1809 (w.) ; Cornet 6th N.C. Adjt. 6th N.C. 5 Apr. 1811 till death.

BYGRAVE, Bulstrode (1802-1873). Major General. 31st N.I.
bapt. Newchurch, I.W., 9 Oct. 1802. Cadet 1820. Admitted 5 June 1821. Ensign 16 Jan. 1821. Lieut. 11 July 1823. Capt. 4 May 1837. Major 8 July 1848. Lt. Col. 15 Nov. 1853. Bt. Col. 28 Nov. 1854. Retired 31 Dec. 1861. Hon. Maj. Gen. 31 Dec. 1861. *d.* 4 Mansfield St., Portland Pl., London, 9 Oct. 1873, aged 71.
Son of George Augustus Bygrave, Bk. Mr., I.W.
Services : Posted as Ensign to 3rd N.I. Transfd. to 2nd N.I. 11 July 1823 ; to 5th N.I. (late 1/2nd) May 1824. Pioneers 26 Dec. 1822. First Burma War ; Sylhet frontier and Arakan ; Lieut. Pioneers (India medal). Adjt. Pioneers 10 May 1826. Paymr. of Native Pensioners, and Adjt. of Native Invalids at Allahabad 2 July 1828. First Afghan War ; joined Army of Indus as Field Paymr. in Nov. 1838, and was employed in Afghanistan as Paymr. Gen. until the end of the campaign ; Ghazni (Medal) ; taken prisoner by Mohd. Akbar during retreat from Kabul ; released 27 Sept. 1842. (Toes of one foot nipped off by frost during the retreat, for which he was awarded a special pension of £80 *p.a.*) Paymr. at Calcutta, and to Queen's troops. Transfd. from 5th N.I.

to newly-raised 3rd Eur. Regt. 15 Nov. 1853 ; to 60th N.I. in Feb. 1857 ; to 31st N.I. in 1857. Fur. s.c. 22 Apr. 1854 till death. Durani, 3 cl.
Refs. : Boase. The Times, 14 Oct. 1873.

BYNG, Hon. Robert Barlow Palmer (1816-1857). Major, 62nd N.I. *b.* Chatham 30 Nov. 1816. Cadet 1832. Arrived in India 16 June 1834. Ensign 16 June 1834. Lieut. 4 Jan. 1836. Capt. 5 July 1844. Major 9 Apr. 1856. *d.* Latu, Assam, 18 Dec. 1857 : kld. in action against the mutineers.

2nd son of George, sixth Viscount Torrington, and Frances Harriet his 2nd wife, dau. of Adm. Sir Robert Barlow, G.C.B. *m.* Hapur, U.P., 11 Feb. 1830, Elizabeth Maria Lowther, eldest dau. of Edward Gwatkin, *q.v.* (*See also* Dacres Fitzherbert Evans.) (She *re-m.* 11 Feb. 1861, and died Rome, 5 Nov. 1868, aged 51.) Father of George Stanley, eighth Viscount Torrington.

Services : Ensign d.d. 10th N.I. 22 July 1834. Posted as Ensign to 62nd N.I. 5 Nov. 1834. Actg. Sub-Asst., Stud Dept., 13 Sept. 1838 till 5 Jan. 1842. Gwalior campaign ; Maharajpur ; Lieut. 62nd N.I. (Bronze star). Mily. Sec. to Dy. Govr. of Bengal Oct. 1848. Offg. in P.W.D. Comdg. Sebundy Corps of S. & M. at Darjeeling 8 Mar. 1849. Comdt. Sylhet L.I. 18 July 1854 till death.

Refs. : Burke's *Peerage,* 1923, p. 2186, *s.n.* Torrington, V. *Howard & Crisp,* ii. 169. *G.M.* 1858, i. 337. *The Times,* 31 Jan. 1858. Will dated 28 June 1856 ; proved 27 Aug. 1858.

BYRES, Patrick (*c.* 1778-1854). Lieut. General. Colonel 33rd N.I. *b. c.* 1778. Cadet 1794. Arrived in India 26 Feb. 1796. Ensign 9 Dec. 1795. Lieut. 30 Oct. 1797. Capt. 12 June 1807. Major 5 Aug. 1816. Lt. Col. 7 Nov. 1822. Lt. Col. Comdt. 13 June 1825. Col. 5 June 1829. Maj. Gen. 28 June 1838. Lt. Gen. 11 Nov. 1851. *d.* Tonley, co. Aberdeen, 1 Feb. 1854, aged 76.

Of Tonley. 2nd son of Robert Byres, of Memil, Prussia, and London, merchant, and Margaret his wife, dau. of James Burnett, of Aberdeen, merchant. *m.* 1st, Dacca, 10 Mar. 1813, Janet Frances Denniss (*possibly* sister of George Gladwin Denniss, *q.v.*). (She died at sea, on board the *Fairlie,* 17 Feb. 1822.) *m.* 2nd, Gadgirth, 25 Apr. 1834, his cousin Margaret, eldest dau. of Joseph Burnett, of Gadgirth, co. Ayr, *q.v.*

Services : Transfd. from Engineers to Inf. at his own request. 1st Bn. Bengal Vols. 1799-1800. Adjt. 1/11th N.I. 1802-6. Second Mahratta War ; Aligarh ; Laswari ; battle of Deig ; siege of Bhurtpore (India medal). To comd. Chittagong Provl. Bn. Aug. 1809. Comdd. Dacca Provl. Bn. 31 Oct. 1812 till 29 Mar. 1816. Siege and capture of Hathras ; Major 2/11th N.I. Lt. Col. Comdt.

272 LIST OF OFFICERS OF THE BENGAL ARMY

20th N.I. 13 June 1825. Fur. s.c. 2 Jan. 1827 till death. Col. 33rd N.I. in 1840.

Refs. : Burke's *Landed Gentry*, 13th edn., p. 257, *s.n.* Moir-Byres, of Tonley, co. Aberdeen. *G.M.* 1854, i. 553. *A.J.* N.S. xiv. 149.

BYRN, John (*d.* 1811 ?). Major. 26th N.I. Cadet (?). Ensign 12 Nov. 1765. Lieut. (?). Capt. 28 Sept. 1771. Major 20 Jan. 1781. Dismissed by G.C.M. Mar. 1782. (? *d.* Manchester St., London, 26 Nov. 1811.)

Services : (? *Probably* resigned during the Batta mutiny in 1766, being re-admitted subsequently.) Raised at Cawnpore in 1778 the 26th Bn. Sepoys, which afterwards formed part of 11th Regt. Second Mysore War ; Major comdg. 26th Bn.

Refs. : *Williams*, p. 161. (? Burke's *Landed Gentry*, 6th edn., p. 245, *s.n.* Byrne, of Allardstown, co. Louth. *G.M.* 1811, ii. 590.)

BYRNE, Thomas Carey (1788-1812). Lieutenant, 19th N.I. *b.* Castlelyons, co. Cork, 6 Dec. 1788. Cadet 1805. Arrived in India 11 July 1806. Ensign 13 Sept. 1806. Lieut. 13 June 1808. *d. unm.* at sea, 23 Sept. 1812, on board the *Helen*.

Late of Ballyclough, co. Cork. Brother of Edward Sweeny Byrne, Eliza Byrne, and Mary, wife of Daniel Geran.

Services : Posted as Ensign to 19th N.I. in 1807. Capture of Java 1811 ; Lieut. 5th Bn. Bengal Vols. Expedition to Sumatra 1812 ; capture of Palembang ; Lieut. 5th Bn. Bengal Vols.

Refs. : Will dated Barrackpore 13 Mar. 1811 ; proved 30 Apr. 1813.

BYRON, George (1805-1834). Lieutenant, 48th N.I. *b.* Haughton-le-Skerne, co. Durham, 10 Aug. 1805. Cadet 1821. Arrived in India 19 Aug. 1822. Ensign 10 Mar. 1821. Lieut. 13 May 1825. *d.* Sitapur, U.P., 23 May 1834, of fever.

2nd son of Rev. Henry Byron, rector of Muston, Leics., and Margaret his wife, eldest dau. of Thomas Powditch. Great grandson of William, fourth Baron Byron. *m.* Calcutta, 16 Nov. 1831, Georgiana Caroline Barbara, youngest dau. of Johan Frederick Meiselback, sometime Col. in the Mahratta service. (*See also* Philip George Cornish, Constantine William Cowley, William Hodgson, Edward Jackson, and George Weyland Moseley.)

Services : Posted as Ensign to 24th N.I. Transfd. to 48th N.I. (late 2/24th) May 1824. No record of active service.

Refs. : Burke's *Peerage*, 1923, p. 414, *s.n.* Byron, B. *G.M.* 1835, i. 221. *A.J.* N.S. xv. 227.

C

CADDELL, Walter (1806-1847). Captain, 36th N.I. *b.* I. of Barbados 21 Mar. 1806. Cadet 1826. Arrived in India 1 June 1827. Ensign 3 Feb. 1827. Lieut. 8 Oct. 1839. Capt. 30 Jan. 1846. *d.* Hoshiarpur, Punjab, 22 June 1847, of apoplexy.

Son of —— Caddell, of Bristol. *m.* Norton Bavant, Wilts., 5 May 1846, Helen, youngest dau. of Hon. John Braithwaite Skeete, president of the council of Barbados.

Services : Posted as Ensign to 36th N.I. Shekhawat expedition ; Ensign 36th N.I. Apptd. to 2nd Inf. Regt., Nizam's army, 9 Jan. 1836. Fur. s.c. 1 Nov. 1843 till Oct. 1846. Rejoined 36th N.I. in 1846.

Refs. : De Rhé-Philipe. Bath. Chron. 2 Sept. 1847.

CADDY, Douglas Truscott (1808-1855). Bt. Major. 70th N.I. *b.* Canada 8 July 1808. Cadet 1823. Arrived in India 31 Mar. 1825. Ensign 10 Sept. 1824. Lieut. 4 June 1826. Capt. 6 Mar. 1841. Bt. Major 11 Nov. 1851. Retired 1 Apr. 1853. *d.* at sea, 3 Jan. 1855, on the voyage to Tasmania.

Son of John Caddy, Lt. Col. R.A. *m.* Simla, 16 July 1853, Hannah Anwer (*alias* Anwer Bibi).

Services : Posted as Ensign to 2nd Extra Regt. (became 70th N.I.). Intr. & Qmr. 70th N.I. 22 Aug. 1837 till 1841. No record of active service.

Refs. : Will dated 23 Oct. 1848 ; codicil dated Simla 2 July 1853 ; proved 8 Mar. 1855.

CADE, William John (1807-1860). Major. 13th N.I. *b.* Wimbledon, Surrey, 27 Apr. 1807. Cadet 1823. Ensign 17 Jan. 1824. Lieut. 13 May 1825. Capt. 6 Sept. 1842. Retired 30 June 1848. Hon. Major 28 Nov. 1854. *d.* London 24 Mar. 1860.

Son of Joseph Cade, purser, E.I.C.N.S.

Services : Posted as Ensign to 13th N.I. Fur. 2 Dec. 1833 till 1837. Adjt. Mhairwara Local Bn. 25 Nov. 1839 ; 2nd in comd. do. 26 Feb. 1842 till retirement.

Refs. : The Times, 2 Apr. 1860. *I.M.* 1860, p. 261.

274 LIST OF THE OFFICERS OF

*CAESAR, Julius. Lieutenant, Infantry. Cadet (?). Ensign (?). Lieut. 6 Dec. 1765.
Services : N.F.P.
Refs. : *B.M. Add. MS.* 6050.

*CAILLAUD, John (1724-1812). Lieut. Colonel comdg. in Bengal. Afterwards C.-in-C. Madras. *b.* 1724. Arrived in India 1753. Arrived in Bengal Nov. 1759. Lt. Col. Jan. 1760. Reverted to Madras 1761. *d.* Aston Rowant, Oxon., 26 Dec. 1812, aged 88.
m. (?). (She died Aston Rowant, Oct. 1808, aged 77.) D.C.L. Oxon. 9 July 1773.
Services : Joined Onslow's Regt. (afterwards the 8th King's) in 1743. Fought at Fontenoy and Culloden. Bt. Capt. Madras Est. 12 May 1753. Capt. 26 June 1753. Apptd. to comd. of Bengal army 25 Feb. 1760. Comdd. during the war in Bihar in 1760. Was succeeded as C.-in-C. by John Carnac, *q.v.* 31 Dec. 1760. Offg. C.-in-C. Madras 1761. Bdr. Gen. 8 July 1763. C.-in-C. Madras 1766. Resigned and returned to England in Jan. 1767. Granted a special pension of £500 *p.a.* by the E.I.Co. on 7 Mar. 1775.
Refs. : *D.I.B.* *E.I.M.C.* ii. 57-9. *Love,* ii. *passim. Alumni Oxon. S.M.* 1813, p. 159.

CALCRAFT, Henry Fox (1756/57-1834). Lieut. General. Colonel 55th N.I. *b.* 1756/57. Cadet 1778. Arrived in India 10 Dec. 1778. Ensign 1778. Lieut. 10 Oct. 1778. Capt. 7 Jan. 1796. Major 29 May 1800. Lt. Col. 13 July 1803. Col. 1 Jan. 1812. Maj. Gen. 4 June 1814. Lt. Gen. 22 July 1830. *d.* Brighton 3 Apr. 1834.
Son of John Calcraft, the army agent (*D.N.B.*), and George Anne Bellamy, the actress. Half-brother of Rt. Hon. John Calcraft, of Rempstone, M.P. co. Dorset (*D.N.B.*). *m.* Calcutta, 19 Feb. 1795, Marianne Elizabeth, only dau. of James Bremer, Capt. R.N., and aunt of Thomas Mountsteven Bremer, *q.v.*
Services : Campaign against the Rajah of Benares 1781. Fur. p.a. 10 Feb. 1785 till 3 Mar. 1792. J.A.G. 7 Nov. 1793 till 26 June 1813. Sec. and A.D.C. to V.P. and Dy. Govr. 27 Feb. 1797 till 13 Mar. 1798. Fort Major, Fort William, 1798 till 1 May 1813. Fur. s.c. 25 July 1813 till death. Served in Bengal Eur. Regt., 21st, 2nd, 1st N.I. Transfd. to 29th N.I. in 1814 ; to 15th N.I. in 1824 ; to 55th N.I. in 1826.
Refs. : Burke's *Landed Gentry,* 10th edn., p. 218, *s.n.* Calcraft, of Rempstone, Dorset. *Hickey,* iii. 204. *G.M.* 1834, ii. 329. Will dated 18 Nov. 1831 ; proved 14 Dec. 1835.

THE BENGAL ARMY, 1758-1834 275

CALDECOTT, John Marriott (1800-?). Lieutenant. 7th N.I. b. Dudleston, Salop., 19 May 1800. Cadet 1818. Ensign (?). Lieut. 17 May 1820. Resigned in India 11 Jan. 1822. d.s.p. (?).

3rd son of Abraham Caldecott, Accountant Gen. at Calcutta, later of Rugby, high sheriff co. Warwick in 1821, and Elizabeth his wife, eldest dau. of Rev. Dr. Marriott, of Cottesbatch, Leics. Ed. Rugby ; entered on the foundation at midsummer 1807.

Services : Ensign d.d. 14th N.I. Posted as Lieut. to 1/7th N.I. in 1820. No record of active service.

Refs. : Burke's *Landed Gentry*, 13th edn., p. 264, *s.n.* Caldecott (now Bolam), of Holbrook Grange, co. Warwick.

CALDWELL, Sir Alexander (1763-1839). Major General, G.C.B. Lt. Col. Comdt. Artillery. b. 1 Feb. 1763. Cadet 1782. Admitted 17 July 1783. Ensign (Inf.) 1782. Fireworker (Art.) 3 Apr. 1783. Lieut. 21 Nov. 1790. Capt. Lt. 23 Aug. 1796. Capt. 25 Dec. 1802. Major 15 May 1807. Lt. Col. 1 Mar. 1812. Lt. Col. Comdt. 4 May 1820. Col. 5 June 1829. Maj. Gen. 10 Jan. 1837. *d.* Upper Berkeley St., London, 6 Dec. 1839.

Son of William Caldwell. Brother of Arthur (? James) Caldwell, *q.v. m.* 1st, Calcutta, 15 May 1793, Miss Ann Miller. *m.* 2nd, in England, 7 July 1835, Elizabeth, 2nd dau. of E. W. Shepheard, of Gt. Russell St., Bloomsbury, London. Ed. R.M.A. Woolwich.

Services : See *D.N.B.* Arrived at Madras in Apr. 1783. Fur. 15 Mar. 1789 till 31 July 1791 ; 4 Apr. 1801 till 1 Dec. 1804 ; 22 Sept. 1806 till 26 Jan. 1810 ; 19 Dec. 1820 till death. C.B. 3 Feb. 1817. K.C.B. 10 Mar. 1837. G.C.B. 20 July 1838.

Refs. : D.N.B. D.I.B. Burke's *Landed Gentry*, 4th edn., p. 198, *s.n.* Caldwell, of Beachlands, I.W. *E.I.M.C.* i. 235. *G.M.* Feb. 1840. *A.J.* N.S. xvii. 279 ; xxxi. 91. *The Times*, 9 Dec. 1839.

CALDWELL, Hugh (1786-1882). Colonel. 61st N.I. b. Kilmarnock 3 Sept. 1786. Cadet 1805. Arrived in India 11 July 1806. Ensign 10 Sept. 1806. Lieut. 15 Aug. 1809. Capt. 1 May 1824. Major 27 May 1830. Lt. Col. 16 Nov. 1835. Retired 9 Aug. 1836. Hon. Col. 28 Nov. 1854. *d.* Palazzo Tittoni, Via Rassella, Rome, 21 Feb. 1882.

4th son of James Caldwell, of High Milton, and Jean Hunter his wife. *m.* (?). (She died Rome *c.* 1876.)

Services : Posted as Ensign to 2/25th N.I. A.D.C. to the Earl of Moira, G.G., 24 Feb. 1815. Third Mahratta War ; A.D.C. to the Marquis of Hastings, G.G. Paymr. at Calcutta 1 May 1819. Transfd. to 1/25th N.I. Extra A.D.C. to Actg. G.G. 15 Jan. 1823 ; do. to Lord Amherst, G.G., 1 Aug. 1823. Transfd. to 49th N.I. (late 1/25th) May 1824. Supt. of Mysore Princes 26 Feb. 1827.

A.D.C. to Lord William Bentinck, G.G., 16 Aug. 1828. Fur. 9 Feb. 1834 till retirement. Transfd. as Lt. Col. to 61st N.I. 1 Mar. 1836.
Refs. : Boase. *The Times*, 27 Feb. 1882, pp. 5, 7.

CALDWELL, James (? Arthur). Lieutenant. Engineers. Cadet 1781. Ensign (?). Lieut. 4 Sept. 1781. Resigned 1793.
(? Brother of Sir Alexander Caldwell, G.C.B., *q.v.*)
Services : N.F.P.
Refs. : (? Burke's *Landed Gentry*, 4th edn., p. 198, *s.n.* Caldwell, of Beachlands, I.W.)

CALDWELL, Robert (1746/47-1778). Ensign, Infantry. *b.* in Ireland 1746/47. Cadet 1777. Arrived in India 2 Nov. 1777. Ensign 4 Jan. 1778. *d.* Berhampore, Bengal, 20 June 1778.
Services : Sailed for India on the *Sea Horse*, 30 Apr. 1777, aged 30. N.F.P.

CALEY, Henry Francis (1792-1866). Major General. Colonel 64th N.I. *b.* Doncaster 15 Mar. 1792. Cadet 1806. Arrived in India 25 Nov. 1807. Ensign 21 Oct. 1807. Lieut. 2 Mar. 1814. Capt. 1 May 1824. Major 21 Jan. 1838. Lt. Col. 16 Apr. 1844. Col. 7 Nov. 1854. Maj. Gen. 18 Mar. 1856. *d.* Rawal Pindi 21 Dec. 1866.

Son of Francis Caley, of Doncaster, surgeon. *m.* Nimach, C.I., 19 Apr. 1823, Margaret Catherine, dau. of John Baillie (1772-1833), *q.v.* (*See also* Thomas Richard Macqueen.)
Services : Barasat C.C. Nov. 1807 till 1 Dec. 1808. Posted as Ensign to 1/1st N.I. 1st Gren. Bn. Dec. 1814. Nepal War 1815 ; Lieut. 1st Gren. Bn. (India medal). Transfd. to 2/1st N.I. in May 1815. Adjt. 4 May 1815 till May 1824. Siege and capture of Hathras ; Lieut. 2/1st N.I. Third Mahratta War ; Dhamoni ; Mandala ; Asirgarh ; Lieut. 2/1st N.I. Transfd. to 4th N.I. (late 2/1st) 1 May 1824. Against the Bhils in 1824 ; Capt. 4th N.I. Comdd. 4th N.I. 1842-4. Comdd. 64th N.I. July 1844 till 1854. Bdr. comdg. Sind Sagar district 1 Sept. 1854 till July 1856. Transfd. to 74th N.I. in Sept. 1854 ; to 50th N.I. in Jan. 1855 ; to 1st Eur. Bengal Fus. in Feb. 1855. Col. 64th N.I. Nov. 1855.
Refs. : De Rhé-Philipe. Boase.

CALL, Thomas (*d.* 1788). Chief Engineer in Bengal. Cadet (?). Ensign 15 Sept. 1771. Lieut. 16 Nov. 1773. Capt. 25 Oct. 1777. Resigned 15 Nov. 1788. *d.* 12 Dec. 1788.

Younger son of Richard Call, of Prestacutt, Launcells, Cornwall, and Mary his wife, of Kenton, nr. Exeter. Cousin-german of Sir John Call, 1st Bart., of Whiteford, Cornwall (*D.N.B.*). *m.* Calcutta, 5 Feb. 1784, Bethia, dau. of John Blackburn, of Sneaton, Yorks.

Services : N.F.P. Author of "A Plan of Fort William and Calcutta . . ."
Refs. : Foster's *Baronetage*, p. 98, *s.n.* Call, Bart. Burke's *Landed Gentry*, 13th edn., p. 149, *s.n.* Blackburne, of Hayne, Devon. Will.

CALLANDER, Adam (1747/48-1815). Captain. Infantry. *b.* 1747/48. Capt. 22 Oct. 1769. Resigned 4 Jan. 1773. *d.* New Cavendish St., London, 14 Aug. 1815, aged 67.
3rd son of John Callander, of Craigforth, co. Stirling, and Mary his wife, eldest dau. of Sir James Livingstone, Bart., of Glentirran and Dalderse. *m.* (?).
Services : N.F.P. Not in Army List of 1 Feb. 1767, so *probably* transfd. as Capt. from H.M.S.
Refs. : Burke's *Landed Gentry*, 13th edn., p. 264, *s.n.* Callander, of Ardkinglass, co. Argyll. *G.M.* 1815, ii. 279.

CALLANDER, Alexander. Ensign. Infantry. Cadet 1770. Ensign 23 Sept. 1770. Resigned 19 Oct. 1771.
Services : N.F.P.

CALVERT, Thomas Palin (1789-1817). Lieutenant. Unposted. Subsequently a Junior Merchant, B.C.S. *b.* 1789. Cadet 1805. Lieut. 11 Apr. 1806. Resigned in England 28 Jan. 1807. *d.* Saharanpur, U.P., 1817.
Of the family of Calvert, of Ockley Court, Surrey. (*Probably* son of Thomas Calvert, B.C.S., and his wife ——, née Philpot.)
Services : Never went to India in a military capacity. Apptd. a Writer, B.C.S., 21 July 1807. Arrived in India 7 Aug. 1807. Admitted to the Coll. at Fort William in Aug. 1807. In charge of the collectorate of Saharanpur in 1817.
Refs. : Burke's *Landed Gentry*, 13th edn., p. 268, *s.n.* Calvert, of Ockley Court, Surrey. Will dated 23 Oct. 1815 ; proved 13 Jan. 1818.
Note : The residuary legatee was Charles Calvert, M.P., of Upper Thames St., London.

CAMAC, George (1765/66-1785). Lieutenant, Infantry. *b.* in Ireland 1765/66. Cadet 1781. Ensign 1781. Lieut. 2 Aug. 1782. *d.* Ramgarh, B. & O., 3 Jan. 1785.
(*Probably* brother of Jacob Camac, *q.v.*)
Services : Apptd. a Cadet on 13 Feb. 1781, aged 17. N.F.P.

CAMAC, Jacob (1744/45-1784 ?). Lieut. Colonel. 24th (Ramgarh) Bn. *b.* 1744/45. Lieut. 14 Oct. 1763. Capt. 18 July 1766. Major 22 Jan. 1777. Lt. Col. 3 Jan. 1781. Resigned 2 Dec. 1782. *d.* in Ireland 1784 ?

Of Greenmount, co. Louth. Son of John Camac, of Lurgan, co. Armagh. Brother of Turner Camac, *q.v.*, of Thomas Camac (to whom he bequeathed Rosehall, co. Down), of George Camac, and of Margaret, wife of William Lane (1753-1814), *q.v.*

Services : Sailed for India on the *Clinton*, 5 Feb. 1762, aged 17. Transfd. to the Bengal army as a Lieut. from H.M. 84th Regt. in 1763. Capt. Lt. 2 Aug. 1765. First Mahratta War 1780-1 ; succeeded Major Popham, *q.v.*, in comd. of the force ; capture of Sipri ; night attack of 24 Mar. 1781. Comdd. the newly-raised 24th Bn. from the end of 1766 till his promotion to Major.

Refs. : E.I.M.C. ii. 101. D.I.B. Williams, p. 70. Will dated 22 Feb. 1781 ; proved 8 July 1785.

CAMAC, Turner. Captain. Infantry. Cadet 1768. Ensign 29 Jan. 1769. Lieut. 28 May 1770. Capt. 9 Oct. 1778. Resigned 23 Dec. 1779.

Of Mount-ross, co. Down. Son of John Camac, of Lurgan, co. Armagh. Brother of Jacob Camac, *q.v.*

Services : N.F.P.

CAMERON, Allan (1799-1821). Lieutenant, Artillery. *b.* Kilmallie, co. Inverness, 15 Nov. 1790. Cadet 1807. Arrived in India 16 Nov. 1808. Fireworker 19 Sept. 1808. Lieut. 16 Oct. 1810. *d.* Mhow 27 Sept. 1821.

Eldest son of Alexander Cameron, of Culcraigie, co. Ross. *m.* Agra, 2 Jan. 1821, Miss Isabella Mackenzie. (She *re-m.* 16 Oct. 1827, Col. Hugh Fraser, Madras Cav.)

Services : Capture of Java 1811 ; Lieut. 1st Coy. 2nd Bn. Art. Capture of Jokyakarta 1812. Capture of Sambas 1813. Posted to 1st Troop H.A. in 1818.

Refs. : S.M. 1822, i. 828.

*CAMERON, Hugh Stronack (*c.* 1702-1782). Bt. Ensign. *b.* Tarbat Ness, co. Ross, *c.* 1702. Bt. Ensign (?). *d.* Chunar, 21 Oct. 1782, aged about 80.

m. (?).

Services : Commissioned from the ranks as Bt. Ensign. N.F.P.

Refs. : Will dated Chunar 28 Sept. 1782. M.I. in the fort cemetery at Chunar.

CAMERON, John (*d.* 1776). Lieutenant, Engineers. Cadet (?). Ensign 10 Apr. 1764. Lieut. 21 Mar. 1765. bur. Calcutta 5 June 1776.

Services : Promoted to Sub-Engineer and Lieut. on 25 Mar. 1765 (subsequently antedated to 21 Mar.). N.F.P.

THE BENGAL ARMY, 1758-1834 279

CAMERON, Kenneth (d. 1766). Lieutenant, Infantry. Cadet 1762. Ensign 5 Nov. 1764. Lieut. 25 Mar. 1765. d. Calcutta 9 June 1766.
Services : N.F.P.

CAMERON, William Neville (1755-1837). Lieut. General. Engineers. b. 1755. Cadet 1772. Ensign 8 May 1775. Lieut. 26 July 1778. Capt. 12 Feb. 1781. Major 15 Nov. 1786. Lt. Col. 24 Feb. 1793. Col. 25 Apr. 1797. Maj. Gen. 1 Jan. 1801. Lt. Gen. 25 Apr. 1808. d. his residence, the Circus, Bath, 13 May 1837, aged 82.
Of New House, nr. Christchurch. Son of Rev. William Cameron and Judith his wife, dau. of Rev. William Somerville, rector of Castlehaven, co. Cork. m. Calcutta, 17 Aug. 1789, Charlotte, 2nd dau. of Sir William Gordon, 7th Bart., of Embo, and sister of Sir John Gordon, 8th Bart., q.v. (*See also* Charles Stewart (1764-1837), and Jabez Mackenzie.) (She died Bath 21 Jan. 1846.)
Services : Nominated an Asst. Engr. and employed at Buxar Fort till 1774, when he joined the "Select Picket" serving with the army in the Rohilla War and was employed under the Field Engr. First Mahratta War 1779-81 ; capture of Gwalior ; Engr. with the force under Major William Popham, q.v. Comdg. Engr., Chunar fort, 1787. Chief Engr. at Fort William 24 Feb. 1793. M.M.B. Fur. 1805 till death.
Refs. : Burke's *Peerage*, 1923, p. 994, s.n. Gordon, Bart., of Embo. E.I.M.C. i. 50. *John Cameron, non-Juror.* G.M. 1837, ii. 209. A.J. N.S. xxiii. 167. Bath Chron., 18 May 1837.

CAMPBELL, Alexander (1780-1825). Lieut. Colonel, 32nd N.I. b. Knockando, co. Moray, 1780. Cadet 1795. Arrived in India 4 Mar. 1797. Ensign 2 Dec. 1796. Lieut. 30 Oct. 1797. Capt. 19 Dec. 1805. Major 22 June 1816. Lt. Col. 1 Sept. 1822. d. Allahabad 13 June 1825.
m. Lambeth, 1809, eldest dau. of John Willis, of Kennington, Surrey, and Whitchurch, Oxon. His dau. m. William John Macvitie, q.v.
Services : Lieut. 4th N.I. Capt. Lt. 4th N.I. 2 May 1805. Second Mahratta War ; Aligarh ; Capt. 1/4th N.I. Fur. 21 Aug. 1808 till 12 Dec. 1810. Capture of Java ; Cornelis 26 Aug. 1811 (w.) ; Capt. 4th Bn. Bengal Vols. 3rd Vol. Bn. in 1816. Major 1/4th N.I. Transfd. to 1/16th N.I. in 1822 ; to 32nd N.I. (late 1/16th) May 1824.
Refs. : *Clan Campbell*, No. 5.

CAMPBELL, Alexander (1788-1850). Cornet. Cavalry. Afterwards Colonel, C.B., K.H., 9th Light Dragoons. *b.* co. Ayr 25 Aug. 1788. Cadet 1804. Arrived in India 13 May 1806. Cornet 1 Apr. 1806. Resigned in India 11 Sept. 1806. *d.* in England 23 Mar. 1850. *bapt.* 30 Aug. 1788. Son of Richard Campbell, of Helentonmains, St. Quivox, co. Ayr.
Services : Lieut. H.M. 25th Light Dns. 4 Sept. 1806. Transfd. to 9th Light Dns. Lt. Col. 16 July 1830. Col. 9 Nov. 1846. Bdr. Comdd. 2nd Cav. Bde. at the battle of Sobraon. C.B. K.H.
Refs. : Clan Campbell, No. 6. *I.M.* 1850, p. 210.

CAMPBELL, Alexander Æneas (1806-1850). Lieutenant, Pension Est. 5th N.I. Subsequently Dy. Supt. of Police, Calcutta. *b.* Poonamallee, nr. Madras, 14 Jan. 1806. Cadet 1821. Ensign 19 June 1822. Lieut. 1 May 1824. Pensioned 16 Mar. 1827. *d.* Calcutta, 22 Apr. 1850, of cholera.

Eldest son of Dr. John Campbell, Madras Est., of the Dunstaffnage family, and Eliza Munro his wife. Brother of Archibald (Charles) Campbell, *q.v.*, and nephew of Alexander Campbell, Capt. of the *Sovereign*, East Indiaman. *m.* Calcutta, 6 Apr. 1830, Miss Eliza Peterson, aged 17.
Services : Posted as Ensign to 19th N.I. Transfd. to 18th N.I. in 1823 ; to 36th N.I. (late 1/18th) May 1824 ; to 37th N.I. in 1825. Siege and capture of Bhurtpore ; Lieut. 37th N.I. Transfd. to 5th N.I. in 1826. After transfer to the pension est. he entered the service of Shah Shuja, of Afghanistan, and comdd. two Bns. of Hindustanis at the defeat of the Shah's army by Dost Muhammad Khan at Kandahar in 1834. He received three wounds on this occasion. After the action he was taken over by Dost Muhammad at double the salary he was getting from the Shah. He was for some time a Dy. Collector, E.I.C.S., and was eventually apptd. Dy. Supt. of Police.
Refs. : Clan Campbell, No. 11. *A.J.* N.S. xvi. 97, 146. *I.M.* 1850, p. 350.

CAMPBELL, Alexander Livingstone (1791-1819). Lieutenant, 4th N.I. *bapt.* Lochgoilhead, co. Argyll, 10 July 1791. Cadet 1807. Arrived in India 25 Mar. 1809. Ensign 17 Feb. 1809. Lieut. 16 Dec. 1814. *d.* Chanda, C.P., 7 Dec. 1819, of a bilious fever.

Son of James Campbell, tacksman of Polchorkan, Lochgoilhead, and Barbara Hare his wife. Brother of Ivie Campbell, *q.v.*, and cousin of Duncan Campbell (1788-1819), *q.v.*, and of Lachlan McLachlan, *q.v.*
Services : Posted as Ensign to 4th N.I. Lieut. 1/4th N.I. Adjt. 1/4th N.I. 4 May 1815 till death. No record of active service.
Refs. : Clan Campbell, No. 17.

THE BENGAL ARMY, 1758-1834

CAMPBELL, Sir Archibald (1739-1791). Lieut. Colonel, Engineers. Chief Engineer of Bengal. Afterwards Major General, K.B. Governor of Madras. *b.* Inverneill, co. Argyll, 21 Aug. 1739. Lt. Col. 1 Sept. 1768. Resigned 19 Sept. 1772. *d.* Upper Grosvenor St., London, 31 Mar. 1791.

2nd son of James Campbell, of Inverneill, commissary of the Western Isles of Scotland, and chamberlain of Argyll, and Elizabeth his wife, dau. of James Fisher, of Durren, provost of Inverary. Grand-uncle of Archibald Lorne Campbell, *q.v.*, of Cornwallis Campbell, *q.v.*, and of George Campbell, *q.v. m.* Marylebone, 7 July 1779, Amelia, eldest dau. of Allan Ramsay, of Kinkell, portrait painter to George III. (She died London, 8 July 1813, aged 58.)

Services : See *D.N.B.* Sailed for India on the *Thames* 21 Mar. 1768. K.B. 30 Sept. 1785.

Refs. : Burke's *Landed Gentry*, 13th edn., p. 277, *s.n.* Campbell, of Inverneill and Ross, co. Argyll. *D.N.B. Clan Campbell*, No. 23. *D.I.B. Thackeray*, p. 7. *Harleian Soc.* x. 448. *Love*, iii. 319-21 (photogravure of the portrait by George Romney).

CAMPBELL, Archibald (1763/64-1821). Lieut. Colonel, 26th N.I. *b.* 1763/64. Cadet 1783. Arrived in India 27 Feb. 1784. Ensign 23 Apr. 1785. Lieut. 26 June 1793. Capt. 21 Sept. 1804. Major 3 Dec. 1813. Lt. Col. 1 Apr. 1818. *d.* Calcutta, 19 Mar. 1821, aged 57.

Son of Dugald Campbell, of Kintarbert, co. Argyll, and fourth in descent from Sir Robert Campbell, 3rd Bart., of Glenorchy.

Services : Sailed for India on the *Besborough* 17 Mar. 1783. Ensign 26th N.I. Lieut. 23rd Bn. Transfd. to 13th Bn. 18 Oct. 1793. (? Second Rohilla War ; Bitaurah ; Lieut. 13th Bn.) Adjt. & Qmr. 5th N.I. in 1803 till 18 Jan. 1805. Fort Adjt. at Fort William 24 Feb. 1807 till 1810. A.C.G. 5 June 1810 till 1818. Capture of Java 1811 ; Comy. Gen. Dy. Comy. Gen. in Java in 1816. Transfd. as Lt. Col. to 26th N.I. in 1818 ; to 9th N.I. in 1819 ; to 26th N.I. in 1820.

Refs.: *Clan Campbell*, No. 24. *S.M.* 1821, ii. 394. M.I. in S. Park St. burial ground, Calcutta.

CAMPBELL, Archibald (Charles) (1807-1845). Bt. Captain, 1st L.C. *b.* Poonamallee, nr. Madras, 26 Aug. 1807. Cadet 1825. Arrived in India 7 July 1826. Cornet 15 Mar. 1826. Lieut. 27 Apr. 1833. Bt. Capt. 15 Mar. 1841. *d.* Cape of Good Hope 23 Oct. 1845.

2nd son of John Campbell, Surgeon, Madras Est., and Eliza Munro his wife. Brother of Osborne Campbell, *q.v. m.* Calcutta,

11 July 1836, Emily, only dau. of J. W. Payter, of Rangpur, Assam, indigo planter.

Services : Posted as Cornet to 1st L.C. 26 Sept. 1826. Adjt. 17 July 1830 till 9 Dec. 1837. First Afghan War 1842 ; re-occupation of Kabul ; Bt. Capt. 1st L.C., with Gen. Pollock's force (Medal). Gwalior campaign ; Maharajpur ; Bt. Capt. 1st L.C. (Bronze star). Fur. m.c. 28 Mar. 1845.

Refs. : Clan Campbell, No. 32.

CAMPBELL, Archibald Lorne (1804-1883). Major General. 2nd European L.C. *b.* Patna 17 Dec. 1804. Cadet 1820. Arrived in India 5 Nov. 1821. Cornet 4 July 1821. Lieut. 13 May 1825. Capt. 12 Jan. 1834. Major 20 Oct. 1852. Lt. Col. 17 Sept. 1855. Bt. Col. 15 Sept. 1857. Retired 31 Dec. 1861. Hon. Maj. Gen. 31 Dec. 1861. *d.* 13 Melville St., Edinburgh, 25 May 1883.

4th and youngest son of Duncan Campbell, of Inverneill, B.C.S., Collector of Govt. customs at Murshidabad, and Elizabeth Cooper his wife, of Gravesend, Kent. Brother of George Campbell, *q.v.*, and grand-nephew of Sir Archibald Campbell, K.B., *q.v. m.* 1st, Calcutta, 3 Apr. 1839, Charlotte Susan, 2nd dau. of Abercrombie Dick, B.C.S. (She died Mian Mir 31 Oct. 1857.) *m.* 2nd, Jemima Janet, dau. of —— Paterson. (She died Brighton, 30 Mar. 1918, aged 81.)

Services : Posted as Cornet to 1st L.C. Fur. p.a. 30 Dec. 1835 till 7 Feb. 1839. First Afghan War 1842 ; re-occupation of Kabul ; Capt. 1st L.C., with Gen. Pollock's force (Medal). Gwalior campaign ; Maharajpur ; Capt. 1st L.C. (Bronze star). First Sikh War ; Aliwal, Bde. Major 2nd Cav. Bde. ; Sobraon (horse shot under him), A.D.C. to Maj.-Gen. Sir Robert Dick (Medal with clasp). Fur. 1855. Transfd. to 10th L.C. in 1856 ; to 9th L.C. 2 Jan. 1857 ; to 3rd Eur. L.C. in 1858 ; to 2nd Eur. L.C. in 1859.

Refs. : Burke's *Landed Gentry*, 13th edn., p. 277, *s.n.* Campbell, of Inverneill and Ross, co. Argyll. Clan Campbell, No. 36. *The Times*, 28 May 1883.

CAMPBELL, Arthur (1802-1833). Lieutenant, Artillery. *b.* Orange Hill, I. of Tobago, 9 Apr. 1802. Cadet 1818. Admitted 11 Sept. 1819. 2nd Lieut. 25 Apr. 1819. Lieut. 27 Oct. 1822. *d.* at sea, 30 May 1833, on his passage out to India.

Son of John Campbell, Lt. Col. 60th Regt., planter in Tobago, and Sophia his wife. Brother of John Campbell, and of Ellen, wife of Henry Walters. Ed. Eton 1814 till (?). Addiscombe Cadet Jan. 1817 till 6 Apr. 1819.

Services : Leave s.c. 12 mos. to China 17 June 1825. Fur. 31 Dec.

1829. Struck off from 25 May 1832, having been absent from India for a period exceeding two years. No record of active service. *Refs. : Clan Campbell*, No. 39. *Eton School Lists*. Will dated 24 May 1833 ; proved 23 Oct. 1833.

CAMPBELL, Charles (1807-1879). Major General. 42nd N.I. *b.* Little Dunkeld, co. Perth, 11 Mar. 1807. Cadet 1823. Arrived in India 9 Oct. 1824. Ensign 23 May 1824. Lieut. 14 July 1825. Capt. 21 Aug. 1843. Major 18 Sept. 1857. Bt. Lt. Col. 28 Nov. 1854. Bt. Col. 25 Oct. 1859. Retired 10 May 1860. Hon. Maj. Gen. 10 May 1860. *d.* 18 Gloucester Pl., Portman Sq., London, 27 Aug. 1879.

Of Kinloch, co. Perth. Eldest son of John Campbell, of Kinloch, and Ann Trapaud his wife, 4th dau. of John Campbell of Melfort. Brother of Ann Livingston, wife of Hope Dick, *q.v.* *m.* Cawnpore, 20 Apr. 1829, Caroline Charlotte, eldest dau. of James Wemyss, B.C.S., Collector at Cawnpore, and sister of James Wemyss, *q.v.* (She died Cawnpore 23 Aug. 1841.)

Services : Posted as Ensign to 42nd N.I. 31 Mar. 1825. First Burma War 1825-6 ; Lieut. 42nd N.I. (India medal). Adjt. 42nd N.I. 15 Jan. 1828 till 12 June 1832. Adjt. Kumaon Local Bn. 18 May 1832 till 9 Jan. 1836. Dy. Paymr. at Cawnpore 9 Jan. 1836. First Afghan War 1839-40 ; Ghazni ; Bt. Capt. 42nd N.I. (Medal). Dy. Paymr. 13 Oct. 1848 till 1857. Second Sikh War ; passage of Chenab ; Sadulapur ; Chilianwala ; Gujerat ; Capt. 42nd N.I., Paymr. to Army of the Punjab (Medal with clasp). Fur. 9 Feb. 1844.

Refs. : Burke's *Peerage*, 1923, p. 2293, *s.n.* Earl of Wemyss. *Clan Campbell*, No. 45. *Lady Login's Recollections*. *The Story of the Campbells of Kinloch*, by E. Dalhousie Login, chart i. *The Times*, 29 Aug. 1879.

CAMPBELL, Charles Hay (1789-1832). Major, Artillery. *b.* Edinburgh, 5 Jan. 1789. Cadet 1804. Arrived in India 10 July 1805. Lieut. 8 May 1805. Capt. Lt. 1 Mar. 1812. Capt. 27 Jan. 1818. Major 28 Sept. 1827. *d.* Fatehgarh, 19 May 1832, after an illness of a few hours only.

bapt. St. Andrews 6 May 1789. 3rd son of William Campbell, of Fairfield, co. Ayr, and Catherine his 2nd wife, dau. of Capt. William Gunning. Brother of Gabriel Napier Christie Campbell, *q.v.* *m.* Madras, 27 Sept. 1824, Jane Wemyss, dau. of Hon. Leveson Granville Keith Murray, Madras C.S., and grand-dau. of John, fourth Earl of Dunmore. (*See also* Christopher Simpson Maling.) Woolwich Cadet ; nominated for R.M.A. 9 Feb. 1803 ; obtained his certificate 4 Mar. 1805.

284 LIST OF THE OFFICERS OF

Services : Sailed for India on the *Surrey.* Second Mahratta War. Capture of Hirapur fort 19 Dec. 1808. Operations in Bundelkhand 1809 ; Rajaoli ; Ajaigarh. Adjt. & Qmr. 3rd Bn. Foot Art. 14 July 1810 till 1816. Siege and capture of Hathras ; Bde. Major to Maj.-Gen. Sir J. Horsford, comdg. the Art., *q.v.* Asst. Sec. to Govt., Mily. Dept., 1 Aug. 1819 ; Dy. do. 17 Apr. 1820. Agent for gun carriages at Cossipore (afterwards at Fatehgarh) 1821 till death. To comd. 1st Troop 3rd Bde. H.A. in 1825, but was seconded and never joined.

Refs. : Burke's *Landed Gentry,* 13th edn., p. 275, *s.n.* Campbell, of Fairfield, co. Ayr. *Clan Campbell,* No. 46. *D.I.B. A.J.* N.S. ix. 142. Will dated 10 Oct. 1831 ; proved 16 Aug. 1832.

CAMPBELL, Colin (1757-1792). Lieutenant, Infantry. *b.* 1757. Cadet 1776. Admitted 6 Mar. 1775. Ensign 23 Mar. 1777. Lieut. 17 Aug. 1778. *d.* Anupshahr, U.P., 15 May 1792.

2nd son of Patrick Campbell, of Ardchattan, co. Argyll, and Lilias Margaret his wife, dau. of John MacFarlane of that ilk. Brother of Robert Campbell (1765-1840), *q.v.*

Services : Sailed for India on the *Triton* 19 Apr. 1776. Removed to the Sepoy Corps, Bombay detachment, Aug. 1777. (? First Mahratta War.) Adjt. 25th Bn. (subsequently 22nd N.I.), in 6th Bde., in 1790.

Refs. : Burke's *Landed Gentry,* 4th edn., p. 204, *s.n.* Campbell, of Ardchattan Priory, co. Argyll. *Clan Campbell,* No. 50.

CAMPBELL, Colin (1775-1819). Major, 4th N.I. *b.* Greenock 13 Aug. 1775. Cadet 1795. Arrived in India 4 Feb. 1797. Ensign 6 Nov. 1796. Lieut. 30 Oct. 1797. Capt. 21 Sept. 1804. Major 14 July 1815. *d.* Gaya, B. & O., 6 June 1819, of jungle fever.

Son of Alexander Campbell, landwaiter, and Susannah his wife. Nephew of Thomas Campbell, of Grenada. *m.* Calcutta, 17 Sept. 1803, Lucy, sister of John Fombelle, B.C.S. (*See also* Henry Templer.) (She died Gaya 8 June 1819.)

Services : Sailed for India on the *Gen. Goddard* 12 Apr. 1796. Ensign 1/5th N.I. Fur. 31 Jan. 1802 till 6 Sept. 1803. Transfd. as Lieut. to 4th N.I. Second Mahratta War; battle of Deig; Capt. 1/4th N.I. Nepal War 1816 ; Major 2/4th N.I., in 4th Bde. Centre Div.

Refs. : Clan Campbell, No. 52. *G.M.* 1820, i. 186. *S.M.* 1820, i. *A.J.* ix. Will dated camp Deig 12 Nov. 1804 ; codicil dated 21 Feb. 1816 ; proved in 1819.

CAMPBELL, Colin (1804-1866). Colonel. 39th N.I. *b.* Ardchattan, co. Argyll, 1 Feb. 1804. Cadet 1819. Admitted 31 July 1820. Ensign 4 Mar. 1820. Lieut. 11 July 1823. Capt. 9 Mar.

1837. Major 23 June 1843. Lt. Col. 15 Dec. 1849. Retired 13 Nov. 1854. Hon. Col. 28 Nov. 1854. d. 28 Mar. 1866, of bronchitis.

Of Cononish, co. Perth. Son of John Campbell, of Auch, cadet of Barcaldine. m. Calcutta, 25 Nov. 1833, Miss Grace Ross. (She died Hansi 29 Oct. 1850.)

Services : Posted as Ensign to 1/30th N.I. 7 Dec. 1821 ; transfd. to 1/26th N.I. 13 Apr. 1822 ; to 27th N.I. 11 July 1823 ; to 53rd N.I. (late 1/27th) May 1824. Fur. p.a. 20 Nov. 1830 till 15 Nov. 1833. First Afghan War 1842 ; forcing of Khyber Pass ; Ali Masjid ; re-occupation of Kabul ; Capt. 53rd N.I., with Gen. Pollock's force (Medal). Second Sikh War ; in garrison at Lahore ; Major 53rd N.I. (Medal). Transfd. to 38th N.I. ; to 28th N.I. Apr. 1850 ; to 29th ; to 31st 18 June 1853 ; to 29th ; to 39th N.I. July 1854.

Refs. : Clan Campbell, No. 53.* Boase. The Times, 31 Mar. 1866.

CAMPBELL, Cornwallis (1788-1819). Bt. Captain, 2nd N.I. b. Benares 14 Jan. 1788. Cadet 1804. Arrived in India 17 Mar. 1805. Ensign 14 Apr. 1805. Lieut. 15 Apr. 1805. Bt. Capt. 1 Jan. 1818. d. Cuttack, 27 Nov. 1819, of fever.

bapt. Calcutta 26 June 1788. 2nd son of James Campbell, M.D., Bengal Medical Est., Apothecary at Calcutta, and Jessy his wife, 2nd dau. of Sir James Campbell, of Inverneill, and niece of Sir Archibald Campbell, K.B., q.v. Brother of James Campbell (1789-1806), q.v.

Services : Posted as Lieut. to 2nd N.I. in 1806. Expedition to Mauritius 1810-1 ; Lieut. 1st Bn. Bengal Vols. Nepal War 1814-5 ; Lieut. Ramgarh Bn., in 4th Div. Continued serving with Ramgarh Bn. till death.

Refs. : Clan Campbell, No. 56. A.J. x. 96.

CAMPBELL, Daniel (1804-1822). Ensign, 19th N.I. b. Greenock 11 May 1804. Cadet 1819. Ensign 19 May 1820. d. Chunar 28 Nov. 1822, of fever and liver complaint.

Son of Daniel Campbell, shipmaster, and Catherine Pagan his wife.

Services : Posted as Ensign to 2/19th N.I. No record of active service.

Refs. : Clan Campbell, No. 60. S.M. 1823, ii. 128. M.I. in old cemetery at Chunar.

CAMPBELL, Dugald Alexander (1813-1837). Ensign, 52nd N.I. b. Dublin 17 Sept. 1813. Cadet 1831. Arrived in India 16 May 1832. Ensign 9 June 1831. d. Nasirabad, Rajputana, 9 Feb. 1837.

Son of Dugald Campbell, of Kildalloig, co. Argyll, deputy keeper of the Privy Seal in Ireland, and Catherine Kingsley his wife. Younger brother of John Eyton Campbell, who assumed the title and style of baronet in 1841, and nephew by marriage of Norman Shairp, *q.v.* Addiscombe Cadet 1829-31.
Services : To do duty with 2nd N.I. 28 June 1832. Posted to 52nd N.I. 19 Oct. 1833. No record of active service.
Refs. : Burke's *Peerage*, 1923, p. 429, *s.n.* Campbell, Bart., of Auchinbreck. *Clan Campbell,* No. 74.

CAMPBELL, Duncan. Cadet, Infantry. Cadet 1772. Resigned 19 Jan. 1773.
Services : N.F.P.
Refs. : Clan Campbell, No. 77.

CAMPBELL, Duncan (1785-1806). Cadet, Infantry. *b.* Mar. 1785. Cadet 1805. Never arrived in India. *d.* Dec. 1806, on his passage to India, in the wreck of the *Skelton Castle.* Struck off with effect from 5 Nov. 1806. (See note to David Allan.)
bapt. Ardnamurchan, co. Argyll, 2 Apr. 1785, " a few days old." Son of Donald Campbell, of Mingary, co. Argyll, and Ann his wife.
Refs. : Clan Campbell, No. 78.

CAMPBELL, Duncan (1788-1819). Lieutenant, 12th N.I. *b.* Artarig, Inverchaolain, Cowal, co. Argyll, 30 Oct. 1788. Cadet 1808. Arrived in India 27 Oct. 1809. Ensign 20 Mar. 1810. Lieut. 16 Dec. 1814. *d.* Agra 20 July 1819.
Son of George Campbell, of Artarig. Cousin of Ivie Campbell, *q.v.,* and of Lachlan McLachlan, *q.v.*
Services : Posted as Ensign to 12th N.I. Lieut. 2/12th N.I. Nepal War 1816 ; Lieut. 5th Gren. Bn., in 2nd Bde., Left Column. Siege and capture of Hathras ; Lieut. 2/12th N.I. Third Mahratta War ; Dhamoni ; Lieut. 2/12th N.I. Operations against the Bhattis of Hariana 1818. Intr. & Qmr. 2/12th N.I. 1818 till death.
Refs. : Clan Campbell, No. 79. Will dated Chittagong 10 Nov. 1812 ; proved 23 Feb. 1820.

CAMPBELL, Sir Edward Alexander (1801-1850). Bt. Lieut. Colonel, Kt., C.B. 3rd L.C. *b.* Vizagapatam, Madras, 4 Aug. 1801. Cadet 1817. Arrived in India 4 July 1818. Cornet (3 Jan. 1818) 28 July 1818. Lieut. 23 Oct. 1818. Capt. 4 Feb. 1825. Bt. Major 19 Jan. 1826. Bt. Lt. Col. 23 Nov. 1841. Retired 16 Nov. 1845. *d.* Argyll Pl., London, 25 Aug. 1850.
2nd son of Sir Robert Campbell, 1st Bart., of Carrick Buoy, co. Donegal, director of the E.I.Co., and Eliza his wife, dau. of Dr. Gilbert Pasley, physician gen. at Madras. Brother of James

THE BENGAL ARMY, 1758-1834

William Henry Campbell, *q.v.*, and cousin-german of Edward Lennox Campbell, *q.v. m.* 1837, Eliza Sophia, eldest dau. of Thomas Parratt, of Lower Grosvenor Pl., London, and of Ramsgate. (She died London, 3 Dec. 1852, aged 46.)
Services : Inf. Cadet ; transfd. to Cav. 4 Mar. 1818. Posted as Cornet to 3rd N.C. A.D.C. to C.-in-C. 14 Jan. 1822. (? Operations in Jodhpur territory 1823 ; capture of Lamba ; Lieut. 3rd L.C.) D.A.A.G. 28 Jan. 1825. Bde. Major 2nd Inf. Bde. 3 Dec. 1825. Siege and capture of Bhurtpore (s.w. in head on 18 Jan. 1826) ; Bde. Major, Capt. 3rd L.C. Fur. s.c. 22 Jan. 1836 till 19 Jan. 1839. First Afghan War 1839 ; Ghazni ; Kabul ; Bt. Major 3rd L.C. (Medal). Fur. s.c. 16 Mar. 1843 till retirement. Recruiting Ofr. at Newry 1847 till death. Kt. 18 July 1838. C.B. 20 July 1838.
Refs. : Burke's *Peerage*, 1905, p. 276, *s.n.* Campbell, Bart., of Carrick Buoy, co. Donegal. *Clan Campbell*, No. 86. *G.M.* 1850, ii. 448. *I.M.* 3 Sept. 1850, p. 530.

*CAMPBELL, Edward Lennox (1805-1833). Cadet, Artillery or Engineers. Subsequently B.C.S., Joint Magistrate and Deputy Collector of Tirhut, B. & O. *bapt.* Trichinopoly 29 Nov. 1805. Never commissioned. *d.* Boalia, Bengal, 10 Mar. 1833.
Son of Edward Campbell, merchant, and Grace Gordon his wife. Brother of James Gordon Campbell, *q.v.*, and cousin-german of Sir Edward Alexander Campbell, Kt., *q.v.* Addiscombe Cadet 1819-21.
Services : Apptd. a Writer B.C.S. 30 Apr. 1824. Arrived in India 17 May 1824.
Refs. : Clan Campbell, No. 89. *A.J.* N.S. xii. 113.

CAMPBELL, Gabriel Napier Christie (1790-1839). Major, Artillery. *b.* Edinburgh 12 June 1790. Cadet 1806. Arrived in India 18 Dec. 1806. Fireworker 14 June 1807. Lieut. 15 Sept. 1809. Capt. 13 Dec. 1820. Major 11 May 1836. *d.* at sea, 20 Oct. 1839, on board the *Hero of Malaun*.
5th son of William Campbell, of Fairfield, co. Ayr, and Catherine his 2nd wife. Brother of Charles Hay Campbell, *q.v. m.* N.S.W., Selina Elizabeth, dau. of William Gore. (*See also* Sir Augustine Fitzgerald, Bart.) (She died Corstorphine 1839.)
Services : 1st Troop H.A. 1810. Nepal War 1814-5 ; Kalanga ; Lieut. 1st Troop in 2nd Div. Transfd. to newly-raised Rocket Troop in 1816. (? Capture of Hathras.) Transfd. to 3rd Troop in 1818. Third Mahratta War 1818. Transferred to 6th Troop in 1819. To comd. 6th Troop 1821. Operations against Maharao Kishor Singh, of Kotah, 1821 ; Mangrol. To comd. 4th Troop 3rd Bde. H.A. 1825. Siege and capture of Bhurtpore ; Capt. comdg. 4th Troop 3rd Bde.

Refs. : Burke's *Landed Gentry*, 13th edn., p. 275, *s.n.* Campbell, of Fairfield, co. Ayr. *Clan Campbell*, No. 91. Will dated Dum-Dum 20 June 1838 ; proved 6 Apr. 1840.

CAMPBELL, George (1803-1882). General, C.B. Colonel Comdt. Artillery. *b.* Nator, Bengal, 16 Sept. 1803. Cadet 1822. Arrived in India 21 Jan. 1824. 2nd Lieut. 6 June 1823. Lieut. 20 Sept. 1826. Capt. 10 July 1840. Major 21 July 1851. Lt. Col. 26 June 1856. Col. 18 Feb. 1861. Col. Comdt. 10 May 1874. Maj. Gen. 4 July 1858. Lt. Gen. 11 Dec. 1868. Gen. 21 July 1874. Retired 1 May 1878. *d.* 1 Byng Pl., Gordon Sq., London, 25 Apr. 1882.

3rd son of Duncan Campbell, of Inverneill, B.C.S., and Elizabeth his wife. Brother of Archibald Lorne Campbell, *q.v. m.* 1st, Calcutta, 12 Jan. 1841, Susan Harriet, dau. of Col. Alexander Campbell, of Possil. (She died 1 Oct. 1855.) *m.* 2nd, Allahabad, 18 Dec. 1858, Isabella, youngest dau. of Capt. James Ryder Mowatt, of Eastbourne, sister of John Lealand Mowatt, *q.v.*, and widow of Roderick Roberts, *q.v.* Addiscombe Cadet 4 Aug. 1820 till 6 June 1823.

Services : 2nd Troop 2nd Bde. H.A. 1825. First Burma War 1824-6 (India medal). To 4th Troop 3rd Bde. in 1828 ; 4th Troop 2nd Bde. in 1829. Fur s.c. 11 Jan. 1836 till 20 Dec. 1838. 3rd Troop 2nd Bde. 21 Feb. 1839. Comdd. 3rd Troop 3rd Bde. 1841-9. Gwalior campaign ; Paniar (Bronze star). First Sikh War ; Ferozshahr ; Sobraon (Medal with clasp). Second Sikh War ; in garrison at Lahore (Medal). To comd. 1st Bde. H.A. 27 Feb. 1855. Bdr. 7 Mar. 1856 ; to comd. at Rawal Pindi 19 July 1856. Indian Mutiny 1857-8 ; comdg. at Rawal Pindi. To comd. Dinapore Div. 6 July 1858. C.B. 13 Mar. 1867.

Refs. : Burke's *Landed Gentry*, 13th edn., p. 277, *s.n.* Campbell, of Inverneill. *Clan Campbell*, No. 97. Boase. *The Times*, 27 Apr. 1882, 10a ; 2 May 1882, 14a.

CAMPBELL, Ivie (1788-1837). Major, 12th N.I. *bapt.* Lochgoilhead, co. Argyll, 23 June 1788. Cadet 1805. Arrived in India 19 Sept. 1806. Ensign 8 Oct. 1806. Lieut. 8 Sept. 1809. Capt. 4 Sept. 1823. Major 19 Oct. 1833. *d.* Calcutta 21 Jan. 1837.

Son of James Campbell, tacksman, and Barbara Hare his wife. Brother of Alexander Livingstone Campbell, *q.v. m.* Bhagulpur, Bengal, 29 June 1816, Eliza Jane, 2nd dau. of Peter Littlejohn, *q.v.* (*See also* Peter Young.) (She died Hyderabad 5 May 1829.)

Services : Barasat C.C. for 9 mos. Posted as Ensign to 2/12th N.I. Adjt. Hill Rangers 29 July 1815 till 1 Jan. 1819. Served with Nizam's army 14 May 1819 till 4 Oct. 1834. Siege of Nowah

THE BENGAL ARMY, 1758-1834

8-31 Jan. 1819 ; Lieut. Nizam's Regular Inf. Fur. s.c. 3 Jan. 1835 till 4 Dec. 1836.
Refs. : Clan Campbell, No. 107. *History of Hyderabad Contingent*, p. 78. M.I. in N. Park St. burial ground, Calcutta. *Calcutta Review*, xi. (1849), 179.

CAMPBELL, James (1789-1806). Cadet, Infantry. *b.* 19 July 1789. Cadet 1805. Never arrived in India. *d.* Dec. 1806, on his passage to India, in the wreck of the *Skelton Castle*. Struck off with effect from 5 Nov. 1806. (See note to David Allan.) *bapt.* Calcutta 19 Oct. 1789. 3rd son of Dr. James Campbell and Jessy his wife. Brother of John Campbell (1789-1875), *q.v.* Woolwich Cadet ; nominated for R.M.A. 25 Apr. 1804 ; obtained his certificate 12 June 1806.
Refs. : Clan Campbell, No. 118.

CAMPBELL, James (1805-?). Lieutenant. 13th N.I. *b* Edinburgh 11 Oct. 1805. Cadet 1823. Arrived in India 7 Oct. 1824. Ensign 20 May 1824. Lieut. 30 Sept. 1826. Resigned 1 June 1834. *d.s.p.* (before 1851).
4th son of Sir Archibald Campbell, 2nd Bart., of Succoth, co. Dumbarton, and Elizabeth his wife, eldest dau. of John Balfour, of Balbirnie, Fife. Cousin-german of Craufurd Tait, *q.v.*
Note : Died before the award of the India medal in 1851.
Services : Posted as Ensign to 29th N.I. 31 Mar. 1825. Transfd. as Ensign to 13th N.I. Siege and capture of Bhurtpore ; Ensign 33rd N.I. Fur. p.a. 3 Feb. 1832 till resignation.
Refs. : Burke's *Peerage*, 1923, p. 433, *s.n.* Campbell, Bart., of Succoth, co. Dumbarton. *Clan Campbell*, No. 121.

CAMPBELL, James Archibald (1800-1821). Ensign, 4th N.I. *b.* Inveresk, Midlothian, 15 Aug. 1800. Cadet 1818. Was already in India when apptd. Cadet. Ensign 15 Sept. 1819. *d.* Partabgarh, U.P., 9 Nov. 1821.
Son of James Campbell, of Glenfeochan, Col. of the 91st Regt., and Margaret his wife, of Campbeltown. Brother of John Campbell (1793-1820), *q.v.*
Services : Was a Local Ensign serving with Champaran L.I. when apptd. a Cadet. Posted as Ensign to 2/4th N.I. No record of active service.
Refs. : Clan Campbell, No. 124. *S.M.* 1822, i. 828. Will dated Mullye 1 Aug. 1820 ; proved 30 Nov. 1821.

CAMPBELL, James Gordon (1808-1859). Lieutenant. 6th L.C. Afterwards B.C.S. ; Controller of Salt Chowkies. *b.* 9 Apr. 1808. Cadet 1823. Cornet 9 July 1824. Lieut. 13 May 1825. Struck off 6 Apr. 1830. *d.* Paris 18 Nov. 1859.

bapt. 23 Apr. 1808. Son of Edward Campbell, of Chillambrum, Madras, merchant, and Grace Gordon his wife. Stepson of Maj. Gen. Sir Charles Deacon, K.C.B., Madras Est. Brother of Edward Lennox Campbell, *q.v.*, and cousin-german of James William Henry Campbell, *q.v.* *m.* Kishunnagar, B. & O., 7 June 1841, Miss Matilda Frances Brown. Addiscombe Cadet 5 Aug. 1822 till 1824.
Services : Posted as Cornet to 7th L.C. 31 Mar. 1825. Transfd. to 6th L.C. 1 May 1825. Siege and capture of Bhurtpore ; Lieut. 6th L.C. (India medal). Fur. p.a. 18 Mar. 1829 till struck off. Apptd. a Writer, B.C.S., 31 Mar. 1830, and returned to India 27 Jan. 1831.
Refs. : *Clan Campbell*, No. 129. *G.M.* 1860, i. 191. *I.M.* 1859, p. 987. Will dated 1 May 1851 ; proved 1 Feb. 1860.

CAMPBELL, James Hunter (1811-1886). Colonel. Artillery. Cadet 1827. Arrived in India 3 June 1828. 2nd Lieut. 13 Dec. 1827. Lieut. 10 May 1835. Capt. 3 July 1845. Major 10 July 1857. Lt. Col. 27 Aug. 1858. Retired 2 Nov. 1858. Hon. Col. 2 Nov. 1858. *d.* 42 Aldridge Villas Rd., Bayswater, 18 Nov. 1886. Of Boulogne. Son of Robert Campbell, of Calcutta, merchant, and Margaret his wife, eldest dau. of Robert Hunter, of Thurston. Brother of Robert Macfarlane Campbell, *q.v.* *m.* Mhow, 15 Sept. 1836, Ann Holland, 2nd dau. of G. Stedman, of Edinburgh, S.S.C. (She died 30 Jan. 1880.) Addiscombe Cadet 1826-7.
Services : Dy. Comy. of Ord. at Chunar 17 June 1840. Leave s.c. to Cape 28 Feb. 1842. Comy. of Ord. 24 June 1843 till 1853. Fur. 1853-5. Indian Mutiny (s.w. before Delhi 11 Sept. 1857) (Medal). After retirement he was gazetted Capt. in 2nd Surrey Rifle Vols. 16 June 1859 ; Capt. Comdt. 17 Mar. 1860 ; Lt. Col. 8 Sept. 1860 ; resigned 28 June 1862.
Refs. : Burke's *Landed Gentry*, 13th edn., p. 952, *s.n.* Hunter, of Thurston, co. Haddington. *Clan Campbell*, No. 130. *The Times*, 22 Nov. 1886.

*****CAMPBELL, James William Henry** (1811-1869). Cadet. Afterwards Deputy Collector, Calcutta. *b.* 16 Nov. 1811. Cadet 1825. *d.* Ramsgate 10 July 1869.
bapt. 6 Jan. 1812. 4th and youngest son of Sir Robert Campbell, 1st Bart., of Carrick Buoy, co. Donegal, and Eliza his wife. Brother of Sir Edward Alexander Campbell, Kt., *q.v.*, and cousin-german of James Gordon Campbell, *q.v.* *m.* 20 Apr. 1857, Anna, dau. of Alexander Greenlaw, and widow of Charles G. Strettell, of Calcutta, attorney. Addiscombe Cadet 2 Feb. 1826. Withdrawn and sent to Civil Coll., Haileybury (Hertford Coll.).
Services : Apptd. a Writer of the China Est. 30 Apr. 1829. Arrived in Macao 1 Oct. 1829. Transfd. to B.C.S. in 1836.

THE BENGAL ARMY, 1758-1834 291

Refs. : Clan Campbell, No. 134. Burke's *Peerage*, 1905, p. 276, *s.n.* Campbell, Bart., of Carrick Buoy. Foster's *Baronetage*, p. 104. *The Times*, 15 July 1869.

CAMPBELL, John (*c.* 1745-1770). Lieutenant, 1st Bn. Sepoys. *b.* in Scotland *c.* 1745. Cadet 1767. Ensign 15 Sept. 1767. Lieut. 13 Apr. 1769. *d.* Monghyr, B. & O., Nov. 1770 : kld. in a duel.
Services : Sailed for India on the *Anson* 6 Apr. 1766. N.F.P.
Refs. : Clan Campbell, No. 140.

CAMPBELL, John (1748 ?-1798 ?). Captain. Comdg. 26th Bn. Sepoys. *b.* in Scotland *c.* 1748. Cadet 1768. Arrived in India 1768. Ensign 14 Feb. 1769. Lieut. 12 June 1770. Capt. 22 Aug. 1779. Resigned 24 Dec. 1791. (? *d.* Irvine 2 July 1798.) (? Of Corraith. *Probably* son of James Campbell.) Brother of William Campbell (died 1779), *q.v.*
Services : Sailed for India on the *Dutton* 31 Jan. 1768. In 1st Bde. in 1775. Comdd. 36th Bn. Sepoys 1786-91.
Refs. : Clan Campbell, No. 142. *S.M.* 1798, p. 575.

CAMPBELL, John (*c.* 1751-1803 ?). Captain. Infantry. *b.* in Scotland *c.* 1751. Cadet 1770. Ensign 13 Apr. 1772. Lieut. 15 Aug. 1776. Capt. Mar. 1781. Struck off 18 Nov. 1786. *d.* 1803 ?
Services : Sailed for India on the *Egmont* 21 Feb. 1770. Posted to Sepoy Corps, Bombay detachment, 12 Mar. 1778. First Mahratta War 1778-82. Transfd. to 10th N.I., 3rd Bde., in 1782. Capt. 1st Bengal Eur. Bn. He appears to have been re-employed after having been struck off, as he was ordered, 28 Nov. 1793, to serve on board the ships that are fitting out against the enemy.
Refs. : Clan Campbell, No. 143. Admon. granted 13 Dec. 1803.

CAMPBELL, John (1754-1780). Lieutenant, Infantry. *b.* 1754. Cadet 1772. Ensign 2 Aug. 1776. Lieut. 20 July 1778. *d.* 8 July 1780, on active service with the Bombay detachment.
Services : Sailed for India on the *Colebrooke* 30 Apr. 1771. Served as a Cadet in the Select Picket. First Mahratta War 1778-80.
Refs. : Clan Campbell, No. 144.

CAMPBELL, John (1764-1833). Lieut. Colonel. 17th N.I. *b.* 1764. Cadet 1780. Arrived in India 27 Apr. 1781. Ensign 1780. Lieut. 6 June 1781. Capt. 1 Nov. 1798. Major 27 Mar. 1804. Lt. Col. 23 Feb. 1807. Retired 8 Sept. 1809. *d.* Clifton, Somerset, 23 Sept. 1833.
Eldest son of James Campbell, of Glasgow.

Services : Lieut. 8th N.I. 25 June 1783. To proceed to N.S.W. on duty 5 Jan. 1796. Capt. 8th N.I. Agent for camels and gram 1803-7. Second Mahratta War; action at Koil 29 Aug. 1803; battle of Delhi; Laswari 1 Nov. 1803 (w.); Capt. 8th N.I., attd. to H.Q. as gram agent. Transfd. to 17th N.I. as Lt. Col. in 1807. Fur. 23 Feb. 1807 till retirement.

Refs. : Clan Campbell, No. 148. *A.J.* N.S. xii. 203. Lord Lake's despatch of 2 Nov. 1803.

CAMPBELL, John (1782-1814). Captain, 6th N.I. *b.* Edinburgh 27 Mar. 1782. Cadet 1798. Arrived in India 1 Sept. 1799. Ensign 9 Sept. 1799. Lieut. 28 Oct. 1799. Capt. 23 June 1809. *d. unm.* 27 Nov. 1814 : kld. in action in the attack on the fort of Kalanga, U.P.

bapt. Edinburgh 30 Apr. 1782. Youngest son of William Campbell, of Duneaves (Cadet of Glenlyon), Capt. Tay Fencibles, and Jean Reed his wife. Half-brother of James Williamson, Civil Surgeon at Calcutta.

Services : Posted as Lieut. to 2/6th N.I. 15 Apr. 1801. Operations in Baghelkhand 1803; Chaukandi; Lieut. 2/6th N.I. Adjt. & Qmr. 6th N.I. 1805-9. Nepal War 1814; Kalanga 27 Nov. 1814 (kld.); Capt. 1/6th N.I., in 2nd Div.

Refs. : Clan Campbell, No. 155. Will dated 9 Nov. 1814; proved in 1815.

CAMPBELL, John (1790-1875). Lieut. Colonel. 59th N.I. *b.* in India 21 Sept. 1790. Cadet 1805. Arrived in India 11 July 1806. Ensign 13 Aug. 1806. Lieut. 13 Jan. 1808. Capt. 1 May 1824. Major 31 Aug. 1831. Retired 1 Mar. 1832. Hon. Lt. Col. 28 Nov. 1854. *d.* his residence, 119 Lansdowne Pl., Brighton, 21 Nov. 1875.

bapt. Calcutta 20 Dec. 1790. 4th son of Dr. James Campbell, Madras Est., and Jessy his wife. Brother of Cornwallis Campbell, *q.v. m.* Dover, 24 July 1832, Emily, dau. of William Leycester, B.C.S., and widow of Charles Byrne Leicester, *q.v.* (She died Brighton, 11 Jan. 1871, aged 61.)

Services : Barasat C.C. for $10\frac{1}{2}$ mos. Posted as Ensign to 14th N.I. Lieut. 30th N.I. Adjt. 2/30th N.I. 16 Dec. 1814 till 1 May 1824. Leave to Cape 21 Apr. 1818 till 29 Mar. 1820. Transfd. as Capt. to 59th N.I. (late 1/30th) May 1824. Bde. Major to troops in Rohilkhand 12 Aug. 1824. No record of active service.

Refs. : Burke's *Peerage*, 1923, p. 1366, *s.n.* Leicester, Bart. Clan Campbell, No. 159. *A.J.* N.S. ix. 51. *The Times*, 24 Nov. 1875. M.I. in St. Andrew's church, Hove.

THE BENGAL ARMY, 1758-1884

CAMPBELL, John (1793-1820). Lieutenant, 10th N.I. *b.* Kilbride, co. Argyll, 29 Aug. 1793. Cadet 1808. Arrived in India 19 July 1809. Ensign 13 Mar. 1810. Lieut. 16 Dec. 1814. *d.* Hoshangabad, C.P., 11 Apr. 1820, of jungle fever.

Son of Lt. Col. James Campbell, of Glenfeochan, and Margaret his wife. Brother of James Archibald Campbell, *q.v.*
Services : Posted as Ensign to 10th N.I. Lieut. 1/10th N.I. 3rd Gren. Bn. in 1816. Third Mahratta War ; Lieut. 1/10th N.I. Comdg. Narbada Local Corps at death.
Refs. : Clan Campbell, No. 160. *S.M.* 1821, i. 189. Will dated Hoshangabad 12 Apr. 1819 ; proved 13 Jan. 1821.

CAMPBELL, John (1805-1826). Lieutenant, 4th Extra Regt. N.I. *b.* Portree, I. of Skye, 21 July 1805. Cadet 1821. Ensign 19 Jan. 1822. Lieut. 27 Oct. 1823. *d.* Mirzapur 25 June 1826.

Son of Rev. Alexander Campbell, minister of Portree, and Margaret his wife, dau. of William Macleod, of Luskintyre, I. of Harris.
Services : Posted as Ensign to 24th N.I. Transfd. to 16th N.I. in 1823 ; to 32nd N.I. (late 1/16th) May 1824. (? First Burma War ; Arakan 1825 ; Lieut. 2nd Gren. Bn.) Transfd. to newly-raised 4th Extra Regt. in 1825.
Refs. : Clan Campbell, No. 163. M.I. in Mirzapur cemetery.

CAMPBELL, John George (1808- ?). 2nd Lieutenant. Artillery. *b.* Dunipace, co. Stirling, 12 Dec. 1808. Cadet 1825. 2nd Lieut. 28 Sept. 1825. Lost 18 steps by G.C.M. Rank postdated to 14 Oct. 1827. Cashiered by sentence of G.C.M. 29 Dec. 1828.

Son of John Campbell, of Annfield, junr., W.S., and Frances his wife, youngest dau. of John Brown, of Glasgow, merchant. Brother of William Hector Campbell, *q.v.* Addiscombe Cadet 1 Aug. 1823 till 1825.
Services : No record of active service.
Refs. : Clan Campbell, No. 175. *A.J.* xxvii. 739, 740.

CAMPBELL, Kenneth (1803-1851). Major, 45th N.I. *b.* Snizort, I. of Skye, 6 May 1803. Cadet 1821. Arrived in India 4 May 1822. Ensign 3 Dec. 1821. Lieut. 17 May 1824. Capt. 8 June 1832. Major 28 July 1850. *d.* Bareilly, U.P., 17 Apr. 1851.

Of Uig, I. of Skye. Son of Donald Campbell, of Lyndale, Snizort. *m.* 21 Aug. 1827, Miss Mary Ann Read.
Services : Posted as Ensign to 23rd N.I. Transfd. to 45th N.I. (late 1/23rd) May 1824. First Burma War ; Chittagong district 1824 ; disaster at Ramu 17 May 1824 (w.), one of three surviving officers ; Lieut. 45th N.I. Adjt. 45th N.I. 8 Oct. 1824. Intr. &

Qmr. 14 Oct. 1824 till 14 Mar. 1828. Dy. Paymr. Lahore Circle 19 May 1846 till 1850.
Refs. : *Clan Campbell*, No. 186. *G.M.* 1851, ii. 217. Will dated 6 Apr. 1834 ; proved 11 Nov. 1851.

CAMPBELL, Neil (1788-1848). Bt. Major. 21st N.I. *b.* 10 Sept. 1788. Cadet 1808. Arrived in India 19 July 1809. Ensign 5 Jan. 1810. Lieut. 1 Oct. 1814. Capt. 6 Mar. 1826. Bt. Major 28 June 1838. Retired in India 1 July 1841. *d.* 11 Jan. 1848.
5th and youngest son of Colin Campbell, " Colin Mhor," of Kilmartin, co. Argyll, and Duncana his wife, dau. of John Campbell, of Combie. *m.* Lochgair House, Argyll, 30 June 1823, Isabella Anne, dau. of Charles Campbell, of Lochgair. (She died 27 Nov. 1880.)
Services : Posted as Ensign to 1/9th N.I. Intr. & Qmr. 1/9th N.I. 11 Sept. 1820. Fur. s.c. 1 Jan. 1821 till 12 June 1824. Transfd. to 21st N.I. (late 2/9th) May 1824. Siege and capture of Bhurtpore ; Capt. 21st N.I.
Refs. : Burke's *Landed Gentry*, 13th edn., p. 279, *s.n.* Campbell, of Kilmartin, co. Inverness. *Clan Campbell*, No. 195. *S.M.* 1823, ii. 254.

CAMPBELL, Osborne (1808-1874). Lieutenant. 43rd N.I. Subsequently in the Indian Postal Service. *b.* Poonamallee, Madras, 6 Sept. 1808. Cadet 1825. Arrived in India 7 July 1826. Ensign 15 Mar. 1826. Lieut. 24 Jan. 1829. Invalided 10 Sept. 1838. Retired 14 Aug. 1861. *d.* 145 Cornwall Rd., Bayswater, London, 28 Apr. 1874.
3rd son of John Campbell, Surgeon, Madras Est., and Eliza Munro his wife. Brother of Alexander Æneas Campbell, *q.v. m.* Edinburgh, 20 June 1837, Isabella Louisa, 4th dau. of Lt. Col. Archibald Campbell (Melfort), and sister of William Frederick Campbell, *q.v.* (She died London 10 Aug. 1886.)
Services : Posted as Ensign to 43rd N.I. Fur. s.c. 30 Nov. 1834 till 19 Feb. 1838. Postmaster at Mainpuri 13 May 1840 ; do. at Landour 1 May 1842 till 1857. Dangerously wounded in a duel with Lieut. Robert Christopher Tytler, 38th N.I., *q.v.*, at Mussoorie in 1844. Fur. 1859 till retirement. No record of active service.
Refs. : *Clan Campbell*, No. 197. *A.J.* N.S. xxii. 331. *I.M.* No. 16, p. 485. *The Times*, 1 May 1874.

CAMPBELL, Peter William (1795-1819). Lieutenant, 11th N.I. *b.* Ardchattan, co. Argyll, 3 July 1795. Cadet 1816. Ensign (?). Lieut. 1 Aug. 1818. *d.s.p.* Calcutta 15 Nov. 1819.
3rd son of Alexander Campbell, of Barcaldine and Glenure, a member of the faculty of advocates, and Mary his wife, dau. of

THE BENGAL ARMY, 1758-1834

John Campbell, of the Citadel, Edinburgh, Dy. Keeper of the Great Seal of Scotland. Younger brother of Sir Duncan Campbell, 1st Bart., of Barcaldine and Glenure.
Services: Posted as Lieut. to 2/11th N.I. No record of active service.
Refs.: Burke's *Peerage*, 1923, p. 437, *s.n.* Campbell, Bart., of Barcaldine, co. Argyll. *Clan Campbell*, No. 202.

CAMPBELL, Robert (1720/21-?). Captain. Infantry. *b.* 1720/21. Madras Cadet 1753. Arrived in Madras 18 June 1754. Ensign 10 June 1754. Lieut. 15 Nov. 1754. Capt. (Bengal) 16 June 1757. Resigned 31 Aug. 1758. Reinstated 8 July 1761. Capt. 20 Dec. 1762. Resigned 23 Jan. 1767.
Of Berwick. *m.* Katherine, dau. of Thomas Frazer, and niece of Alexander Frazer, Lord Strichen.
Services: Sailed for Madras on the *Ilchester* in Oct. 1753, aged 32. Battle of Plassey, when he voted at the council of war for immediate action. His first resignation, in 1758, was due to his supercession by John Gowen, *q.v.* His request for permission to return to Bengal was granted in Nov. 1760. Commended for " spirited conduct in advantage gained over the rebels in Sircar Serang Country " in Jan. 1765, on which occasion he captured a brass gun.
Refs.: Orme *MSS., India*, xiii. 3639. *Clan Campbell*, Nos. 206 and 207. Hill's *Bengal*, iii. 53.

CAMPBELL, Robert (1765-1840). Captain. 2nd N.I. *b.* 1765. Cadet 1782. Arrived in India 1 July 1783. Ensign 23 Jan. 1783. Lieut. 2 July 1789. Capt. 12 Aug. 1801. Retired 10 Feb. 1807. *d.s.p.* 29 Mar. 1840.
Of Ardchattan Priory, co. Argyll. J.P. and D.L. 5th son of Patrick Campbell, of Ardchattan, and Lilias Margaret his wife, dau. of John MacFarlane of that ilk. Brother of Colin Campbell (1757-1792), *q.v. m.* Bruce House, Edinburgh, 29 Mar. 1819, Jean, dau. of Archibald Campbell, writer in Edinburgh.
Services: Sailed for India on the *Rodney* 11 Sept. 1782. Posted as Ensign to 3rd Bengal Eur. Bn. 30 Nov. 1786. Transfd. to Sepoy Corps 14 Feb. 1788. Lieut. 2nd N.I. Fur. 21 Feb. 1795 till 21 Dec. 1798, and 2 Nov. 1803 till retirement.
Refs.: Burke's *Landed Gentry*, 4th edn., p. 204, *s.n.* Campbell, of Ardchattan Priory, co. Argyll. *Clan Campbell*, No. 209.

CAMPBELL, Robert (1800-1889). Colonel. 43rd N.I. *b.* Downpatrick, co. Down, 16 Mar. 1800. Cadet 1819. Admitted 30 May 1820. Ensign 10 Jan. 1820. Lieut. 20 Jan. 1822. Capt. 30 Apr. 1834. Major 14 July 1853. Bt. Lt. Col. 20 June 1854.

Retired 9 Mar. 1855. Hon. Col. 11 May 1855. *d.* Hove, Sussex, 3 Apr. 1889.
2nd son of Colin Campbell, of Edinburgh (Cadet of Barcaldine), Major N. Lowland Fencibles, and Christian Williamson his wife. *m.* Delhi, 29 July 1841, Matilda Mary Susannah, dau. of John Oliver, *q.v.* (*See also* George Moore (1789-1848), Sir Hugh Massy Wheeler, K.C.B., and Astley George Francis John Younghusband.)
Services : Posted as Ensign to 2/10th N.I. Transfd. as Lieut. to 22nd N.I. 11 July 1823 ; to 43rd N.I. (late 1/22nd) May 1824. Intr. & Qmr. 43rd N.I. 28 Dec. 1826 till 8 Nov. 1831. Fur. 9 Jan. 1833 till 22 Oct. 1835. A.D.C. to C.-in-C. 1 Dec. 1835 till 1838. Comdd. Hariana L.I. 22 Feb. 1838 till 16 Oct. 1838. First Afghan War 1839 ; Ghazni ; Capt. 43rd N.I. (Medal). Comdd. Hariana L.I. 25 Dec. 1839 till retirement. Fur. 7 Apr. 1843 till 1845.
Refs. : Clan Campbell, No. 214. M.I. in Hove cemetery.

CAMPBELL, Robert Macfarlane (1805-1832). Lieutenant, 33rd N.I. *b* Calcutta 22 May 1805. Cadet 1824. Arrived in India 6 May 1825. Ensign 1 Jan. 1825. Lieut. 1 Jan. 1826. *d.* Calcutta 8 Apr. 1832.
Son of Robert Campbell, of Calcutta, merchant, and Margaret his wife. Brother of James Hunter Campbell, *q.v.*
Services : Ensign 65th Foot 18 Apr. 1822. Posted as Ensign to 33rd N.I. Siege and capture of Bhurtpore (s.w.) ; Ensign 33rd N.I. Leave for 23 mos. to N.S.W. and Mauritius 11 Apr. 1829.
Refs. : Burke's *Landed Gentry*, 13th edn., p. 952, *s.n.* Hunter, of Thurston, co. Haddington. *Clan Campbell*, No. 220. M.I. in S. Park St. burial ground, Calcutta.

CAMPBELL, Thomas (1763/64-1786). Ensign, Infantry. *b.* in Ireland 1763/64. Cadet 1782. Ensign 5 Apr. 1783. *d.* Dinapore 23 Aug. 1786.
Services : Sailed for India on the *Worcester*, 6 Feb. 1782, aged 18. N.F.P.
Refs. : Clan Campbell, No. 224.

CAMPBELL, Thomas Mackenzie (1796-1834). Captain, 29th N.I. *b.* Balfron, co. Stirling, 1 Dec. 1796. Cadet 1811. Admitted 12 Dec. 1812. Ensign 1 Oct. 1814. Lieut. 1 Aug. 1818. Capt. 15 Jan. 1830. *d.* Jubbulpore, C.P., 12 Oct. 1834, of fever.
bapt. 18 Dec. 1796. Son of Thomas Campbell, of Balfron, surgeon, and Jean McMorran his wife.
Services : Posted as Ensign to newly-raised 2/29th N.I. in 1815. Transfd. to 1/14th N.I. 11 June 1816. (? Third Mahratta War ; Dhamoni ; Mandala ; Garhakota ; Lieut. 1/14th N.I.) Transfd. to

29th N.I. (late 2/14th) May 1824. Fur. p.a. 17 Mar. 1831 till 24 May 1834.
Refs. : Clan Campbell, No. 227. *A.J.* N.S. xvi. 271.

CAMPBELL, William (*c.* 1742-1779). Captain, Infantry. *b. c.* 1742. Cadet 1763. Ensign 14 Sept. 1765. Lieut. 14 Jan. 1767. Capt. 22 Sept. 1770. *d. unm.* 1779, on active service with the Bombay detachment.
Owned the estate of Ballinabir in Islay, co. Argyll. (*Probably son of James Campbell.*) Brother of John Campbell (1748 ?-1798 ?), *q.v.*
Services : Sailed for India on the *Talbot* 19 Jan. 1763. To comd. Invalids at the Presidency 1776. First Mahratta War 1778-9.
Refs. : Clan Campbell, No. 230. Will dated 26 June 1778 ; codicil dated 30 Jan. 1779 ; filed 29 June, proved 15 July 1779.

CAMPBELL, William (*d.* 1769). Ensign, Infantry. Cadet (?). Ensign 21 Feb. 1769. *d.* 1769.
Services : N.F.P.
Refs. : Clan Campbell, No. 232.

CAMPBELL, William. Lieutenant. Infantry. Cadet 1780. Never arrived in India. Ensign 9 Aug. 1780. Lieut. 1 Apr. 1781.
Services : N.F.P.
Refs. : Clan Campbell, No. 234.

CAMPBELL, William (*d.* 1803). Major, 19th N.I. D.Q.M.G., Bengal Army. Cadet 1783. Ensign 3 June 1785. Lieut. 27 Oct. 1793. Bt. Capt. 8 Jan. 1798. Major (official rank only, as D.A.G.) 2 Oct. 1800. *d.* 1 Nov. 1803 : kld. in action at the battle of Laswari.
Son of Maj.-Gen. Duncan Campbell, Royal Marines.
Services : Apptd. in Apr. 1797 to act as D.Q.M.G. and Bde. Major to the detachment under Major Hyndman operating in Hyderabad 1797-8. Adjt. & Qmr. 17th N.I. Apr. 1799. D.A.G. 2 Oct. 1800. D.Q.M.G. Second Mahratta War ; Aligarh ; battle of Delhi ; Agra ; Laswari (kld.) ; D.Q.M.G. of Lord Lake's force.
Refs. : Clan Campbell, No. 235. Lake's despatch of 2 Nov. 1803. Will dated Coel (Koil) 30 Aug. 1803 ; proved in London 27 May 1805.

*****CAMPBELL, William** (1769-?). Ensign, Infantry. *b.* 1769. Cadet (?). Ensign (?).
Services : Arrived in India on the *Defence* (or the *Northumberland*) in 1791. Ensign 14th Bn. Sepoys in 1792-3. N.F.P.
Refs. : Clan Campbell, No. 236.

CAMPBELL, William Charles (1802-1864). Major General. 30th N.I. b. Jamaica 10 Nov. 1802. Cadet 1824. Arrived in India 21 May 1825. Ensign 7 Dec. 1824. Lieut. 27 Dec. 1825. Capt. 13 Oct. 1839. Major 11 Dec. 1851. Lt. Col. 11 May 1857. Bt. Col. 28 Nov. 1857. Retired 31 Dec. 1861. Maj. Gen. 31 Dec. 1861. d. Roorkee, U.P., 21 Jan. 1864.
bapt. St. Catherine, Middlesex, Jamaica, 20 Nov. 1802. Son of Alexander Campbell, of Easdale I., co. Argyll, and Barbara his wife.
Services : Posted as Ensign to 30th N.I. First Afghan War 1842 ; forcing of Khyber Pass ; re-occupation of Kabul ; Capt. 30th N.I., with Gen. Pollock's force (Medal). Second Sikh War ; Sadulapur 3 Dec. 1848 (w.) ; Chilianwala 13 Jan. 1849 (s.w.) ; Capt. 30th N.I., Bde. Major 3rd Inf. Bde. (Medal). Bde. Major 11 Dec. 1849.
Refs. : Clan Campbell, No. 242.

CAMPBELL, William Frederick (1808-1840). Bt. Captain, 64th N.I. b. Melfort 7 May 1808. Cadet 1823. Arrived in India 10 Oct. 1824. Ensign 23 May 1824. Lieut. 24 Apr. 1827. Bt. Capt. 23 May 1839. d. Delhi, 29 Aug. 1840, of fever.
Son of Capt. Archibald Campbell, of Melfort, co. Argyll, and Christian Bruce his wife. His sister m. Osborne Campbell, q.v. m. Largs, 25 Mar. 1834, Anne Moore, youngest dau. of Duncan Campbell, of Achlian (of Greenock). (She died Ryde 1880.)
Services : To do duty with 2nd Bengal Eur. Regt. Oct. 1824. Posted to 50th N.I. Mar. 1825. Transfd. to 64th N.I. July 1825. Actg. Intr. & Qmr. 24 Oct. 1829 till May 1830. Leave s.c. 12 mos. to Nilgiris 16 July 1830. Fur. s.c. 10 Jan. 1832 till 4 Dec. 1834. Intr. & Qmr. 64th N.I. 20 Nov. 1835 till death. No record of active service.
Refs. : Clan Campbell, No. 245. De Rhé-Philipe. A.J. N.S xiv. 59. I.N. i. 127. Will dated Saugor 6 July 1836 ; proved in 1841.

CAMPBELL, William Hector (1806-?). Ensign. Infantry. b. Edinburgh (? Dunipace, co. Stirling) 29 May 1806. Cadet 1824. (? Arrived in India 6 May 1825.) Ensign (?). Resigned 8 July 1825.
Son of John Campbell, of Annfield, junr., W.S., and Frances his wife. Brother of John George Campbell, q.v.
Note : Although his arrival on 6 May is reported in G.O. 142 of 13 May 1825, yet it appears probable that this is a mistake and that he resigned, in fact, in England, not having sailed for India.
Services : To sail for India on the Gen. Kyd, which arrived at Calcutta on 5 May 1825.
Refs. : Clan Campbell, No. 246.

THE BENGAL ARMY, 1758-1884 299

CANDY, Francis (1798-1831). Captain, 64th N.I. *bapt.* Sedgehill, Wilts., 19 Aug. 1798. Cadet 1817. Ensign (?). Lieut. 21 Aug. 1818. Capt. 18 Apr. 1829. *d.* Sloane St., London, 3 Mar. 1831. Son of Robert Candy. Brother of Henry Candy, *q.v. m.* Calcutta, 4 Jan. 1825, Miss Louisa Elizabeth Butler.
Services : Posted as Lieut. to 1/6th N.I. in 1819. Transfd. to 32nd N.I. 11 July 1823 ; to 64th N.I. (late 2/32nd) May 1824. Adjt. 64th N.I. 17 June 1824. Intr. & Qmr. 64th N.I. 10 Aug. 1825 till 1829. Fur. p.a. 11 Dec. 1828 till death. No record of active service.
Refs. : G.M. 1831, i. 282.

CANDY, Henry (1806-1826). Lieutenant, 1st Bengal European Regt. *bapt.* East Knoyle, Wilts., 23 Aug. 1806. Cadet 1822. Ensign 11 July 1823. Lieut. 13 May 1825. *d.* in camp, 27 Jan. 1826, of wounds received at the assault of Bhurtpore on 18 Jan. Youngest son of Robert Candy, of East Knoyle. Brother of Francis Candy, *q.v.*
Services : Posted as Ensign to 1st Bengal Eur. Regt. in 1824. Siege and capture of Bhurtpore 18 Jan. 1826 (s.w.) ; Lieut. 1st Eur. Regt.
Refs. : Bath Chron. 27 July 1826. Will dated camp, before Bhurtpore, 12 Jan. 1826 ; proved 17 June 1826.

CANHAM, R—— S—— (*d.* 1785). Ensign, Infantry. Cadet 1783. Ensign 2 Mar. 1785. *d.* 4 June 1785 : kld. in a duel.
Services : N.F.P.

CANNING, John (1775-1824). Major, 53rd N.I. *bapt.* Ilmington, Worcs., 11 Dec. 1775. Cadet 1799. Arrived in India 7 Jan. 1801. Ensign 12 Aug. 1800. Lieut. 8 Oct. 1800. Capt. 16 Dec. 1814. Major 1 Mar. 1824. *d.* Calcutta 2 Sept. 1824.
3rd and youngest son of Francis Canning, of Foxcote, co. Warwick, and Catherine his wife, dau. of Peter Giffard, of Chillington. *m.* Calcutta, 11 Sept. 1807, Mary Anne, dau. of Sir John Randall Meredyth, Bart., of Newtown, co. Meath, and widow of John Fitzgerald Anster. (She died Hartpury, Gloucs., 2 Sept. 1824.)
Services : Comdd. Murshidabad Provl. Bn. 30 Oct. 1807 till 1819. On embassy to Ava 1812-3. Supy. A.D.C. to G.G. 1814-5. P.A., Aurangabad, 1820-24. Hon. A.D.C. to G.G. 1821-3, and 1824. First Burma War 1824 ; accompanied Bdr.-Gen. Sir Archibald Campbell to Rangoon in May 1824 in a political capacity. Returned to Calcutta owing to ill-health, 1 Sept. 1824, and died within eighteen hours of landing.
Refs. : Burke's *Landed Gentry*, 13th edn., p. 287, *s.n.* Gordon-

Canning, of Hartpury, Gloucs. *E.I.M.C.* iii. 283. Will dated 13 Sept. 1809 ; proved 4 Sept. 1824.

CANNON, Ambrose (*d.* 1774). Cadet, Infantry. Cadet 1771. *d.* Bagaha, B. & O., 2 Dec. 1774.
Services : N.F.P.

CANTLEY, Alexander. Ensign, Infantry. Cadet 1781. Ensign 13 July 1781.
Services : N.F.P.

CAPEL, Edward Samuel (1811-1896). Lieut. Colonel. 53rd N.I. *b.* 16 Jan. 1811. Cadet 1827. Arrived in India 21 Nov. 1828. Ensign 14 June 1828. Lieut. 8 Oct. 1836. Capt. 1 Oct. 1843. Bt. Major 20 June 1854. Retired 20 Apr. 1855. Hon. Lt. Col. 15 June 1855. *d.* Lady's Close, Watford, 28 May 1896.

bapt. Watford 22 Apr. 1811. 3rd and youngest son of Hon. and Rev. William Robert Capel (who was 4th son of William Anne, fourth Earl of Essex), chaplain to Queen Victoria, rector of Raine, Essex, and vicar of Watford, Herts., and Sarah his wife, only dau. of Samuel Salter, of Rickmansworth, Herts. *m.* 5 June 1838, Elizabeth, eldest dau. of James Binnie, of Demarara. (She died 19 Nov. 1851.)

Services : Ensign d.d. 33rd N.I. 14 Jan. 1829. Posted as Ensign to 53rd N.I. 3 June 1829. Fur. p.a. 25 Jan. 1834 till 21 May 1835, and 31 Aug. 1837 till 1839. Adjt. Calcutta Native Mil. 13 May 1840 till 18 Aug. 1843. First Afghan War 1842 ; forcing of Khyber Pass ; re-occupation of Kabul ; Lieut. 53rd N.I. with Gen. Pollock's force (Medal). Fur. 1 Mar. 1845 till 1848. Second Sikh War ; in garrison at Lahore ; Capt. 53rd N.I. (Medal).

Refs. : Burke's *Peerage*, 1923, p. 861, *s.n.* Earl of Essex. *The Times*, 1 June 1896 ; 2 June, p. 10.

CARDEN, William (*d.* 1781). Lieutenant, Bengal European Regt. Cadet 1778. Ensign 1 Sept. 1779. Lieut. 1779. *d.* Madras 1781.

Services : (? Second Mysore War 1781 ; Lieut. 2/1st Bengal Eur. Regt.)

CARDEW, Ambrose (1806-1837). Lieutenant, Artillery. *b.* St. Gluvias, Cornwall, 27 July 1806. Cadet 1822. Arrived in India 28 Dec. 1823. 2nd Lieut. 6 June 1823. Lieut. 28 Sept. 1827. *d.* Agra 17 Nov. 1837.

Son of Rev. John Haydon Cardew, rector of Curry Malet, Somerset, and vicar of Salcombe, Devon, and Anne his wife. *m.* Dinapore, 26 Mar. 1834, Emma Maria, 2nd dau. of John Marshall,

M.R.C.S., physician gen., Bengal. (*See also* Sir George Parker, Bart., and William James Parker.) Addiscombe Cadet 1820-2.
Services : First Burma War ; Arakan 1824-6 ; 2nd Lieut. Art.
Refs. : *G.M.* 1838, i. 447.

CARE or CARR, John. Lieutenant, Infantry. Cadet 1766. Ensign 5 Sept. 1766. Lieut. 15 Sept. 1767.
Services : N.F.P.

CAREW, Henry Holdsworth (1789-1806). Cadet, Infantry. *bapt.* Bickleigh, Devon, 29 Oct. 1789. Cadet 1805. Never arrived in India. *d.* Dec. 1806, on his passage to India, in the wreck of the *Skelton Castle.* Struck off with effect from 5 Nov. 1806. (See note to David Allan.)
2nd son of Rev. John West Carew, rector of Bickleigh (who was 2nd son of Sir John Carew, 5th Bart., of Haccombe, Devon), and Lydson his wife, dau. of Rev. Charles Smallwood.
Refs. : Burke's *Peerage*, 1923, p. 445, *s.n.* Carew, Bart., of Haccombe, Devon. *G.M.* 1808, i. 371.

CAREY, Charles (1795-1820). Lieutenant, 27th N.I. *b.* Aldenham 7 Aug. 1795. Cadet 1811. Ensign 1 Aug. 1814. Lieut. 17 May 1815. *d.* in camp, nr. Udaipur, Rajputana, 3 Nov. 1820.
Son of Richard Carey, of Newmarket, Cambs., and Susannah his wife, née Pope. Brother of George Carey, *q.v.*
Services : Posted as Ensign to 1/27th N.I. Third Mahratta War ; Madhurajpura ; Lieut. 1/27th N.I. Comdg. escort to P.A., Merwara, at death.

CAREY, George (1802-1822). Lieutenant, 24th N.I. *bapt.* St. Mary's, Newmarket, Suffolk, 5 Oct. 1802. Cadet 1818. Ensign (?). Lieut. 13 June 1820. *d.* in England 6 May 1822.
Son of Richard Carey, of Newmarket, Cambs., and Susannah his wife. Brother of Charles Carey, *q.v.*
Services : Ensign d.d. 20th N.I. Posted as Lieut. to 1/24th N.I. in 1820. Fur. 1821 till death. No record of active service.
Refs. : *A.J.* xiii. 629.

CARGILL, Walter (1790-1812). Ensign, 18th N.I. *b.* Dunkeld, co. Perth, 1 Sept. 1790. Cadet 1808. Arrived in India 27 Oct. 1809. Ensign 31 Aug. 1810. *d.* in U.K. 2 Oct. 1812.
Son of Robert Cargill.
Services : Posted as Ensign to 18th N.I. Fur. 1811 till death. No record of active service.

CARIGE, John (1765/66-1813). Captain, Invalid Est. 15th N.I. *b.* 1765/66. Cadet 1783. Arrived in India 16 Oct. 1783. Ensign 26 Jan. 1785. Lieut. 16 Mar. 1791. Capt. 1 May 1804. Invalided 1 Nov. 1805. *d.* Monghyr, Bengal, 21 Apr. 1813, aged 47. *m.* Berhampore, 17 Dec. 1791, Eleanor, dau. of Robert Catts, Dy. Comy. of Ord. at Berhampore, and widow of Lieut. Thomas Smith, *q.v.*† (*See also* Joseph Fletcher.) (She died 21 June 1846, aged 78.)

† *Note :* Probably the one who died 13 Dec. 1788.

Services : Lieut. 1st Bengal Eur. Regt. in 1796. (? Operations in Oudh 1803 ; Sasni ; Bijaigarh ; Kachaura ; Lieut. 15th N.I. Second Mahratta War ; battle of Delhi ; Agra ; Laswari ; battle of Deig ; Capt. 15th N.I.) Comdg. Native Invalids at Monghyr 1805 till death.

Refs. : Will dated Monghyr 5 Apr. 1813 ; proved in 1813. M.I. in Monghyr cemetery.

CARLETON, Charles William (1789-1834). Lieutenant, Pension Est. 1st N.I. *b.* Coolock, co. Dublin, 23 Nov. 1789. Cadet 1805. Arrived in India 13 Dec. 1806. Ensign 18 Dec. 1806. Lieut. 25 Aug. 1811. Pensioned 1 May 1814. *d.s.p.* Monghyr 4 Aug. 1834.

3rd son of Very Rev. Peter Carleton, dean of Killaloe, and Mary Griffin his wife. Brother of Frederick Augustus Carleton, *q.v.*, and 2nd cousin once removed of Henry Alexander Carleton, *q.v.*

Services : Posted as Ensign to 1st N.I.

Refs. : Burke's *Landed Gentry*, 7th edn., p. 300, *s.n.* Carleton, of Clare, co. Tipperary, and Greenfield, co. Cork. *A.J.* N.S. xvi. 137.

CARLETON, Frederick Augustus (1808-1860). Major. 36th N.I. *b.* Aghadowey, co. Londonderry, 7 Aug. 1808. Cadet 1825. Arrived in India 6 May 1826. Ensign 12 Jan. 1826. Lieut. 27 May 1839. Capt. 17 July 1845. Retired 15 Feb. 1853. Hon. Major 28 Nov. 1854. *d. unm.* Saharanpur, U.P., 11 Apr. 1860.

5th son of Very Rev. Peter Carleton, dean of Killaloe, and Mary Griffin his wife. Brother of Henry Peter Carleton, *q.v.*

Services : Posted as Ensign to 36th N.I. Shekhawat expedition 1834 ; Ensign 36th N.I. First Sikh War ; Aliwal ; Capt. 36th N.I. (Medal). Second Sikh War ; Chilianwala 13 Jan. 1849 (s.w.) ; Capt. 36th N.I. (Medal).

Refs. : Burke's *Landed Gentry*, 7th edn., p. 300, *s.n.* Carleton, of Clare, co. Tipperary. Will dated 13 Feb. 1860; proved 28 June 1860.

CARLETON, Henry Alexander (1814-1900). General, C.B. Colonel Comdt. Artillery. Retired List. *b.* London 27 Feb. 1814. Cadet 1829. Arrived in India 16 Mar. 1831. 2nd Lieut. 11 June 1830.

Lieut. 12 Sept. 1839. Capt. 6 Feb. 1848. Major 18 Aug. 1858.
Lt. Col. 14 Oct. 1858. Col. 10 Mar. 1863. Col. Comdt. 26 Apr.
1882. Maj. Gen. 6 Mar. 1868. Lt. Gen. 1 Oct. 1877. Gen.
10 July 1879. *d.* 12 Marlborough Bldgs., Bath, 22 Feb. 1900.
Of Clare, co. Tipperary, and Greenfields, co. Cork. 2nd son of
Francis Carleton (who *s.* to the estates of his uncle, Viscount Carleton,
of Clare) and Charlotte Molyneux his wife, eldest dau. of George
Molyneux Montgomerie, of Garboldisham Hall, Norfolk. 2nd
cousin once removed of Henry Peter Carleton, *q.v.* *m.* Sialkot,
22 Dec. 1855, Elizabeth, dau. of Armor Boyle, of Dundrum. Addiscombe Cadet 1828-30.
Services : Fur. p.a. 5 July 1841 till 1843. Operations against the
Mohmands Oct.-Dec. 1851 (Medal). Mutiny campaign ; siege and
capture of Lucknow Mar. 1858 ; comdg. Bengal Art. Div. siege
train ; Nawabganj June 1858 ; comdg. Art. under Sir Hope Grant
(Medal with clasp). Permitted to reckon 18 mos. leave as service
for pension. C.B. 26 July 1858.
Refs. : Burke's *Landed Gentry of Ireland,* p. 98, *s.n.* Carleton, of
Clare, co. Tipperary. *Boase.* *The Times,* 26 Feb. 1900 ; 27 Feb.
p. 6.

CARLETON, Henry Peter (1787-1844). Major. Bengal European
Regt. *b.* Coolock, co. Dublin, 27 Nov. 1787. Cadet 1805.
Arrived in India 13 Dec. 1806. Ensign 12 Dec. 1806. Lieut.
26 Dec. 1808. Capt. (24 May 1821) 1 May 1824. Major 27 July
1836. Retired in India 25 Feb. 1837. *d.* 6 Mar. 1844.
2nd son of Very Rev. Peter Carleton, dean of Killaloe, and Mary
Griffin his wife. Brother of William Cossart Carleton, *q.v.* *m.*
17 May 1826, Eliza, 2nd dau. of John Cossart. (She died Hyderabad
2 Dec. 1831.)
Services : Barasat C.C. for 11 mos. Posted as Ensign to Bengal
Eur. Regt. Served in Macassar and Amboyna with his Regt.
Resdt. at Laricka (?). Adjt. Bengal Eur. Regt. 4 Nov. 1816 till
1823. Fur. s.c. 23 Apr. 1823 till 22 Oct. 1826. Posted as Capt. to
1st Bengal Eur. Regt. 1 May 1824. Comdt. of escort to Resdt. at
Hyderabad 2 Jan. 1827. Served at Hyderabad till 1836.
Refs. : Burke's *Landed Gentry,* 7th edn., p. 300, *s.n.* Carleton, of
Clare, co. Tipperary. *A.J.* xxi. 817.

CARLETON, William Cossart (1803-1841). Captain, 36th N.I. *b.*
Coolock, co. Dublin, 6 May 1803. Cadet 1819. Admitted 9 Oct.
1820. Ensign 25 May 1820. Lieut. 11 July 1823. Capt.
27 May 1839. *d.* Mymensingh, E. Bengal, 12 Jan. 1841.
4th son of Very Rev. Peter Carleton, dean of Killaloe, and Mary
Griffin his wife. Brother of Charles William Carleton, *q.v.* *m.*

Agra, 22 June 1830, Catherine Louisa, dau. of Capt. John Tritton, 24th Dns., and sister of William Mills Tritton, *q.v.* (*See also* James Henry Ferris, Thomas Fergusson Flemyng, and Charnock Ingleby Harrison.)

Services : Posted as Ensign to 2/3rd N.I. Transfd. as Lieut. to 18th N.I. ; to 36th N.I. (late 1/18th) May 1824. Adjt. Agra Provl. Bn. 28 Oct. 1824. Intr. & Qmr. 36th N.I. 25 Aug. 1825. Siege and capture of Bhurtpore ; Lieut. 36th N.I. Adjt. 36th N.I. 27 June till 29 Sept. 1831. Shekhawat expedition 1834 ; Lieut. 36th N.I.

Refs. : Burke's *Landed Gentry*, 7th edn., p. 300, *s.n.* Carleton, of Clare, co. Tipperary. *I.N.* No. 12, p. 266.

CARLISLE, John (*d.* 1771). Lieutenant, Infantry. Cadet 1768. Ensign 30 Jan. 1769. Lieut. 16 May 1770. *d.* Benares 10 Dec. 1771.

Services : N.F.P.

CARLISLE, Lewis (*d.* 1791). Captain, Infantry. Cadet 1772. Ensign Mar. 1773. Lieut. 21 Mar. 1773. Capt. 14 Oct. 1781. *d.* Berhampore, Bengal, 15 Aug. 1791.

Services : N.F.P.

CARLYON, Charles (1811-1842). Lieutenant, 37th N.I. *b.* Truro 29 Aug. 1811. Cadet 1827. Arrived in India 26 Nov. 1828. Ensign 4 July 1828. Lieut. 18 Sept. 1833. *d. unm.* Jan. 1842 : kld. in action nr. Kabul.

bapt. Truro 22 Nov. 1811. 5th son of Rev. Thomas Carlyon, rector of St. Mary's, Truro, and vicar of Probus, Cornwall, and Mary his wife, 2nd dau. of William Stackhouse, of Trehane, Cornwall.

Services : Ensign d.d. 51st N.I. 14 Jan. 1829. Posted as Ensign to 73rd N.I. 3 June 1829. Transfd. as Lieut. to 37th N.I. 28 Feb. 1833. First Afghan War 1839-42 ; Lieut. 37th N.I.

Refs. : Burke's *Landed Gentry*, 13th edn., p. 207, *s.n.* Carlyon-Britton, of Hanham Court, Gloucs. *Howard & Crisp*, ii. 116.

CARMICHAEL, Alexander (1792-1821). Lieutenant, 5th N.I. *b.* Congash, co. Moray, 30 Nov. 1792. Cadet 1809. Arrived in India 2 Aug. 1810. Ensign 26 Oct. 1811. Lieut. 16 Dec. 1814. *d.* Saharanpur, U.P., 6 Oct. 1821.

Son of Alexander Carmichael, in Congash.

Services : Posted as Ensign to 5th N.I. Operations in Baghelkhand 1813-4 ; Entauri ; Ensign 1/5th N.I. Lieut. 1/5th N.I. Served with Sirmoor Bn. 1819 till death.

CARMICHAEL, Charles Montauban (1790-1870). General, C.B. 5th European L.C. Colonel 20th Hussars. *b.* London 21 Dec. 1790. Cadet 1806. Arrived in India 17 Mar. 1806. Cornet 21 June 1806. Lieut. 12 Apr. 1810. Capt. 8 May 1821. Major 30 Dec. 1833. Lt. Col. 1 Nov. 1838. Col. 6 Sept. 1851. Maj. Gen. 28 Nov. 1854. Lt. Gen. 14 Apr. 1862. Gen. 18 Jan. 1870. *d.* Hotel du Louvre, Boulogne-sur-Mer, 21 Nov. 1870. 4th son of James Carmichael Smyth, M.D., of Aithernie (*D.N.B.*), and Mary his wife, dau. of Thomas Holyland, of Bromley. Brother of George Monro Carmichael Smyth, *q.v.*, and of Sir James Carmichael Smyth, 1st Bart. Discontinued the name of Smyth, by R.L., 17 Aug. 1842. *m.* 4 Mar. 1841, Mary Eliot, dau. of Allan Graham, *q.v.* (She died 29 Apr. 1871.) Ed. Charterhouse 1801-5.

Services : Barasat C.C. for 7 mos. Posted as Cornet to 3rd N.C. Reduction of Kalinjar 1812. Rewah 1813. Alwar 1814. Capture of Hathras 1817. Third Mahratta War. Fur. s.c. 25 Dec. 1818 till 30 Dec. 1822. Against the Bhils 1823-5 ; Bde. Major Meywar F.F. Comdt. 4th Local Horse 16 July 1824 till 17 Oct. 1838. First Afghan War 1838-9 ; Ghazni (Medal). Fur. s.c. 1 Dec. 1840 till 15 Nov. 1843. Transfd. to 4th L.C. in 1843 ; to 9th L.C. 1 Apr. 1844. Fur. 1 Nov. 1844 till 1848, and 5 May 1849 till death. Transfd. to 3rd L.C. ; to 4th L.C. in 1849 ; to 6th L.C. 18 Nov. 1851 ; to 8th L.C. Jan. 1852 ; to 5th Eur. L.C. in 1858. Apptd. Col. of 20th Hrs. 4 Nov. 1862. C.B. 20 Dec. 1839. Durani, 3 cl., 9 Feb. 1841. Author of " A History of the Reigning Family of Lahore," Calcutta and London, 1848 ; " A Rough Sketch of the Rise and Progress of the Irregular Horse of the Bengal Army," by " An Old Cavalry Officer " (? Paris 1854).

Refs. : Burke's *Landed Gentry*, 12th edn., p. 328, *s.n.* Carmichael, of Balmedie. *Boase. Walford. Charterhouse School Register. The Times*, 24 Nov. 1870.

CARNAC, John (1716-1800). Colonel. (Brigadier General.) *b.* 1716. (? 1714/15.) Transfd. as Capt. from H.M. 39th Regt. 1758. Major 11 Oct. 1760. Bdr. Gen. May 1764. Col. 7 May 1765. Resigned 27 Jan. 1767. *d.s.p.* Mangalore, Madras, 29 Nov. 1800, on a sea voyage, aged 84.

(*Possibly* son of Capt. Carnac or Carnae, a Huguenot refugee, who died in Dublin in 1756, aged 91.) Brother of Scipio Carnac, *q.v. m.* 1st, 7 Nov. 1765, Miss Elizabeth Wolleston or Woolaston. (She died 1767.) *m.* 2nd, 20 July 1769, Elizabeth, elder dau. of Thomas Rivett, of Derby, M.P. for that borough. (She died Broach, Bombay, 18 Jan. 1780, aged 28.)

Services : See *D.N.B.*

Refs. : Burke's *Peerage*, 1923, p. 452, *s.n.* Rivett-Carnac, Bart. D.N.B. D.I.B. E.I.M.C. ii. 69.

CARNAC, Scipio (*d.* 1812). Captain. Infantry. Capt. (from H.M.S.) 1 Aug. 1765. Resigned Jan. 1767. *d.* Bristol 24 Oct. 1812. Brother of John Carnac, *q.v.*
Services : N.F.P.

CARNE, John Camin (1789-1824). Captain, Pension Est. Artillery. *b.* Falmouth, Cornwall, 24 Apr. 1789. Cadet 1806. Arrived in India 1 Aug. 1807. Fireworker 8 May 1807. Lieut. 14 Feb. 1808. Capt. 30 Aug. 1819. Pensioned 25 Aug. 1821. *d.* Serampore, Bengal, 7 May 1824.
bapt. Falmouth 15 June 1789. Son of John Carne, H.E.I.C. agent at Falmouth, and Charlotte his wife. *m.* Calcutta, 1 June 1811, Miss Teresa Prendergast. His dau. *m.* James Edward Verner, *q.v.* Woolwich Cadet ; nominated for R.M.A. 7 Dec. 1803 ; obtained his certificate 16 Dec. 1806.
Services : Sailed for India on the *Castle Eden*. Siege and capture of Hathras ; Lieut. 4th Coy. 2nd Bn. Art. Third Mahratta War ; Dhamoni ; Mandala ; Satanwara ; Lieut. 4th Coy. 2nd Bn.
Refs. : Burke's *Landed Gentry*, 4th edn., p. 1737, *s.n.* Carne, of Penzance. Stubbs, ii. 93, note 2.

CARNEGIE, John William (1814-1874). Major, C.B. 15th N.I. *b.* Aberdeen 21 Apr. 1814. Cadet 1832. Arrived in India 30 June 1834. Ensign 23 May 1834. Lieut. 1 Apr. 1838. Capt. 9 Aug. 1848. Major 30 Sept. 1860. Removed from the Army 5 June 1862. *d.* Gipsy Hill, Norwood, 6 Jan. 1874.
bapt. Fetteresso, co. Kincardine, 13 June 1814. Son of David Carnegie, Senior Surgeon, Bombay Est., and Anne his wife. *m.* St. Andrew's, Calcutta, 25 Jan. 1838, Jane, dau. of David Scott. Addiscombe Cadet 2 Mar. 1832 till 13 Dec. 1833.
Services : Posted to 15th N.I. 5 Nov. 1834. Intr. & Qmr. 15 Jan. 1836 till 31 Mar. 1848. Leave s.c. to Cape 27 Oct. 1839 till 10 Aug. 1840. Fur. s.c. 15 Mar. 1848 till 1850. Actg. Cantt. Mgte., Ambala, 26 Apr. till 9 Dec. 1852. Cantt. Mgte., Peshawar, 1855. Special Asst. to D.C. at Lucknow 11 Feb. 1856. Quelled an insurrection in Lucknow on 31 May 1857. Indian Mutiny ; one of the original garrison of the Lucknow Residency (permitted to reckon 1 year's extra service for defence of Residency) ; siege and capture of Lucknow Mar. 1858 (twice hit and horse shot under him) (Medal with two clasps). D.C., 2 cl., Oudh, 23 Mar. 1858. Civil Ofr. with Kapurthala contingent. D.C., 1 cl., Oudh, 15 June 1859. C.B. 18 May 1860.
Refs. : Boase.

CARNEGIE, Nicholas (d. 1824). Major General. Lt. Col. Comdt. Artillery. Country Cadet 1777. Admitted 21 Nov. 1777. Fireworker 31 Mar. 1778. Lieut. 3 Oct. 1778. Capt. Lt. 1 Jan. 1785. Capt. 1 Sept. 1786. Major 1 Jan. 1800. Lt. Col. 15 Nov. 1802. Lt. Col. Comdt. 12 Nov. 1804. Col. 25 July 1810. Maj. Gen. 4 June 1813. d. Coats House, Edinburgh, 30 May 1824.
m. Burdwan, 23 Nov. 1807, Miss Margaret Catherine Boswell. (She died 1 July 1877, aged 91 yrs. and 11 mos.)
Services : Second Mysore War 1781-5 ; Lieut. 5th Coy. 1st Bn. Art. To Madras June-Oct. 1793, for siege of Pondicherry ; Capt. 2nd Coy. 1st Bn. Fur. 24 May 1808 till death.
Refs. : S.M. 1824, ii. 128.

CARNEGY, Alexander (1793-1862). Major General, C.B. 15th N.I. b. 26 Feb. 1793. Cadet 1810. Admitted 22 Oct. 1811. Ensign 20 Aug. 1813. Lieut. 1 Nov. 1815. Capt. 24 Jan. 1826. Major 26 Feb. 1835. Lt. Col. 5 Nov. 1841. Col. 5 Sept. 1851. Maj. Gen. 28 Nov. 1854. d. Meggetland House, Edinburgh, 1 Aug. 1862.

bapt. Forfar 2 May 1793. 2nd son of Patrick Carnegy, of Lour, kinsman of the Earls of Northesk, and Margaret St. Clair his wife, dau. of Alexander Bower, of Kincaldrum, co. Forfar. Brother of William Carnegy, *q.v. m.* Ghazipur, 22 Oct. 1823, Isabella, dau. of William Don. (She died Cawnpore 20 June 1835.)

Services : Posted as Ensign to 2/11th N.I. Nepal War 1815 ; Kumaon ; Ensign 2/11th N.I. (India medal). Capture of Hathras ; Lieut. 2/11th N.I. Third Mahratta War. Adjt. Ramgarh Bn. 21 May 1821. Adjt. 1/11th N.I. 7 Sept. 1821 till 28 Jan. 1822. Transfd. to 15th N.I. (late 1/11th) May 1824. Siege and capture of Bhurtpore ; Lieut. 15th N.I. (Clasp to India medal). Served in Stud Dept. till 14 Aug. 1834. Transfd. to 27th N.I. 14 Feb. 1843. First Sikh War ; Ferozshahr ; Lt. Col. 27th N.I., comdg. 9th Bde. (Medal). Fur. 1846-8. Transfd. to 36th N.I. in 1848. Second Sikh War ; Gujerat ; Lt. Col. 36th N.I., Bdr. comdg. 5th Bde. (Medal). Transfd. as Col. to 24th N.I. 18 Nov. 1851 ; to 42nd N.I. 31 Mar. 1852 ; to 15th N.I. Oct. 1852. Bdr. comdg. at Peshawar 26 June 1852. Fur. s.c. 29 Mar. 1853 till death. C.B. 9 June 1849.

Refs. : Burke's *Peerage*, 1923, p. 1685, *s.n.* Northesk, E. Burke's *Landed Gentry*, 13th edn., p. 296, *s.n.* Carnegy, of Lour and Turin, co. Forfar. *Boase. The Times*, 5 Aug. 1862. *G.M.* 1862, ii. 373.

*CARNEGY, Patrick Ogilvie (or Ogilvy) (1804/05-1861). Cadet. Infantry. Subsequently in Straits C.S. b. 1804/05. Cadet (?). d. Cefn Mine, Pwllheli, 22 Mar. 1861, aged 56.

D.L. co. Carnarvon. Son of (? James) Carnegy, of P.W.I., merchant. *m.* Susan, dau. of Henry Imlach, *q.v.*

… LIST OF THE OFFICERS OF

Services : Never commissioned. Transfd. as Writer to P.W.I., Singapore, and Malacca C.S. in 1820. Subsequently 1st Asst. to Resdt. Counsellor, P.W.I., and Acct. Gen., court of judicature. Retired in 1831.

CARNEGY, William (1803-1880). Captain. 58th N.I. *b.* Forfar 31 Aug. 1803. Cadet 1826. Arrived in India 13 Aug. 1827. Ensign 17 Mar. 1827. Lieut. 17 Sept. 1836. Capt. 17 Mar. 1842. Invalided 3 Mar. 1843. Retired 2 Aug. 1853. *d.s.p.* Clevedon, Somerset, 7 May 1880.

8th son of Patrick Carnegy, of Lour, and Margaret St. Clair his wife. Brother of Alexander Carnegy, *q.v. m.* Kumaon, 16 Sept. 1830, Isabella, dau. of William Newton.

Services : Capt. Forfar Mil. 8 June 1825. Ensign 15th N.I. 1827. Transfd. to 58th N.I. 3 Jan. 1828. Adjt. Kumaon Local Bn. 18 May 1832. Fur. s.c. 30 Aug. 1837 till 17 Dec. 1841. Fur. p.a. 14 Apr. 1843 till 1846. No record of active service.

Refs. : Burke's *Peerage*, 1923, p. 1686, *s.n.* Northesk, E. Burke's *Landed Gentry*, 13th edn., p. 296, *s.n.* Carnegy, of Lour and Turin, co. Forfar. *The Times,* 17 May 1880.

CARPENTER, Edmund Cheese (1783-?). Captain. 19th N.I. *b.* Hereford 6 Nov. 1783. Cadet 1800. Arrived in India 19 Aug. 1801. Ensign 5 Dec. 1801. Lieut. 2 Nov. 1803. Capt. 16 Apr. 1815. Resigned in India 10 Jan. 1818.

Son of Michael Cheese and Elizabeth his wife. Brother of John Cheese, *q.v.* Took the additional name of Carpenter 9 June 1815 (*Lond. Gaz.* 1161).

Note : But appears as Edmund Cheese Carpenter in *E.I.R.* of 15 Aug. 1809 and onwards.

Services : Ensign 19th N.I. Fur. 17 Dec. 1811 till 1815. Capt. 2/19th N.I. No record of active service.

CARPENTER, George (1763/64-1855). General. Colonel 49th N.I. *b.* 1763/64. Cadet (on the Bencoolen Est.) 1780. Ensign (Bencoolen) 25 Sept. 1781. Transfd. to Bengal 10 Nov. 1790. Capt. 29 May 1800. Major 27 Nov. 1805. Lt. Col. 30 Oct. 1811. Lt. Col. Comdt. 29 Apr. 1823. Col. 27 May 1825. Maj. Gen. 10 Jan. 1837. Lt. Gen. 9 Nov. 1846. Gen. 20 June 1854. *d.* Gt. Cumberland Pl., London, 29 Jan. 1855, aged 91.

Of Gt. Cumberland Pl. *m.* Hester, dau. of Robert Moore, of Moore Vale, co. Armagh. (She died 20 Sept. 1855, aged 93.)

Services : Transfd. to Bengal Est. as Lieut. Fur. p.a. 15 Mar. 1796 till 18 Sept. 1800. Second Mahratta War ; Capt. 17th N.I. (India medal). Nepal War 1814-5 ; comdd. 1st column of attack against Kalanga ; Lt. Col. 1/17th N.I., in 2nd Div. (Clasp to India

medal). Transfd. to 29th N.I. in 1816. Third Mahratta War ; Lt. Col. 29th N.I. Transfd. to 3rd N.I. in 1818. Fur. p.a. 21 Jan. 1819 till June 1821. To comd. Cuttack Provl. Bn. 29 Oct. 1821. Comdg. in Cuttack 1821-7. Transfd. to 1/16th N.I. in 1821 ; to 50th N.I. in 1824 ; to 31st N.I. in 1825 ; to 17th N.I. 22 Dec. 1827. To comd. at Delhi 2 July 1827. Bdr. Gen. 7 Nov. 1828. To comd. Benares Div. 8 Nov. 1828. To comd. Cawnpore Div. 22 Nov. 1831. Fur. p.a. 8 Jan. 1834 till death. Transfd. to 49th N.I. in 1837.
Refs. : Boase. *G.M.* 1855, i. 439.

CARR, Charles (1802-1823). Lieutenant, Artillery. *b.* London 6 July 1802. Cadet 1818. 2nd Lieut. 15 Sept. 1818. Lieut. 9 Jan. 1820. *d.* Kamptee, C.P., 27 Sept. 1823.
Son of John Carr. Addiscombe Cadet 1816-8.
Services : No record of active service.

CARR, George (1809-1850). Bt. Major, 21st N.I. *bapt.* Glasgow 3 Dec. 1809. Cadet 1825. Arrived in India 5 May 1826. Ensign 12 Jan. 1826. Lieut. 12 Dec. 1831. Capt. 28 June 1844. Bt. Major 3 Apr. 1846. *d.* Hobart Town, Tasmania, 30 June 1850.
Son of Henry Carr, R.N., and Maria his wife. Ward of Hon. George Cadogan, Capt. R.N. (afterwards Admiral, third Earl Cadogan). *m.* Calcutta, 15 Feb. 1848, Sophia, dau. of George Boulton Mainwaring, and sister of Philip Mainwaring, *q.v.*
Services : Posted as Ensign to 7th N.I. Transfd. to 21st N.I. 7 June 1832. Pioneers 9 June 1832. Adjt. do. 14 June 1832. Adjt. Sylhet L.I. 15 Jan. 1835 till 5 Jan. 1839. A.D.C. to G.G. 5 Jan. 1839. Fur. s.c. 22 Feb. 1840 till 9 Apr. 1842. Actg. D.J.A.G., Sirhind, 15 Mar. 1843, and 27 Sept. 1845. First Sikh War ; Mudki ; Ferozshahr ; Sobraon ; Capt. 21st N.I., D.J.A.G. (Medal with two clasps). D.J.A.G., Nimach (afterwards at Peshawar), 10 Mar. 1846 till death.

CARR, John. (See **CARE, John.**)

CARR, John Frederick (1776-1812). Captain, Pension Est. 24th N.I. *b.* St. Helena 30 Nov. 1776. Cadet 1795. Arrived in India 8 Mar. 1797. Ensign 24 Oct. 1796. Lieut. 30 Oct. 1797. Capt. 22 Feb. 1806. Pensioned 28 Aug. 1806. *d.* 2 Oct. 1812.
bapt. St. Helena 19 Mar. 1777. Son of Rev. Robartes Carr, chaplain at St. Helena and subsequently Bengal Est., and Bridget his wife, née Greentree. Nephew of Rev. Colston Carr, of Twickenham.
Services : Lieut. 11th N.I. Transfd. to newly-raised 24th N.I. in 1805. Capt. Lt. 24th N.I. 26 Oct. 1805. No record of active service.

CARRINGTON, William Henry (1783-1805). Lieutenant, 25th N.I.
b. Ide, Devon, 2 Aug. 1783. Cadet 1798. Arrived in India 23 Nov. 1799. Ensign 4 Oct. 1799. Lieut. 28 Oct. 1799. *d.* Agra, 4 May 1805, of wounds received in action at Adalatnagar on 7 Apr.
bapt. ptely. 3 Sept. 1783; received into the Church at Ide 30 Dec. 1783. Son of William Henry Carrington and Frances his wife.
Services : Posted as Lieut. to 1/10th N.I. 15 Apr. 1801. Transfd. to newly-raised 1/25th N.I. in Oct. 1804. Second Mahratta War ; Adalatnagar 7 Apr. 1805 (s.w.—lost a leg) ; Lieut. 1/25th N.I.
Refs. : Intestate ; admon. granted 30 July 1805.

CARRIQUE, Ponsonby. (See **PONSONBY, Carrique.**)

CARROLL, Christopher (1770-1794). Ensign, Infantry. *b.* 27 Nov. 1770. Cadet 1790. Ensign 1793. *d.* at sea Sept. 1794.
bapt. St. Mary Woolnoth, London, 19 Dec. 1770. Son of Christopher Carroll and Ann his wife.
Services : N.F.P. (*Probably* never arrived in India.)

CARROLL, Thomas (*d.* 1769). Lieutenant, Infantry. Cadet (?). Ensign (?). Lieut. 1 Sept. 1768. *d.* 1769.
Services : N.F.P.

CARRUTHERS, David Alexander (1789-?). Lieutenant. 30th N.I.
b. Everton, nr. Liverpool, 11 May 1789. Cadet 1807. Arrived in India 19 Aug. 1808. Ensign 20 Aug. 1808. Lieut. 11 Sept. 1811. Resigned in India 26 Apr. 1816.
Of Warmanbie, co. Dumfries. Son of James Carruthers, cooper. *m.* Jane, youngest dau. of Rev. Robert Hankinson Roughsedge, rector of Liverpool, and sister of Edward Roughsedge, *q.v.*
Services : Posted as Ensign to 12th N.I. (? Nepal War 1814-5 ; Lieut. Ramgarh Bn., in 4th Div.) Transfd. to newly-raised 1/30th N.I. in 1815. Actg. Adjt. Ramgarh Bn. 1815-6.
Refs. : Burke's *Landed Gentry*, 4th edn., p. 1300, *s.n.* Roughsedge, of Foxghyll, Westmorland.

*CARRUTHERS, Jacob (1776-?). Cadet. Infantry. *b.* Berwick, 20 Sept. 1776. Cadet 1795. Arrived in India 8 Oct. 1797. Dismissed and sent home (?).
Son of John Carruthers, of Berwick, Ensign, Independent Coy. of Invalids.
Services : N.F.P.
Refs. : Philippart MS.

THE BENGAL ARMY, 1758-1884 311

CARRUTHERS, John. Lieutenant. Infantry. Cadet 1783. Arrived in India 17 Sept. 1783. Ensign 6 Apr. 1785. Lieut. 5 May 1793. Retired 20 Jan. 1799.
Of Denbie and Dalton, co. Dumfries. (*Probably* brother of Robert Carruthers, *q.v.*) *m*. Mary Irvine.
Note : His name disappears from the list of Retired Officers in *E.I.R.* after Jan. 1851.
Services: Lieut. 2nd Bengal Eur. Regt. in 1796. N.F.P.

CARRUTHERS, Robert (*d*. 1800). Lieutenant, 14th N.I. Cadet 1783. Arrived in India 4 Aug. 1784. Ensign 27 May 1785. Lieut. 10 Oct. 1793. *d*. Midnapore, Bengal, 28 Nov. 1800.
Son of John Carruthers, of Holmains, surveyor gen. of window lights for Scotland. His sister Rachel *m*. John Peter Wade, M.D., Surgeon Bengal Est.
Services : Adjt. 2/14th N.I. 29 May 1800 till death.
Refs. : Burke's *Landed Gentry*, 13th edn., p. 447, *s.n.* Carruthers, of Dormont, co. Dumfries.

CARSTAIRS, Peter (*d*. 1763). Captain, Bengal European Regt. Cadet (?). Ensign 18 June 1756. Lieut. (?). Capt. Lt. 1757. Capt. 29 Sept. 1757. *d*. Hajipur, nr. Patna, 3 July 1763, of wounds received at the battle of Manjhi two days earlier.
Brother of James Carstairs, nephew of Alexander Wedderburn, of St. Germains, nr. Edinburgh, and of Mrs. Elizabeth Wedderburn.
Services : Siege of Calcutta, wounded at the jail, 18 June 1756, and escaped on board one of the vessels to Fulta. (He may possibly have gone through the ordeal of the Black Hole.) Wounded in the attack on the Nawab's camp 5 Feb. 1757. Battle of Plassey, having voted for immediate action at the preliminary council of war. Resigned 31 Aug. 1758, owing to supercession by John Gowen, *q.v.* Permitted to return to India, and embarked on the *Latham* in 1759 as " Captain—returning to his station." Readmitted 13 Oct. 1760.
Refs. : Orme *MSS.—India*, xiii. 3639. Hill's *Calcutta*, p. 18. Will dated 27 Feb. 1763 ; proved 2 Dec. 1763.

CARSTAIRS, Thomas (1807-1829). Lieutenant, 29th N.I. *b*. Anstruther, co. Fife, 17 Jan. 1807. Cadet 1825. Ensign 25 Sept. 1825. Lieut. 3 Dec. 1826. *d*. Meerut, 11 Oct. 1829.
Son of Rev. Andrew Carstairs, minister of Anstruther.
Services : Posted as Ensign to 29th N.I. No record of active service.

CARTE, Edward (1803-1870). Lieutenant. 63rd N.I. Subsequently vicar of Gentleshaw, Staffs. *b*. Newcastle, co. Limerick, 20 Jan. 1803. Cadet 1820. Arrived in India May 1821. Ensign 16 Jan.

1821. Lieut. 11 July 1823. Resigned 4 Apr. 1826. *d.* Gentleshaw, June 1870.

Son of Edward Carte. T.C.D.; Pensioner 2 Nov. 1818, aged 17. B.A. 1830.

Services : Posted as Ensign to 2/27th N.I. in 1822. Transfd. to newly-formed 32nd N.I. 11 July 1823; to 63rd N.I. (late 1/32nd) May 1824. 2nd Gren. Bn. (? First Burma War; Arakan 1825; Lieut. 2nd Gren. Bn.) Fur. 1825 till resignation. Took holy orders. P.C. Gentleshaw 1837; and Farewell, Staffs. 1838.

Refs. : Alumni Dub. Crockford, 1860 edn.

Note : His name does not figure in the roll of recipients of the India medal.

CARTER, Charles (*d.* 1778/79). Cadet, Infantry. Cadet 1778. Never arrived in India. *d.* at sea 1778/79, on the voyage out to India.

CARTER, Henry (1777-1818). Major, 30th N.I. *b.* London 22 Aug. 1777. Cadet 1793. Arrived in India 30 Oct. 1795. Ensign 6 Oct. 1794. Lieut. 10 June 1796. Capt. 21 Sept. 1804. Major 16 Dec. 1814. *d. unm.* Puri, B. & O., 5 July 1818.

bapt. St. Anne's, Westminster, 18 Sept. 1777. Son of Richard Carter, of Marylebone, and of Foxley, Wilts., and Mary (Eleanor) his wife, née Willington.

Services : Adjt. 1/3rd N.I. 29 May 1800 till 1804. Transfd. as Capt. to newly-raised 25th N.I. in 1804. Operations against Rana of Gohad 1806; Capt. 25th N.I. Expedition to Mauritius 1810-1; Capt. 1st Bengal Vol. Bn. Apptd. to 2/30th N.I., called after him "*Karter-ki-Paltan*," on formation in Jan. 1815.

Refs. : Will dated 23 Jan. 1815; proved 27 Aug. 1818.

CARTER, Henry (1793-1844). Major, 73rd N.I. *b.* Inch, Queen's Co., 29 Sept. 1793. Cadet 1808. Arrived in India 27 Oct. 1809. Ensign 13 Mar. 1810. Lieut. 16 Dec. 1814. Capt. 22 Sept. 1826. Major 17 Sept. 1841. *d.* Delhi, 29 May 1844, of fever.

Son of Michael Carter, of Inch, Rathasbuck, Queen's Co., and Elizabeth his wife. Brother of Samuel Carter, *q.v.,* and nephew of John Peter Boileau, Madras C.S. *m.* Ghazipur, U.P., 19 Jan. 1820, Helen, youngest dau. of Charles Gray, of Carse Gray, and sister of James Coutts Crawford Gray, *q.v.* (*See also* Clements Gillespie Macan.)

Services : Barasat C.C. Jan.-Oct. 1810. Posted as Ensign to 2/7th N.I. Nepal War 1814-5; Malaun; Lieut. 2/7th N.I. A.D.C. to V.P. 18 July 1817. Bk. Mr. at Muttra Sept. 1817; do., Saugor District, June 1819; do., Ghazipur div., June 1823. Posted to

10th N.I. (late 2/7th) May 1824. P.W.D., Ghazipur div., Aug. 1824. Transfd. to newly-raised 5th Extra Regt. (became 73rd N.I. in 1828) in July 1825. P.W.D. Bundelkhand 1831. Fur. s.c. 22 Feb. 1832 till 8 Mar. 1836. Paymr. of Native pensioners at Barrackpore Jan. 1837 till Jan. 1842. Leave to Cape and N.S.W. 9 Jan. 1842 till Nov. 1843.
Refs. : De Rhé-Philipe. A.J. xxviii. 113. I.M. xvi. 497.

CARTER, Henry (1812-1837). Lieutenant, 35th N.I. b. Maidstone, Kent, 29 Feb. 1812. Cadet 1827. Arrived in India 12 Aug. 1828. Ensign (21 Mar. 1828) 4 Nov. 1828. Lieut. 2 Apr. 1834. d. Lucknow 17 Feb. 1837.
Son of Thomas William Carter, of Maidstone, estate agent, and Mary his wife. Ed. Shrewsbury 1822-7.
Services : Ensign d.d. 50th N.I. 8 Sept. 1825. Posted as Ensign to 35th N.I. 4 Nov. 1828. No record of active service.
Refs. : Shrewsbury School List.

CARTER, John William (1813-1867). Lieut. Colonel. 24th N.I. b. 23 July 1813. Cadet 1834. Arrived in India 21 July 1835. Ensign (24 Feb. 1835) 20 Apr. 1835. Lieut. 3 Oct. 1840. Capt. 15 Nov. 1853. Major 27 May 1860. Lt. Col. 3 Aug. 1862. d. Murree 29 Apr. 1867.
bapt. St. Anne Shandon, Cork, 15 Sept. 1813. Son of Benjamin Carter, Capt. R.N., and Anne his wife. Nephew of George Graydon, of Chatham. m. 1st, Calcutta, 30 Dec. 1851, Frances D., widow of G. Turner. m. 2nd, Lyncombe, Bath, 18 Oct. 1865, Sophia, widow of Capt. Edward Herbert Nightingale, 23rd Madras L.I., and youngest dau. of Robert Blackall, q.v. (See also Joseph Graham.)
Services : Posted to 16th N.I. 24 Sept. 1835. First Afghan War 1839-42 ; Ghazni (Medal) ; re-occupation of Kabul ; Lieut. 16th N.I. (Medal). Transfd. to 54th N.I. 14 Dec. 1842. Adjt. 5th Inf. Gwalior Contingent Feb. 1844. First Sikh War ; garrison duty at Ferozepore ; Lieut. 54th N.I. Leave to N.S.W. Mar. 1849 till Nov. 1850. 2nd in comd. 5th Inf., Gwalior Contingent, 8 Jan. 1851. Actg. Comdt. 2nd Inf. 20 May 1856. Comdt. 5th Inf. Apr. 1857. Mutiny campaign 1857-8 (Medal). Comdt. Rohilkhand Mily. Police Bn. June 1858 till Mar. 1861. D.I.G. Police, Rohilkhand div. Apr. 1861 till Dec. 1862. Fur. 1862 till Mar. 1866. Offg. Comdt. 24th N.I. Apr.-Dec. 1866.
Refs. : De Rhé-Philipe. Burke's Peerage, 1923, p. 1666, s.n. Nightingale, Bart. I.M. 1852, p. 96.

CARTER, Samuel (1794-1817). Ensign, 30th N.I. b. Rathasbuck, Queen's Co., 17 Oct. 1794. Cadet 1810. Ensign 3 Aug. 1813. d. Khurda, Bengal, 27 Dec. 1817.

Son of Michael Carter, of Inch, and Elizabeth his wife. Brother of Henry Carter (1793-1844), *q.v.*
Services: Cadet d.d. 2/7th N.I. 1811-3. Posted as Ensign to 8th N.I. in 1813. Transfd. to newly-formed 2/30th N.I. in 1815. No record of active service.

CARTER, Thomas (*d.* 1776). Captain, Infantry. Cadet (?). Ensign 13 Aug. 1765. Lieut. 29 Dec. 1766. Capt. 19 May 1770. *d.* Belgaum, Bombay, 5 Sept. 1776.
Services: Employed on survey work in Bengal under James Rennell, *q.v.* N.F.P.

CARTER, William Charles (1806-1845). Captain, 26th N.I. *b.* London 6 Jan. 1806. Cadet 1823. Arrived in India 1 Oct. 1824. Ensign 1 May 1824. Lieut. 19 May 1825. Capt. 23 June 1842. *d.* Ludhiana 10 Jan. 1845.
Son of George Carter, of the customs. *m.* Calcutta, 6 Dec. 1838, Miss Elizabeth Caroline Boreman.
Services: To do duty with 2nd Bengal Eur. Regt. Posted to 34th N.I. in Mar. 1825. Operations against the Kols and Chuars 1831-3; Lieut. 34th N.I. Fur. s.c. 1 Feb. 1834 till 17 Oct. 1836. The 34th N.I. having been disbanded at Meerut in Mar. 1844, owing to mutiny, he was directed, in Apr., to do duty with 26th N.I.
Refs.: De Rhé-Philipe.

CARTWRIGHT, Edmund (1778-1853). Lieut. General. Colonel 57th N.I. *b.* London 29 Mar. 1778. Cadet 1795. Arrived in India 24 Oct. 1796. Ensign 28 Nov. 1796. Lieut. 30 Oct. 1797. Capt. 22 Feb. 1806. Major 10 Aug. 1816. Lt. Col. 18 Jan. 1823. Col. 5 June 1829. Maj. Gen. 28 June 1838. Lt. Gen. 11 Nov. 1851. *d.* 131 Piccadilly, London, 31 Mar. 1853.
Of 60 New Bond St., London. *bapt.* St. George's, Hanover Sq., London, 26 Apr. 1778. Son of Thomas Cartwright and Catherine his wife, née Moore. Brother of Frances, wife of William Page. *m.* (?).
Services: Posted as Ensign to 1st Bengal Eur. Regt. 4 May 1796. Adjt. 1/5th N.I. 1800-4. Fur. s.c. 19 July 1804; captured by the French, but allowed to return to India on parole. Fur. 21 Mar. 1805 till 5 Oct. 1807. Transfd. to 24th N.I. in 1805. Bde. Major Ludhiana, 13 Mar. 1810; do. 3rd Div., Nepal, 15 Nov. 1814. Nepal War; Capt. 2/24th N.I., Bde Major (India medal). A.D.C. to Sir D. Ochterlony, *q.v.*, 29 Nov. 1815. Capture of Hathras. A.A.G., Rajputana, 23 June 1818. Third Mahratta War; Major 1/24th N.I. Extra Asst. to Resdt. at Delhi 25 Jan. 1821. Fur. s.c. 20 Feb. 1821 till 12 Oct. 1822. Transfd. to comd. 47th N.I. (late 1/24th) May 1824. 47th N.I. mutinied at Barrackpore 31 Oct. 1824. Transfd. to 1st Bengal Eur. Regt. in 1825. Siege and capture of

Bhurtpore ; Lt. Col. 1st Eur. Regt. (Clasp to India medal). Bdr. 4 Feb. 1826. Transfd. to 15th N.I. 28 Dec. 1826 ; to 10th N.I. 22 Mar. 1829. To comd. Agra and Muttra frontier 26 Dec. 1833. Comdt. at Agra 8 Jan. 1835. Col. 57th N.I. Fur. s.c. 14 Feb. 1839 till 18 Dec. 1842. To comd. Presdy. Div. 17 Jan. 1843 ; Dinapore Div. 8 Mar. 1844 ; Presdy. Div. 1 Oct. 1844. Fur. 8 Feb. 1848 till death.
Refs. : Boase. *I.M.* 1853, p. 178. Will dated 9 Sept. 1850 ; proved 17 May 1853.

CARTWRIGHT, John (1791-1840). Bt. Major, Artillery. *b.* London 13 June 1791. Cadet 1809. Arrived in India 20 Oct. 1810. Fireworker 20 Oct. 1810. Lieut. 25 Sept. 1817. Capt. 24 Oct. 1825. Bt. Major 28 June 1838. *d.* Dum-Dum, 9 June 1840, of cholera.

Of Hobart, Tasmania. Son of Thomas Cartwright and Mary his wife. Brother of George Cartwright, of Hobart, solicitor. Addiscombe Cadet 1809-10.

Services : Nepal War 1814-5 ; Malaun ; Lieut. F., with 3rd Div. Nepal War 1816 ; A.D.C. and Sec. to Sir David Ochterlony. Posted to newly-raised Rocket Troop H.A. in 1816. Comy. Ord. 5 Aug. 1824 till 1836. Leave to N.S.W. for 1 yr. 13 Jan. 1825. A.A.G. of Art. May 1835 till death. Leave to Tasmania in 1837.

Refs. : G.M. 1840, ii. 446. *The Times,* 13 Aug. 1840. M.I. in St. Stephen's church, Dum-Dum. Will dated 7 July 1838 ; proved 25 Sept. 1840.

CARTWRIGHT, William Perry (1778-1804). Captain, 20th N.I. *bapt.* Dudley, Worcs., 16 Mar. 1778. Cadet 1794. Arrived in India 2 Feb. 1797. Ensign 23 Nov. 1795. Lieut. 30 Oct. 1797. Capt. 21 Sept. 1804. *d.* Hazaribagh, Bengal, 24 Nov. 1804.

2nd son of Rev. Joseph Cartwright, of Dudley, and Mary his wife. *m.* (?).

Services : Lieut. Marine Regt. (became 20th N.I. in 1803). Second Mahratta War ; occupation of Sambalpur, B. & O., 1803 ; Lieut. Ramgarh Bn.

Refs. : G.M. 1805, ii. 877. Will dated Sambalpur 30 Dec. 1803 ; proved 26 June 1805.

*CARVALHO, John. Capt. Lieutenant. 2nd Troop of European Dragoons. Capt. Lt. 22 Sept. 1760.

A native of Portugal.

Services : Apptd. Capt. Lt. comdg. 2nd Troop of Eur. Dns., with pay at 9s. *p.d.*, 22 Sept. 1760.

Refs. : M.C., Fort William, 22 Sept. 1760. *Journal of the United Service Institution of India,* xlii. 112-3.

CARY, Bernard (1807-1870). Lieut. Colonel. 6th N.I. *b.* London 8 Mar. 1807. Cadet 1827. Arrived in India 5 May 1829. Ensign 4 Dec. 1828. Lieut. 12 Dec. 1837. Capt. (4 Dec. 1843) 17 Nov. 1850. Bt. Major 20 June 1854. Invalided 29 Jan. 1858. Retired Aug. 1860. Hon. Lt. Col. Aug. 1860. *d.* 14 Sept. 1870.

2nd son of John Cary, of Hampstead, barr.-at-law, and Sophia his wife, dau. of Edward Sulyarde. *m.* Calcutta, Nov. 1837, Eliza, 3rd dau. of Marianna Castelli, consul at Lima, Peru.

Services : Ensign d.d. 7th N.I. 10 June 1829. Posted as Ensign to 6th N.I. 14 Sept. 1829. Fur. p.a. 24 Mar. 1835 till 29 Oct. 1837. First Afghan War 1842 ; re-occupation of Kabul ; Lieut. 6th N.I., with Gen. Pollock's force (Medal). Fur. s.c. 15 May 1848 till 1850.

Refs. : Burke's *Landed Gentry*, 13th edn., p. 306, *s.n.* Cary, of Torre Abbey, Devon. *The Devon Carys* (2 vols., ptely. printed, N.Y. 1820), i. 288.

CARY, George Edwin (1802-1832). Lieutenant, 15th N.I. *b.* Canterbury 23 Dec. 1802. Cadet 1819. Admitted 30 May 1820. Ensign 10 Jan. 1820. Lieut. 7 Nov. 1822. *d.* Cheltenham 9 June 1832.

bapt. 13 Jan. 1803. Son of William Robert Cary, Col. R.A., and Susannah his wife. Brother of Henry Vigo Cary, *q.v.*

Services : Posted as Ensign to 2/11th N.I. Adjt. Agra Provl. Bn. 14 Mar. 1825. Transfd. to 15th N.I. (late 1/11th) May 1824. Siege and capture of Bhurtpore ; Lieut. 15th N.I. Fur. s.c. 11 Jan. 1831 till death.

Refs. : G.M. 1832, i. 646.

CARY, Henry Vigo (1800-1825). Lieutenant, 57th N.I. *bapt.* Canterbury 28 Sept. 1800. Cadet 1817. Ensign 26 May 1818. Lieut. 22 Oct. 1819. *d.* at sea, 22 Mar. 1825, on board the *Morley.*

Son of William Robert Cary, Col. R.A., and Susannah his wife. Brother of George Edwin Cary, *q.v.*

Services : Lieut. 1/29th N.I. On fur. in 1820 and again in 1823. Transfd. to 57th N.I. (late 1/29th) May 1824. Adjt. Agra Provl. Bn. till 14 Mar. 1825, when he was succeeded by his brother. No record of active service.

CARY, Oliver (1748/49-1785). Lieutenant, Infantry. *b.* 1748/49. Cadet 1780. Arrived in India 12 Feb. 1780. Ensign 1 Aug. 1780. Lieut. 24 Mar. 1781. *d. unm.* Chunar, U.P., 4 Nov. 1785.

A native of Roscommon, Ireland. Son of —— Cary and Jane his wife. Brother of William, George, James, and Mary Cary.

THE BENGAL ARMY, 1758-1834   317

Services : Sailed for India, as a " soldier," on the *Norfolk*, 7 Mar. 1779, aged 30. " To be appointed a Cadet on arrival in Bengal." N.F.P.
Refs. : Will dated Chunar 28 Sept. 1785.

CASEMENT, George (1788-1823). Captain, 21st N.I. *b.* Larne, co. Antrim, 1 May 1788. Cadet 1804. Arrived in India 18 Mar. 1805. Ensign 4 Mar. 1805. Lieut. 5 May 1805. Capt. 19 Dec. 1820. *d.* Mhow, 1 Nov. 1823.
4th and youngest son of George Casement, Surgeon R.N., and Matilda Montgomery his 2nd wife. Brother of Hugh Casement, *q.v.*, uncle of George Casement, *q.v.*, and cousin-german of John Joseph Casement, *q.v. m.* Bareilly, 16 Apr. 1821, Sarah, 7th dau. of Thomas Chadwick, of Barnascounce, 18th Light Dns., and sister of Thomas Chadwick, *q.v.* (*See also* Charles Hamilton Bell.)
Services : Posted as Lieut. to 2/21st N.I. (? Operations in Bundelkhand 1809-12, and in Rewah 1811.) (? Nepal War 1816; Lieut. 2/21st N.I., in Right Column.) Adjt. 1/21st N.I. 1817. Comdg. 3rd Local Cav. in 1819. Bde. Major Rohilkhand, 1820 ; do., Bareilly, 1821. Bk. Mr. Bareilly div. 1821. Bde. Major at Mhow 1822 till death.
Refs. : Burke's *Landed Gentry of Ireland*, p. 101, *s.n.* Casement, of Magherintemple, co. Antrim. Burke's *Colonial Gentry*, ii. 587, *s.n.* Chadwick. Will dated 3 Aug. 1820 ; proved 22 Nov. 1823.

CASEMENT, George (1811-1830). 2nd Lieutenant, Engineers. *bapt.* Larne, co. Antrim, 13 Jan. 1811. Cadet 1827. Arrived in India 12 Dec. 1828. 2nd Lieut. 21 July 1828. *d.* London 4 June 1830.
Younger son of John Montgomery Casement, of Invermore, Larne, and Mary his wife, dau. of John McGildowny. Nephew of Sir William Casement, K.C.B., *q.v.* Addiscombe Cadet 1825-7.
Services : Fur. s.c. 10 Jan. 1830 till death. No record of active service.
Refs. : Burke's *Landed Gentry of Ireland*, p. 101, *s.n.* Casement, of Magherintemple, co. Antrim.

*CASEMENT, Hugh (1784-1804). Lieutenant, Infantry. *b.* Larne, co. Antrim, 6 Sept. 1784. Cadet 1803. Was already in India when apptd. Ensign 2 Oct. 1804. Lieut. 2 Oct. 1804. *d.* Ceylon, 1804.
3rd son of George Casement, Surgeon R.N., and Matilda Montgomery his 2nd wife. Half-brother of Sir William Casement, K.C.B., *q.v.*, and cousin-german of John Joseph Casement, *q.v.*
Services : Apptd. from H.M. 34th Regt., but never claimed the appt.

Refs. : Burke's *Landed Gentry of Ireland,* p. 101, *s.n.* Casement, of Magherintemple, co. Antrim.

CASEMENT, John Joseph (1791-1825). Bt. Captain, 39th N.I. *b.* Henryville (Harryville), Ballyclugg, co. Antrim, 3 June 1791. Cadet 1807. Arrived in India 19 Aug. 1808. Ensign 4 Sept. 1808. Lieut. 30 Aug. 1814. Bt. Capt. 1 Mar. 1823. *d.* Sydney, N.S.W., 9 May 1825.

Son of Roger Casement, of Harryville, and Catherine his 1st wife, dau. of Julius Cosnahan, of Peel, I. of Man. Cousin-german of Sir William Casement, K.C.B., *q.v.,* and 1st cousin once removed of George Casement (1811-1830), *q.v.*

Services : Ensign 19th N.I. Nepal War 1814-5 ; Lieut. 1/19th N.I., in 1st Div. Baggage Master Nagpur Subsdy. Force 1817-9. (? Third Mahratta War.) Bk. Mr. at Bareilly 1819-21. Transfd. to 2/19th N.I. Bde. Major at Bareilly 1821-5. Transfd. to 39th N.I. (late 2/19th) May 1824.

Refs. : Burke's *Landed Gentry of Ireland,* p. 101, *s.n.* Casement, of Magherintemple, co. Antrim. Will dated Hired Transport *Lady East* 3 May 1825 ; proved 20 June 1826.

CASEMENT, Sir William (1778-1844). Major General, K.C.B. Colonel 23rd N.I. *b.* Larne, co. Antrim, 14 July 1778. Cadet 1795. Arrived in India 26 Sept. 1796. Ensign 17 Oct. 1796. Lieut. 30 Oct. 1797. Capt. 21 Sept. 1804. Major 22 Dec. 1811. Lt. Col. 22 June 1816. Lt. Col. Comdt. 1 May 1824. Col. 5 June 1829. Maj. Gen. 10 Jan. 1837. *d.* Cossipore (Kasipur) 16 Apr. 1844, of cholera.

2nd son of George Casement, Surgeon R.N., and Elizabeth Montgomery his 1st wife. Half-brother of George Casement (1788-1823), *q.v.,* and cousin-german of Thomas Lowry, *q.v. m.* Cawnpore, 21 July 1803, Anne, dau. of Sir George Sackville Browne, K.C.B., *q.v.* (She died Kensington 4 Sept. 1858.)

Services : Approved as Cadet 23 Mar. 1796. Posted as Ensign to 3rd Bengal Eur. Regt. Adjt. 1/4th N.I. 1801-3. Second Mahratta War 1803-4 ; Aligarh ; Deig ; Capt. 4th N.I. D.Q.M.G. 22 Jan. 1810. Nepal War ; Major 1/4th N.I., D.Q.M.G. (G.O.C.C. of 15 Nov. 1814). Transfd. as Lt. Col. to 7th N.I. in 1816. Third Mahratta War ; Lt. Col. 7th N.I., D.Q.M.G. 2nd Div. Sec. to Govt., Mily Dept., 30 Jan. 1819. 2/29th N.I. in 1821. Lt. Col. Comdt. 7th N.I. May 1824. Transfd. to 23rd N.I. in 1837. Mily. Sec. to Govt. of India, and Member of the Supreme Council, 17 June 1839. C.B. 4 June 1815. K.C.B. 10 Mar. 1837.

Refs. : Burke's *Landed Gentry of Ireland,* p. 101, *s.n.* Casement, of Magherintemple, co. Antrim. *D.I.B. G.M.* 1844, ii. 207. *I.M.* No. 14, p. 419. *The Times,* 21 June 1844.

THE BENGAL ARMY, 1758-1834 319

CASSADY, Pierce (*d.* 1799). Lieutenant. Infantry. Cadet 1790. Admitted 8 Nov. 1791. Ensign 17 Mar. 1793. Lieut. 8 Dec. 1794. *d.* Dinapore 18 Aug. 1799.

Services : Apparently commissioned from the ranks. Was " Adjutant with Warrant," and Adjt. 26th Bn. Sepoys in 2nd Bde. in 1790, before receiving a Commission.

CASTELL or CASTIEL, Anthony. Lieutenant. Infantry. Cadet (?). Ensign 11 Nov. 1757. Lieut. 9 Apr. 1759. Dismissed 12 Nov. 1761.

m. Calcutta, 18 Mar. 1760, Mrs. Mary Smith (*probably* widow of Capt. John Smith, Bengal pilot). (She died Calcutta 13 Mar. 1761.)
Note : The name also appears as Casteel and Casteele.
Services : N.F.P.
Refs. : *Orme MSS.—India,* xiii. 3639.

CATANACK, John. Lieutenant. Infantry. Cadet 1764. Ensign 3 Oct. 1764. Lieut. 12 Oct. 1765. Resigned May 1766.

Services : Resigned his Commission during the organized combination against Lord Clive's new batta rules. N.F.P.

CATES, John (1799-1822). Ensign, 19th N.I. *bapt.* Broxbourne, Herts., 3 Nov. 1799. Cadet 1820. Ensign 3 Sept. 1821. *d.* 13 Sept. 1822, on board his budgerow nr. Chunar.

Son of John Cates, farmer.
Services : Posted as Ensign to 19th N.I.

CATHCART, Hugh James Grant Buchanan (1799-1834). Captain, 5th N.I. *b.* Kingston, Jamaica, 21 July 1799. Cadet 1817. Arrived in India 13 Aug. 1818. Ensign 8 Apr. 1818. Lieut. 12 Oct. 1818. Capt. 23 May 1831. *d.* Gauhati, Assam, 21 Dec. 1834.

Son of Hugh Cathcart.
Services : Posted as Ensign to 1/2nd N.I. Transfd. to 5th N.I. (late 1/2nd) May 1824. Intr. & Qmr. 5th N.I. 14 Feb. 1826. Fur. 1 Feb. 1831 till 18 Nov. 1833. Junior Asst. to A.G.G., N.E. frontier, 7 Jan. 1834. No record of active service.
Refs. : M.I. in Gauhati old cemetery. Will dated Gt. Wyrley, Essex, 29 June 1833 ; codicil dated Calcutta 25 Dec. 1833 ; proved 28 Mar. 1835.

CATHCART, James (1764/65-1810). Lieutenant. Infantry. Pensioner on Lord Clive's fund. Subsequently Major 19th Light Dragoons. *b.* 1764/65. Cadet 1781. Ensign 1782. Lieut. 17 Sept. 1782. Pensioned 1790. *d. unm.* 1810.

Eldest son of James Cathcart, of Carbiston, co. Ayr, and Lucretia

his wife, eldest dau. of Robert Colquhoun, of St. Christopher and Santa Cruz.
Services : Apptd. Cadet on 23 Jan. 1781, aged 16. On fur. in 1790. Entered H.M.S. Cornet 19th Light Dns. 26 Mar. 1791. Lieut. 1796. Capt. Lt. 22 June 1799. Capt. 8 Nov. 1799. Major 22 Nov. 1803. Wounded at battle of Assaye 23 Sept. 1803.
Refs. : Burke's *Landed Gentry*, 13th edn., p. 307, *s.n.* Cathcart, of Carbiston, co. Ayr. *The XIXth and their Times*, by Col. John Biddulph, p. 144.

CATLYN (CATYLINE or CATYLYNE), Rowland (*d.* 1771). Captain, Infantry. Cadet 1763. Ensign 23 Feb. 1764. Lieut. 8 Aug. 1765. Capt. 15 Sept. 1767. *d.* at sea, Feb. 1771, on the voyage to Madras.

Brother of Catharina, wife of William Palmer, of Stifford, Essex, and nephew of Jane Catlyn. His Will mentions his "worthy relation Lady Anne Hamilton."
Services : N.F.P.
Refs. : Will dated 18 Jan. 1771 ; proved 12 Mar. 1771.

CATOR, William (*d.* 1800). Ensign. Infantry. Subsequently B.C.S. Cadet (?). Ensign 2 Aug. 1769. Resigned 3 Apr. 1772. *d.* 7 Oct. 1800 : kld. on board the *Kent* in an action with the *Confiance*, French privateer, off the Sandheads in the mouth of the Ganges.

Son of John Cator, of Ross, Hereford, and of Bromley, Kent, and Mary his wife, dau. of John Brough. *m.* Calcutta, 4 Nov. 1780, Miss Sarah Morse.
Services : Resigned the B.C.S. before 1791. "A man of large independent fortune who late in life having lost a material proportion thereof, was induced to return to Bengal, in the hope of increasing his substance, and was killed on board the *Kent* Indiaman in an action with a French privateer close to Balasore Roads." (*Hickey*, iii. 155.)
Refs. : Burke's *Landed Gentry*, 13th edn., p. 308, *s.n.* Cator, of Woodbastwick Hall, Norfolk.

CAULFEILD, Gordon (1816-1894). General. 46th N.I. u.s.l. *b.* Balmaghie, co. Kirkcudbright, 10 Aug. 1816. Cadet 1834. Arrived in India 28 July 1835. Ensign 23 Mar. 1835. Lieut. 3 Oct. 1840. Capt. 8 Oct. 1850. Major 1 Mar. 1861. Lt. Col. 23 Mar. 1861. Col. 23 Mar. 1866. Maj. Gen. 1 Oct. 1877. Lt. Gen. 1 July 1881. Gen. 1 Dec. 1888. *d.* Fairmount, Mottingham, nr. Eltham, 8 Dec. 1894.

Son of Robert Caulfeild, Capt. R.N., and Mary Anne Haverham of Antigua, his wife. Nephew of James Caulfeild, *q.v.*, and cousin-

THE BENGAL ARMY, 1758-1834

german of James Gordon Caulfeild, q.v. m. Dehra Dun, 29 Dec. 1852, Anne, dau. of William Henry Cooper, q.v. (See also Hutton Watkins.) Addiscombe Cadet 1 Feb. 1833 till 12 Dec. 1834.
Services : To do duty with 34th N.I. 8 Aug. 1835. Posted to 46th N.I. 24 Sept. 1835. Actg. Adjt. 2nd Inf. Levy at Jaunpur 4 Nov. 1842. Fur. s.c. 9 Sept. 1845. Second Sikh War ; Chilianwala ; Gujerat ; Lieut. 46th N.I. (Medal with clasp).
Refs. : Burke's *Peerage*, 1923, p. 487, *s.n.* Charlemont, V. Boase. The Times, 8 Dec. 1894 ; 10 Dec. p. 6.

CAULFEILD, James (1783-1852). Lieut. General, C.B. Colonel 10th L.C. *b.* Castle Cosby, co. Cavan, 26 Jan. 1783. Cadet 1798. Arrived in India 10 Sept. 1799. Cornet 13 June 1800. Lieut. 11 Mar. 1805. Capt. 1 Sept. 1818. Major 13 May 1825. Lt. Col. 26 Mar. 1829. Bt. Col. 22 Jan. 1834. Maj. Gen. 23 Nov. 1841. Lt. Gen. 11 Nov. 1851. *d.* Copsewood, co. Limerick, 4 Nov. 1852. M.P. for Abingdon ; director E.I.Co. 4th son of Ven. John Caulfeild, of Benown, Westmeath, archdeacon of Kilmore, and Euphemia Gordon his wife, of Kenmuir, co. Dumfries. *m.* 1st, Cawnpore, 6 Dec. 1814, Letitia, dau. of Hugh Stafford, *q.v.* (See also John Forbes Paton.) (She died 26 Aug. 1826.) Father of James Gordon Caulfeild, *q.v.* *m.* 2nd, Anne Rachel, dau. of William Blake, *q.v.* (She died 17 May 1890.)
Services : Posted as Cornet to 5th N.C. in June 1800. Fur. s.c. 15 Sept. 1807 till 21 Jan. 1812. With G.G.B.G. 16 Mar. 1812 till 1814. Third Mahratta War ; against the Pindaris 1817-8 ; Bt. Capt. 5th N.C. Bde. Major Nagpur Subsdy. Force 14 Nov. 1817. Asirgarh 1819. 1st Asst. to Resdt. at Indore 1819. P.A. in Haraoti 1822-32. Leave s.c. 1829. Transfd. as Lt. Col. to 4th L.C. in June 1829 ; to 3rd L.C. 1 Aug. 1833 ; to 9th L.C. 24 Dec. 1833. Fur. p.a. 4 Nov. 1831 till 21 Dec. 1835. Supt. Mysore Princes 18 Mar. 1836 ; A.G.G., Murshidabad, 1836 ; Resdt. at Lucknow 1839. Col. 10th L.C. Fur. s.c. 27 Feb. 1841 till death. C.B. 27 Sept. 1831. Director E.I.Co. 12 Apr. 1848. Unsuccessfully contested the borough of Abingdon in 1845 and 1847. Pub., Calcutta, 1831, " Observations on our Indian Administration, Civil and Military," 8vo.
Refs. : Burke's *Peerage*, 1923, p. 487., *s.n.* Charlemont, V. Boase. V.B.G. G.M. 1853, i. 201. I.M. 1848, p. 85 ; 1852, p. 658. Will dated 29 Nov. 1850 ; proved 19 June 1855.

*CAULFEILD, James Gordon (1816-1844). Lieutenant, 68th N.I. *bapt.* Cawnpore 18 May 1815. Cadet 1834. Ensign (11 Dec. 1835) 2 July 1836. Lieut. 19 Oct. 1838. *d.* Madeira 21 Sept. 1844.

Eldest son of James Caulfeild, *q.v.*, and Letitia his 1st wife. Ed. Harrow 1829-33. Addiscombe Cadet 1834-5.
Services : Posted as Ensign to 68th N.I. in 1836. First Afghan War 1839-41 ; political employ at Peshawar and with Shah Shuja. Leave s.c. to Cape 8 Mar. 1841. Fur. s.c. 19 Jan. 1843 till death.
Refs. : Burke's *Peerage*, 1923, p. 487, *s.n.* Charlemont, V. *Harrow School Register*.

CAULFEILD, John (*d*. 1782). Ensign, Infantry. Cadet 1772. Ensign 5 Aug. 1776. *d*. Plassey, Bengal, 15 Oct. 1782.
Services : N.F.P.

CAUTLEY, George (1809-1881). Major General. 5th European L.C. *b.* Moulsoe, Bucks., 18 Jan. 1809. Cadet 1824. Arrived in India 23 Feb. 1826. Cornet 22 Sept. 1825. Lieut. 17 May 1829. Capt. 10 July 1844. Major 16 Aug. 1859. Bt. Lt. Col. 28 Nov. 1854. Bt. Col. 28 Nov. 1859. Retired 31 Dec. 1861. Hon. Maj. Gen. 31 Dec. 1861. *d*. Jersey Lodge, Herne Hill, Surrey, 1 Oct. 1881.
Son of Rev. Richard Cautley, of Newport Pagnell. Brother of Richard Cautley, *q.v.* *m*. Dehra Dun, 2 Nov. 1840, Emma Octavia, 4th dau. of George Christopher, of Morton House, Chiswick, and Grangefield, co. Durham, Capt. Middlesex Vols. (*See also* William Beveridge Thomson.)
Services : Posted as Cornet to 8th L.C. Fur. s.c. 4 Dec. 1829 till 7 Nov. 1832. First Sikh War ; Ferozshahr ; Capt. 8th L.C. (Medal). Second Sikh War ; Ramnagar ; Sadulapur ; Chilianwala ; Gujerat ; Capt. 8th L.C. (Medal with 2 clasps). Transfd. to 5th Eur. L.C. in 1858.
Refs. : Burke's *Landed Gentry*, 13th edn., p. 337, *s.n.* Christopher, of Norton. *The Times*, 4 Oct. 1881.

CAUTLEY, Sir Proby Thomas (1802-1871). Colonel, K.C.B. Artillery. *b.* Baydon, Wilts., 3 Jan. 1802. Cadet 1818. Admitted 11 Sept. 1819. 2nd Lieut. 19 Apr. 1819. Lieut. 21 Nov. 1821. Capt. 13 Oct. 1835. Major 3 Oct. 1845. Lt. Col. 5 May 1849. Retired 17 May 1854. Hon. Col. 28 Nov. 1854. *d*. The Avenue, Sydenham Park, 25 Jan. 1871.
Son of Rev. Thomas Cautley, of St. Mary's, Stratford, Suffolk, rector of Baydon. *m*. Landour, U.P., 26 Sept. 1838, Frances, 3rd dau. of Anthony Bacon, of Elcott, Berks. Ed. Charterhouse 1813-8. Addiscombe Cadet 1818 till 6 Apr. 1819.
Services : See *D.N.B.* K.C.B. (Civil) 29 July 1854.
Refs. : D.N.B. D.I.B. Boase. *Vibart*, p. 333. *Charterhouse School List. The Times*, 27 Jan. 1871. Portrait (litho. by C. Baugniet 1846) is in the India Office.

THE BENGAL ARMY, 1758-1834

CAUTLEY, Richard (1807-1868). Lieut. Colonel. 10th L.C. *b.* Moulsoe, Bucks., 3 Nov. 1807. Cadet 1824. Arrived in India 23 Feb. 1826. Cornet 22 Sept. 1825. Lieut. 21 Dec. 1827. Capt. 9 June 1838. Major 27 May 1853. Retired 27 Nov. 1853. Hon. Lt. Col. 28 Nov. 1854. *d.* 4 June 1868.
Son of Rev. Richard Cautley, of Newport Pagnell. Brother of George Cautley, *q.v. m.* 19 Aug. 1841, Elizabeth, 3rd dau. of William Oldfield, of York, and sister of Thomas Wilson Oldfield, *q.v.* (She died York, 28 July 1893, aged 75.)
Services : Posted as Cornet to 10th L.C. Intr. & Qmr. 8 Oct. 1832 till 13 Mar. 1837. Fur. p.a. 20 Jan. 1838 till 30 Dec. 1841. First Afghan War 1842 ; re-occupation of Kabul ; Capt. 10th L.C., with Gen. Pollock's force (Medal). Bde. Major 4th Cav. Bde., Army of Exercise, 11 Dec. 1843. (? Gwalior campaign ; Maharajpur ; Bde. Major.) Offg. in P.W.D., N.W.P., in 1852.

CAUTY, Robert (1787-1819). Lieutenant, 19th N.I. *b.* Westminster 1 Nov. 1787. Cadet 1807. Arrived in India 21 Mar. 1809. Ensign 24 Feb. 1809. Lieut. 3 Nov. 1814. *d.* Nasirabad, 7 July 1819, of cholera.
Son of William Cauty. *m.* Meerut, 6 June 1817, Eliza, dau. of Charles Brietzcke, *q.v.*, and widow of John Frederick Sanford, *q.v.*
Services : Posted as Ensign to 19th N.I. Nepal War 1814-5 ; Lieut. 2/19th N.I. Intr. & Qmr. 2/19th N.I. 4 May 1815 till death. Third Mahratta War ; Lieut. 2/19th N.I.
Refs. : G.M. 1820, i. 186. *A.J.* ix.

CAVE, Edward (*d.* 1767). Lieutenant, Infantry. Cadet (?). Ensign 27 May 1766. Lieut. 15 Sept. 1767. *d.* Bankipore, B. & O., Sept. 1767.
Services : N.F.P.

CAVE, John Henry (1782-1835). Lieut. Colonel, 38th N.I. *b.* London 22 Feb. 1782. Cadet 1798. Arrived in India 24 Oct. 1799. Ensign 18 Oct. 1799. Lieut. 28 Oct. 1799. Capt. 1 June 1813. Major 1 May 1824. Lt. Col. 2 Jan. 1826. *d.* Calcutta 16 June 1835.
bapt. St. George's, Hanover Sq., London, 19 Mar. 1782. Son of John Cave and Rebecca his wife. *m.* Chandernagore, 14 Dec. 1815, Miss Maria De Laval. (*See also* William George Lennox.) His dau. *m.* Nathaniel Joseph Cumberlege, *q.v.*
Services : Posted as Ensign to 2/3rd N.I. 15 Apr. 1801. Transfd. to newly-raised 1/21st N.I. in 1803. (? Second Mahratta War ; pursuit of Holkar 1805-6 ; Lieut. 1/21st N.I.) Actg. Adjt. to five Coys. 1/21st N.I. 5 Dec. 1809. Suptg. bldgs., Hooghly, 1815-6. Comst. Dept., as Supt. of field transport, 1816-24. Third Mahratta

War ; Capt. 1/21st N.I., Supt. field transport 1st Div. Transfd. as Major to 68th N.I. in May 1824. To comd. newly-raised 10th Extra Regt. 1825. Transfd. as Lt. Col. to 6th Extra Regt. (became 74th N.I.) in 1826. Fur. 12 Dec. 1831 till 10 Feb. 1835. Transfd. to 24th N.I. 7 Jan. 1832 ; to 61st N.I. 24 Dec. 1833 ; to 40th N.I. 18 Apr. 1834 ; to 54th N.I. 21 Feb. 1835 ; to 73rd N.I. 2 Mar. 1835 ; to 38th N.I. 8 June 1835. Leave to Tasmania for two yrs. 12 May 1835, but did not live to embark.
Refs. : *A.J.* N.S. xviii. 243. M.I. in Mily. burial ground, Bhowanipore, Calcutta.

CAVE-BROWNE-CAVE, Wilmot (1802-1857). Cadet, Infantry. Unposted. Subsequently vicar of Hope, co. Derby. *b.* 5 Dec. 1802. Cadet 1819. Resigned in India 25 Nov. 1820. *d.s.p.* 6 May 1857.

bapt. Stretton-en-le-Field 21 Dec. 1802. 4th son of Sir William Cave-Browne-Cave, 9th Bart., of Stanford (who assumed the additional surname of Cave on succeeding to the Baronetcy), and Louisa his 2nd wife, 4th dau. of Sir Robert Mead Wilmot, Bart. Nephew of Edward Cave-Browne, *q.v. m.* 1st, 30 Oct. 1824, Mary; eldest dau. of William Eccles, of Davenham. (She was bur. 26 Nov. 1824, aged 20.) *m.* 2nd, Sandal Magna, 27 Oct. 1825, Mary, eldest dau. of Rev. Thomas Westmorland, vicar of Sandal Magna, Yorks. St. Alban Hall, Oxon. ; matric. 3 June 1823.

Services : Took holy orders. P.C. of Altrincham, co. Chester, 14 Feb. 1834 ; of Homerton, Middlesex, 1856. Vicar of Hope and P.C. of Derwent, co. Derby.

Refs. : Burke's *Peerage*, 1923, p. 472, *s.n.* Cave-Browne-Cave, Bart., of Stanford, Northants. *Howard & Crisp*, xi. 156. *Alumni Oxon.*

CECIL, George (1808-1857). Lieut. Colonel, 12th N.I. *b.* Messina, Sicily, 15 Feb. 1808. Cadet 1825. Arrived in India 28 June 1826. Ensign 13 Feb. 1826. Lieut. 3 June 1829. Capt. 24 Jan. 1845. Bt. Major 20 June 1854. Retired 31 Dec. 1854. Hon. Lt. Col. 11 May 1855. *d.* Agra, U.P., 13 Sept. 1857.

Son of an English officer. Ward of Francis Jack, first Earl of Kilmorey, Viscount Newry and Morne.

Services : Ensign d.d. 46th N.I. 8 July 1826. Posted as Ensign to 12th N.I., and served throughout with that Regt. No record of active service.

Refs. : *I.M.* 1857, p. 771.

CHABERT, Thomas (? **Peter**). Lieutenant. Infantry. Cadet 1782. Ensign 29 Mar. 1783. Lieut. 5 Mar. 1790. Resigned 11 Apr. 1790.
Services : N.F.P.

THE BENGAL ARMY, 1758-1834   325

CHADWICK, Thomas (1789-1861). Colonel. Artillery. *bapt.* Tipperary 6 Jan. 1789. Cadet 1805. Arrived in India 13 Dec. 1806. Lieut. 14 Dec. 1806. Capt. Lt. 25 Sept. 1817. Capt. 1 Sept. 1818. Major 21 Oct. 1833. Lt. Col. 24 Apr. 1838. Invalided 31 Dec. 1839. Retired 22 Apr. 1850. Hon. Col. 28 Nov. 1854. *d.* 26 Porchester Terr., London, 25 Jan. 1861, aged 73.

2nd son of Thomas Chadwick, of Barnascounce, 18th Light Dns., and Sarah Lockwood, of Cashel, his wife. His sister *m.* Charles Hamilton Bell, *q.v. m.* Susan. (She died London 2 Mar. 1857.)

Services : Siege and capture of Hathras ; Lieut. 4th Coy. 2nd Bn. Art. Third Mahratta War ; Capt., with Golandaz. Offg. Agent for gun carriages at Fatehgarh 24 Mar. 1818. Comy. of Ord. 1 May 1819 till 22 Nov. 1833. Comdd. Art. at Nimach.

Refs. : Burke's *Landed Gentry of Ireland*, p. 103, *s.n.* Chadwick, of Ballinard, co. Tipperary. Burke's *Colonial Gentry*, ii. 587. *G.M.* 1861, i. 351. *The Times*, 19 Feb. 1861.

*CHAIGNEAU, Christopher Thomas. Cornet. 1st Troop of European Dragoons. Cornet 22 Sept. 1760.

Services : Apptd. Cornet in 1st Troop of Eur. Dns. commanded by Capt. Henry Spelman, *q.v.*, from H.M. 84th Foot.

Refs. : M.C. Fort William, 22 Sept. 1760.

CHAIGNEAU, Peter. Ensign. Infantry. Cadet (?). Ensign 11 June 1759. Resigned 9 Nov. 1761.

Services : N.F.P.

Note : A family of this name, of French origin, was settled in Dublin and in co. Westmeath at about this period. M.I. in French cemetery, Peter St., Dublin. William Chaigneau (1709-1781) was an army agent in Dublin. (*D.N.B.*)

CHALMERS, John (1789-1816). Cornet, 8th N.C. *b.* Airth, co. Stirling, 15 Nov. 1789. Cadet 1809. Cornet 18 Dec. 1813. *d.* in U.K. 25 May 1816.

Son of Andrew Chalmers, of Dunmore, co. Stirling, farmer.

Services : Cadet d.d. 8th N.C. 1811. Posted as Cornet to 8th N.C. in 1813. Fur. 1815 till death. No record of active service.

CHALMERS, John William Collin (1809-1839). Lieutenant, 43rd N.I. *b.* Quilon, Travancore, 15 May 1809. Cadet 1827. Arrived in India 26 Oct. 1828. Ensign 19 May 1828. Lieut. 10 Sept. 1838. *d.* nr. Bhag, Kachhi, Baluchistan, 2 June 1839, of heatstroke.

Only son of Maj.-Gen. Sir John Chalmers, K.C.B., 17th Madras N.I., and Caroline Mary his wife. *m*. Calcutta 16 May 1835, Louisa, youngest dau. of William McQuhae, *q.v.* (*See also* James Tobin Bush.) (She *re-m*. 25 Mar. 1843, Samuel Smith, of Calcutta, merchant.)

Services : Ensign d.d. 33rd N.I. 20 Nov. 1828. Posted as Ensign to 43rd N.I. 4 Mar. 1829. Fur. 6 Feb. 1836 till 31 Dec. 1838. Died whilst on his way to rejoin his Regt. on service in Afghanistan.

Refs. : *G.M.* 1839, ii. 666. *A.J.* N.S. xvii. 240. *From Cadet to Colonel*, by Sir Thomas Seaton, *q.v.*, 1866 edn., i. 134.

CHALMERS, Robert (1788-1840). Lieut. Colonel, 20th N.I. *b.* Dysart, co. Fife, 23 June 1788. Cadet 1806. Arrived in India 30 July 1807. Ensign 25 Aug. 1807. Lieut. 2 Aug. 1813. Capt. 13 May 1825. Major 12 Nov. 1830. Lt. Col. 20 June 1836. *d.* Simla 7 Nov. 1840.

Of Kirkcaldy, co. Fife. Son of Thomas Chalmers. *m.* Edinburgh, 5 Mar. 1822, Miss Jessie Ranken. (She died 14 Jan. 1881, aged 80.) His dau. *m.* Markham Kittoe, *q.v.*

Services : Barasat C.C. Aug. 1807 till Mar. 1808. Posted as Ensign to 2/2nd N.I. Siege and reduction of Kalinjar 1812 ; Ensign 2/2nd N.I. Storm and capture of Entauri 1813 ; Lieut. 2/2nd N.I. To do duty with Rangpur Local Bn. July 1814 till 1815. Fur. s.c. 10 Dec. 1819 till 26 July 1822. Adjt. 1/2nd N.I. 1 Oct. 1823. Transfd. to 22nd N.I. (late 2/2nd) May 1824. Adjt. 22nd N.I. 17 June 1824 till 12 July 1825. Shekhawat expedition 1834 ; Major comdg. 22nd N.I. Fur. 31 Aug. 1835 till 11 Dec. 1837. Transfd. to Bengal Eur. Regt. 30 May 1838 ; to 54th N.I. 10 Oct. 1838 ; to 38th N.I. 10 Mar. 1840 ; to 20th N.I. 5 Oct. 1840.

Refs. : *De Rhé-Philipe*. *S.M.* 1822, i. 559. *G.M.* 1841, i. 222. Will dated 9 Mar. 1822 ; proved 6 Apr. 1841.

CHAMBERS, Frederick James Millbank (1788-1827). Captain, 3rd N.I. *bapt.* Colton, Staffs., 23 Nov. 1788. Cadet 1805. Arrived in India 11 July 1806. Ensign 17 July 1806. Lieut. 23 June 1809. Capt. 11 July 1823. *d.* Calcutta 11 Oct. 1827.

Son of George Chambers (who was son of Sir William Chambers) and Hon. Jane his wife, eldest dau. of George Brydges Rodney, first Baron Rodney.

Services : Ensign 6th N.I. Fur. 1812-3. Nepal War 1814-5 ; Lieut. 2/6th N.I., in 1st Div. Transfd. as Lieut. to 1/6th N.I. (? Third Mahratta War ; Lieut. 1/6th N.I. in Reserve Div.) Adjt. 1/6th N.I. in 1823. Transfd. to 3rd N.I. (late 1/6th) May 1824. Rangpur L.I. in 1824. (? First Burma War ; Assam 1824-5 ; Capt. comdg. Rangpur L.I.) To comd. Champaran L.I. 26 Jan. 1825.

Refs. : Debrett's *Peerage*, 1803, p. 270. Burke's *Peerage*, 1923,

p. 1893, *s.n.* Rodney, B. Will dated 1 May 1818 ; proved 16 Oct. 1827.

CHAMBERS, John (*d.* 1790). Bt. Ensign, Pension Est. Infantry. Cadet 1782. Bt. Ensign (?). *d.* Monghyr, B. & O., 23 May 1790. *Services :* N.F.P.

CHAMBERS, Joseph (1814-1878). Lieut. Colonel. 21st N.I. *bapt.* S. Kilworth, Leics., 12 June 1814. Cadet 1833. Arrived in India 8 July 1834. Ensign 23 May 1834. Lieut. 15 Mar. 1841. Capt. 27 Aug. 1847. Major 25 Aug. 1859. Retired 31 Dec. 1861. Hon. Lt. Col. 31 Dec. 1861. *d.* Oxford, 3 Oct. 1878, aged 64.
Son of Charles William Chambers, of Kilworth, farmer and grazier, and Elizabeth his wife. *m.* Cressing, Essex, 10 June 1847, Maria, eldest dau. of Rev. Sir John Page Wood, 2nd Bart., vicar of Cressing, and sister of F.M. Sir Evelyn Wood, G.C.B., V.C. Ed. Rugby ; entered the school in 1828. Addiscombe Cadet 24 Feb. 1832 till 13 Dec. 1833. Created M.A., Oxon., 3 Nov. 1865.
Services : Posted to 21st N.I. 5 Nov. 1834. Actg. Intr. & Qmr. 27 Apr. 1837. Intr. & Qmr. 22 May 1840 till 16 Dec. 1845. Leave s.c. to Cape 19 May 1844. Fur. s.c. 21 Feb. 1845 till 1847. Cantt. Mgte. at Sialkot 15 Feb. 1856. Fur. 1858 till retirement. No record of active service. University teacher of Hindustani and Persian at Oxford 1859 till death.
Refs. : Burke's *Peerage*, 1923, p. 2360, *s.n.* Wood, Bart., of Hatherley House, Gloucs. *Alumni Oxon. The Times*, 5 Oct. 1878.

CHAMBERS, Robert Ewbank (1790-1842). Lieut. Colonel, 5th L.C. *b.* Newcastle-on-Tyne 23 Apr. 1790. Cadet 1804. Arrived in India 6 Apr. 1806. Cornet 31 Mar. 1806. Lieut. 27 Feb. 1812. Capt. 1 Jan. 1819. Major 9 Sept. 1829. Lt. Col. 10 Oct. 1836. *d.* 12 Jan. 1842 : kld. in action in the Jagdalak Pass during the retreat from Kabul.
Eldest son of Richard Chambers, mayor of Newcastle in 1796. Nephew of Sir Robert Chambers, Kt., C.J., Bengal (*D.N.B.*). *m.* Benares, 13 Sept. 1826, Ellen Mary Frances Margaret, only dau. of Dr. Thomas Yeld, of Benares. (She died 23 Mar. 1881, aged 74.)
Services : Posted as Cornet to 8th N.C. Intr. & Qmr. 8th N.C. 10 Nov. 1814 till 24 May 1819. Third Mahratta War ; Nagpur ; Lieut. 8th N.C. Transfd. to newly-raised 1st Extra Cav. (became 9th L.C.) 17 June 1825. Siege and capture of Bhurtpore (s.w. in hand on 27 Dec. 1825) ; Capt. 9th L.C. Comdd. 9th L.C. 17 Jan. 1837 till 25 Dec. 1838. Transfd. to 5th L.C. 11 Dec. 1838. First Afghan War 1840-2 ; defeat of Ghilzais at Karatu 5 Aug. 1841 ; Lt. Col. 5th L.C., comdg. the force.

Refs. : Burke's *Colonial Gentry,* ii. 766. *Howard & Crisp,* xiv. 24, *s.n.* Comber. M.I. in St. Peter's, Fort William, Bengal. Will proved 26 Jan. 1843.

CHAMBERS, William (*d.* 1769). Lieutenant, Infantry. Cadet 1767. Ensign (?). Lieut. 28 Apr. 1769. *d.* 1769.
Services : N.F.P.

CHAMBRÉ, Christopher (1784-?). Lieutenant. 3rd N.I. *bapt.* Llanfoist, co. Monmouth, 27 June 1784. Cadet 1799. Arrived in India 3 Oct. 1800. Ensign 6 Sept. 1800. Lieut. 4 Feb. 1802. Pensioned on Lord Clive's fund 14 Feb. 1812. Resigned 31 July 1812.
Son of Christopher Chambré and Jane his wife.
Services : Posted as Ensign to 1/3rd N.I. 17 Apr. 1801. (? Operations in Bundelkhand 1809 ; Rajaoli ; Ajaigarh ; Lieut. 1/3rd N.I.) Fur. 22 Jan. 1810 till pensioned.

CHAMPION, Alexander (*d.* 1793). Colonel. Infantry. Commander-in-Chief, Bengal. Cadet (?). Ensign (?). Lieut. 20 Sept. 1757. Capt. 1 Sept. 1758. Major 6 Nov. 1763. Lt. Col. 4 Nov. 1766. Col. 8 Aug. 1770. Retired 29 Dec. 1774. *d.* Bath 15 Mar. 1793. *m.* 11 Feb. 1759, Miss Frances Nynd. (She *re-m.* 4 Jan. 1796, Rev. Thomas Leman, of Wenhaston Hall, Suffolk.)
Services : Served in the campaigns of 1760-1 in Bengal under Majors John Caillaud and John Carnac, *q.v.* ; defeated Kamgar Khan, Nawab of Tirhut, Apr. 1761. 2nd in comd. to Major (afterwards Gen. Sir Hector) Munro when opposed to Shuja-ud-Daulah 1764 ; battle of Buxar. Shortly afterwards comdd. a detached force on the Midnapore frontier. Apptd. to comd. 1st Bengal Eur. Regt. Aug. 1765. First Rohilla War ; battle of St. George ; Col. comdg. 2nd Bde. Succeeded Sir Robert Barker, *q.v.*, as C.-in-C., Bengal army, 18 Jan. 1774, and held this appt. till 27 Oct. 1774. Returned to England in 1775. " He rose, in the course of twenty years' active service in India, to the chief command of the Company's troops in Bengal " (M.I.).
Refs. : *E.I.M.C.* ii. 86. *Orme MSS.—India,* xiii. 3639. *G.M.* 1793, i. 283 ; 1795, ii. 876. Mural tablet, by Nollekens, in Bath Abbey.

CHAMPION, William (1759/60-1780). Cadet, Infantry. *b.* 1759/60. Cadet 1779. *d.* Jan. 1780 : kld. in a duel ; bur. Calcutta 30 Jan. 1780.
A native of Wilts. (*Possibly* son of Alexander Champion, *q.v.*, and Frances his wife.)
Services : Sailed for India on the *Earl Talbot,* 7 Mar. 1779, aged 19.

CHAMPNEYS, Edward Geoffrey John (1813-1884). Colonel. 5th European Inf. *b.* 19 Feb. 1813. Cadet 1828. Arrived in India 27 Aug. 1829. Ensign (29 Mar. 1829) 5 June 1829. Lieut. 30 May 1834. Capt. 24 Jan. 1845. Major 30 Dec. 1852. Lt. Col. 1 July 1857. Retired 31 Dec. 1861. Hon. Col. 31 Dec. 1861. *d. unm.* 22 Apr. 1884.

bapt. Christchurch, Kent, 20 Feb. 1813. 3rd son of Rev. Henry William Champneys, of Ostenhanger, Kent, rector of Badsworth, Yorks. (who assumed the surname of Champneys in lieu of Burt, by R.L., 10 Nov. 1778), and Lucy his wife, eldest dau. of Rev. Geoffry Hornby, rector of Winwick.

Services : Posted as Ensign to 14th N.I. 23 Sept. 1830. A.D.C. to C.-in-C. 6 Dec. 1833. Transfd. to 33rd N.I. 30 May 1834. Sub-Asst. in Stud Dept. 8 Jan. 1835. D.A.Q.M.G., 2 cl., 14 Feb. 1835. A.D.C. to G.G. 7 Mar. 1836. Dy. Paymr., Meerut, 9 Oct. 1837. 2nd Asst. Mily. Auditor Gen.,12 Sept. 1842. Dy. Mily. Auditor Gen. 3 Mar. 1846. Transfd. to 56th N.I. in 1857. Mily. Auditor Gen. 8 Sept. 1857. Transfd. to newly-raised 5th Eur. Regt. in 1858. No record of active service.

Refs. : Burke's *Landed Gentry*, 2nd edn., p. 206, *s.n.* Champneys, of Ostenhanger, Kent. Foster's *Families of Royal Descent*, ii. 624.

CHANCE, Thomas (1787-1805). Lieutenant, Bengal European Regt. *bapt.* Rodborough, Gloucs., 15 Apr. 1787. Cadet 1802. Arrived in India 14 Dec. 1803. Ensign 16 Dec. 1803. Lieut. 21 Sept. 1804. *d.* 6 Mar. 1805, of wounds received in the fourth assault of Bhurtpore on 21 Feb.

Son of Daniel Chance and Elizabeth his wife.

Services : Second Mahratta War (? battle of Deig ; capture of Deig) ; siege of Bhurtpore (s.w.) ; Lieut. Bengal Eur. Regt.

Refs. : Intestate ; admon. granted 14 Oct. 1805.

CHANNER, George Girdwood (1811-1895). Colonel, Artillery. *b.* Heston, Middlesex, 16 Mar. 1811. Cadet 1827. Arrived in India 28 July 1828. 2nd Lieut. 13 Dec. 1827. Lieut. 1 Dec. 1834. Capt. 3 July 1845. Major 4 July 1857. Lt. Col. 27 Aug. 1858. Retired 10 Oct. 1858. Hon. Col. 10 Oct. 1858. *d.* Longleat, Woodville Rd., Ealing, 7 July 1895.

Son of George Channer, of Sutton, near Hounslow. *m.* Plymouth, 24 May 1838, Susan, eldest dau. of Rev. Nicholas Kendall, vicar of Talland and Lanlivery, Cornwall. Father of Gen. George Nicholas Channer, V.C. (*D.N.B.*). Addiscombe Cadet 1826-7.

Services : Fur. s.c. 22 Dec. 1835 till 26 Feb. 1839. Dy Comy. of Ord. 11 Mar. 1840. Comy. of Ord. at Allahabad 17 June 1840 till

1856. Fur. s.c. 4 Apr. 1856 till retirement. No record of active service.
Refs. : *The Times*, 9 July 1895.

CHANNING, Joseph (d. 1817). Major. 12th N.I. Cadet 1772. Ensign 31 July 1776. Lieut. 18 July 1778. Capt. 6 June 1793. Major 1 Nov. 1798. Retired 30 July 1800. d. Charmouth, Dorset, 4 May 1817.
Services : Adjt. 8th Bn., 4th Bde., in 1790. Capt. 2nd Bengal Eur. Regt. Fur. 8 Dec. 1793 till 22 Sept. 1797, and 21 Jan. 1799 till retirement. Transfd. from 2/12th to 1/12th N.I. 29 May 1800.

CHAPMAN, Charles. Colonel. Commander-in-Chief, Bengal. Lt. Col. 5 May 1765. Col. 8 Aug. 1769. Resigned 18 Jan. 1774.
Services : Transfd. as Lt. Col. from H.M.S. in 1765. To comd. 3rd Bengal Eur. Regt., in 3rd Bde., 31 May 1765. Apptd. C.-in-C. 22 Dec. 1773, but held the post for three weeks only.

CHAPMAN, Frederick Wilshire Steer (1817-1839). Cornet, 9th L.C. bapt. Calcutta 13 Dec. 1817. Cadet 1833. Arrived in India 25 Sept. 1834. Cornet 24 May 1834. d.s.p. at sea, 22 July 1839, on board the *Albyn*, on his passage to England, from the effects of sunstroke.
Son of Charles Chapman, B.C.S., Judge of Backergunge, Bengal, and Charlotte his wife. m. Nasirabad, 26 Sept. 1838, Jane, 4th dau. of John Littledale Gale, q.v., and Rebecca his 1st wife. (*See also* Henry Goodwyn and William John Thompson.) (She re-m. twice, and died in India c. 1851/52.)
Services : Cornet d.d. 8th L.C. 20 Oct. 1834. Posted as Cornet to 6th L.C. 9 June 1836. Transfd. to 9th L.C. 13 Oct. 1836. No record of active service.
Refs. : Burke's *Family Records*, p. 258. *Howard & Crisp*, i. 279, s.n. Gale. G.M. 1840, i. 109. A.J. N.S. xxxi. 91.

CHAPMAN, George (1792-1863). Lieut. Colonel. 36th N.I. b. Northampton 31 Aug. 1792. Cadet 1808. Arrived in India 19 July 1809. Ensign 21 Nov. 1809. Lieut. 19 Feb. 1814. Capt. 13 May 1825. Major 28 June 1838. Invalided 14 Nov. 1846. Retired 12 Jan. 1848. Hon. Lt. Col. 28 Nov. 1854. d. his residence, Oaklands, Redhill, Surrey, 16 Jan. 1863.
Son of Timothy Chapman. m. Marion. (She died nr. Monghyr, 21 Aug. 1843, aged 54.) His dau. m. William Anderson (1803-1858), q.v.
Services : Barasat C.C. Posted as Ensign to 2/18th N.I. Fur. s.c. 14 Feb. 1813 till 26 July 1816. Transfd. to 36th N.I. (late

THE BENGAL ARMY, 1758-1834   331

1/18th) May 1824. First Burma War; Ava; Capt. 36th N.I. (India medal). Siege and capture of Bhurtpore; Capt. 36th N.I. (Clasp to India medal). Shekhawat expedition 1834; Capt. 36th N.I. Fur. s.c. 14 Dec. 1843 till 1845.

Refs. : *G.M.* 1863, i. 262. *The Times*, 19 Jan. 1863.

CHAPUSET, Charles Christian Ferdinand (1787-?). Lieutenant. 7th N.C. *b.* Stuttgart, Wurttemberg, 1 Jan. 1787. Cadet 1805. Arrived in India 11 July 1806. Cornet 14 July 1806. Lieut. 3 Feb. 1813. Pensioned in India 1 Oct. 1815. Suspended 1816. Dismissed in England 22 Jan. 1817.

Eldest son of Johann Paul Thomas " Baron Chapuset de St. Valentin," of Stuttgart (said to have been court gardener to the King of Wurttemberg), and the Lady Rosina Magdalena, née Grundgeiger (or Krongeiger), his wife. Nephew by marriage of Warren Hastings, through his 2nd wife.

Services : Obtained his cadetship through the influence of Warren Hastings. Becoming heavily involved in debt, absented himself without leave from his regiment at Muttra in order to avoid his creditors : was arrested by the Bhurtpore Rajah in his territory, and handed over to his Col., who sent him down to Calcutta under a guard. Already under suspension, was sent to England, where he was dismissed by the C.D. Of his subsequent career nothing further is known.

Refs. : *S. C. Grier*, pp. 460-1. *B* : *P.P.* v. 338.

CHARLTON, Andrew (1803-1888). Lieut. Colonel. 74th N.I. *b.* Shawbury, Salop., 27 May 1803. Cadet 1820. Arrived in India May 1821. Ensign 16 Jan. 1821. Lieut. 11 July 1823. Capt. 15 Dec. 1835. Major 16 Mar. 1848. Invalided 1 Dec. 1848. Retired 29 Feb. 1852. Hon. Lt. Col. 28 Nov. 1854. *d.* 21 Oct. 1888.

3rd son of Philip Charlton, of Wytheford Hall, nr. Shrewsbury, J.P. and D.L. for Salop., and Jane Brady his wife, 4th dau. of Hon. William Barnett, of Arcadia, Jamaica. Brother of Henry Charlton, *q.v.*

Services : Posted as Ensign to 2/26th N.I. Transfd. to 24th N.I. ; to 6th Extra Regt. (became 74th N.I.). 2nd Nassiri Bn. 27 Apr. 1826. Adjt. do. 31 Oct. 1827 till 1 Nov. 1829. 2nd in comd. Assam L.I. 27 July 1829 till 14 May 1838. In action against the Singphos in Upper Assam 17 Aug. 1835 (s.w.). Fur. s.c. 9 Apr. 1838 till 9 June 1841 ; to N.Z. 20 Jan. 1844 ; and 5 Mar. 1845 till 1848.

Refs. : Burke's *Landed Gentry*, 2nd edn., p. 208, *s.n.* Charlton, of Wytheford Hall, Salop.

CHARLTON, Henry (1805-1826 ?). Lieutenant, Pension Est. 9th N.I. *b.* Shawbury, Salop., 9 Apr. 1805. Cadet 1820. Ensign 21 May 1821. Lieut. 2 Nov. 1823. Pensioned in England 27 Jan. 1825. *d.* 1826 ?

4th son of Philip Charlton, of Wytheford Hall, Salop., and Jane Brady his wife. Brother of Andrew Charlton, *q.v.*

Note : His name disappears from *E.I.R.* after Oct. 1826.

Services : Posted as Ensign to 6th N.I. in 1822. Transfd. as Lieut. to 8th N.I. in 1823 ; to 9th N.I. (late 1/8th) May 1824. No record of active service.

Refs. : Burke's *Landed Gentry*, 2nd edn., p. 208, *s.n.* Charlton, of Wytheford Hall, Salop.

CHARLTON, John (1802/03-1824). Ensign, 1st Bengal European Regt. *b.* Plumstead, Kent, 1802/03. Cadet 1823. Ensign 26 July 1824. *d.* Hyderabad, Madras, 1824.

Services : Enlisted on 26 Apr. 1822, at the age of 19, as a private in H.E.I.C. Artillery and proceeded to Madras, where he died before he could take up the appt. as a Bengal Cadet. Posted as Ensign to 46th N.I. 31 Mar. 1825, and shortly afterwards transfd. to 1st Bengal Eur. Regt., before intimation of his death had been received in Bengal.

CHARRON, Andrew (1761/62-1811). Lieut. Colonel, 24th N.I. *b.* London 1761/62. Cadet 1781. Arrived in India 23 Oct. 1781. Ensign 9 Apr. 1781. Lieut. 30 July 1782. Capt. 29 May 1800. Major 30 Sept. 1803. Lt. Col. 27 Nov. 1805. *d.* nr. Aligarh, U.P., 10 Mar. 1811.

m. Calcutta, 1 July 1806, Margaret Ledlie, widow, dau. of Mrs. Levague. (She died Rye, Sussex, 1825.)

Note : She describes herself in her Will as " Margaret Charon, alias Charron, alias Ledlie, alias MacInnes, of Lower Dorset St., Dublin." She was *probably* stepmother of Robert and William Ledlie, *q.v.*, both of whom she mentions in her Will.

Services : Apptd. Cadet on 13 Dec. 1780, aged 19. Sailed for India on the *Southampton*, 13 Mar. 1781, aged 19. Capt. Lt. 17th N.I. Capt. 1/17th N.I. Transfd. as Lt. Col. to 19th N.I. in 1805. Fur. 21 Sept. 1806 till 21 Mar. 1809. Transfd. to 23rd N.I. in 1809 ; to 24th N.I. in 1810.

Refs. : Will dated Calcutta 1 Sept. 1806 ; proved 3 Apr. 1811.

CHARTER, James (1789-1847). Lieut. Colonel. 5th N.I. *b.* 5 Nov. 1789. Cadet 1805. Arrived in India 11 July 1806. Ensign 21 Aug. 1806. Lieut. 18 Nov. 1808. Capt. 1 May 1824. Major 23 May 1831. Lt. Col. 24 July 1837. Retired 27 Oct. 1838. *d.* Southwell Lodge, nr. Taunton, 13 Nov. 1847.

Son of Thomas Charter. *m*. 1st (?). (She died 12 Apr. 1812.) *m*. 2nd, Agra, 12 Jan. 1819, Miss Frances Alicia Halhed. (*See also* Edward Carncross Sneyd.) (She died 7 Aug. 1850.)
Services : Barasat C.C. for 9½ mos. Posted as Ensign to 2/2nd N.I. Fur. s.c. 4 Sept. 1811 till 1 Aug. 1814. Adjt. 2nd Gren. Bn. in 1815. Intr. & Qmr. 2/2nd N.I. 4 May 1815 till 1 May 1824. Transfd. as Capt. to 5th N.I. (late 1/2nd) May 1824. Fur. 26 Jan. 1827 till 6 Sept. 1829. To comd. 5th N.I. 13 Sept. 1837. No record of active service.
Refs. : *G.M.* 1848, i. 108.

CHARTERIS, Richard Lowthian Ross (1804-1854). Lieutenant. 65th N.I. *b*. Amisfield, co. Dumfries, 25 July 1804. Cadet 1825. Arrived in India 24 Feb. 1826. Ensign (?). Lieut. 5 July 1826. Retired 15 Sept. 1838. *d*. 8 Mar. 1854 : committed suicide by cutting his throat with a razor during an attack of *delirium tremens*.
4th son of George Charteris, of Amisfield, and Sarah Aglionby his wife, only dau. of George Ross, of Staffold.
Services : Fur. s.c. 15 Mar. 1836 till retirement. Retired on a pension of 4s. *p.d.* No record of active service. "Well known as an Oriental linguist" (*G.M.*).
Refs. : *G.M.* 1854, i. 446.

CHARTERS, Archibald Elijah (1791-1814). Lieutenant, 26th N.I. *b*. 10 Nov. 1791. Cadet 1807. Arrived in India 21 Mar. 1809. Ensign 10 May 1807. Lieut. 29 Nov. 1809. *d*. Java 20 Feb. 1814.
bapt. Calcutta 3 Dec. 1791. Son of Samuel Charters, B.C.S., senior judge of appeal at Patna, and Catherine his 2nd wife. Marlow Cadet.
Services : Posted as Ensign to 26th N.I. Capture of Java 1811 ; Lieut. 5th Bn. Bengal Vols. Continued serving in Java with 5th Vol. Bn. till death.
Refs. : Will proved 22 June 1815.

CHARTERS, Thomas (*d*. 1807). Ensign, Infantry. Subsequently an indigo planter. Cadet 1783. Ensign 24 Feb. 1785. Resigned 20 June 1788. *d*. Calcutta 21 Dec. 1807.
Youngest son of Samuel Charters, solicitor of the customs in Scotland. His dau. *m*. John Irwin, *q.v.*
Services : After resigning the Service he settled at Benares, where he engaged in the manufacture of indigo. "One of H.M. Justices of the Peace."
Refs. : *S.M.* 1808, p. 638.

CHATFIELD, Charles (1750/51-1791). Major, Comdt. 8th Bn. Sepoys. *b.* 1750/51. Cadet 1769. Ensign 6 Jan. 1769. Lieut. 19 Dec. 1769. Capt. 13 July 1778. Major 31 Jan. 1784. *d.* Barrackpore, 8 Oct. 1791, aged 40.

Brother of Robert Allen Chatfield, John, and William. (*Probably* uncle of John Chatfield, *q.v.*)

Services : N.F.P.

Refs. : Will dated 24 July 1791. M.I. in old cemetery at Barrackpore.

CHATFIELD, John (1780-1808). Capt. Lieutenant, Bengal European Regt. *b.* London 19 May 1780. Cadet 1798. Arrived in India 25 Oct. 1799. Ensign 23 Sept. 1799. Lieut. 28 Oct. 1799. Capt. Lt. (?). *d.* Dinapore 29 Apr. 1808.

bapt. St. Olave's, Hart St., London, 9 June 1780. Son of Robert Chatfield and Anne his wife. (*Probably* nephew of Charles Chatfield, *q.v.*)

Services : Posted as Lieut. to 1st Bengal Eur. Regt. 15 Apr. 1801. Second Mahratta War ; Gwalior ; battle of Deig 13 Nov. 1804 (w.) ; Lieut. Bengal Eur. Regt. Qmr. Bengal Eur. Regt. 1804 till death.

CHAUNE, Thomas. Cadet. Infantry. Cadet 1771. Resigned 21 Aug. 1771.

Services : N.F.P.

CHAWNER, Thomas (1763/64-1784). Lieutenant, Infantry. *b.* Stafford 1763/64. Cadet 1780. Ensign 1780. Lieut. 25 July 1781. *d.* Chunar 19 Oct. 1784.

Services : Sailed for India on the *Neptune*, 3 June 1780, aged 16. N.F.P.

CHEAPE, Charles (1806-1890). Colonel. 51st N.I. *b.* co. Fife 27 Sept. 1806. Cadet 1822. Arrived in India 11 Jan. 1824. Ensign 11 July 1823. Lieut. 13 May 1825. Capt. 1 May 1843. Major 27 June 1857. Bt. Lt. Col. 28 Nov. 1854. Retired 10 Sept. 1858. Hon. Col. 10 Sept. 1858. *d.* Killundine 22 Apr. 1890.

Of Killundine, co. Argyll, J.P. 5th son of George Cheape, of Wellfield, co. Fife, and Lilias his wife, dau. of James Guthrie, of Craigie, co. Forfar. 2nd cousin of Sir John Cheape, G.C.B., *q.v. m.* Muttra, 28 Aug. 1833, Caroline Eliza, dau. of George Frederick Harriot, *q.v.*

Services : Posted as Ensign to 51st N.I. Fur. s.c. 4 June 1828 till 22 May 1829. Adjt. Agra Provl. Bn. 16 Feb. 1831. Pioneers 2 June 1831 till 9 July 1832. Bde. Major at Muttra 25 June 1832 ; do. at Lucknow 12 Jan. 1835. Postmaster at Nimach 24 Nov. 1842. Bde. Major Meywar F.F. Second Sikh War ; siege of Multan ;

THE BENGAL ARMY, 1758-1834 335

Gujerat (Medal with clasp). Dy. Paymr. at Lahore 11 Sept. 1850 till retirement. Fur. s.c. 26 Feb. 1856 till retirement.
Refs. : Burke's *Landed Gentry*, 13th edn., p. 326, *s.n.* Cheape, of Strathyrum and Lathockar, co. Fife. *The Times*, 24 Apr. 1890.

CHEAPE, Harry (1763/64-1832). Major. 15th N.I. *b.* in Scotland 1763/64. Cadet 1781. Arrived in India 20 Apr. 1782. Ensign 28 May 1781. Lieut. 11 Sept. 1782. Capt. 13 June 1801. Major 19 Nov. 1807. Retired 25 Apr. 1810. *d.* Edinburgh 12 Sept. 1832.
Services : Apptd. Cadet on 25 Apr. 1781, aged 17. Sailed for India on the *Earl of Hertford*, 26 June 1781, aged 17. Fur. 27 Mar. 1797 till 6 Dec. 1800. Capt. Lt. 1/15th N.I. Capt. 1/15th N.I. Bde. Major Jan. 1801 till 1808 ; Bde. Major at Cawnpore 1804-8. Fur. 17 Feb. 1808 till retirement.
Refs. : *G.M.* 1833, i. 93.

CHEAPE, Henry (1790-1840). Lieutenant, Pensioner on Lord Clive's fund. 19th N.I. *b.* Rossie, co. Fife, 24 June 1790. Cadet 1805. Arrived in India 13 Dec. 1806. Ensign 23 Dec. 1806. Lieut. 3 Feb. 1809. Pensioned on Lord Clive's fund 13 July 1818. *d.* 15 Mar. 1840.
Of Rossie, which place he sold in 1839. Eldest son of John Cheape, of Rossie, Collessie, and Elizabeth his wife, dau. of John Dalyell, of Lingo, co. Fife. Brother of Sir John Cheape, G.C.B., *q.v.*, cousin-german of Thomas Dalyell, *q.v.*, and 2nd cousin of Charles Cheape, *q.v. m.* 1st, 1819, Margaret, dau. of John Carstairs, of Stratford Green, Essex. *m.* 2nd, 1836, Wilhelmina, dau. of George Hathorn, of the Castle Wigg family.
Services : Posted as Ensign to 19th N.I. in 1807. Intr. & Qmr. 2/19th N.I. 1814 ; do. 1/19th N.I. 1815. Nepal War 1814-5 ; Lieut. 19th N.I., in 1st Div. Fur. 1816 till pensioned.
Refs. : Burke's *Landed Gentry*, 13th edn., p. 326, *s.n.* Cheape, of Strathyrum and Lathockar, co. Fife.

CHEAPE, James (1762/63-1794). Lieutenant, Infantry. *b.* in Scotland 1762/63. Cadet 1778. Arrived in India 15 Mar. 1780. Ensign 1779. Lieut. 3 Feb. 1781. *d.* Chunar, U.P., 9 Sept. 1794.
Son of —— Cheape and Mariana his wife. Brother of John Cheape, of Glasgow.
Services : Sailed for India on the *Walpole*, 16 June 1779, aged 16. N.F.P.
Refs. : Will dated 7 Apr. 1794.

CHEAPE, Sir John (1792-1875). General, G.C.B. Colonel Comdt. Engineers. *b.* Rossie, co. Fife, 5 Oct. 1792. Cadet 1809. Ensign 3 Nov. 1809. Lieut. 29 Sept. 1816. Capt. 1 Mar. 1821. Major 25 June 1830. Lt. Col. 22 Jan. 1834. Col. 19 Feb. 1844. Maj.

LIST OF THE OFFICERS OF

Gen. 20 June 1854. Lt. Gen. 24 May 1859. Gen. 6 Dec. 1866. *d.* Old Park, Ventnor, I.W., 30 Mar. 1875.

Of Old Park, Ventnor. 2nd son of John Cheape, of Rossie, and Elizabeth his wife. Brother of Henry Cheape, *q.v. m.* 1st, St. Helena, 5 Mar. 1835, Amelia Frances, eldest dau. of Trevor John Chicheley Plowden, B.C.S., and relict of George Maxwell Batten, B.C.S. (He divorced her in 1841.) *m.* 2nd, Agnes Macpherson. Woolwich Cadet ; nominated for R.M.A. 9 Mar. 1808.

Services : See *D.N.B.* Fur. s.c., 2 yrs. to the Cape, 15 Oct. 1832. Returned finally to England on fur. in 1855. C.B. 20 July 1838. K.C.B. 9 June 1849. G.C.B. 28 Mar. 1865.

Refs. : Burke's *Landed Gentry*, 13th edn., p. 326, *s.n.* Cheape, of Strathyrum amd Lathockar, co. Fife. *D.N.B. D.I.B. Boase. Thackeray*, pp. 68-86. *The Times*, 2 Apr. 1875.

CHEERE, Henry (1807-1874). Major. 74th N.I. *b.* July 1807. Cadet 1824. Arrived in India 10 Mar. 1826. Ensign 13 May 1825. Lieut. 3 Dec. 1827. Capt. 1 Mar. 1838. Invalided 15 Mar. 1844. Retired 15 July 1852. Hon. Major 28 Nov. 1854. *d.* Little Drayton, Salop., 18 Feb. 1874.

Of Papworth Hall, Cambs. *bapt.* Papworth Hall, 22 Aug. 1807, aged 1 month. Son of Charles Madryll, of Papworth (who took the name of Cheere on 12 Feb. 1808), and Frances his wife, dau. of Charles Cheere, and grand-dau. of Sir Henry Cheere, 1st Bart.

Services : Posted as Ensign to 6th Extra Regt. (became 74th N.I.). Fur. s.c. 10 Jan. 1837 till 14 Nov. 1839. No record of active service.

Refs. : G.E.C.'s *Complete Baronetage*, v. 140. Burke's *Extinct Baronetcies*, p. 108, *s.n.* Cheere, Bart., of Westminster. *The Times*, 20 Feb. 1874.

CHEESE, Edmund (1783-?). (*See* **CARPENTER, Edmund Cheese.**)

CHEESE, John (1782-1808). Lieutenant, 1st N.I. *bapt.* All Saints, Hereford, 14 Apr. 1782. Cadet 1799. Arrived in India 9 Dec. 1800. Ensign 12 Oct. 1800. Lieut. 3 Feb. 1803. *d.* Kaitha, Bundelkhand, 3 Sept. 1808.

Son of Michael Cheese and Elizabeth his wife. Brother of Edmund Cheese Carpenter, *q.v.*

Services : Posted as Ensign to 2/1st N.I. 17 Apr. 1801. Operations in Bundelkhand 1806-7 ; Chamir ; Sehlehuganj ; Lieut. 2/1st N.I.

CHEETHAM, John (Edward) (1809-1841). Lieutenant, Invalid Est. 11th N.I. *b.* Woolwich 2 Apr. 1809. Cadet 1825. Arrived in India 13 July 1826. Ensign 3 Mar. 1826. Lieut. 7 Dec. 1827. Invalided 24 June 1839. *d.* Barrackpore 6 May 1841.

Son of John Cheetham. *m.* Dinapore, 7 Dec. 1829, Jane, eldest dau. of Samuel Houlton, *q.v.* (*See also* William Henry Eastfield Colebrooke.)
Services : Posted as Ensign to 21st N.I. Transfd. to 11th N.I. 5 Oct. 1826. (? Wahabi rising 1831 ; Lieut. 11th N.I.) Fur. s.c. 25 Oct. 1831 till 9 Aug. 1834.
Refs. : I.N. 4 Aug. 1841, p. 362.

CHESNEY, Charles Cornwallis (1791-1830). Captain. Artillery. *b.* Kilkeel, co. Down, 14 May 1791. Cadet 1807. Arrived in India 2 Mar. 1809. Fireworker 25 Mar. 1809. Lieut. 1 Mar. 1813. Capt. 2 Aug. 1822. Retired 26 Apr. 1828. *d.* Cheltenham, 3 Apr. 1830, " after a long and painful illness occasioned by exertions in the Nepal War."
2nd son of Alexander Chesney, of Packolet (of Prospect), Kilkeel, coast officer. Brother of John Chesney, *q.v.*, and of Francis Rawdon Chesney *(D.N.B.). m.* St. Helena, 20 July 1818, Sophia Augusta, dau. of —— Cauty. (She died 9 May 1875, aged 75.) Father of Charles Cornwallis Chesney *(D.N.B.),* and of Sir George Tomkyns Chesney *(D.N.B.).* Woolwich Cadet ; nominated for R.M.A. 26 Feb. 1806.
Services : Nepal War 1814-5 ; Adjt. & Qmr. Art. of 2nd Div. Fur. 24 Mar. 1818 till 1822. A.D.C. to Maj.-Gen. Thomas Hardwicke, *q.v.*, 1822-4. Supt. of Cadets at Fort William 1824-5. Fur. 1826 till retirement.
Refs. : G.M. 1830, i. 379. *A.J.* N.S. ii. 56.

CHESNEY, John (1803-1824). Ensign, 28th N.I. *b.* Kilkeel, co. Down, 10 Aug. 1803. Cadet 1821. Ensign 7 Aug. 1822. *d.* Hindaun, Rajputana, 3 Oct. 1824.
Son of Alexander Chesney, of Packolet, Kilkeel, coast officer. Brother of Charles Cornwallis Chesney, *q.v.*
Services : Posted as Ensign to 25th N.I. Transfd. to 14th N.I. in 1823 ;, to 28th N.I. (late 1/14th) May 1824. No record of active service.

CHESTER, Charles (1802-1857). Bt. Colonel, 23rd N.I. *bapt.* Hintlesham, Suffolk, 21 Aug. 1802. Cadet 1820. Arrived in India May 1821. Ensign 13 Jan. 1821. Lieut. 11 July 1823. Capt. 23 Feb. 1836. Major 7 June 1853. Bt. Lt. Col. 7 June 1849. Bt. Col. 28 Nov. 1854. *d.* 8 June 1857 : kld. in action at Badli-ki-Serai.
2nd son of Sir Robert Chester, Kt., of Bush Hall, Herts., Lt. Col. Herts. Mil., J.P. and D.L., Herts., Master of the Ceremonies to George III, George IV, William IV, and Queen Victoria, and

Eliza his wife, 3rd dau. of John Ford, of the Chauntry, nr. Ipswich.
m. Ludhiana, 3 Mar. 1832, Margaret Mundy, 4th dau. of William
Conrad Faithfull, *q.v.* (*See also* John Dickson Dyke Bean.) Ed.
Charterhouse 1814-20 ; admitted scholar 8 Feb. 1816.

Services : Posted to 2/4th N.I. in Oct. 1821. Transfd. to 23rd
N.I. (late 2/4th) May 1824. S.A.C.G. 4 June 1825. First Burma
War 1825-6 ; S.A.C.G. (India medal). Fur. s.c. 2 Apr. 1827 till
10 Aug. 1830. Adjt. 23rd N.I. 27 Jan. 1833 till Oct. 1833. Fur.
s.c. 28 Feb. 1837 till 21 Nov. 1839. Bde. Major E. frontier, at
Sylhet, Dec. 1840 till Mar. 1842. D.J.A.G., Presidency Div., 23 Aug.
1843 till Sept. 1844. Offg. D.A.A.G., Saugor Div., Nov. 1845.
D.A.A.G. May 1846. A.A.G. Jan. 1848. Second Sikh War ;
passage of Chenab ; Chilianwala ; Gujerat ; A.A.G. of Div. and of
the Army (Medal with 2 clasps). 1st A.A.G. of the Army 9 Apr.
1849 ; D.A.G. of Army 6 May 1850. Leave s.c. Jan. 1855 till Mar.
1856. A.G. of Army 6 May 1856. Mutiny campaign ; A.G. of the
Army before Delhi (kld.).

Refs. : Burke's *Landed Gentry*, 4th edn., p. 237, *s.n.* Chester, of
Bush Hall, Herts. *De Rhé-Philipe.* Burke's *Royal Families*, ped.
68. *Alumni Carthusiani*. *G.M.* 1857, ii. 346. M.I. in Winchester
cathedral and in Charterhouse cloisters.

CHESTER, Edward. Cadet. Infantry. Cadet 1770. Resigned
23 Nov. 1771.

Services : N.F.P.

CHETWODE, Robert (1800-1825). Lieutenant, 14th N.I. *bapt.*
Mucklestone, Staffs., 9 Mar. 1800. Cadet 1819. Ensign 3 June
1820. Lieut. 11 July 1823. *d.* Calcutta 28 Aug. 1825.

5th son of Sir John Chetwode, 4th Bart., of Oakley, Staffs., and
Lady Henrietta his wife, eldest dau. of George Harry, fifth Earl of
Stamford and Warrington. Ed. Rugby ; entered at midsummer
1811.

Services : Posted as Ensign to 2/18th N.I. Transfd. as Lieut.
to 10th N.I. 11 July 1823 ; to 14th N.I. (late 1/10th) May 1824.
(? First Burma War ; Cachar 1825 ; Lieut. 14th N.I.)

Refs. : Burke's *Peerage*, 1923, p. 495, *s.n.* Chetwode, Bart., of
Chetwode, Bucks.

CHIENE, Patrick John (1807-1898). Major. 34th N.I. *b.* Penang
20 May 1807. Cadet 1825. Arrived in India 28 June 1826.
Ensign 13 Feb. 1826. Lieut. 6 Aug. 1835. Capt. 24 Jan. 1845.
Retired 1 Feb. 1850. Hon. Major 28 Nov. 1854. *d.* 16 June
1898.

Son of Patrick Chiene, of Penang, shipbuilder. *m.* Calcutta,

21 Apr. 1834, Eliza, dau. of "the late Lieut. Cunningham, Bengal Est." (*See also* Arthur Quin Hopper.)
Services : Ensign d.d. 42nd N.I. 8 July 1826. Posted as Ensign to 34th N.I. Adjt. 3rd Local Horse 16 June 1830. Operations against the Kols 1832-3 ; Ensign 34th N.I. Fur. s.c. 8 Apr. 1841 till 28 Nov. 1843. 34th N.I. disbanded at Meerut, for mutiny, 20 Mar. 1844 ; re-embodied 4 July 1846. Comdg. Meerut Police Bn. 18 Apr. 1844 till 1846 (appt. cancelled on 18 May 1844, but confirmed from 11 Sept. 1844). Apptd. Postmaster at Meerut 26 Aug. 1844. Capt., City of Edin. Art. Mil., 11 Nov. 1854.
Refs. : *I.M.* 1850, pp. 316, 571, 575.

CHILCOTT, Joseph (1807-1869). Major. 74th N.I. *bapt.* Bristol 1 Aug. 1807. Cadet 1826. Arrived in India 15 Aug. 1827. Ensign 7 Jan. 1827. Lieut. 27 Apr. 1833. Capt. 15 Mar. 1844. Invalided 3 Oct. 1845. Retired 25 May 1858. Hon. Major 25 May 1858. *d.* Mussoorie, U.P., 13 Mar. 1869, aged 62.

Son of Thomas Chilcott, of Bristol. *m.* Warminster, Wilts., 1 Mar. 1837, Hannah Buckler, only dau. of John Hoare, of Warminster, surgeon.
Services : Posted as Ensign to 74th N.I. Fur. s.c. 7 Jan. 1836 till 17 Nov. 1838. Intr. & Qmr. 74th N.I. 16 Jan. 1839 till 17 Sept. 1842. Fur. s.c. 2 Dec. 1856. No record of active service.
Refs. : *Bath Chron.* Mar. 1837. *The Times,* 19 Mar. 1869.

CHINN, Philip Sinckler (1806-1885). Major. 51st N.I. *b.* Cathedral Close, Lichfield, Staffs., 27 Apr. 1806. Cadet 1824. Arrived in India 18 Mar. 1826. Ensign 28 Sept. 1825. Lieut. 28 May 1829. Capt. 24 Jan. 1845. Retired 1 July 1846. Hon. Major 28 Nov. 1854. *d.* Westgate Cottage, Lichfield, 17 June 1885.

Son of Henry Chinn, of Lichfield, proctor. *m.* Emma, dau. of —— Sergeant. Ed. Shrewsbury 1817-22.
Services : Posted as Ensign to 51st N.I. First China War ; Lieut. 1st Bn. Bengal Vols. 15 Feb. 1840 till 1 June 1841 (Medal).
Refs. : *Shrewsbury School Register.* *The Times,* 20 June 1885.

CHITTY, Aynott (1798-1827). Lieutenant, 4th N.I. *bapt.* Deal, Kent, 19 Jan. 1798. Cadet 1817. Ensign (?). Lieut. 1 Aug. 1818. *d.* Cawnpore 22 Aug. 1827.

Son of Richard Chitty, of Deal, miller. Brother of Richard Chitty, *q.v.* *m.* Cawnpore, 14 Sept. 1821, Maria Jane, dau. of John Jenkins Bird, *q.v.* (*See also* John Holbrow and Frederick Young.)
Services : Posted as Lieut. to 1/1st N.I. Operations in Rohilkhand against Bhoja Singh Mar. 1820 ; distinguished himself in an engagement on the banks of the Chuka nullah ; Lieut. comdg. a

detachment of 1st Rohilla Cav. Transfd. to 4th N.I. (late 2/1st) May 1824. Adjt. Murshidabad Provl. Bn. 1823. Adjt. Cawnpore Provl. Bn. 1824 till death.

Refs. : Will dated Cawnpore, 21 Aug. 1827 ; proved 29 Apr. 1828.

CHITTY, Richard (1836-?). Lieutenant. Infantry. *b.* Chichester, Sussex, 1736. Cadet 1763. Ensign 21 June 1763. Lieut. 24 Feb. 1764. Resigned 13 Dec. 1765.

Services : Sailed for India on the *Deptford*, 2 Jan. 1763, aged 26. N.F.P.

CHITTY, Richard (1806-1871). Lieut. Colonel. 40th N.I. *b.* Deal, Kent, 19 Apr. 1806. Cadet 1821. Arrived in India 14 Oct. 1822. Ensign 18 Oct. 1822. Lieut. 2 Oct. 1823. Capt. 1 Sept. 1841. Bt. Major 11 Nov. 1851. Retired 6 Aug. 1854. Hon. Lt. Col. 28 Nov. 1854. *d.* Stow Villa, Oldfield Rd., Bath, 10 Apr. 1871.

Son of Richard Chitty, of Deal, miller. Brother of Aynott Chitty, *q.v. m.* Maria Jane. (She died 4 June 1827.)

Services : Posted as Ensign to 1st N.I. 18 Oct. 1822. With 2/9th N.I. in Malacca in 1823. Transfd. as Lieut. to 20th N.I. 2 Oct. 1823 ; to 40th N.I. (late 2/20th), May 1824. Intr. & Qmr. 40th N.I. 20 Nov. 1830 till 1841. Fur. p.a. 28 May 1843 till 1845. Second Burma War 1852 ; operations in vicinity, and capture of Rangoon ; Bt. Major 40th N.I. (Medal). To comd. 4th Sikh Local Inf. Dec. 1853.

Refs. : *The Times*, 17 Apr. 1871.

CHOWNE, formerly TILSON, James Henry (1812-?). Captain. 66th N.I. Subsequently in holy orders. *b.* London 13 Jan. 1812. Cadet 1828. Arrived in India 2 Oct. 1829. Ensign (12 Dec. 1828) 14 Sept. 1829. Lieut. 8 May 1832. Capt. 24 Nov. 1842. Retired 5 Aug. 1845.

Of Wheatleigh Lodge, Taunton, and of Slape House, Netherbury, Dorset. Son of James Tilson, of Goring, Oxon., and Frances his wife, dau. of William Sanford, of Walford, Somerset. Assumed, by R.L., the surname of Chowne only, on the demise of Gen. Christopher Chowne in 1835, in compliance with the Will of Mary, Countess De Bruhl (*Lond. Gaz.* 24 Feb. 1836, p. 403). *m.* Calcutta, 19 Aug. 1835, Mary Maynard, eldest dau. of William Braddon, of Skisdon, Cornwall, and Blacklands, Devon, B.C.S., and niece of Richard Braddon, *q.v.* St. Peter's Coll., Camb. ; B.A. 1847 ; M.A. 1850.

Services : Posted as Ensign to 66th N.I. Adjt. Arakan Local Bn. 8 Apr. 1834. Adjt. 66th N.I. 15 Nov. 1834 till 19 Jan. 1843. Fur. p.a. 5 Feb. 1843 till retirement. No record of active service. Took holy orders ; Deacon 1847 ; Priest 1849. Apptd. to St.

James's, Taunton, 1852 ; curate of Netherbury, Beaminster, Dorset, 1854.
Refs. : Burke's *Landed Gentry*, 4th edn., p. 244, *s.n.* Chowne, of Wheatleigh Lodge, Taunton. *Walford. Crockford. Graduati Cantab.*

CHRISTIAN, Hugh Holmes (1810-1830). Cornet, 7th L.C. *b.* London 21 Nov. 1810. Cadet 1826. Arrived in India 31 Oct. 1827. Cornet (18 Jan. 1827) 1 Oct. 1827. *d.* Kaitha, Bundelkhand, 31 Dec. 1830.
Son of Hood Hanway Christian, Rear Adm. of the White, and Harriet his wife, 2nd dau. of Samuel Shute, of Fernhill, I.W. Grandson of Rear-Adm. Sir Hugh Cloberry Christian, K.B. (*D.N.B.*).
Services : Was at the Cape when nominated to a Cadetship. Posted as Supy. Cornet to 7th L.C. 1 Oct. 1827. No record of active service.
Refs. : Burke's *Landed Gentry*, 13th edn., p. 334, *s.n.* Christian, of West Huntingdon Hall, Yorks.

CHRISTIE, Andrew (1788-1821). Bt. Captain, 6th N.I. *b.* Cupar, co. Fife, 20 Sept. 1788. Cadet 1804. Arrived in India 16 May 1806. Ensign 4 Mar. 1806. Lieut. 1 Feb. 1807. Bt. Capt. 1 Jan. 1819. *d.* in camp at Bandarej, Rajputana (or Sikandra, nr. Agra), 21 Nov. 1821.
bapt. Cupar 25 Sept. 1788. Eldest son of Andrew Christie, of Cupar, writer, and Margaret Dempster his wife, of Ferrybank. Twin brother of Charles Christie (1788-1870), *q.v. m.* St. Andrew's, Calcutta, 2 June 1817, Miss Jane Dempster.
Services : Posted as Ensign to 2/6th N.I. On fur. in 1812. Nepal War 1814-5 ; Lieut. 2/6th N.I., in 1st Div. Actg. Intr. & Qmr. 2/6th N.I. in 1815. Adjt. 2/6th N.I. 21 Oct. 1815 till death. Operations in Kotah 1821 ; Mangrol ; Bt. Capt. 2/6th N.I.
Refs. : *S.M.* 1822, i. 828. Will dated Moradabad 4 June 1819 ; proved 12 Apr. 1822.

CHRISTIE, Charles (*d.* 1805). Captain, 2nd N.I. Cadet 1781. Arrived in India 8 Feb. 1781. Ensign 16 Aug. 1781. Lieut. 4 June 1783. Capt. 4 Sept. 1800. *d.* on left bank of Jumna, between Agra and Muttra, 30 Apr. 1805.
Son of James Christie. *m.* Harriet. (She *re-m.* Edward William Butler, *q.v.*)
Services : Capt. Lt. 2/2nd N.I. 29 May 1800. Operations in Jumna Doab 1803 ; Kachaura. Second Mahratta War ; battle of Delhi ; Agra ; Bde. Major 3rd Bde. Bde. Major at Fatehgarh in 1804. Raised at Fatehgarh a corps of levies which became 2/25th

N.I. in Oct. 1804. This Corps, which he comdd. from Oct. 1804 till death, was called after him " Cristeen-ki-Paltan."
Refs. : Williams, pp. 372-4. *Pester.* Will dated Fatehgarh 20 Oct. 1802 ; proved 20 June 1805.

CHRISTIE, Charles (1788-1870). Lieut. Colonel. 7th N.I. *b.* Cupar, co. Fife, 20 Sept. 1788. Cadet 1805. Arrived in India 11 July 1806. Ensign 6 Sept. 1806. Lieut. 19 Dec. 1809. Capt. 1 May 1824. Major 12 Dec. 1831. Retired 9 July 1835. Hon. Lt. Col. 28 Nov. 1854. *d.* 26 Gt. King St., Edinburgh, 10 Mar. 1870.

bapt. Cupar 25 Sept. 1788. Son of Andrew Christie, of Cupar, writer, and Margaret Dempster his wife. Twin brother of Andrew Christie, *q.v.*, and brother of John Christie, *q.v.*

Services : Posted as Ensign to 1/4th N.I. Capture of Java 1811 ; Lieut. 4th Bn. Bengal Vols. (Medal). Reposted to 4th Vol. Bn. 27 July 1815, and served in Java till 1816. Fur. p.a. 31 Dec. 1816 till 25 May 1821. Bk. Mr. Saugor Div. Dy. Paymr., Muttra, 11 Mar. 1822 till 1 Jan. 1832. Transfd. as Capt. to 7th N.I. (late 1/4th) May 1824. Siege and capture of Bhurtpore ; Capt. 7th N.I. (India medal). Fur. s.c. 9 Jan. 1833 till retirement.

Refs. : The Times, 14 Mar. 1870.

CHRISTIE, Charles Robert Hewell (1811-1846). Bt. Captain, 6th L.C. *b.* Ealing 5 May 1811. Cadet 1828. Arrived in India 5 May 1829. Cornet 4 May 1829. Lieut. 28 Dec. 1838. Bt. Capt. 8 Jan. 1844. *d.* Muzaffarpur, Bengal, 29 Oct. 1846.

Son of Charles Christie, of Halliford, nr. Shepperton, Middlesex, Capt. E.I.C.S., and Thomasine his wife. *m.* Calcutta, 23 Aug. 1839, Margaret, eldest dau. of Benjamin Lindsay, of Scotland.

Services : To do duty with 2nd L.C. ; do. with 8th L.C. 13 Dec. 1832. Posted to 9th L.C. 19 Jan. 1833. Transfd. to 6th L.C. 9 June 1836. No record of active service.

CHRISTIE, Edward (1810-1849). Bt. Major, Artillery. *b.* Twickenham, Middlesex, 2 June 1810. Cadet 1826. Arrived in India 15 June 1827. 2nd Lieut. 28 Sept. 1827. Lieut. 30 Nov. 1833. Capt. 3 July 1845. Bt. Major 19 June 1846. *d.* in camp at Chilianwala, 15 Jan. 1849, of wounds received at the battle of Chilianwala on 13 Jan.

Son of Thomas Christie, of Cheltenham, physician. Addiscombe Cadet 1824-6.

Services : Posted to 3rd Troop 2nd Bde. H.A. in Aug. 1827. Transfd. to 1st Troop 2nd Bde. Dec. 1828 ; to 2nd Troop 3rd Bde. Mar. 1831 ; to 2nd Troop 1st Bde. Oct. 1837. Adjt. of Art. at Ludhiana June 1843 till July 1845. D.A.A.G. of Art. 1 Jan. 1846.

First Sikh War; Sobraon (Medal). To comd. 3rd Troop 2nd Bde.
H.A. Aug. 1847. Second Sikh War; passage of Chenab; Sadulapur; Chilianwala (s.w.); Bt. Major comdg. 3rd Troop 2nd Bde.
H.A.
Refs. : *De Rhé-Philipe.*

CHRISTIE, John (1806-1869). Major General, C.B. 1st European L.C. *b.* Cupar, co. Fife, 13 Nov. 1806. Cadet 1822. Arrived in India 14 May 1823. Cornet (4 Jan. 1823) 1 May 1824. Lieut. 18 May 1824. Capt. 1 Jan. 1846. Major 3 Apr. 1846. Lt. Col. 7 June 1849. Bt. Col. 28 Nov. 1854. Maj. Gen. 21 Feb. 1861. *d.* San Remo, Italy, 7 May 1869.

Son of Andrew Christie, of Cupar, agent of the British Linen Co., and Margaret Dempster his wife. Brother of Andrew Christie, *q.v.* *m.* Sept. 1846, Charlotte Augusta, eldest dau. of Colin Lindsay, B.C.S., judge at Delhi, of the Balcarres family.

Services : Posted as Cornet to 3rd L.C. 1 May 1824. Siege and capture of Bhurtpore; Lieut. 3rd L.C. (India medal). Adjt. 3rd L.C. 10 June 1826 till 9 May 1831. Fur. s.c. 9 May 1831 till 6 Nov. 1834. Comdt. Shah Shuja's 1st Cav. 28 Aug. 1838. First Afghan War 1839-42; Ghazni (Medal); Pashut; with Kandahar force under Gen. Nott; re-occupation of Kabul; taking of Istalif (Medal). Comdt. 8th Irreg. Cav. 2 Jan. 1843. Gwalior campaign; Paniar (Bronze star). Comdt. 9th Irreg. Cav. 27 Apr. 1844 till 28 Apr. 1854. First Sikh War; Mudki; Ferozshahr; Sobraon (Medal with 2 clasps). Second Sikh War; passage of Chenab; Chilianwala; Gujerat (Medal with clasp). Resumed comd. of 9th Irreg. Cav. 1 May 1854. Fur. 1855-6. To be Bdr., 2 cl., for special service, 29 Oct. 1857. Transfd. to 1st Eur. L.C. in 1858. Fur. 1859. C.B. 13 Mar. 1867. Durani, 3 cl. A.D.C. to Queen Victoria 7 Mar. 1856 till 21 Feb. 1861.

Refs. : Burke's *Peerage*, 1923, p. 614, *s.n.* Earl of Crawford. *Boase. D.I.B. The Times,* 14 May 1869.

CLANCEY, George (*d.* 1800). Captain, 18th N.I. Country Cadet 1779. Admitted 15 May 1779. Ensign 15 Oct. 1779. Lieut. 25 May 1781. Bt. Capt. 7 Jan. 1796. Capt. 1798. *d.* at sea 31 May 1800, on board the *Marquess of Lansdowne,* on the voyage to England.

Services : Transfd. from 1st Bengal Eur. Regt. to 2/18th N.I. 29 May 1800. N.F.P.

CLARK, Charles (*d.* 1778). Capt. Lieutenant, Artillery. Cadet (?). Fireworker 5 July 1770. Lieut. 18 May 1772. Capt. Lt. 31 Mar. 1778. bur. Calcutta 21 Dec. 1778.

Son of —— Clark(e) [1] and Elizabeth his wife. Brother of John, Burton, George, Anthony, Frances, and Sophia.
Services : First Rohilla War ; battle of St. George ; Lieut. Art.
Refs. : Will dated 22 Apr. 1774 ; proved 16 July 1779.
[1] *Note* : In both his Will and the burial register the name is given as Clarke.

CLARK, Charles (1809-1846). Captain, 1st European L.I. *bapt.* Dorchester 14 July 1809. Cadet 1825. Arrived in India 27 June 1826. Ensign (13 Feb. 1826) 12 Mar. 1827. Lieut. 15 Jan. 1829. Capt. 10 Nov. 1843. *d.* Sabathu, Punjab, 13 Oct. 1846, of wounds received at the battle of Ferozshahr on 21 Dec. 1845.
Son of George Clark, of Cornhill, Dorchester, bookseller.
Services : Ensign d.d. 6th Extra Regt. 8 July 1826. Posted as Ensign to 1st Extra Regt. in Sept. 1826. Transfd. to 1st Bengal Eur. Regt. 12 Mar. 1827. Adjt. Eur. Regt. Jan. 1837 till Jan. 1838. Fur. s.c. 22 Jan. 1838 till 12 Dec. 1840. With the Army of Reserve (for Afghanistan) at Ferozepore 1842. First Sikh War ; Ferozshahr (s.w.) ; Capt. 1st Bengal Eur. L.I.
Refs. : *De Rhé-Philipe. G.M.* 1847, i. 110. M.I. in Winchester cathedral.

CLARK, Edward (*d.* 1804). Lieutenant, 18th N.I. Cadet 1794. Arrived in India 22 Oct. 1796. Ensign 1 Nov. 1795. Lieut. 25 Apr. 1797. *d.* Bundelkhand 24 May 1804.
Formerly of S. Lopham, Norfolk, later of London.
Services : Ensign 1st Bengal Eur. Regt. Lieut. do. Transfd. as Lieut. to 1/18th N.I. 29 May 1800. Second Mahratta War ; Bundelkhand 1803 ; operations to S.W. of Delhi 1803 ; Narnaul ; Kanun ; Lieut. 1/18th N.I.

CLARK, Elias. Lieutenant. Infantry. Cadet 1767. Ensign 15 Sept. 1767. Lieut. 5 Apr. 1769. Resigned 13 Dec. 1770.
Services : N.F.P.

CLARK, George Quintin (1792-1813). Ensign, 25th N.I. *b.* Putney, Surrey, 2 Aug. 1792. Cadet 1807. Arrived in India 14 Sept. 1808. Ensign 3 Oct. 1808. *d.* Cuttack 5 July 1813.
Services : Posted as Ensign to 1/25th N.I. No record of active service.
Refs. : M.I. in Cuttack cemetery.

CLARK, James (1780-1854). Lieut. Colonel. 7th N.I. *b.* Holmes, Galston, co. Ayr, 18 Dec. 1780. Cadet 1799. Arrived in India 23 Oct. 1800. Ensign 17 Sept. 1800. Lieut. 4 June 1801. Capt. 22 Dec. 1811. Major 1 Sept. 1822. Lt. Col. 1 May 1824. Retired in India 21 Jan. 1826. *d.* 14 Jan. 1854.

bapt. Galston 25 Dec. 1780. Son of Peter Clark, of Holmes.
Services : On the voyage out to India in 1800 was captured in H.C.S. *Kent* off the Sandheads by a French privateer. Posted as Ensign to 1/4th N.I. 17 Apr. 1801. Second Mahratta War ; storm of Aligarh ; Lieut. 1/4th N.I. ; defence of Delhi Oct. 1804 ; Lieut. 2/4th N.I. Adjt. 2/4th N.I. Feb. 1804 till 1810. Capture of Java ; Cornelis ; Lieut. 4th Bn. Bengal Vols. (Medal). Served in Java till Sept. 1816, when he returned to Bengal in comd. of 4th Vol. Bn. Fur. 1817-9. Major 1/4th N.I. Transfd. as Lt. Col. to 7th N.I. (late 1/4th) May 1824.
Refs. : E.I.M.C. ii. 341.

CLARK, John (1802-1821). Ensign, Infantry. *b.* Kingussie, co. Inverness, 21 May 1802. Cadet 1820. Ensign (?). *d.* on the river, nr. Benares, 31 Aug. 1821.
Son of Alexander Clark.
Services : N.F.P.

CLARK, Otto (1781/82-1840). Lieutenant. 5th N.C. *b.* 1781/82.[1] Cadet 1797. Arrived in India 22 Sept. 1798. Cornet 25 Jan. 1799. Lieut. 29 May 1800. Retired 4 June 1813. *d.* Mar. 1840.
Services : Posted as Ensign to 2nd Bengal Eur. Regt. in Oct. 1798. Transfd. as Cornet to 3rd N.C. ; as Lieut. to newly-raised 5th N.C. 29 May 1800. (? Second Mahratta War ; Lieut. 5th N.C.) Fur. 10 Feb. 1808 till retirement.

[1] *Note :* " Aged 16, he believes." (Affidavit sworn on 16 Feb. 1798.)

CLARK, Thomas (1782-1804). Lieutenant, 18th N.I. *bapt.* Tower chapel, London, 5 Nov. 1782. Cadet 1798. Arrived in India 22 Nov. 1799. Ensign 3 Sept. 1799. Lieut. 28 Oct. 1799. *d.* Kalpi, 2 June 1804.
Son of Thomas Clark and Hannah his wife.
Services : Posted as Lieut. to 1/18th N.I. 15 Apr. 1801. Second Mahratta War ; Bundelkhand 1803 ; Kapsa ; capture of Kalpi ; Lieut. 1/18th N.I.

CLARK, William (1787-1817). Lieutenant, Invalid Est. 23rd N.I. *bapt.* Wetheral, Cumberland, July 1787. Cadet 1805. Arrived in India 13 Nov. 1806. Ensign 26 Dec. 1806. Lieut. 5 Jan. 1810. Invalided 15 Sept. 1816. *d.* Chunar 1817.
Son of Robert Clark, of Warwick Bridge, Cumberland, yeoman, and Catherine his wife. *m.* Agra, 11 Feb. 1811, Miss Anne Wilson, of Mainpuri.
Services : Posted as Ensign to 1/23rd N.I. (? Operations against

Dhundia Khan 1807; Komona; Ganauri; Ensign 1/23rd N.I.) Intr. & Qmr. 3rd Gren. Bn. 1815-6.

CLARKE, Andrew (1804-?). Lieutenant. 55th N.I. *b.* 14 Sept. 1804. Cadet 1820. Ensign 13 Jan. 1821. Lieut. 11 July 1823. Resigned 29 June 1824.

Son of Robert Clarke, of Cowrie, Culross, co. Fife.

Services : Posted as Ensign to 1/4th N.I. Fur. 1822-3. Transfd. as Lieut. to 28th N.I. 11 July 1823; to 55th N.I. (late 1/28th) May 1824. Fur. 1824 till resignation.

CLARKE, Edward (*d.* 1812). Major General. Colonel 9th N.I. Cadet 1766. Arrived in India 14 June 1767. Ensign 15 Sept. 1767. Lieut. 28 Sept. 1769. Capt. 13 May 1777. Major 30 July 1781. Lt. Col. 1 Mar. 1794. Col. 1 Jan. 1798. Maj. Gen. 1 Jan. 1805. *d.* Richmond, Surrey, 3 May 1812.

m. 1st, Eliza, dau. of Edward Ives, of Titchfield House, Hants. (She died Kalkapur, Murshidabad, 19 Aug. 1783, aged 23.) *m.* 2nd, a sister of John Carrington Smith, of Richmond (of St. Margaret's, Gloucs.), Lt. Col. 19th Foot.

Services : Lt. Col. 1st Bengal Eur. Regt. 4 May 1796; Col. do. 1 Jan. 1798. Col. 9th N.I. 1 Feb. 1799. Maj. Gen. comdg. at Dinapore 1805-10. Fur. 22 June 1810 till death.

Refs. : Burke's *Commoners,* iv. 740, *s.n.* Carrington Smith, of St. Margaret's, Gloucs. Burke's *Landed Gentry,* 13th edn., p. 1373, *s.n.* Partridge, late of Bishop's Wood, co. Hereford. Will dated 17 Sept. 1810; proved in 1813.

CLARKE, Edward (1758/59-1810). Lieut. Colonel, Artillery. *b.* 1758/59. Country Cadet 1778. Admitted 29 Sept. 1778. Fireworker 5 Nov. 1778. Lieut. 7 July 1784. Capt. 5 Dec. 1794. Major 1 Jan. 1805. Lt. Col. 30 May 1805. *d.* Calcutta 7 Dec. 1810, aged 51.

m. Point de Galle, Ceylon, Jan. 1799, Miss Cara Beta de More ("Clara Beata, *ci-devant* Demoor").

Services : Third Mysore War; Bangalore; Seringapatam; Lieut. 4th Coy. 2nd Bn. Art. Fourth Mysore War; siege and capture of Seringapatam; Capt. comdg. 5th Coy. 2nd Bn. (Medal). Served in Ceylon from 19 Sept. 1796 till (?) Oct. 1804.

Refs. : Will dated Colombo 30 Jan. 1799; proved 26 Dec. 1810. M.I. in N. Park St. burial ground, Calcutta.

CLARKE, James (1761/62-1818). Major. 6th N.I. *b.* 1761/62. Cadet 1780. Arrived in India 30 Apr. 1781. Ensign 22 Mar. 1780. Lieut. 27 July 1781. Capt. 31 July 1799. Major 21 Sept. 1804. Retired 21 Aug. 1805. *d.* 25 Feb. 1818.

A native of Suffolk.
Services : Sailed for India on the *Bellmont,* 3 Apr. 1780, aged 18.
Was on fur. in 1803. N.F.P.

CLARKE, John (1810-1895). Major General. 25th N.I. *b.* Clanville, Hants, 11 Nov. 1810. Cadet 1827. Arrived in India 11 Aug. 1828. Ensign 21 Jan. 1828. Lieut. 5 Jan. 1837. Capt. 15 Aug. 1844. Major 27 June 1857. Bt. Lt. Col. 28 Nov. 1854. Col. 12 Aug. 1861. Retired 31 Dec. 1861. Hon. Maj. Gen. 31 Dec. 1861. *d.* Melbourne, Australia, 23 Feb. 1895.

Son of Ralph Clarke, R.N., of Fishbourne, nr. Chichester, and May Christian his wife. Brother of Ralph Richard Clarke, *q.v.*
m. 5 Nov. 1846, Frances Rice, dau. of Rev. Charles Brown, rector of Whitestone, Devon.
Services : Ensign d.d. 57th N.I. 8 Sept. 1828. Posted as Ensign to 69th N.I. 4 Nov. 1828. Transfd. to 25th N.I. 4 Nov. 1834. Intr. & Qmr. 16 Dec. 1836 till 1841. Fur. s.c. 4 Jan. 1841 till 17 Mar. 1843. Intr. and Qmr. 24 May 1843 till 15 Aug. 1844. Second Sikh War ; Sadulapur ; Chilianwala ; Gujerat ; Capt. 25th N.I. (Medal with 2 clasps). D.C., Lahore Div., 13 Apr. 1849. D.C., 2 cl., 28 Apr. 1854. Comr. Khairabad Div., Oudh, 15 Apr. 1858 till retirement. Mutiny campaign ; comr. in Oudh (Medal). Permitted to reckon leave from 10 Jan. 1859 till 26 Sept. 1859 as service for pension.
Refs. : The Times, 26 Feb. 1895.

CLARKE, Ralph Richard (1808-1829). Cornet, 6th L.C. *bapt.* Chilbolton, Hants, 28 Jan. 1808. Cadet 1824. Cornet 25 Sept. 1825. *d.* Sultanpur, Benares, 28 July 1829, of spasmodic cholera.

Son of Ralph Clarke, R.N., of Clanville, Weyhill, Hants, and May Christian his wife. Brother of John Clarke, *q.v.* Addiscombe Cadet 1823-4.
Services : Posted as Cornet to 6th L.C. in 1826. No record of active service.
Refs. : A.J. N.S. i. 96.

CLARKE, Richard (1772-1824). Lieut. Colonel, C.B. Comdt. 4th L.C. *b.* St. Mary's, Islington, Middlesex, 2 July 1772. Cadet 1793. Admitted 29 Sept. 1794. Cornet 1794. Lieut. 27 July 1796. Capt. 4 Aug. 1801. Major 27 Feb. 1812. Lt. Col. 1 Oct. 1819. Lt. Col. Comdt. 1 May 1824. *d.* Karnal 7 Oct. 1824.

bapt. 17 Aug. 1772. Son of Richard Clarke and Sarah his wife. *m.* (before 1799) Mary Elizabeth. His dau. *m.* Patrick Martin Hay, *q.v.*
Services : Posted as Lieut. to newly-raised 5th N.C. 29 May 1800.

348 LIST OF THE OFFICERS OF

Capt. Lt. 5th N.C. 17 July 1801. (? Second Mahratta War ; Capt. 5th N.C.) Third Mahratta War ; Chanda ; Major 5th N.C. Transfd. as Lt. Col. to 1st L.C. in 1819 ; to 4th L.C. in 1823. C.B. 23 July 1823.

CLARKSON, James Oram (1786-1848). Lieut. Colonel, 48th N.I.
b. London 6 Aug. 1786. Cadet 1805. Arrived in India 20 July 1807. Ensign 30 June 1807. Lieut. 1 June 1811. Capt. 1 May 1824. Major 24 July 1837. Lt. Col. 21 Aug. 1843. *d.* York St., Portman Sq., London, 21 Nov. 1848.

Son of James Oram Clarkson. *m.* 1st, a sister of Hyder Young Hearsey, a near relation of Andrew Wilson Hearsey, *q.v.* (*See also* Arthur Owen, and Sir William Richards, K.C.B.) *m.* 2nd, 3 Nov. 1818, Miss Mary Price. (She died 16 Mar. 1862.)

Services : Ensign 2/21st N.I. Attack on Bhapawi fort 1811 ; Lieut. 2/21st N.I. Operations against Rajah of Boni, in Celebes, 1816 ; Macassar 26 Apr. 1816 (w. gunshot wound in right thigh); Lieut. 4th Bengal Vol. Bn. Operations in Oudh 1818 (w.). Transfd. to 1/21st N.I. Adjt. Chittagong Provl. Bn. Transfd. to 42nd N.I. (late 2/21st) May 1824. First Burma War ; Arakan 1825 ; Capt. 42nd N.I. A.D.C. to Bdr.-Gen. Price, comdg. Benares Div., 2 Mar. 1825. D.A.A.G., Benares Div., 11 July 1825. Fur. p.a. 13 Jan. 1829 till 11 Oct. 1830. First Afghan War 1839-42 ; Kandahar ; Istalif : Major 42nd N.I. (Medal). Transfd. to 47th N.I. 18 Dec. 1844 ; to 10th N.I. 27 Dec. 1844 ; to 48th N.I. 11 Feb. 1848. Fur. 1847 till death. Durani, 3 cl.

Refs. : *G.M.* 1849, i. 103. Will dated 14 Jan. 1847 ; proved 10 Jan. 1850.

CLARKSON, John Horatio (1801-1884). Lieut-Colonel. 6th N.I.
b. Sculcoates, Yorks., 28 Mar. 1801. Cadet 1819. Admitted 14 June 1820. Ensign 10 Jan. 1820. Lieut. 19 May 1823. Capt. 5 Oct. 1832. Bt. Major 9 Nov. 1846. Retired 28 Feb. 1850. Hon. Lt. Col. 28 Nov. 1854. *d.* 5 Carlton St., Edinburgh, 14 July 1884.

Son of John Clarkson, merchant, and Ann his wife. *m.* 1st, St. John's, Calcutta, 10 May 1823, Miss Sophia Martindell. (She died Bareilly, 6 Nov. 1841, aged 37.) *m.* 2nd, Clonmel, co. Tipperary, 25 Sept. 1850, Miss Helen Melville.

Services : Posted as Ensign to 1/6th N.I. Transfd. as Lieut. to 3rd N.I. ; to 6th N.I. (late 1/3rd) May 1824. Intr. & Qmr. 2nd Extra Regt. 23 July 1825. Siege and capture of Bhurtpore ; Lieut. 6th N.I. (India medal). Adjt. 6th N.I. 25 Apr. 1826. Intr. & Qmr. 6th N.I. 21 Aug. 1829 till 9 Feb. 1833. Fur. p.a. 18 Apr. 1843 till 1845.

Refs. : *The Times,* 16 July 1884.

THE BENGAL ARMY, 1758-1834

CLARKSON, Robert Graham (1773-1807). Captain, 14th N.I. *b.* 4 Mar. 1773. Cadet 1794. Arrived in India 23 Feb. 1796. Ensign 4 Oct. 1795. Lieut. 3 Oct. 1796. Capt. 21 Sept. 1804. *d.* Lucknow 18 Mar. 1807.
m. Eliza. (She died Bath, 6 Feb. 1828.)
Services : Lieut. H.M. 58th Regt. 30 Sept. 1790. Lieut. 14th N.I. Capt. Lt. 14th N.I. 27 Mar. 1804. Second Mahratta War.
Refs. : S.M. 1808, p. 398.

CLAY, John (*d.* 1784). Ensign, Infantry. Cadet 1783. Ensign 3 Feb. 1784. *d.* 26 Sept. 1784.
Services : N.F.P.

CLAYTON, Charles Edward (1788-1808). Lieutenant, 17th N.I. *bapt.* Calcutta 31 Dec. 1788. Cadet 1804. Arrived in India 10 Dec. 1805. Ensign 17 Oct. 1804. Lieut. 19 Feb. 1806. *d.* Muttra 8 Sept. 1808 : drowned whilst attempting to cross the Jumna R.
Son of Thomas William Clayton, *q.v.*, and Emma Maria his wife.
Services : Posted as Lieut. to 17th N.I. Apptd. a Cadet for the Cav. in 1807, and had probably recently joined a Cav. regt. at Muttra when his death occurred.

CLAYTON, Edward (*d.* 1799). Captain, Infantry. Cadet 1778. Arrived in India 10 Dec. 1778. Ensign 1778. Lieut. 1 Dec. 1778. Bt. Capt. 7 Jan. 1796. Capt. 1796. *d.* Fatehgarh, U.P., 16 Nov. 1799.
Son of Edward Clayton, of Gort. His dau. *m.* David Lyons, *q.v.*
Services : Lieut. 5th Bn. Sepoys in 1787. N.F.P.
Refs. : Will dated 12 Nov. 1799.

CLAYTON, Henry (1804-1869). Major General. 3rd European L.C. *b.* Ely 8 Sept. 1804. Cadet 1820. Arrived in India May 1821. Cornet 16 Jan. 1821. Lieut. 6 Mar. 1823. Capt. 16 June 1835. Major 6 Sept. 1851. Lt. Col. 28 Nov. 1854. Bt. Col. 18 May 1856. Retired 31 Dec. 1861. Hon. Maj. Gen. 31 Dec. 1861. *d.* 4 Cedars Rd., Clapham Common, 17 May 1869.
2nd son of George Clayton, of Stonehall, Surrey (who was younger brother of Sir William Clayton, 4th Bart.), Col. 3rd Fus. Gds., and Frances his wife, dau. of Right Rev. John Hinchcliffe, bishop of Peterborough. *m.* 9 Aug. 1826, Jean Henrietta, dau. of Sir Robert Blair, K.C.B., *q.v.* (*See also* William Kennedy, Thomas Reynolds, William Swinton, and John Waterfield.) (She died 1 Feb. 1880.)
Services : Posted as Cornet to 4th L.C. With G.G.B.G. 25 Nov. 1824 till Aug. 1825. Siege and capture of Bhurtpore ; Lieut. 4th

L.C. (India medal). S.A.C.G. 30 Dec. 1826. Dy. Paymr., Benares, 2 July 1828 till 1839. Gwalior campaign; Maharajpur; D.Q.M.G. of Cav. Div. (Bronze star). Transfd. to newy-raised 3rd Eur. L.C. in 1858. Fur. 1858 till retirement.
Refs.: Burke's *Peerage*, 1923, p. 804, *s.n.* Clayton-East, Bart. Foster's *Families of Royal Descent*, ii. 813. *V.B.G. The Times*, 24 May 1869.

CLAYTON, Thomas William (1763/64-1804). Lieut. Colonel, 18th N.I. *b.* 1763/64. Cadet 1771. Arrived in India 10 Dec. 1771. Ensign 30 Mar. 1773. Lieut. 27 May 1778. Capt. 21 Jan. 1784. Major 1797. Lt. Col. 29 May 1800. *d.* Barrackpore, 22 Sept. 1804, aged 50.
m. 10 Nov. 1787, Miss Emma Maria Jenkins. Father of Charles Edward Clayton, *q.v.*, and of Emma Maria, wife of George Barker (1786-1819), *q.v.*
Services: Capt. 3rd Bengal Eur. Regt. in 1796. Major 2/1st N.I. Transfd. as Lt. Col. to 2/18th N.I. 29 May 1800; to 20th N.I. Second Mahratta War; reduction of Cuttack 1803; capture of Barabati fort; Lt. Col. 20th N.I.
Refs.: Will dated Barrackpore 1 Aug. 1803; proved in 1804. M.I. in Barrackpore cemetery records the fact that " he saved the forfeited lives of three hundred men at the assault of Barrahbutty Fort, Cuttack, A.D. 1803."

CLEARIHUE, James (*d.* 1770). Capt. Lieutenant, Artillery. Cadet 1764. Fireworker 11 Oct. 1764. Lieut. 8 July 1769. Capt. Lt. 11 July 1770. *d.* Monghyr (? Calcutta) 9 Sept. 1770.
Son of John Clearihue, of Edinburgh, and Jane his wife. Brother of Janet, wife of Lachlan McBane, and of Mary, wife of James Hutchison, of Edinburgh.
Services: Resigned his Commission during the Batta mutiny in May 1766; re-admitted 19 Oct. 1766. N.F.P.
Refs.: Will dated 8 Sept. 1770; proved 25 Sept. 1770.

*CLELAND, David. Ensign, Infantry. Cadet (?). Ensign 7 Sept. 1766.
Services: N.F.P.
Refs.: *B.M. Add. MS.* 6050.

CLELOW or CLEWLOW, Charles (1758/59-1782). Lieutenant, Infantry. *b.* in Ireland 1758/59. Cadet 1766. Ensign 9 Apr. 1777. Lieut. 25 Aug. 1778. *d.* Bijegarh, U.P., 25 Oct. 1782.
Services: Sailed for India on the *Egmont*, 1 Jan. 1777, aged 17. N.F.P.

THE BENGAL ARMY, 1758-1834 351

CLEMENT, Francis William (1808-1830). Lieutenant, Engineers. *b.* Montreal, Canada, 26 Mar. 1808. Cadet 1827. 2nd Lieut. (?). Lieut. 28 Sept. 1827. *d.* Aligarh 24 June 1830.
Son of John Alcock Clement, Col. R.A., and Margaret his wife. Addiscombe Cadet 1825-6.
Services : Serving with Sappers at Aligarh at date of death. No record of active service.
Refs. : A.J. N.S. iv. 37. Will dated Aligarh 23 June 1830; proved 27 Aug. 1830.

CLEMENTS, Daniel. Cadet. Infantry. Cadet 1768. Resigned 1769.
Services : N.F.P.

CLEOBURY, Christopher (1755/56-1802). Captain, Bengal European Regt. *b.* 1755/56. Cadet 1780. Arrived in India 27 Sept. 1780. Ensign 22 Mar. 1781. Lieut. 4 July 1781. Capt. 1799. *d. unm.* Dinapore 21 Oct. 1802.
A native of Bucks. Brother of William Cleobury, of Gt. Marlow, Bucks., surgeon, and of Rev. John Cleobury, of Abingdon, Berks. Uncle of Mortimer Cleobury.
Services : Sailed for India on the *Duke of Portland*, 12 Feb. 1780, aged 24. Fur. 31 Oct. 1786 till 28 Aug. 1788. Bt. Capt. 5th N.I. in June 1798.
Refs. : Will dated Dinapore 26 Sept. 1801 ; proved 23 Jan. 1803.

CLEPHANE, George (1775-1799). Ensign, Engineers. *b.* Kirkness 8 Oct. 1775. Cadet 1793. Ensign 17 Oct. 1794. *d.* Baragaon, nr. Dinapore, 14 Jan. 1799 : kld. in action against a refractory rajah.
bapt. Kirkness 18 Oct. 1775. Son of George Clephane, of Carselogie, and Jean Ann Douglas his wife.
Services : " We mention with concern, the loss of a very promising young officer, Ensign Clephane, of the Engineer Corps. This gentleman being at Dinapore, and not particularly employed, volunteered his services to go against a refractory rajah, in the vicinity of Burragong. A party was sent out, which Ensign Clephane headed ; and in the execution of this duty, he was repulsed by numbers, with the loss of his own and other lives." (*A.A.R.* i. 114.)
Refs. : Anderson, i. 651, *s.n.* Clephane, of Carselogie.

CLERK, Henry (1803-1838). Captain, Artillery. *b.* Pilton, Somerset, 17 Aug. 1803. Cadet 1819. Arrived in India Feb. 1821. 2nd Lieut. 16 June 1820. Lieut. 1 May 1824. Capt. 27 Jan. 1837. *d. unm.* Saugor 20 Apr. 1838.
3rd son of Thomas Clerk, of Westholme, Somerset, Capt. Madras

Est., and Dorothy his wife, widow of Jeremiah Adderton, and dau. of John Taylor, of Townhead, Lancs. Cousin-german of John Clerk, *q.v.* Addiscombe Cadet 1818-20.

Services : Siege and capture of Bhurtpore ; Lieut. and Adjt. 6th Bn. Foot Art. (Golandaz). Fur. s.c. 31 Dec. 1829 till 19 Oct. 1833.

Refs. : Burke's *Landed Gentry*, 13th edn., p. 353, *s.n.* Clerk, of Westholme, Somerset. Foster's *Families of Royal Descent*, i. 284. Will dated 15 Feb. 1836 ; proved 30 Mar. 1839.

CLERK, John (1802-1821). Lieutenant, 4th L.C. *b.* Worting, Hants, 19 Nov. 1802. Cadet 1818. Cornet (?) Lieut. 16 Mar. 1820. *d.* 1 Oct. 1821 : kld. in action at Mangrol, Rajputana.

bapt. Worting 23 Dec. 1802. 2nd son of John Clerk, of Worthy (Worting), Hants, and Anne his 2nd wife, 2nd dau. of Carew Mildmay, of Shawford House, Hants, and of Mildmay Park, Stoke Newington. Younger brother of Sir George Russell Clerk, G.C.S.I. (*D.N.B.*), and cousin-german of Henry Clerk, *q.v.* Educ. Sandhurst. " Permitted to proceed to Bengal as passenger on the *General Hewett* under charge of Col. Campbell, with a view to his being appointed a Cadet of Cavalry upon his attaining the age of 16, which will take place in November next." (Resolution of C.D. dated 6 Mar. 1818.)

Services : Cornet d.d. 4th L.C. in 1819. Adjt. 4th L.C. 1820 till death. Operations in Kotah ; Mangrol (kld.) ; Lieut. 4th L.C.

Refs. : Burke's *Landed Gentry*, 13th edn., p. 353, *s.n.* Clerk, of Westholme, Somerset. Foster's *Families of Royal Descent*, i. 288. Will proved 10 Nov. 1821. M.I. in Cheltenham parish church.

CLERKSON, Henry Chambers (1796-1827). Lieutenant, 41st N.I. *b.* Calcutta 22 May 1796. Cadet 1811. Ensign 7 Oct. 1814. Lieut. 24 June 1817. *d.* on the Ganges, off Bhagulpur, 20 May 1827.

Son of John Clerkson, *q.v.*, and Aurora Catherine his wife.

Services : Posted as Ensign to 1/21st N.I. Transfd. to 42nd N.I. (late 2/21st) May 1824 ; to 41st N.I. Aug. 1824. Adjt. 41st N.I. 21 Aug. 1824 till death. Siege and capture of Bhurtpore ; Lieut. 41st N.I.

CLERKSON, John (*d.* 1801). Lieut. Colonel, 4th N.I. Cadet 1772. Arrived in India 3 Oct. 1772. Ensign 15 July 1776. Lieut. 4 July 1778. Capt. 15 Jan. 1793. Major 31 Aug. 1798. Lt. Col. 8 Jan. 1801. *d.* Cawnpore 13 June 1801.

m. Calcutta, 23 Nov. 1793, Miss Aurora Catherine Maxwell. Father of Henry Chambers Clerkson, *q.v.*

Services : First Rohilla War ; battle of St. George ; Cadet, with 2nd Bn. Sepoys. A.D.C. to Col. George Bolton Eyres, *q.v.*, in 1790.

THE BENGAL ARMY, 1758-1834

Capt. 3rd Bengal Eur. Regt. in 1796. Major 8th N.I. Transfd. as Lt. Col. to 4th N.I. in 1801.
Refs. : *S.M.* 1802, p. 372.

CLEWLOW, Charles. (*See* **CLELOW, Charles.**)

CLIFFORD, Robert Wigram (1812-?). Cornet. Cavalry. *b.* Wexford 11 May 1812. Cadet 1828. Arrived in India 4 May 1829. Cornet 8 Jan. 1829. Resigned 15 Jan. 1831. *d.* 1858 (?).
bapt. 12 May 1812. Son of John Clifford, of Wexford, yeoman, and Ann his wife.
Note : The following is conjectural only : (? Of Carn Cottage, Belturbet, co. Cavan. *m.* Mary, dau. of Rev. Thomas Williams, Army chaplain. (She died 1876.))
Services : Cornet d.d. 4th L.C. 10 June 1829.
Refs. : (? *Walford*, 1900 edn., p. 203.)

CLIFFORD, William (1799-1837). Captain, 39th N.I. *b.* Wexford 21 Nov. 1799. Cadet 1820. Arrived in India 7 Mar. 1822. Ensign 3 Sept. 1821. Lieut. 1 May 1824. Capt. 1 Oct. 1832. *d.* Nimach 27 Sept. 1837.
Son of James Clifford, of Wexford, master builder.
Services : Posted as Ensign to 19th N.I. Transfd. to 39th N.I. (late 2/19th) 1 May 1824. Adjt. 39th N.I. 1 May 1829 till 24 Nov. 1831. Fur. s.c. 31 Jan. 1832 till 17 July 1835. No record of active service.

CLIFTON, Charles. Capt. Lieutenant. Artillery. Cadet (?). 2nd Lieut. 4 Sept. 1763. Lieut. 5 Oct. 1763. Capt. Lt. 13 Mar. 1765. Resigned 6 May 1766.
m. Margaret Jones.
Services : N.F.P. *Probably* resigned his Commission in connexion with the mutinous combination against Lord Clive's new batta regulations.

CLODE, William. Major. Infantry. Cadet 1766. Ensign 11 Dec. 1766. Lieut. 5 Apr. 1768. Capt. 1 July 1776. Major 29 Jan. 1781. Struck off 1793.
Services : On fur. in 1790. N.F.P.

CLOSE, Frederick Alfred (1811-1891). Lieut. Colonel. 65th N.I. *b.* Ripon, Yorks., 1 May 1811. Cadet 1828. Arrived in, India 5 May 1829. Ensign 4 Dec. 1828. Lieut. 15 Oct. 1834. Capt. 21 June 1843. Bt. Major 20 June 1854. Retired 1 Oct. 1855. Hon. Lt. Col. 1 Oct. 1855. *d.* 22 Clanricarde Gdns., London, 4 June 1891.
bapt. 29 May 1811. Son of John Close, consul at Charente,

France, originally of Easby, Yorks. Nephew of Leonard Currie, of Stanlake, Berks. m. St. James's, London, 2 Nov. 1859, Eliza Millbank, 2nd dau. of William J. Thompson, M.D.
Services : Ensign d.d. 50th N.I. 10 June 1829. Posted as Ensign to 65th N.I. 14 Sept. 1829. Tempy. Asst. to Resdt. at Indore Jan. 1833. Fur. s.c. 19 Sept. 1838 till 28 Aug. 1841. Comdt. 2nd Cav., Gwalior Contingent, 8 Jan. 1846. Comdt. 1st Cav., Gwalior Contingent, 30 Mar. 1855 till retirement.
Refs. : Burke's *Landed Gentry,* 13th edn., p. 443, *s.n.* Currie, late of Seafield Park. Foster's *Baronetage,* p. 166, *s.n.* Currie, Bart. *The Times,* 6 June 1891.

CLOUGH, Henry Butler (1789-1823). Bt. Captain, 17th N.I. *b.* 1789. Cadet 1804. Arrived in India 28 Feb. 1806. Ensign 4 May 1806. Lieut. 4 Apr. 1807. Bt. Capt. 1 Jan. 1819. *d.* Calcutta 16 May 1823.

bapt. Henllan, co. Denbigh, 20 Apr. 1789. 3rd son of Rev. Roger Clough, of Bathafern Park, co. Denbigh, canon of St. Asaph and rector of Llansannan, co. Denbigh, and Anna Jemima his wife, eldest dau. of James Butler, of Warminghurst Park, Sussex. Ed. Eton ; K.S. 1802.
Services : Posted as Ensign to 2/17th N.I. Nepal War 1814-5 ; Lieut. 2/17th N.I., in 3rd Div. Bt. Capt. 2/17th N.I.
Refs. : Burke's *Landed Gentry,* 13th edn., p. 359, *s.n.* Clough, of Llwyn Offa, co. Denbigh. *Eton School Lists.*

COATES, Humphrey (*d.* 1782). Lieutenant, Artillery. Cadet (?). Fireworker 1776. Lieut. 24 Sept. 1778. *d.* in China 1782.
Services : First Mahratta War 1778-81 ; with Gen. Goddard's detachment. Was probably on sick leave in China at date of death.

COATES, Philip. Lieutenant. Infantry. Cadet 1769. Ensign 3 Sept. 1769. Lieut. 7 Feb. 1773. Resigned 22 July 1773.
Services : N.F.P.

*COATS, John (*d.* 1765). Ensign, Infantry. Cadet (?). Ensign (?). *d.* 1765.
Stepson of James Langdale, of N. Alington (? Northallerton), Yorks., grocer. Brother of Thomas and William Coats.
Services : N.F.P.
Refs. : Will dated " before Bannass " 16 Nov. 1764 ; proved 5 Nov. 1765.

COBBE, Charles Henry (1803-1871). Major. 60th N.I. *b.* Colchester 13 Aug. 1803. Cadet 1820. Admitted 5 June 1821. Ensign 16 Jan. 1821. Lieut. 11 July 1823. Capt. 12 July 1833.

Invalided 15 Apr. 1842. Retired 10 Oct. 1850. Hon. Major 28 Nov. 1854. d. Jersey 20 Nov. 1871.

Elder son of George Cobbe, Gen. R.A., and Amelia his wife, dau. of Rev. Royston Barton. Nephew of Thomas Alexander Cobbe, q.v. m. 1st, Berhampore, 3 Oct. 1832, Sarah, dau. of Col. James Dennis, H.M. 49th Regt. m. 2nd, Woolwich, 15 Oct. 1835, Anne, eldest dau. of Col. William Gravatt, R.E. m. 3rd, Lewisham, 2 July 1864, Louisa, youngest dau. of John Knox, of Greenwich.

Services : Posted as Ensign to 1/7th N.I. Transfd. as Lieut. to 2/30th N.I. ; to 60th N.I. (late 2/30th) May 1824. Siege and capture of Bhurtpore; Lieut. 60th N.I. (India medal). Fur. s.c. 14 Dec. 1833 till 8 July 1837. Offg. D.J.A.G. in 1839.

Refs. : Burke's *Landed Gentry of Ireland*, p. 118, *s.n.* Cobbe, of Newbridge House, co. Dublin. *Howard & Crisp's Ireland*, iv. 2, *s.n.* Heaton-Armstrong, of Roscrea, King's Co. *A.J.* N.S. xviii. 195. *G.M.* 1864, ii. 236. *The Times*, 23 Nov. 1871.

COBBE, Thomas Alexander (1788-1836). Lieut. Colonel, 37th N.I. *b.* Bath 31 Aug. 1788. Cadet 1804. Arrived in India 10 Sept. 1805. Ensign, rank not assigned. Lieut. 25 Aug. 1804. Capt. 9 Sept. 1817. Major 25 Dec. 1827. Lt. Col. 1 Dec. 1832. *d.* at sea, 27 July 1836, on board the *Robarts*, of a paralytic stroke.

bapt. Walcot, Bath, 17 Jan. 1789. 4th son of Charles Cobbe, of Newbridge House, co. Dublin, M.P., and Anne Power Trench his wife, sister of William, first Earl of Clancarty, and aunt of Hon. Luke Henry Trench, *q.v.* Uncle of Charles Henry Cobbe, *q.v.* *m.* Nuzzeer Begum, dau. of Aziz Khan, of Kashmir. Marlow Cadet.

Services : Lieut. 2/6th N.I. A.D.C. to the G.G., the Earl of Moira, 4 Oct. 1813. (? Nepal War 1814-5 ; Lieut. 2/6th N.I., in 1st Div.) Dy. Paymr. Nagpur Subsdy. Force 12 Aug. 1817. Garrison Storekeeper, Fort William, 28 Oct. 1818. Sec. to Mily. Board 28 Feb. 1820. Transfd. to 18th N.I. (late 2/6th) May 1824. P.A. at Udaipur 1822-31. A.G.G. at Murshidabad 4 Mar. 1831 till 29 Jan. 1836. Leave s.c. 5 mos. to Mauritius 31 July 1833. Posted as Lt. Col. to 37th N.I. 29 July 1833. Fur. s.c. 15 Mar. 1836.

Refs. : Burke's *Landed Gentry of Ireland*, p. 118, *s.n.* Cobbe, of Newbridge House, co. Dublin. *A.J.* N.S. xxi. 53. Will dated on board *Indian Oak* 11 Aug. 1833 ; proved 23 Dec. 1836.

COCHRAN, Dewar (*d.* 1785). Ensign, Infantry. Cadet 1782. Ensign 14 Jan. 1783. *d.* Calcutta 11 Mar. 1785.
Services : N.F.P.

COCHRANE, George D——. *See* **COCKRIN.**)

356 LIST OF THE OFFICERS OF

*COCHRANE, —— (d. 1760). Captain, Bengal European Regt. Cadet (?). Ensign 23 May 1757. Lieut. (?). Capt. (?). d. 9 Feb. 1760 : kld. in action at the battle of Masimpur, nr. Patna.
Services : N.F.P.
Refs. : Orme MSS., India, xiii. 3639. *Broome,* pp. 280, 282. *Innes,* p. 114.

COCK, Alexander (1786-1823). Captain, Invalid Est. 6th L.C. *b.* London 1 Feb. 1786. Cadet 1800. Arrived in India 14 Oct. 1801. Cornet 14 Mar. 1803. Lieut. 1 Nov. 1809. Capt. 27 Oct. 1818. Invalided 15 Aug. 1823. *d.* Buxar 21 Sept. 1823.

bapt. St. Margaret Lothbury and St. Christopher-le-Stocks, London, 25 Feb. 1786. Son of James Cock and Elizabeth his wife. Brother of Henry Cock, *q.v.*, and nephew of John Cock, of Bengal. *m.* St. John's, Calcutta, 10 Dec. 1822, Charlotte Frederica Sherin, widow.

Services : Posted as Cornet to 6th L.C. and served with that Regt. throughout. (? Second Mahratta War ; Laswari ; pursuit of Holkar. Settlement of Hariana 1809 ; Bhawani. Third Mahratta War ; Sitabaldi ; Nagpur.)
Refs. : Will dated 17 Sept. 1823 ; proved 18 Oct. 1823.

COCK, Henry (1787-1851). Colonel, C.B. 64th N.I. *b.* London 14 Dec. 1787. Cadet 1804. Arrived in India 10 Sept. 1805. Ensign 24 Aug. 1804. Lieut. 25 Aug. 1804. Capt. 1 Aug. 1818. Major 29 Apr. 1826. Lt. Col. 4 June 1831. Col. 10 Apr. 1843. *d.* Hopton Hall, nr. Lowestoft, Suffolk, 17 Feb. 1851.

bapt. St. Margaret Lothbury, London, 12 Jan. 1788. Son of James Cock and Elizabeth his wife. Brother of James Cock, *q.v. m.* St. George's, Hanover Sq., London, 22 Oct. 1828, Mary, 3rd dau. of John Deane, of the Rectory, Gt. Marlow, Bucks. Marlow Cadet.

Services : Posted as Lieut. to 2/4th N.I. Adjt. 2/4th N.I. 1811-4. Intr. & Qmr. 1 July 1814 till 30 Jan. 1818. Nepal War 1816 ; Lieut. 2/4th N.I., in 4th Bde., Centre Column. Third Mahratta War 1817-8 ; in Bdr.-Gen. W. Toone's Bde. 1st Ceylon Vol. Bn, 10 Aug. 1818. Bde. Major at Dinapore 18 Dec. 1820. Leave s.c. 30 May 1821 till 28 Jan. 1824. Transfd. to 23rd N.I. (late 2/4th) May 1824. Siege and capture of Bhurtpore ; Capt. 23rd N.I. Returned from fur. 5 Nov. 1832. Transfd. to 32nd N.I. 7 Jan. 1832 ; to 23rd N.I. 1 Dec. 1832 ; to 30th N.I. 2 Oct. 1833. Bdr. 2 cl., comdg. in Rohilkhand, Jan.-Feb. 1835. Transfd. to 29th N.I. 29 Nov. 1836 ; to 23rd N.I. 29 Apr. 1837 ; to 52nd N.I. ; to 64th N.I. in 1850. Fur. 21 Jan. 1838 till 24 Aug. 1842, and 17 June 1843 till death. C.B. 20 July 1838.
Refs. : Boase. G.M. 1828, ii. 462 ; 1851, i. 452.

THE BENGAL ARMY, 1758-1834 357

COCK, James (1780-1851). Major General. Colonel 9th N.I. *b.* Glasgow 16 July 1780. Cadet 1795. Arrived in India 2 Feb. 1797. Ensign 11 Oct. 1796. Lieut. 30 Oct. 1797. Capt. 27 Sept. 1807. Major 17 May 1815. Lt. Col. 20 Mar. 1821. Lt. Col. Comdt. 30 May 1824. Col. 5 June 1829. Maj. Gen. 28 June 1838. *d.* Hopton Hall, nr. Lowestoft, Suffolk, 17 Mar. 1851. Of Hopton Hall. *bapt.* Glasgow 19 July 1780. Son of James Cock and Elizabeth his wife. Brother of Alexander Cock, *q.v. m.* Whitsbury, Hants, 27 Aug. 1829, Georgiana Mary, youngest dau. of Rev. Thomas Baker, of Rollesby, Norfolk. (She died on board the *London* 3 Apr. 1840.)
Services : To do duty on the voyage out with a detachment of recruits at the Cape. Posted to 7th N.I. Transfd. as Lieut. to 1/18th N.I. 29 May 1800. Operations in Bundelkhand 1803 ; Lieut. 1/18th N.I., with force under Lt.-Col. Peregrine Powell, *q.v.* Second Mahratta War ; capture of Deig ; siege of Bhurtpore ; Lieut. 1/18th N.I. Transfd. to 2/21st N.I. Nepal War 1814-5. Nepal War 1816 ; action at Harriharpur ; Major comdg. Left Wing of 2/21st N.I. (India medal, but died before it was issued). Transfd. as Lt. Col. to 1/12th N.I. Lt. Col. Comdt. 12th N.I. (late 1/12th) May 1824. Col. 12th N.I. in 1829. Fur. 21 Jan. 1828 till 24 Jan. 1836. Col. 51st N.I. in 1838 ; 9th N.I. in 1846. Bdr. comdg. Benares Div. 25 Apr. 1838. Fur. 17 Mar. 1843 till death.
Refs. : Boase. A.J. xxviii. 509. *G.M.* 1851, i. 571.

COCK, Robert (1784-1816). Capt. Lieutenant, 26th N.I. *b.* Madeira 17 Nov. 1784. Cadet 1800. Arrived in India 14 Oct. 1801. Ensign 29 Oct. 1801. Lieut. 13 July 1803. Capt. Lt. 16 Dec. 1814. *d.* at sea, 30 Sept. 1816, on board the transport *Mary Anne*, on his passage from Java.
Son of Robert Cock, vice-consul at Madeira.
Services : Posted as Ensign to 9th N.I. (? Second Mahratta War ; Lieut. 9th N.I.) Transfd. to newly-raised 1/26th N.I. in Oct. 1804. Operations in Bundelkhand 1807 ; Sehlehuganj. Capture of Java 1811 ; Lieut. 4th Bengal L.I. Bn. Adjt. L.I. Bn. in 1814. Comdg. Left Wing of L.I. Bn. in 1816.
Refs. : A.J. iii. 622.

COCKAY, Peter. Ensign. Infantry. Cadet 1761. Ensign 11 Oct. 1761. Dismissed 30 June 1762.
Services : N.F.P.

COCKBURN, Henry De Waal (1808-1831). Lieutenant, Artillery. *bapt.* Chelmsford 18 July 1808. Cadet 1824. Arrived in India 11 June 1825. 2nd Lieut. 16 Dec. 1824. Lieut. 21 Apr. 1828. *d.* in camp nr. Agra 20 Jan. 1831.

Son of John Cockburn, Col. R.A. Addiscombe Cadet 1823-4.
Services : No record of active service.
Refs. : *A.J.* N.S. vi. 20.

COCKBURN, James (*d.* 1770). Lieutenant, Artillery. Cadet (?). Fireworker Sept. 1768. Lieut. 10 Mar. 1770. *d.* Bankipore, B. & O., 10 May 1770.
Services : N.F.P.

COCKBURN, John (1789-?). Lieutenant. Bengal European Regt. *b.* London 13 Oct. 1789. Cadet 1806. Arrived in India 1 Aug. 1807. Ensign 25 July 1807. Lieut. 22 Jan. 1812. Resigned in India 16 Apr. 1814.
Son of James Cockburn.
Services : Posted as Ensign to Bengal Eur. Regt. in 1808. Served in Java 1812-3.

COCKER, John. (*See* **COKER.**)

COCKERELL, John (1753-1798). Bt. Colonel. Infantry. *b.* 10 Aug. 1753. Cadet 1764. Ensign 22 May 1766. Lieut. 15 Sept. 1767. Capt. 26 June 1771. Major 18 Jan. 1781. Lt. Col. 2 Feb. 1788. Bt. Col. 1795. Retired May 1796. *d. unm.* Conduit St., London, 6 July 1798.
Eldest son of John Cockerell, of Bishop's Hull, nr. Taunton, and Frances his wife, dau. of John Jackson, of Clapham, Surrey. Elder brother of Sir Charles Cockerell, 1st Bart., B.C.S.
Services : Went out to India in 1764 in the suite of Sir Robert Barker, *q.v.* Mily. Sec. to Sir Robert Barker, C.-in-C., Bengal, 1767-74, whom he accompanied to England in the latter year. Returned to India in 1776. With the Bombay detachment in the first Mahratta war under Cols. Leslie and Goddard, 1779-84, as Q.M.G. Third Mysore War ; Bangalore ; Seringapatam ; Lt. Col. comdg. the Bengal detachment. Returned to England in 1793.
Refs. : Burke's *Peerage*, 1923, p. 1926, *s.n.* Rushout, Bart. *E.I.M.C.* i. 114. *G.M.* 1798, ii. 635.
Note : Although 1753 is given as the year of his birth by Burke, yet it appears more probable that he was born *c.* 1749/50.

COCKRIN (? COCHRANE), George D—— (*d.* 1783). Lieutenant, Infantry. Cadet 1776. Ensign 7 May 1777. Lieut. 5 Aug. 1778. *d.* at sea, 1783, on his passage from Bombay.
Services : (? First Mahratta War.) N.F.P.

CODRINGTON, Christopher (1807-1841). Bt. Captain, 49th N.I. *b.* Jersey 27 June 1807. Cadet 1825. Arrived in India 16 May 1826. Ensign 5 Nov. 1825. Lieut. 27 May 1830. Bt. Capt.

5 Nov. 1840. *d.* 5 Nov. 1841 : kld. in action during the defence of Charikar, Kohistan.

Son of Christopher Codrington, Surgeon on the Staff, and Martha his wife, of Portsea. Brother of Robert Codrington, *q.v.* *m.* Karnal, 19 Mar. 1832, Julia Isabella, dau. of Mark Carter Webber, *q.v.* (She died 25 Mar. 1894.)

Services : Posted as Ensign to 49th N.I. Adjt. 8 Oct. 1829 till 17 Sept. 1838. Adjt. Shah Shuja's 2nd Inf. 17 Aug. 1838. First Afghan War ; defence of Charikar Nov. 1841 (kld.) ; comdg. 4th (Gurkha) Inf., Shah's army. Durani, 3 cl., 12 Sept. 1841.

Refs. : *Howard & Crisp,* xvi. 25. Will dated 27 Aug. 1837 ; proved 1 Feb. 1843.

CODRINGTON, Robert (1805-1847). Bt. Lieut. Colonel, 49th N.I. *bapt.* Colchester 13 Mar. 1805. Cadet 1820. Arrived in India 19 Nov. 1821. Ensign 4 July 1821. Lieut. 1 May 1824. Capt. 4 Aug. 1829. Bt. Major 23 Dec. 1842. Bt. Lt. Col. 3 Apr. 1846. *d.* at sea, 22 Jan. 1847, on board the *Wellesley,* as the result of wounds received at the battle of Mudki on 18 Dec. 1845.

Son of Christopher Codrington and Martha his wife. Brother of Christopher Codrington, *q.v.* *m.* Kilve, Somerset, 11 Nov. 1834, Susan Elizabeth, 3rd dau. of Rev. John Matthew, rector of Kilve and Stringston. (She died Simla 21 June 1841.)

Services : Posted to 2/7th N.I. in Apr. 1822. Transfd. to 2/20th N.I. 19 Apr. 1822 ; to 49th N.I. May 1824. First Burma War 1824-6 ; disaster at Ramu ; Lieut. 40th N.I. (late 2/20th), one of three surviving officers ; Arakan 1825 ; with tempy. corps of Pioneers. Adjt. tempy. Pioneers 11 Feb. 1825. Bde. Major L.I. Bde. in Arakan 5 Aug. 1825. Adjt. 49th N.I. 14 Feb. 1826 till Oct. 1829. Fur. 5 Feb. 1832 till 24 July 1835. D.A.Q.M.G., 2 cl., 10 Apr. 1837 ; do., 1 cl., 1 Dec. 1838. 1st A.Q.M.G. of the Army 13 Jan. 1842. First Afghan War 1842 ; forcing of Khyber Pass ; Tezin ; Haft Kotal ; re-occupation of Kabul ; with Gen. Pollock's force (Medal). First Sikh War ; Mudki (s.w.) ; A.Q.M.G. (Medal). Leave s.c. to Cape Dec. 1846.

Refs. : *De Rhé-Philipe.* *A.J.* N.S. xv. 240. *G.M.* 1849, i. 679. Will dated 10 Nov. 1846 ; proved 13 July 1847.

COKE, Sir John (1806-1897). Major General, K.C.B. 10th N.I. Comdt. 1st Punjab Inf. *b.* 17 Nov. 1806. Cadet 1827. Arrived in India 1 June 1828. Ensign 3 Dec. 1827. Lieut. 29 Aug. 1835. Capt. 28 Mar. 1848. Major 18 Nov. 1857. Bt. Lt. Col. 19 Jan. 1858. Bt. Col. 20 July 1858. Retired 31 Dec. 1861. Hon. Maj. Gen. 31 Dec. 1861. *d.* Lemore, Eardisley, 18 Dec. 1897.

Of Lemore House, co. Hereford, J.P. and D.L. co. Hereford, High

Sheriff 1879. *bapt.* Eardisley 27 Feb. 1807. 4th son of Rev. Francis Coke, J.P., rector of Gladestry, co. Radnor, vicar of Selack and Caple, co. Hereford, and prebendary of Hereford, and Anne his wife, dau. of Robert Whitcombe, of Kington.
Services : Posted as Ensign to 10th N.I. 29 Nov. 1828. Adjt. 10th N.I. 9 Sept. 1835 till 10 Mar. 1845. Fur. 21 Feb. 1845 till 1848. Second Sikh War ; Chilianwala (horse shot under him) ; Gujerat ; Capt. 10th N.I., as a volunteer with 2nd Irreg. Cav. (Medal with clasp). Raised 1st Punjab Inf. at Peshawar 18 May 1849, and comdd. that Regt. till 1858. Against Yusafzais 1849-50 and 1852. Against the Afridis, nr. Kohat, Nov. 1853 ; Orakzais 1855 ; Miranzai 1855-6 ; Bozdars 1857 (w.). Mutiny campaign ; comdd. Moveable Column at Delhi 4 July till 12 Aug. 1857 ; wounded at capture of the guns at Ludow Castle ; comdd. a Bde. in Rohilkhand 1858 (Medal with clasp). C.B. 21 Jan. 1858. K.C.B. 24 May 1881.
Refs. : Burke's *Landed Gentry*, 10th edn., p. 298, *s.n.* Coke, of Lemore, co. Hereford. *D.I.B. The Times*, 20 Dec. 1897. The *Pioneer*, Allahabad, 10 Nov. 1912.

COKER or COCKER, John (1737/38-?). Captain. Infantry. *b.* Stepney, Middlesex, 1737/38. Cadet 1760. Ensign 8 July 1762. Lieut. 13 Oct. 1763. Capt. 9 Aug. 1765. Resigned May 1766.
Services : Sailed for India on the *Norfolk* in 1760, aged 22. Resigned his Commission during the " Batta mutiny " of 1766.
Note : John R. Cocker, of Lower Grosvenor St., London, *d.* 10 Mar. 1820.

COLE, William (1804-1833). Lieutenant, 67th N.I. *bapt.* Whitwell, I.W., 4 Oct. 1804. Cadet 1823. Arrived in India 3 Sept. 1824. Ensign 24 Apr. 1824. Lieut. 2 Oct. 1827. *d.* Banda, U.P., 22 Sept. 1833.
3rd son of Robert Cole, of Newport, I.W., banker, Capt. of the Niton Inf., Major I.W. Vols., and Elizabeth his wife, dau. of Henry Dennett, of Newport.
Services : Posted as Ensign to 67th N.I. First Burma War 1825.
Refs. : Burke's *Landed Gentry*, 7th edn., p. 376, *s.n.* Cole, of Hill House, Brading, I.W. *G.M.* 1834, ii. 335.

COLEBROOKE, Philip (1761/62-1782). Lieutenant, Infantry. *b.* London 1761/62. Cadet 1778. Ensign 1778. Lieut. 16 Oct. 1778. *d.* Madras 1782.
Services : Sailed for India on the *Gatton*, 27 Apr. 1778, aged 16. (? Second Mysore War.) N.F.P.

THE BENGAL ARMY, 1758-1834   361

COLEBROOKE, Richard (1800-1868).   Captain.   26th N.I.   *b.*
Calcutta 30 Dec. 1800. Cadet 1817. Ensign (?). Lieut. 1 Aug.
1818. Capt. 26 May 1825. Invalided 30 Dec. 1826. Retired
13 Aug. 1831. *d.* 23 Feb. 1868.

Son of Robert Hyde Colebrooke, *q.v.*, and Charlotte his wife.
Addiscombe Cadet 1817-8.

Services : Posted as Lieut. to 1/13th N.I. Transfd. to 27th N.I.
(late 2/13th) May 1824. Adjt. 27th N.I. 22 June 1824. Transfd.
as Capt. to 26th N.I. May 1825. At Chunar in 1827 ; at Monghyr
1827-8. Fur. s.c. 9 Jan. 1829 till retirement. No record of active
service.

COLEBROOKE, Robert Hyde (1762/63-1808). Lieut. Colonel, 22nd
N.I. Surveyor General, Bengal. *b.* in Switzerland 1762/63.
Cadet 1778. Arrived in India 10 Dec. 1778. Ensign 1778.
Lieut. 9 Nov. 1778. Capt. 7 Jan. 1796. Major 21 Feb. 1801.
Lt. Col. 2 Nov. 1803. *d.* Bhagulpur, B. & O., 21 Sept. 1808.

(*Probably* son of Robert Colebrooke, of Chilham Castle, Kent,
minister to the Swiss cantons 1762-4, and Elizabeth his 2nd wife,
dau. of John Thresher, of Bradford, Wilts.) *m.* Calcutta, 31 July
1795, Miss Charlotte Bristow. (*See also* James Tillyer Blunt.)
(She died Bath 2 July 1833.) Father of Richard Colebrooke, *q.v.*,
and of Frances Henrietta, 2nd wife of Joseph Taylor (1790-1835),
q.v.

Services : Second Mysore War 1781-5. Apptd. by Col. T. D.
Pearse, *q.v.*, on 15 Nov. 1783 to be surveyor to the detachment.
On the return march from Madras to Calcutta in 1785 he made a
survey of the route. The remainder of his service was passed in the
Survey Dept. Surveyor Gen. from before 1800 till death. Capt.
13th N.I. Major 13th N.I. Transfd. as Lt. Col. to 20th N.I. in
Nov. 1803 ; to 22nd N.I. in 1805.

Refs. : (? Burke's *Peerage*, 1923, p. 554, *s.n.* Colebrooke, B.)
Bath Chron. 4 May 1809. Will dated Lucknow 24 Dec. 1807 ;
proved 6 Oct. 1808.

COLEBROOKE, Thomas Elliot (1812-1864). Lieut. Colonel. 13th
N.I. Comdt. Ferozepore Sikhs. *b.* Madras 19 May 1812. Cadet
1828. Arrived in India 23 July 1829. Ensign 12 Dec. 1828.
Lieut. 2 Aug. 1836. Capt. 15 July 1845. Bt. Major 20 June
1854. Retired 10 Mar. 1855. Hon. Lt. Col. 11 May 1855. *d.*
Beechwood, Painswick, Gloucs., 9 Dec. 1864, of paralysis.

Son of Lt. Col. James Colebrooke, 8th Madras N.I., and Henrietta
his wife. Brother of William Henry Eastfield Colebrooke, *q.v.*, and
nephew of Thomas Cockburn. *m.* Allahabad, 14 July 1838, Mrs.
Eliza H. Wall. Addiscombe Cadet 1827-8.

Services : Posted as Ensign to 13th N.I. Fur. s.c. 5 Dec. 1832 till 5 Sept. 1835. Adjt. Hariana L.I. 5 Aug. 1836 till 1844. Operations in Bundelkhand 1842 ; Lieut. 13th N.I. Postmaster at Hansi 9 Mar. 1842. 2nd in comd. Hariana L.I. 11 Oct. 1844 till 27 Mar. 1849. Mily. Sec. to Presdt. of Council of India 15 Apr. 1850. Comdt. Ferozepore Sikhs 13 Jan. 1852 till retirement.
Refs. : *G.M.* 1865, i. 124. *The Times*, 13 Dec. 1864.

COLEBROOKE, William Henry Eastfield (1810-1835). Lieutenant, 66th N.I. *b.* Walajabad, Madras, 2 Aug. 1810. Cadet 1827. Arrived in India 30 Jan. 1829. Ensign 19 June 1828. Lieut. 21 Aug. 1834. *d.* Sikraul, Benares, 2 Apr. 1835.

Son of Lt. Col. James Colebrooke, 8th Madras N.I., and Henrietta his wife. Brother of Thomas Elliot Colebrooke, *q.v. m.* Calcutta, 2 Mar. 1830, Louisa, 2nd dau. of Samuel Houlton, *q.v.* (*See also* John (Edward) Cheetham.) (She *re-m.* Calcutta, 29 July 1835, John Castello.)

Services : Ensign d.d. 58th N.I. 23 Feb. 1829 ; do. 14th N.I. 3 Mar. 1829 ; do. 63rd N.I. 1829. Posted as Ensign to 14th N.I. 21 July 1829. Transfd. to 66th N.I. 22 Dec. 1832. No record of active service.
Refs. : *A.J.* N.S. xviii. 243.

COLEBY, Richard L—— (*d.* 1792). Brevet Ensign, Infantry. Cadet 1781. Bt. Ensign 1782. *d.* Moradbag, nr. Murshidabad, Bengal, 5 Feb. 1792.
Services : N.F.P. (*Probably* commissioned from the ranks.)

COLEMAN, James (1769-?). Ensign. Infantry. *bapt.* St. Andrew's, Holborn, Middlesex, 29 Nov. 1769. Cadet 1790. Ensign 17 Oct. 1792. Resigned 11 Mar. 1793.

Son of John Coleman and Elizabeth his wife.
Services : Entered H.M.S. Ensign 77th Foot 27 Sept. 1792.

COLERIDGE, Francis Syndercombe (1770-1792). Lieutenant, Infantry. *b.* 1770. Cadet 1782. Ensign 13 May 1783. Lieut. 5 June 1790. *d. unm.* Madras presidency, 21 Jan. 1792, aged 21.

7th son of Rev. John Coleridge, vicar of Ottery St. Mary, Devon, and Anne his 2nd wife, dau. of Roger Bowden. Brother of John Coleridge, *q.v.*, and of Samuel Taylor Coleridge, the poet (*D.N.B.*).
Services : Third Mysore War.
Refs. : Burke's *Peerage*, 1923, p. 555, *s.n.* Coleridge, B.

COLERIDGE, John (1755/56-1787). Captain, Infantry. *b.* 1755/56. Cadet 1770. Ensign 24 Nov. 1771. Lieut. 7 Aug. 1776. Capt. 28 Feb. 1781. *d. unm.* Tellicherry, Madras, Dec. 1787, aged 31.

Eldest son of Rev. John Coleridge, vicar of Ottery St. Mary, Devon, and Anne his 2nd wife. Brother of Francis Syndercombe Coleridge, q.v.
Services : First Mahratta War ; comdd. 6th Bn. Sepoys (became subsequently 3rd N.I.) and brought it back to Bengal in 1784.
Refs. : Burke's *Peerage*, 1923, p. 555, *s.n.* Coleridge, B.

COLES, John (1783-1802). Lieutenant, 9th N.I. *b.* Bridgwater, Somerset, 21 Feb. 1783. Cadet 1799. Arrived in India 13 Jan. 1801. Ensign 18 Aug. 1800. Lieut. 23 Nov. 1800. *d.* Calcutta 6 Mar. 1802.
bapt. Bridgwater 19 Mar. 1783. Son of James Coles and Mary his wife.
Services : Posted as Ensign to 1/9th N.I. No record of active service.

COLES, Thomas Hayes (1794-?). Lieutenant. Bengal European Regt. *b.* Kelso, co. Roxburgh, 3 May 1794. Cadet 1810. Ensign 13 Nov. 1813. Lieut. 4 Mar. 1816. Struck off 2 Mar. 1820.
Son of Thomas Coles, one of the Pages of H.M. Bedchamber.
Services : Cadet d.d. 9th N.I. 1811-3. Posted as Ensign to Bengal Eur. Regt. On fur. in 1817 till struck off. No record of active service.

COLLIER, Charles (1782-1818). Cornet, 1st N.C. *b.* London 19 Aug. 1782. Cadet 1808. Arrived in India 21 Oct. 1809. Cornet 14 Nov. 1812. *d. unm.* Muttra 23 May 1818.
5th and youngest son of Sir George Collier, Kt., of Foyle, Hants, Vice-Adm. of the Blue, M.P. for Honiton 1784 (*D.N.B.*), and Elizabeth his 2nd wife, dau. of William Fryer, of Exeter.
Services : Barasat C.C. Cornet d.d. 3rd N.C. 1811-2. Posted as Cornet to 7th N.C. 14 Dec. 1812. Transfd. to 1st N.C. 13 Mar. 1813. Mily. student at Coll. of Fort William 1813-4. Third Mahratta War ; Cornet 1st N.C., in Right Div.
Refs. : Burke's *Family Records*, p. 172.

COLLIER, James (*d.* 1801). Bt. Captain, Artillery. Country Cadet 1781. Admitted 10 Apr. 1781. Fireworker 11 Sept. 1781. Lieut. 6 Aug. 1787. Bt. Capt. 7 Jan. 1796. Capt. Lt. 8 Jan. 1796. *d. unm.* I.W. Sept. 1801.
Services : To Madras for siege of Pondicherry June-Oct. 1794. Served in Ceylon with 5th Coy. 2nd Bn. Art. from 19 Sept. 1796 till he proceeded on sick leave towards the end of 1797. Fur. 11 Jan. 1799 till death.
Refs. : Will dated 5 Feb. 1799 ; proved 24 Mar. 1802.

COLLINGS, William. (*See* **COLLINS.**)

COLLINS, Charles (*d.* 1769). Lieutenant, Engineers. Cadet 1765. Ensign 12 Nov. 1765. Lieut. 23 Jan. 1767. *d.* Nov. 1769.

Note : It appears probable that this officer, whose name is included in *Dodwell & Miles*, is identical with the following. There was only one officer of this name, a Lieut. of Inf., on the Bengal Est. on 1 Feb. 1767.

COLLINS, Charles (*d.* 1770). Lieutenant, Infantry. Cadet (?). Ensign 17 Aug. 1765. Lieut. 1 Jan. 1767. *d.* Calcutta 1 Feb. 1770.

Services : N.F.P.

COLLINS, Charles James Colin (1804-1833). Lieutenant, 25th N.I. *b.* Swansea 16 Feb. 1804. Cadet 1823. Arrived in India 7 Oct. 1824. Ensign 20 May 1824. Lieut. 20 July 1825. *d.* Malacca 2 July 1833.

Son of John Charles Collins, of Swansea, physician, and Elizabeth his wife. Brother of Colin MacFarquhar Collins, *q.v.*

Services : Posted as Ensign to 40th N.I. 31 Mar. 1825. (? First Burma War.) Fur. s.c. 1 Jan. 1826 till 1827. Transfd. to 25th N.I. in 1827. To comd. escort of Resdt. at Ava Feb. 1832. Leave s.c. to Straits 9 Apr. 1833.

Refs. : Will dated on board *Will Watch*, to Penang, 26 Apr. 1833 ; proved 10 Sept. 1833.

COLLINS, Colin MacFarquhar (1813-1896). Captain, Invalid Est. 25th N.I. *b.* Swansea 1 Jan. 1813. Cadet 1828. Arrived in India 5 May 1829. Ensign 8 Jan. 1829. Lieut. 7 Aug. 1834. Capt. 7 Nov. 1840. Invalided 3 May 1841. *d.* Mussoorie, 28 Feb. 1896.

Son of John Charles Collins, of Swansea, physician, and Elizabeth his wife. Brother of Charles James Colin Collins, *q.v.*

Services : Ensign d.d. 25th N.I. 10 June 1829. Posted as Ensign to 25th N.I. 14 Sept. 1829. Fur. s.c. 2 Dec. 1833 till 24 Nov. 1836. Whilst on reserve duty at Fort William in Apr. 1840, having stepped over a railing of a window, he fell from the top storey of the Royal barracks, a height of over 40 ft., on the pavement below, and was picked up with his jawbone smashed to pieces, his knee broken, and otherwise seriously injured. Leave s.c. 6 mos. to Straits 26 Mar. 1833. No record of active service.

Refs. : A.J. July 1840. *I.N.* vol. i. 12.

COLLINS, Henry John (1793-?). Ensign, Infantry. Never joined a Regt. *b.* Calcutta 30 Aug. 1793. Cadet 1810. Ensign 3 Mar. 1813. Struck off in England 1815.

Son of John Ulric Collins, *q.v.*, and Charlotte his wife.

THE BENGAL ARMY, 1758-1884 865

Services : Fur. s.c., as Cadet, 1811-5, when he was struck off as insane. Posted as Ensign to 24th N.I. in 1813. Transfd. to 1/30th N.I.
Refs. : Burke's *Colonial Gentry,* ii. 862.

COLLINS, James (*c.* 1756-1803). Lieut. Colonel, Infantry. *b.* Dublin *c.* 1756. ("Aged 38 and upwards" on 16 July 1794.) Cadet 1776. Arrived in India 16 July 1776. Ensign 19 Mar. 1777. Lieut. 14 Aug. 1778. Capt. 29 Oct. 1794. Major 31 July 1799. Lt. Col. 12 Aug. 1802. *d. unm.* Fatehgarh, U.P., 11 Jan. 1803.
Brother of John and Francis Collins, of Dublin, merchants, and nephew of John Darragh, lord mayor of Dublin 1781-2, and Mary his wife.
Services : Capt. 1st Bengal Eur. Regt. in 1796. Capt. 5th N.I. in 1798. N.F.P.
Refs. : Will dated Hazaribagh, 16 July 1794 ; proved 1 Apr. 1803.

COLLINS, John Ulric (*d.* 1807). Colonel, 19th N.I. Resident at Lucknow. Cadet 1769. Arrived in India 26 July 1769. Ensign 26 July 1769. Lieut. 17 Nov. 1772. Capt. 20 Nov. 1780. Major 1794. Lt. Col. 27 July 1796. Col. 29 May 1800. *d.* Lucknow 11 June 1807.
Descended from the ancient line of Collins, of Devon. *m.* Calcutta, 24 Nov. 1790, Miss Charlotte Wrangham (*probably* dau. of William Wrangham, member of council at St. Helena). (She died London, 5 Feb. 1857, aged 84.) Father of Henry John Collins, *q.v.*
Services : See *D.N.B.*
Refs. : Burke's *Colonial Gentry,* ii. 862. *D.N.B. D.I.B.* Will dated Lucknow 25 Nov. 1805 ; proved Aug. 1807.

COLLINS or COLLINGS, William (1742/43-1765). 2nd Lieutenant, Artillery. *b.* 1742/43. Cadet 1762. Fireworker 6 Sept. 1763. 2nd Lieut. 1 Aug. 1765. *d.* Bankipore, B. & O., 30 Oct. 1765, aged 22.
Son of Marmaduke Collins or Collings.
Services : N.F.P.
Note : The name, as given in his Will and in the inscription on his tomb in the churchyard adjoining St. Joseph's convent at Bankipore, is Collings.

COLLINSON, William Clinton Peter (1810-1840). Lieutenant, 37th N.I. *b.* Sproughton, Suffolk, 7 Jan. 1810. Cadet 1827. Arrived in India 1 Aug. 1828. Ensign (3 Mar. 1828) 4 Nov. 1828. Lieut. 30 June 1833. *d.* 30 Jan. 1840, of wounds received in action at the fort of Pashut, Afghanistan, on 18 Jan.

LIST OF THE OFFICERS OF

2nd son of Charles Streynsham Collinson, of The Chantry, Suffolk, B.C.S., sometime commercial resident at Bauleah, Bengal, and Maria his wife, eldest dau. of John Sowerby, of Puttridge Bury, Herts. Ed. Harrow 1821-7.
Services : Ensign d.d. 24th N.I. 8 Sept. 1828. Posted as Ensign to 37th N.I. 4 Nov. 1828. First Afghan War 1839-40 ; Ghazni ; storm of Pashut (s.w.) ; Lieut. 37th N.I.
Refs. : Burke's *Commoners,* ii. 538, *s.n.* Collinson, of The Chantry, Suffolk. *Harrow School Register. G.M.* 1840, ii. 332.

COLLYER, Frederick (1804-1842). Bt. Captain, 5th L.C. *b.* Gislingham, Suffolk, 19 Apr. 1804. Cadet 1825. Arrived in India 9 May 1826. Cornet 18 Jan. 1826. Lieut. 2 Dec. 1831. Bt. Capt. 18 Jan. 1841. *d.* nr. Jalalabad, Afghanistan, 14 Jan. 1842 : found murdered about 3 miles from Jalalabad, on the Kabul road.

Son of Rev. Thomas Collyer, rector of Gislingham. *m.* Emily. (She died in India, 10 July 1840, aged 23.)
Services : Posted as Cornet to 5th L.C. 26 Sept. 1826. Fur. p.a. 20 Jan. 1837 till 21 Jan. 1840. First Afghan War 1840-2 ; Bt. Capt. 5th L.C.
Refs. : M.I. in St. Peter's, Fort William, Bengal.

COLLYER, William (1779-1861). Colonel. 67th N.I. *b.* Wroxham, Norfolk, 20 Aug. 1779. Cadet 1798. Arrived in India 27 Aug. 1799. Ensign 9 Nov. 1799. Lieut. 21 Apr. 1800. Capt. 21 Apr. 1809. Major 20 Apr. 1818. Lt. Col. 11 July 1823. Retired 24 Dec. 1825. Hon. Col. 28 Nov. 1854. *d.* Norwich 24 Oct. 1861.

Of Gimingham, Norfolk ; a mgte. for Norfolk and Norwich. *bapt.* Wroxham 22 Aug. 1779. 3rd son of Rev. Daniel Collyer, of Wroxham Hall, and Catherine his wife, dau. of John Bedingfield, of Caistor, Norfolk. *m.* Harriet, dau. of Rev. Charles Collyer, of Gunthorpe Hall.
Services : Posted as Lieut. to 2/18th N.I. 15 Apr. 1801. Second Mahratta War ; occupation of Bundelkhand 1803 ; Gwalior ; Jaitpur 1804 ; Lieut. 2/18th N.I. Operations in Bundelkhand 1809 ; Rajaoli ; Ajaigarh ; Capt. 1/18th N.I. Capture of Java 1811 ; Capt. 5th Bn. Bengal Vols. (Medal). Fur. 1816-7. Major 2/18th N.I. Transfd. as Lt. Col. to 67th N.I. in May 1824.
Refs. : Burke's *Landed Gentry,* 13th edn., p. 371, *s.n.* Collyer, of Cormiston, co. Lanark. *G.M.* 1861, ii. 693. *The Times,* 26 Oct. 1861.

COLNETT, James Richard (1792-1859). Lieut. Colonel. 17th N.I. *b.* London 19 Jan. 1792. Cadet 1806. Arrived in India 1 Aug. 1807. Ensign 7 Aug. 1807. Lieut. 31 Aug. 1810. Capt. 1 May

THE BENGAL ARMY, 1758-1834 367

1824. Major 9 July 1840. Invalided 8 Sept. 1843. Retired 28 Aug. 1852. Hon. Lt. Col. 28 Nov. 1854. *d.* Valetta, Malta, 12 Jan. 1859, of bronchitis.
Of Southwick Cresc., Hyde Park Sq., London. Son of Richard Colnett. *m.* 22 Apr. 1822, Miss Ann Duncan.
Services : Barasat C.C. for 12 mos. Posted as Ensign to 1/11th N.I. Adjt. Purnea Provl. Bn. 1818 till 17 June 1824. Transfd. to 17th N.I. (late 2/11th) May 1824. Dy. Paymr. to forces in Cachar and Assam. Asst. Executive Ofr. P.W.D. Bk. Mr. at Fort William, and Supt. of Gent. Cadets 23 Dec. 1830 till 1839. Fur. s.c. 23 Dec. 1839 till 11 Oct. 1842. No record of active service.
Refs. : *G.M.* 1859, i. 328. *The Times,* 25 Jan. 1859. Will dated 30 Mar. 1857 ; proved 14 June 1860.

COLQUHOUN, Joseph William (1805-1826). Lieutenant, 32nd N.I. *b.* Luss, co. Dumbarton, 3 Feb. 1805. Cadet 1820. Ensign 9 Mar. 1821. Lieut. 11 July 1823. *d.* Malacca 4 July 1826.
2nd son of Lt. Col. Ludovic Colquhoun (who was 3rd and youngest son of Sir James Grant or Colquhoun, 1st Bart., of Luss), of Ross Lodge, and Barbara Camilla his wife, dau. of Rev. Dr. Joseph McIntyre. Cousin-german of Sir William Baillie, Bart., *q.v.*
Services : Posted as Ensign to 2/19th N.I. 2nd Nassiri Bn. in 1823. Transfd. as Lieut. to 16th N.I. 11 July 1823 ; to 32nd N.I. (late 2/16th) May 1824. Leave s.c. 18 Feb. 1825 till death. No record of active service.
Refs. : Burke's *Peerage,* 1923, p. 559, *s.n.* Colquhoun, Bart., of Luss, co. Dumbarton. *Misc. Gen. et Her.* N.S. ii. (1877) 539. *A.J.* xxiii. 278. Will dated Malacca 26 Feb. 1826 ; proved 5 Dec. 1826.

COLQUHOUN, Sir Robert David, tenth baronet (1786-1838). Bt. Major, 44th N.I. *b.* Edinburgh 15 May 1786. Cadet 1806. Arrived in India 21 July 1807. Ensign 24 July 1807. Lieut. 11 Mar. 1811. Capt. 1 May 1824. Bt. Major 10 Jan. 1837. *d.s.p.* at sea, 2 June 1838, on board the *Reliance,* on his passage to India.
Tenth Baronet, of Tilliquhoun, co. Dumbarton. *s.* June 1812; 3rd and youngest son of Sir George Colquhoun, 7th Bart., and Charlotte his 2nd wife, dau. of David Barclay. *m.* Calcutta, 14 Feb. 1822, Anna Maria, 2nd dau. of James Colvin, of Calcutta.
Services : Barasat C.C. for 10 mos. Posted as Ensign to 22nd N.I. Operations in Bundelkhand against Gopal Singh ; action at Bhamori 19 Nov. 1810. A.D.C. to G.G. 11 Sept. 1813 till 24 June 1815. Lieut. 1/22nd N.I. Comdt. Gorakhpur Provl. Bn. 24 Feb. 1815. Comdt. Kumaon Bn. 26 Aug. 1815 till 1828. 2/22nd N.I. in 1822. Transfd. to 44th N.I. (late 2/22nd) May 1824. Comdt.

LIST OF THE OFFICERS OF

Calcutta Native Mil. 6 Dec. 1828. Town and Fort Major of Fort William 1 Jan. 1831. Supt. of Mysore Princes 4 Mar. 1831. Leave to Cape for 2 yrs. 16 Dec. 1831 till 18 Nov. 1833. Fur. s.c. 21 Feb. 1835 ; permitted to return to India 4 Apr. 1838.

Refs. : Burke's *Peerage*, 1832, i. 274, *s.n.* Colquhoun, Bart., of Tilliquhoun, co. Dumbarton. *S.M.* 1822, ii. 267. *G.M.* 1838, ii. 671. *A.R.* 1838. Will dated Calcutta 14 Feb. 1832 ; proved 21 Sept. 1838.

COLT, William Arnold (1778-1816). Captain, 14th N.I. *bapt.* Kington, co. Hereford, 16 June 1778. Cadet 1798. Arrived in India 22 Oct. 1800. Ensign 18 Sept. 1799. Lieut. 28 Oct. 1799. Capt. 13 Jan. 1808. *d.* Java 1 Feb. 1816.

2nd son of Sir John Dutton Colt, 3rd Bart., of Westminster, Middlesex, and Mallet his wife, eldest dau. of John Langley, Capt. R.M. *m.* Sitapur, 5 July 1804, Miss Margaret Leathert.

Services : Second Mahratta War ; Lieut. 14th N.I. Adjt. Burdwan Provl. Bn. 1805-7. Capt. Lt. 14th N.I. 24 Sept. 1807. Comdg. Java Inf. Vols. 1812. Comdg. 4th Vol. Bn. in Java at death.

Refs. : Burke's *Peerage*, 1923, p. 561, *s.n.* Colt, Bart., of Westminster. Will dated 6 Jan. 1816 ; proved 6 May 1818.

COLVILL, Thompson (1779-1827). Lieutenant. 5th N.I. *b.* Dublin 1 Aug. 1779. Cadet 1799. Arrived in India 9 Dec. 1800. Ensign 27 Sept. 1800. Lieut. 2 Jan. 1802. Retired 11 Mar. 1812. *d.* Dublin Apr. 1827.

bapt. St. Nicholas Within, Dublin, 10 Aug. 1779. 2nd (twin with Robert) son of Robert Colvill, of Ahadagh-Youghall, and Sarah his wife, dau. of Clotworthy Lennox, of Derry.

Services : Posted as Ensign to 2/5th N.I. 17 Apr. 1801. Fur. 4 Sept. 1809 till retirement. No record of active service.

Refs. : Burke's *Landed Gentry*, 2nd edn., iii. 71, *s.n.* Colvill, of Ireland.

COLVIN, John (1794-1871). Colonel, C.B. Engineers. *b.* Glasgow 20 Aug. 1794. Cadet 1809. Admitted 26 Sept. 1810. Ensign 15 Sept. 1810. Lieut. 15 Dec. 1817. Capt. 18 May 1821. Major 18 June 1831. Lt. Col. 20 Apr. 1835. Retired 4 Sept. 1839. Hon. Col. 28 Nov. 1854. *d.* Leintwardine, co. Hereford, 27 Apr. 1871.

4th son of Thomas Colvin, merchant, and his wife, formerly Miss Rennie. *m.* Ludlow, Salop., 27 Feb. 1838, Josephine Puget, eldest dau. of Capt. Joseph Baker, R.N., and sister of Sir William Erskine Baker, *q.v.* Addiscombe Cadet 23 Jan. 1809 till 22 Dec. 1809.

Services : Third Mahratta War ; siege of Mandala. Supt. of

THE BENGAL ARMY, 1758-1834

canals in Delhi territory Sept. 1820. Siege and capture of Bhurtpore ; Capt. Engrs. (India medal). Supt. of canals in Delhi territory 20 Jan. 1827 ; do. in N.W.P. The original projector of the Ganges canal. C.B. 20 July 1838.
Refs. : *Thackeray*, p. 33. Boase. G.M. 1838, i. 539. *The Times*, 29 Apr. 1871.

COLYEAR, Martin Thomas (1807-1827). 2nd Lieutenant, Artillery. *b.* Shepperton, Middlesex, 26 May 1807. Cadet 1825. 2nd Lieut. 22 Sept. 1825. *d.* Dum-Dum 13 Feb. 1827.
Natural son of Thomas Charles Colyear, Viscount Milsington, afterwards fourth and last Earl of Portmore, and Harriet Jackson. Brother of Thomas David Colyear, *q.v.* Addiscombe Cadet 1822-5.
Services : Posted to 4th Troop 1st Bde. H.A. in 1826. No record of active service.

COLYEAR, Thomas David (1805-1875). Lieut. Colonel. 7th L.C. *b.* Shepperton, Middlesex, 14 May 1805. Cadet 1822. Arrived in India 22 Oct. 1823. Cornet 8 May 1823. Lieut. 13 May 1825. Capt. 23 Apr. 1839. Major 6 Sept. 1851. Retired 20 Dec. 1851. Hon. Lt. Col. 1856. *d.* Dukhani, nr. Simla, 8 Aug. 1875.
Natural son of Thomas Charles Colyear, Viscount Milsington, and Harriet Jackson. Brother of Martin Thomas Colyear, *q.v.*
Services : To do duty with 6th L.C. Nov. 1823. Posted as Cornet to 7th L.C. in Jan. 1824. Shekhawat expedn. 1834 ; Lieut. 7th L.C. With Army of Reserve (for Afghanistan) at Ferozepore Oct. 1842 till Jan. 1843. Second Sikh War ; Jullundur Doab ; Capt. 7th L.C. with Bdr. Wheeler's force (Medal).
Refs. : *De Rhé-Philipe.*

COMBAULD, Peter (1754/55-1786). Lieutenant, Infantry. *b.* London 1754/55. Cadet 1780. Arrived in India 12 Feb. 1780. Ensign 1780. Lieut. 4 Mar. 1781. *d.* Dacca 4 Sept. 1786.
Services : Sailed for India on the *Norfolk*, 7 Mar. 1779, aged 24. N.F.P.

COMBE, Harvey Terrick (1811-1877). Lieut. Colonel. 1st European Bengal Fusiliers. *b.* Edmonton, Middlesex, 30 June 1811. Cadet 1829. Arrived in India 1 May 1830. Ensign 23 Apr. 1830. Lieut. 27 July 1836. Capt. 1 Nov. 1844. Bt. Major 1 Dec. 1848. Retired 10 May 1854. Hon. Lt. Col. 28 Nov. 1854. *d.s.p.* Henfield, Sussex, 19 Nov. 1877.
Elder son of Harvey Combe, M.C.S., and Elizabeth his wife, dau. of Charles Harris. *m.* Anne, dau. of ——.
Services : Ensign d.d. 13th N.I. 7 June 1830. Posted as Ensign to Bengal Eur. Regt. ; to Right Wing, do., 20 Aug. 1833. Intr. &

Qmr. 18 Apr. 1840 till 1845. First Afghan War 1839-40 ; Ghazni (Medal) ; operations in Waziri valley ; Lieut. 1st Eur. L.I. First Sikh War ; Ferozshahr ; Sobraon ; Capt. 1st Eur. L.I. (Medal with clasp). Leave s.c. to Cape 11 Jan. 1852.
Refs. : Burke's *Landed Gentry*, 13th edn., p. 378, *s.n.* Combe, of Oaklands, Sussex. *The Times*, 21 Nov. 1877.

COMFORT, Thomas (*d.* 1773). Lieutenant, 6th Bn. Sepoys. Cadet 1768. Ensign 14 Jan. 1769. Lieut. 19 Dec. 1769. *d.* Cooch Behar, June 1773.
Services : Operations against the Bhutias in Cooch Behar 1772-3 ; storm and capture of Cooch Behar ; Lieut. 6th Bn.

COMMELINE, Charles (1804-1855). Major. 13th N.I. *b.* Gloucester 4 Feb. 1804. Cadet 1820. Arrived in India 3 Nov. 1821. Ensign 20 May 1821. Lieut. 11 Sept. 1823. Capt. 1 July 1842. Bt. Major 9 Nov. 1846. Major 1849. Retired 15 June 1849. *d.* Banbury, 30 Mar. 1855, from the effects of a fall from his horse whilst hunting with the Warwickshire Hounds on 26 Mar.
Son of Thomas Commeline, of Gloucester, attorney.
Services : Posted as Ensign to 1/23rd N.I. Transfd. to 1/7th N.I. ; to 13th N.I. (late 1/7th) May 1824. Adjt. Orissa Provl. Bn. 27 Nov. 1826. Fur. p.a. 19 Mar. 1832 till 4 Dec. 1834. Adjt. 13th N.I. 24 Dec. 1841 till 6 Sept. 1842. Sub-Asst. in Stud Dept. 7 Dec. 1846 till retirement. Second Sikh War ; Gujerat ; Bt. Major 13 N.I. (Medal).
Refs. : *G.M.* 1855, i. 548.

COMPTON, Herbert (1803-1821). Ensign, 16th N.I. *b.* London 6 Sept. 1803. Cadet 1819. Ensign 13 July 1820. *d.* Indore 3 Nov. 1821 : drowned in a well whilst on the line of march.
Son of Sir Herbert Abingdon Draper Compton, Kt., C.J. of Bombay 1831-9 (*D.N.B.*), by his 1st wife.
Services : Posted as Ensign to 1/16th N.I.

COMYN, Powell Thomas (1780-1832). Lieut. Colonel, 33rd N.I. *b.* Royal Hospital, Chelsea, 16 Feb. 1780. Cadet 1798. Arrived in India 9 Nov. 1799. Ensign 22 Oct. 1799. Lieut. 28 Oct. 1799. Capt. 8 Jan. 1810. Major 7 Oct. 1821. Lt. Col. 1 May 1824. *d.* at sea, 4 Apr. 1832, on board the *Marquis of Camden*.
Of Bush Lane, London, E.C. Son of Rev. Thomas Comyn, vicar of Tottenham, Middlesex, and Harriet Charlotte Staples his wife. Brother of Sir Robert Buckley Comyn, Kt. (*D.N.B.*). *m.* Calcutta, 1 May 1805, Jane Harris De Courcy, natural dau. of John De Courcy, *q.v.* (She died Cawnpore, 30 Jan. 1831, aged 40.) His dau. *m.* William Burlton, *q.v.*

Services : Posted as Ensign to 1/7th N.I. 15 Apr. 1801. Operations against the Garrows 1807 ; Lieut. 1/7th N.I. Capt. 2/7th N.I. Against the Rajah of Bardhi, in Rewah, 1811-2. Nepal War 1814-5 ; Capt. 7th N.I. Third Mahratta War 1817-9 ; Major 2/7th N.I., in Reserve Div. Transfd. as Lt. Col. to 24th N.I. ; to 53rd N.I. ; to 37th N.I. 22 Dec. 1826 ; to 53rd N.I. 19 Jan. 1827 ; to 33rd N.I. 14 Oct. 1831. Leave s.c. for 15 mos. to Cape and N.S.W. 15 Feb. 1832. (? First Burma War.)
Refs. : *E.I.M.C.* iii. 398. *A.J.* N.S. viii. 171.

COMYN or CUMMINE, William (1755/56-1785). Lieutenant, Infantry. *b.* London 1755/56. Cadet 1780. Ensign 1780. Lieut. 6 Aug. 1781. *d.* Fatehgarh, U.P., 29 July 1785.
Services : Sailed for India on the *Lascelles*, 12 Feb. 1780, aged 24. N.F.P.

COMYN, William (1774-1840). Major General. Colonel 33rd N.I. *b.* London 7 Mar. 1774. Cadet 1793. Arrived in India 13 Oct. 1794. Ensign 1 Oct. 1794. Lieut. 8 Jan. 1796. Capt. 21 Sept. 1804. Major 5 Nov. 1812. Lt. Col. 22 Jan. 1817. Lt. Col. Comdt. 1 May 1824. Col. 5 June 1829. Maj. Gen. 10 Jan. 1837. *d.* Carnarvon 9 July 1840.
bapt. St. Gregory by St. Paul's, London, 30 Mar. 1774. Son of Stephen Comyn and Mary his wife. *m.* Elizabeth. (She died 23 Feb. 1845, aged 62.)
Services : Posted to 17th N.I. Capt. Lt. 17th N.I. 9 Mar. 1804. Fur. p.a. Dec. 1806 till Oct. 1810. Nepal War 1814-5 ; Major 2/17th N.I., in 3rd Div. Comdt. Gorakhpur Hill Corps. Transfd. as Lt. Col. to 29th N.I. in 1817. Siege of Asirgarh ; Lt. Col. 29th N.I. Transfd. to 2/8th N.I. 5 June 1822 ; to 24th N.I. (late 2/8th) May 1824. Fur. 2 Jan. 1827 till death. Col. 33rd N.I. 14 Oct. 1831.
Refs. : *A.J.* N.S. xxxii. 360. *G.M.* 1840, ii. 331. *The Times*, 15 July 1840.

CONGALTON, David (*d.* 1772). Lieutenant, Infantry. Cadet 1768. Ensign 18 Jan. 1769. Lieut. 16 Mar. 1770. *d. unm.* Berhampore, Bengal, 12 Feb. 1772.
2nd son of William Congalton, of that ilk, in E. Lothian, and Mary his wife, younger dau. of David Bethune, 16th laird of Balfour.
Services : N.F.P.
Refs. : Burke's *Commoners*, iii. 381, *s.n.* Bethune, of Balfour, co. Fife. *S.M.* 1772, p. 517.

CONINGHAM, Daniel. (*See* **CONYNGHAM.**)

CONINGHAM, John (*d.* 1784). Captain, 3rd N.I. Cadet 1772. Ensign 13 Feb. 1773. Lieut. 10 Mar. 1778. Capt. 6 Oct. 1781. *d.* Cawnpore 15 Sept. 1784.
Services : N.F.P.

CONNELLAN, Martin (1792-1811). Ensign, Infantry. Unposted. *bapt.* co. Galway 9 Jan. 1792. Cadet 1807. Arrived in India 21 Mar. 1809. Ensign 12 Feb. 1809. Suspended 20 Nov. 1809. *d.* London 9 Apr. 1811.
Son of Patrick Connellan and Elizabeth his wife.
Services : Whilst an unposted Ensign undergoing instruction at the Barasat C.C., was suspended for a serious breach of discipline and sent back to the U.K. He was still under suspension when his death occurred.

CONNELLAN, Peter (1745-1820). Lieutenant. Infantry. *b.* 1745. Cadet 1769. Ensign 23 July 1769. Lieut. 20 Nov. 1772. Resigned 14 Dec. 1778. *d.* 1820.
6th and youngest son of Martin Connellan and his wife, formerly Miss Butler. *m.* Miss Marguerite Galhie, a lady of French extraction.
Services : First Rohilla War ; battle of St. George.
Refs. : Burke's *Landed Gentry of Ireland*, p. 128, *s.n.* Connellan, of Coolmore, co. Kilkenny.

CON(N)OLLY, Dennis (*d.* 1790). Lieutenant, Infantry. Cadet 1781. Ensign 20 July 1782. Lieut. 16 Jan. 1785. *d.* Fatehgarh, U.P., 30 June 1790.
Services : N.F.P.

CONNER, James (*d.* 1792 ?). Ensign. Infantry. (? Subsequently Mate in the Bengal Pilot service.) Cadet 1782. Ensign 1783. Dismissed by C.M. 4 Dec. 1783. (? bur. Calcutta 8 June 1792.)
Services : N.F.P.
Refs. : (? Will dated 6 June 1792 ; proved 11 June 1792.)
Note : One James Conner, described as "European inhabitant not in the Service," was living at Chunar in Aug. 1798.

CONOLLY, Arthur (1807-1842 ?). Bt. Captain, 6th L.C. *b.* London 2 July 1807. Cadet 1823. Arrived in India 3 Feb. 1824. Cornet 30 July 1823. Lieut. 13 May 1825. Bt. Capt. 30 July 1838. *d.* on or about 17 June 1842 : murdered whilst in captivity at Bokhara by Amir Nasirulla.
3rd son of Valentine Conolly, of 37 Portland Pl., London, formerly Surgeon Madras Est., and Matilda his wife, dau. of Sir William Dunkin, Kt., of Clogher, sometime a puisne judge of the supreme

court at Calcutta. Brother of Edward Barry Conolly, *q.v.*, and cousin-german of Sir William Hay Macnaghten, 1st Bart. (*D.N.B.*). Ed. Rugby ; entered the school in 1820. Addiscombe Cadet 1822-3.
Services : See *D.N.B.* Sailed for India on H.C.S. *Thomas Grenville* 16 June 1823. Fur. s.c. 26 Jan. 1827 till Mar. 1831. Leave 9 mos. in India 27 Apr. 1836. Pub. in 1834 a description of his overland journey (1829-31) to India.
Refs. : *D.N.B.* *D.I.B.* *Vibart,* p. 375. *Rugby School List.*

CONOLLY, Edward Barry (1809-1840). Bt. Captain, 6th L.C. *b.* London 2 Mar. 1809. Cadet 1824. Arrived in India 5 Oct. 1825. Cornet (?). Lieut. 25 May 1825. Bt. Capt. 25 May 1840. *d.* 29 Sept. 1840 : kld. in action at Fort Tutamdara, north of Kabul.

4th son of Valentine Conolly and Matilda his wife, dau. of Sir William Dunkin, Kt., of Clogher, and of Arlingham Court, Gloucs. Brother of John Balfour Conolly, *q.v.*, and nephew of Edward Dunkin, *q.v.*
Services : Posted as Lieut. to 6th L.C. Siege and capture of Bhurtpore ; Lieut. 6th L.C. Leave s.c. 6 mos. to Mauritius 2 Sept. 1831. First Afghan War 1840 ; comdg. escort with envoy to Shah Shuja.
Refs. : *D.N.B.* *D.I.B.*

CONOLLY, John Balfour (1815-1842). Lieutenant, 20th N.I. *b.* London 28 Feb. 1815. Cadet 1833. Arrived in India 30 Sept. 1834. Ensign 14 June 1834. Lieut. 31 July 1839. *d.* Kabul, 7 Aug. 1842, of fever, whilst a hostage in Bala Hissar.

6th and youngest son of Valentine Conolly and Matilda his wife. Brother of Arthur Conolly, *q.v.* Brasenose Coll., Oxon. ; matric. 15 Mar. 1832.
Services : Ensign d.d. 13th N.I. 9 Oct. 1834. Posted to 42nd N.I. 2 Mar. 1835. Transfd. to 20th N.I. 26 Mar. 1836. Adjt. Shah Shuja's 4th Inf. 3 Sept. 1838. First Afghan War ; Mily. Asst. and comdg. escort of envoy and minister at Kabul 28 Oct. 1840.
Refs. : *D.N.B.* *Alumni Oxon.*

CONRAL, Christopher (*d.* 1794). Ensign, Infantry. Cadet (?). Ensign 6 Mar. 1793. *d.* at sea, 20 Sept. 1794, on the voyage from Penang.
Services : N.F.P.

CONRAN, Henry Marcell (1813-?). Major. Artillery. *b.* Hopton, Suffolk, 26 June 1813. Cadet 1831. Arrived in India 22 Dec. 1832. 2nd Lieut. 14 June 1832. Lieut. 10 July 1840. Capt.

1 Oct. 1849. Retired 29 May 1855. Hon. Major 10 Aug. 1855. Living in 1897.

2nd son of Capt. James Samuel Conran, 17th Light Dns., and Penelope his wife, dau. of Rev. William Baynes. Brother of James William Conran, *q.v.* Addiscombe Cadet 20 Apr. 1830 till 16 June 1832.

Services : Disturbances in Bundelkhand 1840-1 ; capture of Chirgaon. First Sikh War ; Sobraon ; Lieut. 1st Coy. 6th Bn. Art. (Medal). Second Sikh War ; in garrison at Lahore ; Bt. Capt. 1st Coy. 6th Bn. (Medal).

Refs. : Burke's *Family Records*, p. 176.

CONRAN, James William (1810-1832). Lieutenant, 64th N.I. *b.* Bickeringhall Inferior, Norfolk, 4 Sept. 1810. Cadet 1826. Arrived in India 17 June 1827. Ensign 5 Jan. 1827. Lieut. 18 Apr. 1829. *d.* Calcutta 25 Aug. 1832.

Eldest son of Capt. James Samuel Conran, 17th Light Dns., and Penelope his wife. Brother of Henry Marcell Conran, *q.v.*

Services : Posted as Ensign to 64th N.I. No record of active service.

Refs. : Burke's *Family Records*, p. 176. *A.J.* N.S. x. 80 (Feb. 1833). M.I. in Mily. burial ground, Bhowanipore, Calcutta.

Note : Both Burke and the inscription on his grave give the date of his death incorrectly as 25 Aug. 1833.

CONROY, Llewellyn (1788-1825). Captain, 12th N.I. *b.* N. Wales 31 Jan. 1788. Cadet 1803. Arrived in India 29 Apr. 1805. Ensign 12 May 1805. Lieut. 13 May 1805. Capt. 25 Aug. 1818. *d.* Alipore, Calcutta, 4 Sept. 1825, of cholera.

3rd son of John Ponsonby Conroy, barr.-at-law, and Margaret his wife, dau. of Francis Vernon Wilson, of Tully, co. Longford. Brother of Sir John Conroy, K.C.H., 1st Bart., of Llanbrynmair, co. Montgomery. *m.* St. John's, Calcutta, 10 Jan. 1822, Claudine Anne, dau. of John Palmer, of Calcutta, banker, widow of —— Kerr, and sister of Francis Charles Palmer, *q.v.* (*See also* Robert Castle Jenkins.)

Services : Posted as Lieut. to 2/12th N.I. Operations in Oudh 1807-8 ; Akbarpur ; Pathar-serai Oct. 1808 ; Lieut. 2/12th N.I. Java Inf. Vols. in 1812. L.I. Vol. Bn. in 1815. A.A.G. in Java. Fur. 1816-8. Capt. 1/12th N.I. Bde. Major in Oudh 1819. A.D.C. to G.G. 1820-2. Agent for army clothing, Presidency Div., 1821. Comdg. Calcutta Native Mil. 1822 till death. Reposted to 12th N.I. (late 1/12th) May 1824.

Refs. : Burke's *Commoners*, i. 492, *s.n.* Conroy, of Llanbrynmair, co. Montgomery. Foster's *Baronetage*, p. 137, *s.n.* Conroy, Bart., of Llanbrynmair.

THE BENGAL ARMY, 1758-1834 375

*CONSTABLE, Charles George (*d*. 1820). Lieutenant, 26th N.I. Cadet 1806. Arrived in India 28 Dec. 1807. Ensign 12 Oct. 1807. Lieut. 8 July 1810. *d*. Delhi 27 Sept. 1820. Son of George Constable, *q.v.*
Services : Transfd. to Bengal army from H.M. 53rd Regt. Posted as Ensign to 27th N.I. Transfd. to 2/26th N.I. in 1810. Adjt. 1/26th N.I. 1818 till death. No record of active service.
Refs. : Will dated 8 Jan. 1818 ; proved 10 Nov. 1821.

CONSTABLE, George (1756/57-1838). Lieut. Colonel. Artillery. *b*. 1756/57. Country Cadet 1781. Admitted 5 Nov. 1781. Fireworker 26 July 1782. Lieut. 26 June 1788. Capt. Lt. 8 Jan. 1796. Capt. 18 Feb. 1802. Major 28 Feb. 1806. Lt. Col. 5 Dec. 1809. Retired 17 Jan. 1816. *d*. New Rd., London, 12 July 1838, aged 81.
Brother of Rev. Dr. Thomas Constable, of Liff, co. Forfar. *m*. (?). Father of Charles George Constable, *q.v.*
Services : Carnatic, under Sir Eyre Coote, 1783. Reduction of fort of Dastampur, nr. Etah, U.P., May 1800 ; detached with 7th N.I. under Col. James Morris. Operations in Jumna Doab 1802-3 ; Sasni ; Bijaigarh (w.) ; Kachaura, Second Mahratta War ; Aligarh ; Delhi ; Agra ; Laswari ; Capt. comdg. 1st Coy. 2nd Bn. Art. Fur. 18 Dec. 1804 till 22 Aug. 1808. Whilst on fur. was employed under the Board of Ordnance on experimental work in connexion with the forging and casting of brass ordnance on the Asiatic principle. Fur. 17 Dec. 1811 till retirement.
Refs. : E.I.M.C. i. 55. *Stubbs*, ii. 241. *G.M.* 1838, ii. 337. *A.J.* N.S. xxvi. 285.

BROWN-CONSTABLE, Charles (1807-1887). Lieut. Colonel. 18th N.I. *b*. Petrograd 20 Mar. 1807.' Cadet 1825. Arrived in India 25 June 1826. Ensign 4 Feb. 1826. Lieut. 26 July 1827. Capt. 15 Apr. 1840. Major 31 Jan. 1853. Bt. Lt. Col. 28 Nov. 1854. Retired 1 Jan. 1855. *d*. Cheltenham 10 Feb. 1887.
Of Wallace Craigie, Dundee, co. Forfar. Formerly Brown : added the surname of Constable 27 Jan. 1853 (*Lond. Gaz.* p. 229). Son of Lawrence Constable Brown, Russia merchant. Brother of Lawrence Constable Brown, *q.v. m*. 1st, Saugor, 8 June 1830, Helen Eliza, only dau. of Capt. Rowland Dennilon. *m*. 2nd, Ferozepore, 14 Dec. 1849, Mary Christian, dau. of Kenneth Francis Mackenzie, *q.v.*
Services : Posted as Ensign to 68th N.I. Transfd. to 18th N.I. in 1826. Intr. & Qmr. 18th N.I. 21 Aug. 1829 till 3 Mar. 1835. Asst. to Gen. Supt. of operations for suppression of *thagi* 11 May

1835. Asst. to A.G.G., Saugor and Narbada territories, 14 May 1849 till 1853. Fur. 1853.
Refs. : *A.J.* N.S. iii. 209. *I.M.* 1850, p. 70. *The Times,* 14 Feb. 1887.

CONWAY, Edward Sayer (1762-1799). Captain, 2nd N.I. *b.* London 1762. Cadet 1778. Admitted 1778. Ensign 1778. Lieut. 25 Nov. 1778. Capt. 7 Jan. 1796. *d.* Benares, 14 Jan. 1799, aged 37 : kld. during Wazir Ali's revolt.
Services : Sailed for India on the *Gatton,* 27 Apr. 1778, aged 15. N.F.P.
Refs. : *G.M.* 1799, ii. 620.

CONWAY, John Edward (1790-1823). Bt. Captain, 6th N.I. *b.* nr. Troyes, France, 11 Jan. 1790. Cadet 1805. Arrived in India 27 Sept. 1806. Ensign 12 Sept. 1806. Lieut. 28 Feb. 1810. Bt. Capt. 27 Mar. 1821. *d.* 11 Sept. 1823 : drowned.
m. St. John's, Calcutta, 21 Dec. 1822, Paulina Anne Bertram, widow.
Services : Posted as Ensign to 6th N.I. Nepal War 1814-5 ; Lieut. 1/6th N.I., in 2nd Div. (? Third Mahratta War ; Lieut. 1/6th N.I., in Reserve Div.) Intr. & Qmr. 2/6th N.I. 5 Oct. 1818 till death. Operations in Kotah 1821 ; Mangrol ; Bt. Capt. 2/6th N.I.

*CONWAY, Thomas. Ensign. Infantry. Cadet (?). Ensign 3 Aug. 1766.
Services : N.F.P.
Refs. : *B.M. Add. MS.* 6050.

CONWAY, William. (*See* **CONWAY-GORDON, William.**)

CONYNGHAM or CONINGHAM, Daniel (*d.* 1816). Major General. Colonel 26th N.I. Cadet 1772. Arrived in India 3 Feb. 1772. Ensign 24 Feb. 1773. Lieut. 18 Mar. 1778. Capt. 11 Oct. 1781. Major 1 Mar. 1794. Lt. Col. 21 Apr. 1800. Lt. Col. Comdt. 14 Nov. 1805. Col. 25 Apr. 1808. Maj. Gen. 4 June 1811. *d.* Cheltenham 22 June 1816.
Services : Apptd. to comd. newly-raised 2/14th N.I. on its formation in 1797. Transfd. to 2/11th N.I. ; as Lt. Col. to 1/11th N.I. 21 Apr. 1800. Second Mahratta War ; comdd. garrison at Shikohabad which capitulated on 2 Sept. 1803 (w.) ; Lt. Col. comdg. 1/11th N.I. Transfd. as Lt. Col. Comdt. to 26th N.I. 14 Nov. 1805. Fur. 23 Feb. 1807 till death.
Refs. : *S.M.* 1816, p. 559.

THE BENGAL ARMY, 1758-1834 377

COOK, Charles (1804-1880). Lieutenant. 21st N.I. *b.* London 8 Oct. 1804. Cadet 1823. Arrived in India 22 Sept. 1824. Ensign 2 May 1824. Lieut. 18 Feb. 1826. Invalided 27 Feb. 1834. Retired 6 July 1836. *d.* 13 Feb. 1880.
Son of Thomas Bewsher Cook, of Bath, and Harriet his wife.
Services : Sailed for India on the *David Scott* 2 May 1824. Posted as Ensign to 21st N.I. 31 Mar. 1825. Siege and capture of Bhurtpore ; Ensign 21st N.I. (India medal). Granted an extra pension of £27 *p.a.* in addition to his h.p. of 4s. *p.d.* " in consideration of the peculiar and distressing nature of his malady, which has been brought on by the climate of India." Returned from fur. in July 1828. Fur. s.c. 21 Aug. 1834 till retirement.

COOK, William (*d.* 1814). Lieut. Colonel. Infantry. Cadet 1765. Ensign 19 Oct. 1765. Lieut. 4 Jan. 1767. Capt. 20 May 1770. Major 14 Jan. 1781. Lt. Col. 17 July 1787. Struck off 1793. *d.* Wimpole St., London, 7 Feb. 1814. *m.* (before 1780) Esther.
Services : On fur. in 1790. N.F.P.
Refs. : G.M. 1814, i. 409.

COOKE, Bryan William Darwin (1806-1850). Captain, Pension Est. 56th N.I. *b.* Wadworth, Yorks., 21 July 1806. Cadet 1823. Arrived in India 29 Oct. 1824. Ensign 23 May 1824. Lieut. 13 May 1825. Capt. 13 Jan. 1842. Pensioned 18 Mar. 1847. *d.* Dehra Dun, U.P., 19 Apr. 1850.
2nd son of Bryan William Darwin Cooke, of Alverley Grange, Yorks., and Catherine his wife, dau. of John Griffith. Brother of William Augustus Cooke, *q.v. m.* Calcutta, 21 July 1835, Harriette, youngest dau. of Charles Scott, of Trewadreva, Cornwall. Addiscombe Cadet 1821-4.
Services : Sailed for India on the *Cornwall* 23 May 1824. Posted as Ensign to 56th N.I. 31 Mar. 1825. Fur. s.c. 9 May 1831 till 30 Jan. 1835. Suspended for 12 mos. from 8 Aug. 1842. No record of active service.
Refs. : Burke's *Peerage*, 1923, p. 572, *s.n.* Cooke, Bart., of Wheatley, Yorks.

COOKE, George Martin (1801-1828). Captain, Pension Est. 31st N.I. *b.* Walcot, Somerset, 8 Mar. 1801. Cadet 1817. Ensign (?). Lieut. 1 Aug. 1818. Capt. 1827. Pensioned 8 June 1827. *d.* Presidency hospital, Calcutta, 28 Sept. 1828.
Son of John Cooke.
Services : Posted as Lieut. to 2/15th N.I. in 1818. A.D.C. to G.G. 1821-2. Bde. Major at Berhampore 1822 till 2 Mar. 1827. Leave s.c. 6 mos. to Singapore 26 July 1826. No record of active service.

COOK(E), Loftus (1742/43-1768). Fireworker, Artillery. *b.* in Ireland 1742/43. Bencoolen Cadet 1760. Bengal Cadet 1767. Fireworker 1 Dec. 1767. *d.* Calcutta 16 Apr. 1768.
Services : Sailed for Bencoolen on the *Worcester,* 15 Mar. 1761, aged 18. N.F.P.

COOKE, Thomas (1799-1881). Major. 17th N.I. *b.* Queen's Co. 1 Sept. 1799. Cadet 1819. Admitted 27 May 1820. Ensign 10 Jan. 1820. Lieut. 11 July 1823. Capt. 28 Aug. 1833. Major 8 Sept. 1843. Dismissed by G.C.M. 31 Oct. 1849. *d.* in England 11 Mar. 1881.
Son of Robert Cooke, of Queen's Co., farmer. *m.* Calcutta, 6 May 1844, Mrs. Grace Carey Boulton.
Services : Posted as Ensign to 1/26th N.I. Transfd. as Lieut. to 11th N.I. ; to 17th N.I. (late 2/11th) May 1824. Fur. p.a. 10 Mar. 1840 till 10 Oct. 1842. Having lost Rs. 26,000 at cards, he was dismissed the Service for gambling. No record of active service.
Refs. : I.M. 1850, p. 23. *The Times,* 22 Mar. 1881.

COOKE, William Augustus (1808-1864). Colonel. 2nd N.I. *b.* Wadworth, Yorks., 14 May 1808. Cadet 1828. Arrived in India 25 Sept. 1829. Ensign 7 June 1829. Lieut. 30 Apr. 1835. Capt. 8 Nov. 1844. Major 17 May 1853. Lt. Col. 3 Sept. 1857. Retired 24 Apr. 1860. Hon. Col. 24 Apr. 1860. *d. unm.* Hall Gate, Doncaster, 1 June 1864.
3rd son of Brian William Darwin Cooke, of Alverley Grange, Yorks., and Catherine his wife. Brother of Bryan William Darwin Cooke, *q.v.*
Services : To do duty with 12th N.I. 30 Dec. 1830 ; do. 38th N.I. 6 Feb. 1832. Actg. Ensign 27 Oct. 1831 (having been more than 2 yrs. in India). Posted to 2nd N.I. 23 Dec. 1832. Operations against the Kols 1832. Fur. s.c. 26 Sept. 1832 till 26 Oct. 1835. First Afghan War 1840-2 ; Lieut. 2nd N.I., with Gen. Nott's force (Medal). Adjt. 2nd N.I. 14 Feb. 1843 till 23 July 1845. Fur. s.c. 23 Feb. 1845 till 1847, and 1858 till retirement.
Refs. : Burke's *Peerage,* 1923, p. 572, *s.n.* Cooke, Bart., of Wheatley, Yorks. *The Times,* 4 June 1864.

COOKE, William Percy (1782-1831). Major, 6th N.I. *b.* Cathay, psh. of St. Mary Redcliffe, Bristol, 11 Nov. 1782. Cadet 1803. Arrived in India 18 Mar. 1805. Ensign 2 Apr. 1805. Lieut. 3 Apr. 1805. Capt. 11 July 1823. Major 1 Apr. 1829. *d.* Cawnpore 18 July 1831.
m. Meerut, 10 Aug. 1818, Miss Fanny Steuart. (She died Cawnpore, 26 Oct. 1830, aged 30.)

THE BENGAL ARMY, 1758-1834

Services: (? Operations in Bundelkhand 1809; Rajaoli; Ajaigarh; Lieut. 1/3rd N.I.) Nepal War; Actg. Dy. Paymr. 2nd Div. D.J.A.G. 2nd and 3rd Divs. of Field Army 16 Dec. 1816. Third Mahratta War; Lieut., D.J.A.G. Transfd. to 6th N.I. (late 1/3rd) May 1824. Siege and capture of Bhurtpore; Capt. 6th N.I., D.J.A.G. Ceased to be D.J.A.G. on promotion 15 May 1829. Comr. with Baji Rao, the ex-Peshwa, at Bithur, nr. Cawnpore.
Refs.: *G.M.* 1832, i. 94. *A.J.* N.S. vii. 42.

COOKNEY, Frederick (1803-?). Ensign. 26th N.I. *b.* London 17 June 1803. Cadet 1824. Ensign 27 Dec. 1825. Struck off in India 23 Jan. 1828.

Son of Charles Cookney, of Castle St., Holborn, London, attorney and solicitor. Ed. St. Paul's school; admitted 17 Apr. 1811, aged 7.

Services: Posted as Ensign to 26th N.I. 14 July 1826. No record of active service.
Refs.: *Gardiner.*

COOKSON, George Bryan (1789-1813). Lieutenant, 8th N.I. *b.* Petersfield, Hants, 30 Mar. 1789. Cadet 1805. Arrived in India 13 Nov. 1806. Ensign 27 Dec. 1806. Lieut. 16 July 1808. *d.* Dinapore 17 Mar. 1813.

Son of Rev. James Cookson, master of Churcher's college, Petersfield (*D.N.B.*). Brother of John Cookson, *q.v.*

Services: Posted as Ensign to 8th N.I. Lieut. 1/8th N.I. No record of active service.

COOKSON, George James (1805-1838). Lieutenant, Artillery. *b.* Woolwich 21 July 1805. Cadet 1821. Arrived in India 2 Jan. 1823. 2nd Lieut. 10 May 1822. Lieut. 25 May 1826. *d.* Karnal, 20 Feb. 1838, of smallpox.

Son of Charles Norris Cookson, of co. Derby, Lieut. Gen. R.A., and Mary Margaret his 1st wife, 2nd dau. of Dr. Thomas Weir, of Jamaica. Cousin-german of William Cookson, *q.v. m.* Karnal, 8 June 1832, Catherine Theresa, dau. of P. Murray, of co. Wicklow. Addiscombe Cadet 1820-2.

Services: Siege and capture of Bhurtpore; 2nd Lieut. 3rd Coy. 4th Bn. Foot Art.
Refs.: *A.J.* N.S. x. 41.

COOKSON, John (1787-1819). Captain, Artillery. *b.* Petersfield, Hants, 3 June 1787. Cadet 1803. Arrived in India 17 Mar. 1805. Lieut. 30 Aug. 1804. Capt. Lt. 6 Dec. 1809. Capt. 25 Sept. 1817. *d.* in England 30 Aug. 1819.

bapt. Petersfield 5 Oct. 1787. Son of Rev. James Cookson

(*D.N.B.*) and Sarah his wife. Brother of George Bryan Cookson, *q.v.*
  Services: Fur. 24 Oct. 1807 till 1810. Serving in P.W.I. in 1816. Fur. 1818 till death. No record of active service.

COOKSON, William (1808-1843). Bt. Captain, 9th L.C. *bapt.* London 17 Apr. 1808. Cadet 1826. Arrived in India 11 May 1827. Cornet (20 Jan. 1827) 28 Dec. 1827. Lieut. 10 Oct. 1836. Bt. Capt. 1842. *d.* 17 Feb. 1843 : kld. in action at the battle of Miani. Eldest son of George Cookson, Lieut. Gen. R.A. (*D.N.B.*), and Margaret his 3rd wife, only dau. of William Remington. Cousin-german of George James Cookson, *q.v. m.* Karnal, 6 Feb. 1834, Elizabeth Lucy, 2nd dau. of Col. John Goulston Price Tucker, 5th W.I. Regt., and sister of Auchmuty Tucker, *q.v.* Ed. Harrow 1821/22 till 1823 ; at E.I.C. Hertford Coll. (Haileybury) 5 Jan. 1825 till 1826.
  Services: Posted as Cornet to 2nd L.C. 28 Dec. 1827. Transfd. to 9th L.C. 17 Aug. 1832. Adjt. 9th L.C. 10 June 1833 till death. Campaign in Sind ; Miani (kld.) ; Bt. Capt. 9th L.C.
  Refs.: *Harrow School Register.* *G.M.* 1843, i. 556. Will dated 17 Jan. 1835 ; proved 14 Aug. 1843.

COOPER, Charles (1806-1879). Colonel. 23rd N.I. *b.* Seaborough, Somerset, 29 Nov. 1806. Cadet 1823. Arrived in India 12 Oct. 1824. Ensign (4 May 1824) 13 May 1825. Lieut. 12 Apr. 1826. Capt. 10 June 1840. Major 8 June 1857. Bt. Lt. Col. 4 July 1858. Retired 31 Dec. 1861. Hon. Col. 31 Dec. 1861. *d.* Abergavenny 8 Jan. 1879.
  3rd son of John Allen Cooper, Lieut. 1st Life Gds., Knight of Windsor, and Ann his wife, younger dau. of John Collins, of Hatch Court, Somerset. *m.* Moradabad, 17 Feb. 1855, Alethea Rosamond, 2nd dau. of Capt. Francis William Stehelin, H.M. 13th L.I.
  Services: Sailed for India on the *Lord Amherst* 4 May 1824. Posted as Ensign to 23rd N.I. 13 May 1825. Siege and capture of Bhurtpore ; Ensign 23rd N.I. (India medal). Adjt. 23rd N.I. 5 Feb. 1840 till 27 Oct. 1840. Against the Kohat Pass Afridis Feb. 1850 ; Capt. 23rd N.I. (Medal). Fur. 1858 till retirement.
  Refs.: Burke's *Landed Gentry*, 2nd edn., p. 245, *s.n.* Collins, of Hatch Beauchamp, Somerset. *The Times*, 11 Jan. 1879.

COOPER, George (1780-1847). Major General. Colonel 34th N.I. *bapt.* Gravesend, Kent, 26 Aug. 1780. Cadet 1798. Arrived in India 15 Dec. 1799. Ensign 20 Oct. 1799. Lieut. 28 Oct. 1799. Capt. 22 Feb. 1809. Major 11 July 1823. Lt. Col. 21 Oct. 1824. Col. 2 Apr. 1834. Maj. Gen. 28 June 1838. *d.* Dinapore 27 Aug. 1847.

THE BENGAL ARMY, 1758-1834

Son of George Cooper, surgeon, and Elizabeth his wife. *m.* 1st, Jane. (She died 20 Feb. 1823, aged 43.) Father of George Lewis Cooper, *q.v. m.* 2nd, Jamalpur, Bengal, 19 Dec. 1830, Miss Jessy Besseterre. (She died 27 Sept. 1844, aged 28.) *m.* 3rd, Barrackpore, 13 Feb. 1845, Eliza Frances Henrietta, eldest dau. of Thomas Haslam, *q.v.*

Services : Posted to 2/5th N.I. 15 Apr. 1801 ; to Vol. Corps under Major James Maclean, *q.v.*, 21 Dec. 1801. Adjt. 2/5th N.I. 1806-8. Fur. 21 Jan. 1809 till 1811. Capt. 1/5th N.I. 2nd Ceylon Vol. Bn. 1819. Dy. Paymr. at Dinapore 10 July 1820. Comdd. Champaran L.I. 18 Sept. 1820 till 26 Jan. 1825. First Burma War 1824-5 ; Rangpur ; capture of stockade at Burragong 19 Mar. 1824. Transfd. to 20th N.I. (late 2/5th) May 1824 ; to 69th N.I. 18 Feb. 1825 ; to 54th N.I. ; to 25th N.I. ; to 34th N.I. 1 Dec. 1832. Maj. Gen. comdg. at Barrackpore 26 Jan. 1842. Bdr., 2 cl., 7 Apr. 1843. Comdg. Dinapore Div. 30 Sept. 1845 till death. Transfd. to 54th N.I. in 1847.

Refs. : G.M. 1847, ii. 670. Burke's *Patrician*, iv. 589. Will dated 7 Aug. 1847 ; proved 11 Nov. 1847.

COOPER, George Lewis (1812-1857). Bt. Major, Artillery. *b.* London 2 Feb. 1812. Cadet 1827. Arrived in India 1 Aug. 1828. 2nd Lieut. 2 Feb. 1828. Lieut. 23 Nov. 1835. Capt. 18 Dec. 1845. Bt. Major 20 June 1854. *d.* 25 Sept. 1857 : kld. in action at the first relief of Lucknow.

Eldest son of George Cooper, *q.v.*, and Jane his 1st wife. Nephew of Duncan Campbell. *m.* 1st, Meerut, 9 Nov. 1834, Catherine Mary, only dau. of Robert Chamberlain, B.C.S. *m.* 2nd, Lucknow, 8 Oct. 1846, Miss Mary Ann Griffin. Addiscombe Cadet 1826-7.

Services : Posted to 3rd Troop 2nd Bde. H.A. in 1833 ; to Shah Shuja's Troop in 1838. First Afghan War 1838-42 ; capture of Kalat ; against the Duranis July 1841 ; Kandahar ; comdd. Art. with Gen. England's column from Kandahar to the Indus ; Ghazni (Medal). D.C. Ord. 24 June 1843 ; Comy. of Ord. 24 July 1845. Posted to 1st Troop 3rd Bde. H.A. 24 July 1845. To comd. 2nd Troop 2nd Bde. in 1856. Mutiny campaign ; comdd. Art. of Gen. Havelock's force for relief of Lucknow (kld.).

Refs. : The *Times*, 12 Jan. 1858.

COOPER, Henry Edward Gilbert. (*See* **GILBERT-COOPER, Henry Edward.**)

COOPER, John (*d.* 1782). Captain, Infantry. Cadet 1770. Ensign 6 Dec. 1771. Lieut. 24 July 1776. Capt. 18 Feb. 1781. *d.* 1782, whilst on active service with the Bombay detachment.

Services : First Mahratta War 1778-82.

COOPER, John Chamier (1809-1857). Lieut. Colonel, 51st N.I. *b.* Madras 21 Dec. 1809. Cadet 1825. Arrived in India 24 June 1826. Ensign 5 Feb. 1826. Lieut. 24 Nov. 1832. Capt. 14 Mar. 1845. Major 24 Jan. 1851. Lt. Col. 22 May 1856. *d.* Peshawar, 28 Aug. 1857, of sunstroke.

Son of Lt. Col. Leonard Cooper, 21st Madras N.I. *m.* Bombay, 19 Dec. 1854, Frances, dau. of S. Smith, of Twickenham.

Services : To do duty with 49th N.I. 8 July 1826. Posted as Ensign to 49th N.I. 26 Oct. 1826. Intr. & Qmr. 49th N.I. 1 Jan. 1835 till Mar. 1845. Offg. S.A.C.G. 22 Aug. 1848. Second Sikh War ; siege of Multan ; Gujerat ; Capt. 49th N.I., S.A.C.G. (Medal with 2 clasps). Fur. s.c. 9 Apr. 1851 till Oct. 1853. To comd. 51st N.I. July 1856. Mutiny campaign ; in comd. of 51st N.I. at Peshawar. Having been disarmed in May, the 51st mutinied on 28 Aug. 1857, and made for the Khyber Pass. During the operations in pursuit of the mutineers on that day, he succumbed to heatstroke.

Refs. : De Rhé-Philipe. *I.M.* 1855, p. 99.

COOPER, John Samuel (*d.* 1788). Ensign, Infantry. Cadet 1782. Ensign 3 Feb. 1783. *d.* St. Helena, 29 July 1788, on his passage to Europe.

Services : N.F.P.

COOPER, Richard (*d.* 1783). Lieutenant, Infantry. Cadet 1779. Ensign 12 Feb. 1780. Lieut. 13 Feb. 1781. *d.* Madras 12 Jan. 1783.

Services : Second Mysore War.

COOPER, Samuel (1759-1794). Lieutenant, Infantry. *b.* 1759. Cadet 1780. Ensign 17 May 1781. Lieut. 31 Aug. 1782. *d.* Ramu, Chittagong, 21 Dec. 1794.

A native of Oxfordshire. Brother of Thomas Cooper, of Henley-on-Thames, and nephew of Rev. Samuel Cooper, of Loxley, co. Warwick. " Bound an apprentice to Messrs. Clarkes, of the city of Coventry."

Services : Apptd. Cadet on 20 Feb. 1781, aged 21. Sailed for India on the *Blandford,* 26 June 1781, aged 22. Adjt. & Qmr. 5th Bde. in 1790. N.F.P.

Refs. : Will proved in 1795.

COOPER, William George (1801-1843). Captain, 71st N.I. *b.* Bengal 9 Oct. 1801. Cadet 1819. Arrived in India 6 Jan. 1821. Ensign 16 July 1820. Lieut. 11 July 1823. Capt. 7 Jan. 1836. *d.* Sikraul, Benares, 28 May 1843.

THE BENGAL ARMY, 1758-1834

Natural son of William Henry Cooper, *q.v.*, and Mrs. Mary Ridley, whom he afterwards married. His sister *m.* Hutton Watkins, *q.v.*
Services : Posted as Ensign to 2/16th N.I. Transfd. as Lieut. to 4th N.I. 11 July 1823 ; to 20th N.I. 9 Feb. 1824 ; to 40th N.I. (late 2/20th) May 1824. First Burma War 1824 ; Lieut. 40th N.I. Transfd. to 3rd Extra Regt. (became 71st N.I.) in 1825. Adjt. Burdwan Provl. Bn. 22 Feb. 1826 ; do. Farrukhabad Provl. Bn. 26 May 1829. Bde. Major 28 Dec. 1829. D.A.A.G., Benares Div., 13 June 1837 till 3 Apr. 1838. A.A.G., 2nd Div. Army of the Indus, 11 Jan. till 14 Apr. 1839. D.A.A.G., Sirhind Div., 1839 ; do. Benares 1840. A.A.G., Benares Div., 1 Sept. 1841 till death.
Refs. : *G.M.* 1843, ii. 334. Will dated 21 May 1843 ; proved 13 Oct. 1843.

COOPER, William Henry (1762-1822). Lieut. Colonel, C.B. Invalid Est. 1st N.I. *b.* 30 Apr. 1762. Country Cadet 1780. Admitted 3 Apr. 1780. Ensign 1 Feb. 1781. Lieut. 7 Oct. 1781. Capt. 29 May 1800. Major 20 Oct. 1805. Lt. Col. 25 Aug. 1811. Invalided 4 Apr. 1818. *d.* Dacca, 8 May 1822, aged 60 years and 8 days.

m. 8 Jan. 1808, Mary, dau. of Hercules Skinner, *q.v.*, and widow of William Ridley, *q.v.* (She died Dehra Dun, 3 Dec. 1853, aged 76.) Father of William George Cooper, *q.v.*, Maria, wife of Hutton Watkins, *q.v.*, and Anne, wife of Gordon Caulfeild, *q.v.*
Services : Capt. 1/1st N.I. (? Operations in Bundelkhand 1804-5 ; Capt. 1/1st N.I.) Operations in Bundelkhand 1806-9 ; Chamir ; Sehlehuganj ; Rajaoli ; Ajaigarh ; Major 2/1st N.I. Transfd. as Lt. Col. to 9th N.I. in 1811 ; to 2/1st N.I. in 1812. Nepal War 1814-5 ; Lt. Col. comdg. 2/1st N.I., in 1st Div. (? Capture of Hathras 1817 ; Lt. Col. 2/1st N.I.) Comdg. at Fatehgarh 1817-8. Comdd. Dacca Provl. Bn. 6 Feb. 1819 till death. C.B. 3 Feb. 1817.
Refs. : Will dated Kaitha 10 July 1808 ; proved 28 May 1822. M.I. in English cemetery at Dacca.
Note : *G.M.* 1810, i. 182, has the following : " William Henry Cooper, late Capt., E.I.C.S., d. at Barampore (Berhampore), 1 July 1809." Presumably this is a premature obit. notice of the foregoing, no other individual of these names having been traced.

*COOPER, —— (*d.* 1763). Lieutenant, Infantry. Cadet (?). Ensign (?). Lieut. (?). *d.* Murshidabad, July 1763 : kld. by the troops of Nawab Kasim Ali.
Services : N.F.P.
Refs. : MS. list preserved at the India Office entitled, " List of Persons killed in the Massacre at Patna, and at other places during

the Troubles, 1763," signed by "J. Graham, Secretary, Fort William, 20 Feb. 1764." Forrest's *Clive*, ii. 237. *Firminger*, p. 71.

GILBERT-COOPER, Henry Edward (1784-1831). Lieut. Colonel, 48th N.I. *b.* Southwell, Notts., 20 Feb. 1784. Cadet 1800. Arrived in India 24 Oct. 1801. Ensign 4 Nov. 1801. Lieut. 12 Sept. 1803. Capt. 25 Apr. 1810. Major 13 Jan. 1823. Lt. Col. 2 May 1824. *d.* at his residence, Claverton Hill, Bath, 10 Dec. 1831.

bapt. Southwell 27 Feb. 1784. Son of John Gilbert Cooper, of Thurgarton Priory, Notts., and Catherine his wife. Uncle of Sir Daniel Lysons, G.C.B. (*D.N.B.*). *m.* 1st, Calcutta, 21 July 1810, Caroline, dau. of —— Collins, and widow of George William Wiggens or Wiggins, *q.v.* (She died Dacca 11 June 1811.) *m.* 2nd, Calcutta, 10 Mar. 1814, Miss Mary Anne Muckle. (She died 19 Jan. 1874, aged 76.)

Services : Second Mahratta War 1803-5 ; Aligarh ; Delhi ; Laswari ; Deig ; Bhurtpore ; Lieut. 15th N.I. Adjt. 2/15th N.I. in 1810. Nepal War 1814-5 ; Capt. 2/15th N.I., in 4th Div. Nepal War 1816 ; Capt. 2/15th N.I., in 4th Bde., Centre Column. Bde. Major at Penang 22 July 1816 ; do. to troops in Oudh 28 Nov. 1818. Bk. Mr., Agra district, 1 Aug. 1819. Fort Adjt. at Buxar 22 Jan. 1821. Supt. of telegraphs 7 Mar. 1822 till 26 July 1824. Transfd. as Lt. Col. to 63rd N.I. in May 1824. Siege and capture of Bhurtpore ; Lt. Col. 63rd N.I. Fur. s.c. 1 Feb. 1829 till death. Transfd. to 48th N.I. 5 Dec. 1829.

Refs. : E.I.M.C. iii. 376. *A.J.* N.S. vii. 68. *Bath Chron.* 15 Dec. 1831. Will dated 5 Feb. 1831 ; proved 25 July 1832.

Note : John Gilbert took the surname of Cooper in 1735.

COOTE, George Chidley (1793-1819). Lieutenant, 20th N.I. *b.* Ipswich 15 Sept. 1793. Cadet 1809. Ensign 1 June 1812. Lieut. 1 Oct. 1815. *d.* nr. Budge-Budge, Bengal, 24 July 1819.

bapt. ptely., St. Peter's, Ipswich, 18 Sept. 1793. Son of George Coote, Capt. h.p. 24th Foot (who was nephew of Sir Eyre Coote (*D.N.B.*), and Margaret Hunt his wife.

Services : Barasat C.C. Cadet d.d. 15th N.I. 1811. Posted as Ensign to 1/20th N.I. in 1812. Nepal War 1816 ; Lieut. 8th Gren. Bn., in 2nd Bde., Left Column. Lieut. 1/20th N.I.

Refs. : Foster's *Baronetage*, p. 141, *s.n.* Coote, Bart.

COPE, Robert Wright Cope (1809-1858). Bt. Captain. 12th N.I. *b.* Clifton, Gloucs., 2 Feb. 1809. Cadet 1827. Ensign 3 June 1829. Lieut. 21 Jan. 1837. Bt. Capt. 16 June 1843. Resigned 19 Feb. 1845. *d.* Paris 23 Apr. 1858.

THE BENGAL ARMY, 1758-1834

Of Loughall Manor, co. Armagh, J.P. and D.L. Formerly Doolan : assumed the surname and additional arms of Cope, by Warrant from Dublin Castle, 14 June 1844 (*Dublin Gaz.* 389, 397). *bapt.* 12 Apr. 1809. Elder son of Lt. Col. Richard Doolan, Bombay Est., of Blagdon, nr. Bristol, and Mary his wife, 3rd and youngest dau. of Arthur Cope, of Loughall. *m.* Ardrahan, 6 June 1848, Cecilia Philippa, eldest dau. of Capt. Shawe Taylor, of Castle Taylor, co. Galway.

Services : Posted as Ensign to 12th N.I. Asst. to A.G.G., Saugor and Narbada territories, 1836-43. Fur. s.c. 12 Aug. 1843 till resignation. No record of active service.

Refs. : Burke's *Landed Gentry of Ireland*, p. 134, *s.n.* Cope, of Loughall Manor, co. Armagh. *Howard & Crisp's Ireland*, vi. 138, *s.n.* Shawe-Taylor.

COPELAND, George (*d.* 1820). Ensign, Pension Est. Cadet 1783. Ensign 30 Apr. 1785. Invalided (?). Pensioned 1808. *d.* in England, 10 Dec. 1820, insane.

Services : Invalided on some date between 1790 and 1804. N.F.P.

COPPINGER, John (*d.* 1792). Lieutenant, Infantry. Cadet 1782. Ensign 14 Apr. 1783. Lieut. 14 Mar. 1790. *d.* Dinapore 2 Oct. 1792.

Services : N.F.P.

COPSON, William (1788-1811). Ensign, 16th N.I. *b.* Rytor-on-Dunsmore, co. Warwick, 11 Mar. 1788. Cadet 1808. Arrived in India 27 Oct. 1809. Ensign 16 Mar. 1810. *d.* Muttra 5 Sept. 1811.

Son of William Copson and Anne his wife.

Services : Posted as Ensign to 16th N.I. (? Operations in Bundelkhand 1810-1.)

CORBET, Samuel (1785-1811). Lieutenant, 27th N.I. *b.* 21 Apr. 1785. Cadet 1800. Arrived in India 22 Aug. 1801. Ensign 7 Nov. 1801. Lieut. 13 July 1803. *d.* in India 6 Nov. 1811.

bapt. New Ross, co. Wexford, 23 May 1785. 3rd and youngest son of Robert Corbet, of Corbet Hill, co. Wexford, and Susannah his wife, dau. of —— Woodward, of Drumbarrow, co. Meath.

Services : Posted as Ensign to Bengal Eur. Regt. Transfd. as Lieut. to newly-raised 27th N.I. in 1804. Operations against Dhundia Khan 1807 ; Komona ; Ganauri ; Lieut. 27th N.I. Actg. Adjt. 1/27th N.I. 1810 till death.

Refs. : Burke's *Landed Gentry of Ireland*, p. 639, *s.n.* Singleton, of Aclare, co. Meath.

CORBETT, Sir Stuart (1802-1865). Major General, K.C.B. Colonel 16 N.I. *b.* Tankersley, Yorks., 1802. Cadet 1818. Admitted 11 Sept. 1819. Ensign 7 Sept. 1819. Lieut. 9 Apr. 1822. Capt. 18 Aug. 1825. Major 19 Sept. 1840. Lt. Col. 26 Dec. 1846. Col. 18 May 1856. Maj. Gen. 4 Feb. 1859. *d.* Naini Tal, U.P., 1 Aug. 1865.

bapt. Wortley, Yorks., 17 Oct. 1802. Eldest son of Rev. Stuart Corbett, curate of Wortley, afterwards archdeacon and canon of York, rector of Kirk Bramwith, Yorks., and Ann his wife (née King), of Loughborough. *m.* 1st, Penang, 13 Mar. 1822, Miss Charlotte Britten ("sister to G. Ernst, of Fairbrook Cottage, Gloucester, and gt. niece to Count von Hahn, of Mecklenburg-Strelitz." *Probably* sister of George Ernst Britten, *q.v.*). (She died Lohoo Ghat, nr. Almora, 19 Apr. 1840.) *m.* 2nd, Calcutta, 1 Sept. 1845, Mary Augusta, dau. of Henry Kellett.

Note: George Ernst de Hahn was naturalized in 1775.

Services: Posted as Ensign to 1/20th N.I. Leave to China 1821. Transfd. to 25th N.I. (late 1/20th) May 1824. Comdt. Kumaon Local Bn. 8 Dec. 1828 till 1 Nov. 1842. Second Sikh War; Sadulapur; Chilianwala; Gujerat; Lt. Col. comdg. 25th N.I. (Medal with clasp). Transfd. to 24th N.I. Jan. 1854; to 16th N.I. July 1856. Bdr. comdg. Lahore station 8 Aug. 1856. Mutiny campaign (Medal). Fur. 1859. Comdg. Benares Div. 6 July 1863. C.B. 9 June 1849. K.C.B. 28 Jan. 1862.

Refs.: Boase. D.I.B. G.M. 1866, i. 141.

CORFIELD, Alfred Henry (1810-1866). Major. 2nd Bengal European Regt. *b.* Bridewell, London, 12 Oct. 1810. Cadet 1828. Arrived in India 13 Feb. 1829. Ensign 23 Aug. 1828. Lieut. 18 June 1834. Capt. 23 Aug. 1843. Invalided 6 Jan. 1849. Retired 16 Oct. 1856. Hon. Major 16 Oct. 1856. *d.* Pulteney Villa, Bath, 28 Feb. 1866.

Son of John Corfield and Sophia Keates his wife. Brother of William Corfield, of Old Bond St., London, solicitor.

Services: Posted as Ensign to 21st N.I. 3 June 1829. Transfd. to 2nd Bengal Eur. Regt. 8 Oct. 1839. Fur. s.c. 28 Feb. 1840 till 13 Dec. 1842. Intr. & Qmr. 18 Apr. 1843 till 1847.

Refs.: G.M. 1866, i. 605. *The Times*, 6 Mar. 1866.

CORFIELD, Charles (1807-1883). Lieut. Colonel. 47th N.I. *b.* Cawnpore 30 Aug. 1807. Cadet 1824. Arrived in India 29 June 1825. Ensign 8 Jan. 1825. Lieut. 15 Aug. 1826. Capt. 15 Dec. 1838. Bt. Major 19 June 1846. Retired 3 Nov. 1852. Hon. Lt. Col. 28 Nov. 1854. *d.* 27 Hove Villas, Brighton, 28 Apr. 1883.

THE BENGAL ARMY, 1758-1834

bapt. Cawnpore 16 Sept. 1807. 3rd son of Charles Corfield, of Knowle Lodge, Taunton, sometime Surgeon 17th, 76th, and 38th Foot, and Cordelia his wife. Brother of Frederick Brooke Corfield, *q.v. m.* Cawnpore, 14 Mar. 1835, Mary Jane, eldest dau. of Samuel Lightfoot, Surgeon, Bengal Est. (She died London, 17 Sept. 1853.) *Services :* Posted as Ensign to 69th N.I. Transfd. to 47th N.I. in 1828. Magh Sebundy Corps Mar. 1831. Adjt. 47th N.I. 22 July 1834 till 19 Jan. 1839. First Sikh War ; Aliwal ; Sobraon ; Capt. 47th N.I. (Medal with clasp). Fur. s.c. 18 Sept. 1850 till retirement.
Refs. : The Times, 1 May 1883.

CORFIELD, Frederick (*d.* 1826). Captain. Infantry. Dy. Mily. Auditor Gen., Bengal. Cadet 1783. Arrived in India 20 Sept. 1783. Ensign 28 Jan. 1785. Lieut. 3 Nov. 1791. Capt. 8 Jan. 1798. Retired 8 July 1802. *d.* Cheltenham 16 Feb. 1826.
Services : N.F.P.
Refs. : S.M. 1826, i. 511.

CORFIELD, Frederick Brooke (1803-1884). General. Colonel 5th European Inf. *b.* Calcutta 4 Dec. 1803. Cadet 1819. Admitted 22 Aug. 1820. Ensign 3 Apr. 1820. Lieut. 11 July 1823. Capt. 22 Apr. 1831. Major 14 Mar. 1843. Lt. Col. 3 Sept. 1849. Col. 26 Apr. 1859. Maj. Gen. 18 Nov. 1860. Lt. Gen. 25 June 1870. Gen. 1 Oct. 1877. *d.* at his residence, Knowle House, Upper Norwood, 2 Sept. 1884.

Son of Charles Corfield, of Knowle Lodge, Taunton, Surgeon 17th Foot, and Cordelia his wife. Brother of William Robert Corfield, *q.v. m.* Kishnaghur, 27 Apr. 1825, Annie, dau. of Robert Nairne, *q.v.*
Services : Posted as Ensign to 1/28th N.I. Transfd. as Lieut. to 5th N.I. ; to 20th N.I. (late 2/5th) May 1824. Adjt. Purnea Provl. Bn. 11 Sept. 1826. Pioneers 27 July 1829. Adjt. Calcutta Native Mil. 5 June 1830 till 14 Oct. 1831. Pioneers 14 Nov. 1831. Bde. Major at Delhi 13 Nov. 1835. Comdd. 20th N.I. 7 Mar. 1842. Second Sikh War ; Chilianwala ; Gujerat ; Major 20th N.I. (Medal with clasp). Transfd. to 70th N.I. ; to 49th N.I. Mar. 1851 ; to 17th N.I. 23 Sept. 1853 ; to 48th N.I. 13 Jan. 1854 ; to 55th N.I. in Mar. 1854. Fur. p.a. 17 Mar. 1854. Transfd. to 2nd N.I. in July 1855 ; to 6th N.I. 26 Sept. 1857 ; to 5th Eur. Regt. in 1859.
Refs. : Boase. The Times, 4 Sept. 1884. *I.L.N.* vol. 85 (1883), p. 225 (portrait).

CORFIELD, Joseph (1804-1881). Colonel. 61st N.I. *b.* London 26 June 1804. Cadet 1819. Arrived in India 22 Jan. 1821. Ensign 8 July 1820. Lieut. 11 July 1823. Capt. 14 Nov. 1832. Major 14 Nov. 1849. Lt. Col. 16 Jan. 1855. Retired 31 May

1857. Hon. Col. 31 May 1857. *d.* Greatham House, Henrietta St., Bath, 24 Apr. 1881.

Son of Joseph Corfield, of Coram St., Russell Sq., London, solicitor, and Martha his wife. *m.* 1st, Anne Martha, dau. of Charles Poole, *q.v.* (She died 1838, aged 34.) *m.* 2nd, Calcutta, 29 July 1843, Mary, dau. of T. C. Hogan. (She died Calcutta, 20 Nov. 1845, aged 18.)

Services : Posted as Ensign to 2/4th N.I. Transfd. as Lieut. to 12th N.I. 11 July 1823 ; to 1st N.I. (late 2/12th) May 1824. Fur. s.c. 22 Feb. 1826 till 2 Feb. 1828. Fur. 20 Jan. 1830 till 18 July 1832. Second Sikh War ; Bt. Major 1st N.I. (Medal). Fur. s.c. 30 Mar. 1855 till retirement. Transfd. to 61st N.I. in Sept. 1855.

Refs. : G.M. 1839, i. 333. *Bath Chron.* 28 Apr. 1881.

CORFIELD, William Robert (1805-1882). General. 22nd N.I. *b.* Calcutta 23 July 1805. Cadet 1821. Arrived in India 4 May 1822. Ensign 3 Dec. 1821. Lieut. 11 Sept. 1823. Capt. 30 July 1832. Major 2 Feb. 1845. Lt. Col. 31 Mar. 1851. Col. 18 Nov. 1860. Maj. Gen. 30 Jan. 1861. Lt. Gen. 25 June 1870. Gen. 1 Oct. 1877. *d.* 128 Lexham Gdns., Earls Court, London, 30 Nov. 1882.

Son of Charles Corfield and Cordelia his wife, née Smith. Brother of Charles Corfield, *q.v.,* and of Augusta, wife of Alexander Mercer, *q.v.* Ed. Blundell's, 14 Aug. 1817 till 29 June 1821.

Services : Posted as Ensign to 1/14th N.I. Transfd. to 15th N.I. ; to 31st N.I. (late 2/15th) May 1824. Siege and capture of Bhurtpore ; Lieut. 31st N.I. (India medal). Pioneers 17 Feb. 1826. Operations in the Kol country 1836-7. First Afghan War 1838-40 ; Kalat ; Ghazni ; Capt. 31st N.I. (Medal). 1st L.I. Bn. Gwalior campaign ; Maharajpur ; Capt. 31st N.I. (Bronze star). Second Sikh War ; Sadulapur ; Chilianwala ; Gujerat ; Major 31st N.I., comdg. 30th N.I. (Medal with clasp). Against the Kohat Pass Afridis Feb. 1850 ; Bt. Lt. Col. 31st N.I. (Medal). Transfd. to 29th N.I. 13 Apr. 1853 ; to 31st N.I. 18 June 1853. Fur. s.c. 13 Aug. 1855 till 1857. Transfd. to 30th N.I. in Sept. 1855 ; to 34th N.I. 4 July 1857 ; to 22nd N.I. in 1857.

Refs. : Boase. *The Times,* 5 Dec. 1882, 7f.

CORNER, Frederick (1804-?). Captain. 1st N.I. *b.* London 1 July 1804. Cadet 1821. Arrived in India 19 Aug. 1822. Ensign 10 Mar. 1822. Lieut. 1 May 1824. Capt. 18 Aug. 1834. Resigned 12 July 1837.

Son of Lieut.-Gen. Charles Corner, Madras N.I.

Services : Posted as Ensign to 12th N.I. Transfd. to 1st N.I. (late 2/12th) May 1824. Fur. p.a. 2 Feb. 1835 till resignation. No record of active service.

THE BENGAL ARMY, 1758-1834

CORNISH, Charles (*d.* 1784). Lieutenant, Infantry. Cadet 1772. Ensign 15 Feb. 1774. Lieut. 3 June 1778. *d.* in India Jan. 1784.
Son of James Cornish, of Teignmouth, and Margaret his wife, dau. of Rev. William Floyer. Brother of James Cornish, of Totnes, surgeon, and of Charlotte, wife of John, first Lord Teignmouth.
Services : First Mahratta War. N.F.P.
Refs. : Burke's *Landed Gentry*, 13th edn., p. 181, *s.n.* Cornish-Bowden, of Zaire, Devon. Will dated 2 May 1783.

CORNISH, Charles John (1802-1879). Lieutenant. 4th L.C. *b.* Salcombe Regis, Devon, 7 Apr. 1802. Cadet 1819. Admitted 31 July 1820. Cornet 4 Mar. 1820. Lieut. 1 Oct. 1821. Retired 15 Dec. 1832. *d.* Salcombe House, nr. Sidmouth, Devon, 29 Mar. 1879.
Of Salcombe House, Devon, J.P. and D.L. for Devon. 2nd son of George Cornish, of Sidmouth, and Sarah his wife, dau. of J. Kestell. *m.* his cousin, Elizabeth Rhodes, 4th and youngest dau. of James Cornish, of Black Hall, Devon. (She died 5 Nov. 1853.)
Services : Posted as Cornet to 4th L.C. Adjt. 4th L.C. 25 Apr. 1823 till 12 July 1825. D.J.A.G. 11 June 1825. Fur. 31 July 1830 till retirement. No record of active service.
Refs. : Burke's *Landed Gentry*, 13th edn., p. 181, *s.n.* Cornish-Bowden, of Zaire, Devon. *Walford. The Times*, 3 Apr. 1879.

CORNISH, Frederick William (1810-1851). Captain, Artillery. *bapt.* Staverton, Devon, 29 Oct. 1810. Cadet 1827. Arrived in India 10 June 1828. 2nd Lieut. 13 Dec. 1827. Lieut. 2 July 1835. Capt. 3 July 1845. *d.* at sea, 20 May 1851, on board the *Sutlej* off Cape Agulhas, Cape Colony.
Son of Charles Cornish, Surgeon Bengal Est., and Emily Reybaud his wife (*probably* dau. of the govr. of (Dutch) Chinsura, and sister of Helena Louisa, wife of Nathaniel Brassey Halhed (*D.N.B.*)). Brother of Henry Hubert Cornish, *q.v. m.* 1st, 13 July 1835, Margaret Olympia, youngest dau. of Thomas Ephraim Monsell, B.C.S. (*See also* Edmund Trant Spry.) (She died Jubbulpore, 13 July 1836, aged 17.) *m.* 2nd, Sarah Baker, only child of William Orchard, of Ashbridge House. Addiscombe Cadet 1826-7.
Services : 2nd Troop 3rd Bde. H.A. in 1830. Asst. to A.G.G., Saugor and Narbada territories, 26 Sept. 1835. Fur. p.a. 9 Feb. 1837 till 17 Apr. 1839. First Afghan War 1840-2 ; Ghazni ; Kabul ; Lieut. 3rd Coy. 2nd Bn. Foot Art. (Medal). Capt. 2nd Coy. 3rd Bn.

CORNISH, Henry Hubert (1812-1887). 2nd Lieutenant. Artillery. Subsequently Principal of New Inn Hall, Oxford. *b.* 14 Feb. 1812. Cadet 1827. Arrived in India 10 June 1828. 2nd Lieut. 14 Feb. 1828. Resigned 15 July 1835. *d.* Oxford 9 June 1887.

bapt. Totnes, Devon, 10 Mar. 1812. 2nd son of Charles Cornish, of Gatcombe House, Totnes, and Emily Reybaud his wife. Brother of Philip George Cornish, *q.v.*, and nephew of Philip Gould Cornish, *q.v. m.* Dacca, 4 June 1832, Mary, eldest dau. of Sir William Dick, Bart., *q.v.* Addiscombe Cadet 1826-7. Magdalen Hall, Oxon.; B.A. 1841; M.A. 1842; D.D. 1866.

Services : Posted to 1st Troop 2nd Bde. H.A. 1830. Fur. 5 June 1834 till resignation. Took holy orders. Deacon 1842; Priest 1843. Chaplain of C.C.C. Principal of New Inn Hall 1866.

Refs. : Boase. Alumni Oxon. The Times, 13 June 1887.

CORNISH, Philip George (1813-1880). Major. 10th N.I. *b.* 24 Dec. 1813. Cadet 1831. Arrived in India 14 Sept. 1832. Ensign 19 May 1832. Lieut. 8 Sept. 1840. Capt. 8 Dec. 1846. Invalided 1 Oct. 1852. Retired 26 Aug. 1865. Hon. Major 26 Aug. 1865. *d.* 23 Sept. 1880.

bapt. Totnes, Devon, 31 Jan. 1814. Son of Charles Cornish, of Gatcombe House, Totnes, and Emily Reybaud his wife. Brother of Frederick William Cornish, *q.v. m.* Benares, 24 Dec. 1834, Mary Anne, 3rd dau. of Johan Frederick Meiselback, formerly Col. in the service of Himmat Bahadur, afterwards pensioned and employed by the British Govt. in India. (*See also* George Byron.) Addiscombe Cadet 5 Feb. 1830 till 8 Dec. 1831.

Services : Ensign d.d. with 53rd, 48th, 24th, and 33rd N.I. Posted as Ensign to 38th N.I. 19 Dec. 1833. Transfd. to 10th N.I. 24 Sept. 1835. Fur. s.c. 13 Mar. 1843 till 1845. No record of active service.

CORNISH, Philip Gould (*d.* 1806). Lieutenant, 1st N.C. Cadet 1798. Arrived in India 25 Sept. 1799. Cornet 9 June 1800. Lieut. 15 Feb. 1803. *d.* Saharanpur, U.P., 12 Oct. 1806.

Son of James Cornish, of Totnes, M.D., and Sarah his wife. Nephew of Charles Cornish, *q.v.*, and uncle of Frederick William Cornish, *q.v.*

Services : Second Mahratta War; Laswari 1 Nov. 1803 (w.); Lieut. 1st N.C.

Refs. : Burke's *Landed Gentry*, 13th edn., p. 181, *s.n.* Cornish-Bowden, of Zaire, Devon. Will dated 7 Sept. 1801; proved 31 Dec. 1806.

CORNISH, Richard Samuel (1781-1805). Lieutenant, 23rd N.I. *bapt.* St. Mary's, Newington, Surrey, 14 Sept. 1781. Cadet 1798. Arrived in India 8 Nov. 1799. Ensign 23 Dec. 1799. Lieut. 29 May 1800. *d.* Bareilly, U.P., 2 Sept. 1805.

Son of M. (*probably* Mark) Cornish and Frances his wife.

THE BENGAL ARMY, 1758-1834

Services : Posted as Lieut. to 2/18th N.I. 15 Apr. 1801. Second Mahratta War ; occupation of Bundelkhand 1803 ; Lieut. 2/18th N.I. Transfd. to newly-raised 23rd N.I. in 1804.
Refs. : *G.M.* 1806, i. 180.

CORRI, Anthony Albert Lambert (1800-1842). Captain, 54th N.I. *b.* London 17 Feb. 1800. Cadet 1819. Admitted 27 Mar. 1820. Ensign 26 Oct. 1819. Lieut. 11 July 1823; Capt. 24 Feb. 1835. *d.* Jan. 1842 : kld. in action nr. Kabul.
Eldest son of Philip Anthony Corri, musician, and Augusta his wife, dau. of —— Albert, of Cecil St., London. Grandson of Domenico Corri (*D.N.B.*). *m.* 1st, Banda, 10 June 1823, Miss Emily Jane Bathurst. (She died 24 Jan. 1826.) *m.* 2nd, Benares, 15 June 1830, Miss Maria Eliza Whish. Addiscombe Cadet 1816-7.
Services : Posted as Ensign to 1/2nd N.I. Transfd. as Lieut. to 27th N.I. ; to 54th N.I. (late 2/27th) May 1824. First Burma War ; Arakan 1825 ; Lieut. 2nd L.I. Bn. Intr. & Qmr. 54th N.I. 7 Aug. 1828. First Afghan War 1840-2 ; Capt. 54th N.I.

CORRY, John (1787-1806). Lieutenant, 16th N.I. *b.* Derryvullen, co. Fermanagh, Nov. 1787. Cadet 1803. Arrived in India 2 Dec. 1804. Ensign 21 Nov. 1804. Lieut. 21 Nov. 1804. *d. unm.* Cawnpore 21 May 1806 : kld. in a duel by Charles Ryan, *q.v.*
Natural son of Armar, first Earl of Belmore, and Margaret Begby.
Services : Lieut. 1/16th N.I. No record of active service.
Refs. : Burke's *Peerage*, 1923, p. 255, *s.n.* Earl of Belmore. Will dated Cawnpore 13 May 1806 ; proved 5 Dec. 1806.

CORSAR, Colvin (1815-1852). Captain, 64th N.I. *b.* London 6 Dec. 1815. Cadet 1833. Arrived in India 15 Aug. 1834. Ensign 22 May 1834. Lieut. 8 Oct. 1839. Capt. 3 June 1848. *d.* Barnstaple, 25 Nov. 1852.
Son of John Corsar, of Edinburgh, coal merchant, formerly of the firm of Colvin, Bazett & Co., Calcutta, and Anna Ludivina his wife. Brother of Henry Fotheringham Corsar, *q.v.* Addiscombe Cadet 3 Feb. 1832 till 13 Dec. 1833.
Services : Ensign d.d. 54th N.I. 20 Aug. 1834. Posted to 64th N.I. 5 Nov. 1834. First Afghan War 1842 ; Ali Masjid ; Kabul ; Lieut. 64th N.I. (Medal). Adjt. 64th N.I. 11 Oct. 1844 till 28 July 1848. Fur. s.c. 19 Apr. 1852 till death.
Refs. : *G.M.* 1853, i.

CORSAR, Henry Fotheringham (1809-1828). 2nd Lieutenant, Artillery. *b.* Calcutta 24 Feb. 1809. Cadet 1826. 2nd Lieut. 19 Nov. 1826. *d.* Dum-Dum 16 Dec. 1828.
Son of John Corsar, merchant, of the firm of Colvin, Bazett & Co.,

Calcutta, and Anna Ludivina his wife, née Pringle. Brother of Colvin Corsar, *q.v.* Addiscombe Cadet 1825-6.
Services : ? Posted to H.A. No record of active service.

COSBY, William (*d.* 1773). Captain, Infantry. Capt. 18 Aug. 1760. *d.* Calcutta 25 Jan. 1773.
(? *Possibly* of the family of Cosby, of Stradbally Hall, Queen's Co.)
Services : N.F.P. *Probably* transfd. from H.M.S.

COSTLEY, William Robert Clayton (1780-1866). General. Colonel 9th N.I. *b.* Dublin 24 Dec. 1780. Cadet 1801. Arrived in India 16 Oct. 1802. Ensign 6 Aug. 1802. Lieut. 4 June 1804. Capt. 9 Dec. 1817. Major 27 Jan. 1826. Lt. Col. 2 Jan. 1831. Col. 22 Oct. 1842. Maj. Gen. 20 June 1854. Lt. Gen. 2 Apr. 1856. Gen. 13 June 1865. *d.* 6 Fitzwilliam Sq., Dublin, 16 Sept. 1866.

Of Templeogue, Dublin. *bapt.* St. Nicholas Within, Dublin, 30 Dec. 1780. Son of John Costley and Ann his wife. *m.* Jaunpur, 17 July 1811, Miss Eleanora McCarthy. His dau. *m.* Henry Gardiner Nash, *q.v.*

Services : Ensign 1/4th N.I. Second Mahratta War ; battle and capture of Deig ; pursuit of Holkar from Muttra ; Lieut. 1/4th N.I. (India medal). Nepal War ; Lieut. 4th N.I. (Clasp to India medal). Transfd. to 7th N.I. (late 1/4th) May 1824. Comdt. Calcutta Native Mil. 12 Sept. 1825 till 6 Dec. 1828. Leave s.c. 12 mos. to St. Helena 26 Jan. 1827. Transfd. to 56th N.I. 24 Sept. 1831 ; to 29th N.I. 17 Sept. 1833 ; to 18th N.I. 26 Aug. 1834 ; to 32nd N.I. 29 Mar. 1844. Bdr., 2 cl., comdg. at Ambala, 13 Sept. 1844 ; do. Barrackpore and Presdy. Div. 1846. Col. 9th N.I. 20 May 1851. Fur. p.a. 3 Feb. 1853 till death.

Refs. : Boase. *The Times,* 19 Sept. 1866.

COTES, William (1790-1826). Bt. Captain. 28th N.I. *bapt.* Bedlington, Northumberland, 13 Aug. 1790. Cadet 1805. Arrived in India 11 July 1806. Ensign 27 July 1806. Lieut. 24 Sept. 1807. Bt. Capt. 27 Mar. 1821. Struck off in England 23 June 1820. *d.* Buitenzorg, nr. Batavia, Java, 7 Oct. 1826.

Latterly of Salatiga, Java. Son of Henry Cotes, of Bedlington.
Services : Posted as Ensign to 14th N.I. Capture of Java 1811 ; Lieut. 3rd Bn. Bengal Vols. Was still serving with 3rd Vol. Bn. in Java in 1816. Transfd. to newly-raised 28th N.I. in 1815.
Refs. : A.J. xxiv. 253.

COTTON, Henry (1808-1857). Bt. Colonel, 67th N.I. *b.* co. Chester 29 Aug. 1808. Cadet 1824. Arrived in India 17 Nov. 1825. Ensign 13 May 1825. Lieut. 19 Jan. 1828. Capt. 30 Mar. 1837.

Major 5 Dec. 1855. Bt. Lt. Col. 9 Dec. 1853. Bt. Col. 22 Aug. 1857. *d.* Dehra Dun, U.P., 28 Nov. 1857.

Son of Henry Cotton. *m.* Sophia B. (She died Dinapore 2 Dec. 1853.)

Services : Posted as Ensign to 67th N.I. Adjt. 4 Mar. 1836 till 19 June 1837. Fur. s.c. 22 Nov. 1837 till 17 May 1839. D.J.A.G. 18 Feb. 1843 till 1856. Second Burma War ; taking of Rangoon ; capture of Pegu June 1852 ; operations against the rebel chief Mayat-Toon ; with 40th N.I. (Medal). Mutiny campaign ; action nr. Agra 10 Oct. 1857. Comdg. Agra and Muttra districts.

Refs. : *I.M.* 1858, p. 5.

COTTON, Henry Perry (1806-1881). Lieutenant. 7th L.C. *b.* Thanet 14 Dec. 1806. Cadet 1825. Arrived in India 18 Mar. 1826. Cornet 28 Sept. 1825. Lieut. 13 June 1827. Resigned 16 Mar. 1831. *d.* Quex Park, I. of Thanet, Kent, 21 Nov. 1881.

Of Quex Park, Birchington, Kent. Eldest son of Charles Bowland Cotton, of Kingsgate, Kent, formerly R.N., and afterwards Capt. E.I.C.N.S., and Harriot his 1st wife, dau. of William Roberts, of Park House, Fulham. *m.* Calcutta, 25 Mar. 1828, Georgina, youngest dau. of George Hanbury Pine, *q.v.*

Services : Posted as Cornet to 7th L.C. A.D.C. to Maj.-Gen. George Hanbury Pine 16 Oct. 1827 till 1829. Fur. s.c. 17 Feb. 1829. No record of active service.

Refs. : Burke's *Landed Gentry*, 13th edn., p. 404, *s.n.* Powell-Cotton, of Quex Park, Thanet. *The Times*, 24 Nov. 1881.

COULL, Archibald Dunbar (1809-1852). Ensign. 4th N.I. Subsequently an indigo planter. *b.* Ashgrove, nr. Elgin, co. Moray, 5 June 1809. Cadet 1825. Ensign 15 Mar. 1826. Resigned 9 Mar. 1827. *d.* Dacca 29 Oct. 1852.

Son of James Coull, of Ashgrove, and Jean his wife, only dau. of Sir Alexander Dunbar, 4th Bart. of Northfield. Cousin-german of Charles Cumming Dunbar, *q.v.*

Services : No record of active service. After resigning the Service he became an indigo planter, first at Mymensingh, later at Jumalpore. In 1849 he was Sec. to the Dacca bank.

Refs. : Burke's *Peerage*, *s.n.* Dunbar, Bart., of Northfield. Will dated Dacca 29 Oct. 1852 ; proved 30 Nov. 1852.

COULSEY, Peter (1761/62-1782). Lieutenant, Infantry. *b.* 1761/62. Cadet 1779. Ensign 12 Feb. 1780. Lieut. 20 Mar. 1781. *d.* Madras 30 June 1782.

A native of Norfolk.

Services : Sailed for India on the *True Briton*, 16 June 1779, aged 17. Second Mysore War 1781-2.

COULTHARD, Samuel (1789-1866). Captain, Artillery. *b.* 29 Aug. 1789. Cadet 1805. Arrived in India 3 Oct. 1807. Fireworker 30 Apr. 1807. Lieut. 1 May 1807. Capt. Lt. 7 Oct. 1817. Capt. 1 Sept. 1818. Struck off 24 May 1831. Retired 11 Nov. 1837. *d.* 13 King St., Portman Sq., London, 3 Oct. 1866. 5th son of Thomas Coulthard, of Burkham House, Hants (late of Farleigh, Hants). Woolwich Cadet ; nominated for R.M.A.13 June 1804 ; obtained his certificate 7 July 1806.

Services : Sailed for India on the *Union.* Fur. 3 Mar. 1809 till 1812. Actg. Asst. Professor of Persian at Coll. of Fort William Feb. 1815 till 17 Jan. 1816. Siege and capture of Hathras ; Lieut. 6th Coy. 2nd Bn. Foot Art. Third Mahratta War ; Dhamoni ; Garhakota ; Capt. 5th Coy. 1st Bn., afterwards 4th Coy. 2nd Bn. Fur. 28 Dec. 1828 till struck off.

Refs. : G.M. 1866, ii. 702.

COUNSELL, William (1794-1831). Captain, Artillery. *b.* Calcutta 5 Aug. 1794. Cadet 1812. Admitted 21 Aug. 1813. Fireworker 16 Aug. 1813. Lieut. 1 Sept. 1818. Capt. 3 Mar. 1831. *d.* 25 July 1831 : drowned at sea nr. Ramri I., Lower Burma, by the capsizing of a boat, along with Edmund McIntosh Nugent, *q.v.*

bapt. Calcutta 23 Aug. 1794. Son of William Counsell, master mariner, and Petronella Sebastiana his wife. *m.* 12 Sept. 1826, Miss Susannah Elizabeth Wiltshire. (*See also* William Vernon Mitford.) (She *re-m.* Henry Palmer, *q.v.*) Addiscombe Cadet 1811-2.

Services : Nepal War 1814-5 ; Lieut. F. 6th Coy. 2nd Bn. Art., in 1st Div. Nepal War 1816 ; Lieut. F. 6th Coy. 2nd Bn. Third Mahratta War ; siege of Asirgarh (w.) ; Lieut. 6th Coy. 2nd Bn. First Burma War ; operations of Sir A. Campbell's force in Burma.

Refs. : Will proved 30 Sept. 1831.

COURTENAY, Frederick Eardley Bellenden (1804- ?). Cadet, Infantry. *b.* London 2 Apr. 1804. Cadet 1823. Never arrived in India.
Services : N.F.P.

COURTNEY, John Lees (1772-1794). Cadet, Artillery or Engineers. *b.* Islington, Middlesex, 2 July 1772. Cadet 1794. *d.* Dum-Dum 13 Dec. 1794.

bapt. Islington 17 Aug. 1772. Son of Richard Courtney and Sarah his wife.
Services : N.F.P.

COVENTRY, Charles (1793-1854). Colonel, 70th N.I. *b.* Douglas, co. Lanark, 31 Dec. 1793. Cadet 1808. Arrived in India 27 Oct. 1809. Ensign 10 Oct. 1810. Lieut. 16 Dec. 1814. Capt. 24 Apr. 1824. Major 19 Sept. 1836. Lt. Col. 19 Dec. 1842. Col. 7 June 1853. *d.* Barrackpore 7 May 1854.

Son of John Coventry, of Newtonhead, Douglas. Brother of Frederick Coventry, *q.v.*
Services : Posted as Ensign to 1/16th N.I. Served in Alwar 1813. Fur. s.c. 18 Dec. 1819 till 28 Oct. 1824. Transfd. to 32nd N.I. (late 1/16th) May 1824. Siege and capture of Bhurtpore ; Capt. 32nd N.I. (India medal). To comd. 32nd N.I. 2 Jan. 1843. Transfd. to 9th N.I. ; to 63rd N.I. in Nov. 1852 ; to 10th N.I. in July 1853 ; to 70th N.I. 4 Aug. 1853.
Refs. : Boase. *I.M.* 1854, p. 346.

COVENTRY, Frederick (1799-1855). Bt. Lieut. Colonel, 6th L.C. *b.* Douglas, co. Lanark, 8 Aug. 1799. Cadet 1820. Admitted 4 Aug. 1821. Cornet 2 Feb. 1821. Lieut. 1 May 1824. Capt. 19 Nov. 1835. Major 4 Nov. 1852. Bt. Lt. Col. 7 June 1849. *d.* at sea, 24 Dec. 1855, on board the *Hindostan,* between Calcutta and Madras, on the voyage to England.
Son of John Coventry, of Newtonhead, Douglas. Brother of Charles Coventry, *q.v. m.* Anna M. (She died Nowgong, 20 Aug. 1855, aged 26.)
Services : Posted as Cornet to 6th L.C. 21 Nov. 1821. Adjt. 6th L.C. 6 Aug. 1823 till 14 July 1825. Siege and capture of Bhurtpore ; Lieut. 6th L.C. (India medal). Intr. & Qmr. 6th L.C. 20 July 1825 till 4 May 1832. Fur. p.a. 12 Jan. 1838 till 26 Feb. 1841. Sub-Asst. in Stud Dept. 22 Apr. 1843 till 1852 ; Asst., 2 cl., do., 16 Apr. 1852 till 1853. Second Sikh War ; Chilianwala ; Gujerat ; Bt. Major comdg. 6th L.C. (Medal with clasp). Fur. 1855.
Refs. : G.M. 1856, i. 545. *I.M.* 1856, p. 60. Will dated 21 Dec. 1855 ; proved 5 Feb. 1856.

COWARD, Thomas. Ensign. Infantry. Cadet 1782. Ensign 21 Mar. 1783. Struck off 1788.
Services : N.F.P.

COWE, John (*d.* 1818). Captain. 2nd Bengal European Regt. Cadet 1769. Ensign 2 July 1770. Lieut. 3 Apr. 1771. Capt. 6 Sept. 1779. Resigned before 1790. *d.* Edinburgh 15 Dec. 1818.
Services : Lieut. R.N. 17 June 1757. " At Dacca (*c.* 1778) I made acquaintance with my venerable friend John Cowe. He had served in the Navy so far back as the memorable siege of Havannah, was reduced when a lieut. at the end of the American War, went out in the Company's military service, and here I found him in command of a regiment of Sebundees, or native militia."
Refs. : Lives of the Lindsays, iii. 161. *S.M.* 1819, i. 96.

COWE, Peter (*d.* 1785). Captain, Infantry. Cadet 1769. Ensign 11 Aug. 1769. Lieut. 24 Jan. 1773. Capt. 16 Jan. 1781. *d. unm.* Cawnpore 25 Jan. 1785.
Brother of Christian Ann Cowe.

Services : N.F.P.
Refs. : Will dated 24 Jan. 1785.

COWIE, John (*d.* 1779). Fireworker, Artillery. Cadet 1778. Fireworker 1 Oct. 1778. *d.* Budge-Budge, Bengal, 19 Aug. 1779.
Services : N.F.P.

COWLEY, Constantine William (1793-1848). Major, Invalid Est. 35th N.I. *b.* Dysert, co. Clare, 1 May 1793. Cadet 1811. Admitted 12 Dec. 1812. Ensign 30 Sept. 1814. Lieut. 3 Mar. 1818. Capt. 20 Nov. 1827. Major 4 Jan. 1841. Invalided 17 Feb. 1841. *d.* Dehra Dun, U.P., 13 Sept. 1848.

Son of William Cowley. *m.* Calcutta 17 Mar. 1831, Catherine, 6th dau. of Col. J. F. Meiselback. (*See also* George Byron.)
Services : Posted as Ensign to 1/17th N.I. 30 Sept. 1814. Served with Mirzapur Local Bn. Transfd. to 2/17th N.I.; to 34th N.I. (late 1/17th) May 1824. Adjt. 34th N.I. 23 Mar. 1825. Adjt. 35th N.I. (late 2/17th) 28 June 1825. Siege and capture of Bhurtpore; Lieut. 35th N.I. First Afghan War 1839; Ghazni; Capt. 35th N.I. (Medal).
Refs. : I.M. 1848, p. 656.

COWLEY, Thomas (1753/54-1797). Captain, Infantry. *b.* 1753/54. Cadet 1782. Arrived in India 28 Aug. 1783. Ensign 20 Mar. 1783. Lieut. 28 Feb. 1790. Capt. 1796. *d.* Mangee, nr. Dinapore, 6 June 1797, *en route* from Chunar to Calcutta.

A native of Cumberland. *m.* Hannah Parkhouse, the dramatist (*D.N.B.*), dau. of Philip Parkhouse, of Tiverton, Greek scholar and bookseller. His dau. *m.*, as 2nd wife, Rev. David Brown (*D.N.B.*).
Services : Apptd. Cadet on 25 June 1782, aged 28. Adjt. 6th Bengal Eur. Bn. in 1790. Lieut. 3rd Bengal Eur. Regt. in 1796.
Refs. : Burke's *Landed Gentry*, 4th edn., p. 1151, *s.n.* Parkhouse, of Eastfield Lodge, Hants. *G.M.* 1798, i. Will dated Chunar 4 July 1794.
Note : If his age is given correctly here, his marriage with Hannah Parkhouse could hardly have taken place " *c.* 1768," as stated in *D.N.B.*

COWLISHAW, Elias (*d.* 1793). Brevet Ensign. Cadet 1781. Bt. Ensign 1782. *d.* Buxar 11 Jan. 1793.
Services : N.F.P.

COWLISHAW, Richard (1758/59-1799). Captain, Infantry. *b.* Northampton 1758/59. Cadet 1778. Arrived in India 12 Feb. 1780. Ensign 27 June 1779. Lieut. 18 Feb. 1781. Capt. 7 June 1796. *d.* Chittagong (? Calcutta) 17 Mar. 1799.
Services : Sailed for India on the *Norfolk*, 7 Mar. 1779, aged 20. N.F.P.

COWPAR, Archibald (1807-1840). Lieutenant, 59th N.I. *bapt.* Kirriemuir, co. Forfar, 15 Oct. 1807. Cadet 1826. Arrived in India 14 Aug. 1827. Ensign 17 Mar. 1827. Lieut. 4 Feb. 1833. *d.* Ludhiana 9 Nov. 1840.

Son of Thomas Cowpar and Charlotte his wife, dau. of James Galloway, of Perth, and sister of Sir Archibald Galloway, K.C.B., *q.v.*

Services : Posted as Ensign to 59th N.I. No record of active service.

COWPER, Gilbert (1791-1814). Lieutenant, 15th N.I. *b.* Wantage, Berks., 13 Jan. 1791. Cadet 1806. Arrived in India 1 Aug. 1807. Ensign 23 July 1807. Lieut. 16 Apr. 1810. *d.* Java 14 Oct. 1814.

Son of Gilbert Cowper and Catherine his wife.

Services : Posted as Ensign to 1/15th N.I. Expedition to Mauritius 1810-1 ; Lieut. 1st Bn. Bengal Vols. Java Inf. Vols. in 1812.

COWPER, Isaac (1800-1825). Lieutenant, 2nd N.I. *bapt.* Sandside (? Ulverston), Lancs., 9 Nov. 1800. Cadet 1819. Arrived in India Jan. 1821. Ensign 8 July 1820. Lieut. 11 July 1823. *d.* Chittagong 20 Oct. 1825.

3rd son of Thomas Cowper, of Saltcoats, yeoman, and Mary his wife, dau. of James Swainson, of the Castle, Hawkshead, Lancs.

Services : Midshipman E.I.C.N.S. 1818. Posted as Ensign to 1/11th N.I. Transfd. as Lieut. to 1st N.I. 11 July 1823 ; to 2nd N.I. (late 1/1st) May 1824. First Burma War ; Arakan 1825 ; Lieut. 2nd Gren. Bn. Intr. & Qmr. 2nd Gren. Bn. 7 June 1825 till death.

Refs. : Burke's *Landed Gentry*, 13th edn., p. 578, *s.n.* Cowper-Essex, of Keen Ground, Hawkshead, Lancs. *Howard & Crisp*, vi. 12, *s.n.* Cowper-Essex.

COWSLADE, John (1787-1858). Colonel. 72nd N.I. *bapt.* Reading 16 July 1787. Cadet 1805. Arrived in India 19 Aug. 1806. Ensign 19 July 1806. Lieut. 25 Dec. 1807. Capt. (1 May 1824) 13 May 1825. Major 8 Oct. 1839. Lt. Col. 23 Oct. 1845. Retired 8 July 1848. Hon. Col. 28 Nov. 1854. *d.* 14 Notting Hill Sq., Bayswater, 29 Oct. 1858.

Of Gothic Villa, Queen's Rd., Reading. Son of Thomas Cowslade, of Donnington, Berks., and Mary Anne his wife. Brother of Thomas Carnan Cowslade, *q.v.*, and nephew of John Cowslade, gentleman usher to Queen Charlotte.

Services : Posted as Ensign to 2/19th N.I. Nepal War 1814-5 ; Lieut. 2/19th N.I., in 2nd Div. (India medal). Adjt. 2/19th N.I. 2 Nov. 1818 till 13 July 1824. Third Mahratta War ; Lieut. 2/19th N.I. Transfd. as Capt. to 39th N.I. (late 2/19th) May 1824. Transfd. to newly-raised 2nd Extra Regt. (became 70th N.I.) May

1825. Fur. s.c. 31 Dec. 1829 till 7 Feb. 1833. Bde. Major at Barrackpore 13 June till 25 Nov. 1837. Comdd. 70th N.I. 15 Nov. 1837 till Nov. 1839. Transfd. as Major to 2nd Bengal Eur. Regt. 21 Oct. 1839. With Army of Reserve (for Afghanistan) 25 July 1842 till Jan. 1843. Fur. 15 Mar. 1845 till 1847. Transfd. to 52nd N.I. ; to 42nd N.I. ; to 72nd N.I. 5 Feb. 1848.
Refs. : *G.M.* 1792, ii. 962. The Times, 2 Nov. 1858.

COWSLADE, Thomas Carnan (1788-1826). Captain, 43rd N.I. *bapt.* St. Lawrence's, Reading, 16 Dec. 1788. Cadet 1803. Arrived in India 5 Dec. 1804. Ensign 11 Oct. 1804. Lieut. 11 Oct. 1804. Capt. 25 Dec. 1817. *d.* on the river nr. Cawnpore, 9 Nov. 1826, aged 38.

Son of Thomas Cowslade, of Donnington, Berks., and Mary Anne his wife. Brother of John Cowslade, *q.v.*

Services : Posted as Lieut. to 2/22nd N.I. in 1805. Nepal War 1816 ; Lieut. 2/22nd N.I., in 3rd Bde., Centre Column. Capt. 1/22nd N.I. Transfd. to 43rd N.I. (late 1/22nd) May 1824. First Burma War ; Arakan 1825 ; Capt. 1st Gren. Bn.
Refs. : *A.J.* xxiii. 857.

COX, George (1806-1855). Major, Invalid Est. 60th N.I. *b.* Sandford, Oxon., 14 May 1806. Cadet 1821. Arrived in India 19 Dec. 1822. Ensign 6 Nov. 1822. Lieut. 30 Oct. 1824. Capt. 7 Jan. 1836. Major 9 Nov. 1846. Invalided 15 Nov. 1849. *d.* Graythwaite, Westmorland, 23 Sept. 1855.

Son of Samuel Cox, *q.v.*, and Caroline his wife. Brother of William Cox, *q.v. m.* Wolston, co. Warwick, 5 Nov. 1840, Mary Elizabeth, widow of A. C. Orme, of the Inner Temple. (She died 8 Jan. 1879, aged 59.)

Services : Posted as Ensign to 30th N.I. Transfd. to 60th N.I. (late 2/30th) May 1824. Cashiered by sentence of G.C.M. ; sentence remitted 16 June 1824. Siege and capture of Bhurtpore ; Lieut. 60th N.I. (India medal). Fur. s.c. 31 Jan. 1840 till 12 Oct. 1842. Leave s.c. to Cape and N.S.W. 21 Feb. 1852. Fur. 1854 till death.
Refs. : *A.J.* N.S. xxxiii. 315. *G.M.* 1855, ii. 556.

COX, George Hamilton (1800-1841). Captain, Invalid Est. 62nd N.I. *b.* Newfoundland 11 Aug. 1800. Cadet 1819. Admitted 15 Nov. 1820. Ensign 29 May 1820. Lieut. 27 Aug. 1822. Capt. 30 Mar. 1832. Invalided 2 Nov. 1835. *d.* Calcutta 29 Apr. 1841 : committed suicide by shooting himself with a revolver at his rooms in the Bengal Club : verdict, *felo de se.*

Youngest son of Lt. Col. William Cox, R.A. *m.* Walcot, Bath, 21 June 1824, Eliza Kearton, 4th dau. of John Horne, of St. Vincent, W.I., planter. (She died Bath, 4 Jan. 1858, aged 51.) Father of Rev. George William Cox, nominated bishop of Natal in 1886.

Services : Posted as Ensign to 2/13th N.I. Transfd. as Lieut. to 31st N.I. 11 July 1823 ; to 62nd N.I. (late 2/31st) May 1824. Fur. s.c. 20 Aug. 1823 till 16 Jan. 1825. First Burma War ; Arakan 1825 ; Lieut. 62nd N.I. After transfer to the Invalid Est. he became actuary to the Calcutta Fire Insurance Co.
Refs. : Bath Chron. June 1824. *I.N.* vol. i. No. 15, p. 335. B : *P.P.* vol. ii. p. 499.

COX, Henry Chambers Murray (1789-1876). General. 58th N.I. *bapt.* Calcutta 11 Aug. 1789. Cadet 1805. Arrived in India 7 Feb. 1807. Ensign (24 May 1806) 2 Jan. 1807. Lieut. 30 Aug. 1809. Capt. 1 May 1824. Major 17 Sept. 1836. Lt. Col. 22 Oct. 1842. Col. 5 June 1853. Maj. Gen. 28 Nov. 1854. Lt. Gen. 18 Jan. 1867. Gen. 9 Dec. 1871. *d.* St. Ann's, Burnham, Somerset, 22 July 1876, aged 87.

Son of Hiram Cox, *q.v.*, and Mary his wife. *m.* 1st, Ann, widow of Andrew Fraser (*d.* 1812), *q.v.* (She died Jamalpur 8 Dec. 1837.) *m.* 2nd, St. Saviour's, Bath, 28 June 1842, Catherine, 3rd dau. of Rev. Thomas Esbury Partridge, of Hilsley, Gloucs., rector of Uley, Gloucs. (She died 11 Dec. 1879, aged 65.)

Services : Barasat C.C. for 11 mos. Ensign 22nd N.I. 5th Vol. Bn. 1811-3. Capture of Java 1811 ; Cornelis ; Lieut. 5th Vol. Bn. (Medal). Adjt. 2/22nd N.I. 18 Feb. 1814. Adjt. 1/29th N.I. 4 May 1815 till 15 Dec. 1818. Siege and capture of Hathras ; Lieut. 1/29th N.I. Fur. 15 Dec. 1818 till 9 July 1821. Operations in Oudh 1822. Transfd. to 58th N.I. (late 2/29th) May 1824. To raise and comd. Bundelkhand Provl. Bn. 21 Mar. 1825. Fur. 30 Dec. 1832 till 10 Dec. 1833. Transfd. to 31st N.I. in 1842. Fur. s.c. 11 Jan. 1842 till 24 Nov. 1843. Leave m.c. 1 yr. to Ceylon June 1846. Transfd. to 58th N.I. 15 Nov. 1843 ; to 21st N.I. 24 Nov. 1847 ; to 32nd N.I. June 1851 ; to 13th N.I. Feb. 1852 ; to 33rd N.I. Dec. 1852 ; to 34th N.I. 2 Feb. 1853 ; to 58th N.I. 4 Aug. 1853.
Refs. : Boase. The Times, 26 July 1876.

COX, Henry Digby (1798-1847). Lieut. Colonel. 25th N.I. *b.* Lisbon, Portugal, 23 Nov. 1798. Cadet 1814. Admitted 1 Jan. 1815. Ensign 16 Dec. 1814. Lieut. 1 Aug. 1818. Capt. 13 May 1825. Major 17 Jan. 1834. Lt. Col. 19 Sept. 1840. Retired 22 Dec. 1842. *d.* 11 May 1847.

Son of H. D. Cox, of Sherborne. Ward of Sir Henry Digby, G.C.B., Adm. R.N. (whose mother was Charlotte, dau. of Joseph Cox), father of the ninth Baron Digby. *m.* St. Margaret's, London, 1 Feb. 1832, Miss Jane Elizabeth Wilkinson.

Services : Posted as Ensign to 2/13th N.I. Third Mahratta War ; Ensign 2/13th N.I. Transfd. as Lieut. to 2/20th N.I. First Burma War 1825 ; Ramri I. ; comdg. Light Coy. 40th N.I. (late

2/20th). Transfd. as Capt. to 25th N.I. (late 1/20th) in 1825.
Fur. p.a. 4 Dec. 1829 till 7 Nov. 1832. Comdd. 25th N.I. 29 Aug.
1833 till 30 Nov. 1833, and 6 Jan. till 28 Apr. 1837. Suspended for
12 mos. by sentence of G.C.M. 27 Dec. 1834. Fur. s.c. 25 Nov. 1842.
Removed from the Service and permitted to retire 22 Dec. 1842.
Refs.: A.J. N.S. vii. 166; N.S. xvii. 125. The Times, 14 Nov. 1831.

COX, Hiram (1759/60-1799). Bt. Captain, Infantry. b. 1759/60.
Cadet 1779. Arrived in India 14 Sept. 1779. Ensign 18 Sept.
1780. Lieut. 29 May 1781. Bt. Capt. 7 Jan. 1796. d. Chittagong, 2 Aug. 1799, of fever, aged 39.
m. Mary, dau. of Alexander Fraser, of Fairfield, Inverness, and gt.-grand-dau. of eighth Lord Lovat. (See also Allan Macpherson.) Father of Henry Chambers Murray Cox, q.v.
Services : Resigned 11 Apr. 1785. Readmitted 29 Oct. 1790. Lieut. 3rd Bengal Eur. Regt. in 1796. The town of Cox's Bazaar, Chittagong, is named after him. At this place he established in 1798 a colony of Maghs, who sought shelter in British territory after the conquest of Arakan by the Burmese. Author of " Journal of a Residence in the Burman Empire . . .," produced by his son H. C. M. Cox, q.v., pub. London, 1821.
Refs. :, District Gazetteer of Chittagong. G.M. 1800, i. 485.

COX, Sir Richard, fifth baronet (1769-1786). Ensign, Infantry.
b. 6 June 1769. Cadet 1783. Ensign 16 Apr. 1785. d.s.p.
9 Sept. 1786 : lost in the Severn packet in the mouth of the Hooghly, a little below Contai, on his passage to England.
Fifth Baronet, of Dunmanway, co. Cork. s. his cousin, Sir Richard Eyre Cox, 4th Bart., who was accidentally drowned 16 Sept. 1784. Eldest son of Michael Cox, Lt. Col. in the Guards, and Anna Maria his wife, dau. of Daniel Shea, a W.I. planter.
Services : N.F.P.
Refs. : Foster's Baronetage, p. 680, s.n. " Chaos." Burke's Landed Gentry of Ireland, p. 670, s.n. Villiers-Stuart, of Castletown, co. Kilkenny. S.M. 1787, p. 148.

COX, Robert (1740/41-1778). Captain, Infantry. b. Cirencester, Gloucs., 1740/41. Cadet (?). Ensign (?). Lieut. 24 Sept. 1765. Capt. 9 June 1767. d. Calcutta 12 July 1778.
Services : Sailed for India on the Britannia, 6 May 1762, aged 21. N.F.P.

COX, Samuel (d. 1810). Lieut. Colonel. 1st Bengal European Regt.
Cadet 1771. Arrived in India 19 Sept. 1771. Ensign 17 Feb. 1773. Lieut. 13 Mar. 1778. Capt. 6 Oct. 1781. Major 1 Mar. 1794. Lt. Col. 21 Apr. 1800. Retired 21 Feb. 1801. d. Sandford, nr. Enstone, Oxon., 21 Dec. 1810.

Of Sandford Park, Oxon., J.P. *m.* Calcutta 18 Dec. 1794, Caroline, dau. of John Fortnom, *q.v.* (*See also* Patrick Douglas, Alexander Orme, and Andrew Pringle.) (She died Clifton 6 Feb. 1850.) Father of George Cox, *q.v.*, and of William Cox, *q.v.*
Services : Fur. 14 Dec. 1792 till 29 Dec. 1794. Major 5th N.I. Transfd. as Lt. Col. to 1st Bengal Eur. Regt. 21 Apr. 1800.
Refs. : G.M. 1810, ii. 665.

COX, William (1809-1827). Ensign, 19th N.I. *bapt.* Sandford, Oxon., 26 Mar. 1809. Cadet 1825. Ensign 21 June 1826. *d.* Nasirabad, Rajputana, 19 May 1827.
Son of Samuel Cox, *q.v.*, and Caroline his wife. Brother of George Cox, *q.v.*
Services : Posted as Ensign to 19th N.I.

COX, William Beckford (*d.* 1814). Captain, Invalid Est. 7th N.I. Cadet 1796. Arrived in India 7 Apr. 1797. Ensign 23 Oct. 1797. Lieut. 10 Sept. 1798. Capt. 22 Sept. 1808. Invalided 4 Jan. 1811. *d.* Fort Marlborough, Sumatra, 8 Feb. 1814.
m. Ann. (She died Calcutta, 6 Mar. 1838, aged 63.)
Services : The greater part of his service was spent at Bencoolen, at which place he held the adjtcy. from 1805 till invalided on the Bencoolen Est.

COXWELL, William (1780-1803). Cornet, 1st N.C. *b.* Barnsley, Gloucs., 30 Sept. 1780. Cadet 1800. Arrived in India 17 Sept. 1801. Cornet 15 Feb. 1803. *d.* 1 Nov. 1803 : kld. in action at the battle of Laswari.
bapt. Barnsley 4 Nov. 1780. Son of Rev. Charles Coxwell, of Ablington House, Gloucs., rector of Barnsley, and Mary his wife, dau. of Joseph Small, of Cirencester.
Services : Second Mahratta War ; Laswari (kld.) ; Cornet 1st N.C.
Refs. : Burke's *Landed Gentry*, 13th edn., p. 1517, *s.n.* Coxwell-Rogers, of Dowdeswell, Gloucs.

COZENS, Francis (*d.* 1763). Captain, Infantry. Cadet (?). Ensign 10 Nov. 1757. Lieut. 8 Apr. 1760. Capt. 2 Aug. 1763. *d.* Kasim Bazar, Bengal, 15 Sept. 1763.
m. (?).
Services : At the date of his death was Qmr.
Refs. : Proceedings, Fort William, 26 Sept. 1763. Will dated 1 Sept. 1763 ; proved 18 Nov. 1763.

COZENS, Thomas. (*See* **CUSSONS, Thomas.**)

CRABB, William. Ensign. Infantry. Cadet 1783. Ensign 25 Mar. 1785. Struck off 1788.
Services : N.F.P.

CRABB(E), William Joseph (*d.* 1791). Lieut. Colonel. Infantry. Capt. 14 Aug. 1768. Major 26 Oct. 1773. Lt. Col. 22 Dec. 1781. Resigned Feb. 1782. *d.* Tamerton, Devon, 14 June 1791.
m. Sarah, youngest dau. of John Raggett, surgeon dispenser of the Royal Naval Hospital, Stonehouse, Devon. (She died Southampton, 6 Aug. 1852, aged 90.)
Services: Transfd. as Capt. from H.M. 84th Foot. First Rohilla War; battle of St. George; Capt. 2nd Bn. Sepoys. Campaign against the Rajah of Benares 1781; actions at Lora and Sukrut Pass; occupation of Latifpur; Major comdg. a force of 1,800 Art. and Inf.
Refs.: E.I.M.C. iii. 221, 222, 223. *G.M.* 1791, i. 588. *Eur. Mag.* 1791, i. 480.

CRACKLOW, George (1789-1832). Captain, 6th N.I. *b.* Southwark, Surrey, 31 Oct. 1789. Cadet 1811. Admitted 8 Aug. 1812. Ensign 30 Apr. 1814. Lieut. 19 July 1816. Capt. 21 Nov. 1826. *d.* Jaunpur, U.P., 5 Oct. 1832.
Son of Henry Cracklow, of Tooley St., Southwark, hatmaker. *m.* St. James's, Westminster, 13 Apr. 1826, Suzette, eldest dau. of D. Gill, of Cork St., London.
Services: Posted as Ensign to 2/3rd N.I. Nepal War 1814-5; Ensign 2/3rd N.I., in 1st Div. Transfd. as Lieut. to 1/3rd N.I.; to 6th N.I. (late 1/3rd) May 1824. Fur. p.a. 13 Mar. 1823 till 17 Nov. 1826.
Refs.: G.M. 1833, i. 479. *A.J.* xxi. 698. Will dated Jaunpore, 3 Oct. 1832; proved 17 Nov. 1832.

CRACROFT, Edmund (1761/62-?). Lieutenant. Infantry. *b.* 1761/62. Cadet 1781. Ensign 1781. Lieut. 16 Sept. 1782. Resigned 1791.
9th and youngest son of Robert Cracroft, of Hackthorn, Lincs., and Rebecca Waldegrave his 2nd wife.
Services: Apptd. Cadet on 19 Dec. 1780, aged 19. Sailed for India on the *Chapman,* 13 Mar. 1781, aged 19. N.F.P.
Refs.: Burke's *Landed Gentry,* 11th edn., p. 385, *s.n.* Cracroft, of Hackthorn, Lincs.

***CRAGG, William** (*d.* 1784). Cadet. Cadet (?). bur. Calcutta 5 July 1784.
Services: N.F.P.
Refs.: Calcutta burial register.

CRAGGS, William (*d.* 1802). Major, 7th N.I. Country Cadet 1770. Admitted 11 Jan. 1770. Ensign 18 Sept. 1770. Lieut. 13 Feb. 1779. Capt. 7 Jan. 1796. Major 4 Jan. 1801. *d.* Calcutta 18 Nov. 1802.

Services : Resigned 7 Sept. 1777 ; readmitted in 1779. Capt. 7th N.I. Major 1/7th N.I.
Refs. : Will dated 3 Nov. 1802 ; proved 19 Nov. 1802.

CRAIG, Edward (1784-1822). Captain, 16th N.I. *bapt.* Carrickfergus, co. Antrim, 10 Oct. 1784. Cadet 1800. Arrived in India 23 Sept. 1801. Ensign 8 Sept. 1801. Lieut. 11 July 1803. Capt. 13 Aug. 1815. *d.* New South Wales 22 Feb. 1822.
Son of Edward Craig. Brother of Thomas Craig, *q.v. m.* Carrickfergus, 13 May 1819, a dau. of William Mortimer Kirk, and niece of Sir William Kirk, Kt., sometime mayor of Carrickfergus.
Services : Posted as Ensign to 1/6th N.I. Operations in Jumna Doab 1803 ; Thathia 30 Sept. 1803 (w.) ; Lieut. 1/16th N.I. 3rd Vol. Bn. in 1814-5. Capt. 2/16th N.I. and comdg. at Banda, Amboyna, in 1816. Fur. 1818-20. Transfd. to 1/16th N.I. Leave to N.S.W. 1821.
Refs. : A.J. ix. 317.

CRAIG, James. Lieutenant. Infantry. Cadet (?). Ensign (?). Lieut. 19 Dec. 1766. Dismissed 8 Dec. 1767.
Services : N.F.P.

CRAIG or CRAIGIE, John. Ensign. Infantry. Cadet 1769. Ensign 1769. Resigned 29 May 1772. Brother of Thomas Craig or Craigie, *q.v.*
Services : N.F.P.

CRAIG or CRAIGIE, Thomas (*d.* 1777). Ensign. Infantry. Cadet (?). Ensign 23 May 1766. Resigned 7 Dec. 1766. *d.* Patna 1777. Brother of John Craig or Craigie, *q.v.*
Services : N.F.P. (? *Probably* one of those who received Commissions from Lord Clive in order to fill the vacancies caused by the defection amongst officers during the " Batta mutiny.")
Refs. : Will dated 3 Feb. 1770 ; proved 29 Nov. 1777.

CRAIG, Thomas (1786-1807). Cornet, 3rd N.C. *b.* Carrickfergus, co. Antrim, 6 Jan. 1786. Cadet 1804. Arrived in India 13 May 1806. Cornet 27 Mar. 1806. *d.* Ghazipur, U.P., 10 June 1807.
Son of Edward Craig. Brother of William Craig, *q.v.*
Services : Posted as Cornet to 3rd N.C. No record of active service.

* **CRAIG, William** (1787-1805). Cadet, Artillery. *b.* Carrickfergus, co. Antrim, 11 Aug. 1787. Cadet 1805. Never arrived in India. *d.* at sea, 1 Feb. 1805 : lost in the *Earl of Abergavenny,* off Portland.
bapt. 12 Aug. 1787. Son of Edward Craig and Mary his wife. Brother of Thomas Craig, *q.v.*
Refs. : Stubbs's *List of Officers of the Bengal Art. Philippart MS.*

CRAIG, William Millar (1812-1831). 2nd Lieutenant, Artillery. b. Glasgow 24 Mar. 1812. Cadet 1828. Arrived in India 3 Feb. 1829. 2nd Lieut. 12 June 1828. d. 2 Aug. 1831, on board the *Mountstuart Elphinstone*, nr. Diamond Harbour, Bengal.

Son of John Craig, of Gt. King St., Edinburgh, merchant. Addiscombe Cadet 1826-8.

Services : Fur. s.c. 29 July 1831. No record of active service.

Refs. : A.J. N.S. vii. 68.

CRAIGIE, Edmund Buchan (1784-1850). Lieut. Colonel. 13th N.I. b. Bengal 7 Dec. 1784. Cadet 1802. Arrived in India 6 July 1802. Ensign 16 July 1802. Lieut. 11 Oct. 1803. Capt. 18 Feb. 1815. Major 1 May 1824. Lt. Col. 21 Mar. 1828. Retired 22 May 1830. d. Mount Radford, nr. Exeter, 14 June 1850 : committed suicide by cutting his throat.

m. Agra, 17 Dec. 1810, Sarah, dau. of Alexander Manson, of Woodecock Hill, co. Kirkcudbright.

Services : Apptd. Cadet on 20 Feb. 1802, aged 17. Posted as Lieut. to 9th N.I. Transfd. to newly-raised 2/24th N.I. in 1804. Adjt. 2/24th N.I. 18 Jan. 1805 till 1813. Second Mahratta War 1805 ; Adalatnagar. Operations against the Rana of Gohad 1806 ; capture of Gohad. Settlement of Hariana 1809 ; capture of Bhawani. D.J.A.G., 1st Div. of Field Army at Cawnpore, 19 May 1815 till 1821. Leave to Cape 1821. Fur. 1822-3. Transfd. as Major to 47th N.I. (late 1/24th) May 1824. This Regt. having mutinied at Barrackpore the following Nov., he was transfd. to newly-raised 69th N.I. (became 47th). First Burma War ; Arakan 1825 ; Major comdg. 2nd Gren. Bn. Fur. 1 Dec. 1826 till retirement. Transfd. as Lt. Col. to 13th N.I. in 1828.

Refs. : S.M. 1811. G.M. 1850, ii. 225.

CRAIGIE, Henry Halkett. (*See* **CRAIGIE-HALKETT, Henry.**)

CRAIGIE, James (1787-1875). Major. 37th N.I. b. 23 Dec. 1787. Cadet 1805. Arrived in India 13 Dec. 1806. Ensign 2 Dec. 1806. Lieut. 20 Nov. 1809. Capt. 1 May 1824. Retired 30 June 1833. Hon. Major 28 Nov. 1854. d. 26 Albyn Pl., Aberdeen, 29 Mar. 1875.

Son of Rev. John Craigie, minister of St. Fergus, co. Aberdeen, and Mary Burnet his wife. Brother of John Craigie (1780-1811), q.v. m. Elizabeth, 5th dau. of Rev. Alexander Farquhar, of Old Pitsligo, co. Aberdeen.

Services : Barasat C.C. for 8 mos. Posted as Ensign to 2/18th N.I. Operations in Hariana 1809 ; capture of Bhawani 29 Aug. 1809 (w.) ; Ensign 2/18th N.I. Nepal War 1816 ; Lieut. 2/18th N.I., in 2nd Bde., Left Column (India medal). Adjt. Patna Provl. Bn. 1818 till 31 May 1824. Transfd. as Lieut. to 1/18th N.I. ; as

Capt. to 37th N.I. (late 2/18th) May 1824. Fur. 9 Dec. 1825 till 3 Jan. 1829, and 24 Jan. 1832 till retirement.
Refs. : The Times, 1 Apr. 1875.

CRAIGIE, James (1805-1826). Lieutenant, 13th N.I. *b.* Quebec 27 Nov. 1805. Cadet 1821. Ensign 10 Mar. 1822. Lieut. 13 May 1825. *d.* Biswanath, Assam, 8 Oct. 1826.
bapt. Quebec 5 Jan. 1806. Son of John Craigie, Commissary and Storekeeper Gen. in the Canadas, and Susannah Coffin his wife, widow of James Grant. Grandson of John Craigie, of Kilgraston, Dumbarnie, co. Perth, and nephew of Robert, Lord Craigie, a Lord of Session.
Services : Posted as Ensign to 29th N.I. Transfd. to 7th N.I. 10 Mar. 1823 ; to 13th N.I. (late 1/7th) May 1824. No record of active service.
Refs. : Anderson, iii. 702. (*See also* Burke's *Landed Gentry*, *s.n.* Craigie-Halkett, of Cramond.)

CRAIGIE, John (1780-1811). Lieutenant, 6th N.C. *b.* St. Fergus, co. Aberdeen, 14 Oct. 1780. Cadet 1799. Arrived in India 8 Dec. 1800. Cornet 8 June 1800. Lieut. 13 Mar. 1803. *d.* Muttra 17 Jan. 1811.
bapt. St. Fergus 26 Oct. 1780. Son of Rev. John Craigie, minister of St. Fergus, later of Deer, co. Aberdeen, and Mary Burnet his wife. Brother of James Craigie (1787-1875), *q.v.*
Services : Posted as Cornet to 6th N.C. and remained with that Regt. throughout his service. Operations in Jumna Doab 1802-3 ; Sasni ; Bijaigarh ; Kachaura. Second Mahratta War ; Laswari ; pursuit of Holkar. (? Operations against Dhundia Khan 1807 ; Komona ; Ganauri. Settlement of Hariana 1809 ; Bhawani.)
Refs. : S.M. 1811, p. 716.

CRAIGIE, John (1786-1840). Lieut. Colonel, 41st N.I. *b.* Glasgow 12 Jan. 1786. Cadet 1803. Arrived in India 14 Aug. 1804. Ensign 4 Sept. 1804. Lieut. 21 Sept. 1804. Capt. 11 May 1816. Major 13 May 1825. Lt. Col. 18 July 1829. *d.* Hatchett's Hotel, Piccadilly, 23 Nov. 1840 : committed suicide by taking poison during a fit of temporary insanity.
Son of Lawrence Craigie, of the Kilgraston branch of the family, merchant. *m.* in England, 2 Jan. 1823, Emily, dau. of Henry Churchill, of Gloucester Pl., London. (*See also* Sir Jeremiah Bryant, Kt.)
Services : Posted to 1/24th N.I. Adjt. 1/24th N.I. 27 Aug. 1807 till 4 May 1815. Mily. Sec. to V.P. 28 Dec. 1814. Asst. Mily. Sec. Offg. Sec. to Govt., Mily. Dept., and Pte. Sec. to V.P. 10 July 1817. Dy. Sec. to Govt., Mily Dept., 16 Sept. 1817. Pte. Sec. to V.P. 23 Mar. 1818. Garrison Storekeeper at Calcutta 17 Apr. 1820.

Sec. to Mily. Board 22 July 1822. On duty in England 1819-23. Transfd. to 48th N.I. (late 2/24th) May 1824 ; to 22nd N.I. 31 Mar. 1830 ; to Bengal Eur. Regt. 24 Sept. 1831 ; to 48th N.I. 1 Jan. 1832. Leave s.c. to Cape 23 Feb. 1834 till 19 Dec. 1835. Transfd. to 69th N.I. 11 Dec. 1835 ; to 41st N.I. 12 Jan. 1836. Fur. p.a. 4 Mar. 1837 till death.

Refs.: *Howard & Crisp*, v. 155, *s.n.* Lyte. *G.M.* 1823, i. 82 ; 1841, i. 215. *A.J.* N.S. xxxiii. 316. *I.N.* vol. i. 166. *The Times*, 25 Nov. 1840.

CRAIGIE, John Halkett. (*See* **CRAIGIE-HALKETT, John.**)

CRAIGIE, Patrick (1799-1843). Bt. Major, 38th N.I. D.A.G., Bengal. *b.* Montrose, co. Forfar, 28 Apr. 1799. Cadet 1817. Admitted 19 Sept. 1818. Ensign 26 May 1818. Lieut. 26 Oct. 1819. Capt. 31 Dec. 1830. Bt. Major 23 July 1839. *d.* Dinapore, 3 Oct. 1843.

Son of Patrick Craigie, of Montrose, provost and merchant. *m.* Dacca, 16 Aug. 1824, Eliza (née Olivier, of Spanish descent), widow of Ensign Edward Gilbert, of Limerick, H.M. 44th Foot. (She died 1875.) Step-father of " Lola Montez " (*D.N.B.*), who *m.* Thomas James, *q.v.*

Services : Posted as Ensign to 2/19th N.I. Transfd. to 38th N.I. (late 1/19th) May 1824. First Burma War ; Bde. Major 4th Bde., Sylhet frontier, 21 July 1824 ; Baggage Mr. to Bdr.-Gen. Shuldham's Div. 16 Jan. 1825. Siege and capture of Bhurtpore ; Lieut. 23rd N.I. D.A.A.G., Meerut, 24 Oct. 1826. A.A.G. Meerut Div. 29 Dec. 1829. 1st Asst. A.A.G. of the Army 21 May 1832. D.A.G. of the Army, with the official rank of Major, 18 Dec. 1837. First Afghan War 1839 ; Ghazni ; D.A.G., Army of the Indus (Medal). Durani, 2 cl., 26 Mar. 1841. Said to have been the inventor of " Craigie Toast." [1]

Refs. : *Autobiography of Lola Montez. Seven Splendid Sinners,* by W. H. R. Trowbridge. *A.J.* 3S. ii. 554. *I.M.* No. 8, p. 240. Will dated 29 Sept. 1843 ; proved 2 Jan. 1844.

[1] *Note* : A savoury compounded of tomatoes, eggs, Worcester sauce, and other condiments, well known in (old style) Anglo-Indian households.

CRANCH, Peter (*d.* 1793). Lieutenant, Artillery. Cadet 1779. Fireworker 3 Oct. 1780. Lieut. 30 May 1786. *d.* Madras 17 Sept. 1793.

Son of Elizabeth Cuningham, of Highgate, Middlesex. (*Perhaps* son of Capt. Peter Cranch, Madras Est., who died Trichinopoly, 27 Aug. 1768, aged 31.)

Services : Third Mysore War ; siege and capture of Nandidrug 18 Oct. 1791 (w.) ; Bangalore ; Seringapatam ; Lieut. 5th Coy.

THE BENGAL ARMY, 1758-1834   407

2nd Bn. Art. To Madras Aug. 1793, in order to take part in the siege of Pondicherry ; Lieut. 2nd Coy. 1st Bn.
Refs. : Will dated 20 June 1792.

CRANE, Charles Joshua (1793-1869). Major. 23rd N.I. *b.* Islington, Middlesex, 13 May 1793. Cadet 1811. Admitted 4 Aug. 1812. Ensign 16 Apr. 1814. Lieut. 9 Dec. 1817. Capt. 15 Apr. 1828. Invalided 17 Dec. 1832. Retired 29 Apr. 1846. Hon. Major 28 Nov. 1854. *d.* Bath Pl., Kensington, 22 July 1869. Son of Rev. Charles Theomartyr Crane, rector of Stockton, co. Warwick. *m.* Calcutta, 26 Oct. 1816, Miss Sophia Athanass. Ed. Rugby ; entered, on the foundation, midsummer 1806.
Services : Posted as Ensign to 2/4th N.I. (? Nepal War 1816 ; Ensign 2/4th N.I., in 4th Bde., Centre Column.) Transfd. to 23rd N.I. (late 2/4th) May 1824. First Burma War ; Arakan 1825 ; Lieut. 2nd L.I. Bn. (India medal). Fur. s.c. 2 May 1826 till 4 May 1829.
Refs. : *Rugby School Register. The Times,* 10 Aug. 1869.

CRANSTON, Andrew (1746-1776). Lieutenant, Infantry ; also an Assistant Surgeon. *b.* 1746. Cadet 1769. Asst. Surgeon Oct. 1769. Ensign 5 Oct. 1769. Lieut. 28 Mar. 1773. *d.* Berhampore 5 Sept. 1776.
Services : Surgeon on the *Northumberland,* which sailed from the Downs 31 Dec. 1766, and returned on 29 May 1768. He held a combatant Commission in addition to his rank as Asst. Surgeon, and at the date of his death was still doing double duty, his turn not having come for promotion either to Capt. or to Surgeon.
Refs. : *Crawford,* i. 226, 230, 231.

CRANSTON, Andrew (1764/65-1785). Lieutenant, Infantry. *b.* in Ireland 1764/65. Cadet 1781. Ensign 28 Mar. 1781. Lieut. 20 July 1782. *d.* Ramgarh, B. & O., 10 Oct. 1785.
Services : Apptd. Cadet on 9 Jan. 1781, aged 16. Sailed for India on the *Chapman,* 13 Mar. 1781, aged 16. N.F.P.

CRANSTON(E), John (*d.* 1771). Lieutenant, Artillery. Cadet 1767. Fireworker 15 Sept. 1767. Lieut. 8 Mar. 1770. *d.* Monghyr, B. & O., 31 Oct. 1771.
Services : N.F.P.

*****CRAUFURD, Charles Henry Gregan** (1803-1876). Cadet. Subsequently rector of Old Swinford, Worcs. *b.* London 14 Jan. 1803. Cadet (?). Did not proceed to India. *d.* 24 Feb. 1876.
Eldest son of Maj.-Gen. Robert Craufurd (*D.N.B.*) and Mary Frances his wife, dau. of Henry Holland, of Hans Pl., Chelsea. *m.* 2 Mar. 1836, Eliza, dau. of Richard Hickman, of Old Swinford House, Worcs. Magdalen Hall, Oxon. ; B.A. 1831 ; M.A. 1833.

Took holy orders ; Deacon 1830 ; Priest 1831. Rector of Old Swinford 7 Oct. 1835.
Refs. : Burke's *Peerage*, 1923, p. 608, *s.n.* Craufurd, Bart., of Kilbirney, co. Stirling. Boase. *Alumni Oxon.* Foster's *Index Ecclesiasticus*, 1800-1840. *G.M.* 1803, i. 81.

CRAUFURD, Patrick (1803-1821). Ensign, 10th N.I. *b.* Chelsea, Middlesex, 14 Jan. 1803. Cadet 1819. Ensign 24 May 1820. *d.* Barrackpore 26 Sept. 1821.
Son of Patrick Craufurd.
Services : Posted as Ensign to 1/10th N.I. No record of active service.
Refs. : M.I. in old cemetery, Barrackpore.

CRAVEN, Daniel (*d.* 1785). Captain, Infantry. Cadet 1772. Ensign 1 Apr. 1773. Lieut. 31 May 1778. Capt. 25 Feb. 1784. *d.* Cawnpore 26 Aug. 1785.
Services : N.F.P.

CRAWFORD, Archibald (1762-1786). Lieutenant, Infantry. *bapt.* psh. of St. Andrew, Holborn, Middlesex, 23 Dec. 1762. Cadet 1781. Admitted 24 May 1781. Ensign 25 June 1781. Lieut. 29 Sept. 1782. *d.* Chunar 9 Dec. 1786.
Son of Archibald Crawford and Caroline his wife. Admitted a Poor Scholar of Charterhouse 29 June 1773.
Services : Apptd. Cadet on 3 Jan. 1781, aged 18. N.F.P.
Refs. : *Alumni Carthusiani.*

CRAWFORD, Charles (1760-1836). Colonel. 25th N.I. *b.* 1760. Cadet 1779. Arrived in India 12 Feb. 1780. Ensign 23 July 1779. Lieut. 15 Mar. 1781. Capt. 30 Oct. 1797. Major 13 July 1803. Lt. Col. 14 Nov. 1805. Col. 4 June 1814. Retired 10 June 1818. *d.* Bivia House, Goodrich, co. Hereford, 23 Dec. 1836, aged 76.
Services : Campaign against the Rajah of Benares ; siege and capture of Bijaigarh, in the Kaimur Hills, 10 Nov. 1781 ; served as an Engineer and erected the batteries. Fur. 31 Aug. 1785 till 21 Sept. 1789. Resigned 8 Feb. 1793 ; readmitted 21 Dec. 1795. Comdd. escort of the Resident in Nepal 1802-5, when he was able to carry out some valuable surveys. Comdd. 4th N.I. Apptd. Surveyor Gen. in 1813. Transfd. to 24th N.I., subsequently to 25th N.I. Fur. 1815 till retirement.
Refs. : *E.I.M.C.* ii. 302. *Bath. Chron.* 5 Jan. 1837. *G.M.* 1837, i. 220.

CRAWFORD, James (*d.* 1778). Captain, comdg. 4th Bn. Sepoys. Cadet 1763. Ensign 26 Feb. 1764. Lieut. 11 Aug. 1765. Capt. 1 Dec. 1767. *d.* nr. Kalpi, U.P., 3 June 1778, of sunstroke.

THE BENGAL ARMY, 1758-1834

Services : Dismissed 16 Feb. 1767 ; restored to the Service 7 July 1767. Apptd. in 1768 to comd. 5th Bn. (became 4th in 1775), and held comd. till his death, which occurred whilst *en route* to Bombay to take part in first Mahratta War, with the force under Lt.-Col. Matthew Leslie. Was known throughout the Bengal army as " Caesar Crawford."
Refs. : *E.I.M.C.* iii. 447.

CRAWFORD, James (*d.* 1787). Major, Infantry. Cadet 1767. Ensign 20 July 1767. Lieut. 19 Apr. 1769. Capt. 9 Apr. 1777. Major 26 July 1781. *d.* Madras 24 Aug. 1787.
Brother of Capt. Arthur Crawford, Madras Est., and of John Crawford. Brother-in-law of James Alexander.
Services : Raised at Ramgarh in July 1778 the Ramgarh L.I. Bn., which became 31st Bn. in 1786, 23rd N.I. in May 1824. This Bn. was named after him " Chota Crawford-ki-Paltan."
Refs. : *Williams*, p. 94. Will.

CRAWFORD, Robert (1803-1875). Ensign. 27th N.I. *b.* Cork 31 Mar. 1803. Cadet 1824. Ensign 6 Apr. 1825. Resigned in India 30 Dec. 1826. *d. unm.* 1875.
3rd son of William Crawford, of Lakelands, co. Cork, and Mary his 2nd wife, dau. of James Uniacke, of Castletown, co. Cork. T.C.D. ; Fellow Commoner 6 Nov. 1820 ; B.A. 1824.
Services : Posted as Ensign to 27th N.I. No record of active service.
Refs. : Burke's *Landed Gentry of Ireland,* p. 141, *s.n.* Sharman-Crawford, of Crawfordsburn, co. Down. *Alumni Dub.*

*CRAWFORD, William (*d.* 1763). Ensign, Bengal European Regt. Cadet (?). Ensign (?). *d.* 1 July 1763 : kld. in action at the battle of Manji (*or* massacred at or near Patna by order of Nawab Mir Muhammad Kasim on 5th, 6th or 11th Oct. 1763). (See note to Benjamin Adamson.)
Services : N.F.P.
Refs. : MS. list in India Office entitled, " List of Persons killed in the Massacre at Patna, and at other places during the Troubles, 1763." *Broome*, p. 365. *Innes*, p. 169.

CRAWFORD, William (1745/46-1782). Lieutenant, Infantry. *b.* Edinburgh 1745/46. Cadet 1777. Ensign 23 Sept. 1778. Lieut. (?). *d.* Ramgarh, B. & O., 7 Jan. 1782.
Half-brother (*or* brother-in-law) of John Wotherspoon, of Edinburgh, printer.
Services : Campaign against the Rajah of Benares 1781.
Refs. : Will dated Buxar 2 Sept. 1781.

CRAWFORD, William (1793-1818). Lieutenant, 16th N.I. *b.* Straiton, co. Ayr., 23 Oct. 1793. Cadet 1808. Arrived in India

15 Dec. 1809. Ensign 13 Aug. 1811. Lieut. 19 May 1815. *d.* Calcutta 16 Apr. 1818.

Son of Rev. William Crawford, minister.

Services : Barasat C.C. 1810-1. Posted as Ensign to 1/16th N.I. in 1811. Adjt. 1/16th N.I. 4 May 1815 till death. No record of active service.

Refs. : Will dated Chittagong 19 Feb. 1818 ; proved 27 Apr. 1818. M.I. in S. Park St. burial ground, Calcutta.

CRAWFURD, Gavin Ralston (1793-1849). Lieut. Colonel, Artillery. *b.* Greenock 7 July 1793. Cadet 1809. Admitted 17 Nov. 1810. Fireworker 13 Nov. 1810. Lieut. 25 Sept. 1817. Capt. 28 Sept. 1827. Major 28 Feb. 1842. Lt. Col. 3 July 1845. *d.* Mussoorie, U.P., 5 May 1849.

Only son of Hugh Crawfurd, of Kilblain, merchant of Greenock, and Annabella his wife, elder dau. of Gavin Ralston, of that ilk. *m.* (?). Woolwich Cadet ; nominated for R.M.A. 7 Oct. 1807.

Services : Nepal War 1814-5 ; Lieut. F. 5th Coy. 2nd Bn. Foot Art., in 4th Div. Nepal War 1816 ; Lieut. F. 5th Coy. 2nd Bn. Transfd. to 6th Troop H.A. in 1817. Third Mahratta War ; Chanda ; Lieut. and Adjt. Nagpur Subsdy. Force. Civil Comr. in Chanda district June 1818 till 1825. Nagpur service 1826. Asst. to A.G.G., Saugor and Narbada territories, 9 July 1830 till 1834. Fur. s.c. 29 Mar. 1834. Comdd. 1st Troop 2nd Bde. H.A. 1837-42. Lt. Col. comdg. 1st Bn. Foot Art. Pub., Calcutta, 1830, " Suggestions regarding the Management of part of the Nagpore Territories." Fcap. folio, with plates.

Refs. : Burke's *Landed Gentry,* 3rd edn., p. 999, *s.n.* Ralston, of Ralston, N.B.

CRAWFURD, Moses (1745-1794). Major. Infantry. *b.* 1745. Asst. Surgeon 1764. Cadet 1766. Ensign May 1766. Lieut. 30 Aug. 1767. Capt. 28 Nov. 1772. Major 22 Jan. 1781. Resigned 14 Oct. 1782. *d.* Newfield, co. Ayr, 3 Mar. 1794.

Of Newfield. 2nd son of Robert Crawfurd and Marion Brison his wife, co-heiress of the lands of Groatholme, in the psh. of Kilwinning. *m.* 1785, Margaret, eldest dau. of John McKerrell, of Hillhouse.

Services : Asst. Surgeon in 1764, exact date unknown. Campaign against the Rajah of Benares 1781 ; capture of Bijaigarh, Kaimur Hills, as 2nd in comd. to Major William Popham, *q.v.* On his return to Scotland in 1783 he purchased the estate of Newfield.

Refs. : Burke's *Landed Gentry,* 2nd edn., p. 279, *s.n.* Crawfurd, of Crawfurd. *Anderson,* i. 704. *Crawford,* i. 242. *S.M.* 1794, p. 178.

CREAGH, William Bagwell (1782-1804). Lieutenant, 18th N.I. *b.* Doneraile, co. Cork, 2 Feb. 1782. Cadet 1799. Arrived in

India 13 Jan. 1801. Ensign 13 Aug. 1800. Lieut. 25 Oct. 1800. d. Kalpi, U.P., 12 Sept. 1804, " of fatigue, after a series of engagements with the forces under Holkar."

4th son of Arthur Gethin Creagh, of Laurentinum, co. Cork, and Isabella his wife, dau. of William Bagwell, M.P., of Clonmel, co. Tipperary.

Services : Posted as Lieut. to 2/18th N.I. 17 Apr. 1801. Second Mahratta War 1803-4 ; occupation of Bundelkhand ; Kapsa ; Kalpi ; Gwalior ; action of 2 July 1804 ; Jaitpur ; Lieut. 2/18th N.I.

Refs. : Burke's *Landed Gentry of Ireland*, p. 144, *s.n.* Creagh, of Bally Andrew, co. Cork. Intestate ; admon. granted 11 Sept. 1805.

CREDLAND, James (*d.* 1769). Lieutenant, Engineers. Cadet 1767. Ensign 15 Sept. 1767. Lieut. 1 Apr. 1769. *d.* Dec. 1769.
Services : N.F.P.

CREIGHTON, Thomas. (*See* **CRICHTON, Thomas.**)

CRESTIE, William. Cadet. Infantry. Cadet 1768. Resigned 6 Apr. 1769.
Services : N.F.P.

CRESWELL, William (*c.* 1765/66-1794). Lieutenant, 27th Bn. Sepoys. *b.* Worcester 1764/65 or 1766/67. Cadet 1780. Arrived in India 30 Apr. 1781. Ensign 1780. Lieut. 4 June 1781. *d. unm.* Goalpara, Assam, 14 Apr. 1794, aged 27, of a wound received in action the preceding day.

Services : Sailed for India on the *Belmont*, 3 Apr. 1780, aged 15. Expedition to Assam 1793-4 ; recapture of Gauhati ; skirmish nr. Goalpara 13 Apr. 1794 (kld.) ; Lieut. 27th Bn.

Refs. : Will dated 12 Apr. 1794 ; proved in 1794. M.I. at Goalpara, where his age at death is given as 27 years.

CREW, Josiah (1791-1812). Cornet, 8th N.C. *bapt.* Tetbury, Gloucs., 24 Feb. 1791. Cadet 1810. Cornet (?). *d.* (? Partabgarh, Oudh) 1812.

Son of John Crew, of Tetbury, farmer.
Services : Cadet d.d. 8th N.C. Posted as Cornet to 8th N.C.

CREWE, Francis Glynne (1790-1811). Ensign, 4th N.I. *b.* Hawarden, co. Flint, 10 Aug. 1790. Cadet 1806. Arrived in India 25 Nov. 1807. Ensign 23 Oct. 1807. *d.* Sikraul, Benares, 22 Apr. 1811.

Only son of Rev. Randolph (Ranulphe) Crewe, LL.B., rector of Hawarden, and Frances his wife, dau. of Sir John Glynne, 6th Bart., of Hawarden Castle, Flint.

Services : Posted as Ensign to 4th N.I. No record of active service.
Refs. : Burke's Landed Gentry, 12th edn., p. 1590, *s.n.* Crewe-Read, late of Llandinam Hall, co. Montgomery.

CRICHTON, Charles (1787/88-1812). Lieutenant, 7th N.I. *b.* 1787/88. Cadet 1805. Arrived in India 7 Feb. 1807. Ensign 6 Jan. 1807. Lieut. 8 Jan. 1810. *d.* Java 15 Jan. 1812.
Brother of Thomas Crichton, of Daleton, co. Dumfries. (*Probably* brother of David Crichton, *q.v.*)
Services : Passed as Cadet on 18 Apr. 1806, aged 18. Posted as Ensign to 7th N.I. Capture of Java 1811 ; Lieut. 4th Bn. Bengal Vols.
Refs. : Will dated 9 Jan. 1812 ; proved 9 Aug. 1817.

CRICHTON, David (1782-1845). Lieut. Colonel. 38th N.I. *b.* co. Kirkcudbright 16 Mar. 1782. Cadet 1804. Arrived in India 6 Apr. 1806. Ensign 9 Sept. 1805. Lieut. 10 Sept. 1805. Capt. 1 Aug. 1818. Major 26 Aug. 1829. Lt. Col. 29 June 1835. Retired 1 Feb. 1840. *d.* 7 Aug. 1845.
Son of Robert Crichton. (*Probably* brother of Charles Crichton, *q.v.*) *m.* Agra, 24 Apr. 1843, Miss Sarah Thornton. (She died Edinburgh 9 Mar. 1881.)
Services : Lieut. Dumfries North British Mil. Posted as Ensign to 1/15th N.I. Capture of Mauritius ; Lieut. 1st Bn. Bengal Vols. Capt. 1/15th N.I. Transfd. to 31st N.I. (late 2/15th) May 1824 ; to newly-raised 1st Extra Regt. (became 69th N.I.) 23 July 1825. Fur. s.c. 14 Dec. 1831 till 14 June 1833. To comd. 69th N.I. 28 Oct. 1835. Transfd. to 64th N.I. 22 Oct. 1836 ; to 38th N.I. 14 May 1839.
Refs. : Will dated 29 Jan. 1840 ; proved 31 July 1851.

CRICHTON or CREIGHTON, Thomas (*d.* 1820). Lieutenant. Infantry. Cadet 1778. Ensign 1778. Lieut. 9 Sept. 1779. Resigned 15 Mar. 1791. *d.* Burnside, co. Linlithgow, 28 July 1820.
Services : Adjt. 5th Bn. 3rd Bde. in 1790. N.F.P.

CRISPIN, George Charles (1805-1840). Lieutenant, 2nd L.C. *b.* Chatham 24 Nov. 1805. Cadet 1825. Arrived in India 26 Oct. 1826. Cornet 22 May 1826. Lieut. 19 May 1838. *d.* Ghorband Pass, Afghanistan, 2 Nov. 1840 : kld. in action owing to the misbehaviour of two sqdns. of 2nd L.C.
Son of George William Crispin, an officer of the Royal dockyard at Chatham.
Services : Posted as Cornet to 2nd L.C. 9 Nov. 1826. Adjt.

23 Jan. 1839. A.D.C. to Maj.-Gen. Thackwell, comdg. Cav., Army of the Indus. First Afghan War 1839-40 ; Ghazni ; action at Parwandara 2 Nov. 1840 ; Lieut. and Adjt. 2nd L.C.
Refs. : A.J. N.S. xxxiv. *The Times,* 13 Feb. 1841.

CROFT, Edward Nugent (1814-1837). Ensign, 65th N.I. *b.* Calcutta 5 Oct. 1814. Cadet 1832. Arrived in India 22 July 1834. Ensign 9 Feb. 1834. *d.* at sea, 26 Sept. 1837, in the wreck of the brig *Motichund Amichund,* which was lost by the pilot on the voyage to Singapore.
Only son of James William Croft, sealer of the supreme court of Calcutta, and clerk to the C.J., and Anna Eliza his wife, only dau. of Sir Edward Hyde East, 1st Bart., C.J. of Bengal. Nephew of John Thomas Croft, *q.v.* Ed. Winchester ; scholar 1828 ; left 9 July 1832.
Services : Ensign d.d. 44th N.I. 1 Aug. 1834. Posted to 65th N.I. 5 Nov. 1834. Leave s.c. 6 mos. to Singapore 26 Sept. 1837. No record of active service.
Refs. : Burke's *Landed Gentry,* 6th edn., p. 392, *s.n.* Croft, of Greenham Lodge, Berks. *Kirby.*

CROFT, John Thomas (1794-1859). Lieut. Colonel. 34th N.I. *b.* 1794. Cadet 1812. Admitted 3 Sept. 1813. Ensign 1 Nov. 1814. Lieut. 1 Aug. 1818. Capt. 1 July 1825. Bt. Major 28 June 1838. Retired 1 Aug. 1841. Hon. Lt. Col. 28 Nov. 1854. *d.* 15 Regent St., London, 11 Nov. 1859.
bapt. London 4 Aug. 1794. 3rd son of James Croft (formerly Woodcock), of Berkhampstead, and Charlotte Elizabeth his wife, eldest dau. and co-heir of Sir Archer Croft, 3rd Bart., of Croft Castle, co. Hereford. Uncle of Edward Nugent Croft, *q.v.*
Services : Posted as Ensign to 1/17th N.I. (? Nepal War 1814-5 ; Ensign 1/17th N.I., in 2nd Div.) Adjt. 1/17th N.I. 11 Jan. 1820. Transfd. to 34th N.I. (late 1/17th) May 1824. Adjt. 34th N.I. 28 June till 10 Aug. 1825. Operations against the Chuars 1832 ; Capt. 34th N.I. Bde. Major 21 Mar. 1833. Fur. 7 Jan. 1836 till 3 Aug. 1839. Bde. Major at Agra 18 Apr. 1840.
Refs. : Burke's *Peerage,* 1923, p. 621, *s.n.* Croft, Bart., of Croft Castle, co. Hereford. Burke's *Landed Gentry,* 6th edn., p. 392, *s.n.* Croft, of Greenham Lodge, Berks. *G.M.* 1859, ii. *The Times,* 14 Nov. 1859.

CROFTON, Robert (1801-1871). Lieutenant, Pension Est. 73rd N.I. *b.* Dublin 31 Oct. 1801. Cadet 1821. Arrived in India 17 Aug. 1822. Ensign 23 Aug. 1822. Lieut. 1 May 1824. Pensioned 28 Apr. 1831. *d.s.p.* 31 Dec. 1871.

4th son of Morgan Crofton, barr.-at-law (who was 3rd and youngest son of Sir Morgan Crofton, 1st Bart., of Mohill Castle, co. Leitrim), and Mary his wife, dau. of William Dun. *m.* Calcutta, 2 Jan. 1832, Miss Eliza Reid. (*m.* the dau. of —— La Trobe: *Burke.*) T.C.D.; Pensioner 6 July 1818.

Services : Posted as Ensign to 2nd Bengal Eur. Regt. First Burma War 1824 ; Lieut. 2nd Bengal Eur. Regt. Transfd. to 51st N.I. 20 Dec. 1827 ; to 5th Extra Regt. (became 73rd N.I.) 8 Mar. 1828.

Refs. : Burke's *Peerage*, 1923, p. 625, *s.n.* Crofton, Bart., of Mohill Castle, co. Leitrim. *Alumni Dub.*

Note : His name appears in the Burma prize roll, but not in the roll of those to whom the " India Medal " was awarded in 1851.

CROFTS, William. Cadet. Infantry. Cadet 1769. Resigned 25 Aug. 1771.
Services : N.F.P.

CROKATT, James (1755/56-1804). Captain, 9th N.I. *b.* London 1755/56. Cadet 1780. Arrived in India 23 Oct. 1781. Ensign 1780. Lieut. 11 June 1781. Capt. 1 Nov. 1798. *d.* 24 Aug. 1804 : kld. in action on the banks of the Banas R. during Col. Monson's retreat.

Services : Sailed for India on the *Hillsborough*, 27 July 1780, aged 24. This ship having been captured by the combined fleets of France and Spain off the N.W. coast of Africa on 9 Aug. 1780, he spent some time as a prisoner of war in Spain. Second Mahratta War ; siege and capture of Gwalior ; Monson's retreat (kld.) ; Capt. 2/9th N.I. " James Crockett, whom I recollected a dissipated London dasher. He had run through an independent fortune, being finally obliged like many other spendthrifts, to seek refuge from his creditors' attacks by accepting a commission in the East India Company's service."

Refs. : Hickey, iii. 210. Will dated camp nr. Agra 26 July 1804 ; proved in 1804.

CROMMELIN, George Russell (1803-1844). Major, C.B. 1st L.C. *b.* Ghazipur, 2 Sept. 1803. Cadet 1819. Admitted 8 May 1820. Cornet 25 Nov. 1819. Lieut. 4 May 1823. Capt. 7 Dec. 1827. Major 12 Nov. 1838. *d.* in camp, 1 Jan. 1844, from wounds received in action at the battle of Maharajpur on 29 Dec. 1843.

Son of Charles Russell Crommelin, Senior Merchant, B.C.S., collector of land revenue at Contai, Bengal, and Ann his 2nd wife. Brother of James Arden Crommelin, *q.v. m.* Johanna Maria. (She *re-m.* Simla, 6 Oct. 1845, George Elliot Voyle.) Ed. Harrow 1814/15 till 1819.

Services : Posted as Cornet to 1st L.C. To do duty with G.G.B.G. until further orders 8 May 1820. To continue to do duty with G.G.B.G. 21 Feb. 1821. To comd. escort of Resdt. at Lucknow 27 May 1825. Adjt. 1st L.C. 6 Oct. 1825. Fur. s.c. 9 Dec. 1829 till 7 Mar. 1833. Comdt. 3rd Local Horse 11 Sept. 1838 till 2 Aug. 1839. First Afghan War 1842 ; Tezin ; re-occupation of Kabul ; Major 1st L.C. (Medal). Gwalior campaign ; Maharajpur (s.w.) ; Major comdg. 1st L.C. C.B. 24 Dec. 1842.

Refs. : Harrow School Register. G.M. 1844, i. 446. Will dated 19 Feb. 1842 ; proved 16 Apr. 1844. Name on cenotaph " To the Memory of the Brave " in Barrackpore Park. *V.B.G.*

CROMMELIN, James Arden (1801-1893). Lieut. Colonel. Engineers. *b.* Calcutta 2 Feb. 1801. Cadet 1820. Admitted 24 Nov. 1821. Ensign (?). Lieut. 1 May 1824. Capt. 12 Jan. 1834. Major 22 Oct. 1841. Retired 1 Jan. 1843. Hon. Lt. Col. 28 Nov. 1854. *d.* 30 Jan. 1893.

bapt. Calcutta 1 Mar. 1801. Son of Charles Russell Crommelin, B.C.S., and Ann his 2nd wife. Half-brother of John Dethick Crommelin, *q.v. m.* Darjeeling, 20 Aug. 1851, Mary Anne Rajendra. Ed. Harrow ; entered the school 1814/15 ; left 1816/17. Addiscombe Cadet 1817-9.

Services : First Burma War ; Lieut. Engineers (India medal). Adjt. Engineers 1823-30. In the service of the King of Oudh 16 May 1828 till 3 Apr. 1829. Fur. 12 Feb. 1830 till 6 Mar. 1833. Executive Engr., Dum-Dum Div., 19 Oct. 1833. Leave to Cape 18 Mar. 1837. Suptg. Engr., N.W.P., 10 Mar. 1841 till retirement.

Refs. : Harrow School Register.

CROMMELIN, John Dethick (1795-1830). Lieutenant, Artillery. *b.* Calcutta 8 June 1795. Cadet 1812. Arrived in India Nov. 1813. Fireworker 9 Nov. 1813. Lieut. 1 Sept. 1818. *d.* Karnal 7 Sept. 1830.

Son of Charles Russell Crommelin, B.C.S., and Juliana his 1st wife. Half-brother of George Russell Crommelin, *q.v. m.* Meerut, 10 Mar. 1828, Isabella, youngest dau. of Rev. Thomas Pennington, and sister of Gervaise Pennington (1795-1835), *q.v.* (She died Wragby, Lincs., 30 May 1853.) Ed. Charterhouse 1807-11. Addiscombe Cadet 1811-2.

Services : Siege and capture of Hathras 1817 ; Lieut. F. 4th Coy. 2nd Bn. Foot Art. Third Mahratta War ; Dhamoni ; Mandala ; Garhakota ; Lieut. 4th Coy. 2nd Bn. Fur. Jan. 1824 till Oct. 1825. Transfd. to 2nd Troop 2nd Bde. H.A. (Rocket Troop) Dec. 1826 ; to 1st Troop 2nd Bde. Dec. 1828.

Refs. : De Rhé-Philipe. Charterhouse School List. A.J. xxvi. 486.

CROOKE, Samuel Cantwell (d. 1824). Captain, 40th N.I. b. I. of St. Christopher. Cadet 1805. Arrived in India 13 Dec. 1806. Ensign 10 Dec. 1806. Lieut. 3 Aug. 1811. Capt. 26 Aug. 1822. d. Penang 26 Sept. 1824.

Services : Posted as Ensign to 2/20th N.I. (? Capture of Java 1811 ; Lieut. 2/20th N.I.) Transfd. to 40th N.I. (late 2/20th) May 1824.

CROOKS, William (1788-1811). Lieutenant, 23rd N.I. b. Ayr 27 July 1788. Cadet 1805. Arrived in India 27 June 1807. Ensign 13 July 1807. Lieut. 10 Oct. 1810. d. Calcutta 30 Aug. 1811.

Son of William Crooks, writer in Ayr.

Services : Posted as Ensign to 23rd N.I. in 1808.

Refs. : S.M. 1812, p. 316.

CROSSDILL, Richard. Ensign, Infantry. Subsequently Madras Est. Cadet 1780. Ensign 26 Feb. 1781.

Services : Transfd. to Madras Est. Out of the Service before 1787. N.F.P.

CROSSLEY, Francis (1786-1846). Captain. 62nd N.I. *bapt.* Lisburn, co. Antrim, 5 Apr. 1786. Cadet 1805. Arrived in India 13 Nov. 1806. Ensign 4 Jan. 1807. Lieut. 5 Sept. 1811. Capt. 1 May 1824. Retired 4 Jan. 1836. d. 18 Sept. 1846.

Of Glenburn, Lisburn. Son of John Crossley, of Lisburn. m. (before 1811) (?).

Services : Barasat C.C. for $7\frac{1}{2}$ mos. Ensign Bengal Eur. Regt. Served at Macassar and Amboyna with his Regt. Supt. of spices in Banda Is. Fur. s.c. 27 Dec. 1820 till 26 July 1825. Transfd. as Capt. to 62nd N.I. in May 1824. Served with Nizam's army 14 Feb. 1827 till 30 July 1833. Action at Wanpati Jan. 1831. Fur. to China and England 30 July 1833. Retired on a pension of 10/6 *p.d.*

Refs. : Burton, p. 117.

CROSSMAN, Crawford (*or* **Craufurd**) (1811-1874). Major. 7th N.I. b. West Monkton, Somerset, 18 Oct. 1811. Cadet 1828. Ensign 12 June 1828. Lieut. 8 Oct. 1839. Bt. Capt. 12 June 1843. Invalided 5 Dec. 1845. Retired 30 Sept. 1861. d. 17 Nov. 1874.

Son of Rev. Francis Geach Crossman, of Bath. m. St. Mark's, Kennington, 6 Dec. 1836, Elizabeth Henrietta Craggs, only g.-child of Thomas Holland, *q.v.* Addiscombe Cadet 1826-8.

Services : Ensign d.d. 2nd Bengal Eur. Regt. 10 June 1829. Posted as Ensign to 7th N.I. 12 June 1832. Fur. s.c. 8 Sept. 1834 till 1837. Leave s.c. 1844 till 15 Nov. 1845. Fur. s.c. 30 Jan. 1847 till 1849. No record of active service. After being invalided he

THE BENGAL ARMY, 1758-1884

resided at Barrackpore until retirement. Postmaster at Barrackpore Jan. 1850.
Refs. : A.J. N.S. xxii. 68.

CROTTY, John (*d.* 1768). Lieutenant, Infantry. Cadet (?). Ensign 1 Aug. 1766. Lieut. 15 Sept. 1767. *d.* 1768.
Services : N.F.P.

CROUDACE, James (1793-1883). Lieut. Colonel. 11th N.I. *b.* Chester-le-Street, co. Durham, 10 Mar. 1793. Cadet 1809. Admitted 15 Dec. 1810. Ensign 16 July 1812. Lieut. 29 May 1817. Capt. 8 Sept. 1827. Bt. Major 23 Nov. 1841. Retired 20 Nov. 1845. Hon. Lt. Col. 28 Nov. 1854. *d.* Holland Rd., Kensington, 29 Jan. 1883.

Son of Thomas Croudace, of Lambton (Castle), agent (to the Earl of Durham).
Services : Barasat C.C. for 8 mos. Posted as Ensign to 2/5th N.I. (? Nepal War.) Third Mahratta War ; Lieut. 2/5th N.I. Adjt. 2/5th N.I. 1 Oct. 1823. Transfd. to 11th N.I. (late 1/5th) May 1824. Adjt. 11th N.I. 17 June 1824 till 11 Oct. 1827. Siege and capture of Bhurtpore ; Lieut. 11th N.I. (India medal). Fur. s.c. 2 yrs. to Cape and Tasmania 19 Dec. 1833. Fur. s.c. 7 Jan. 1836 till 17 Dec. 1838. A.D.C. to Maj.-Gen. G. R. Penny, *q.v.*, comdg. Dinapore Div., 29 Mar. 1839 till 4 Dec. 1840. Bde. Major at Cawnpore 27 Oct. 1843.
Refs. : The Times, 1 Feb. 1883.

CROW, John (*d.* 1819). Colonel, 26th N.I. Country Cadet 1778. Admitted 10 Aug. 1778. Ensign 28 Apr. 1779. Lieut. 8 Jan. 1781. Capt. 7 Jan. 1796. Major 5 Nov. 1802. Lt. Col. 21 Sept. 1804. Col. 4 June 1813. *d.* Dundee 24 Jan. 1819.

Of Amelia Bank, nr. Dundee. *m.* Barbara Kirkaldy. (She died Dundee 18 Apr. 1819.)
Services : Capt. 2/6th N.I. Major 7th N.I. Lt. Col. 7th N.I. Fur. 25 Dec. 1809 till 1812. Transfd. to 1/23rd N.I. in 1812. Fur. 1815 till death. Col. 26th N.I. 4 Nov. 1817.
Refs. : S.M. 1819, i. 286. Will dated Forfar 20 June 1818 ; proved 16 July 1819.

CROWE, Philip (1778/79-1831). Lieutenant. 2nd N.C. *b.* 1778/79. Cadet 1798. Arrived in India 23 Oct. 1799. Cornet 10 June 1800. Lieut. 11 Mar. 1805. Retired 22 May 1815. *d.* Montagu Sq., London, 23 Oct. 1831, aged 52.

bapt. Earl Soham, Suffolk, 26 Aug. 1782. Son of Philip Crowe and Margaret his wife. *m.* Matilda Ann, dau. of William Willis, of Lombard St. and Battersea Rise. (She died 18 Apr. 1844, aged 63.)

Services : Posted as Cornet to 2nd N.C. Second Mahratta War; battle of Delhi 11 Sept. 1803 (w.); Cornet 2nd N.C. Bk. Mr. at Dinapore 1804 till Dec. 1811. Fur. 17 Dec. 1811 till retirement.
Refs. : G.M. 1831, ii. 473. N. & Q. 12S. ii. 126. M.I. in St. Mary's, Battersea.

CROXTON, Lane. Lieutenant. Infantry. Cadet 1769. Ensign 16 June 1770. Lieut. 5 Apr. 1773. Resigned 10 Aug. 1775.
Services : N.F.P.

CROXTON, Thomas (1791-1851). Major. Artillery. b. 17 Apr. 1791. Cadet 1807. Arrived in India 14 Sept. 1808. Fireworker 23 Sept. 1808. Lieut. 12 July 1811. Capt. 10 Dec. 1821. Major 28 Apr. 1837. Retired 1 Mar. 1841. d. 32 Upper Baker St., London, 28 May 1851.

bapt. Gt. Catworth, Hunts., 3 July 1791. Son of William Croxton and Mary his wife. Brother of William Croxton, *q.v.* *m.* Gt. Houghton, Northants., 1 June 1824, Charlotte, 2nd dau. of Rev. Richard Williams, rector of Gt. Houghton and preby. of Lincoln. (She died 5 Mar. 1856.)

Services : Nepal War 1814-5; Lieut. 2nd Coy. 2nd Bn. Foot Art. (d.d. 5th Coy. 2nd Bn.), in 4th Div. Siege and capture of Hathras; Lieut. 2nd Coy. 2nd Bn. Third Mahratta War; Lieut. and Adjt. of Art. with Right Div. Fur. s.c. 8 Nov. 1822 till 29 Oct. 1824. To comd. 3rd Troop 3rd Bde. H.A. 1827; 2nd Troop 1st Bde. 1832-7. Fur. 25 Jan. 1839 till 30 Jan. 1841.
Refs. : A.J. xviii. 99. I.M. 1851, p. 339.

CROXTON, William (1776-1844). Major General. Colonel 21st N.I. b. Gt. Catworth, Hunts., 31 Mar. 1776. Cadet 1793. Arrived in India 9 Dec. 1794. Ensign 4 Oct. 1794. Lieut. 8 Jan. 1796. Capt. 21 Sept. 1804. Major 4 May 1812. Lt. Col. 19 Sept. 1816. Lt. Col. Comdt. 1 May 1824. Col. 5 June 1829. Maj. Gen. 10 Jan. 1837. d. Wadenhoe House, nr. Oundle, 26 Dec. 1844.

Son of William Croxton and Mary his wife. Brother of Thomas Croxton, *q.v.* *m.* St. Matthew's, Brixton, 10 Apr. 1833, Susannah Elizabeth, eldest dau. of Knight Spencer, of West Brixton.

Services : Apptd. Cadet on 19 Mar. 1794. Adjt. 1/1st N.I. 22 Apr. 1799 till 19 Jan. 1804. Transfd. to 2/23rd N.I. in 1804. Adjt. 1804. (? Operations in Hariana 1809; Bhawani; Capt. 2/23rd N.I.) Major 2/23rd N.I. Fur. s.c. 19 Feb. 1817 till 9 Oct. 1820. Lt. Col. 2/8th N.I. Transfd. to 1/17th N.I. 5 June 1822; to 34th N.I. (late 1/17th) May 1824. Tempy. comdg. troops on E. frontier 4 July 1826. Transfd. to 3rd N.I. 7 July 1826; to 10th N.I. 20 Dec. 1826; to 46th N.I. 2 Apr. 1827; to 21st N.I. 9 Feb.

1828. Bdr. 21 Feb. 1828. To comd. Muttra and Agra frontier 23 Feb. 1828. Fur. 8 Jan. 1829 till death.
Refs. : *A.J.* N.S. xi. 42. *G.M.* 1845, i. 218. *The Times*, 28 Dec. 1844.

CRUICKSHANK, George (1808-1833). Ensign, 9th N.I. *b.* Fordyce, co. Banff, 9 July 1808. Cadet 1827. Arrived in India 10 Oct. 1828. Ensign 10 May 1828. *d.* in the U.K. 23 Dec. 1833.
Son of William Cruickshank, master of the grammar school at Fordyce, and Margaret Davidson his wife.
Services : Ensign d.d. 13th N.I. 5 Nov. 1828. Posted as Ensign to 9th N.I. 18 Apr. 1829. Fur. s.c. 26 Sept. 1832. No report of his death having been received, he was promoted to the rank of Lieut. on 31 Mar. 1835. This promotion was subsequently cancelled. No record of active service.

CRUIKSHANK, John (1789-1820). Bt. Captain, 24th N.I. *b.* London 10 Dec. 1789. Cadet 1804. Arrived in India 13 May 1806. Ensign 3 Apr. 1806. Lieut. 1 Feb. 1807. Bt. Capt. 1 Jan. 1819. *d.* Cawnpore 30 Nov. 1820 : kld. by the accidental discharge of a pistol while drawing the charge.
Son of B. Cruikshank. Brother of Kenneth Cruikshank, *q.v.*
Services : Posted to 24th N.I. Lieut. 1/24th N.I. Capture of Java 1811 ; Lieut. 3rd Bn. Bengal Vols. Adjt. 3rd Vol. Bn. 1812-4 ; Qmr. do. 1815-6. Third Mahratta War ; Lieut. 1/24th N.I., d.d. with 2/10th N.I. Was in comd. of a detachment of 130 Cav. and 180 Inf. which destroyed a large band of the enemy at Junagarhi in Aug. 1818. D.A.Q.M.G., 3 cl., 1819 till death.
Refs. : *S.M.* 1821, ii. 93. Will dated 17 Aug. 1818 ; proved 13 Apr. 1821.

CRUIKSHANK, Kenneth (1791-1820). Lieutenant, Artillery. *b.* Lambeth, Surrey, 24 Oct. 1791. Cadet 1807. Arrived in India 21 Mar. 1809. Fireworker 1 Apr. 1809. Lieut. 1 Aug. 1814. *d.* Mhow 30 Sept. 1820.
Son of B. Cruikshank. Brother of John Cruikshank, *q.v.*
Services : Nepal War 1814-5 ; Adjt & Qmr. of Art. with 3rd Div. Posted to 6th Troop H.A. in 1818 ; transfd. to 1st Troop in 1819.
Refs. : *G.M.* 1821, i. 378. Will dated Mhow 6 Sept. 1820 ; proved 13 Apr. 1821.

CRUMP, Philip (*d.* 1806). Captain, 9th N.I. Cadet 1782. Arrived in India 15 July 1783. Ensign 8 Feb. 1783. Lieut. 26 Jan. 1790. Bt. Capt. 7 Jan. 1796. Capt. 2 Sept. 1803. *d. unm.* at sea, 30 Oct. 1806, on board the *Union* on the voyage to England.

Son of —— Crump and Keturah his wife. Brother of Robert Crump.
Services : Capt. Lt. 2/9th N.I. Adjt. 2/9th N.I. in 1803. Second Mahratta War ; Capt. 9th N.I. Fur. 19 Sept. 1806.
Refs. : Will dated 25 July 1804 ; proved 8 Nov. 1808.

CRUTTEN, Philip (*d.* 1769). Cadet, Infantry. Cadet 1769. *d.* 1769.
Services : N.F.P.

CRUTTENDEN, George (1767-1822). Bt. Major. 7th N.I. Subsequently a merchant in Calcutta. *b.* London 1767. Cadet 1781. Ensign 29 June 1781. Lieut. 2 Oct. 1782. Capt. 4 Jan. 1801. Bt. Major 25 Apr. 1808. Resigned 5 Aug. 1809. *d.* Macao, China, 23 Mar. 1822.
bapt. St. Martin's, Ludgate, 9 Jan. 1768. Grandson of Robert Cruttenden (*d.* 1763), accountant of the Penny P.O. Winchester scholar 1778 ; left in 1780.
Services : Apptd. Cadet on 9 Apr. 1781 (when he gave his age as 15). Sailed for India on the *Lord Mulgrave* 26 June 1781 (when he gave his age as 14). Capt. Lt. 7th N.I. Capt. 2/7th N.I. Comdg. Moradabad Provl. Bn. 1804-6 ; comdg. Patna Provl. Bn. in 1806 ; comdg. Dacca Provl. Bn. 1807 till resignation. He subsequently joined the firm of Cruttenden, Mackillop & Co. (formerly Downie & Co.), Calcutta agents and merchants.
Refs. : *Hickey*, iii. 138, 278 ; iv. 491. *Kirby*. *S.M.* 1823, i. 383. *N. & Q.* 8S. vii. 106. Will proved 29 June 1822.

CUBITT, William (1790-1840). Major, 18th N.I. *b.* 20 July 1790. Cadet 1805. Arrived in India 11 July 1806. Ensign 28 Aug. 1806. Lieut. 13 Dec. 1809. Capt. 1 May 1824. Major 3 Sept. 1839. *d.* Calcutta 15 Apr. 1840.
bapt. ptely., Catfield, Norfolk, 26 July 1790. 5th son of George Cubitt, of Catfield Hall, Norfolk, J.P. and D.L., and Mary his 1st wife, dau. of Rev. Justice Finlay, of Burton upon Stather, Lincs. *m.* Calcutta, 8 Feb. 1834, Harriet Harcourt.
Services : Barasat C.C. for 10 mos. Posted as Ensign to 2/6th N.I. Nepal War 1814-5 ; Lieut. 2/6th N.I., in 1st Div. Operations against Maharao Kishor Singh, of Kotah ; action at Mangrol 1 Oct. 1821 ; Lieut. 2/6th N.I. Transfd. as Capt. to 18th N.I. (late 2/6th) May 1824. First Burma War ; Arakan 1825 ; Capt. 1st Gren. Bn. Actg. S.A.C.G. of Arakan force 1 Dec. 1825. Sec. to Clothing Board 13 June 1828. Leave to Tasmania 7 Feb. 1833 till 1 Jan. 1834. Asst. Sec. to Govt., Mily. Dept., 3 July 1834. Dy. Mily. Sec., Govt. of India, 1839.
Refs. : Burke's *Landed Gentry*, 13th edn., p. 434, *s.n.* Cubitt.

formerly of Catfield Hall, Norfolk. *Howard & Crisp*, xviii. 36. *I.N.* vol. i. No. i. pp. 12, 15.

CUDMORE, John. Captain. Infantry. Capt. 12 Sept. 1756. Resigned 31 Aug. 1758.
(*Perhaps* father of Paul Cudmore, *q.v.*)
Services : Was a Lieut. in comd. at Dacca at the time of the Black Hole disaster, when he was kept a prisoner in the French factory at that station. Battle of Plassey, when he voted at the council of war for immediate action. Resigned owing to supercession by John Gowen, *q.v.*
Refs. : *Orme MSS.*, *India*, xiii. 3639.

CUDMORE, Paul (1764/65-1781). Ensign, Infantry. *b.* in Ireland 1764/65. Cadet 1781. Never arrived in India. Ensign 20 May 1781. *d.* St. Helena, on the voyage out to India, and was bur. there, 27 Oct. 1781.
(*Perhaps* son of John Cudmore, *q.v.*)
Services : Apptd. Cadet on 20 Mar. 1781, aged 16. Sailed for India on the *Lord Mulgrave*, 26 June 1781, aged 16.
Refs. : (? Burke's *Colonial Gentry*, ii. 674.) St. Helena burial register.

CULIN, Robert (*d.* 1773). Cadet, Infantry. Cadet 1772. *d.* June 1773.
Services : N.F.P.

CULLEN, George Downie (1806-1823). Ensign, 11th N.I. *b.* Glasgow 22 May 1806. Cadet 1821. Ensign (?). *d.* Barrackpore 30 June 1823.
Son of James Cullen, of Stockbridge, Edinburgh, merchant.
Services : Posted as Ensign to 11th N.I.
Refs. : *S.M.* 1824, i. 255. M.I. in old cemetery at Barrackpore.

CULLEN, John (1799-1830). Lieutenant, Artillery. *b.* London 10 Sept. 1799. Cadet 1816. 2nd Lieut. 25 Sept. 1817. Lieut. 1 Sept. 1818. *d.* Dacca 25 Oct. 1830.
Son of William Cullen. *m.* St. George's, Hanover Sq., London, 30 Aug. 1828, Isabella, 3rd dau. of James Watson, of Edinburgh, W.S. (She died Jamaica 3 Apr. 1834.) Addiscombe Cadet 1814-7.
Services : Posted to 6th Troop H.A. in 1819. Siege and capture of Bhurtpore ; Lieut. 4th Troop 2nd Bde. H.A. Fur. 1827-9.
Refs. : *A.J.* xxvi. 517.

CULLEN, John Peter (*d.* 1793). Captain, Infantry. Cadet 1776. Ensign 7 July 1776. Lieut. 28 June 1778. Capt. 23 Oct. 1792. *d.* Fatehgarh 13 July 1793.

Son of Dr. William Cullen.
Services : Bde. Major of Art. (although an Infantryman) Apr. 1787 till 26 Mar. 1788. Bde. Major at Dinapore in 1790.
Refs. : *G.M.* 1794, i. 278. *S.M.* 1794, p. 178. Will dated 13 July 1793.

CULLEN, William (*d.* 1768). Lieutenant, Infantry. Cadet 1766. Ensign 31 Dec. 1766. Lieut. 10 Apr. 1768. *d.* 1768.
Services : N.F.P.

CULLEY, Thomas (1791-1830). Captain, 2nd N.I. *b.* Newry, co. Down, 28 May 1791. Cadet 1807. Arrived in India 14 Aug. 1808. Ensign 23 Sept. 1808. Lieut. 10 June 1814. Capt. 1 May 1824. *d.* Singapore 30 Sept. 1830.
Son of James Culley.
Services : Posted as Ensign to 1st N.I. Lieut. 2/1st N.I. Siege and capture of Hathras ; Lieut. 2/1st N.I. Third Mahratta War ; Dhamoni ; Asirgarh ; Lieut. 2/1st N.I. Transfd. as Capt. to 2nd N.I. (late 1/1st) May 1824. Leave s.c. 1 yr. to Mauritius 28 Mar. 1828 ; s.c. 6 mos. to Singapore 23 July 1830.

CUMBERLAND, William (1808-1860). Major. 11th N.I. *b.* July 1808. Cadet 1825. Arrived in India 7 Aug. 1826. Ensign 11 Feb. 1826. Lieut. 8 Sept. 1827. Capt. 11 Feb. 1841. Invalided 27 Mar. 1846. Retired 18 Mar. 1855. Hon. Major 11 May 1855. *d.* 25 New King St., Bath, 6 Dec. 1860, suddenly.
bapt. Westerham, Kent, 29 Aug. 1808. Eldest son of William Cumberland, Rear Adm. of the Blue (who was youngest son of Richard Cumberland, the dramatist (*D.N.B.*)). *m.* Cheltenham, 13 Dec. 1837, Amelia Ann, dau. of —— Cossens, of Cheltenham, merchant.
Services : Posted as Ensign to 11th N.I. Wahabi rising 1831 ; Lieut. 11th N.I. Fur. p.a. 8 Sept. 1836 till 21 June 1838. Disturbances in Bundelkhand 1842. First Sikh War ; Ferozshahr ; Capt. 11th N.I. (Medal). Fur. s.c. 10 Dec. 1847 till 1850.
Refs. : Foster's *Families of Royal Descent*, i. 180. *Bath Chron.* 13 Dec. 1860. *G.M.* 1861, i. 114. *The Times*, 12 Dec. 1860.

CUMBERLEGE, Edward Altham (1803-1873). Lieut. General. 40th N.I. *b.* Shikohabad, U.P., 2 Feb. 1803. Cadet 1819. Admitted 1 July 1820. Ensign 31 Dec. 1819. Lieut. 11 July 1823. Capt. 29 Nov. 1834. Major 4 Apr. 1845. Lt. Col. 7 Apr. 1851. Bt. Col. 28 Nov. 1854. Maj. Gen. 22 Nov. 1862. Lt. Gen. 17 Sept. 1871. *d.* 23 Burlington Rd., Westbourne Pk., London, 28 Dec. 1873.
Son of Nathaniel Altham Cumberlege, *q.v.*, and Catherine his 1st

THE BENGAL ARMY, 1758-1834

wife. Brother of John Cumberlege, *q.v.*, and half-brother of Henry Altham Cumberlege, *q.v.* m. Calcutta, 23 May 1838, Charlotte, 3rd dau. of Capt. George Hunter.

Services : Posted as Ensign to 1/4th N.I. Transfd. as Lieut. to 29th N.I. 11 July 1823 ; to 58th N.I. (late 2/29th) May 1824 ; to 5th Extra Regt. (became 73rd N.I.) in 1825. To comd. Delhi Police Bn. 18 Apr. 1844. First Sikh War; Sobraon ; Major 73rd N.I. (Medal). Second Sikh War ; in garrison at Lahore ; Major 73rd N.I. (Medal). Comdd. 6th N.I. 1 Nov. 1851 till Nov. 1855. Suspended for 6 mos. (G.O. of 13 Nov. 1855). Transfd. to 40th N.I. in 1856.

Refs. : Boase. *I.M.* 1856, p. 4. *The Times*, 1 Jan. 1874.

CUMBERLEGE, Henry Altham (1811-1833). Ensign, 74th N.I. *b.* Dinapore 19 Feb. 1811. Cadet 1827. Arrived in India 11 June 1828. Ensign 21 Dec. 1827. *d.* Calcutta 14 Nov. 1833.

Son of Nathaniel Altham Cumberlege, *q.v.*, and Fanny his 2nd wife. Half-brother of John Cumberlege, *q.v.*, and nephew of Mrs. Mary Brown, of Shacklewell Green, Middlesex.

Services : Posted as Ensign to 43rd N.I. 4 Nov. 1828. Transfd. to 74th N.I. 23 Dec. 1828. Fur. s.c. 8 Sept. 1829 till 25 Jan. 1833. No record of active service.

Refs. : M.I. in Mily. burial ground, Bhowanipore, Calcutta.

CUMBERLEGE, John (1799-1852). Major, 41st N.I. *bapt.* Cawnpore 29 Sept. 1799. Cadet 1819. Admitted 14 June 1820. Ensign 31 Dec. 1819. Lieut. 11 July 1823. Capt. 17 Oct. 1838. Major 25 May 1852. *d.* at sea, 8 Dec. 1852, on board the *Queen*.

Son of Nathaniel Altham Cumberlege, *q.v.*, and Catherine his 1st wife. Brother of Nathaniel Joseph Cumberlege, *q.v.* m. Hazaribagh, Bengal, 27 Mar. 1835, Maria Sophia, 3rd dau. of Sir Henry Maturin Farrington, 3rd Bart.

Services : Posted as Ensign to 2/23rd N.I. 10 Jan. 1820. Transfd. as Lieut. to 21st N.I. ; to 41st N.I. (late 1/21st) May 1824. Intr. & Qmr. 1st L.I. Bn. 7 Dec. 1824. First Burma War ; Arakan 1825 ; Lieut. 1st L.I. Bn. (? India medal). Adjt. 1st L.I. Bn. 19 Nov. 1825. Fur. 4 Feb. 1831 till 28 Dec. 1833. Adjt. 41st N.I. 14 Apr. 1835 till 14 Feb. 1839. Comdd. Police Bn. at Ambala 14 May 1844. First Sikh War ; Sobraon ; Capt. 41st N.I. (Medal). Fur. s.c. 17 Dec. 1851.

Refs. : Burke's *Peerage*, 1923, p. 887, *s.n.* Farrington, Bart., of Blackheath.

CUMBERLEGE, Nathaniel Altham (1770-1823). Lieut. Colonel, 2nd N.I. *b.* 1770. Cadet 1783. Arrived in India 26 Sept. 1783. Ensign 15 Apr. 1785. Lieut. 2 June 1793. Capt. 21 Sept. 1804. Major 24 Jan. 1809. Lt. Col. 18 Aug. 1814. *d.* Kalpi 17 Aug. 1823.

Younger son of John Cumberlege, of Doctors' Commons, proctor, and Mary Hodges his wife. *m.* 1st, Miss Catherine Leadbeater, sister of William Edward Leadbeater, *q.v.* (*See also* John Boujannar.) (She died 29 Aug. 1806.) Father of John, *q.v.*, Nathaniel Joseph, *q.v.*, and Edward Altham, *q.v. m.* 2nd, Dinapore, 1 Feb. 1809, Miss Fanny Friend. (She died at sea 23 Jan. 1819.) Father of Henry Altham, *q.v.*, and of Fanny Agnes, wife of William John Baptist Knyvett, *q.v.* Ed. St. Paul's; admitted 14 May 1776.

Services : Operations in Jumna Doab 1802-3; Sasni; Bijaigarh; Kachaura; Thathia; Bde. Major to force under Lt. Col. Robert Blair, *q.v.* Second Mahratta War; Koil; Aligarh; battle of Delhi; battle and siege of Agra; Lieut. 2nd N.I. Apptd. Actg. Fort Adjt. at Agra. Reduction of Kalinjar 1812; Major 2/2nd N.I. Lt. Col. comdg. 2/2nd N.I. Fur. 14 Dec. 1818 till 1822.

Refs. : E.I.M.C. i. 216. *Gardiner.* Will dated on board *Coldstream,* 8 July 1822; proved 23 Dec. 1824.

Note : His brother, Capt. John Cumberlege, E.I.C.S., was ancestor of the present family of Cumberlege-Ware, of Poslingford Hall, Suffolk.

CUMBERLEGE, Nathaniel Joseph (1799-1848). Major, 74th N.I. *b.* Chunar 9 July 1799. Cadet 1819. Admitted 12 Sept. 1820. Ensign 7 Jan. 1820. Lieut. 22 July 1823. Capt. 28 June 1835. Major 22 Dec. 1844. *d.* Mhow 16 Mar. 1848.

bapt. Jaunpur, U.P., 21 Jan. 1800. Son of Nathaniel Altham Cumberlege, *q.v.*, and Catherine his 1st wife. Brother of Edward Altham Cumberlege, *q.v. m.* 1st, Mullye, B. & O., 17 Nov. 1827, Lucy, dau. of John Henry Cave, *q.v.* (She died Bareilly 2 Mar. 1835.) *m.* 2nd, Calcutta, 15 Nov. 1836, Fanny, youngest dau. of William Knyvett, of Ryde, I.W., and sister of William John Baptist Knyvett, *q.v.* (She died Calcutta, 26 June 1844, aged 33.)

Services : Was already in India when apptd. Cadet. Posted as Ensign to 2/12th N.I. Transfd. to 24th N.I. 27 Oct. 1823; to 6th Extra Regt. (became 74th N.I.) 13 May 1825. Adjt. 6th Extra Regt. 12 July 1825. Comdd. Calcutta Native Mil. 4 June 1835 till 24 Jan. 1845. Leave s.c. to Cape for 2 yrs. 11 June 1842; s.c. to Cape for 2 yrs. 26 Jan. 1845. No record of active service.

Refs. : Burke's *Family Records,* p. 364, *s.n.* Knyvett. Will dated 21 Sept. 1847; proved 22 July 1848.

CUMINE, George (1799-1834). Captain, 61st N.I. *b.* Monquhitter, co. Aberdeen, 31 Mar. 1799. Cadet 1820. Admitted 19 Jan. 1822. Ensign 14 Mar. 1821. Lieut. 20 July 1823. Capt. 13 June 1833. *d.* Nimach 13 Oct. 1834.

Son of Archibald Cumine, of Monquhitter.

Services : Was already in India when apptd. Cadet by G.O. of 15 Aug. 1821. Posted as Ensign to 1/12th N.I. Transfd. to 31st N.I. ; to 61st N.I. (late 1/31st) May 1824. Adjt. 61st N.I. 18 Nov. 1825 till 16 July 1833. No record of active service.
Refs. : *A.J.* N.S. xvi. 272.

CUMING, Hugh (1801-1829). Lieutenant, 18th N.I. *b.* Keady, co. Armagh, 28 Nov. 1801. Cadet 1818. Ensign 20 Sept. 1819. Lieut. 29 Aug. 1822. *d.* Calcutta 28 Dec. 1829.
Son of George Cuming.
Services : Posted as Ensign to 1/6th N.I. Transfd. to 18th N.I. (late 2/6th) May 1824. Siege and capture of Bhurtpore ; Lieut. 18th N.I. Fur. s.c. Dec. 1829, but did not live to embark.
Refs. : Will dated camp, Bhurtpore, 17 Jan. 1826 ; proved 1 May 1832.

CUMINGS, Andrew. (*See* **CUMMING, Andrew.**)

CUMMINE, Stuart or Stewart. (*See* **CUMMINGS, Stuart.**)

CUMMINE, William. (*See* **COMYN, William.**)

CUMMING, Alexander (1780-1836). Colonel, 4th L.C. *b.* Edinburgh 15 May 1780. Cadet 1795. Arrived in India 15 Feb. 1797. Cornet 11 Nov. 1796. Lieut. 29 May 1800. Capt. 11 Mar. 1805. Major 27 Feb. 1812. Lt. Col. 16 Aug. 1822. Lt. Col. Comdt. 13 May 1825. Col. 5 June 1829. *d.* Casterton House, Midlothian, 25 Mar. 1836.
3rd son of Sir John Cumming, Kt., *q.v.*, and Mary his wife. *m.* Middleton House, Scotland, 3 Dec. 1828, Jane Hepburne, dau. of A. H. Mitchelson, of Middleton. (She died 3 Apr. 1861, aged 52.) His dau. *m.* Alexander Cumming Dewar, *q.v.*
Services : Posted as Cornet to 2nd N.C. Lieut. 6th N.C. 1800. Operations in Jumna Doab 1802-3 ; Sasni ; Bijaigarh ; Kachaura ; Lieut. 6th N.C. Second Mahratta War ; Agra ; Laswari. Fur. 4 Mar. 1804 till 15 Sept. 1806. Transfd. as Capt. to newly-raised 7th N.C. 11 Mar. 1805. Operations in Oudh 1807-8, under Lt. Col. Robert Bourke Gregory, *q.v.*, and Major Henry Anderson O'Donnell, *q.v.* ; Pathar-serai Oct. 1808 (w.) ; Capt. 7th N.C. Nepal War 1814 ; Kalanga ; Major 7th N.C., in 2nd Div. Siege and capture of Hathras ; comdd. Cav. Bde. Third Mahratta War ; in Bundelkhand under Maj.-Gen. Dyson Marshall, *q.v.* ; Mandala ; operations against Apa Sahib of Nagpur 1818, under Bdr.-Gen. John Withington Adams, *q.v.* ; recapture of Multai. Fur. s.c. 18 Sept. 1820 till 29 Aug. 1823, and 21 Nov. 1823 till death. Transfd. to 1st L.C. in 1822 ; to 4th L.C. in 1825.
Refs. : *E.I.M.C.* iii. 31. *A.J.* xxvii. 125. *G.M.* 1836, i. 678.

CUMMING or CUMINGS, Andrew (*d.* 1794). Lieutenant, 18th Bn. Sepoys. Cadet 1778. Ensign 24 May 1778. Lieut. 27 Jan. 1781. *d.* 26 Oct. 1794 : kld. in action against the Rohillas at the battle of Bitaurah.

Son of Anne Mitchell, of Gerder House, Shetland I. Brother of Gifford Cumming, Thomas Cumming, and Agatha Buchan.
Services : Second Rohilla War ; battle of Bitaurah (kld.) ; Lieut. 18th Bn. Sepoys.
Refs. : Will dated Chunar Ghur 15 July 1792 ; proved in 1795. M.I. in St. John's churchyard, Calcutta.

CUMMING, Hugh (*d.* 1793). Lieutenant, 12th Bn. Sepoys. Cadet 1779. Ensign 18 Sept. 1780. Lieut. 27 May 1781. *d.* Cawnpore 19 Oct. 1793.

Brother of Samuel, Alexander, and George Cumming, and of Jane, wife of James Kyd. Cousin of David and John Colvin.
Services : Adjt. 12th Bn. 3rd Bde. in 1790. N.F.P.
Refs. : Will dated Oct. 1793.

CUMMING(S), James (*d.* 1806). Captain, 10th N.I. Cadet 1783. Arrived in India 21 Aug. 1784. Ensign 12 Jan. 1785. Lieut. 27 Dec. 1790. Bt. Capt. 8 Jan. 1798. Capt. 27 Jan. 1804. *d.* Bhagulpur, B. & O., 27 June 1806.
Services : Adjt. 2/10th N.I. 29 May 1800.

CUMMING, Sir John (*d.* 1786). Colonel, Kt. Infantry. Capt. 13 Nov. 1763. Major 1 Jan. 1768. Lt. Col. 30 Nov. 1769. Col. 10 June 1779. *d.* St. Helena, 26 Aug. 1786, on his passage to England.

m. Calcutta, 22 Jan. 1770, Mary, dau. of Capt. Henry Wedderburn, of Gosford. Father of Alexander Cumming, *q.v.*
Services : Transfd. as Capt. from H.M. 84th Regt. in 1763. On fur. in 1780. Apptd. to comd. all the Coy.'s troops in the service of the Nawab Wazir of Oudh 18 Apr. 1771. Knight Bachelor 31 May 1780.
Refs. : G.M. 1787, i. 189. *S.M.* 1787, p. 50.

CUMMING, Robert (*d.* 1797). Captain, Infantry. Country Cadet 1778. Admitted 9 Mar. 1778. Ensign June 1778. Lieut. 17 Nov. 1780. Capt. 7 Jan. 1796. *d.* Monghyr 23 May 1797.

m. Frances. (She died Midnapore, 30 Mar. 1791, aged 22.) Father of Robert Cumming, *q.v.*
Services : Fur. 28 Dec. 1785 till 24 July 1788. N.F.P.
Refs. : Will dated 20 May 1797 ; proved in 1797.

THE BENGAL ARMY, 1758-1834   427

CUMMING, Robert (1788- ?). Ensign, Infantry. *b.* Edinburgh 9 Jan. 1788. Cadet 1804. Arrived in India 4 Aug. 1806. Ensign 30 Apr. 1806. Resigned 10 Sept. 1806.

Son of Robert Cumming, *q.v.*, and Frances his wife.

Services : Sentenced by the C.D. to lose 28 days' seniority for having, " whilst proceeding to his appointment on the *Glory*, incurred our severe displeasure by persisting to sleep on shore while the ship remained at Falmouth, contrary to our express orders." N.F.P.

Refs. : G.O. by G.G. in Council 13 Feb. 1806.

CUMMING, Robert Hugh (1801-1822). Lieutenant, Artillery. *b.* Edinkillie, co. Moray, 3 Sept. 1801. Cadet 1817. 2nd Lieut. 8 Aug. 1818. Lieut. 16 Apr. 1819. *d.* Kamptee, C.P., 19 Sept. 1822, of fever.

2nd son of Robert Cumming, of Logie.

Services : Was serving with the Nagpur Subsdy. Force at the date of his death.

Refs. : S.M. 1823, i. 519.

CUMMINGS, David. Captain. Infantry. Cadet (?). Ensign (?). Lieut. 24 June 1763. Capt. 9 Feb. 1764. Resigned 1 Sept. 1764.

Services : N.F.P.

CUMMINGS or CUMMINE, Stuart (1745/46-1791). Captain, Artillery. *b.* 1745/46. Cadet 1771. Fireworker 2 Dec. 1771. Lieut. 31 Jan. 1774. Capt. Lt. 20 Sept. 1779. Capt. 1 July 1782. Resigned on pension 15 Jan. 1783. *d.* London 16 Apr. 1791. aged 45.

4th son of Charles Cummings, of Kininmont, co. Aberdeen, and Sophia his wife, eldest dau. of James, 15th Lord Forbes.

Services : First Rohilla War ; battle of St. George.

Refs. : Burke's *Peerage*, 1904, p. 625, *s.n.* Forbes, B. *Misc. Gen. et Her.* 2S. iii. 313. M.I. in burial ground of St. George's, Hanover Sq., London.

Note : His Christian name is variously given as Stuart and Stewart, and his surname as Cummine, Cummings, Cumine, and Cumming.

CUMMING, William (1762/63 ?-1805 ?). Ensign. Infantry. Cadet 1782. Ensign 5 Sept. 1782. (? *d.* Calcutta 13 May 1805, aged 42.)

Services : N.F.P. (*Possibly* resigned and became a schoolmaster in Calcutta till death.)

CUNINGHAME, Alexander (*d.* 1784). Lieutenant, Infantry. Cadet 1772. Ensign 26 July 1776. Lieut. 12 July 1778. *d.* Berhampore, Bengal, 23 Apr. 1784.

2nd son of George Cuninghame, of Bandalloch, and Esther his

wife, dau. of Alexander Jolly, of the high court of Admiralty, Edinburgh.
Services : N.F.P.
Refs. : Burke's *Landed Gentry*, 7th edn., p. 449, *s.n.* Cuninghame, of Bandalloch. *S.M.* 1785, p. 257.

CUNINGHAME or CUNNINGHAM, George (1783-1838). Major. 7th N.I. Subsequently an Especial Judge in Mauritius. *bapt.* English church, The Hague, 22 June 1783. Cadet 1798. Arrived in India 22 Dec. 1799. Ensign 10 Sept. 1799. Lieut. 28 Oct. 1799. Capt. 2 Jan. 1810. Major 3 Dec. 1819. Retired 7 Oct. 1821. *d.* Mauritius 30 July 1838.

Son of George Cunningham or Cuninghame, of the Cuninghames of Entricken, Col. Scots Bde., and Charlotte Elizabeth Macalister his wife. Brother of John Cuninghame (1788-1814), *q.v. m.* Calcutta, 16 Mar. 1814, Ann Helen, 2nd dau. of Sir Joseph O'Halloran, *q.v.* (*See also* Thomas Vallencey Lysaght and Sir George Moyle Sherer.) (She died St. Leonards-on-Sea 30 May 1856.)

Services : Posted as Lieut. to 1/7th N.I. 15 Apr. 1801. Adjt. & Qmr. 10th N.I. 1803 till 23 Jan. 1810. A.D.C. to Maj.-Gen. James Morris, *q.v.*, comdg. at Berhampore, 1812-5. Capt. 1/7th N.I. Apptd. to comd. newly-raised 2nd Rohilla Cav. 26 July 1815. Bareilly insurrection 1816. Siege and capture of Hathras ; comdg. 2nd Rohilla Cav. Fur. s.c. 9 Jan. 1818 till retirement. Granted by the C.D. in May 1828 a special pension of £200 *p.a.* in order to bring his total pension up to £503, in consideration of the important services rendered to the Coy. during the Bareilly insurrection in 1816, from which his health suffered severely. After retirement he was, for some years, an especial judge in the I. of Mauritius.

Refs. : Burke's *Colonial Gentry*, i. 83, *s.n.* O'Halloran. *A.J.* xxvi. 97-100. *G.M.* 1839, i. 223.

CUNINGHAME, John (*d.* 1843). Lieut. General. Colonel 48th N.I. Country Cadet 1780. Admitted 25 Apr. 1782. Ensign 29 May 1781. Lieut. 2 Oct. 1781. Capt. 29 May 1800. Major 27 Mar. 1804. Lt. Col. 3 Mar. 1808. Col. 14 June 1814. Maj. Gen. 27 May 1825. Lt. Gen. 28 June 1838. *d.* in England 10 Apr. 1843.

Services : Abroad when nominated Cadet on 27 Mar. 1781. Capt. Lt. and Capt. 1st Bengal Eur. Regt. Fur. s.c. 29 Jan. 1800 till 4 Dec. 1804. Lt. Col. 21st N.I. 1808. Transfd. to Bengal Eur. Regt. ; to 18th N.I. in 1815. Fur. s.c. 2 Jan. 1815 till Jan. 1818, and 5 Feb. 1820 till death. Was borne at various times on the rolls of 17th, 1st, and 6th N.I. Transfd. to 44th N.I. in 1824 ; to 48th N.I. 7 July 1826.

CUNINGHAME, John (1783-1806). Lieutenant, 10th N.I. b. 31 Jan. 1783. Cadet 1799. Arrived in India 8 Dec. 1800. Ensign 2 Oct. 1800. Lieut. 2 Dec. 1802. d. Fatehgarh, U.P., 12 Mar. 1806. bapt. Stevenston, co. Ayr, 11 Feb. 1783. Son of Robert Reid Cuninghame, of Auchenharvie. Kinsman of John Cuninghame (1790-1816), q.v.
Services : Posted as Ensign to 2/10th N.I. 17 Apr. 1801. On fur. in 1803.
Refs. : Burke's *Peerage*, 1923, p. 636, s.n. Fairlie-Cuninghame Bart., of Robertland and Fairlie, co. Ayr.

CUNINGHAME or CUNNINGHAM, John (1788-1814). Lieutenant, 13th N.I. b. Springfield, S. Leith, 23 Sept. 1788. Cadet 1803. Arrived in India 15 Aug. 1804. Ensign 30 Aug. 1804. Lieut. 21 Sept. 1804. d. 27 Nov. 1814 : kld. in action in the attack on Kalanga fort.
Son of Col. George Cunningham or Cuninghame, Scots Bde. Brother of George Cuninghame, q.v.
Services : Posted as Lieut. to 1/13th N.I. (? Operations against Dhundia Khan 1807 ; Komona ; Ganauri ; Lieut. 1/13th N.I.) Nepal War 1814 ; Kalanga (kld.) ; Lieut. 1/13th N.I., in 2nd Div.

CUNINGHAME, John (1790-1816). Lieutenant, 17th N.I. b. Irvine, co. Ayr, 5 July 1790. Cadet 1807. Arrived in India 1 Nov. 1808. Ensign 11 Nov. 1808. Lieut. 16 Dec. 1814. d. Muttra 2 June 1816.
Younger son of Alexander Cuninghame, collector of customs at Irvine (who was younger son of Sir William Cuningham, 5th Bart.), and Sarah his wife, dau. of John Reid. Brother of William Cunningham, q.v., who altered the spelling of his name. Kinsman of John Cuninghame (1783-1806), q.v.
Services : Posted as Ensign to 2/17th N.I. Nepal War 1814-5 ; Jitpur ; Lieut. 2/17th N.I., in 3rd Div. Actg. A.D.C. to Maj.-Gen. J. S. Wood, comdg. 3rd Div., in 1815. Bk. Mr. at Cawnpore 1815-6.
Refs. : Burke's *Peerage*, 1923, p. 636, s.n. Fairlie-Cuninghame, Bart., of Robertland and Fairlie, co. Ayr. Will dated Gorakhpur 18 Nov. 1814 ; proved 27 June 1816.

CUNLIFFE, George (1813-1834). Cornet, Cavalry. b. Cawnpore 26 Nov. 1813. Cadet 1830. Arrived in India 7 May 1831. Acting Cornet 6 June 1833. d. Meerut 18 Oct. 1834.
2nd son of Sir Robert Henry Cunliffe, Bart., q.v., and Louisa his 1st wife.
Services : To do duty with 1st L.C. 28 June 1831. No record of active service.

Refs. : Burke's *Peerage*, 1923, p. 640., *s.n.* Cunliffe, Bart., of Liverpool. *Howard & Crisp*, xvi. 75. *A.J.* N.S. xvi. 272.

CUNLIFFE, Sir Robert Henry, fourth baronet (1783-1859). General, Kt. and C.B. Colonel 4th N.I. *b.* 28 Sept. 1783. Cadet 1798. Arrived in India 9 Dec. 1800. Ensign 25 Sept. 1799. Lieut. 28 Oct. 1799. Capt. 1 May 1808. Major 17 Oct. 1818. Lt. Col. 30 Jan. 1824. Col. 5 June 1829. Maj. Gen. 28 June 1838. Lt. Gen. 11 Nov. 1851. Gen. 13 Oct. 1857. *d.* Acton Park, Wrexham, co. Denbigh, 10 Sept. 1859.

Fourth Baronet, of Liverpool. *s.* 15 June 1834. *bapt.* St. John Baptist's, Chester, 13 Oct. 1783. 2nd son of Sir Foster Cunliffe, 3rd Bart., and Harriet his wife, dau. of Sir David Kinloch, Bart. *m.* 1st, Lucknow, 15 Dec. 1805, Louisa, widow of Major Arthur Forrest. (She died 4 May 1822.) Father of George Cunliffe, *q.v.*, and of Louisa Harriot, wife of Hippisley Marsh, *q.v. m.* 2nd, Calcutta, 2 Apr. 1825, Susan Emily, dau. of John Paton (1760/61-1824), *q.v.* (She died 11 Nov. 1856.)

Services : Posted to 2/1st N.I. 15 Apr. 1801. Adjt. 2/1st N.I. 1804. Jumna Doab 1804. Adjt. & Qmr. 2/1st N.I. 1806-8. S.A.C.G. 1 June 1811. Kalinjar 1812. A.C.G. 6 Mar. 1813. Nepal War 1814-5 (India medal). Siege of Hathras 1817. Third Mahratta War 1818 ; Capt. 2/1st N.I., A.C.G. 2nd Div. Offg. Dy. Comy. Gen. 18 Nov. 1820. Dy. Comy. Gen. 2 July 1821. Transfd. to 1/1st N.I. Comy. Gen. 27 Nov. 1823. Transfd. to 24th N.I. in 1824 ; to 4th Extra Regt. 28 Dec. 1826 ; to 4th N.I. 10 Sept. 1828. Fur. 10 Jan. 1833 till death. Kt. 16 Sept. 1829. C.B. 20 July 1838.

Refs. : Burke's *Peerage*, 1923, p. 640, *s.n.* Cunliffe, Bart. *Howard & Crisp*, xvi. 73. *E.I.M.C.* i. 310. *Boase. G.M.* 1859, ii. 434, 541. *The Times*, 15 Sept. 1859. Will dated 21 Mar. 1857 ; proved 4 May 1860.

Note : All the above authorities give the date of his birth as 22 Apr. 1785 ; his obit. notice in *The Times* gives his age at death as 74, and in the obit. notice of Miss Emily Cunliffe, his 6th dau., who died so recently as 22 June 1926, it is stated that her father was born on 22 Apr. 1785. The copy of his birth and baptismal certificate in the India Office, however, clearly shows that the dates as given here are correct ; it is, moreover, unlikely that he could have obtained his Lieutenancy at the age of $14\frac{1}{2}$.

CUNNINGHAM, Sir Alexander (1814-1893). Major General, K.C.I.E. Engineers. *b.* Westminster 23 Jan. 1814. Cadet 1832. Arrived in India 9 June 1833. 2nd Lieut. 9 June 1831. Lieut. 20 May 1839. Capt. 15 Jan. 1851. Major 13 Aug. 1858. Lt. Col. 27 Aug. 1858. Col. 16 June 1860. Retired 30 June 1862. Hon.

Maj. Gen. 30 June 1862. *d.* 2 Cranley Mansions, S. Kensington, 28 Nov. 1893.
2nd son of Allan Cunningham, miscellaneous writer (*D.N.B.*), and Jean Walker his wife. Brother of Joseph Davey Cunningham, *q.v. m.* Simla, 30 Mar. 1840, Alicia Mary, dau. of Martin Thomas Whish, B.C.S. Ed. Christ's Hospital. Addiscombe Cadet 1 Aug. 1829 till 9 June 1831. Chatham 13 Aug. 1831 till 30 Aug. 1832.
Services : See *D.N.B.* A.D.C. to G.G. 4 Mar. 1836. Author of " Ancient Geography of India," 1871, etc. C.S.I. 1871. C.I.E. 1 Jan. 1878. K.C.I.E. 15 Feb. 1887.
Refs. : D.N.B. D.I.B. Vibart, p. 455. *The Times,* 1 Dec. 1893, p. 10.

CUNNINGHAM, Benjamin. Cadet. Infantry. Cadet 1768. Resigned 14 Mar. 1769.
Services : N.F.P.

CUNNINGHAM, George. (*See* **CUNINGHAME, George.**)

CUNNINGHAM, John. (*See* **CUNINGHAME, John.**)

CUNNINGHAM, Joseph Davey (1812-1851). Captain, Engineers. *b.* Lambeth 9 June 1812. Cadet 1831. Arrived in India 13 June 1832. 2nd Lieut. (10 Dec. 1830) 3 Feb. 1839. Lieut. 20 May 1839. Capt. 13 Nov. 1849. *d.* in camp, nr. Ambala, 28 Feb. 1851.
bapt. Christchurch, Surrey, 4 June 1813. Eldest son of Allan Cunningham and Jean Walker his wife. Brother of Sir Alexander Cunningham, K.C.I.E., *q.v.* Addiscombe Cadet 6 Feb. 1829 till 10 Dec. 1830. Chatham 10 Feb. 1831 till 3 Jan. 1832.
Services : See *D.N.B.* Author of " History of the Sikhs," 1849.
Refs. : D.N.B. D.I.B. Boase. Vibart, p. 453. *Thackeray,* p. 40. *G.M.* 1851, i. 555. *I.M.* 1851, p. 230.

CUNNINGHAM, William (1787-1838). Major. 54th N.I. *b.* Irvine, co. Ayr., 4 Apr. 1787. Cadet 1804. Arrived in India 30 Sept. 1805. Ensign (?). Lieut. 15 Aug. 1805. Capt. 18 Oct. 1822. Major 6 Jan. 1832. Retired 18 May 1833. *d.* 11 Aug. 1838.
Of South Lodge, Ayr. Originally Cuninghame : altered the spelling of his name. Elder son of Alexander Cuninghame and Sarah his wife. Brother of John Cuninghame (1790-1816), *q.v.*, and kinsman of John Cuninghame (1783-1806), *q.v. m.* 1st, Calcutta, 27 Dec. 1813, Miss Anna Elizabeth Buchanan Stewart. (She died Muttra, 17 June 1815, aged 18½.) *m.* 2nd, Bengal, 31 Dec. 1816, Rebecca, dau. of William Armstrong, B.C.S., Comr. of Nadia, Bengal. (She died 19 Apr. 1875.)

Services : Posted as Lieut. to 1/27th N.I. With the escort to the mission to Ranjit Singh at Amritsar 1809. Dy. Paymr. at Muttra 1814-22. Third Mahratta War ; Field Paymr. 1st Div. Garrison Storekeeper at Calcutta 21 Jan. 1822 till 5 July 1830. Transfd. to 54th N.I. (late 2/27th) May 1824. Fur. 5 July 1830 till retirement.

Refs. : Burke's *Peerage*, 1923, p. 636, *s.n.* Fairlie-Cuninghame, Bart., of Robertland and Fairlie, co. Ayr.

CUNNINGHAM, William S. (or L.) [1] (*d.* 1795). Lieutenant, Artillery. Country Cadet 1781. Admitted 10 Apr. 1781. Fireworker 5 Sept. 1781. Lieut. 26 Nov. 1786. *d.* at sea, 5 Feb. 1795.

Services : N.F.P.

[1] *Note :* Phillipart *MS.* and *Stubbs* give the second initial as S. ; *Dodwell & Miles* and the *East India Kalendar*, 1791, as L.

CUNYNGHAME, Robert South Thurlow (1807-1829). Ensign. 25th N.I. *b.* 27 Mar. 1807. Cadet 1824. Ensign 8 Jan. 1825. Resigned in India 26 July 1826. *d.* Bruges, Belgium, 13 Mar. 1829.

bapt. Church Oakley, Hants, 28 Mar. 1807. 3rd son of Sir David Cunynghame, 5th Bart., of Milncraig, Col. 82nd Foot, and Maria his 1st wife, natural dau. of Edward, Lord Thurlow, lord-chancellor of England.

Services : Posted as Ensign to 25th N.I. No record of active service.

Refs. : Burke's *Peerage*, 1923, p. 643, *s.n.* Cunynghame, Bart., of Milncraig, co. Ayr. *G.M.* 1829, i. 382.

CUPPAGE, William (*d.* 1819). Lieut. Colonel, Invalid Est. 22nd N.I. Country Cadet 1781. Admitted 15 Jan. 1781. Ensign 15 Aug. 1781. Lieut. 3 June 1783. Capt. 13 July 1803. Major 30 Dec. 1807. Lt. Col. 16 Jan. 1814. Invalided 13 July 1815.

d. unm. Fatehgarh, U.P., 1 July 1819.

Services : Adjt. 1st Vol. Bn. 26 Nov. 1798. Fourth Mysore War ; Lieut 1st Vol. Bn. (? Medal). Lieut. 1st N.I. in 1800. Capt. Lt. 1st N.I. 30 June 1802. Transfd. as Capt. to newly-raised 21st N.I. Comdd. a detachment which captured Hirapur, a small fort in Tehri district, C.I., 19 Dec 1808. Transfd. as Lt. Col. to 22nd N.I. in 1814. Comdg. Farrukhabad Provl. Bn. 1815 till death.

Refs. : *Stubbs*, i. 311-2. Will dated 21 July 1818 ; proved 19 July 1819.

CURFY, Edward (1746/47-1791). Major, Infantry. *b.* in Ireland 1746/47. Cadet 1767. Ensign 15 Sept. 1767. Lieut. 3 Oct. 1769. Capt. 4 Jan. 1778. Major 20 Sept. 1781. *d.* Barrackpore 20 Nov. 1791.

m. Calcutta, 19 Dec. 1769, Miss Flora Campbell. Father of Edward Curfy, *q.v.*
Services : Sailed for India on the *Anson,* 2 Apr. 1764, aged 17. N.F.P.

CURFY, Edward John (1774-1800). Lieutenant, Invalid Est. Infantry. *b.* Calcutta Nov. 1774. Cadet 1793. Arrived in India 16 Oct. 1795. Ensign 22 Oct. 1794. Lieut. 3 Oct. 1796. Invalided (?). *d.* Chunar 25 May 1800.
bapt. Mission church, Calcutta, 19 Dec. 1774, aged one month. Son of Edward Curfy, *q.v.*, and Flora his wife.
Services : N.F.P.

CURGENVEN, John Francis (1802-1823). Lieutenant, 30th N.I. *b.* psh. of St. Michael, Penkevil, Cornwall, 27 Dec. 1802. Cadet 1819. Ensign 7 Apr. 1820. Lieut. 11 July 1823. *d.* Delhi 4 Sept. 1823.
Son of Rev. William Curgenven, rector of Lamorran, Cornwall, and Laura his wife.
Services : Posted as Ensign to 2/28th N.I. Transfd. as Lieut. to 30th N.I. 11 July 1823, but did not live to join this Regt.

CURPHEY, William (1786-1856). Lieut. Colonel. Artillery. *b.* psh. of St. Paul, Dublin, 26 Dec. 1786. Cadet 1804. Arrived in India 12 Sept. 1805. Lieut. 12 May 1805. Capt. Lt. 26 Aug. 1813. Capt. 1 Sept. 1818. Major 28 Sept. 1827. Retired 28 Jan. 1832. Hon. Lt. Col. 28 Nov. 1854. *d.* Kensington 24 Sept. 1856.
Son of Anne Alexander, *alias* Curphey. *m.* Kensington, 2 Mar. 1836, Christina, 6th dau. of Jonathan Bell, of Hornsey.
Services : (? Storm and capture of Chamir fort 29 Jan. 1807.) Nepal War (India medal). Siege and capture of Hathras ; Capt. Lt. 3rd Coy. 2nd Bn. Art. Siege and capture of Bhurtpore ; Capt. comdg. 1st Coy. (Field Battery) 3rd Bn. Art. (Clasp to India medal).
Refs. : Foster's *Families of Royal Descent,* ii. 674. *G.M.* 1836, i. 424 ; 1856, ii. 659.
Note : Stubbs does not record the fact of his having served in the Nepal campaign, although the India Medal roll does.

CURRAN, James (1787-1815). Lieutenant, 29th N.I. *b.* Newmarket, co. Cork, 15 Jan. 1787. Cadet 1804. Arrived in India 10 Sept. 1805. Ensign 1 Oct. 1805. Lieut. 25 Oct. 1805. *d.* Bareilly, 4 Sept. 1815.
Services : Posted as Lieut. to 27th N.I. in 1806. Operations against Dhundia Khan 1807 ; Komona ; Ganauri ; Lieut. 27th N.I. Transfd. to newly-raised 29th N.I. in 1815.

CURRIE, George Alfred (1798-?). Lieutenant. 51st N.I. *b.* Ganjam, Madras, 12 Aug. 1798. Cadet 1819. Ensign 20 Sept. 1819. Lieut. 25 Dec. 1821. Resigned 19 June 1824.

(*Probably* brother of John Armstrong Currie, *q.v.*)
Services: Ensign 2/26th N.I. Fur. 1821 till resignation. Transfd. to 51st N.I. (late 1/26th) May 1824. Entered H.M.S. Ensign H.M. 67th Foot 1 Sept. 1825. Lieut. do. 16 Mar. 1832. Capt. do. 24 Nov. 1843; h.p. 23 Feb. 1844.

CURRIE, John Armstrong (1790-1856). Captain. 14th N.I. Subsequently a merchant in Calcutta. *b.* Trichinopoly, Madras, 22 May 1790. Cadet 1806. Arrived in India 1 Aug. 1807. Ensign 3 Aug. 1807. Lieut. 25 Feb. 1813. Capt. 21 Feb. 1824. Resigned 23 Feb. 1827. *d.* Garden Reach, Calcutta, 17 May 1856.

bapt. Trichinopoly 21 July 1790. Son of Thomas Currie, Ensign 1st Bn. Madras Eur. Inf., and Jane his wife. *m.* St. John's, Calcutta, 24 June 1820, Frances Sophia, 2nd dau. of H. Williams.

Services: Posted as Ensign to 10th N.I. in 1808. Capture of Java 1811; Lieut. Pioneers (Medal). Nepal War 1814-5; Lieut. 2nd Coy. Pioneers (? India medal). Served with Pioneers 1811-20. Lieut. 2/10th N.I. Dy. Paymr. at Dinapore 1820-3. Transfd. to 14th N.I. (late 1/10th) May 1824. (? First Burma War; Cachar 1825; Capt. 14th N.I.) Bde. Major at Barrackpore Sept. 1825 till resignation. After quitting the Service he became a merchant in Calcutta, and was for some time Registrar of the Merchant Seamen's Office in that city.

Refs.: A.J. xi. 62. Will dated 6 July 1847; proved 17 June 1856.

CURSEY, Alexander. Ensign. Infantry. Cadet 1771. Ensign 21 Mar. 1773. Dismissed by G.G. and Council 30 Apr. 1774.
Services: N.F.P.

CURSEY, Thomas Francis. Cadet. Infantry. Cadet 1771. Resigned 19 Jan. 1773.
Services: N.F.P.

CURTIS, James Gray William (1809-1870). Colonel, C.B. 37th N.I. *b.* Booterstown, co. Dublin, 10 Jan. 1809. Cadet 1826. Arrived in India 28 Oct. 1827. Ensign 1 July 1828. Lieut. 27 Feb. 1833. Capt. 13 Jan. 1842. Bt. Major 30 Apr. 1844. Bt. Lt. Col. 3 Apr. 1846. Retired 8 Dec. 1850. Hon. Col. 28 Nov. 1854. *d.* Oaklands, Shepherd's Bush, Middlesex, 16 Nov. 1870.

Son of Joseph Curtis, of Cross Avenue, Booterstown, and Eugenia Maria his wife. Brother of Robert Ruddock Curtis, *q.v. m.*

Dublin, 19 Jan. 1831, Mary Grace, youngest dau. of John Shaw, of Bohomer, co. Dublin.
Services : Posted as Ensign to 61st N.I. Transfd. to 36th N.I. 2 May 1828; to 37th N.I. 1 July 1828. Fur. 17 Jan. 1829 till 22 Oct. 1831. Intr. & Qmr. 37th N.I. 14 Dec. 1833. S.A.C.G. 9 Mar. 1840. First Afghan War 1839-40; Ghazni; S.A.C.G. (Medal). Gwalior campaign; Maharajpur; Capt. 37th N.I., S.A.C.G. (Bronze star). First Sikh War; Mudki; Ferozshahr; Sobraon; Bt. Major 37th N.I., S.A.C.G. (Medal with 2 clasps). D.A.C.G., 2 cl., 3 Mar. 1847; do., 1 cl., 27 Mar. 1849. C.B. 9 June 1849.
Refs. : Boase. The Times, 19 Nov. 1870.

CURTIS, John (1788-1821). Captain, Artillery. *b.* Birmingham 28 Nov. 1788. Cadet 1 Feb. 1806. Arrived in India 11 July 1806. Lieut. 5 Apr. 1806. Capt. Lt. 25 Sept. 1817. Capt. 1 Sept. 1818. *d.* Mhow 10 Dec. 1821.
bapt. St. Martin's, Birmingham, 7 Feb. 1789. 3rd son of Rev. Charles Curtis, rector of St. Martin's, Birmingham, and of Solihull, co. Warwick, and Dorothy his wife, dau. of Rev. John Wylde, of Bell Broughton, Worcs. Nephew of Sir William Curtis, Bart., lord mayor of London (*D.N.B.*). *m.* (?).
Services : Posted to newly-raised 2nd Troop H.A. in 1809, and served with it till 1817. Transfd. to newly-raised 4th (Native) Troop in 1817; to 2nd Troop in 1818. Third Mahratta War; Capt. 2nd Troop (d.d. 4th Troop).
Refs. : Foster's *Baronetage,* p. 169, *s.n.* Curtis, Bart., of Culland's Grove, Middlesex. Will dated Mhow 8 Dec. 1821; proved 27 Apr. 1822.

*CURTIS, Robert Ruddock (1805-1838 ?). Cadet. Never arrived in India. Lieut. H.M. 84th Foot. *b.* Booterstown, co. Dublin, 11 June 1805. *d.* 1838 ?
Son of Joseph Curtis, of Cross Avenue, Booterstown, and Eugenia Maria his wife. Brother of James Gray William Curtis, *q.v.* T.C.D.; Pensioner 20 Oct. 1823.
Services : Lieut. H.M. 84th Foot 13 Sept. 1831.

CUSACK, James Charles (1793-1820). Lieutenant, 3rd N.I. *b.* Dublin 24 July 1793. Cadet 1810. Ensign 17 Nov. 1813. Lieut. 22 May 1815. *d.* Saugor 28 Sept. 1820.
Son of Ignatius Cusack, "a country gentleman, near Dublin." T.C.D.; Pensioner 3 July 1809.
Services : Cadet d.d. 9th N.I. 1811-3. Posted as Ensign to 1/3rd N.I. Lieut. 2/3rd N.I. No record of active service.

CUSSONS or COZENS, Thomas (1747/48-1802). Lieutenant, Invalid Pension Est. *b.* York 1747/48. Cadet 1780. Arrived in India 27 Sept. 1780. Ensign 27 Sept. 1780. Lieut. 25 Aug. 1781. Invalided and pensioned (before 1791). *d.* Chunar, U.P., 1 Jan. 1802.
Services : Sailed for India on the *York,* 12 Feb. 1780, aged 32.
N.F.P.

CUST, Thomas (*d.* 1795). Captain, Infantry. Cadet 1769. Ensign 28 June 1770. Lieut. 19 Mar. 1773. Capt. 19 Jan. 1781. *d. unm.* Barrackpore 10 Dec. 1795.
Services : Capt. 2/15th N.I. in 1781. N.F.P.
Refs. : Will.

CUTHBERT, Alexander (*d.* 1813 ?). Ensign. Infantry. Cadet 1771. Ensign 10 Mar. 1773. Resigned 5 Sept. 1773. (*d.* Chandos St., Cavendish Sq., London, 16 Aug. 1813 ?)
Services : N.F.P.
Refs. : (? *G.M.* 1813, ii. 300.)

CUTHBERT, Benjamin (*d.* 1823). Lieut. Colonel. 15th N.I. Country Cadet 1778. Admitted 19 Aug. 1778. Ensign 23 May 1779. Lieut. 26 Jan. 1781. Capt. 13 Sept. 1797. Major 13 July 1803. Lt. Col. 28 Sept. 1804. Retired 13 May 1806. *d.* Henrietta St., Bath, 6 Mar. 1823.
Services : Lieut. 1st Bengal Eur. Regt. in 1796. Major 15th N.I. Fur. 22 Dec. 1803 till retirement.
Refs. : Bath Chron., 13 Mar. 1823.

CUTHBERT, Peter (*d.* 1769). Cadet, Infantry. Cadet 1769. *d.* Calcutta 23 Sept. 1769.
m. Martha. (She died Aberdeen, 26 Mar. 1807, aged 73.)
Services : N.F.P.
Refs. : Calcutta burial register.

www.ingramcontent.com/pod-product-compliance
Lightning Source LLC
Chambersburg PA
CBHW052055230426
43662CB00037B/1786